Trekking in the Nepal Himalaya

Western
Nepal
p248

Annapurna
Region
p124

Langtang,
Helambu &
Manaslu
p196

Kathmandu
p46

Everest
Region
p62

Eastern
Nepal
p218

THIS EDITION WRITTEN AND RESEARCHED BY

Bradley Mayhew,
Lindsay Brown, Stuart Butler

PLAN YOUR TRIP

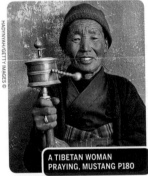

A TIBETAN WOMAN PRAYING, MUSTANG P180

HADYNYAH/GETTY IMAGES ©

GOKYO RI P96

FENG WEI PHOTOGRAPHY/GETTY IMAGES ©

ON THE ROAD

Contents

Post-Earthquake Update

Lonely Planet's Nepal authors updated the 10th edition of this *Trekking in the Nepal Himalayas* guidebook shortly before the first tremor. We have updated our coverage since the disaster using local sources, but with some areas off-limits to trekkers and more landslides expected in the 2015 monsoon, it will be some time before the full extent of the damage becomes clear, particularly in rural areas. For all the treks in this book, you should seek local advice before setting off to make sure that all stages are open and that food and accommodation is available for all overnight stops. If you discover anything that is incorrect or out of date in this guidebook, please let us know via the following link: www.lonelyplanet.com/contact/guidebook_feedback/new.

Welcome to the Nepal Himalaya

The bottom line: if you love the mountains, life simply doesn't get any better than on a trek through the Nepal Himalaya.

The High Life

With its magnificent peaks and glacial valleys, it's no surprise the Nepal Himalaya hosts some of the world's best trekking. The world's highest mountain range defines everything in Nepal, from its topography and development to its weather and religion. Even after the devastating earthquakes of April and May 2015, most of Nepal's trekking routes are open, serving up the kind of views normally reserved for mountaineers. Nothing rivals these mountains. 'In a hundred ages of the gods,' rhapsodises Skanda Purana, the ancient Hindu text, 'I could not tell thee of the glories of the Himalaya.'

The Apple-Pie Trail

Nepal sets the global standard for spectacular, hassle-free trekking, especially in the teahouse trekking regions of Everest and the Annapurnas. You can hike for weeks into the very heart of a mountain range, safe in the knowledge that at the end of the day you can count on a clean bed, a hot meal and a slice of warm apple pie. While some lodges were damaged in the 2015 earthquakes, the sheer profusion of lodges has ensured that the Apple Pie Trail is still alive and well – so leave the leaky tent, sputtering stove and freeze-dried goulash at home and enjoy the world's most accessible trekking.

Off the Beaten Trek

Away from the popular teahouse treks lie dozens of adventures. Treks to Nar-Phu and Makalu Base Camp can now be done in high season by staying in simple teahouses, and Manaslu is likely to regain its status as the 'best new teahouse trek in Nepal' once earthquake damage to its teahouses has been repaired. Beyond these regions you need to camp and cook and probably need staff to support you, but the scope is limitless. The far west in particular offers endless adventures into remote and timeless pockets of Tibetan culture.

Aside from Mountains

Beyond the famous mountain views, Nepal's mountains are rivalled only by its people and its superb trek staff – porters, sherpas and guides. Get to know your porters or lodge owners over a game of cards or cup of butter tea and you'll find that many have fascinating stories to tell. Whether overnighting in bamboo Rai villages, visiting Tibetan monasteries in Mustang, greeting Sherpa yak herders or haggling with Manangi traders, what you will soon realise is that the rich culture and customs of Nepal's myriad peoples and their unswerving good humour are as big a draw as the peaks themselves.

Why I Love Trekking in the Nepal Himalaya

By Bradley Mayhew, Author

Trekking research is the very best kind of research there is. No pesky bus stations, no tricky backstreets to map, just moments of bliss watching the evening alpenglow linger on a frozen peak or enjoying a silent section of trail alone in the early morning light. For me it's all about the settling of the mind that comes on a multiday trek, the sense of scale and perspective that only the big mountains can bring. I can't think of a better way to spend a couple of weeks of your life.

For more about our authors, see page p376

Above: Marsyangdi River (p144), close to the Annapurna Range

Trekking in the Nepal Himalaya

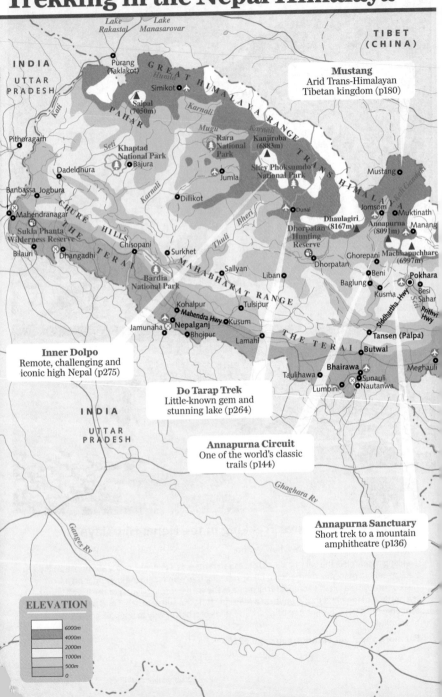

Mustang
Arid Trans-Himalayan Tibetan kingdom (p180)

Inner Dolpo
Remote, challenging and iconic high Nepal (p275)

Do Tarap Trek
Little-known gem and stunning lake (p264)

Annapurna Circuit
One of the world's classic trails (p144)

Annapurna Sanctuary
Short trek to a mountain amphitheatre (p136)

TIBET (CHINA)

INDIA
UTTAR PRADESH

INDIA
UTTAR PRADESH

Lake Rakastal
Lake Manasarovar

Purang (Taklakot)
Simikot
Saipal (7050m)

GREAT HIMALAYA RANGE

PAHAR

Pithoragarh
Dadeldhura
Banbassa Jogbura
Mahendranagar
Sukla Phanta Wilderness Reserve
Bilauri
Dhangadhi

Khaptad National Park
Bajura

CHURE HILLS
THE TERAI

Chisopani
Surkhet

Rara National Park
Jumla
Dillikot

Kanjiroba (6883m)
Shey Phoksumdo National Park

Mustang

Dunai
Dhaulagiri (8167m)
Dhorpatan Hunting Reserve

Jomsom
Muktinath
Annapurna (8091m)
Manang

Ghorepani
Machhapuchhare (6997m)

Dhorpatan
Beni
Baglung
Kusma

Pokhara
Besi Sahar

MAHABHARAT RANGE
Sallyan
Liban

Kohalpur
Mahendra Hwy
Kusum
Tulsipur

Jamunaha
Nepalganj
Bhojpur
Lamahi

THE TERAI

Tansen (Palpa)
Butwal

Bhairawa
Taulihawa
Lumbini
Sunauli
Nautanwa

Meghauli

Siddhartha Hwy
Prithvi Hwy

Ghaghara Rv

Ganges Rv

Karnali
Humli
Karnali
Mugu
Karnali
Seti
Bheri
Thuli
Seti

ELEVATION

	6000m
	4000m
	2000m
	1000m
	500m
	0

Around Manaslu
Spectacular views on Nepal's new favourite trek (p211)

TIBET (CHINA)

Three Passes
The ultimate Everest trek (p97)

Everest Base Camp
Iconic but crowded must-do trek (p68)

Manaslu (8156m)

Ganesh Himal (7406m)

Himalchuli (7892m)

Langtang Lirung (7246m)

Dorje Lakpa (6966m)

Cho Oyu (8153m)

Mt Everest (8848m)

Gauri Shankar (7145m)

Lhotse (8516m)

Makalu (8462m)

Nuptse (7879m)

Kanchenjunga Conservation Area

Kanchenjunga (8598m)

Marsyangdi

Buri Gandaki

Trisuli

Bhote Kosi

Gorkha

Dhunche

Langtang National Park

Langtang

Kodari

Barabise

ROLWALING

Sagarmatha National Park

Namche Bazaar

Lukla

GREAT HIMALAYA RANGE

Dumre

Trisuli Bazaar

Nuwakot

Shivapuri National Park

Nagarjuna

Charikot

Mugling

Bandipur

KATHMANDU

Bhaktapur

Jiri

Phaplu

Tamba Kosi

Sun Kosi

Dudh Kosi

Arun

Tamur

Kanchenjunga Conservation Area

Narayangarh

Naubise

Patan

Dolalghat

PAHAR

Taplejung

INDIA

Bharatpur

Daman

Dhulikhel

Panauti

Ramechhap

Tumlingtar

Basantapur

SIKKIM

Sauraha

MAHABHARAT

Chitwan National Park

Hetauda

RANGE

Sindhuli

Lamidanda

Hile

Dhankuta

Kalimpong

Parsa Wilderness Reserve

CHURE HILLS

THE TERAI

Darjeeling

Pathlaiya

Bardibas

Mahendra Hwy

Koshi Tappu Wildlife Reserve

Chatara

Dharan

Ilam

Simara

Birganj

Kosi

Itahari

Kakarbhitta

Raxaul Bazaar

Janakpur

Mahanpur

Rajbiraj

Panitanki

Jaleshwar

Jaynagar

Birpur

Biratnagar

Bhadrapur

Jogbani

BANGLADESH

Kanchenjunga
Get far from the crowds in Nepal's wild east (p233)

INDIA
BIHAR

INDIA
WEST BENGAL

Tribhuvan Hwy

Plan Your Trip

Nepal & the 2015 Earthquakes

At 11.56am on 25 April 2015, Nepal was hit by a massive earthquake measuring 7.8 on the Richter scale, causing devastation to many parts of the country. This chapter is intended to provide an overview of what happened, how this has affected travel to Nepal, and how we deal with the disaster in this guidebook.

A Dark Day for Nepal

The morning of 25 April 2015 brought destruction to central Nepal. Thousands of buildings collapsed in the initial tremor and in subsequent aftershocks, killing more than 8500 people, and leaving thousands more homeless. Landslides destroyed entire villages and an avalanche at Everest Base Camp killed 18 climbers in Nepal's worst mountaineering disaster. Aftershocks followed for weeks, including a major tremor on 12 May, which killed hundreds more. Around the epicenter in Gorkha district, and across the Kathmandu Valley, communities were devastated and centuries-old monuments were reduced to rubble. Many of Nepal's most famous tourist sights were damaged beyond recognition. The earthquake has been described as the worst disaster to hit Nepal since the deadly Bihar-Nepal earthquake of 1934.

A huge international response has helped Nepal to cope with the immediate aftermath of the crisis, but rebuilding lost homes, monuments and livelihoods is likely to be a slow and drawn-out process. Tourism has been severely affected by the disaster, and this comes at a time when Nepal is desperately in need of the revenue from tourism to rebuild. It is our hope at Lonely Planet that this guidebook will inform travellers about the damage caused by the earthquake, and encourage people to return and help the people of Nepal as they rebuild their lives after the crisis.

Counting the Cost

While the earthquake is one of the worst disasters to ever hit the Himalayan region, it is important to note that damage was localised. Kathmandu and other towns in the Kathmandu Valley were badly affected, but little damage was recorded in Pokhara and the Annapurna region, and only mild shocks were felt in the Terai and in eastern and western Nepal. Damage to trekking regions was similarly patchy; whole villages were destroyed by landslides and avalanches in Langtang, Helambu, Manaslu, Rolwaling and parts of the Everest region, and many traditional buildings were damaged in Mustang, but other trekking areas were mostly untouched by the disaster.

It's also important to note that the devastation was not total, despite media reports from tourist sites such as Kathmandu's Durbar Square. While dozens of historic temples, palaces and monuments were reduced to piles of bricks and broken timbers, many more escaped undamaged. Much was lost but Nepal is still recognisably Nepal. The historic towns of the Kathmandu Valley still overflow with medieval architecture and the foothills of the Himalaya are still dotted with immaculate stone villages and criss-crossed by carefully maintained walking trails.

Where Now For Nepal?

The question asked by most travellers in the aftermath of the earthquake was not 'Where can I go instead of Nepal?' but 'When will it be safe to go back to Nepal?' In the days immediately following the disaster, aftershocks were a daily occurrence and millions slept outside under canvas fearing further building collapses. The initial advice was for travellers to stay away, to avoid using valuable resources and impeding the relief effort.

Since then, the aftershocks have largely subsided and the relief effort has moved on to reconstruction and housing people left homeless by the disaster. The authorities in Nepal are now appealing to tourists to return and help Nepal rebuild its economy by spending money with local business and supporting the livelihoods of local people. Nevertheless, the damage is severe and it will be some time before Nepal returns to the position it was in before the disaster.

Trekking Today

While the vast majority of Nepal's trek-king routes are still open following the 2015 disaster, trekkers should expect some disruption as a result of the earthquake. Damage from the tremor is plainly visible in many mountain areas, and some regions are off-limits while emergency relief work continues. Across the country, thousands of buildings are structurally unsound and can no longer be used, and others will need extensive repairs. Bridges and trekking trails also need repairs in many areas, and many trails now detour around landslides from the disaster. Nepal is engaged in a massive program of reconstruction but many people remain in temporary accommodation, and transport links, power supplies and communications may all be disrupted. Even where trails are open, you should expect to find that some trekking lodges are closed for restoration or because of lack of customers.

Despite all this, Nepal remains the same captivating, fascinating and welcoming destination it always was. If you go trekking in Nepal today, and spend your money with local businesses, you will be contributing directly to the reconstruction effort, providing valuable revenue that has the potential to change lives. The Nepalis are a resilient people but now more than ever they need the world to remember Nepal after the headlines have faded.

REGIONS AFFECTED

Different regions were affected to differing levels by the 2015 disaster.

Kathmandu Severe damage to buildings and monuments, particularly in Kathmandu Durbar Square, but many districts escaped with only minor damage.

Kathmandu Valley Widespread damage to buildings and monuments, particularly in the historic cities of Patan and Bhaktapur, but some areas escaped damage.

Pokhara & Around The area around Pokhara was mostly unaffected but there was some minor damage in rural areas; the road to Jomsom was also affected.

Everest Region Trekking routes are open but a major avalanche killed climbers at Base Camp and there was damage to older buildings across Solukhumbu, particularly close to Lukla and Namche Bazaar.

Annapurna Region Most areas saw only minor damage but older buildings collapsed in Jomsom and many historic monuments and village homes were damaged in Mustang; all trails in this area are open.

Langtang, Helambu & Manaslu The earthquake caused catastrophic damage to Langtang, Manaslu and stages of the treks to Manaslu and Tsum. Whole villages were destroyed and most treks in this region are expected to be off-limits for some time. The Manaslu trek may reopen as a camping trek while infrastructure is restored.

Eastern Nepal Some damage to early stages of the Lukla to Tumlingtar and Makalu treks, but most trails were not seriously affected. All routes are expected to be open following the 2015 monsoon.

Western Nepal Western Nepal saw only minor damage from the earthquake and there are no reports of trails being closed after the disaster.

The Nepal Himalaya's
Top 9

Annapurna Circuit

1 The Annapurna Circuit (p144) is the most popular trek in Nepal, offering more cultural variety and a clearer sense of journey than the Everest Base Camp trek but still offering amazing (though slightly less close up) mountain views. The trail follows the Marsyangdi Valley to some spectacular mountain views, high lakes, glacier viewpoints and Buddhist pilgrimage sites around Manang, before crossing the 5416m Thorung La high pass to Jomsom. Road-building is nibbling away at the trail in sections, but it remains without doubt one of the world's classic treks.

Everest Base Camp

2 Number one on most people's wish list is the Everest Base Camp trek (p68), a 16-day scenic tour de force that climbs through Sherpa villages and glacial valleys into unparalleled high-mountain scenery. You'll get the best views of the great peak from the hill of Kala Pattar, before visiting Everest Base Camp itself. What you will soon realise, however, is that Everest itself isn't all that impressive from this angle. Far more stirring are the mountains you may not have heard of: Kantega, Ama Dablam and Pumori.

FENG WEI PHOTOGRAPHY/GETTY IMAGES ©

CHRISTIAN KOBER/GETTY IMAGES ©

BARTOSZ HADYNIAK/GETTY IMAGES ©

GOINYK/GETTY IMAGES ©

NICRAM SABOD/SHUTTERSTOCK ©

Mustang

3 One of the most remote but fastest-changing enclaves of Tibetan culture in Nepal is the kingdom of Mustang, a restricted area where a 10-day trek (p184) winds through arid, desert-like canyons to the fabled walled city of Lo Manthang. The scenery in these areas is spectacular – white snow peaks, barren brown and yellow eroded cliffs, and red-walled gompas, all set against a cobalt-blue sky – but the real draws are the medieval-style villages and Tibetan monasteries. There's only one catch: a US$100 permit fee. Top left: Novice monks at a monastery in Mustang (p180)

Everest Three Passes

4 For the ultimate high-altitude Himalayan roller-coaster ride, head to the Everest region to try the challenging Three Passes trek (p97). It's a tough option, taking you over the region's three most spectacular trekking passes, each over 5000m. The epic views of Makalu from the Kongma La, and the panorama of glacial highway and turquoise lakes filling the Gokyo Valley from Gokyo Ri, are perhaps the most impressive vistas nonclimbers will ever get. Bottom left: Gokyo Valley

Annapurna Sanctuary

5 The Annapurna Sanctuary (p136) is a teahouse trek that gets you right into a high mountain amphitheatre, surrounded on three sides by the massive peaks of Annapurna, Hiunchuli, Fluted Peak and Machhapuchhare. For a relatively short trek (10 days) it packs an incredible scenic punch as well as amazing diversity, journeying from rhododendron forests and bamboo groves up to glacial moraines. The teahouses are excellent and the Gurung village of Ghandruk is one of the region's nicest. Come prepared to climb plenty of stone steps.

ZVEV/GETTY IMAGES ©

RICHARD I'ANSON/GETTY IMAGES ©

Inner Dolpo

6 For something even more remote, Tibet-ophiles should head to Dolpo (p275), known among trekking aficionados for its spectacularly remote gompas, colourful yak caravans and dramatic high-desert scenery. For an off-the-map adventure, the ultimate goal for fans of Peter Matthiessen's *The Snow Leopard* is Shey Gompa, try the insanely remote trek to the gompas of Saldang, Nam-gung and Yangtser, across the roof of Nepal, from Shey Gompa to Jomsom. You'll need to join a group for this challenging expedition-style trek. Top: Bon stupa, Saldang village

Kanchenjunga

7 Little-visited eastern Himalaya is wetter, lusher and more forested than the west. The star is the world's third tallest peak, a huge massif of summits on the Indian bor-der. Offering a fine mix of village life and high alpine splendour, this incredibly varied trek (p233) is for connoisseurs who don't mind the long travel times or a camping-style trek, though simple teahouses now line most of the route. Budget a month to combine the northern and southern approach routes into one of Nepal's most epic adventures. Above: Trekking the Tamur Kosi Valley in Kanchenjunga (p234)

Around Manaslu

8 A challenger to Everest and Annapurna, this epic 16-day walk (p211) circles around the world's eighth highest peak. Before the 2015 earthquake, this was a tea-house classic; while rebuilding is underway, camping may be the only way to go. Expect fantastic scenery, lots of exciting side trips and a dramatic high pass crossing. The heart of the walk is the Tibetan region of Nupri, long considered a *baeyul* (hidden Himalayan valley). Throw in the option of a week-long detour to the neighbouring Tsum Valley and you have one of Nepal's most exciting trekking regions.

Phoksumdo Lake via Do Tarap

9 This camping trek (264) in Nepal's wild west involves ascending the barren Tarap gorge to the Trans-Himalayan villages, Tibetan monasteries and unique *chortens* (stupas) of Do Tarap village. From here it's a simply mind-blowing three days of achingly beautiful wilderness, before reaching the shores of Phoksumdo Lake, Nepal's most beautiful lake. Dotted with Bön monasteries, it's one of Nepal's hidden gems. Better still, avoid the domestic flight and trek in on the superb and little-walked Beni to Dolpo trek.

Need to Know

For more information, see Survival Guide (p323)

Currency
Nepali rupee (Rs)

Language
Nepali

Visas
Tourist visas (15, 30 or 90 days) available on arrival; bring two photos and cash in US dollars.

Money
Easy to change cash and access ATMs in Kathmandu, Pokhara and other cities but almost impossible in rural areas or on treks.

Mobile Phones
Buy SIM cards at Kathmandu airport on arrival, or at Nepal Telecom (Namaste) or Ncell outlets across the country.

Time
Five hours and 45 minutes ahead of GMT.

When to Go

Subtropical warm winters, hot wet summers
Cool winters, warm wet summers
High altitude freezing winters, cool summers

Dolpo
TREK May–Oct

Mustang
TREK May–Oct

Around Manaslu
TREK Mar–May
Oct–Nov

Annapurna Circuit
TREK Mar–Apr
Oct–Nov

Everest Base Camp
TREK Mar–May
Oct–Dec

Kangchenjunga
TREK Mar–Apr
Oct–Nov

High Season
(Oct–Nov)

➡ Clear skies and warm days make autumn the peak trekking season.

➡ Thousands of people hit the trails in the Everest and Annapurna regions.

➡ Accommodation in Kathmandu gets booked up as prices peak.

Shoulder
(Mar–Apr)

➡ Spring brings warm weather and spectacular rhododendron blooms.

➡ High passes can be blocked before mid-March.

Low Season
(Jun–Sep)

➡ The monsoon rains bring landslides, and clouds often obscure mountain views.

➡ Rain, mud and leeches deter most trekkers.

➡ A good time to visit Mustang, Dolpo, Limi and Nar-Phu.

Useful Websites

Great Himalaya Trail (http://thegreathimalayatrail.org) Details the various sections of the epic trail, with articles and a forum.

Nepal Tourism Board (www.welcomenepal.com) Government site.

TAAN (www.taan.org.np) The Trekking Agencies' Association of Nepal website details current trekking regulations.

Trekking Partners (www.trekkingpartners.com) Useful for finding trek partners and guides, plus some helpful articles.

Lonely Planet (www.lonelyplanet.com/nepal) Find trail updates and track down trekking partners on the designated Nepal and Trekking branches of the Thorn Tree forum.

Important Numbers

Ambulance	☏102
Country code	☏977
International access code	☏00
Police	☏100
Tourism hotline	☏4225709
Tourist police	☏4247041

Exchange Rates

Australia	A$1	Rs 75
Canada	C$1	Rs 78
China	Y1	Rs 16
Europe	€1	Rs 112
India	₹1	Rs 1.60
Japan	¥10	Rs 8
UK	£1	Rs 158
US	US$1	Rs 102

For current exchange rates see www.xe.com.

Daily Costs

**Budget:
Less than US$50**

➡ Food and accommodation in trekking lodge: US$15–20 per day

➡ Trekking porter/guide: US$15/25 per day

➡ TIMS permit: US$20

**Midrange:
US$50–150**

➡ Agency-organised teahouse trek: US$40–50 per person per day

➡ Flight to Lukla: US$165

➡ Manaslu permit: US$50–70 for seven days

**Top end:
More than US$150**

➡ Top-end lodge in Everest region: US$90–150

➡ Organised camping trek: US$60–100 per person per day

➡ Mustang trekking permit: US$500 for 10 days

Trek Ratings

Treks in this guide are rated according to difficulty in the box preceding each trek description. Our authors have used the following guidelines:

Easy Shorter walks following well-travelled trails through villages with facilities for trekkers. Most days are less than six hours and ascend less than 500m.

Medium Involves some steep climbs and perhaps exposed cliffs, at altitudes up to 5500m. Some long days and a high pass crossing may be involved.

Hard May require basic mountaineering skills out of season or after heavy snowfall. There may be stretches without decent camping spots and navigation can be tricky in places.

Arriving in Nepal

Kathmandu's Tribhuvan International Airport (p337) Prepaid taxis are available inside the terminal. Many midrange hotels offer free pick-ups from the airport. Long queues at immigration can slow things if you are getting your visa on arrival.

Sunauli (Indian border; p339) For Kathmandu and Pokhara take a direct bus from the border. Golden Travels offers the most comfortable service. For other destinations take a 4WD or rickshaw to nearby Bhairawa and change there.

Getting Around

Transport in Nepal is reasonably priced and accessible. Roads are often narrow, overcrowded and poorly maintained and delays should be expected. Remote treks are only accessible by flight.

Air Flights to/from major centres are efficient, whereas mountain flights to trail heads are highly weather dependent and frequently delayed. Safety is an issue.

Bus Tourist class buses are comfortable, usually air-conditioned, and relatively safe and reliable. Local buses are generally uncomfortable, crowded and slow.

Vehicle hire The best way to get to a trailhead but pricey.

Road construction You may find that the first day or two of treks such as the Annapurna Circuit or Shivalaya to Lukla trek have changed as roads progress through the Middle Hills.

For much more on **getting around**, see p340

PLAN YOUR TRIP NEED TO KNOW

If You Like...

Low-Altitude Treks

The following treks are perfect for winter trekking, or if your time is limited or you just can't face the cold and headaches of high altitude.

Annapurna Panorama Great views, lots of knee-bruising steps, photogenic Gurung villages and comfortable trekking lodges mark the foothills of the Annapurna range. (p129)

Lukla to Tumlingtar With the lowest altitude of any trek in this book (320m), expect warm temperatures even in winter, despite passes of 3350m. (p220)

Shivalaya to Lukla Despite earthquake damage, the classic approach to Everest is a good teahouse option when other treks are snowed in, with three passes to help you acclimatise en route. (p104)

Namche Bazaar & Around A wonderful low-altitude loop from Lukla will take you to a string of fascinating Sherpa villages around Namche Bazaar, though earthquake damage means some route changes. (p68)

Khopra Ridge A week at lower elevations, passing culturally fascinating villages, with a climb up to 3660m for a grandstand view of the Annapurnas. (p133)

Epic Views

Gokyo Ri Probably the best single view in the Everest region, taking in a turquoise lake, a glacial highway and views of Mt Everest. (p96)

Phoksumdo Lake Nepal's most scenic lake boasts a lakeshore Bön monastery and views towards forbidden Dolpo. (p262)

Jalja La A little-known pass four days west of Beni, with astonishing sunset views of Dhaulagiri and the Annapurnas. (p269)

Chhukung Ri Huge views of the Lhotse wall, Ama Dablam and Island Peak, from this high mountain cul-de-sac. (p68)

Ghorepani to Ghandruk Long-distance views come no better than the distinctive fishtail curve of Machhapuchhare from Tadapani or Ghandruk. (p131)

Religious Sites

Muktinath The natural springs and gas flames here are sacred to both Hindus and Buddhists. (p144)

Tengboche Monastery Shaken but not destroyed in the 2015 earthquake, the Everest region's largest Buddhist monastery bursts into life during the masked festival dances of Mani Rimdu. (p78)

Shey Gompa Dolpo's Crystal Monastery is a pilgrimage destination for locals and foreigners, elevated to near mythological status by *The Snow Leopard*. (p285)

Lo Manthang The four ancient Tibetan monasteries in Mustang's capital unfurl giant thangkas during May's Tiji festival. (p188)

Do Tarap's Bon Monasteries Discover tantalising traces of the culture that preceded Tibetan Buddhism in the ancient Bon sanctuaries of Do Tarap. (p267)

IF YOU LIKE...YETIS

Visit Khumjung Monastery to see its yeti scalp, or Pangboche Monastery for its replica yeti hand. To actually see a yeti (p82), the remote peaks of Gaurishankar (7134m) and Melungtse (7181m) are said to be the best places.

Top: Tiji festival (p22) in Lo Manthang, Mustang
Bottom: A Buddhist statue on top of Gokyo Ri (p96)

Side Trips

Annapurna Circuit Don't miss day trips from Manang to Milarepa's Cave or Praken Gompa, or the gorgeous section of trail around Ngawal and Ghyaru. (p144)

Everest Base Camp Side trips to Ama Dablam Base Camp and the upper Gokyo Valley offer better views than you'll get from Base Camp itself. (p68)

Jomsom A comfortable base from which to visit the timeless Mustang-style villages of Jhong, Kagbeni and Tiri, as well as the Bön-influenced Lubra valley. (p144)

Tilicho Lake The trails to this high-altitude lake are particularly hairy, but it's an adventurous Annapurna add-on if you are experienced and acclimatised. (p157)

Village Culture

Annapurna Circuit The villages of Bragha, Marpha and Kagbeni are delightful places to overnight, full of winding stone backstreets, hidden shrines and traditional architecture. (p144)

Khopra Ridge Community lodges and homestays give you a deeper connection with the locals and ensure local communities benefit collectively from your visit. (p133)

Phu This timeless Himalayan village huddles on a conical hill, making it one of the most photogenic in Nepal. (p175)

Lo Manthang Life is changing fast in this remote pocket of Tibetan culture, but it still retains a wonderful centuries-old lifestyle. (p180)

Namche Bazaar Drink *rakshi* (fortified rice wine) with your Sherpa guide or overnight in Kunde or

Khumjung villages to get an authentic taste of the Khumbu's Sherpa culture. (p68)

High Passes

Three Passes This outrageous itinerary combines the Kongma La, Cho La and Renjo La into what is perhaps the single most scenic trek in this book. (p97)

Thorung La You need to be well acclimatised and have an eye on the weather to cross this 5416m pass, the highest on any teahouse trek. (p149)

Do Tarap Loop The sublime wilderness passes Numa La and Baga La rank as two of the least visited and most beautiful in this guide. (p264)

Kagmara La The remotest pass in this book links Phoksumdo Lake with remote Jumla in the far western corner of the country. (p261)

Ganja La A challenging, camping-only crossing that conveniently links the Langtang and Helambu treks, offering fabulous views. (p204)

Solitude

To really get away from it all, ditch the teahouse crowds of Annapurna and Everest for these lonesome gems.

Shivalaya to Lukla The old expedition approach to the Khumbu is still in business despite the

earthquake, with a fraction of the Everest crowds and abundant trekking lodges – a fine warm-up to a Base Camp trip. (p104)

Lukla to Tumlingtar A rough-and-ready way to finish an Everest trek, hiking through Sherpa and Rai communities to finish in the eastern lowlands. (p220)

Beni to Dolpo A largely unsung but incredibly scenic trek across the breadth of central Nepal, a favourite of those in the know. (p269)

Rara Lake Remote and untouched, this wilderness walk takes you through an uninhabited national park in Nepal's remote far west. (p251)

Jumla to Dunai Large sections of Western Nepal never see a foreign trekker and this is a great place to start, linking Dolpo with the far west. (p258)

Tibetan Culture

Large parts of northern Nepal are an extension of the Tibetan plateau, sheltering some of the last bastions of traditional Himalayan culture.

Mustang The last Himalayan Buddhist kingdom boasts horse-racing festivals, Tibetan forts, stunning Buddhist frescos and a deeply traditional lifestyle. (p180)

Nar-Phu A pocket of pristine Tibetan culture, just off the Annapurna Circuit, with permit

fees a fraction of those in Mustang. (p174)

Do Tarap Dolpo is one of the most traditional Tibetan-influenced areas in Nepal, where border trading and yak herding remains the norm. (p264)

Limi Valley Hidden in the furthest corner of Nepal, bordering Tibet's Mt Kailash, Limi offers remote Tibetan-style villages and the chance to hike into Tibet. (p279)

Nupri The upper parts of the Manaslu region are lined with mani walls, building-sized prayer wheels and chortens (Tibetan stupas). (p211)

Base Camp Views

Kangchenjunga Views of the world's third-highest mountain from Pang Pema rank among the most impressive in the Himalaya. (p234)

Annapurna Sanctuary For a short trek, the 360-degree views of Annapurna, Hiunchuli and Machhapuchare give an unrivalled sense of being in the heart of the big peaks. (p136)

Everest Base Camp You don't actually get to see Everest from base camp but the views of the Khumbu Icefall and of expedition tents are worth the trip. (p68)

Ama Dablam Few trekkers make it up here on a side trip from Pangboche but the views are superb and there's even a lodge at nearby Mingbo. (p83)

Makalu Base Camp Splendid isolation and views that could inspire religions are the rewards for trekkers who climb to the base camp for ascents of the world's fifth-highest mountain. (p229)

Plan Your Trip
Planning Your Trek

Trekking in Nepal is logistically as easy as it gets, but it still requires some planning. It's possible to turn up in Kathmandu and set off on a teahouse trek two days later, but for more logistically complex treks booked through an agency you should allow a week. For the lowdown on teahouse versus camping treks, independent or organised trekking, porters and permits, read on.

When to Trek

The trick to choosing when to start a trek is striking a balance between the period of best weather for the area you wish to trek and the crowds that this good weather attracts.

October to November The first two months of the dry season offer the best weather for trekking and the main trails are heaving with trekkers at this time, for good reason. The air is crystal clear, the mountain scenery is superb and the weather is still comfortably warm during the day (though nights fall below freezing in the mountains). The climate is becoming less predictable. Monsoon rains are lingering into late September and freak winter storms are becoming increasingly common in October

December to February These are good months for trekking, but the cold can be bitter and dangerous at high altitudes. Getting up to the Everest Base Camp can be a real endurance test. High passes such as the Thorung La (Annapurna Circuit) and Laurebina La (Gosainkund trek) are usually closed from mid-December to late February, as are treks to the remote regions of Dolpo, Mustang, Makalu Base Camp and Humla. The Christmas period brings a temporary spike in group treks. Some high-altitude lodges on popular trekking routes, particularly at Gorak Shep, the Annapurna Sanctuary and Gosainkund, close in December and February, though there is always something open.

Trail Essentials

Altitude sickness supplies A good briefing on altitude sickness and an emergency supply of Diamox.

Something to read A good paperback, useful for passing long evenings in a lodge or tent.

Necessary permits A fistful of permits, including a TIMS card and either an ACAP permit, national park ticket or restricted-area permit.

Get to know your trekking partner Spend at least one day on a trail or a night in a tent with your potential trekking partner, to experience the full range of snoring, farting, unusual smells and bad jokes that you may have to face on the trail.

First-aid kit A good medical kit and blister padding and tape, to be carried on your person at all times, alongside an emergency stash of toilet paper.

Earplugs Sanity-savers for travel on noisy turboprop planes, noisy local buses and noisy hotel rooms.

Photocopies Passport photos and passport copies for visa and permit applications.

FESTIVALS

Nepal has dozens of colourful festivals throughout the year so there's a good chance your trek will coincide with one of them. Festivals can complicate treks, however, as government offices close and porters disappear back home. Popular mountain festivals like Tiji in Mustang or Tengboche monastery's Mani Rimdu festival are very popular with groups, so you can expect local lodges and campsites to be overflowing during these times. Festivals are scheduled in accordance with the Nepali and Tibetan lunar calendars, so they can vary over a period of almost a month with respect to the Gregorian (Western) calendar.

The most popular festivals along Nepal's trekking trails include the following:

➡ **Gyalpo Losar** (February) Two weeks of revelry ushers in the Tibetan New Year in Tibetan communities from Dolpo to the Khumbu. Tamangs celebrate their Losar (Sonam Losar) a month earlier, while Magar, Loba and Gurung communities celebrate Tolo Losar a further month or so before that.

➡ **Saga Dawa** (May–June) Celebrates the full moon of Buddha's birth, enlightenment and death and is held in Tibetan areas, as well as in Lumbini, the birthplace of Buddha. Tibetan Buddhist monasteries hold special prayers and processions. Outside of Tibetan areas it's known as Buddha Jayanti.

➡ **Mani Rimdu** (May–June; p65) Religious festival at Thame Gompa, a day's walk west of Namche Bazaar.

➡ **Tiji Festival** (May) Three-day festival in Mustang celebrating the victory over drought and a demon, with monk dances, an exorcism ceremony and the unfurling of a giant thangka (Tibetan religious painting).

➡ **Janai Purnima** (July–August) Up to 20,000 pilgrims flock to sacred Gosainkund Lake in the Langtang region during the full-moon Festival of the Sacred Thread. Devotees also head to Dudh Kund in the Solu region and Gokyo in the Khumbu. Elsewhere in the hills, locals descend upon Shiva temples with a *jhankri* (medicine man) leading the throngs.

➡ **Dasain** (October–November) This 10-day festival is Nepal's biggest and much of the country comes to a stop (p333). All creeds and castes participate as 100,000 animals are sacrificed across Nepal in honour of Durga (Kali). It is difficult to start a trek during Dasain because all of the buses and planes are jammed, and porters are impossible to find in the countryside. On your trek you'll see the bamboo swings and simple Ferris wheels that are erected in every village.

➡ **Tihar** (Diwali; October–November) The Festival of Lights is the second-most important festival in Nepal. Hindus pay homage to Laxmi (the goddess of wealth). Houses are given new coats of paint, hundreds of oil lamps and candles are lit, firecrackers are recklessly tossed into the streets and most houses are packed with men gambling the night away.

➡ **Mani Rimdu** (October–November; p65) This popular three-day Sherpa festival at Tengboche Monastery features masked dances and dramas, which celebrate the victory of Buddhism over the existing Tibetan Bön religion.

In addition to these national events, there are many regional festivals, as well as local religious dances or ceremonies marked by specific monasteries.

Teahouse owners often close their lodges on less visited routes such as Makalu Base Camp, Tsum Valley and Manaslu, as they head down to lower altitudes for winter.

March to May Dry weather and dust means poorer Himalayan views but the compensations are several: fewer crowds, warm weather and spectacular spring rhododendron blooms. Mustard fields colour the farmlands with bright yellow flowers in February/March. This is the second most popular period for trekking. Trekking tapers off by May, the hottest month of the year, when it starts to get very hot, dusty and humid at lower altitudes.

June to September Monsoon rains bring land-slides – expected to be particularly severe following the 2015 earthquakes – plus slippery trails and hordes of *jukha* (leeches). Raging rivers often wash away bridges and stretches of trail. Trekking is difficult but still possible and there are hardly any trekkers on the trails. Good for Trans-Himalayan regions like Mustang, Dolpo and around Jomsom. Some lodges close during the monsoon.

There are three excellent times to trek when you will often have campsites or lodges to yourself and can usually rely on good weather. These little-known trekking seasons are the first two weeks of December, the entire month of February, and the second half of September.

What Kind of Trek?

There are many different treks to suit your budget, fitness level and available time, but most walks fall into two categories: teahouse treks and camping treks.

If you stick to the established trails in the Annapurna, Langtang, Everest or Manaslu regions, you can depend on frequent lodges to offer food and accommodation every few hours, which makes everything a lot simpler. To head into remoter areas or to beat the crowds you will have to camp.

Most independent trekkers plan to sleep and eat in lodges every night and forgo the complications of camping. You can carry your own pack and rely on your own navigation skills and research; or you might find it makes sense to hire a local porter to carry your main backpack so that you can enjoy walking with only a daypack. A good guide can make life easier (especially if you become ill) and can enhance your trekking experience by offering additional security and cultural insight, though a bad one will just make life more complicated. Most popular trails are not hard to follow in good weather, so you don't strictly need a porter or guide for route-finding alone.

Independent trekking does not mean solo trekking; in fact, we advise trekkers not to walk alone. It simply means that you are not part of an tour organised by a trekking agency.

To save time, many people organise a trek through a trekking agency, either in Kathmandu or in their home country. Such organised treks can be simple lodge-to-lodge affairs or extravagant expeditions with the full regalia of porters, guides, portable kitchens, dining tents and even toilet tents.

Trekking is physically demanding. Some preparation is recommended, even for shorter treks. You will need stamina and a certain fitness level to tackle the steep ascents and descents that come with trekking in the highest mountain range in the world. It makes sense to start on some kind of fitness program at least a month or two before your trek. That said, Nepal's treks are well within the range of most active people.

Teahouse Trekking

The main trekking trails have lodges (also called teahouses; p324) along their entire length, meaning you can walk for weeks carrying only the bare minimum of equipment.

By arranging your accommodation and food locally, on the spot, you can move at your own pace, set your own schedule and take impromptu side trips or days off that are not possible with an organised group. You also know that your money is going directly to local lodge owners rather than wealthy companies in Kathmandu or abroad.

On the down side, because you are relying on finding food and accommodation every day, you are limited to the better-known routes and will be trekking in the company of other tourists. Teahouse treks are sociable events, which can be great, but much of your cultural interaction will be with foreign trekkers rather than Nepalis. Most lodge owners on the main routes are too busy being short-order cooks to allow them much opportunity to talk to trekkers.

Still, teahouse trekking in Nepal is a luxury that few other places in the world can match. It's an unrivalled way to trek in freedom and comfort right into the heart of the mountains. Most of the routes in the Everest and Annapurna regions can be done as comfortable teahouse treks. More routes around Langtang, Gosainkund, Helambu and Manaslu were teahouse treks before the 2015 earthquake, but damage in these areas is severe and many routes will only be possible as camping treks until infrastructure is restored.

Outside the most popular routes, lodges are generally simpler and only open seasonally. The Makalu Base Camp, Lukla to Tumlingtar and Hinku Valley treks are feasible as teahouse treks, but you will

TREKS SUMMARY

TREK	DAYS	DIFFICULTY	MAXIMUM ELEVATION	TREKKING SEASON
Everest Region				
Everest Base Camp	16	medium-hard	5545m	Feb-May, Oct-Dec
Gokyo	12	medium-hard	5360m	Feb-May, Oct-Dec
Three Passes	20	hard	5535m	Mar-May, Oct-Nov
Shivalaya to Lukla	6	medium	3530m	Oct-May
Annapurna Region				
Annapurna Panorama	6	easy-medium	3210m	Oct-May
Khopra Ridge	5-6	medium	3660m	Oct-Nov, Mar-Apr
Annapurna Sanctuary	10	medium	4095m	Mar-Apr, Oct-Nov
Annapurna Circuit	12-18	medium-hard	5416m	Mar-Apr, Oct-Nov
Nar-Phu	7	medium-hard	5320m	May-Oct
Mustang	10	medium-hard	4325m	May-Oct
Langtang, Helambu & Manaslu				
Langtang Valley	7-8	medium	3870m	Sep-May
Ganja La	5	hard	5106m	Mar-May, Oct-Nov
Gosainkund	8	medium-hard	4610m	Mar-Apr, Oct-Nov
Helambu Circuit	6	easy-medium	3640m	Oct-Apr
Around Manaslu	18	medium	5100m	Oct-May
Eastern Nepal				
Lukla to Tumlingtar	7-9	medium	3350m	Oct-Apr
Makalu Base Camp	13	hard	5000m	Mar-May, Oct-Nov
Kanchenjunga North	18-20	hard	5140m	Mar-May, Oct-Nov
Kanchenjunga South	14	hard	4800m	Mar-May, Oct-Nov
Western Nepal				
Rara Lake	9	medium	3710m	Mar-Oct
Jumla to Dunai	6	medium	3820m	Mar-Oct
Kagmara La	4	medium-hard	5115m	Mar-Oct
Phoksumdo Lake	3	medium	3730m	May-Oct
Phoksumdo Lake via Do Tarap	9	hard	5290m	May-Oct
Beni to Dolpo	12	medium-hard	4420m	May-Oct
Phoksumdo Lake to Shey Gompa	7 or more	medium-hard	5160m	May-Oct
Limi Valley	17	medium-hard	4988m	mid-May–early Oct

TEAHOUSES	OTHER INFORMATION	PAGE
excellent	Potential altitude problems; flight hassles in Lukla; some earthquake damage	p68
excellent	Extraordinary scenery but potential altitude problems; some earthquake damage	p91
excellent	Dramatic mountain passes, but high altitude; some earthquake damage	p97
mostly good	Lots of ups and downs; allow 22 days to visit base camp; some earthquake damage	p104
excellent	Outstanding views from Poon Hill	p129
good	Community-run lodges and outstanding views	p133
very good	Spectacular mountain amphitheatre; danger of avalanches	p136
excellent	Classic scenery; one very high pass; excellent side trips	p144
simple	Scenic villages and a preserved pocket of Tibetan culture	p175
simple	Walled city; Tibetan culture and scenery; some earthquake damage	p184
very good	High alpine valley and glaciers; close to Kathmandu; severe earthquake damage	p199
none	May require technical mountaineering skills in snow; severe earthquake damage	p204
mostly good	Sacred lakes and Himalayan views; some earthquake damage	p205
very good	Good transport from Kathmandu; cheap and easy; severe earthquake damage	p208
good	cliffside trails, mountain views, Tibetan culture; severe earthquake damage	p211
primitive	Hot in Arun Valley; alternative exit, or approach, from Khumbu; some earthquake damage	p220
simple	Steep climb to Barun Valley; rain or snow likely; some earthquake damage	p229
patchy	Long, hot approach; remote base camp	p234
primitive	Flights to/from Suketar (Taplejung); excellent mountain scenery	p241
none	Complicated logistics but an outstanding trek; lots of birds	p251
minimal	Deep forests; interesting villages with unique culture	p258
none	High, remote and potentially dangerous	p261
basic	Spectacular high-altitude lake and dramatic scenery	p262
none	Through a steep gorge to Tibetan villages and high passes	p264
none	A true journey and wide range of scenery; great views of Dhaulagiri	p269
none	Lots of mystique surrounding Crystal Mountain	p275
none	Remote triangular walk on the borders of Tibet; some earthquake damage	p279

sometimes be limited to dormitory accommodation and daal bhaat for dinner. There are also some homestays established for trekkers in regions such as Tsum Valley and the Tamang Heritage Trail.

Outside popular trekking regions there is often a network of fledgling lodges or simple *bhatti* (local-style inns), which cater mostly to porters. A few experienced trekkers travel with just a sleeping bag and sleep and eat daal bhaat in these local *bhatti*, but life can be pretty uncomfortable at times and you'll need good language skills to pull this off. It's far more common for foreigners to travel through these areas with a contingent of guide and porters.

Teahouse trekking is generally inexpensive. A reasonable daily budget for food and accommodation in the Annapurna and Everest regions is US$20 per person per day, without a guide or porter. Add on another US$10 for wi-fi access and the occasional hot shower. For more on teahouses and food, see those sections in the Directory chapter.

Camping Treks

In more remote areas you cannot rely on finding accommodation so you'll need to arrange a full camping trek. You can arrange this independently, hiring a couple of porters and a cook through a trekking agency but providing your own tents and food, or you can let a trekking agency arrange the whole thing, from porters to a dining tent.

There are few completely empty areas in Nepal and people live in even the most remote trekking areas, so the completely self-sufficient trekking style of carrying all your own gear, a stove, food, water and a tent is usually unnecessary.

Even if you plan to travel light in a small group of two or three, you'll still need a minimum number of crew. You'll likely need a porter to carry some of your gear, and that porter will also need to carry his own gear and tent, so you'll need another porter to help him carry that, as well as his gear and probably a stove for them. Two trekkers can just about get away with two porters and a cook-porter, but it's harder to travel any lighter than that.

Your staff will carry a kerosene stove, kitchen gear and a certain amount of dried foods, restocking with rice and fresh vegetables in local villages as you go. Because you'll carry tents and a stove for the crew,

you do not have to camp near villages, and can trek comfortably to remote regions and high altitudes, enjoying the solitude of remote valleys and your own private Himalayan views.

On the flip side, because itineraries and camping spots are quite standardised on many treks, you may find yourself sharing sites with other camping groups and even in competition with other groups to get to the best sites first. Just because you are on a camping trek or in a restricted area, don't think that you'll necessarily have the place to yourself.

There's little point camping on a teahouse trek, unless you have a large group in high season, when finding enough rooms in a lodge can be a problem.

Guides & Porters

If you don't want to carry all your gear, have children or elderly people in your party, or if you plan to walk in regions where you have to carry in food, fuel and tents, you should consider hiring a porter (*bhaaria* in Nepali) to carry your baggage.

Even if you are teahouse trekking you will still have to carry a certain amount of gear (warm clothes, camera, medical kit, chocolate supply) and many teahouse trekkers employ a porter to help carry it, freeing you up to take photos and simply enjoy the trails. The freedom of carrying your own pack may appeal, but remember that that pack will weigh a lot more at 4500m than it does in your living room. Most people find it's well worthwhile hiring a porter, though there are currently no requirements to do so.

There is a distinct difference between a guide and a porter. A guide should speak English, know the terrain and the trails, and supervise porters, but probably won't carry a load or do menial tasks such as cooking or putting up tents. Porters are generally only hired for load-carrying, although an increasing number speak some English and know the trails well enough to act as porter-guides. A *sirdar* is a head guide who organises a group of porters and camp assistants.

Professional porters employed by camping groups usually carry their loads in a bamboo basket known as a *doko*. Porter-guides used to dealing with independent trekkers normally prefer to carry your backpack on their shoulders. They will likely carry a daypack for their own gear, packed on top of your pack or worn on their front.

If you make arrangements with one of the small trekking agencies in Kathmandu, expect to pay around US$25 per day for a guide and US$15 for a porter. These prices generally include your guide/porter's food and lodging.

Finding Guides & Porters

To hire a guide, look on bulletin boards, check out forums (such as www.lonely-planet.com/thorntree or www.trekking-partners.com), hire someone through a trekking agency, or check with the office of KEEP (p31). It's not difficult to find guides and porters, but it is hard to be certain of

their reliability and ability. Don't hire a porter or guide you meet on the street in Kathmandu or Pokhara.

If during a trek you decide you need help, because of illness, problems with altitude, blisters or weariness, it will generally be possible to find a porter. Most lodges can arrange a porter, particularly in large villages or near an airstrip or roadhead, where there are often porters who have just finished working for a trekking party and are looking for another load to carry.

Whether you're making the arrangements yourself or dealing with an agency, make sure you clearly establish your itinerary (write it down and go through it day by day), how long you will take, how much you are going to pay and whether that

---

TREK DESCRIPTIONS IN THIS GUIDE

Each trek account in this guide includes a general explanation of the lay of the land, but these are not self-guiding trail descriptions. If you are not travelling with a Nepali guide, you will sometimes need to ask about the correct path. The treks in this guide were researched just before the 2015 earthquakes and have been updated since using local sources, but it will be some time before the full extent of the damage caused by the disaster becomes clear. On any route, it is a sensible precaution to seek local advice on the current state of trails and infrastructure before starting your trek.

The route descriptions are separated into daily stages, thus giving an overview of the number of days required for each trek. Your actual stopping place will depend on your fitness, health, the weather, trail conditions, arrangements with the porters and personal preference. Any moderately fit trekker can accomplish the suggested daily stages in one day.

It is notoriously difficult to determine distance in Nepal. With the many gains and losses of altitude and twists and turns of the trails in Nepal, pure map measurements of trekking routes become virtually meaningless.

At high altitudes, in order to avoid altitude sickness, you should proceed no faster than the ascent times recommended in the trek descriptions, even if that means ending the day's walk before lunch.

Bear in mind the following conventions used in this guide:

➡ The terms 'true left' or 'true right' are used to describe the banks of a stream or river. The 'true left' bank simply means the left bank as you look downstream.

➡ Walking times are based on actual walking time and do not include time for snacks, photography or side trips.

➡ To help you plan a teahouse trek that offers alternative night stops, we've included a table with walking times between accommodation for each major trek in the Everest Region, Annapurna Region and Langtang & Helambu chapters.

➡ The elevations given in the trek descriptions are composites based on our measurements with an altimeter or GPS unit and the best available maps.

➡ Trek profiles give a rough indication of the steepness of the trail and the duration of the trek. Major high and low points are marked for each day, but some of the smaller ascents and descents are not shown. The vertical scale is the same on each chart, so it's easy to compare treks.

includes your porter's food and accommodation. It's always easier to agree on a fixed daily inclusive rate for your guide and porter's food and accommodation rather than pay their bills as you go. Note that you will have to pay your porter/guide's transportation to and from the trailhead and will have to pay their daily rate for the time spent travelling.

It's standard policy to pay up to 50% of your porter's wages up front, though naturally you have to be careful when hiring a porter you've just met at a trailhead.

Obligations to Guides & Porters

An important thing to consider when you decide to trek with a guide or porter is that you become an employer. This means that you may have to deal with disagreements over trekking routes and pace, money negotiations and all the other aspects of being a boss. Be as thorough as you can when hiring people and make it clear from the beginning what the requirements and limitations are.

Porters often come from the lowland valleys, are poor and poorly educated, and are sometimes unaware of the potential dangers of the areas they are being employed to work in. Stories abound of porters being left to fend for themselves, wearing thin cotton clothes and sandals when traversing high mountain passes in blizzard conditions.

When hiring a porter you are morally responsible for the welfare of those you employ. Many porters die or are injured each year and it's important that you don't contribute to the problem. If you hire a porter or guide through a trekking agency, the agency will pocket a percentage of the fee but it should provide insurance for the porter (check with the agency).

There are some trekking companies in Nepal, especially at the budget end of the scale, who simply don't look after the porters they hire.

The following are the main points to bear in mind when hiring and trekking with a porter:

➡ Ensure that adequate clothing is provided for any staff you hire. Clothing needs to be suitable for the altitudes you intend to trek to and should include adequate footwear, headwear, gloves, windproof jacket, trousers and sunglasses.

➡ Ensure that whatever provision you have made for yourself for emergency medical treatment is available to porters working for you.

➡ Ensure that porters who fall ill are not simply paid off and left to fend for themselves (it happens!). They should be taken down in order to access medical treatment and accompanied by someone who speaks the porter's language and also understands the medical problem.

➡ If you are trekking with an organised group using porters, be sure to ask the company how they ensure the well-being of porters hired by them.

In order to prevent the abuse of porters, the **International Porter Protection Group** (www.ippg.net) was established in 1997 to improve health and safety for porters at work, to reduce the incidence of avoidable illness, injury and death, and to educate trekkers and travel companies about porter welfare.

You can learn a lot about the hardships of life as a porter by watching the excellent BBC documentary *Carrying the Burden,* shown daily at 2pm at KEEP.

If you're hiring your own porters, contact the Porters' Clothing Bank at KEEP, a scheme that allows you to rent a set of protective gear for your porter for Rs 500 (with a Rs 1500 deposit). **Porters' Progress UK** (www.portersprogressuk.org) operates a similar clothing bank (p118) at Lukla. If you've got gear left over at the end of your Everest trek, consider donating it there.

Organised Trekking

There are more than 300 trekking agencies in Nepal, ranging from those connected to international travel companies down to small agencies that specialise in handling independent trekkers. Organised treks can vary greatly in standards and costs so it's important you understand exactly what you are getting for your money.

A number of companies offer escorted teahouse treks. Porters carry your gear, and a guide travels with the group during the day and handles all of the arrangements for meals and deals with the bureaucracy. You'll generally pay a per-day inclusive fee that includes food and accommodation (but not beer), but this is open to negotiation. This arrangement works best with single trekkers or groups of fewer than five.

If you want to organise your own private camping trek, you would do best to contact a Nepal trekking company well in advance. It takes a day or more to organise the gear and logistics for a camping trip, longer for

Top: Annapurna Himal (p129)

Right: Lobuche (p102), Everest

a remote trek that involves flight bookings, permits and logistical issues such as pre-arranging supplies of kerosene and yaks. If you have not organised the trek in advance, you should be prepared to spend up to a week choosing a company, settling the details, waiting for permits and meeting your trekking crew.

Organised treks normally cost US$60 to US$100 per person per day for a fully equipped camping trek, or US$40 to US$60 for a teahouse trek, depending on the itinerary, group size and level of service.

If you plan to trek in areas damaged by the 2015 earthquakes, particularly Langtang, Gosainkund, Helambu and Manaslu, you may need to join an organised trek until infrastructure is restored.

International Trekking Agencies

At the top of the price range are foreign adventure-travel companies with glossy brochures. If you just have three week's holidays, an organised trek from abroad will give you the best bang for your time, if not your buck.

A fully organised trek provides virtually everything: tents, sleeping bags, food and porters, as well as an experienced English-speaking *sirdar* (trail boss), Sherpa guides and sometimes a Western trek leader. You'll trek in real comfort with tables, chairs, dining tents, toilet tents and other luxuries. All you need worry about is a daypack and camera.

The cost will probably include accommodation in Kathmandu before and after the trek, tours and other activities, as well as the trek itself. Organised treks generally charge solo travellers a supplement if you don't want to share a tent or room.

Foreign-run companies based in Nepal include the excellent **Project Himalaya** (www.project-himalaya.com) and **Kamzang Treks** (www.kamzang.com).

Local Trekking Agencies

It's quite possible (and it can save a lot of money) to arrange a fully organised trek when you get to Nepal. There are hundreds of trekking agencies in Nepal but many are fly-by-night operators with little first-hand knowledge of the trails. Always ask your prospective agency about its environmental and social policies.

➡ You gain a measure of protection by booking with an agency that is a member of the **Trekking Agencies' Association of Nepal** (TAAN; ☏01-4427473; www.taan.org.np; Maligaun Ganeshthan, Kathmandu). You are always better off booking through a recognised trekking agency than through a trekking guide you meet on the streets of Thamel or Pokhara.

➡ Several agencies run specialist treks: **Nature Treks** (☏01-4381214; www.nature-treks.com) focuses on wildlife, birdwatching and community ecolodge treks, while **Purana Yoga & Treks** (☏061-465922; www.nepalyogatrek.com) is one of several agencies that run yoga treks on all the main trails.

➡ **3 Sisters Adventure Trekking** (☏061-462066; www.3sistersadventure.com)

➡ **Adventure Pilgrims Trekking** (☏01-4424635; www.trekinnepal.com)

➡ **Adventure Treks Nepal** (☏9851065354; www.adventurenepaltreks.com)

➡ **Alpine Adventure Club Treks** (☏01-4260765; www.alpineadventureclub.com)

➡ **Ama Dablam Trekking** (☏01-4415372; www.amadablamadventures.com)

➡ **Asian Trekking** (☏01-4424249; www.asian-trekking.com)

➡ **Crystal Mountain Treks** (☏01-4428013; www.crystalmountaintreks.com)

➡ **Earthbound Expeditions** (Map p56; ☏01-4701051; www.enepaltrekking.com)

➡ **Explore Himalaya** (Map p51; ☏01-4418100; www.explorehimalaya.com)

➡ **Explore Nepal** (☏01-4226130; www.xplorenepal.com) Trek and tour agency with commendable ethical policies; money from trips helps to fund litter clearing and other environmental projects.

➡ **Firante Treks & Expeditions** (☏01-4000043; www.firante.com)

➡ **Friends in High Places** (☏01-5525656; www.fihp.com)

➡ **High Spirit Treks** (☏01-4701084; www.allnepaltreks.com)

➡ **Himalaya Journey** (☏01-4383184; www.himalayajourneys.com)

➡ **Himalayan Encounters** (Map p56; ☏01-4700426; www.himalayanencounters.com; Kathmandu Guest House courtyard, Thamel) This company has a solid reputation. Its overnight Trisuli trips stay at the Trisuli Center camp, near Big Fig beach, while its Seti trips hike in from Bandipur. It also arranges treks.

➡️ **Himalayan Glacier** (☎️01-4411387; www.himalayanglacier.com)

➡️ **International Trekkers** (☎️01-4371397; nepal@intrek.wlink.com.np)

➡️ **Journeys International** (☎️01-4414662; journeys@mos.com.np)

➡️ **Langtang Ri Trekking & Expedition** (☎️014423360, 014424268; www.langtang.com)

➡️ **Mountain Travel Nepal** (☎️01-4361500; www.mountaintravelnepal.com)

➡️ **Multi Adventure** (☎️01-4257791; www.multiadventure.com.np)

➡️ **Nepal Social Treks** (☎️01-4701573; www.nepalsocialtreks.com)

➡️ **Shangri-la Nepal Trek** (☎️01-4810373; www.shangrilanepal.com)

➡️ **Sherpa Society** (☎️01-4249233; www.sherpasocietytrekking.com)

➡️ **Sherpa Trekking Service** (☎️01-4421551; www.sts.com.np)

➡️ **Sisne Rover Trekking** (☎️061-462208, 061-461893; www.sisnerover.com; Pokhara)

➡️ **Thamserku Trekking** (☎️01-4000701; www.thamserkutrekking.com)

➡️ **Trek Nepal International** (☎️01-4701001; www.treknepal.com)

Information

The following organisations in Kathmandu offer free, up-to-date information on trekking conditions, health risks and minimising your environmental impact. They are also excellent places to visit and advertise for trekking companions.

Himalayan Rescue Association (HRA; Map p56; ☎️01-4701223; www.himalayanrescue.org; 1st fl, Mandala St, Thamel; ⊙2-5pm Sun-Fri) Runs health posts at Pheriche, Macchhermo (with a porters' shelter), Gokyo and Manang and hopes to eventually run a post at Thorung Phedi on the Annapurna Circuit. Free lectures on altitude sickness are held at the Thamel office upstairs at 3pm Monday to Friday, as well as at the various health posts. You can buy T-shirts and patches to support their work.

Kathmandu Environmental Education Project (KEEP; Map p56; ☎️01-44100952; www.keepnepal.org; Thamel; ⊙10am-5pm Sun-Fri; 🛜) Has a library, some vaguely useful notebooks, an excellent noticeboard and a small cafe. It also sells iodine tablets (Rs 1000), biodegradable soap,

trekking garbage bags and other environmentally friendly equipment. It's a good place to find a trek partner or to donate clothes to the Porters' Clothing Bank. It shifts location frequently, so check before heading out.

Trekking Agencies' Association of Nepal Details trekking regulations, oversees the TIMS card program and can mediate in disputes with trekking agencies.

Maps

Most trekkers are content to get one of the trekking route maps produced locally by **Himalayan Map House** (www.himalayan-maphouse.com) or Nepa Maps. They are relatively inexpensive (Rs 400 to Rs 800) and adequate for the popular trails, though not for off-route travel. They are found everywhere in map and bookshops in Thamel. Be aware that there is a great deal of repackaging going on; don't buy two maps with different covers and names assuming you are getting significantly different maps.

The best series of maps of Nepal is the 1:50,000 series produced by Erwin Schneider and now published by Nelles Verlag. They cover the Kathmandu Valley and the Everest region from Jiri to the Hongu Valley, as well as the Khumbu region. You may also find older 1:100,000 Schneider maps of Annapurna and Langtang.

National Geographic produces 1:125,000 trekking maps to the Khumbu, Everest Base Camp, Annapurna and Langtang areas, as part of its Trails Illustrated series.

All of these maps are available at bookshops in Kathmandu and at some speciality map shops overseas, including the following:

Stanfords (www.stanfords.co.uk)

Omni Resources (www.omnimap.com)

Melbourne Map Centre (www.melbmap.com.au)

Documents & Fees
TIMS Card

All trekkers are required to register their trek by obtaining a **Trekking Information Management System** (TIMS; www.timsnepal.com) card, administered by the Trekking Agencies' Association of Nepal. The card costs the equivalent of US$20

BARTOSZ HADYNIAK/GETTY IMAGES ©

PICTUREGARDEN/GETTY IMAGES ©

Top: Ama Dablam
(p83), in Mount
Everest National Park

Left: Annapurna Himal
(p129)

for individual trekkers or US$10 if you are part of a group. Trekkers from SAARC countries pay US$6 (US$3 for groups). You currently need to show the TIMS card at the start of the Annapurna, Langtang and Everest treks. You can sometimes fill one out on the spot, but you may have to pay double so it's better to get one in advance.

There were rumours that the requirements would be tightened before the 2015 earthquakes, and rumours afterwards that the rules would be relaxed to encourage more trekkers – enquire about the latest rules and regulations when you visit.

The easiest place to get a TIMS card is from the Tourist Service Centre (p59) in Kathmandu, mainly because you can also get conservation area and national park tickets in the same building. Bring two passport photos (though you can currently get free digital photos on the spot). The card is issued on the spot; green for individuals and blue for group trekkers.

If you just need a TIMS card there's a more central **TIMS Centre office** (Map p56; Manang Plaza; ☺7am-6pm Sun-Fri, 10am-noon Sat), also in Kathmandu, on the eastern side of Thamel, opposite Osho Travels. Bring a copy of your passport and two photos.

Authorities occasionally consider putting an end to solo independent trekking, possibly by requiring a guide or porter as part of TIMS registration. As yet there are no plans to follow through on this, though this could certainly change in the future.

National Park & Conservation Fees

If your trek enters a national park such as Langtang, Sagarmatha (Everest), Makalu-Barun, Rara Lake or Shey-Phoksundo, you will need to pay a national park fee. You can pay the fee at the entry to the parks, or in advance from the **national parks office** (☑4224406 www.dnpwc.gov.np; ☺9am-2pm Sun-Fri), which is located at the Tourist Service Centre, a 20-minute walk from Thamel in Kathmandu. The fee is Rs 3000 for each park, and there is talk of adding tax onto this. No photo is required.

If you are trekking in the Annapurna, Manaslu or Gauri Shankar (Rolwaling) regions, you must pay a conservation area fee to the **Annapurna Conservation Area Project** (ACAP; ☑01-4222406; www.ntnc.org.np; Bhrikuti Mandap; ☺9am-4pm), which is also

at the Tourist Service Centre. Bring Rs 2000 and two photographs. The permit is issued on the spot. For Manaslu you will need to already have your restricted-area permit.

Conservation fees for the Annapurna area are also payable in Pokhara at the **ACAP** (☑061-463376; ☺10am-5pm Sun-Fri, 4pm Sat, to 4pm winter), at Damside inside the Nepal Tourism Board (NTB) office, or in Besi Sahar. Note that if you arrive at an ACAP checkpoint without a permit you will be charged double for the permit.

Restricted-Area Trekking Permits

Restricted-area trekking permits are not required for the main treks in the Everest, Annapurna and Langtang regions.

The following treks require restricted-area trekking permits, which can only be obtained through registered trekking agencies. The level of services you book through the agency is up for discussion; for some treks you can just hire a porter and/or guide, others require the trek to be fully organised. Permits are only available for groups of two and up, so if you want to trek alone you'll have to pay for two permits. Note that the Mustang and Upper Dolpo permits were reduced in price after the 2015 earthquakes; no end date has been given for this arrangement so check the current rates as part of your trek planning.

AREA	TREKKING FEE
Humla	US$50 for 1st week, then US$7 per day
Kanchenjunga & lower Dolpo	US$10 per week
Manaslu	US$70 for 1st week, then US$10 per day Sep-Nov; US$50 per week then US$7 per day Dec-Aug
Nar-Phu	US$90 per week Sep-Nov, US$75 per week Dec-Aug
Tsum Valley	US$35 for first eight days Sep-Nov; US$25 for first eight days Dec-Aug
Upper Mustang & upper Dolpo	US$100 for 1st 10 days (reduced from US$500 after the 2015 earthquakes), then US$50 per day

Responsible Trekking

The trekking industry has brought many benefits to Nepal, from employment opportunities and wealth generation among marginalised rural people to funding for schools and health centres, but it has also brought problems, largely in terms of environmental degradation and the loss of traditional culture.

There are many ways you can lessen your impact; for example, by choosing an environmentally and socially responsible company and being responsible with garbage, water and firewood. For tips on how to be an environmentally responsible trekker see p321. KEEP (p31) is also a good resource for tips on responsible trekking. For cultural tips see the People & Culture chapter (p307).

➡ Don't hand out money, sweets (candy) or presents indiscriminately to children, as this merely encourages begging.

➡ If you want to give something, consider gifts like Nepali school books, pens and paper, biodegradable soap and toothbrushes, and hand them to teachers or community leaders.

➡ Respect local culture by wearing modest clothing, asking permission before taking photographs, behaving appropriately at religious sites and respecting local customs.

➡ After your trek consider making a donation to a local or international NGO that is working in rural Nepal.

Trekking For a Cause

A number of trekking agencies use the proceeds of trekking trips to support charitable projects and some offer volunteering options as part of a trek. Some travellers undertake sponsored treks and climbing expeditions in Nepal to raise money for specific projects.

Following is a list of organisations offering volunteering treks in Nepal; but Lonely Planet does not endorse any organisations that we do not work with directly, so it is essential that you do your own thorough research before agreeing to volunteer with anyone.

➡ **Australian Himalayan Foundation** (www. australianhimalayanfoundation.org.au) Offers fundraising treks to its aid projects.

➡ **Community Action Treks** (www.catreks. com) Offers various treks that contribute to the work of Community Action Nepal.

➡ **Crooked Trails** (www.crookedtrails.com) Runs fundraising treks and volunteer programs.

➡ **Dolma Ecotourism** (www.dolmatours.com) Runs cultural-immersion treks that provide income for a remote village in Langtang.

➡ **Global Vision International** (www.gvi.co.uk) Offers one-month volunteer placements on educational and conservation projects as part of an Everest Base Camp trek.

➡ **Himalayan Healthcare** (www.himalayan-healthcare.org) Arranges medical and dental treks around Nepal.

➡ **Himalayan Travel** (www.himalayantravel. co.uk) UK agency offering treks to support the Nepal Trust (www.nepaltrust.org).

➡ **Restoration Works International** (www. restorationworksinternational.org) Offers paid volunteer treks to Mustang to help with the restoration of Chairro Gompa.

➡ **Summit Climb** (www.summitclimb.com) Runs an annual service trek providing health care in remote parts of Solu Khumbu.

➡ **Umbrella Trekking Nepal** (www. umbrellatrekkingnepal.com) Offers internships to disadvantaged youth and provides funding for a children's charity.

Trekking Peaks

None of the treks in this guide requires any mountaineering skills. If you want to cross the line between trekking and mountaineering, your best bet is to try one of Nepal's trekking peaks. The name 'trekking peak' can be quite deceiving; few of the trekking peaks are 'walk-ups', and some of them, such as Kusum Kangru and Lobuche East, offer technically demanding and potentially dangerous mountaineering challenges.

Permits

To climb one of Nepal's 33 trekking peaks you need to organise permits from the **Nepal Mountaineering Association** (NMA; ☎01-4434525; www.nepalmountaineering.org; Nag Pokhari). The peaks are classified into two groups, with fees ranging from US$70 to US$400 per person, depending on the peak and the season. See the association website for a list of peaks and fees.

All people ascending trekking peaks must be accompanied by a *sirdar* (leader) who is registered with the NMA. You must insure any Nepali who goes beyond base camp. All peaks require a refundable garbage deposit of US$250.

Organised Climbs

Because of the bureaucracy involved, it is easiest to use an adventure travel company to organise the climb, rather than do the running around yourself. Trip permit fees are included in all of the prices listed in this guide but you will have to hire your own plastic climbing boots (Rs 200 to Rs 350 per day in Namche Bazaar, double this in Chhukung). For details on individual trekking peaks see the relevant destination chapters of this guide.

The most popular trekking peak in Nepal is Island Peak (Imja Tse; 6189m) in the Everest region. Trips run weekly in season (mid-October to mid-November, and the end of March to May) and cost around US$700. Mera Peak (6476m) is another popular choice, and the highest of the trekking peaks, but involves 10 days of trekking to get there. For details see p85.

Other popular trekking peaks are Chulu West (6419m) and Pisang Peak (6091m) in the Annapurna region, and Naya Kangri (5846m) in the Langtang region.

Several companies run trekking peaks as part of a standard trek. In the Everest region this includes the Everest Base Camp trek and Island Peak (21 to 23 days) or Lobuche East (25 days). Pisang Peak or Chulu West can be combined with the Annapurna Circuit trek in around 25 days.

Foreign mountaineering companies such as **Jagged Globe** (www.jagged-globe.co.uk) and **Adventure Consultants** (www.adventure.co.nz) also operate trekking peak

trips to Island Peak, Lobuche East and Pokalde (5806m), as well as guided mountaineering ascents of more technical peaks such as Ama Dablam and Baruntse.

Trekking companies in Kathmandu that organise ascents of trekking peaks include the following:

Climb High Himalaya (Map p56; ☏01-4701398; www.climbhighhimalaya.com; Mandala St)

Equator Expeditions (Map p56; ☏01-4700854; www.equatorexpeditionsnepal.com; Thamel, Kathmandu) This company specialises in long participatory rafting/kayaking trips and kayak instruction but also offers treks.

Himalayan Ecstasy (Map p56; ☏01-4700001; www.himalayanecstasynepal.com) One of the best for well-run tuition and peak climbing. In addition to the main trekking peaks, they also offer Island and Lobuche Peaks together in one trip for US$1350.

Mountain Monarch (☏01-4373881; www.mountainmonarch.com; Hattigauda)

Peak Promotion (☏01-4263115; www.peak-promotionnepal.com) Top-end company.

Information

Bill O'Connor's comprehensive guidebook *The Trekking Peaks of Nepal* includes photographs, maps, trekking information and climbing routes on 18 trekking peaks.

Trekking peak maps available in Kathmandu include *Paldor* (1:34,000), *Island Peak and Mera Peak* (1:30,000), Ganja La (1:80,000), *Chulu Peaks* (1:50,000) and *Pisang Peak* (1:50,000).

The designated Mountaineering section of the Ministry of Tourism in the Bhrikuti Mandap's Tourist Service Centre (p59) in Kathmandu maintains information files about expeditions, approach routes and other aspects of mountaineering in Nepal.

Plan Your Trip
Clothing & Equipment

The task of kitting yourself out for a trek and then packing it can feel almost overwhelming at times, but preparing for a trek in Nepal is essentially no more complicated than equipping yourself for a weekend backpacking trip. Pack light and right with the following tips.

Top Tips

Dress in Layers

A wickable base layer next to the skin, an insulating fleece, and a waterproof shell.

Avoid Cotton

T-shirts and shirts made from synthetic material such as polypropylene are expensive but wick moisture away from the body, dry quickly and reduce chilling.

Equipment in Kathmandu

Kathmandu's trek shops sell everything, including excellent-value down jackets, fleeces and trekking poles.

Know your Gear

You can rent or buy trekking gear in Nepal but it's much better to know your gear and break it in beforehand, especially your boots.

Pack Light

The key to packing light is to take things that can fulfil more than one purpose: a down jacket can act as a camping pillow.

Smell Fresh

Tip: put a couple of dryer sheets in your laundry bag to keep your dirty clothes smelling fresh.

Clothing

The type of gear you need depends largely on the type of trek you are planning. If you intend to stay in teahouses you won't need camping equipment, which makes life a lot easier. On a wilderness camping trek, you will need more equipment for a DIY trip than you will for an organised camping trek, where the company will provide tents, mats, cutlery etc. Treks above 4000m require you to be better equipped than a lowland trek.

Some people teahouse trek with almost nothing. When the weather is good, the hotels aren't full and you have no health problems, this arrangement can work. But the mountains are not always kind, and you may find yourself lost or caught in a snow- or rainstorm a long way from a hotel. It's always best to be prepared for the worst in Nepal.

If you are on a group trek, have your entire kit organised in advance because you won't have much time in Kathmandu to shop for gear (plus there are more interesting things to do here). Porters carry a maximum of 30kg, and it is expected that a porter will carry the luggage of two trekkers. Domestic flights also limit you to a 15kg luggage allowance (plus 5kg carry on).

Waterproof Jacket, Poncho or Umbrella

It is likely to rain at some time during your trek. A waterproof jacket is useful as an outer layer but be sure it's breathable otherwise the condensation inside can leave you wetter than the rain. Fabrics such as Gore-Tex are supposed to be breathable, but in lowland Nepal it's usually so warm, and the hills so steep, they don't always work as advertised. Armpit vents and map pockets are things to look for. Most of the 'Gore-Tex' equipment sold in Kathmandu is not genuine.

Ponchos can be a low-tech alternative as they give better air circulation and can keep your backpack dry. Inexpensive ponchos, umbrellas and waterproof pack covers are available in Kathmandu.

Umbrellas can double as a sunshade, a walking stick, an emergency toilet shelter and a dog deterrent.

Trousers, Shorts & Skirts

Almost any long, comfortable, quick-drying trousers will do except jeans, which take too long to dry.

The early stages of your trek will likely be hot and humid and many trekkers wear pants with zip-off legs that become shorts. Skimpy track shorts are culturally unacceptable throughout Nepal.

Many women recommend trekking skirts for trailside toilet stops, in conjunction with leggings.

A set of thermal underwear doubles as a warm pair of pyjamas and is also useful during late-night toilet trips. Silk thermals are warmest and lightest but less hard-wearing than other materials.

A swimsuit, sarong or pair of shorts can be useful for washing in rivers or bathing in hot springs.

Footwear

The most important item you will bring is proper footwear and you should bring these from home, wearing them on the plane in case your baggage gets lost or delayed. Lightweight hiking shoes are fine, even for long treks, if there is no snow. For rockier trails and scree, the ankle support offered by boots is invaluable, though these are hotter and heavier than low-cut shoes. Hard, nonslip soles, such as Vibram, provide the best grip and protection.

Gore-Tex waterproofing is essential for snow and rain but limits breathability, so bring a pair of odour-eaters or slip a car air-freshener under your insole.

Buy boots in warm conditions or go for a walk before trying them on, so that your feet can expand slightly, as they would on a walk. Make sure also that you try them on wearing thick socks. It's essential to break in your shoes on several hikes (particularly up and down hills) before you come to Nepal. Be sure your shoes provide enough room for your toes. There are many long and steep descents during which short boots can painfully jam your toes, causing the loss of toenails.

If you are travelling with porters, you have the luxury of carrying two sets of shoes. Trekking sandals, light trainers and even thongs (flip-flops) are comfortable to change into for the evening, can serve as trail shoes if you get blisters and are useful if you expect to be fording streams.

Miniature crampons like **Microspikes** (www.kahtoola.com) and **Yaktrax** (www.yaktrax.com) can make a huge difference when crossing icy high passes, especially during winter.

Equipment
Backpack & Duffle Bag

If you have porters, they will carry your main bag, leaving you to carry a daypack containing your camera, water bottle, extra clothing and a small first-aid kit (everything you need for that day). A 35L to 45L daypack with a foam waistband is most versatile and can double as an overnight backpack.

Professional porters generally carry their loads in a bamboo basket called a *doko*, which is carried suspended from the forehead with a tumpline called a *naamlo*. In this case it's a good idea to carry your gear in a lockable duffle bag, which some foreign trekking companies will provide for you if you book their tour. Duffles are also the way to go if you will be using horses or yaks to carry your gear. End-loading duffles are less practical than top-loaders. Expect your duffle bag to age 20 years over the course of a two-week trek.

Porter-guides and some freelance porters may actually prefer to carry your

CLOTHING & EQUIPMENT CHECKLIST

This list is a general guide to the things you might take on a trek. Your list will vary depending on the type of trek and on the terrain, weather conditions and time of year.

Clothing

➡ Trekking boots and spare laces
➡ Hat (warm), scarf and gloves
➡ Waterproof jacket, poncho or umbrella
➡ Hiking shoes, sandals or thongs (flip-flops)
➡ Wool-blend socks (for snow), Cool-max socks (for warmer weather) and underwear (three pairs)
➡ Sunhat with strap and wide brim
➡ Fleece jacket
➡ Quick-drying T-shirts (two or three) and long-sleeved shirt with collar

Equipment

➡ Backpack and daypack
➡ Sleeping bag and silk liner
➡ Maps, compass and guidebook
➡ Water bottle, plus collapsible bladder if camping
➡ LED head torch (flashlight) and spare batteries
➡ Duffle bag (if on an organised trek)

Self-Organised Camping

➡ Trowel (if no toilet tent)
➡ Tent and sleeping mat
➡ Cooking, eating and drinking utensils
➡ Dishwashing items
➡ Stove (with wind screen and maintenance kit) and fuel

Miscellaneous Items

➡ Toiletries (in travel-size bottles with screw-on lids)

➡ Quick-drying camp towel
➡ Biodegradable laundry soap
➡ Toilet paper and cigarette lighter
➡ Sunscreen (SPF 20plus) and lip balm
➡ Polarising sunglasses and hard case
➡ Water-purification (p348) tablets, filter or Steripen
➡ Medical kit (p346)
➡ Blister kit (moleskin, tape, scissors) on hand at all times
➡ Insect repellent (for lower elevations)
➡ Emergency kit including a whistle and waterproof matches/lighter
➡ Locks for bags and lodge rooms
➡ Stuff sacks and Ziploc bags
➡ Gaffer/duct tape for repairs

For Treks above 4000m

➡ Thermal underwear and down jacket
➡ Gaiters

Optional Equipment

➡ Camera, memory card and battery charger (or spare batteries)
➡ GPS unit
➡ Smart phone or tablet/Kindle and charger
➡ Small duffle bag (to leave behind in Kathmandu)
➡ Backpack cover (waterproof, slip-on)
➡ Trekking poles
➡ Antibacterial gel or premoistened towelettes (baby wipes)
➡ Pocket knife

backpack and may have trouble with a duffle bag, so try to ascertain how your porter will carry your bag before packing it.

Waterproof nylon or plastic bags inside your bag will protect your belongings (especially your sleeping bag) from the rain, as will a waterproof backpack cover.

Bring a small collapsible and lockable bag to leave your city clothes and other items at your hotel in Kathmandu.

Tent

A three-season tent will fulfil the requirements of most trekkers. The floor and the outer shell, or fly, should have taped or sealed seams and covered zips to stop leaks. Free-standing dome-shaped tents are most popular because they are easy to put up on rocky ground, generally have enough head room to sit up in and handle windy conditions well. Look for a tent that is well venti-lated and that has a decent-sized vestibule.

Sleeping Bag

This is one item you should consider bring-ing from home. Down bags are warmer than synthetic for the same weight and bulk but, unlike synthetic fillings, do not retain warmth when wet. Mummy bags are the best shape for weight and warmth. The manufacturer's bag ratings (-5°C, for instance) are generally optimistic, so err on the side of warmth. If you are camping above 4000m bring a 0°F (-18°C) bag.

The loft in down sleeping bags varies from 550 to 800 cubic inches; the higher the fill, the lighter (but more expensive) your bag will be for the same warmth rat-ing. Compression straps will ensure down items take up the least space possible.

An inner sheet helps keep your sleeping bag clean, as well as adding an insulating layer. Silk liners are lightest and warmest and you can use them instead of a sleeping bag in the warm lowlands.

When camping, an inflatable sleeping mat is essential to insulate you from the cold. Three-quarter-length mats provide the best combination of weight versus warmth. Foam mats are a low-cost, but less comfortable, alternative. You don't need a mat on the more popular teahouse treks.

Heavy dews on mid-altitude treks can cause a lot of condensation in your tent so bring a small camp towel.

Stove

If you are organising your own camping trek you will need a stove. If you organise porters and cook staff through an agency, they will normally provide their own stove.

A multifuel stove is small and efficient but the poor quality of Nepali kerosene means that they regularly clog up with soot, so bring a cleaning kit. The frequent main-tenance can drive you mad and will leave your hands covered in soot and kerosene for days. The clunky low-tech Nepali stoves are much more reliable with local kerosene.

Butane gas canisters are available in Kathmandu, Pokhara and Namche Bazaar (Rs 500 to 900) but you can't take them on planes. At altitudes above 3500m a butane/propane mix is preferable. Canisters are hard to dispose of responsibly and you never quite know how much gas you have left.

Cheap Chinese-made, Primus-style burners are available in Kathmandu for around US$20 to US$40. Kerosene is avail-able at most trailheads and towns.

When it comes to cookware, titanium pots are lighter than aluminium and steel and just as durable. A 'spork' saves weight by doubling as a spoon and a fork.

Buying & Hiring Locally

It is helpful to have all your gear before you leave home, but if you're just slotting a teahouse trek into a longer trip through Asia, you could theoretically pick up all the gear you need in Kathmandu or Pokhara.

Buying Gear in Nepal

Kathmandu's Tridevi Marg, to the east of Thamel, has a collection of imported gear shops selling everything from Therm-a-Rests and MSR stoves to Deuter backpacks and Black Diamond climbing harnesses, and even imported trekking boots, all at prices comparable to those in the West.

Kathmandu also has a wide range of inexpensive, locally produced trekking and climbing gear. Most items are reasonably well made and will probably last through a short trek. Many items are copies of high-tech brand-name equipment, right down to the fake labels, so don't be fooled into thinking that you are getting a bargain on genuine brand-name equipment.

The best 'fake' gear is made from real materials, ie imported Gore-Tex and fleece, but produced in Nepal. Some of the best buys include locally made down jackets and vests, duffle bags, waterproof back-pack covers and fleece jackets.

Namche Bazaar has fantastic trekking equipment shops because many expedi-tions jettison their gear there. You can find items like sunscreen in shops in Manang and Jomsom.

Hiring Equipment

You can rent most things you need in Kathmandu, from down jackets to sleep-ing bags and tents, although you should bring your own trekking shoes or boots. All shops require a deposit to ensure you return the equipment in good condition.

A limited supply of equipment is availa-ble for rent in Pokhara and Namche Bazaar.

Plan Your Trip
Trekking Safely

Nepal's devastating earthquakes in April and May 2015 were a powerful reminder that trekking in mountainous terrain carries inherent risks. While only a tiny proportion of trekkers have any problems in Nepal, a small number of people do die or go missing on Nepal's trekking trails every year, and it's important to be aware of the risks and take steps to avoid becoming another statistic.

Golden Rules

Never Trek Alone

Almost all deaths, disappearances and incidents of violent crime in Nepal have involved trekkers travelling alone. Unless you are an experienced trekker or have a friend to trek with, you should at least take a porter or guide.

Crossing Passes

Keep an eye on weather reports if planning to cross a high pass, and never cross a pass with less than three people.

Altitude Sickness

Be aware of the symptoms of altitude sickness (p349) and never ascend more than 500m per day above 3000m.

Let Someone Know

Register with your embassy (p329) and carry the contact details of your embassy and trekking company with you. Leave your itinerary with someone at home.

Carry an Emergency Kit

Your day pack should always include water purification supplies, a blister kit, a whistle, a torch, a map, snacks, a spare T-shirt and a raincoat.

Be Prepared for Emergencies

Carry suitable clothing for adverse weather conditions and emergency food and water (or a means of purifying water). A plastic survival bag weighs little but can keep you warm and dry in the worst conditions.

On The Trail

Once you are on the trail in Nepal you will quickly realise just how far you are from medical help and how responsible you are for your own well-being. Even a twisted ankle or sore knee can become a serious inconvenience if you are several days away from help and your companions need to keep moving. Remember to always travel with your own medical kit (p346) so you can deal with minor medical problems.

Always trek with a partner – you'll really appreciate having someone around when you're lost, sick or suffering from altitude sickness. It's also useful to have someone to occasionally watch your pack or valuables when you visit the bathroom or take a shower. To find a fellow trekking companion, check the bulletin board at KEEP (p31) in Kathmandu or post a message on www.trekinfo.com, www.trekkingpartners.com or www.lonelyplanet.com/thorntree.

Despite the apparent ease and convenience of teahouse trekking, it's important to have a healthy respect for the mountain environment. Bear the following in mind:

➡ Many of the trails are in more remote areas are exposed, with steep drop-offs. Keep your eyes firmly on the narrow, slippery trails and not the stellar mountain views.

➡ You will be sharing the trail with porters, mules and yaks, all usually carrying heavy loads, so give them the right of way. If a mule or yak train approaches, always move to the high side of the trail to avoid being knocked over the edge. Be very cautious of dogs in Tibetan areas.

NATURAL DISASTERS IN NEPAL

Nepal has suffered more than its fair share of deadly disasters in recent years, with avalanches and landslides that claimed the lives of dozens of trekkers and mountaineers in 2014 and 2015, and devastating earthquakes on 25 April and 12 May 2015. Trekking routes in Langtang, Helambu, Manaslu and Tsum were particularly badly affected, and further tremors, avalanches and landslides remain a possibility.

However, it's important to keep these disasters in perspective. Earthquakes, landslides and avalanches are a risk in any mountainous region in the world, and while it's hard to predict when a natural disaster will occur, you can take steps to minimise the risks if you get caught in one of these events. Carrying emergency food and water, and appropriate clothing for the conditions is always a sensible policy, and you are more likely to be rescued in the event of a disaster if you let people know your itinerary and where you are going. By following the advice in this chapter, you will be taking the most important steps to stay safe in the mountains.

➡ High passes have particular dangers including rockfalls, snow, avalanches and high altitude. All members of the party, including sherpas and porters, must have good equipment before attempting these routes. The chance of snow increases from December to April, but at any time of year snow on a pass might force you to turn back.

➡ In recent years sudden storms have struck the mountains with increased frequency, especially during the peak trekking months of October and November. In October 2014, over 20 trekkers were killed in the Thorung La region of the Annapurna Circuit during a cyclone-induced blizzard. Never underestimate the changeability of the weather and seek shelter promptly if conditions deteriorate. It is never wise to leave a safe location in bad weather just to keep to your planned itinerary.

➡ If you cross fresh landslides or avalanches, do so one person at a time, with someone keeping an eye on falling objects from above.

➡ On a different topic, fires do occasionally break out in trekking lodges (most of which are made of wood), so it's worth keeping your escape route in the back of your mind.

Altitude Sickness

At least three trekkers die each year in Nepal from altitude illness; such deaths are preventable if trekkers follow the appropriate steps to avoid this life-threatening condition. See the Health chapter (p349).

The good news is that most people can travel safely up to a height of around 2800m without getting ill. As long as you don't ascend with altitude illness symptoms, and you descend promptly if your symptoms appear to be worsening, you have almost no chance of dying from altitude illness in Nepal.

Eighty percent of altitude-sickness deaths occur in organised trekking groups (even though only 40% of people trek in an organised group). Since people on an organised trek don't want to be left behind on a 'trip of a lifetime', they will often hide or minimise their symptoms. Even if their symptoms become apparent, an inexperienced trek leader may minimise their importance to avoid the logistical complications of splitting up the group. If you feel ill, make sure your trekking companions are aware of this.

Always bear the following in mind when crafting your itinerary:

➡ Most of the treks in this guide reach over 4000m, and many over 5000m. On high treks like these ensure adequate acclimatisation by limiting altitude gain above 3000m to 500m per day.

➡ The maxim of 'walking high, sleeping low' is good advice; your night halt should ideally be at a lower level than the highest point reached in the day.

➡ Make a point to catch the free altitude lectures given by the Himalayan Rescue Association (p349) in Kathmandu, or at their Manang and Pheriche aid posts on the Annapurna and Everest treks respectively.

Crime

Theft is a rarity in the hills of Nepal, though it's not unknown on popular trekking routes. It pays to be cautious anywhere within a day or two from a road.

A number of trekkers have disappeared in recent years from Chhukung and Dingboche in Everest, from Langtang and Gosainkund and from the Sikles region of the Annapurnas and it's suspected that some of these cases involve foul play.

ASKING DIRECTIONS

It isn't easy to get totally lost in the hills of Nepal but finding the exact trail you want, particularly through a large village or on an exposed scree slope, can sometimes be a challenge. Watch for the footprints of other trekkers and for arrows or dots marked on rocks by guides. Fresh yak dung is always a good sign when crossing a pass.

Trek routes can change from season to season. The routes described in this guide were the main trails in use during the peak trekking season, but in the monsoon, seasonal bridges are often washed away and lower trails flooded, so you'll have to find the established alternative routes. This is likely to be an even bigger issue following the 2015 earthquakes so it is always worthwhile asking locals about current trail conditions.

When asking directions be sure to phrase the question in a way that forces people to point the way. '*Kun baato Namche Bazaar jaanchha?*' ('Which trail goes to Namche Bazaar?') will usually do the job. If you point to a trail and ask if it goes where you want to go, most Nepalis will say yes, because they want to please you. This will be much easier if you hire a guide or porter who can translate for you.

➡ Solo women trekkers should choose male guides particularly carefully.

➡ If you are camping, be warned that thieves have been known to cut tents in the night and reach inside to grab whatever is handy. Minimise opportunistic theft by not leaving your boots near the door of your tent or outside a hotel room, or your clothing hanging on a line outside at night.

➡ While trekking, carry your money yourself, either in a money belt or hidden in an interior zipped pocket of the pack you are carrying. Never store valuables or money in your hotel room. Flashing a pile of money around at a tea stall invites night-time theft.

➡ One of the most common forms of theft is when backpacks are rifled through when they're left on the roof of a bus. Try to make your pack as theft-proof as possible – small padlocks and cover bags are a good deterrent.

Emergencies

The remoteness of most treks in Nepal means trekkers have to be well prepared for the possibility they could become sick or injured on the trail and need to return to Kathmandu. In recent years, communication from the mountains to Kathmandu has improved dramatically with the presence of both mobile (cell) phones and satellite phones. The police and the army posts throughout the country also have radio capability.

An emergency helicopter rescue can cost US$6000, and medical evacuation by air ambulance to Bangkok costs in excess of US$75,000, so it's essential that you have insurance (p331) that will cover evacuation. If you need evacuation from the mountains, payment must be cleared in advance, normally through your credit card. On established teahouse trekking routes, lodge owners may be able to call for the rescue, process your credit card, and pay the helicopter company for you. Other options for arranging rescue include through your trekking company (make sure they have your insurance details) or via your embassy, which will help contact a family member. In the event of a natural disaster, the government will usually organise emergency rescue teams to search for people caught up in the disaster.

Rescue time can vary from as short as an hour to as long as two days (if weather is a problem). Once a request is sent, stay put for at least two days, or make it clear in the message where and how you will be travelling. If you see the helicopter, make an effort to signal it. It is very difficult to pick out people on the ground from a helicopter moving at 145km/h, especially if you are unsure where to look. Try to locate a field large enough to land a helicopter safely, but do not mark the centre of the field with cloth, as this can fly up and wreck the rotors on landing.

While helicopters can fly as high as 6000m, they are rarely able to land and take off above 5500m, as the air is too thin to give the rotors sufficient lift. In most areas of Nepal, horses or yaks will be available to help transport a sick or injured trekker. In mild cases of altitude sickness, your lodge should be able to find some porters to help get you and your belongings down the mountain quickly.

Regions at a Glance

Everest Region

Teahouses
Scenery
Passes

Teahouses

The Sherpa-run lodges in the Everest region are the best in Nepal, with many offering pizza, hot showers and wi-fi, and most survived the 2015 quake. You'll never be more than an hour away from a hot cup of tea. The downside? Lots of company in high season.

Mountain Views

Everyone comes here for a glimpse of the world's highest peak but the Khumbu's other peaks are equally alluring. Views of Ama Dablam, Cho Oyu and the Gokyo lakes or views from the top of Chhukung Ri are the real highlights here.

The High Himalaya

For the ultimate trekking challenge, the roller-coaster Three Passes trek links the Everest region's four main valleys via three 5000m-plus passes, offering jaw-dropping views over glaciers, frozen lakes and a skyline of peaks.

p62

Annapurna Region

Villages
Culture
Scenery

Gurung & Thakali Villages

Mostly beyond the earthquake's reach, the Annapurna region is no wilderness, but treks wind through fascinating villages, from the former trading centres of Manang, Jomsom and Thukche to the medieval Tibetan-style hamlets of Bragha and Kagbeni.

Sacred Sites

Trails here are lined with chortens, mani walls, prayer wheels and village monasteries. Muktinath ranks as one of the holiest pilgrimage sites in the Nepal Himalaya, while sacred caves and pre-Buddhist shrines dot the sacred landscape.

Annapurna & Machhapuchhare

These two giants capture the eye from almost everywhere in the Annapurna region. Our favourite views are those from Ngawal (on the Annapurna Circuit) or from Annapurna Base Camp.

p124

Langtang, Helambu & Manaslu

Scenery
Detours
Proximity

Mountain Views

The earthquake devastated villages and teahouses, but the scenery endures. The views near Kyanjin Gompa and along the trails around Manaslu are stupendous, but likely to be reserved for camping groups until infrastructure is restored.

Scenic Detours

Before the quake, this region was famous for the scenic detours that could easily be tacked on to the end of a trek around Langtang or Helambu – such as the Ganja La and treks to the sacred lakes at Gosainkund. These may become the new focus for trekking.

Proximity

The big perk of trekking in central Nepal is the proximity to Kathmandu. No long approach treks or alarming flights to remote airstrips are needed, making the routes ideal for trekkers with tight schedules. However, massive work is underway to help these areas rebuild after the earthquakes.

p196

Eastern Nepal

Culture
Scenery
Nature

An Ethnic Mosaic

Mostly untouched by the 2015 earthquakes, the east is a patchwork of Sherpa, Rai, Limbu and Walung villages. Family-run teahouses between Lukla and Tumlingtar offer the chance to overnight in remote villages and share a *tongba* (millet beer) with mountain-dwellers.

High Peaks

Views of the world's third and fifth highest mountains from Kangchenjunga and Makalu Base Camps rival anything in the country, but little-known peaks like Jannu, Peak 4 and Chamlang also put on an incredible show.

Flora & Fauna

The Himalaya's wettest and lowest corner also offers its greatest natural diversity. Expect to hike past rhododendrons, orchids and bamboo, through the habitat of red panda and blue sheep into high glacial valleys, all on the same trek!

p218

Western Nepal

Solitude
Tibetan Culture
Nature

Off the Beaten Trek

Hardly touched by the earthquakes, the west is the place to get away from the teahouse crowds. Difficult access, limited supplies and a scarcity of lodges mean you'll get the trails to yourself. Dolpo and Limi in particular feel like the end of the world.

Monasteries & Mani Walls

Dolpo is essentially an extension of the Tibetan plateau. Here you'll find pristine Tibetan culture, lovely villages, remote pockets of Bon belief, unique styles of chortens and plenty of wizened old Tibetans swinging their prayer wheels.

Wilderness

The west is scarcely inhabited and contains some of Himalaya's last untouched corners. This is a land of blue sheep and snow leopards, where you need to be fully self-supporting, camping in remote valleys far from the nearest civilisation.

p248

On the Track

Western
Nepal
p248

Annapurna
Region
p124

Langtang,
Helambu &
Manaslu
p196

Kathmandu
p46

Everest
Region
p62

Eastern
Nepal
p218

Kathmandu

♪ 01 / POP 1 MILLION / ELEV 1337M

Best Places to Eat

➡ Gaia Restaurant (p55)

➡ Third Eye (p55)

➡ Kaiser Cafe (p55)

Best Places to Stay

➡ Hotel Ganesh Himal (p53)

➡ Dwarika's (p54)

➡ Kantipur Temple House (p53)

Why Go?

For many, stepping off a plane into Kathmandu is a pupil-dilating experience, a riot of sights, sounds and smells that can quickly lead to sensory overload. Whether you're barrelling through the traffic-jammed alleyways of the old town in a rickshaw, marvelling at the medieval temples or dodging trekking touts in the backpacker district of Thamel, Kathmandu can be an intoxicating, amazing and exhausting place.

The 2015 earthquake brought devastation to parts of the city – including Kathmandu's Unesco-listed Durbar Square – but many areas emerged unscathed, and the soul of the city endures. Stroll through the backstreets and Kathmandu's timeless cultural and artistic heritage will reveal itself in hidden temples overflowing with marigolds, courtyards full of drying chillies and rice, and tiny hobbit-sized workshops.

This endlessly fascinating, sometimes infuriating city has enough sights to keep you busy for a few days, but you'll soon be longing to breathe some fresh mountain air. When you come back after your trek, the backpacker comforts will feel like heaven.

When to Go

➡ Autumn (October to November) is the most popular time to visit, with fine mountain views and warm days but also peak-season crowds, so reserve hotels and restaurants ahead. Trekkers will be interested in December's Kathmandu International Mountain Film Festival.

➡ Spring (March to May) brings comfortable temperatures, though days can be hot in May. Time a March trek with Kathmandu's Seto Machhendranath festival or Nepali new year celebrations in Bhaktapur.

➡ Winter (December to February) is a quiet time but nights can be chilly. Pashupatinath's Maha Shivaratri Festival attracts thousands of sadhus (Hindu holy men) in February/March.

➡ The monsoon months (June to September) are considered low season but include September's Indra Jatra festival.

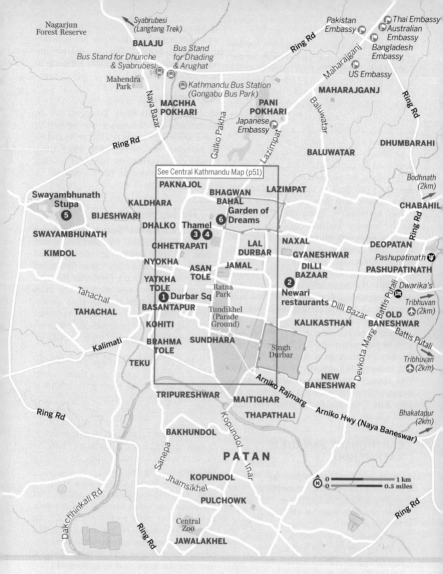

Kathmandu Highlights

1 Admiring the amazing architectural monuments that defied the earthquake in **Durbar Sq** (p48), whose artistic and architectural legacy rivals the great cities of Europe.

2 Dining on momos (dumplings) and wild boar to the beat of *madal* (drums)

and *bansari* (flutes) at one of the city's classy **Newari restaurants** (p55).

3 Ensuring the love of friends and family by snapping up the bargains in **Thamel's shops** (p58).

4 Chilling out in one of **Thamel's garden restaurants** (p54) with a good book, a pot

of masala tea and a slice of chocolate cake.

5 Taking a day trip to the nearby Unesco World Heritage Site of **Swayambhunath** (p52).

6 Escaping the traffic in the peaceful and beautifully restored Rana-era **Garden of Dreams** (p50).

History

The history of Kathmandu is really a history of the Newars, the main inhabitants of the Kathmandu Valley. The foundation of Kathmandu itself dates from the 12th century AD, during the time of the Malla dynasty. The original settlement grew up around the trade route to Tibet. Traders and pilgrims stayed at rest houses such as the Kasthamandap, which later lent its name to the city.

Originally known as Kantipur, the city flourished during the Malla era, and the bulk of its superb temples and other monuments date from this time. In the 15th century the valley divided into three independent kingdoms: Kathmandu, Patan and Bhaktapur. Rivalry between the three city-states led to a series of wars that left each state vulnerable to the 1768 invasion of the valley by Prithvi Narayan Shah.

The ensuing Shah dynasty unified Nepal and made the expanded city of Kathmandu its new capital – a position the city has held ever since. A massive earthquake in 1934 destroyed much of the old city.

During the Maoist uprising (1996–2005), tens of thousands of Nepalis flooded into the rapidly growing city to escape the political violence. Infrastructure in Kathmandu was already over-stretched when a series of massive earthquakes struck in April and May 2015. Thousands were killed and many

EARTHQUAKE DAMAGE IN KATHMANDU

Sitting on a bed of vulnerable clay, Kathmandu bore the full force of the earthquake on 25 April 2015, but not all parts of the city were affected equally. Thamel, the most popular district for accommodation, eating and nightlife, saw relatively little damage, and Bodhnath and Pashupatinath also escaped with only minor damage.

The most serious damage was reported in districts with many old buildings, including Kathmandu's famous Durbar Square, but even here, damage was uneven – temples at the south end of the square toppled while those to the north were almost untouched by the disaster. Other badly affected areas include Gongabu, near the main Kathmandu bus station, and Kalanki, at the start of the road to Pokhara.

of Kathmandu's most famous monuments were reduced to rubble. While life is slowly returning to normal after the disaster, the repercussions of the earthquake are likely to be felt for generations.

◉ Sights

Most of the interesting things to see in Kathmandu are clustered in the old part of town, around the majestic Durbar Sq and its surrounding backstreets. With more time, consider a trip out to the medieval cities of **Patan** and **Bhaktapur**, both accessible by local bus.

◉ Durbar Square

Kathmandu's **Durbar Square** (Map p51; foreigner/SAARC Rs 750/150, no student tickets) was where the city's kings were once crowned and legitimised, and from where they ruled (*durbar* means 'palace'). Even after the 2015 earthquakes, which saw many of the most famous temples tumble from their pedestals, the square remains the traditional heart of the old town and preserves Kathmandu's most spectacular legacy of traditional architecture.

A Unesco World Heritage Site, Durbar Square is actually made up of three loosely linked squares. To the south is the open **Basantapur Sq** area, a former royal elephant stables that now houses souvenir stalls, but this area took the full force of the earthquake, and several temples were completely destroyed, including the landmark Maju Deval temple and Kasthamandap, the pavilion that gave the city its name.

The main Durbar Square area is to the west. Running northeast is a second part of Durbar Sq, which contains the entrance to the **former palace of Hanuman Dhoka** and an assortment of historic statues and spectacular temples with ornate carved timbers. From this open area, **Makhan Tole**, at one time the main road in Kathmandu and still the most interesting street to walk down, continues northeast. Here you'll find some of Kathmandu's most eye-catching monuments, including the towering **Taleju Temple**, the giant mask of **Seto (White) Bhairab** and the fearsome statue of **Kala (Black) Bhairab**.

It's easy to spend hours wandering around the interlinked squares, marvelling at the temples and watching the world go by. An offering at the **Ashok Binayak shrine** is thought to ensure safety on a forthcoming journey, so come here before departing on your trek.

★Hanuman Dhoka
PALACE, MUSEUM
(Map p51; admission free with Durbar Sq ticket; ⊙10.30am-4pm Tue-Sat Feb-Oct, to 3pm Tue-Sat Nov-Jan, to 2pm Sun) Kathmandu's royal palace, known as the Hanuman Dhoka, was originally founded during the Licchavi period (4th to 8th centuries AD) but the compound was expanded considerably by King Pratap Malla in the 17th century. Sadly, the sprawling palace was hit hard by the 2015 earthquake and damage was extensive. At the time of research, the palace was closed for reconstruction, but once this work is complete, visitors should again be able to access the beautiful royal courtyards and royal museum.

Kumari Bahal
COURTYARD
(Map p51) At the junction of Durbar and Basantapur Sqs, this red-brick, three-storey building is home to the Kumari, the girl who is selected to be the town's living goddess until she reaches puberty and reverts to being a normal mortal. The goddess is regarded as a living symbol of *devi* - the Hindu concept of female spiritual energy. Inside the building is Kumari Chowk, a three-storey courtyard. It is enclosed by magnificently carved wooden balconies and windows, making it quite possibly the most beautiful courtyard in Nepal. Amazingly, the *bahal* escaped with only minor damage despite the devastation all around – a sign perhaps of the Kumari's benign influence.

◉ North of Durbar Square

Hidden in the fascinating backstreets north of Durbar Sq is a dense sprinkling of colourful temples, courtyards and shrines. Visit the following sights on a backstreet wander from Thamel to Durbar Sq.

Kathesimbhu Stupa
BUDDHIST STUPA
(Map p51) The most popular Tibetan pilgrimage site in the old town is this lovely stupa, a small copy dating from around 1650 of the great Swayambhunath complex. The stupa is set in a hidden courtyard, which saw only minor damage in the 2015 earthquake. Just as at Swayambhunath, there is a two-storey pagoda to Hariti, the goddess of smallpox, in the northwestern corner of the square. In the northeast corner is the Drubgon Jangchup Choeling Monastery. It's just a couple of minutes' walk south of Thamel.

BEAUTIFUL BODHNATH

Head east from the centre by taxi or local bus to see **Bodhnath Stupa** (foreigner/SAARC Rs 200/50), Kathmandu's most spectacular stupa.

The first stupa at Bodhnath was built sometime after AD 600, when the Tibetan king, Songtsen Gampo, converted to Buddhism. In terms of grace and purity of line, no other stupa in Nepal comes close to Bodhnath. From its whitewashed dome to its gilded tower painted with the all-seeing eyes of the Buddha, the monument is perfectly proportioned. The stupa had a lucky escape in the 2015 earthquake and repairs to the tower were underway at the time of writing.

★Asan Tole
SQUARE
(Map p51) From dawn until dusk the junction of Asan Tole is jammed with vegetable and spice vendors selling everything from yak tails to coconuts. It's the busiest square in the city and a fascinating place to linger, if you can stand the crowds. Cat Stevens wrote his hippie-era song 'Kathmandu' in a smoky teahouse in Asan Tole.

★Seto Machhendranath Temple (Jan Bahal)
TEMPLE
(Map p51) Southwest of Asan Tole at the junction known as Kel Tole, this temple attracts both Buddhists and Hindus – Buddhists consider Seto (White) Machhendranath to be a form of Avalokiteshvara, while to Hindus he is a rain-bringing incarnation of Shiva. The temple's white-faced god is taken out during the Seto Machhendranath festival in March/April each year and paraded around the city in a chariot. The temple's age is not known but it was restored during the 17th century.

★Indra Chowk
SQUARE
(Map p51) The busy street of Makhan Tole spills into Indra Chowk, the courtyard named after the ancient Vedic deity, Indra. Locals crowd around the square's newspaper sellers, scanning the day's news. Indra Chowk is traditionally a centre for the sale of blankets and cloth, and merchants cover the platforms of the Mahadev Temple to the north. The next-door stone Shiva Temple to the northeast is a smaller and simplified version of Patan's Krishna Temple.

East of Thamel

★Garden of Dreams　　　　　　GARDENS
(Swapna Bagaicha; Map p56; ☑01-4425340; www.
gardenofdreams.org.np; adult/child Rs 200/100;
☺9am-10pm, last entry 9pm) Despite some
damage from the 2015 earthquake, the beautifully restored Swapna Bagaicha, or Garden
of Dreams, remains one of the most serene
and beautiful enclaves in Kathmandu. It's
two minutes' walk and one million miles
from central Thamel.

Narayanhiti Palace Museum　　　MUSEUM
(Map p51; ☑01-4227844; foreigner/SAARC Rs
500/250; ☺11am-4pm Thu-Mon, closes 3pm Nov-
Jan) Few things speak clearer to the political
changes that have transformed Nepal
over the last decade than this walled palace
at the northern end of Durbar Marg. King
Gyanendra was given 15 days to vacate the
property in 2007 and within two years the
building was reopened as a people's museum by then Prime Minister Prachandra, the
very Maoist guerrilla leader who had been
largely responsible for the king's spectacular
fall from grace.

🏃 Activities

Mountain Flight　　　　　SCENIC FLIGHTS
(flights US$206) A popular activity from Kathmandu is to take an early morning scenic
mountain flight along the spine of the Himalaya for close-up views of Mt Everest and other peaks from a distance of just five nautical
miles. Major airlines like Buddha Air and
Yeti Airlines offer the hour-long flights and
each passenger on the six- to 30-seat turbo
props is guaranteed a window seat.

Seeing Hands　　　　　　　MASSAGE
(Map p56; ☑01-4253513; www.seeinghandsnepal.
org; massage 60/90min Rs 1800/2800; ☺10am-
6pm) A branch of the Pokhara-based organisation that offers massage from blind
masseurs, providing employment to some
of Nepal's 600,000 blind people. Choose
between a relaxing post-trek Swedish massage or remedial sports therapy for specific
issues.

🤝 Tours

Social Tours　　　　　　COOKING COURSE
(Map p56; ☑01-4412508; www.socialtours.com)
This innovative company runs a half-day
Nepali cookery course that involves a trip

Central Kathmandu

to a local market to get ingredients for momos, spinach curry, *alu gobi* (potato and
cauliflower), tomato pickle and *alu paratha*
(fried chapatti with potato). Pay what you
think the experience is worth and then eat
your homework.

Central Kathmandu

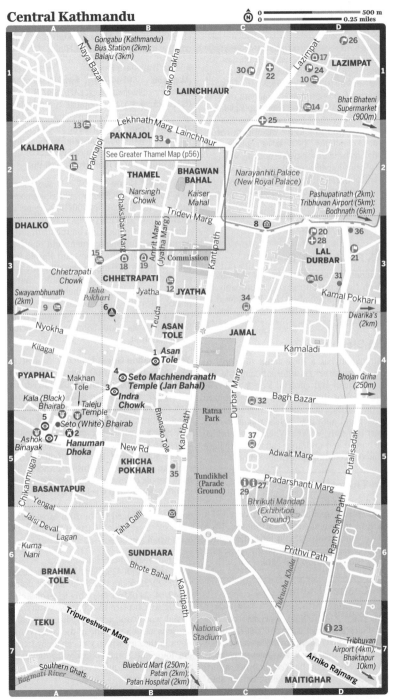

THE 'MONKEY TEMPLE'

The **Swayambhunath Stupa** (foreigner/SAARC Rs 200/50), west of Kathmandu city, is one of the crowning glories of Kathmandu Valley architecture. This perfectly proportioned monument rises through a whitewashed dome to a gilded spire, from where four faces of the Buddha stare out across the valley in the cardinal directions. The noselike squiggle below the piercing eyes is actually the Nepali number *ek* (one), signifying unity, and above is a third eye signifying the all-seeing insight of the Buddha. The site was shaken severely by the 2015 earthquake but the main stupa sustained only superficial damage.

✷ Festivals & Events

Kathmandu has many religious festivals, of which the most outrageous is probably Indra Jatra in September, closely followed by the Seto Machhendranath chariot festival in March/April.

🛏 Sleeping

Kathmandu has a huge range of places to stay, from luxurious international-style hotels to cheap and cheerful lodges, and only a handful of them suffered severe damage in the earthquakes. Bear in mind that for budget and midrange hotels, rooms in each hotel can vary widely. When hotels bridge the budget and midrange categories we have grouped according to their lowest price.

🛏 Thamel

For budget and midrange places, the tourist ghetto of Thamel is the main local and it escaped the worst in the earthquake. It's a convenient area to stay in for a short time, but you are likely to tire of the noise and congestion in a couple of days.

🛏 Central Thamel

Hotel Potala GUESTHOUSE $

(Map p56; ☑01-4700159; www.potalahotel.com; s/d US$12/18, without bathroom US$8/13, deluxe US$15/20; @🛜) Bang in the beating heart of Thamel, this small backpacker place is a good option, and has free internet, a nice rooftop area and a convenient momo restaurant overlooking Thamel's main drag. Rooms

are simple but clean and decent, with sunny corner deluxe rooms the best. It's down an alleyway near the Maya Cocktail Bar. Don't confuse it with Potala Guest House.

Karma Travellers Home GUESTHOUSE $

(Map p56; ☑01-4417897; www.karmatravellershome.com; Bhagawati Marg; s/d US$14/18, deluxe US$20/25; ✳🛜) This popular central place has decent rooms, several nice terrace sitting areas and helpful owners. The air-con deluxe rooms are more spacious and some rooms come with a balcony. You can get a 20% discount online and a free airport pick-up.

Hotel Silver Home GUESTHOUSE $

(Map p56; ☑01-4262986; www.hotelsilverhome.com; dm Rs 300, s/d Rs 700/1100, deluxe Rs 1200/1500; @🛜) Plus points here include a quiet but central location on the main drag, friendly helpful management and one free airport pick-up. The rooms are simple but come with proper mattresses and hot water in the bathroom, and the hotel shares a little garden with two other good budget places, including the Pokhara Peace Hotel (which has good corner deluxe rooms from Rs 1200 to Rs 1500). Sunny south-facing rooms are best.

★**Kathmandu Guest House** HOTEL $$

(Map p56; ☑01-4700800; www.ktmgh.com; r US$60-100, without bathroom US$2-16, deluxe US$120-180; ✳@🛜) The KGH is an institution. A former Rana palace, it was the first hotel to open in Thamel in the late 1960s and still serves as the central landmark. Everyone from Jeremy Irons to Ricky Martin has stayed here. In strictly dollar terms you can get better rooms elsewhere, but most people enjoy the atmosphere here and it's often booked out weeks in advance. Note that the atmospheric heritage wing of the hotel was damaged in the 2015 earthquake, so check to see which parts of the hotel are open when you book.

International Guest House HOTEL $$

(Map p51; ☑01-4252299; www.ighouse.com; s/d US$29/31, deluxe US$38/43, superior deluxe US$49/54, ste US$60; 🛜) This is a solid and quietly stylish place that boasts century-old carved woodwork, terraced sitting areas, a spacious garden and one of the best rooftop views in the city, which you can enjoy in the sun loungers. Some rooms were damaged by the 2015 earthquake so ask to see a few before deciding.

Hotel Holy Himalaya
HOTEL **$$**

(Map p56; 📞01-4263172; www.holyhimalaya. com; 117 Brahmakumari Marg; s/d US$35/40, deluxe US$45/55, ste US$75/85; ❄@🛜) This is a good midrange find frequented by small in-the-know tour groups. The rooms are simple but reassuring and some come with a balcony. Perks include organic coffee, a nice rooftop garden and free guided meditation in the mornings. The spacious deluxe rooms in the new building across the road offer the best value. Rates include tax and breakfast.

★Kantipur Temple House
BOUTIQUE HOTEL **$$$**

(Map p51; 📞01-4250131; www.kantipurtemple-house.com; s/d US$70/80, deluxe US$110/140) 🌿 Hidden down an alley on the southern edge of Thamel, this Newari-temple-style hotel has been built with meticulous attention to detail. The spacious rooms are tastefully decorated, with traditional carved wood, terracotta floor tiles, window seats and fair-trade *dhaka* (hand-woven) cloth bedspreads. Due to the traditional nature of the building, rooms tend to be a little dark.

Paknajol (Northern Thamel)

This area to the northwest of central Thamel has half a dozen pleasant guesthouses grouped together in a district known as Sorakhutte. They're away from traffic but only a short walk from Thamel.

Nirvana Peace Home
GUESTHOUSE **$**

(Map p51; 📞01-4383053; www.nirvanapeace-home.net; Sorakhutte; s Rs 800, d Rs 1000-1300, r with shared bathroom Rs 700; 🛜) New management has revitalised this superior place in budget-friendly Paknajol. Simple but clean rooms, a nice garden and upstairs lounge hang-out make it one of the best options in this area.

Bhagwan Bahal (Northeastern Thamel)

Alobar 1000
HOSTEL **$**

(Map p56; 📞01-4410114; www.alobar1000; dm Rs 350-550, r Rs 1700-2700) If you are looking to hook up with other young backpackers, this well-run and oddly named place (taken from a Tom Robbins novel) is the most popular hostel in the city. The travel desk offers treks, language classes and city walks, and there's fair-priced laundry and airport

transfers. The sociable rooftop hang-out and restaurant is the place to meet a trekking buddy.

Mi Casa
BOUTIQUE HOTEL **$$**

(Map p56; 📞01-4415149; www.micasanepal. com; r US$50-70) For a stylish, cosy option this place has just nine rooms with splashes of colour from Nepali fabrics and potted plants. The pricier rooms come with kitchenette and terrace; others are smallish. There are a couple of small terraces and a courtyard cafe serving breakfast. The location is useful for both Thamel and the new town. Prices include tax.

Chhetrapati (Southwest Thamel)

This area is named after the important five-way intersection (notable for its distinctive bandstand) to the southwest of Thamel. The further you get from Thamel the more traditional the surroundings become.

★Hotel Ganesh Himal
HOTEL **$$**

(Map p51; 📞01-4263598; www.ganeshhimal. com; s/d US$20/25, deluxe US$30/35, super deluxe r US$40-45; ❄@🛜) Our pick for comfort on a budget is this well-run and friendly place. The rooms are among the best value in Kathmandu, with endless hot water and lots of balcony and garden seating. Throw in free airport pick-up and this place is hard to beat, even if the booking system gets a bit overwhelmed at times.

Tibet Guest House
HOTEL **$$**

(Map p51; 📞01-4251763; www.tibetguesthouse. com; s/d US$16/20, standard US$40/45, deluxe US$50/60, superior US$70/80, ste US$90/100; ❄@🛜) This busy, efficient and popular

---

EARTHQUAKE WARNING STICKERS

After the 2015 earthquakes, the government of Nepal surveyed thousands of buildings to make sure they were safe for human habitation. Look out for prominent stickers indicating if a building is safe, unstable or dangerous:

➡ **Green** Building is safe

➡ **Orange** Some structural problems; only enter if absolutely necessary

➡ **Red** Building is unsafe

hotel gets heavy use and things are looking a bit worn in places, but it's a solid choice, so book in advance. There's a lovely breakfast patio, a lobby espresso bar and the superb views of Swayambhunath from the rooftop just cry out to be appreciated at sunset with a cold beer.

🛏 Elsewhere

★Hotel Tibet   HOTEL $$$
(Map p51; ☎01-4429085; www.hotel-tibet.com. np; s/d US$80/90, ste US$110-120; ❄️🛜) Tibetophiles and tour groups headed to or from Tibet like the Tibetan vibe of this recommended place. The 56 quiet and comfortable rooms are plain compared to the opulent lobby, but several of the larger front-facing rooms have a balcony. There's also a great rooftop terrace bar and a side garden cafe.

★Dwarika's   BOUTIQUE HOTEL $$$
(☎01-4479488; www.dwarikas.com; Battis Putali; s/d US$275/295, ste from US$400; 🛜☀️) For stylish design and sheer romance, this outstanding hotel is unbeatable; if you're on your honeymoon, look no further. Over 40 years the owners have rescued thousands of woodcarvings from around the valley and incorporated them into the hotel design. The end result is a beautiful hybrid – a cross between a museum and a boutique hotel, with a lush, pampering ambience.

Yak & Yeti Hotel   HOTEL $$$
(Map p51; ☎01-4248999; www.yakandyeti.com; d US$240-280; ❄️🛜☀️) This hotel is probably the best known in Nepal, due to its connections with the near-legendary Boris Lissanevitch (known as the godfather of tourism in Nepal), who ran the original restaurant. The hotel is centred on a Rana-era

palace that was slightly damaged in the 2015 earthquake, but the actual rooms are in two modern wings which were not affected. The recently renovated Newari wing incorporates woodcarvings, oil brick walls and local textiles, while the deluxe rooms in the Durbar wing are fresh, modern and stylish.

Shanker Hotel   HISTORIC HOTEL $$$
(Map p51; ☎01-4410151; www.shankerhotel.com. np; s/d US$105/121; ❄️🛜☀️) There's nowhere in town quite like this creaky 19th-century former Rana residence – the kind of place where you expect to bump into some whiskered old Rana prince shuffling around one of the wooden corridors. The entry columns of neoclassical whipped cream overlook a palatial manicured garden and one of the city's nicest swimming pools. The historic lobby area was damaged in the 2015 earthquake, but repairs were underway at the time of writing and rooms were unaffected.

🍴 Eating

Kathmandu has an astounding array of restaurants. Indeed, with the possible exception of the canteen at the UN building, there are few places where you have such a choice of cuisines. After weeks trekking in the mountains, Kathmandu feels like a culinary paradise. Most restaurants in the city are in modern buildings that survived the 2015 earthquakes.

Most midrange restaurants in Kathmandu have tax and service charges totalling 24%. A bottle of beer will double your bill in most places. Make reservations during October's high season. Almost all the following restaurants are in Thamel.

Apart from those listed here, good midrange places include **La Dolce Vita** (Map p56; ☎01-4700612; pastas Rs 310-385, mains

---

KATHMANDU IN...

Two Days

Start off the day exploring Kathmandu's old town south from Thamel to **Durbar Sq** (p48), where you can spend a couple of hours soaking up the architectural grandeur of the city's traditional heart. In the afternoon head out to **Swayambhunath** (p52). If this is your first day back from trekking, head to **K-Too Steakhouse** for a celebratory pepper steak and a cold beer.

Unless you are on an organised trek you'll likely need to spend half a day getting your TIMS card and national park or ACAP permits (p59). Budget the rest of the day for shopping for last-minute trekking snacks, equipment, maps and a bus ticket to your trailhead. For your final meal, splurge at a traditional Newari restaurant like **Bhojan Griha**.

Rs 500-850, house wine per glass Rs 375; ⏰11am-10pm) for Italian, **Yin Yang** (Map p56; ☎01-4425510; www.yinyangrestaurantbar.com; curries Rs 580; ⏰11am-10pm) for Thai and **Or2K** (Map p56; www.or2k.net; mains Rs 180-400; ⏰8am-10pm; 🖉) for vegetarian Middle Eastern food.

⭐**Gaia Restaurant**   INTERNATIONAL **$$**
(Map p56; mains Rs 350-480; ⏰7am-9pm; 🛜) This popular and dependable place combines good breakfasts, salads, sandwiches and organic coffee in a pleasant garden courtyard with global music, reasonable prices (tax included) and good service. The Thai red curry is surprisingly good and the chicken *choiyla* (spicy barbecued meat) packs a punch; you're bound to find something good in a menu that ranges from daal bhaat to carrot cake.

Roadhouse Cafe   PIZZERIA **$$**
(Map p56; ☎01-4262768; Arcadia Bldg; pizzas Rs 350-475; ⏰11am-10pm) The big attractions at this well-run place are the pizzas from the wood-fired oven and the warm and intimate decor, with an open-air courtyard located out the back. The salads, soups, sandwiches, desserts (sizzling brownie with ice cream) and espresso coffees are all top-notch and there are some good Newari snacks, including smoked chicken *sandekho* (marinated with spices).

New Orleans Cafe   INTERNATIONAL **$$**
(Map p56; ☎01-4700736; mains Rs 450; ⏰8am-10pm; 🖉) Hidden down an alley near the Kathmandu Guest House, New Orleans boasts an intimate candlelit vibe and live music on Wednesdays and Saturdays. It's a popular spot for a drink, but the menu also ranges far and wide, from Thai curries and good burgers to Creole jambalaya and oven-roasted vegies. You need to book a table in the high season.

⭐**Fire & Ice Pizzeria**   PIZZERIA **$$$**
(Map p56; ☎01-4250210; www.fireandicepizzeria.com; 219 Sanchaya Kosh Bhawan, Tridevi Marg; pizzas Rs 480; ⏰8am-11pm) This excellent and informal Italian place serves the best pizzas in Kathmandu (wholewheat crusts available, as well as combo pizzas), alongside breakfasts, smoothies, crêpes and good espresso, to a cool soundtrack of Cuban son or Italian opera. The ingredients are top-notch, from the imported anchovies to the house-made tomato sauce.

ℹ️ **LOAD SHEDDING**

Electricity cuts ('load shedding') are a fact of life in Kathmandu; they last for up to 16 hours a day in winter when hydro-power levels are at their lowest. Electricity is currently rationed across the city, shifting from district to district every eight hours or so. Try to choose a hotel with a generator and make sure your room is far away from it.

⭐**Third Eye**   INDIAN **$$$**
(Map p56; ☎01-4260289, 4260160; www.thirdeyerestaurant.com; JP School Rd; mains Rs 475-650; ⏰11am-10pm) This long-running favourite is popular with well-heeled tourists. Indian food is the speciality and the tandoori dishes are especially good, even if the portions are a bit small. Spice levels are set at 'tourist' so let the efficient (if not friendly) suited waiters know if you'd like extra heat.

⭐**Kaiser Cafe**   INTERNATIONAL, AUSTRIAN **$$$**
(Map p56; ☎01-4425341; Garden of Dreams, Tridevi Marg; mains Rs 600-1650; ⏰9am-10pm) This cafe-restaurant in the Garden of Dreams is run by Dwarika's, so quality is high. It's a fine place for a light meal (such as savoury crêpes or build-your-own sandwiches), a quiet breakfast or to linger over a pot of tea or something stiffer. More than anything else, it's one of the city's most romantic locations, especially at dusk.

K-Too Steakhouse   STEAKHOUSE **$$$**
(Map p56; ☎01-4700043; www.kilroygroup.com; mains Rs 450-615; ⏰10am-10pm) The food and warm, buzzy atmosphere here are excellent. Dishes range from chip butties (sandwiches) to healthy salads, but it's really all about the steaks. The pepper steak sizzler followed by fried apple momos and an Everest Beer is a post-trekking classic. For a quieter vibe, head for the garden.

Bhojan Griha   NEPALI **$$$**
(☎01-4416423; www.bhojangriha.com; Dilli Bazaar; set menus Rs 997; ⏰11am-2pm & 5-10pm) 🖉 The most ambitious of the city's traditional Newari restaurants, Bhojan Griha is located in a restored 150-year-old mansion in Dilli Bazaar, just east of the city centre. It's worth eating here just to see the imaginative renovation of this beautiful old building, once the residence of the caste of royal priests. There's a cultural show at 7pm.

Greater Thamel

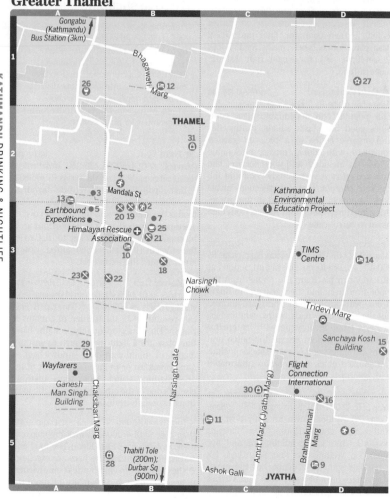

Self-Catering

For trekking supplies, there are several extensive supermarkets grouped around central Thamel Chowk. For larger supermarkets, try the various branches of **Bluebird Mart** (www.bluebirdmart.com.np; ⊙9am-9pm), including one by the main bridge across the Bagmati River to Patan; **Big Mart** (Map p51; ⊙7am-9pm) in Lazimpat, near the Radisson Hotel; and **Bhat Bhateni Supermarket** (☑01-4419181; www.bbsm.com.np; ⊙7.30am-8.30pm), south of the Chinese embassy.

Drinking & Nightlife

There are a few bars scattered around Thamel, all within a short walk of each other. Most places have a happy hour between 5pm and 8pm, with two-for-one cocktails. Nepal is an early-to-bed country and even in Kathmandu you'll find few people on the streets after 10pm.

Himalayan Java   CAFE
(Map p56; ☑01-4422519; www.himalayanjava.com; Tridevi Marg; coffee Rs 110, snacks Rs 300; ⊙7am-9pm) The various branches of this modern and buzzing coffeehouse are the

place to lose yourself in a sofa, a laptop and a pulse-reviving Americano. There are also breakfasts, paninis, salads and cakes. The main Tridevi Marg branch has a balcony, lots of sofas and big-screen TV for the football, but feels a bit like a hotel foyer; the smaller Mandala St branch (Map p56) in Thamel is quiet and popular.

Sam's Bar   BAR
(Map p56; ⊙4-11pm) A long-time favourite with trek leaders, mountain guides and other Kathmandu regulars. There's reggae every Saturday.

House of Music   LIVE MUSIC
(Map p56; ☑9851075172; cover Rs 200-400; ⊙11am-11pm Tue-Sun) This beery bar is the best place in Kathmandu to listen to original Nepali rock, reggae and R 'n' B music, mostly on Friday and Wednesday. It's in northern Thamel but miles away from the cover bands of the centre. Upcoming concerts are posted on the venue's Facebook page. It's part-owned by the drummer of 1974AD, one of Nepal's biggest bands.

🔒 Shopping

Thamel offers the best collection of shops in the country, selling everything from Kashmiri carpets to trekking poles and yak-milk soap. Bring an extra bag and stock up on Christmas presents. Some of the best buys include tea, spices, jewellery, clothing such as pashmina shawls, and yak-hair blankets and scarves. Trekkers often commission embroidered badges and T-shirts commemorating their trek.

Kathmandu has dozens of excellent bookshops with a great selection of Himalaya titles, including books that are not usually available outside the country.

Pilgrims Book House   BOOKS
(Map p56; ☑01-4221546; www.pilgrimsonline-shop.com) Kathmandu's best bookstore tragically burned down in 2013. Hopefully it will reincarnate phoenix-like, but in the meantime its branch location contains as many of the saved books as possible.

Amrita Craft Collection   HANDICRAFTS
(Map p56; ☑01-4240757; www.amritacraft.com) This broad collection of crafts and clothing is a good place to start your Thamel shopping. Quality isn't top-notch but subtract 20% from its fixed prices and you get a good benchmark for what you should aim to pay on the street if you don't mind haggling.

Outdoor Gear

Kathmandu has an excellent selection of outdoor gear these days, from top-priced imported gear to locally made or Chinese knock-offs. Make sure you know what you are getting when making a purchase. The impossibly cute baby-sized 'North Face' fleeces and down jackets are particularly hard to pass by.

PRAYER FLAGS

If you want to buy a string of prayer flags to hang on a pass during your trek, the best place to visit is the street in front of the **Kathesimbhu Stupa** (p49) south of Thamel. Most feature an image of the Lungta, or Wind Horse, who carries the mantras to heaven, though Buddhist deities and even mythological animals are also popular designs. Choose between cheaper polyester and better-quality, biodegradable cotton flags and remember, this is your karma we're talking about.

Shona's Alpine Rental   OUTDOOR EQUIPMENT
(Map p56; ☑01-4265120) Reliable rentals and gear shop that makes its own sleeping bags and offers advice on the best trek gear for your trip. Get a season warmer than they recommend. Sleeping bags and down jackets cost Rs 80 to Rs 100 each per day to rent. You can make a deposit in any combination of currencies.

North Face   OUTDOOR EQUIPMENT
One of several *pukka* (not fake) gear shops on Tridevi Marg, offering imported gear at foreign prices. These shops sell everything from Black Diamond climbing gear to US Thermarests. Other brands, such as Mountain Hard Wear, Marmot, and locally made Sherpa, are nearby.

Holyland Hiking Shop   OUTDOOR EQUIPMENT
(Map p51; ☑01-4248104) The better trekking gear shops are at the southern end of Thamel. Both this and the nearby **Sonam Gear** (Map p51; ☑01-4259191) have been recommended.

Sports Wear International OUTDOOR EQUIPMENT
(Map p56; www.hi-himal.com) Several trekkers have recommended this friendly gear shop for equipment rental.

ℹ️ Information

EMERGENCY

Ambulance Service (☑01-4521048, 102) Provided by Patan Hospital.

Police (☑01-4223011, 100; www.nepalpolice.gov.np)

Tourist Police (☑in Bhrikuti 01-4247041, in Thamel 01-4700750)

INTERNET ACCESS

There are a few cybercafes in Thamel, though almost all cafes, restaurants and hotels offer free wi-fi.

LAUNDRY

Several laundries across Thamel will machine wash laundry for Rs 50 per kilo. Get it back the next day or pay double for a three-hour service. Amazingly, it all comes back relatively clean, even after a three-week trek. Power cuts can delay wash times so don't cut it too fine by handing in your laundry the day before your flight.

MEDICAL SERVICES

Dozens of pharmacies on the fringes of Thamel offer all the cheap antibiotics you can pronounce. Diamox tablets (to help with altitude sickness) are widely available.

ℹ DANGERS & ANNOYANCES

As well as the erratic electricity supply, be aware of the following problems.

➡ Post-earthquake repairs are ongoing across the city and there is lots of rubble piled up in the streets; some of Kathmandu's historic bahals (courtyards) are inaccessible because of debris. Look out for the stickers indicating if buildings are safe after the disaster.

➡ The combination of ancient vehicles, low-quality fuel and lack of emission controls makes the streets of Kathmandu particularly dirty, noisy and unpleasant. After a few days in the city you will likely feel the onset of a throat infection.

➡ Traffic rules exist, but are rarely enforced; remember that pedestrians account for over 40% of all traffic fatalities in Nepal.

➡ Other annoyances in Thamel are the crazy motorcyclists, and the barrage of flute and chess-set sellers, tiger-balm hawkers, musical-instrument vendors, travel-agency touts, hashish suppliers, freelance trekking guides and over-eager rickshaw drivers.

➡ Note that the colourful sadhus (itinerant holy men) who frequent Durbar Sq and Pashuputinath will expect baksheesh (a tip) if you take a photo, as will the Thamel 'holy men' who anoint you with a tika on your forehead.

CIWEC Clinic Travel Medicine Center (Map p51; ☎ 01-4424111, 01-4435232; www. ciwec-clinic.com; ☺ 24hr emergency, clinic 9am-noon & 1-4pm Mon-Fri) In operation since 1982 and has an international reputation for research into travellers' medical problems. Staff are mostly foreigners and a doctor is on call around the clock. A consultation costs around US$65. Credit cards are accepted and the centre is used to dealing with insurance claims.

CIWEC Dental Clinic (Map p51; ☎ 01-4440100, emergency 01-4424111; www. ciwec-clinic.com; Lazimpat) US dentist on the top floor of CIWEC Clinic.

Healthy Smiles (Map p51; ☎ 01-4420800; www.smilenepal.com; Lazimpat) UK-trained dentist, opposite the Hotel Ambassador.

Nepal International Clinic (Map p51; ☎ 01-4435357, 01-4434642; www.nepalinternationalclinic.com; Lal Durbar; ☺ 9am-1pm & 2-5pm) Just south of the New Royal Palace, east of Thamel. It has an excellent reputation and is slightly cheaper than the CIWEC Clinic. Credit cards accepted.

MONEY

There are dozens of licensed moneychangers in Thamel. Their hours are longer than those of the banks (generally until 8pm or so) and rates are similar, perhaps even slightly better if you don't need a receipt.

Useful ATMs in the Thamel area are located beside Yin Yang Restaurant, Roadhouse Cafe and in the compound of the Kathmandu Guest House.

Himalayan Bank (Map p56; ☎ 01-4250208; www.himalayanbank.com; Tridevi Marg; ☺ 10am-3pm Sun-Fri, 10am-1pm Sat) The

most convenient bank for travellers in Thamel, this kiosk on Tridevi Marg changes cash and travellers cheques until 3pm; after this head to the main branch in the basement of the nearby Sanchaya Kosh Bhawan shopping centre. Cash advances on a Visa card are possible and there's a prominent ATM next to the kiosk. It's in front of the Three Goddesses Temples.

There is no commission for changing cash but travellers cheques incur a charge of 0.75% (minimum Rs 250).

POST

Most bookshops in Thamel sell stamps and deliver postcards to the **main post office** (Map p51; Sundhara; ☺ 7am-6pm Sun-Thu, to 3pm Fri), beside the collapsed Dharahara tower, which is much easier than making a special trip to the post office yourself.

TELEPHONE

If you don't have a mobile phone or access to Skype or Viber, you can make international telephone calls from internet cafes for around Rs 20 per minute.

There are dozens of Ncell offices around town where you can buy or top up a SIM card.

TOURIST INFORMATION

Tourist Service Centre (Map p51; ☎ 01-4256909 ext 223, 24hr tourism hotline 01-4225709; www.welcomenepal.com; Bhrikuti Mandap; ☺ 10am-1pm & 2-5pm Sun-Fri, TIMS card 7am-7pm daily, national parks tickets 9am-2pm Sun-Fri) On the eastern side of the Tundikhel parade ground; has an inconvenient location but is the place to get trekking permits and a TIMS card, and pay national park fees.

TRAVEL AGENCIES

Flight Connection International (Map p56; ☑ 01-4258282, international flights 01-4233111; www.flightconnectionintl.com; Jyatha, Thamel) Good for flight tickets. The international department is in Gaia Restaurant (p55).

Wayfarers (Map p56; ☑ 01-4266010; www.wayfarers.com.np; JP School Rd, Thamel; ⏰9am-6pm Mon-Fri, to 5pm Sat & Sun) For straight-talking ticketing, bespoke tours and Kathmandu Valley walking trips.

VISA EXTENSIONS

Visa extensions of 30 to 60 days are fairly painless to obtain at the **Central Immigration Office** (☑ 01-4429659; www.nepalimmigration.gov.np; Kalikasthan, Dilli Bazaar; ⏰10am-4pm Sun-Thu, 10am-3pm Fri, 11am-1pm Sat). You need to make your application online before arriving (up to 15 days beforehand) at the office, though there is currently a computer in the hall in case you haven't done so.

ℹ️ Getting There & Away

AIR

It's a good idea to reconfirm the departure time of your return flight, especially if travelling with the notoriously unreliable Nepal Airlines.

Domestic Airlines

Kathmandu is the main hub for domestic flights. It's easiest to buy tickets through a travel agency.

Nepal Airlines domestic office (Map p51; ☑ 01-4227133; ⏰9.30am-1pm & 2-5pm) has flights to remoter airstrips but only has computerised booking on some of its flights. The office is to the side of the main Nepal Airlines international booking centre. The other domestic carriers are much more reliable: Yeti Airlines, Tara Air and Buddha Air are the best choices. See p341 for details.

BUS

Long-Distance Buses

The **Gongabu bus station** (Ring Rd, Balaju) is north of the city centre. It is also called the Kathmandu Bus Terminal, or simply 'new bus park'. This bus station is for most long-distance buses. Bookings for long trips should be made a day in advance – Thamel travel agents will do this for a fee. A taxi from Thamel costs around Rs 200. Note that travel to some destinations may be disrupted by landslides following the 2015 earthquakes – check before you travel.

For the Langtang region, the bus stand for **Pasang Lhamo Transport** (☑ 01-4356342) is at Machha Pokhari (Fish Pond), diagonally across the Ring Rd from Gongabu bus station. However, this region was devastated by the 2015 earthquakes and the area is unlikely to be fully open to trekkers for some time. Before the disaster, there was a daily tourist bus (Rs 500, 7am) and local services (Rs 340, 6.20am, 6.50am, 7.30am) to Syabrubesi via Dhunche.

Buses for Arughat (Rs 385, seven hours, 6am, 8am) depart from the lime green Buddha Mahal depot, on the south side of the ring road, 100m west of Gongabu bus station.

The main exceptions to these are the comfortable **tourist buses** (Map p56) to Pokhara (Rs 800, seven hours) and Sauraha for Chitwan National Park (Rs 600, six hours) that depart daily at 7am from a far more convenient location at the Thamel end of Kantipath.

BUSES FROM GONGABU BUS STATION

Check timings of buses before you travel in case of schedule changes following the 2015 earthquakes.

DESTINATION	DISTANCE (KM)	FARE (RS)	DURATION (HR)	FREQUENCY	TICKET WINDOW
Besi Sahar	150	450	6	tourist bus 7am, 8am & 10am	25, 32
Bhairawa/ Sunauli	282	550 (tourist bus 960)	8	ordinary bus every 15 min, tourist bus 8am	23, 24, 29
Birganj	300	550	8	7am, 8am & 7.15pm	16
Gorkha	140	300	5	6am-noon	27, 43
Hile (via Dharan)	635	1250	14	3pm	39
Kakarbhitta	610	1150-1380	14	4.30am, 4-5pm	26 & 39
Nepalganj	530	1180-1230	12	deluxe 6am & 6pm, ordinary 4pm, 5pm & 7pm	24, 20, 36
Pokhara	200	425 (tourist bus 500)	6-8	tourist bus 8.30am, 10am & 11am, others every 15 min to 1pm	27, 28

ⓘ GETTING TREKKING PERMITS

The **Tourist Service Centre** (p59) is the place to get a TIMS card, a national park permit (eg for the Everest or Langtang regions) or a conservation area permit (eg for Annapurna). All three desks are in the same room but have different opening hours. If you just need a TIMS card, it's easiest to go to the TIMS Centre office in Thamel.

See p31 for details of fees and any requirements.

Greenline (Map p56; ☎01-4253885; www.greenline.com.np; Tridevi Marg; ☺7am-5.30pm) offers air-con deluxe services at 7.30am to Pokhara (US$23, six hours) and Chitwan (US$20, six hours). Book a day or two in advance.

Golden Travels (Map p51; ☎01-4220036; Woodlands Complex, Durbar Marg) runs similar services, departing at 7am from Kantipath to Pokhara (US$15 with lunch), Sunauli (US$15) and Lumbini (US$15, nine hours). Buy tickets at any travel agency.

To/From the Kathmandu Valley

Buses for most destinations within the Kathmandu Valley, and for those on or accessed from the Arniko Hwy (for Shivalaya, Barabise and Kodari on the Tibetan border), operate from the **Ratna Park bus station** (Map p51), also known as the old or city bus stand, in the centre of the city on the eastern edge of Tundikhel parade ground. The station is a bit of a horror, but keep shouting out your destination and someone will eventually direct you to the right bus.

ⓘ Getting Around

Most of the sights in Kathmandu itself can easily be covered on foot, and this is by far the best way to appreciate the old town, even if the traffic is atrocious.

TO/FROM THE AIRPORT

Getting into town from Kathmandu's Tribhuvan Airport (p337) is quite straightforward. Both the international and domestic terminals offer a fixed-price prepaid taxi service, currently Rs 700 to Thamel.

Many hotels will pick you up for free if you've booked a room in advance for more than one night.

From Kathmandu to the airport you should be able to get a taxi for Rs 500, or a bit more for a late or early flight.

CYCLE-RICKSHAW

Cycle-rickshaws cost around Rs 60 for short rides around Thamel or the old town but expect to have to haggle hard. It's essential to agree on a price before you go.

TAXI

Taxis are quite reasonably priced, though few taxi drivers use the meters these days. Shorter rides around town cost about Rs 200. Most taxis are tiny Suzuki Marutis, which can just about fit two backpackers and their luggage.

Everest Region

Best Side Trips

➜ Ama Dablam Base Camp (p83)

➜ Upper Bhote Kosi Valley (p103)

➜ Chhukung Ri (p84)

➜ Hillary Memorial Stupas (p76)

Best Sherpa Villages

➜ Phortse (p97)

➜ Upper Pangboche (p79)

➜ Khunde (p76)

Why Go?

Mt Everest has been calling out to trekkers and climbers since it first appeared in the telescopes of mountain surveyors. Like the Annapurna region, the districts of Solu and Khumbu boast well-maintained trails and comfortable lodges, but the trekking routes here start higher and stay higher, offering unrivalled views of the world's highest peaks. The 2105 earthquakes caused some damage here, but the trails were surveyed following the quake and all routes are expected to be open by the time you read this.

Solu Khumbu is the homeland of the Sherpa people, who have become synonymous with guiding and mountaineering. The Buddhist monuments of the Sherpas – stone stupas, carved mani walls (built of stones carved with Buddhist prayers) and Tibetan-style monasteries – add a further layer of charm to the landscape.

A regular on many people's bucket lists, Everest is what most trekkers are naturally fixated on. The real draws of the region, though, are its side valleys, mountain passes and lesser-known (but far more beautiful) surrounding peaks. Don't overlook these in your rush to the world's highest peak.

When to Go

➜ The best weather and the biggest crowds are in autumn (October and November), when skies are clear and temperatures are bearable at higher altitudes.

➜ Spring (March and April) is a quieter time to visit, though cloud and rain become more frequent in the build-up to the monsoon.

➜ It is theoretically possible to trek in the Khumbu year-round. The most serious obstacle to trekking in winter is the cold. Days can be comfortable but nights are freezing.

➜ At some time during the season from October to March there is certain to be a storm or two that will blanket the countryside with snow. Check the weather conditions locally before attempting any high-altitude passes.

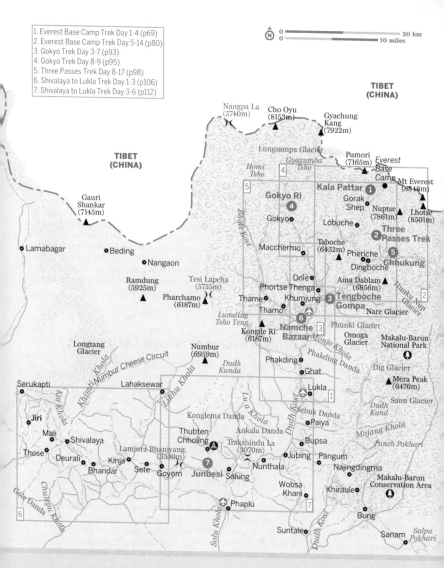

0   20 km
0   10 miles

TIBET (CHINA)

Nangpa La (5740m)   Cho Oyu (8153m)   Gyachung Kang (7922m)

Lungsampa Glacier   Pumori (7165m)   *Everest Base Camp*

TIBET (CHINA)

Homi Tsho   *Gyazumba Tsho*   Mt Everest (8848m)

Gauri Shankar (7145m)   **Kala Pattar**   Gorak Shep   Nuptse (7861m)   Lhotse (8501m)

Gokyo Ri   Gokyo   Lobuche   **Three Passes Trek**

Lamabagar   Beding   *Bhote Kosi*   Macchermo   Taboche (6452m)   Pheriche   **Ghhukung**

Nangaon   Dole   Dingboche

Ramdung (5925m)   Tesi Lapcha (5755m)   Phortse Thenga   Ama Dablam (6856m)   *Hunku Nup Glacier*

Pharchamo (6187m)   Thame   Khumjung   **Tengboche Gompa**

Lumding Tsho Teng   Thamo   Nare Glacier

Kongde Ri (6187m)   **Namche Bazaar**   Phunki Glacier   Omoga Glacier   Makalu-Barun National Park

Longtang Glacier   Numbur (6959m)   *Monjo Khola*

Serukapti   *Khunti Mumbur Cheese Circuit*   Lahaksewar   Dudh Kunda   Phakding   *Phakding Danda*   Dig Glacier   Mera Peak (6476m)

Jiri   *Kor Khola*   Ghat   Lukla   *Dudh Kund*

Mali   Shivalaya   *Likhu Khola*   *Liu a Khola*   Konglema Danda   *Ssebuk Danda*   Sanu Glacier

Those   Deurali   Thubten Chholing   Ankala Danda   Paiya   *Mojang Khola*   *Punch Pokhari*

Lamjura Bhanjyang (3530m)   Trakshindu La (3070m)   Bupsa   *Dudh Kosi*

Bhandar   Kinja   Sete   Goyom   **Junbesi**   Salung   Jubing   Pangum   Najingdingma

Chaurikharka Khola   Nunthala   Wobsa Khani   Khiraule   Makalu-Barun Conservation Area

Gole Danda   Phaplu   *Solu Khola*   Suntale   Bung   Sanam   *Salpa Pokhari*

Everest Highlights

1 Sneaking a peek at the highest peak on earth from **Kala Pattar** (p88).

2 Scrambling over the rugged Kongma La pass for views of Makalu on the challenging **Three Passes trek** (p100).

3 Joining the monks for morning prayers at **Tengboche Gompa** (p77).

4 Viewing the turquoise Gokyo Lake and the Ngozumpa Glacier from **Gokyo Ri** (p96).

5 Detouring off the main trail and exploring the excellent excursions from **Chhukung** (p84).

6 Enjoying the cafes, pizza parlours and gear shops of **Namche Bazaar** (p119).

7 Escaping the crowds and exploring the monasteries around **Junbesi** (p109) on the Shivalaya to Lukla trek.

Environment

The mountains of the Khumbu are so large that they create their own local climate. As you climb through the hills, mixed deciduous forests and scattered rice terraces give way to pine forests, then rhododendrons, then scrub junipers, before finally the only vegetation is low alpine shrubs and grasses. As you walk, scan the skies and the undergrowth for golden eagles and the spectacular Himalayan monal (danphe or impeyan pheasant), with its regal, shimmering green, blue and purple plumage.

In forested areas around Namche Bazaar, Thame, Phortse and Tengboche, keep your eyes peeled for Himalayan tahr and musk deer, often spotted beside trails early in the morning. You may also hear the strange, hoarse call of the muntjac, or barking deer. The predators of the Himalaya are rarely seen but they are out there – the Khumbu is home to both leopards and snow leopards, and, allegedly, the fearsome yeti.

Planning

ACCOMMODATION

Few independent trekkers bother to camp in the Khumbu region because there are so many excellent lodges along the trails. You rarely have to walk more than an hour to find another place to stay.

Most lodges are broadly identical stone houses with tiny box rooms separated by plywood partitions. A few have indoor toilets shared between two rooms, which can be a mixed blessing when you consider that few walls are soundproof. Restaurant menus are extensive and prices are generally fixed in each village.

Many lodges in the Everest region suffered damage in the 2015 earthquake but most were quickly repaired. However, some lodges collapsed completely and others may no longer be habitable after the disaster. At the time of writing, it was not possible to confirm that all the lodges listed in this chapter were open and more lodges may close because of lack of business. On any trek in this area, ask locally to confirm that accommodation will be available for all your planned overnight stops.

TREKKING IN THE EVEREST REGION AFTER THE EARTHQUAKES

Just northeast of the main earthquake zone, the Everest region suffered a fair bit of damage during the 2015 tremors, particularly at lower elevations. While major settlements such as Lukla and Namche Bazaar saw little damage, a deadly avalanche swept over the tent city at Everest Base Camp on 25 April killing 18 trekkers and guides – the worst mountaineering disaster in Everest's history – and buildings were damaged all along the trekking routes to Base Camp, Gokyo and Lukla. However, Solukhumbu avoided the devastation seen in the Langtang Valley. In most villages, buildings escaped with only minor cracks and a post-quake survey by specialist engineers found little serious structural damage to either buildings or trekking trails.

Reconstruction is underway throughout the Everest region and all the trails in this area are expected to be open by the time you read this. However, some villages saw quite serious damage, and it is likely that some lodges will be forced to close. Trekkers may need to pick alternative places to break for the night while restoration work is ongoing. The villages of Thame, Khumjung and Pheriche on the Everest Base Camp route, Dole and Machhermo on the Gokyo track, and Jiri, Shivalaya and Kinja on the trail to Lukla were particularly badly hit. On some routes, you may need to detour to avoid landslips, and there is an ongoing risk of further landslides where land has been destabilised by the earthquake.

The trek descriptions in this chapter were researched shortly before the earthquakes hit, and we have updated since using local sources. However, we do not claim to have captured every change since the earthquakes. At the time of writing, it was not possible to confirm that all the lodges listed in this chapter were open, and there may be further closures because of the reduced number of people trekking in this area following the disaster. Enquire locally if any of the lodges mentioned in this chapter are locked up when you arrive.

The monsoon may bring further problems and it will be some time before the full extent of damage becomes clear. On any trek in this region, seek local advice on the current status of trails – including if any detours are required – and confirm that food and accommodation will be available for all overnight stops before you set off from the trailheads.

ⓘ BEATING THE CROWDS

Around 35,000 foreigners trek in the Everest region each year, with just under a third of them arriving in October. Even if there's a downturn in numbers due to the earthquakes, but at the peak of the season, you may still face stiff competition for a bed. The most popular months to trek in the Everest region are October, November, April and March, in that order, with crowds peaking during the second and third weeks of October. If you want to combine the best high season weather with fewer crowds, consider the following tips:

➡ The second half of November is generally a good time to trek. It's not too cold and the crowds are abating. Early December is also good, though lodges in smaller trekking centres start to close and water supplies freeze in higher lodges.

➡ One good way to beat the crowds is to break your trek at a different place from the main trekking groups – there are dozens of villages with trekking lodges dotted between the more established stops.

➡ If you can budget a couple of extra days to explore side trips, you'll find you can have the trails to Ama Dablam Base Camp and the east valley route from Gokyo to Phortse all to yourself, even in high season.

EVEREST REGION PLANNING

Throughout the Khumbu, rooms with shared bathroom cost Rs 200, though singles might snag a room for Rs 100. In Namche Bazaar, you can also find rooms with private bathrooms for Rs 500 to US$50. Expect to pay upwards of Rs 400 for a meal, with prices rising to Rs 700 for a daal bhaat at Everest Base Camp.

Many lodges now offer wi-fi (Rs 500 to Rs 1000 per day) and most lodges offer solar-heated hot showers (Rs 300 to Rs 500).

Outside of Namche Bazaar, many of the region's bakeries and internet cafes close in winter (December to February) and during the monsoon (June to September).

ELECTRICITY

Hydroelectricity in the lower Solu Khumbu region is reliable, though solar power in the upper regions is sometimes too weak to charge smartphones and tablets. Lodges charge between Rs 150 and Rs 350 per hour to charge batteries.

RESOURCES

In Namche Bazaar and Lukla, drop into the offices of the **Sagarmatha Pollution Control Committee** (SPCC; Map p120; www.spcc.org.np; ⊙10am-5pm Mon-Fri) for information on responsible travel and conservation in the Khumbu. The website www.namchebazar.info has lodge listings.

FESTIVALS

There are four major festivals in Solu Khumbu, all linked to Tibetan Buddhism and the Tibetan lunar calendar.

Gyalpo Losar (Tibetan New Year)

Tibetan New Year is celebrated with masked dances, performances of *lhamo* (Tibetan opera) and other festivities at gompas and shrines throughout the Khumbu. The festival is held at the end of the 12th month of the Tibetan calendar, which usually falls in late February or early March.

Buddha Jayanti

Also known as Saga Dawa, Buddha Jayanti celebrates the birthday of Siddhartha Gautama Buddha (the historical Buddha), with parades to stupas and gompas, and the lighting of butter lamps at sacred sites. The festival falls on the full moon of the fourth Tibetan month, normally in May.

Mani Rimdu

The most famous Sherpa festival, Mani Rimdu is celebrated for three days at the monasteries of Tengboche, Thame and Chiwang (near Phaplu). On the second day of the festival, monks don elaborate masks and costumes and perform ritualistic *chaam* dances that symbolise the triumph of Buddhism over the ancient animistic religion of the mountains. Sherpas from all over the Khumbu flock to attend the spectacle.

At Tengboche the celebrations start on the full moon of the ninth lunar month, which normally falls in October or November. As large crowds of Westerners attend the ceremony, both hotel and tent space is hard to come by and the monastery charges for tickets. For details see www.tengboche.org.

Similar festivals are held at Chiwang (near Phaplu) in the 10th Tibetan month, typically in November or December, and at Thame on the full moon of the fourth Tibetan month, which normally falls in May.

Dumje

Sherpas celebrate the birth of Guru Rinpoche (Padmasambhava), the Himalayan saint who introduced Buddhism to Tibet, with six days of rituals and feasting in the fifth Tibetan lunar month, normally in June or July. The largest celebrations are at Namche Bazaar, Pangboche, Khumjung and Thame.

GUIDES & PORTERS

Most people organise porters and guides before flying to Lukla, but sherpas crowd around the exit gate to Lukla airstrip every morning offering their services. Most are every bit as professional as guides and porters hired in Kathmandu and they often have better local knowledge. Lodges in Lukla can also connect you with a guide, at a slightly higher price.

MAPS

Nepa Maps produces a series of superior maps of the Everest region – so many, in fact, that other publishers rarely get a look-in. Useful maps include the 1:50,000 *Lukla to Everest Base Camp* and *Trekking Lukla to Gokyo* maps, and the handy-sized 1:60,000 *Lukla to Everest Base Camp Pocket Map* and *Lukla to Gokyo Pocket Map*.

For an overview of the entire region, the 1:100,000 *Jiri to Everest* map covers the trails from Jiri all the way to Everest Base Camp and Gokyo.

Nelles has reproduced updated versions of Erwin Schneider's original maps of the Solu-Khumbu region. Most useful is the 1:50,000 *Khumbu Himal* map, covering Namche Bazaar to Mt Everest.

National Geographic prints a 1:50,000 *Everest Base Camp* map and a 1:125,000 *Khumbu* map, which shows the walk in from Jiri. For a bit of mountaineering nostalgia, pick up the reprint of the 1:90,000 *Mt Everest 50th Anniversary Map*, which shows the ascent paths of famous mountaineering groups.

MEDICAL FACILITIES

The Khumbu has better medical facilities than most mountain districts, and while many health posts saw some earthquake damage, most were promptly repaired. There is only one proper hospital convenient for trekkers – the Khunde Hospital (p123) just north of Namche Bazaar, built by Sir Edmund Hillary in 1965. The hospital has a decompression chamber. You can donate medicines here at the end of your trek.

Above Namche, the health post at Pheriche is run by the **Himalayan Rescue Association** (www.himalayanrescue.org). If you do need

---

LUXURY ACCOMMODATION IN THE EVEREST REGION

The Everest region has the most luxurious lodges in the country. Rooms at the top-end places are generally overpriced, but you will get a private bathroom, a proper mattress and some stylish decor. Almost all the guests in the following resorts book in advance through a trekking agency.

The Yeti Mountain Home lodge at Kongde (4250m) is particularly interesting, as it lies well off the main trail and is only accessible along tough trails from Toktok (four hours) or Thame (six hours), or by expensive chartered helicopter. Mountain views from the two lodges are as exclusive as they are superb, but you need to be extremely careful about acclimatisation. If your itinerary includes Kongde, visit at the end of your trek, not the beginning.

However, some of these luxury properties saw some earthquake damage and lodges may be closed for repairs – contact the following lodges in advance if you plan to stay.

Himalayan Eco Resorts (☑ Kathmandu 01-4413732, Lobuche 9841984132; www.himalayanecoresort.com; d US$15-25) Chain of mid-priced lodges at Phakding, Khumjung, Lobuche and Gokyo, operated by Asian Trekking.

Yeti Mountain Home (Map p120; ☑ 01-4000711; www.yetimountainhome.com; r US$115-185) This upmarket chain operates attractive stone lodges in Lukla, Phakding, Namche Bazaar, Thame and Kongde ridge.

Everest Summit Lodges (☑ 01-4371537; www.nepalluxurytreks.com; r US$150-225) Runs the superior Everest Summit Lodges in Lukla, Monjo, Mende (near Thame) and Pangboche. Their property at Tashinga (near Phortse) was damaged and may still not be open. Priority is given to guests on the company's treks.

Beyul Hermitage & Farm (☑ 9813766450; www.thebeyul.com; Chhuserma; r per person with three meals US$95) A stylish and secluded luxury lodge, 30 minutes off the main trekking trail, across the river, between Ghat and Phakding. It's below a hermitage, with six rooms and a private helipad. Contact Nyima Sherpa or Caryl Sherpa.

Hotel Everest View (☑ 038-540118, in Kathmandu 01-5011648; www.hoteleverestview.com; s/d US$115/180) On the ridge above Namche Bazaar, this famous hotel is one of the highest hotels in the world and popular with Japanese guests.

KHUMBU ROUTE OPTIONS

The minimum timescale for a trek from Lukla to Everest Base Camp or Gokyo and back is two weeks – any less and you will be exposing yourself to the risk of acute mountain sickness (AMS).

Rather than walking the same way twice, you can trek to Everest Base Camp or Kala Pattar, then climb over the 5420m Cho La to Gokyo, returning to Namche Bazaar via Machhermo or Phortse (17 days). Another interesting option is to loop around from Lobuche over the 5535m Kongma La to Chhukung and Dingboche (17 days). You can combine both these options as part of the outstanding Three Passes trek (20 days).

You can also link the Everest and Gokyo trails without crossing a high pass by following the little-used trail from upper Pangboche to the earthquake damaged village of Phortse. On the descent from Gokyo avoid repetition by taking the surprisingly remote east bank route via Konar.

For a shorter 10-day loop, avoiding high altitudes and therefore a good option in winter, trek to Pangboche and then return via Phortse and Khumjung.

emergency treatment, a consultation here is US$65, and the clinic has access to Gamow bags and bottled oxygen. Similar health posts are set up at Machhermo and Gokyo (the latter in October only). All three have resident foreign doctors during high season. There was some earthquake damage to these facilities by they should be open by the time you read this.

Chartered helicopters shuttle up and down the Khumbu all day, taking the well-heeled on sightseeing tours or bringing sick or injured trekkers down.

PERMITS & REGULATIONS

Treks north of Lukla pass through Sagarmatha National Park, so you must pay a Rs 3000 entry fee, either in advance at the **Department of National Parks and Wildlife Conservation** (☑ 4227926, 01-4222406; www.dnpwc.gov.np; Pradarhshanti; ☉ 9am-2pm Sun-Fri) office in Kathmandu or at the park entry checkpoint at Monjo.

You must also obtain the usual TIMS trekking permit for all treks in this chapter.

Under national park rules, trekkers are banned from using firewood for heating or cooking meals.

SUPPLIES & EQUIPMENT

Shops in Namche Bazaar sell almost anything you could want, including a full range of trekking and climbing equipment. As you head further north lodges and the occasional shop sell batteries, sunscreen and chocolate. Books are in short supply. Prices for everything shoot up dramatically the further you get from the airstrip at Lukla.

There's no need to carry ice axes or crampons for any of the treks listed in this chapter, though Microspikes (www.kahtoola.com) or Yaktrax (www.yaktrax.com) can be very useful in icy conditions on the Cho La, Renjo La or Kongma La passes.

ⓘ Towns & Facilities

Lukla (p117) is the main trailhead for treks into the Everest region, with various routes branching out from the Sherpa centre of Namche Bazaar (p119). Both towns escaped serious damage in the 2015 earthquakes.

Trekkers taking the approach trek into the Everest region generally begin in the trailhead village of Shivalaya (p119), but this village, and the nearby village of Jiri, were badly damaged in the earthquakes.

ⓘ Getting There & Away

Most visitors to the Khumbu fly into the tiny airstrip at Lukla (US$165) and the airstrip here was not affected by the earthquakes. Because flights to Lukla do not always take off as planned, always allow a few spare days for your flight back to Kathmandu, particularly in winter and during the monsoon. For more on flight safety at Lukla, see the boxed text, p118.

Alternative airstrips in the Khumbu region include Phaplu (US$154 from Kathmandu, weekly), a three-day walk southwest from Lukla, and Lamidanda (US$133 from Kathmandu, weekly), a five-day walk south of Lukla. Both are served by Tara Air.

You can also access the Khumbu region on foot, avoiding the crowds and improving your fitness and acclimatisation for the high mountain trails. The original 1953 Everest expedition had to start walking in Bhaktapur in the Kathmandu Valley; these days buses run from Kathmandu to Shivalaya, the start of a six-day hike to Lukla.

A remoter exit route from the Khumbu is the nine-day trek to Tumlingtar, connecting with buses and flights to Kathmandu or the eastern Terai.

Everest Base Camp Trek

Duration 16 days

Max Elevation 5545m

Difficulty Medium to hard

Season October to December & February to May

Start/Finish Lukla

Permits TIMS card, Sagarmatha National Park permit

Summary The definitive Himalayan trek, flying into Lukla and climbing to the foot of Mt Everest through breathless high alpine landscapes.

Iconic Mt Everest has exerted a powerful draw for a century now. By following this route, you will be following in the footsteps of great mountaineers like Reinhold Messner, Edmund Hillary and Tenzing Norgay. As you climb through the foothills of the world's highest mountain, the terrain soars on all sides like jagged shards of glass. The trails are steep and the altitude hangs on your muscles like a diving belt, but the sense of achievement at the end of the trek is quite profound.

However, this is not a mountaineering expedition or a wilderness hike. There are trekking lodges every few hundred metres along the trails and tens of thousands of trekkers storm the trails ever year. Competition for accommodation can be fierce during the peak months of October to November, and March to May.

This area saw some damage in the 2015 earthquake. Many lodges suffered minor damage, and houses and trekking lodges collapsed completely in the villages of Thame, Pheriche and Khumjung. Until lodges are repaired, trekkers may need to choose alter-

---

> ### ⓘ WARNING
>
> Be alert for the symptoms of altitude sickness on this trek, and follow the recommended rest days. These are very important for acclimatisation and will allow you to see much more of the Khumbu region than you'll see if you rush directly to Base Camp. The trek to Base Camp is not especially strenuous; the trekkers who fail to reach their goal are usually those who don't allow enough time for acclimatisation.

---

native overnight stops. At the time of writing, it was not possible to confirm that all the lodges on this trek were open. As a sensible precaution, check locally to make sure accommodation will be available for all your overnight stops before starting your trek.

You should also be aware that the views of Everest are neither brilliant or guaranteed. Many trekkers climb to the viewing summit of Kala Pattar, only to find the peaks have vanished into a swirling mass of vapour.

Because of the risk of acute mountain sickness (AMS), it takes a minimum of two weeks to climb to Everest Base Camp and return to Lukla. You don't have to sit around on rest days – there are lots of interesting side hikes to fabulous places like Thame and Chhukung and these will improve your fitness and acclimatisation before you head to the base camp.

The main downside to the simple Base Camp trail is that you return along the same route. To mix up the return section consider heading back via Phortse and Khunde. For loop options see the Gokyo (p91) and Three Passes (p97) treks.

🏃 The Trek

Day 1: Lukla to Phakding

3 HOURS / 200M DESCENT / 50M ASCENT

It's an easy and gentle first day from Lukla to Phakding, but you will see some evidence of earthquake damage along this route and some lodges may not be operating – check locally to see what accommodation is available at each stop before setting off from Lukla.

After arriving in Lukla, sorting out your porter(s) and repacking, most people head off mid-morning. As you head through the north end of Lukla, you pass a tourism police checkpost where you must register your TIMS card and list any valuables. You finally leave Lukla through the Pasang Lhamo Memorial Gate, named after the first Nepali woman to summit Everest. Just below is a white chorten dedicated to the 18 victims of the 2008 Yeti Airlines air crash at Lukla.

Leaving Lukla, the trail drops, keeps right at an unsigned junction to Chaurikharka, then runs level above the village of Kyangma. About 40 minutes from Lukla, you'll enter the village of **Cheplung** (Chablung; 2700m), where a side trail from Shivalaya and Chaurikharka joins near the Hilltop View Lodge. There are several places to stay along the trail, but some have been damaged

EVEREST REGION EVEREST BASE CAMP TREK

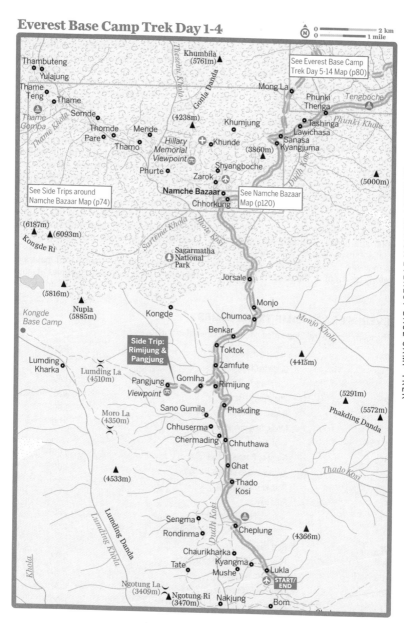

EVEREST REGION EVEREST BASE CAMP TREK

in the quake. Before the disaster, the Khumbila Guesthouse and Amadablam Lodge were good choices for their pleasant front terraces, while the imposing Norbu Linkha Guesthouse had good rooms and valley views from its overhanging balconies. Ten minutes' walk above the village, squeezed into a cave at the bottom of soaring cliffs, is the tiny **Cheplung (Taktag) Gompa**; however, Cheplung village was badly damaged in the quake; ask at Norbu Linkha Guesthouse to see if it is possible to visit the gompa.

As you continue north from Cheplung, you'll catch your first views of the Dudh Kosi roaring along the bottom of the valley. The trail descends through a community forest, past the pleasant Mountain View Restaurant, before crossing a swaying metal suspension bridge above the Thado Kosi Khola. Just beyond the bridge in **Thadokoshi** is another cluster of trekking lodges, but earthquake damage was widespread. Before the quake, Kusum Kangkaru View Lodge was a good choice for its views of **Kusum Kangru** (6367m), the most difficult of the Khumbu's trekking peaks, which rises at the east end of the side valley here.

It's a short climb around the ridge to **Ghat** (Yulning; 2590m), on the edge of the Dudh Kosi. Before the quake, this was a good alternative overnight stop, but earthquake damage was severe, and some lodges may not be operating after the disaster. Before the tremor, the stone-built Eco Vil-

lage Lodge, Himalayan Sherpa Lodge and Chamalungma Garden Lodge were all cosy and well run. Good choices further uphill included the Kongde View Lodge and Lama Lodge, which faced onto a small private red-walled gompa. In the village, note the shrine and mani wall dedicated to Green Tara.

A side trail from the Eco Village Lodge crosses the river to the west bank and runs for 30 minutes to the exclusive Beyul Hermitage & Farm (p66), before eventually rejoining the main trail just north of Phakding.

If you have more time, the owner of Eco Village Lodge is full of ideas on local hikes, including a detour across the Dudh Kosi to a collection of mani stones, a rock painting of Buddha and a *shabje* (footprint) of Guru Rinpoche. This west bank trail was the one used by Hillary on the 1951 Everest reconnaissance trek.

Leaving Ghat, the main trail passes a school and enters a curious complex of mani

EVEREST BASE CAMP TREK – TIMES

The following are trekking times only; stops are not included.

DAY	SECTION	HOURS
1	Lukla to Cheplung	1:15
	Cheplung to Phakding	1:45
2	Phakding to Benkar	1:30
	Benkar to Monjo	1:00
	Monjo to Namche Bazaar	3:00
3	Rest day	
4	Namche Bazaar to Kyangjuma	1:00
	Kyangjuma to Phunki Thenga	1:00
	Phunki Thenga to Tengboche	1:30
5	Rest day	
6	Tengboche to Pangboche	1:30
	Pangboche to Pheriche/Dingboche	2:00
7	Rest day	
8	Pheriche/Dingboche to Dughla	2:00
9	Dughla to Lobuche	2:30
10	Lobuche to Gorak Shep	2:30
11	Gorak Shep to Everest Base Camp	6:00
	Gorak Shep to Kala Pattar	4:00
12	Gorak Shep to Lobuche	2:00
13	Lobuche to Pheriche/Dingboche	3:00
14	Pheriche/Dingboche to Tengboche	2:30
15	Tengboche to Namche Bazaar	4:30
16	Namche Bazaar to Lukla	6:00

walls, chortens, boulders carved with black and white Tibetan mantras, and brightly painted prayer wheels. The focal point for this sacred Buddhist site is a small rock with strata in the shape of a lama's hat, worshipped as a symbol of Guru Rinpoche.

The trail climbs over an old landslide to the hamlet of **Chhuthawa** (2591m) and then winds through forest beside the Dudh Kosi, passing the large, red-roofed Yeti Mountain Home.

Follow the path up into the village of **Phakding**, a collection of more than a dozen lodges, straddling the Dudh Kosi at 2610m. Many buildings here saw damage in the earthquake but owners are rebuilding and most lodges are expected to be operating as normal for the 2015-2016 trekking season. Top picks before the disaster included the Snowland Lodge, Buddha Lodge, Royal Sherpa Resort, Sherpa Eco-Home, Shangri-la Guesthouse and Khumbu Travellers Guesthouse, all lined up on the main street. Across the small stream is another collection of lodges, including the large Namaste Lodge. The Liquid Bar and Reggae Bar are just two of several bars and pool joints in this surprisingly raucous section of the trail.

The path runs north across a long, sinuous suspension bridge over the Dudh Kosi to a smaller, quieter and nicer group of lodges; there was more earthquake damage here but restoration is underway. Good choices before the quake included the excellent Phakding Star Lodge and Sunrise Lodge, both with big gardens, large terraces, real coffee and some rooms with attached bathrooms (Rs 500). Behind these two lodges, a small track runs south to Jo's Garden Lodge, a collection of stone cottages on the riverbank, one of the Himalayan Eco Resorts (p66).

If you find Phakding too busy and crowded, you may be able to find accommodation in Zamfute (25 minutes), Benkar (90 minutes) or Monjo (three hours), but note that all three villages saw some earthquake damage – check that accommodation will be available before leaving Phakding.

SIDE TRIP: RIMIJUNG & PANGJUNG
2–5 HOURS / 300M ASCENT / 300M DESCENT

Just north of Phakding, a yellow signposted side trail leads steeply up the ridge for 15 minutes to the Sherpa village of **Rimijung** (also known as Thulo Gumelha), set on a plateau overlooking the valley and untouched by the trekking crowds below. This part of the valley is known as Pharak. Check

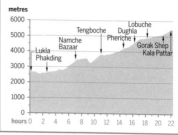

Lukla to Everest Base Camp

that the trails are open before setting off from Phakding.

Assuming all is well, swing left past fields of buckwheat to reach the 350-year-old **Pema Choling Gompa**, under restoration following the earthquake, which enshrines statues of Guru Rinpoche, Red Mahakala and the snow-lion-faced goddess Senge Dongma. Just above the gompa is the smaller Thaktul Gompa, the residence of a local *rinpoche* (reincarnate lama). Allow about 30 minutes each way for the walk from Phakding.

With more time to spare, you can climb for 40 minutes above the gompa to a small retreat for nuns at **Gomlha**. En route you might meet monks from Pema Choling surfing down the hillside on planks of wood.

Die-hards can continue steeply up the hillside for another hour to a hillside viewpoint at **Pangjung** (three hours total), which offers splendid views of the valley from Lukla to Khumjung, including the tip of Everest. Give yourself two hours to return to Phakding.

Day 2: Phakding to Namche Bazaar
5½ HOURS / 1000M ASCENT / 100M DESCENT

From Phakding the trail follows the Dudh Kosi Valley north, meandering through the pines about 100m above the west bank of the river. The village of **Zamfute** had a number of good lodges before the earthquake, including the large new Sherpa Shangrila Lodge, Kongde Peak Guesthouse (with some attached bathrooms) and River View Lodge, but some of these may be closed because of earthquake damage. Check that accommodation will be available before planning an overnight stop here. A second trail to Rimijung runs uphill from the Kongde Peak Guesthouse.

ℹ MIND THE YAK

Within a few minutes of leaving Lukla, you'll probably spot your first yaks hauling gear for trekking groups – these beasts of burden will not give way to pedestrians so always step to the hill side of the trail (never the river side) to let them pass.

Crosing the Ghatte Khola by a small hydroelectric project, the trail climbs up over the ridge to the tiny village of **Toktok**, also damaged in the quake, where you may be able grab a bed or a bite at the Amadablam Lodge. Earthquake engineers have suggested moving the houses of Toktok across the river because of the risk of further rockfalls. The trail then descends through pines to a pretty, multilevel waterfall and restaurant.

From here it's a short climb to a fine view of Thamserku, the 6608m peak that rises to the east of Namche Bazaar. The trail climbs to the agreeable Benkar Guesthouse and passes a small waterfall before cresting a miniature pass and dropping into **Benkar** at 2710m. Look up to the cliffs above Benkar to see a rock painting of Guru Rinpoche marking the entrance to a meditation retreat.

Before the earthquake, Benkar was a popular alternative stop to Phakding, but a number of lodges here were damaged in the earthquake, and engineers have suggested moving the village because of the risk of further landslides. Check that accommodation will be available before planning an overnight stop here.

Assuming lodges are open, the Everest Mini Guesthouse and Hotel Waterfall straddle the pass just before the village. Dotted among walled potato fields in the main village are half a dozen more lodges, including the Himalayan Guesthouse. The Tashi Guesthouse makes its own incense and has an incredible outdoor table on a stone platform that must rank as the most memorable lunch location in the Khumbu.

You are now about four hours' walk from Namche Bazaar, but what a walk it is! Heading north from Benkar, the trail crosses back to the east bank of the Dudh Kosi by the River Side Lodge.

After 10 minutes you'll reach **Chumoa** (2820m), where you will need to present your TIMS card to the checkpost. This village was also shaken by the tremor. Before the quake, there were five lodges in Chumoa, including the good Chumoa Guesthouse, but you will find more choice just minutes along the trail at Monjo.

Along this stage of the trek, villages are interspersed with magnificent forests of rhododendron, magnolia and fir. From Chumoa, it's another short climb to the outskirts of **Monjo** at 2840m. The village has a pretty setting beside the Dudh Kosi, and you can visit the small Utse Choling Gompa set on a rocky outcrop next to the village school.

Some lodges here were damaged in the earthquake, but most are expected to be open for business by 2016; ask locally to see who has rooms available. As you enter the village you'll find the large but welcoming **Monjo Guesthouse** (r without/with bathroom Rs 200/1000), set around a kitchen garden that provides plenty of fresh organic vegetables and apples for the kitchen. There are more lodges uphill, including the wi-fi-enabled Mount Kailash Lodge, which is enlivened by flowers growing in old tin cans. At the top end of the village is the upmarket Everest Summit Lodge (p66) and the Mountain View Lodge.

Just above Monjo is the entrance checkpoint for the **Sagarmatha National Park** (adult Rs 3000; ⊙ 6am-6pm), where your TIMS card and national park receipt will be checked. If you did not pay in advance, you can pay the national park fee at the counter. The attached information centre has a 3D map of the Khumbu Himalaya and displays on responsible trekking.

Beyond the national park checkpoint, the trail passes through a *kani* (stupa-shaped gateway) signifying your entry to a *baeyul*, or hidden land, and drops down next to an enormous granite bluff, carved with mantras in huge Tibetan characters. The trail cuts across to the west bank of the Dudh Kosi on another suspension bridge then runs north to **Jorsale** (Thumbug; 2830m). This is the last settlement before the big climb to Namche Bazaar and a good place to charge your fuel cells with a decent helping of daal bhaat. However, the village was badly affected by the earthquake – check ahead to make sure food and/or accommodation will be available.

Before the quake, Jorsale had six almost identical lodges lined up along the trail – the Boudha Lodge was recommended, as was the River View Restaurant with its back verandah overlooking the river. If open, the alpine-style **Nirvana Lodge** (www.kazi-sherpa.

com) is a good choice for its charming garden; the kitchen serves Austrian treats like home-baked bread and *kaiserschmarrn* (shredded pancake). The German-speaking owner acts as a guide. You will have to stop briefly at the end of town to register with the army.

Just above the checkpoint is the ruined former *tsamkhang* (meditation retreat) of the local lama, set in a huge cave above the village. The interior murals painted on planks of wood are exquisite. The tricky 10-minute trail here runs from behind the Sherpa Lodge. Check that it's open at the Bouddha Lodge, which is run by the lama's grandson.

Above Jorsale the trail recrosses the Dudh Kosi on yet another suspension bridge. Follow the lower riverbank trail over gravel and boulders before climbing back into the forest. Before long, you'll see the confluence of the rivers Bhote Kosi and Dudh Kosi – the trail to Namche Bazaar climbs directly up the spur between these two watercourses, a continuous ascent of around two hours.

Grit your teeth and climb to a drooping suspension bridge floating above the Dudh Kosi (if any yak or pony trains are already on the bridge, let them pass – you don't want to be tipped into the gorge by a pushy bovine). There is a powerful sense that this is where the mountains really begin.

From here to **Namche Bazaar** (p119), it's a torturous, zigzagging ascent through dense pine forests, with only a handful of water-pipes to fill your drinking bottle. About halfway up is a public toilet where you can get your first partial glimpse of Everest.

Eventually, the path levels out and climbs gently out of the forest to a checkpoint at Mislung, where you must present your TIMS card and national park receipt. The main trail continues to climb, branching right up stone steps for central and upper Namche Bazaar or continuing along the main trail for the lower or western village.

You'll be glad to set down your pack once you reach Namche, which is the closest the Khumbu region has to a city. Thankfully, Namche saw only minor damage in the earthquake. This climb has taken you to an elevation where you may feel the first symptoms of altitude sickness – be alert for the warning signs.

Day 3: Acclimatisation in Namche

Trekkers should schedule an 'acclimatisation day' in Namche to avoid symptoms of

WORTH A TRIP

CHHORKHUNG

One easy acclimatisation walk is the 15-minute climb to the village of **Chhorkung** (3540m), which sprawls along the ridge east of Namche. Climb up past the Panorama Lodge to a memorial gateway, from where you can visit the **Sagarmatha National Park Visitor Centre** (p120) and **Sherpa Culture Museum** (p120); both are expected to be open for the 2015-2016 season. Figure on two-hour return trip.

AMS further up the trail. This doesn't mean you have to stop walking – there are numerous short walks through the hills around Namche that will improve your fitness and help you adjust to the altitude without any dangerous increases in elevation.

You could easily spend a day exploring the shops and sights of Namche and Chhorkung. A shorter alternative to the two side trips described here is to hike up via Zarok to the runway at Shyangboche and then drop back down the zigzag path to Chhorkung for a hike of around 90 minutes.

You could also consider spending your second night at Khunde, Khumjung or Kyangjuma, or spending the day trekking out to Thame, though this village was badly affected by the earthquake.

SIDE TRIP: NAMCHE BAZAAR TO THAME

6–7 HOURS / 330M ASCENT / 330M DESCENT

The most ambitious acclimatisation trek around Namche takes you west along the valley of the Bhote Kosi to the secluded village of **Thame** (3750m), set among fields beneath the mountain wall of Kongde Ri. However, the Thame Valley was severely affected by the 2015 earthquake and many houses collapsed completely in Thame and other villages along the route. Villagers are rebuilding but seek local advice about the availability of food and accommodation before setting off from Namche Bazaar.

Assuming the route is open, it should take about 3½ hours to trek from Namche Bazaar to Thame. If you are in good shape and well acclimatised, it is possible to make the trip to Thame and back to Namche Bazaar in one long day. However, if accommodation is available, staying the night at Thame will provide the opportunity to enjoy the clear mountain views in the morning.

EVEREST REGION EVEREST BASE CAMP TREK

KHUMBILA

The mountain that rises above Namche is Khumbila (5761m). Sherpas worship this mountain as the abode of the protector of the Khumbu region. The Sherpa name Khumbu Yul Lha translates as 'God of the Khumbu territory'. On thangkas (Buddhist paintings) and monastery murals, Khumbu Yul Lha is depicted as a white-faced being riding on a white horse.

The trail to Thame begins by Namche Gompa and climbs around the ridge through a quarry, passing some enormous **mani boulders**, with carved mantras picked out in black and white paint.

After passing a turn-off to Shyangboche, the trail enters a pretty forest of pines and rhododendrons, where you'll hear the jangling bells of grazing yaks. Keep an eye out for musk deer among the trees as you skirt around the ridge to an ancient mud-plastered stupa at **Phurte** (3390m). If open, the small Kongde View Lodge by the stupa is a good choice for clean rooms and snacks.

Follow a forest path dotted with flowering irises around the ridge to a boulder with a painted image of Guru Rinpoche at **Samshing**, then swing past a large chorten. Pass underneath a *kani* and cross a crystal-clear stream at **Tesho** (Thesiyo), where the lovely side valley of the Thesebu Khola beckons invitingly. If open, the simple Khumbila Restaurant makes a handy tea stop.

Just beyond the bridge, a side trail branches right up stone steps to **Mende** (3700m), a patchwork of stone-walled fields on a small plateau. A 20-minute walk above Mende is **Lawudo Gompa** (☑ 9851070922; www.lawudo.com), a monastic school and meditation retreat used by students from Kopan Monastery near Bodhnath. The monastery was badly damaged by the earthquake and reconstruction work is underway; depending on the status of the works, it may be possible for Buddhist-minded trekkers to overnight here – contact them in advance to check. Also damaged, but expected to open for the 2015-2016 trekking season, the chalet-style Everest Summit Lodge (p66) offers luxury accommodation on the edge of the ridge at Mende.

Continuing west from Tesho, climb through rhododendrons to the ridge. About an hour after leaving Phurte, you'll roll into **Thamo** (3440m), also damaged in the quake. Check ahead to make sure lodges are open before planning a stop here. Before the quake, the neat and tidy Maya Lodge at the beginning of the village was a good choice and used home-grown organic vegetables in the kitchen. Other options were the friendly Thamo Guesthouse and Tashi Dele Lodge, next to the large mani wall and stupa in the middle of the village.

At the top end of Thamo, the trail reaches a *kani* and a junction – ignore the path that drops down to the Bhote Kosi, and climb past the Valley View Lodge and the **Khari Gompa** (now under reconstruction for the second time following the earthquake), which is used mostly by nuns.

Above Thamo, the landscape is drier and dustier, like something from California's Sierra Nevada. The path ascends steadily above the stone village of **Thomde**, meeting a side

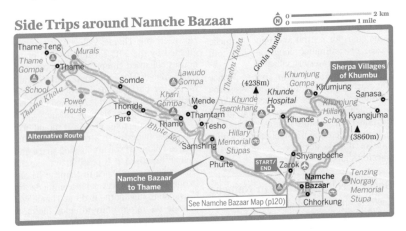

Side Trips around Namche Bazaar

ADVENTUROUS SIDE TRIPS FROM THAME

The valley east of Thame leads to the Rolwaling Valley over the Tesi Lapcha pass. The difficult pass crossing should only be attempted by well-equipped groups with experienced guides, ropes and crampons, and may be closed completely because of earthquake damage. Check ahead to make sure the route is open to trekkers.

If you are not headed to Rolwaling but fancy an adventurous taste of the approach to the pass, it's possible to overnight in Thame and then head west from the gompa up the valley for two hours to **Thyangbo** (4230m), near the pastures of Khure Kharka, where a simple lodge serves as a base camp to explore the trio of lakes at the base of Pachhermo peak and Tashi Labtsa wall. Figure on a two-day trip from Thame.

Another side trip for the fully committed and acclimatised is to the top of **Sunder Peak** (5360m), the toughest of all the viewpoints in the Khumbu. You'll need to leave Thame at dawn to give yourself time for the relentlessly steep 1500m climb and its knee-crushing descent. The trail leads up from behind the gompa and ascends the ridgeline steeply. Your reward is a view of almost the entire Khumbu.

trail that climbs back along the valley to Mende. Continue west to **Somde** (3580m), another cluster of stone-built houses, chortens and mani stones, which also saw extensive damage in the earthquake. If it is open, the spotless Sunshine View Lodge offers views of Kongde Ri and Pharchamo (6187m).

After another steep climb, the trail dives down to the river by a cliff wall with enormous **murals** of Green Tara, Guru Rinpoche and Thangtong Gyalpo, a 14th-century mystic who constructed a series of iron chain bridges across the Himalaya (note the length of chain depicted in his right hand). Below the murals, you cross the raging Bhote Kosi over a narrow cleft in the rock.

From the bridge, it's a steep final 20-minute climb up to the village of **Thame** (3820m), whose earthquake-damaged houses are scattered across a broad, flat flood-plain. The soft sediments beneath the village made Thame particularly vulnerable to earthquakes, and many houses here were destroyed. While villagers are rebuilding, it is essential to check that accommodation will be available here before setting out from Namche Bazaar, or from Gokyo if attempting the Three Passes trek.

Thame lies at an important junction, with trails running west towards Tesi Lapcha, the 5755m pass leading to the Rolwaling Valley (also severely affected by the earthquake), and north towards the Renjo La (5345m) and the Nangpa La (5716m) crossing to Tibet. The fang-like ridge of Kongde Ri (6187m) rises sheer above the valley.

Most lodges in the village were damaged in the earthquake, and some are beyond repair. It is not clear which of the following

lodges will be open by the time you read this; ask locally for advice. Before the quake, the first lodge in the village was the Chooyo Thame Lodge on the right, while straight on was the popular Everest Summiteer Lodge. The nearby Valley View Lodge and Sunshine Lodge were recommended for offering some rooms with attached bathrooms, while the Tibet Guest House was notable for owner Pasang Sonam Sherpa, who made 10 successful summits of Everest. if you plan to overnight in Thame, check ahead to see what accommodation is available.

A 25-minute trek up the sandy ridge behind the Valley View Lodge will get you to **Thame Gompa**, wedged into a crack in the rock at 3970m; keep to the left as you pass the chortens and mani walls. Set in a compound of slate-roofed stone houses, the gompa survived the earthquake, but many structures were damaged and restoration work is underway. The gompa (properly known as Dechen Chekhorling) was founded in 1667 but it has been renovated many times and the murals inside were retouched by local artists in 1998. The main chapel enshrines images of Chenresig, Guru Rinpoche and Sakyamuni, but the views over the valley are even more impressive than the Tibetan iconography inside. A single lodge here offers the chance to spend a serene night above the hubbub of Thame.

To return to Namche from Thame, you can either retrace your steps or follow a quieter short cut along the south bank of the Bhote Kosi. From the Tibet Guest House, cross the stream to the reservoir, then follow the new wide trail just below the ridge. At the end of the spur, the trail drops steeply to a hydro-electric powerhouse, then turns left to cross the Bhote Kosi on a small bridge. Rise gently along the north bank to the stupa at Thomde and finally the *kani* at Thamo. From here it's a pleasant two-hour stroll back to Namche.

SIDE TRIP: SHERPA VILLAGES OF KHUMBU
4–5 HOURS / 460M ASCENT / 460M DESCENT

Another rewarding acclimatisation trek is the full-day circuit through Shyangboche, Khunde and Khumjung and back to Namche, but all three villages saw some earthquake damage so check that the route is OK to trek before you set off.

Pick up the trail above Namche Gompa and make a tiring ascent of the ridge on a steep, zigzagging path to the boulder-strewn village of **Zarok**, where the lonely but peaceful Sunshine Lodge is under reconstruction following the earthquake. Small quarries below here provide the stone for all the lodge construction going on in the valley.

Continue climbing past a signposted trail to Thame to the small Phinjo Lodge and the grass airstrip at **Shyangboche** (3790m). This lofty runway was built to serve the Hotel Everest View, but no airlines currently have planes that can climb to this lofty altitude.

Pass the runway and follow the signposted path to Khunde, which rises up a sandy gully between wind-twisted juniper bushes, passing a turn-off for a direct route to Khumjung. At the top of the ridge, the path enters a wonderland of carved boulders, chortens, junipers and rhododendrons, where a fairy-tale stairway drops to a *kani* and Bodhnath-style chorten on the edge of **Khunde** (3840m), two hours from Namche Bazaar. The views of Khumbila, Ama Dablam and Thamserku peaks are wonderful.

The village is famous as the location of the first hospital in the Khumbu, built by the Himalayan Trust in 1966, which played a major role in the relief effort following the earthquakes. A number of village houses collapsed in the disaster, but reconstruction work is underway. Above the village is the friendly **Khunde Tsamkhang**, a Buddhist temple founded by a lama who fled here from Tingri in Tibet in the 1970s; it's currently being restored following the earthquake.

A side trail leaves the temple to gently traverse the ridge to the left. In 30 minutes you can reach the **Hillary Memorial Viewpoint**, offering 360-degree views over Khunde, Namche Bazaar, Ama Dablam and

Pachermo peak behind Thame. Two minutes further up the ridge are three memorial chortens to Edmund Hillary, and to his wife Louise and daughter Belinda who both died in an aeroplane accident in the Khumbu. It's possible to continue to the top of the ridge for wonderful views down over Khumjung.

If you want to spend the night there are several quiet lodges in the tangle of stone lanes near the hospital but it is unclear which are still operating after the earthquake. Before the quake, these included the pleasant Sonam Norwegian Lodge, Khunde Guest House and Green Valley Lodge; check locally to see what accommodation is available if you intend to stop overnight.

From Khunde, follow the obvious cobbled trail east for 15 minutes through potato fields to **Khumjung** (3780m), the largest village in the Khumbu, which sprawls below the peak of Khumbila (5761m). The houses here are large and impressive, and many locals own tracts of land further north along the valley. Sadly, the earthquake caused a fair amount of damage in the village and some houses were destroyed.

In the south of Khumjung is the original Hillary school, established by Sir Edmund Hillary in 1961, just eight years after the conquest of Everest. Now under reconstruction following the earthquake, the school provides primary and secondary education for more than 350 children from surrounding villages. The mani wall here is said to be the longest in the Khumbu region.

Khumjung has a small and atmospheric **gompa**, damaged but not destroyed in the earthquakes, reached by a winding path that starts near the Mountain View Lodge. One of the treasures kept here is a 'yeti skull' that was transported to America for analysis by Sir Edmund Hillary and village headman Konchok Chumbi. Tests concluded that the scalp was made from the skin of a serow, a member of the antelope family, but the legend continues.

Before the disaster, there were at least 15 lodges in Khumjung, all offering rooms with shared bathrooms for the standard Khumbu rates, but some were damaged in the earthquakes; check locally to see which lodges are currently open. Before the disaster, the Khumbiye-La Garden Lodge, Hidden Village Lodge, Sherpaland Lodge and Panorama In Eco-Lodge by the village school were all good choices. In the eastern village, consider the large **Khumjung Hotel** (☏038-540041; r Rs 300); at first glance the building looks

SHERPAS

The Solu-Khumbu region is the homeland of the Sherpas, a Buddhist people who migrated to Solu Khumbu from the Tibetan plateau around the 15th century. Sherpas still follow similar customs to the Buddhists of Tibet and they speak a language derived from Tibetan. The Sherpas call themselves 'Shar-wa', meaning 'people from the East'. Sherpas can be divided into 18 ancient clans, but most Sherpa men take their names from the day of the week on which they were born – Lhakpa (Wednesday), Phurba (Thursday) etc. Sherpas often add the prefix 'Ang' to their name (similar to the English suffix 'son' or abbreviation 'Jr').

The term 'sherpa' is applied to porters throughout Nepal, but only the people of Solu Khumbu and Helambu can properly be called Sherpas. Ever since the climbing expeditions of the 1950s, the Sherpas have been famous for their skills as mountaineers and high-altitude porters. In fact, they have a unique advantage in this regard – thanks to hundreds of years of living at high altitude, the blood of Sherpas is chemically more efficient at carrying oxygen than the blood of people from the lowlands.

large and impersonal, but there's a sunny conservatory at the back.

For views and afternoon sun, try the Valley View Lodge and Khumjung Hilltop View Lodge in the upper part of Khumjung, near the gompa. There are many more lodges with similar facilities – just stroll through the village and see which places take your fancy.

For lunch, the long-established Everest Bakery is a local institution and the deep-filled apple pie is often said to be the best in the Khumbu; there are reports that the bakery was badly damaged so check locally to see if they are still baking.

Several paths lead on from Khumjung. If you are not returning to Namche Bazaar, the main trail drops over the eastern edge of the ridge on wide stone steps to Sanasa and Phortse Thenga (passed on Day 4 of the Everest Base Camp trek). To return directly to Namche Bazaar, take the path behind the Hillary school to the north end of the runway at Shyangboche.

For a scenic route, take the small track that climbs south near the Everest Bakery for 10 minutes to the white Hillary Memorial Stupa. Continue uphill into a delightful forest and then bear right to reach the perimeter wall of the famous Hotel Everest View (p66). The hotel used to fly guests into Shyangboche directly from Kathmandu, using pressurised rooms and piped oxygen to avoid their heads exploding from AMS. Needless to say, this is no longer regarded as a sensible policy.

Follow the trail south from the Everest View as it winds around the steep hillside, then drop down to the southern end of the airfield, passing the seven-roomed Khumbu Mountain View Lodge and the laughably overpriced **Everest Sherpa Resort** (☑ 01-447884; www.everestresort.com; s/d US$127/150), which was damaged in the earthquake but is being restored.

Follow the path down through the junipers and cross the airfield, then take the steep trail that zigzags past a prayer-flag-strewn lookout down to the huge carved mani stone at Chhorkung (3540m).

Day 4: Namche Bazaar to Tengboche

4 HOURS / 350M DESCENT / 750M ASCENT

There are several routes from Namche to Tengboche. One excellent option is to climb to Shyangboche and Khumjung; the advantage of this is that it avoids repetition on the way back. Most trekkers instead opt for the more direct, level trail that cuts around the ridge from Chhorkung.

Pick up the path by the giant mani boulder in Chhorkung, and trek north around a long, denuded ridge. This slope was once covered by dense juniper forests, but locals have stripped the hillside for firewood to supply the demands of trekkers for cooked food, warm rooms and hot water. At the end of the bluff a memorial chorten to Tenzing Norgay frames a grand panorama of peaks, from Thamserku to Ama Dablam, Lhotse and Everest.

Every spur you gain seems to bring the mountains closer. At **Kyangjuma** (Kenjoma; 3550m), which escaped serious damage in the earthquake, several lodges offer a tea stop or a wonderfully quiet acclimatisation night – our picks are the professionally run **Ama Dablam Lodge** (☑ 038-540013; r Rs 200-1500) with wi-fi, bakery, a sun terrace and warm restaurant, or the quieter and more intimate Dream Garden Lodge, which sells yak cheese.

TENGBOCHE MONASTERY

A powerful mythology has grown up around the monastery at Tengboche (Thyangboche) as a result of the writings of explorers and mountaineers, but the gompa is not as ancient as you might expect. The first gompa at Tengboche was constructed in 1916 by Lama Gulu, a monk from Khumjung, but the building was destroyed in the earthquake of 1934, which also killed its founder. A second gompa on the site lasted until 1989, when an electrical fire burned the stone-and-timber structure to the ground.

Fortunately, most of the gompa's valuable books, paintings and religious relics were saved. Using donations from Sherpas, foreign aid organisations, Buddhist groups and mountaineering and trekking companies, Tengboche was painstakingly reconstructed, reopening its doors in 1993. The main hall enshrines a 4m-high statue of Sakyamuni, flanked by the bodhisattvas Dorje Sempa (Vajrasattva) and Jampelyang (Manjushri) and backed by an ornate original wooden frieze that was rescued from the fire.

Sadly, Tengboche sustained further earthquake damage in the 2015 quake. Restoration work is underway, but many of the monks' cells and outlying buildings were damaged and some parts of the compound may be inaccessible. Assuming you can explore, look out for the stone with a foot-shaped imprint in the entryway to the monastery courtyard; this was allegedly left by Lama Sange Dorje as he travelled around the Himalaya in the 17th century. The fifth reincarnate lama of Rongbuk Gompa in Tibet, Sange Dorje is credited with bringing Buddhism to the Khumbu.

The monastery courtyard is the setting for the famous Mani Rimdu festival in the ninth Tibetan month (normally October or November), with whirling masked *chaam* dances and plenty of eating, drinking and making merry. See www.tengboche.org for dates and details.

Visitors are welcome to attend the daily puja (prayer) ceremonies at 6am and 3pm, but sit to the right so as not to interrupt the resident monks as they chant the scriptures. Wearing shoes or shorts, smoking and taking photos are all prohibited inside the monastery.

An important trail junction at **Sanasa** (3600m) is 10 minutes further on. Signposted trails climb the hillside to Khumjung (30 minutes) and Gokyo, while the trail to Tengboche runs gently downhill towards the river. There are three lodges at Sanasa, but most trekkers are put off by the over-enthusiastic souvenir vendors.

From Sanasa, the Tengboche trail drops gradually to **Lawichasa** (Labisyasa; 3450m), which has the Pokhara Lodge and a few smoky teashops. As you descend, the thumb-like peak of Ama Dablam soars into view above the trail.

A minor side trail branches north from Lawichasa to **Tashinga** (3380m), a grid of stone-walled fields on a flat bluff and the red-roofed luxury Everest Summit Lodge (p66), which was damaged in the quake and expected to open in 2016.

Below Lawichasa, the Tengboche trail drops on steep stone steps to **Phunki Thenga** (3250m), a cluster of lodges and a bakery by a wood-and-stone bridge across the river, all of which escaped serious earthquake damage. From here it's a draining two-hour climb to Tengboche, so make the most of the eating options – Evergreen Lodge and Cozy Garden Lodge both serve hearty meals.

From the bridge, stop briefly at the army checkpost and then climb past some water-powered prayer wheels on a sustained 90-minute climb through a forest of tall, mature rhododendrons. Look out for musk deer and Himalayan tahr among the trees. On the way, there are several chautara (porter rest stops) and springs where you can set down your pack and enjoy the views towards Kantega. Kantega means 'horse saddle', and from here it's clear how the mountain got its name.

Eventually you'll reach a *kani* and a pair of chortens marking **Tengboche** (3870m). The village is scattered across a wide, grassy saddle below a crescent-shaped ridge covered by scrub pines and dwarf rhododendrons. The focal point of Tengboche is the famous **Tengboche Gompa**, the largest and most active monastery in the Khumbu, which is currently being restored after taking some damage in the earthquake. Taking photos is not allowed inside.

Across the meadow from the monastery is the eratically open **Eco Centre** (www.sacred-land.net; admission Rs 100; ☉7-10.30am & noon-

5.30pm Mar, Apr, Jun-Aug, Oct & Nov, 7-9.30am & 1-5pm Sep, Dec & May, 3-5pm Jan & Feb), with some thought-provoking displays on the history of Tengboche, the culture of the Sherpas and the environmental issues facing the Khumbu.

The lodges at Tengboche get extremely crowded during the trekking season and there was some damage here from the earthquake, so check locally to see which lodges are currently operating. Before the disaster, one good choice was the ramshackle backpacker Trekkers Lodge, by the start of the side trail to Phortse, with fine views looking back down the valley. In the meadow below the gompa, the fancy Tashi Deleck Lodge and Himalayan View Lodge have carpeted rooms and wi-fi and are popular with groups. At the lower end of the saddle are the simpler tin-roofed Tengboche Guest House and the run-down Gomba Lodge. Between these two lodges, the monastery-owned **Tengboche Bakery** (cakes Rs 400, mains Rs 500-600; ☺6am-8pm) serves big mugs of tea and coffee, huge slices of cake and portions of lasagne and pizza. It's a great place to escape the chilly breezes that blow across the saddle. Depending on connections, you may be able to check email at nearby Tengboche Cyber.

A quieter alternative to Tengboche is to continue for 20 minutes down the main trail to Debuche, where there are several excellent lodges.

Day 5: Acclimatisation Day in Tengboche

You will do much better in the high country if you spend another day acclimatising at Tengboche, though you could feasibly replace this with an alternative extra day in Thame or Khumjung, or a night in Pangboche. You can explore the monastery, climb the prayer-flag-strewn hill above the Hotel Himalayan or take a hike to the nunnery at Debuche.

Day 6: Tengboche to Pheriche

3½ HOURS / 70M DESCENT / 450M ASCENT

From Tengboche, follow the trail below the bakery through a lovely forest of dwarf conifers and rhododendrons, keeping an eye out for monal pheasants and musk deer. After 15 minutes the stone path reaches **Debuche** (3820m). There are several lodges here, but some were damaged in the quake so check locally to see which are currently operating. Before the disaster, the excellent **Rivendell**

Lodge (☑ 9803527894; www.khumburivendell. org; r with shared/private bathroom Rs300/3000) scored points for its hot showers and rooms with attached bathrooms and electric blankets. Also good were the smaller Everest Rhododendron Lodge and 10 minutes further along the track, the friendly Paradise Lodge, Ama Dablam Garden Lodge and fancy new Hotel Himalayan Culture Home, set in a copse of pines.

While you are here, drop into the **Debuche Nunnery**, which suffered some exterior damage in the earthquake but still has some impressive old thangkas (Buddhist paintings) and murals painted on wooden panels inside. Photos are allowed. The nunnery is beside the main track, near the chorten.

The trail continues through a dense rhododendron forest, dripping with Spanish moss. About 15 minutes past Debuche you'll reach **Milinggo**, where the the path drops past a ruined metal bridge to a wooden bridge crossing the surging white waters of the Imja Khola.

On the far side take care climbing the eroded hillside (don't take the dangerous shortcut) to reach a white chorten decorated with Buddha eyes. After 100m you'll reach a great photo opportunity – a stupa crowns an exposed bluff, mirroring the soaring tower of Ama Dablam at the end of the valley. East of the stupa is a footprint of Khumbu's patron saint Lama Sange Dorje, preserved in stone.

You'll soon reach a *kani* on the outskirts of **Pangboche** (3860m) where the trail splits. The lower path drops to a cluster of trailside lodges, while the upper trail climbs to the charming upper village and monastery. Some buildings sustained minor earthquake damage, but most lodges are open as normal. Most trekkers take the lower path on the way to Everest Base Camp, and the upper path on the way back down.

In the upper part of the village, **Pangboche (Pal Rilbu) Gompa** (requested donation Rs 100; ☺8am-5pm) is the oldest monastery in the Khumbu, founded by Lama Sange Dorje in the 17th century but restored by the Mountain Institute in 2010. The most famous relics are the supposed skull and hand of a yeti displayed by the donations box. The originals were stolen in 1991 and what you see now are replicas. Just above the nearby Hillary school is a small shrine to Guru Rinpoche.

There is no shortage of accommodation. There are six similar lodges lining the lower

TIBET (CHINA) (6150m)

Khumbutse (6639m)

(6822m)▲

Chumbu (6859m)

Pumori (7165m) Mahalangur Himal

Everest Base Camp (5340m)

Khumbu

Side Trip: Kala Pattar

Gyubanar Glacier

Gyubanar Glacier

Kala Pattar (5545m)

(6027m)▲

▲(5962m)

Changri Shar Glacier

Changri La (5697m)

(6063m)▲

Nirekha Peak (6169m)▲

(5690m)

Changri Nup Glacier

Gorak Shep

Khumbu Glacier

Paugungayan Tsho

Lobuche (6135m)

(5865m)▲

▲(5672m)

(5656m)

Sagarmatha National Park

Niro Tsho

▲(5963m)

Italian Pyramid

Cho La (5420m)

Lobuche East (Abi) (6119m)▲

Lobuche Glacier

Nuptse Glacier

▲(5666m)

Lobuche

Kongma Tse (Mehra Peak) (5820m)▲

▲(5729m)

Cholatse Khola

Alternative Route

▲(5939m)

Naktok Tsho

Dzonglha

Kongma La (5535m)

▲(5798m)

Tsholo Og

Niyang Khola

Cholatse Tsho

Alternative Route

Dughla

Pokhalde (5745m)

Pokhalde (5806m)▲

Tsusam Khola

Cholatse (6443m)▲

Chola Glacier

Cholatse Glacier

Phalang Karpo

Dusa

Nangkartshang (5090m)▲

Nangkartshang Hermitage

Bibre

(6367m)▲

(6432m)▲

Pheriche

Dingboche

Sanjo

Konar Glacier

(5724m)▲

Taboche (6542m)▲

Duwo

Amphu Gyabjen (5650m)▲

▲(5610m)

Duwo Glacier

Mingbo Glacier

▲(5477m)

(5375m)▲

Orsho

Taboche

Shomare

Ralha

▲(5055m)

Ama Dablam (6856m)▲

Kandu Khola

▲(5202m)

Lhabarma

Mingbo Glacier

Konar

See Everest Base Camp Trek Day 1-4 Map (p69)

Pangboche

Yarai

Mingbo

Side Trip: Ama Dablam Base Camp

Dudh Kosi

Milinggo

Imoga Khola

▲(5178m)

Cholungche Khola

Phortse Thenga

Phortse

Debuche

Mong La

Phunki Thenga

Tengboche

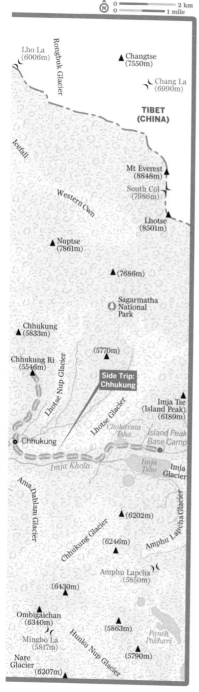

trail, and there are a couple more in upper Pangboche village, but it is not clear if all the lodges will be open by the time you read this; enquire locally for the latest news.

Good choices before the disaster included the Buddha Lodge, on the main trail through the lower village, and Highland Sherpa Resort, which has wi-fi, oxygen and a mountain rescue service. At the far end of the village, the popular **Om Kailash Hotel** (☑038-540226; r without/with bathroom Rs 200/1500) offers simple rooms facing down the valley. Nearby Everest View Lodge is also good. A little further on is Sonam Lodge and the good new Wind Horse Inn, opposite to which is Hermann Bakery, offering wi-fi, telephone calls, coffee and a fine apple strudel.

Upper Pangboche has a collection of atmospheric lodges in traditional village houses scattered around the gompa. The best option is the Trekker's Holiday Inn Lodge, overlooking the gompa and run by 12-time Everest summiteer Phutashi Sherpa.

Heading north from Pangboche, the main trail and upper Pangboche trail join after 10 minutes. From here you'll climb above the treeline, entering an arid landscape of glacial boulders and alpine meadows. You won't see another proper tree until you drop below the treeline on your way back from Everest Base Camp.

Follow the path of the Imja Khola past a rock mural of Guru Rinpoche to Shomare (4010m), which was hit by sliding debris in the earthquake. Before the quake, there were five good lodges operating here, plus the Sunshine Lodge, sitting in glorious isolation a little further on in the Orsho plain; check locally to see which are currently offering accommodation. Note that a landslide risk has been identified on this stretch of trail.

Beyond Orsho the trail divides. You have two options for the night – you can take the lower, more obvious-looking trail along the Imja Khola to Dingboche, which is the better location for a day or two exploring some side trips, or follow the smaller left-hand path to Pheriche, which has medical facilities but was badly damaged in the earthquake. Traditionally, most trekkers have opted to stay in Pheriche, as the village is 130m lower than Dingboche, but this may change because of the destruction caused by the 2015 disaster.

To reach Pheriche, the trail climbs to a minor ridge topped by stupas and memorials to lost climbers and then crosses the small but fast-flowing Khumbu Khola on a small bridge that gets washed away and replaced every other monsoon.

The houses of **Pheriche** (4240m) are scattered along the broad valley of the Khumbu Khola, which drains from the Khumbu Glacier at the foot of Everest. Icy winds scour down the valley, wicking away moisture and body heat – wrap up warmly and wear plenty of lip balm on this stage of the trek.

The village itself was hit very badly by the 2015 earthquake. Around 70% of buildings were damaged and while restoration work is underway, the difficulty of getting building materials to this remote location is impeding progress. It was not clear at the time of

YETIS

Countries all around the world have legends of hairy human-like animals that live in areas untouched by modern explorers. In Nepal and Tibet, this mythical figure is known as the yeti, from the Tibetan *yeh* (meaning 'snow valley') and *teh* ('man'). You may also hear the Tibetan name *mehton kangmi,* which translates as 'abominable snowman'. Reports from western Nepal talk of the *lamkarna,* or 'long-eared' monster.

There have been dozens of cases of local sightings. Villagers in the Rongbuk region of Tibet apparently discovered a drowned yeti corpse in 1958. In 1998 the official police report on the murder of a Sherpa woman near Dole on the Gokyo trek in Nepal cited 'yeti attack' as the cause of death.

First-hand accounts of the yeti describe it as having reddish fur, a conical head, a high-pitched cry and strange body odour that smells of garlic, but a sign at Khumjung Monastery outlines the different types of yeti in more subtle and, more importantly, cultural terms. The apelike *dre-ma* and *tel-ma* are messengers of calamity, it says, while the *chu-ti* moves on all fours and preys on goats, sheep and yaks. Worst of all is the *mi-te,* a man-eater, 6ft to 8ft tall, with 'a very bad temperament'.

Before you throw your arms up in the air and storm out of the room, bear in mind that the pro-yeti camp has some serious proponents. In 1938 mountaineer Bill Tilman tracked yeti footprints for over a mile, later writing that their 'existence is surely no longer a matter for conjecture'. Edmund Hillary led an expedition to Rolwaling in 1960 to track the yeti, as did Chris Bonington in 1986 and travel writer Bruce Chatwin. Reinhold Messner claimed to have seen a yeti in Tibet in 1986 and wrote a book about the subject called *My Quest for the Yeti.*

Hillary even carried a 'yeti skull' from Khumjung to America to be studied in 1960. The relic turned out to be made from a serow, a type of goat/antelope. However, in 2014 DNA tests conducted on a 'yeti' hair sample gave a match with a type of prehistoric polar-bear-like creature thought to have died out 40,000 years ago.

Here are some pivotal moments in yeti history:

1889 – Major LA Wassell finds a set of mysterious footprints in northeastern Sikkim, the first recorded sighting of a yeti by a Westerner.

1923 – British mountaineer Alan Cameron spots humanoid creatures walking along a ridge near Everest.

1937 – Lord Hunt and Tilman find yeti tracks on the Zemu Glacier in Sikkim.

1939 – German professor Ernst Schaefer visits Tibet in search of the yeti, allegedly on the orders of the Nazi SS.

1951 – Eric Shipton discovers yeti tracks during a reconnaissance mission to Everest, later revealed as a practical joke.

1970 – Don Whillans hears weird cries and watches a yeti through binoculars while climbing Annapurna.

1984 – Tim Macartney-Snape and Greg Mortimer find unexplained tracks near the summit of Everest.

2008 – A Japanese expedition to Dhaulagiri IV finds yeti footprints, but fails to capture a yeti on film.

writing when the lodges would reopen, and for the time being at least, trekkers might do better staying in Dingboche.

If you do stay here, check locally to see which lodges are currently operating. Before the disaster, Pheriche's central and well-run Panorama Lodge was a good choice and slightly cheaper than other options. Former US President Carter stayed here in 1985. Also popular was the Himalayan Hotel next door, with a bakery and internet cafe. Slightly above the village, the large White Yak Mountain Hut offered cosy rooms with Tibetan curtains, Western-style toilets,hot showers and slightly pricey meals. Other popular lodges included the long-established Snowland Lodge, Pheriche Resort, and Mountain Guides Lodge. Assuming lodges are operating, it should be possible to make international satellite phone calls here; expect to pay upwards of Rs 150.

Pheriche is famous as the location of the emergency health centre run by the **Himalayan Rescue Association** (☑ 038-540214; consultation US$65, Visa cards accepted for 5% fee; ☉ 9am-noon & 1.30pm-5pm), which is dedicated to the treatment and prevention of altitude sickness. The centre played a major role in the rescue operation following the 2015 earthquake. Western doctors are usually in attendance during the trekking season, and there is a highly recommended free presentation every day at 3pm to educate trekkers about the risks of AMS.

In front of the Panorama Lodge is the modern cone-shaped Everest Memorial Sculpture, inscribed with the names of those who have died climbing Everest.

SIDE TRIP: AMA DABLAM BASE CAMP
5 HOURS / 720M ASCENT / 720M DESCENT

If you are fit and well acclimatised it's possible to make an incredibly scenic but fairly strenuous half-day return trip from Pangboche to meadows at Ama Dablam Base Camp (4580m), from where you'll get superb views of expedition tents camped at the base of the iconic peak. It's a minimum two-hour ascent and the first half is steep. However, check locally to see if this route is currently trekkable.

Branch off the main trail at the far end of Pangboche next to the Sonam Lodge and descend to cross the bridge over the Dudh Kosi. The trail is steep, then flat, then steep again, passing a stupa to the left offering fine views of Pumori. The gorge of the gla-

CEREMONIAL SCARVES

Throughout the Khumbu, you will see Sherpas presenting each other with *kata* – silk scarves bearing woven images of the eight lucky Buddhist symbols. Sherpas offer *kata* to high lamas, relatives, friends, guests and the gods as a gesture of respect – when you finish your trek, your guide may drape a *kata* around your neck to wish you luck on the rest of your travels. If you plan to present a *kata* to a lama (Buddhist teacher), place the scarf in their hands, rather than putting it around their neck.

cial Chhulungche Khola thunders to the right. The trail continues through sandy sections to eventually pop up at meadows at the base of 6856m Ama Dablam, one of the Khumbu's most sublime peaks.

There are normally lots of expedition tents at base camp, many more than you will find at Everest in October, and there are stunning views of Ama Dablam's east face. A short detour behind the moraine hill to the south takes you the Ama Dablam Summit Lodge at Mingbo (4600m), offering food and lodging in eight simple rooms. If you are experienced and acclimatised to these altitudes (ie on the way *down* from Everest Base Camp) then you could use the lodge as a base to explore advanced base camp or even the glaciers around Mingbo La at the head of the valley.

From base camp it's a 90-minute descent back to Pangboche.

ALTERNATIVE ROUTE: TENGBOCHE TO DINGBOCHE
3–4½ HOURS / 70M DESCENT / 580M ASCENT

Dingboche is a popular alternative overnight stop to Pheriche, and is likely to be even more popular now because of the earthquake damage in Pheriche. Few buildings in Dingboche were damaged in the quake, but the village is 130m higher than Pheriche, which can increase the risk of AMS. Even if you don't stay here, you can visit Dingboche as part of the acclimatisation trek to Chhukung.

Coming from Tengboche, follow the Pheriche trail as far as Orsho, and take the lower path along the west bank of the Imja Khola. The trail drops to a small bridge over the Khumbu Khola at 4130m and then climbs beside the river for about 30 minutes to the scattered houses of **Dingboche** (4360m). Looking east from the

RECYCLING, HIMALAYAN STYLE

Above Tengboche, you will start to see the detritus of past climbing expeditions being sold on by shops and lodges. The average Everest team carries 24 tonnes of equipment, loaded onto 600 porters, and much of this gear is never used. As a result, the lodges and shops of the Khumbu are piled high with hand-me-downs from climbing expeditions. You'll find mountain gear being recycled in all sorts of imaginative ways – elderly women use technical trekking poles as walking sticks, scarecrows wear bright Gore-Tex jackets and old oxygen cylinders are used as dinner bells and monastery gongs.

Almost every lodge north of Tengboche has a cabinet full of bashed and bent tin cans that are sold on to locals and campers. You can find all sorts of oddities in these cabinets: tins of sardines, Italian pasta, French snails, condensed Russian borscht, processed cheese – often without labels. It's a bit like Russian roulette, but with canned goods.

village, you'll see the snowcapped summits of Island Peak (Imja Tse; 6189m), Peak 38 (7591m) and Lhotse (8501m).

In many ways, Dingboche is a more pleasant place to stay than Pheriche – the sun stays here longer each evening and the wind blows gently instead of roaring down the valley. You can check emails on a reasonably fast connection at the **Dingboche Internet Café** (per min Rs 20; ⊙ 7am-8pm), at the Peak 38 View Lodge.

There are at least 10 lodges down in the lower village – the recommended Snow Lion Lodge has a cafe-bakery, a pharmacy and good food, while the Peaceful Lodge opposite is also good, as long as you get a room with an exterior window. The Green Tara Guesthouse and Everest Resort are also good choices. In the upper village, Valley View Lodge and Peak 38 View Lodge are typical mountain lodges with good views. This part of the village enjoys longer afternoon sun.

Day 7: Acclimatisation Day in Pheriche/Dingboche

It is very important to spend an additional night at Pheriche or Dingboche to aid the acclimatisation process. Many trekkers are happy to spend the day exploring Pheriche and Dingboche (the two villages are just 30 minutes apart), but there are several interesting day hikes in this area.

One enjoyable short walk is the hour-long climb past prayer flags and chortens to **Nangkartshang Hermitage**, a collection of retreats built around the meditation cave of Sange Dorje, on the ridge north of Dingboche. The trail continues up the hillside for another 90 minutes to a **viewpoint** at 5070m that offers fantastic views north to Cholatse (6443m) and Taboche (6542m), south to the lakes at the foot of Ama Dablam

and east to Chhukung and Makalu (8463m), the fifth-highest mountain in the world. Check locally to make sure that the trail is intact before you set off.

SIDE TRIP: CHHUKUNG
5–6 HOURS / 490M ASCENT / 490M DESCENT

A longer acclimatisation trek is the full-day hike to Chhukung in the upper Imja Valley. This side valley escaped serious damage in the earthquake but the status of the lodges here is unclear – check locally to make sure meals and accommodation are available before leaving Dingboche or Pheriche. Assuming all is open, the views are stupendous, even by Khumbu standards, but the glacial winds will cut you to the bone without multiple clothing layers. This trek forms part of the approach to Island Peak, one of Nepal's most popular trekking peaks.

Starting from Pheriche, pick up the trail to Dingboche on the moraine slope southeast of the village. From the crest of the hill, pause to admire the snow-wrapped peaks of Taboche and Cholatse and the north face of Ama Dablam, which is almost unrecognisable from this angle.

The upper path passes two chortens (the second marks the turn-off to Nangkartshang Peak) before dropping to the upper village and Peak 38 View Lodge. From here it's a steady climb over barren moraines to a series of stepping stones over the Niyang Khola and a lonely teashop at **Bibre** (4570m), one hour from Dingboche.

About 30 minutes west of Bibre, you'll reach **Chhukung** (4730m), the barest smudge of a village nestling among ridges of moraine. Before the earthquake, the largest lodge was the well-run **Chukung Resort** (☑ 038-540145; hoteltibet@gmail.com; ☎), with hot showers and wi-fi, owned by the Hotel

Tibet in Namche Bazaar. Also popular were the Khangri Resort and Sunrise Eco Guesthouse, both of which rented climbing gear such as plastic boots (Rs 600 per day). Check locally to see which lodges are operating.

Mountains and glaciers surround Chhukung and there are some great side trips here. The most popular half-day trip is the stiff climb up the 5546m **Chhukung Ri** (four hours return) for views over a fairy-tale panorama of peaks, including Ama Dablam, Baruntse (7220m) and Makalu (8463m).

Using Chhukung as an overnight base, you can make a challenging day trip to **Island Peak Base Camp** (4970m; six to seven hours return) along the moraine of the Lhotse Glacier, passing the bloated waters of Imja Tsho. This glacial lake has

swelled to dangerous levels because of global warming, and scientists are watching it carefully after the 2015 earthquake, though no specific risks have been identified.

Instead of branching left before Imja Tsho towards Island Peak Base Camp, it is also possible to branch right, crossing the stream over a wooden bridge to pass Imja Tsho on its southern side and then swing south up to the base of serrated **Amphu Lapcha**. The perilous 5850m Amphu Lapcha pass crosses this knife-edge of ice and rock to access the high glaciers of Makalu-Barun National Park. From this high mountain cul-de-sac there are fine views of Imja Tsho, Island Peak, Lhotse Shar, Cho Polu and Buruntse peaks. Figure on a seven-hour return day trip from Chhukung.

TREKKING PEAKS

The most popular trekking peak in the Khumbu is **Island Peak**, properly known as Imja Tse (6189m), and accessed from a base in Chhukung. Although one of the smaller trekking peaks, it is still a challenging ascent requiring ice axes and crampons. The reward for all this exertion is an unparalleled view of Ama Dablam and the south face of Lhotse. It makes sense to trek to Everest Base Camp first to help with acclimatisation. All indications are that the peak will be open as normal by the time you read this.

After acclimatisation, briefing, training and a half-day hike to base camp, the peak is generally climbed in a single eight-hour day, departing as early as 1am. It's physically demanding but apart from one steep and exposed 100m ice or snow climb, is considered a nontechnical snow climb. Companies like **Himalayan Ecstasy** (p35) operate six-day courses and ascents weekly in season (mid-October to mid-November, and the end of March to May), with training at the base of Ama Dablam, at a cost of US$700.

A good step after Island Peak is to the false summit of **Lobuche East** (6119m), a more technically difficult ascent that requires two days of training. The top is exposed and often covered with rotten snow; there's also an exposed knife ridge and some crevasses; check that the route is open before setting off. Climbers generally depart from a high camp at 1.30am and are back by noon. The six-day return trip from Dzonglha costs around US$700. Himalayan Ecstasy offers Island and Lobuche Peaks together in one trip for US$1350. Trips operate in November and from mid-April to mid-May.

For details of the trip from Lukla to Mera Peak, the highest of the trekking peaks, see the Eastern Nepal boxed text on p226.

See p34 for details of the permit requirements for trekking peaks.

More advanced trekking peaks in the Everest region include:

➡ **Kongma Tse** (5820m) A rock and ice climb that's not difficult from either the Imja Valley or Lobuche. It used to be called Mehra Peak.

➡ **Kusum Kangru** (6367m) The most difficult of the trekking peaks; it means 'Three Snowy Peaks' in Tibetan. It's the large squarish peak just south of Thamserku that you can see from the trail from Lukla to Namche.

➡ **Kwangde** (6187m) The north face (seen from Namche Bazaar) is a difficult climb; the southern side (from Lumding Kharka above Ghat) is a moderately technical climb (allow about two to three weeks).

➡ **Pharilapche** (6017m), **Machhermo** (6273m) and **Kyajo Ri** (6186m) All in the stunning Gokyo Valley.

➡ **Pokhalde** (5806m) Short, steep snow climb from the Kongma La above Lobuche.

You will need to overnight at Chhukung if you want to attempt these excursions, and this is only advisable if you've spent two nights at Dingboche. If you don't feel like stopping overnight, it's an easy two-hour descent back to Dingboche or Pheriche.

A trail leads from Chhukung over the Kongma La (5535m) to Lobuche. See the Three Passes (p100) trek for details.

Day 8: Pheriche/Dingboche to Dughla

2 HOURS / 400M ASCENT

If you head straight to Lobuche (4930m), you will almost double the recommended daily gain in elevation. For this reason, we strongly advise breaking the journey overnight at Dughla (4620m) or Chhukung (4730m) to aid with acclimatisation.

Coming from **Pheriche**, follow the wide trail north along the valley floor. Within an hour you'll reach the seasonal village of **Phulaji Kala** (4343m), with its scattered stone goths (herders' shacks). In this huge bowl of a valley, other trekkers appear as insignificant dots along the trail.

From **Dingboche**, you can cross to Pheriche via the stupas at the top of the ridge, or take an alternative path to Dughla that climbs slowly along the ridge through the village of **Dusa** (4503m). On either trail, there are outstanding views of the rugged twin peaks of Taboche and Cholatse above a desolate landscape sculpted by vanished glaciers. Ama Dablam appears as a perfect pyramid, while the true summit of Kantega is visible far to the left of the prominent saddle seen from Tengboche.

The Pheriche and Dingboche trails meet and drop down to a glacial stream, rising up the other side to **Dughla** (Tukla), set in a small depression. Half of the village was washed away in 2007 floods but there was no major damage in the 2015 earthquake; accommodation is limited to the inviting

Yak Lodge, with a sunny courtyard restaurant, or the new, clean and slightly pricier Kala Pathar Lodge. Beds are limited here so it's a good idea to arrive early or send your porter ahead to secure accommodation.

If you have time and energy for a half-day hike, continue up along the main trail over the pass to the bridge over the Dudh Kosi and the junction with the trail to Dzonglha (see Day 9 for details). Instead of bearing right upstream along the main trail, take the left trail towards Dzonglha and follow the Day 13 alternative route to Cholatse Tsho and back to Dughla (p89).

Day 9: Dughla to Lobuche

2½ HOURS / 300M ASCENT

Again, altitude will limit you to a short ascent today. From Dughla, the trail goes directly up the gravelly terminal moraine of the Khumbu Glacier for about one hour.

The path bears left at the top of the ridge, which is covered with memorials to lost climbers and sherpas. The largest memorial commemorates Babu Chhiri Sherpa, who summitted Everest 10 times, but died after falling into a crevasse on his 11th attempt at the peak in 2001. A smaller stone chorten stands in memory of Scott Fischer, who perished in the 1996 Everest disaster.

As you cross the ridge, the perfect peak of Pumori (7165m) soars into view. The air is heavy with the scent of ground-hugging rhododendron bushes. To the west, across a shallow gravel gully, you can trace the route of the side trail to Dzonglha and the Cho La pass.

After meeting the junction with this trail, make a laboured ascent to the north over loose moraine to the tangle of lodges at **Lobuche** (4930m). Originally a summer village for herders, Lobuche now exists solely to service the trekking industry. It's not the most appealing rest stop, and the bitter cold keeps most people inside around the dung-

THE ITALIAN PYRAMID

Just north of Lobuche, tucked into a side valley at the foot of the Lobuche Glacier, the curiously named **Ev-K2-CNR** (www.evk2cnr.org) was constructed in 1990 by Italian mountaineer Agostino da Polenza and the geologist Ardito Desio, who led the first ascent of K2 in 1954. Housed inside a striking glass pyramid, which amazingly survived the 2015 earthquake, the research station was established to measure the exact height of Everest and K2. Today, it is used for scientific research into mountain conservation, climate change, mountaineering technology and the effects of altitude on the human body. Most people know the station by its nickname, the 'Italian Pyramid'.

fuelled stoves. Food at Lobuche is the most expensive in the Khumbu, with a daal bhaat costing Rs 700.

Many buildings were damaged here, and it is not clear which lodges will be operating by the time you read this. Before the quake, the very similar Alpine Inn, Sherpa Lodge and Above the Clouds Lodge were good choices. The large **High Altitude Homes** (www.lobuche.com; r Rs 300-2000), formerly Mother Earth House, has three grades of rooms, all with good mattresses, but the end of the building collapsed in the quake and repair work is ongoing. One superior choice is the smart and tidy Himalayan Eco Resort (p66), set away from the other lodges at the top of the village. The 'eco' part refers to the stone and aluminium (not timber) used to build the three lodge buildings. Rooms have shared bathrooms, but carpets make them feel cosy.

You can climb the ridge east of the village for your first views of the Khumbu Glacier, with Everest mostly obscured by Lhotse and Nuptse (7861m). Alternatively, take a stroll north for 20 minutes along the moraine to the intriguing Italian Pyramid.

Day 10: Lobuche to Gorak Shep

2½ HOURS / 250M ASCENT

The effects of altitude will really become apparent on the climb to Gorak Shep. Few people sleep comfortably above Lobuche and many people start to suffer headaches and other mild symptoms of AMS on the climb to Gorak Shep. To avoid a night at high altitude, some fit trekkers make a day trip past Gorak Shep to Kala Pattar and back to Lobuche for the night, but it's a very long day. The good news is that there was no serious earthquake damage at Gorak Shep, so there'll be a warm meal waiting for you when you arrive.

The first section of the trail from Lobuche follows the narrow gap between the glacial moraine and the mountain wall, past the turn-off to the Italian Pyramid. To the right, the Khumbu Glacier gurgles and moans under a blanket of ground-up rocks and gravel.

As you climb, take time to detour (carefully!) to the edge of the moraine to look out over the Khumbu Glacier. This enormous tongue of ice marches down the slopes of Everest at a rate of up to a metre per day, breaking off into brittle seracs – towers of ice – at the Khumbu Icefall. Crossing the ice-fall is one of the most perilous stages of the Everest ascent.

Eventually, after a couple of short but steep climbs and a 45-minute traverse of the terminal moraine of the Changri Shar Glacier, you'll reach **Gorak Shep**, a flat, sandy bowl at 5160m, at the foot of Kala Pattar. This was the base camp for the 1952 Swiss Everest expedition but subsequent expeditions have used the advanced base camp just below the Khumbu Icefall.

Gorak Shep has better lodges than Lobuche but few people sleep soundly because of the altitude, the cold and the noise of other trekkers coming through the paper-thin walls.

The sandy patch below the lodges is actually the bed of a vanished lake. Arranged around this sandbox are the recommended **Himalayan Lodge** (✉9803282237; ☎), with 50 rooms and a huge restaurant, the cosier **Buddha Lodge** (✉9841069395; ☎) and **Snowland Highest Inn** (✉9841581552; ☎). Amazingly, all offer wi-fi! All rooms in Gorak Shep are Rs 300 to Rs 500. The **Yeti Resort** (☎) is building a new hotel here.

Where you stay will largely depend on which lodges have space. If you get a late start from Lobuche, you may have to make do with what you can find. Lodges run a skeleton staff between December and February but you'll always find something open.

You cannot actually see Everest from Gorak Shep as the peak is hidden by the shoulder of Nuptse, but there are grand views over the Khumbu Glacier from the top of the moraine. As you look north you can see (from left to right) Pumori (7165m), Lingtren (6713m), Khumbutse (6639m) and Changtse (7550m), the last of these poking its head over the Lho La pass from inside Tibet.

Dotted around the ridge above Gorak Shep are a number of memorials to expedition members lost during various ascents of Everest. Since 1921 more than 250 climbers, sherpas and porters have perished here, either on the peak or in helicopter crashes at Base Camp. Climbers Rob Hall and Andy Harris, who perished in the 1996 Everest disaster, are both commemorated in a collection of chortens 15 minutes' walk from Gorak Shep.

Most trekkers stop for lunch at Gorak Shep and arrange a room or bed space for the night, before continuing to Kala Pattar or Everest Base Camp. Because of the exhaustion and lethargy experienced at this altitude, many people only visit one of these two options. If you want to see both, use the afternoon of the first day to visit Base Camp, and climb to Kala Pattar the next morning when views are more reliable.

Day 11: Gorak Shep to Everest Base Camp

6 HOURS RETURN / 200M ASCENT / 200M DESCENT

The walk to Base Camp from Gorak Shep is a draining scramble over an ever-changing path across the Khumbu Glacier, starting at the north end of the sandpit at Gorak Shep. Look out for tiny pika (mouse-hares) scurrying between the boulders on the path.

Your destination is a semi-permanent village of brightly-coloured dome tents and prayer flags wedged between rocks at the bottom of the Khumbu Icefall at 5340m. In April and May the atmosphere at Base Camp can be fascinating, with groups from dozens of different nations playing cards, gambling, eating, reading, strumming guitars and doing everything possible to fill their time while they wait for the green light to climb to the summit. The periodic groans of the seracs in the icefall only add to the tension in the air. In October or November you'll find the place mostly deserted.

On 25 April 2015, this was the scene of Everest's worst ever mountaineering disaster, as avalanches triggered by the earthquake surged down from the slopes of Pumori and Nuptse, killing 18 climbers and guides. The disaster came almost exactly a year after a similar avalanche killed 16 Sherpas on the Khumbu Icefall. The 2015 climbing season was promptly abandoned. If climbing is still suspended, you may find nothing at Base Camp but the debris from past expeditions.

Many people have unrealistic expectations of Base Camp and end up being disappointed. Visiting is an interesting cultural experience, but there are no views of Everest – the mountain lurks somewhere beyond the icefall – and cloud often rolls down from the peaks, obscuring everything in a grey fog. The main reason to go there is to say you have been there. If you are specifically after a view of Everest, climb Kala Pattar instead.

SIDE TRIP: KALA PATTAR

4 HOURS RETURN / 200M ASCENT / 200M DESCENT

The summit of Kala Pattar (5545m) hill provides perhaps the best view of Mt Everest in the Nepal Himalaya. Mornings are usually sparkling clear, and this is the best time to make the ascent. For many people this is the highlight of their trek, but cloud can roll in quickly, obscuring the peaks. For the best chance of an Everest photo opportunity, start this trek as soon as it gets light. This route was not affected by the 2015 earthquake.

The path to Kala Pattar climbs up the grassy ridge above Gorak Shep. You can't miss the path – just look for the long line of Gore-Tex-clad trekkers snaking up the hillside. It takes 1½ to two hours to gain the summit (5545m), which is marked by a tangle of wind-lashed prayer flags. As you climb, the peak of Pumori looms dramatically ahead.

Having reached the summit, sit back and be amazed. By climbing 200m, you have placed yourself in front of one of the most

EXTREME SPORTS IN THE EVEREST REGION

In case you didn't find walking through the Khumbu hard enough, you can race through it on an ever-expanding number of extreme runs in the region. All are expected to run as normal after the earthquake.

The **Everest Marathon** (www.everestmarathon.org.uk) follows a downhill route from Gorak Shep to Tengboche and Namche Bazaar. The winners usually complete the 42km (26.2-mile) course in close to four hours, but participants must spend two weeks trekking as part of their training. The race is run every two years in November as a charitable venture and proceeds go to development projects around the Khumbu.

The similar but for-profit **Tenzing Hilary Everest Marathon** (www.everest marathon.com) is held every year at the end of May.

If all that seems too tame, check yourself in for counselling and consider the **Everest Ultra** (www.everestultra.com), a one-day 65km race, or the **Solukhumbu Trail** (www. dawasherpa-races.com/en/solukhumbu-trail.html), a 16-day race from Jiri to Base Camp, over the Renjo La and Cho La Passes.

For a completely different view of Everest, those with a spare US$25,000 can even **parachute jump** over the peak. See www.everest-skydive.com for details of the epic drop.

MT EVEREST

Everest has gone by a number of different names over the years. The Survey of India christened the mountain 'Peak XV', but it was later named Everest after Sir George Everest, the surveyor general of India in 1865 (who pronounced his name 'Eve-Rest').

It was later discovered that the mountain already had a name – Sherpas call the peak Chomolungma (Chomo Miyo Langsangma), after the female guardian deity of the mountain who rides a red tiger and is one of the five sisters of long life. There was no Nepali name for the mountain until 1956 when the historian Babu Ram Acharya invented the name Sagarmatha, meaning 'head of the sky'.

Using triangulation from the plains of India, the Survey of India established the elevation of the summit of Everest at 8839m. In 1954 this was revised to 8848m using data from 12 different survey stations around the mountain. In 1999 a team sponsored by National Geographic used GPS data to produce a new elevation of 8850m, but in 2002 a Chinese team made measurements from the summit using ice radar and GPS systems and produced a height of 8844.43m.

So is Everest shrinking? Not exactly: the Chinese calculated the height of the bedrock of the mountain, without the accumulated snow and ice. In fact, Everest is growing and moving northeast at a rate of 6cm a year as plate tectonics drive the Indian subcontinent underneath Eurasia.

The earthquakes that hit Nepal in 2015 forced another frantic round of remeasuring, but the official verdict was that the height of Everest was unchanged, though the entire mountain moved 3cm southwest!

astonishing views on earth – a 360-degree panorama of Himalayan giants from Pumori and Lobuche West (6145m) to Nuptse, Lhotse and Everest. Even Gorak Shep seems impossibly distant, a tiny speck next to the frozen river of the Khumbu Glacier.

From this elevation, the true height of Everest becomes clear. The entire south face is clearly visible, as well as Lho La (the pass between Nepal and Tibet, named the Western Cwm by George Mallory in 1921) and most of the West Ridge route climbed by Unsoeld and Hornbein in 1963. On the north side of the peak, you may be able to spot the North Ridge and the first and second steps, prominent obstacles during the first attempts on the mountain in the 1920s and 1930s.

On your way back down to Gorak Shep, detour south to the lower ridge to look down over the two glacial lakes that form the base camp for Pumori.

Day 12: Gorak Shep to Lobuche

2 HOURS / 250M DESCENT

If you didn't visit Kala Pattar yesterday you can grab an early start today, have lunch in Gorak Shep and then start heading down the valley. It can feel like you are wearing ten-league boots as you skip down the mountainside, losing all the altitude you have gained in the last two days. You can easily reach Lobuche in two hours and many people continue downhill to Pheriche or Dingboche. Just retrace your steps along the moraine of the Khumbu Glacier.

Day 13: Lobuche to Pheriche/Dingboche

3 HOURS / 700M DESCENT

If you overnight again in Lobuche, you can take your time over the downhill stroll to Pheriche or Dingboche. Continue down the moraine to Dughla and drop to the bridge over the gushing stream that flows out of the glacier. The path forks on the other side: for Pheriche, follow the low path that drops along the wide valley; for Dingboche, follow the upper path that runs along the valley wall through Dusa.

ALTERNATIVE ROUTE: VIA CHOLATSE TSHO

3½ HOURS / 700M DESCENT

To take an alternative route back to Dughla, follow the main trail down the valley for 20 minutes, then stay on the northern side of the river when the main trail branches left to follow the trail to Dzonglha (see p102 for details of the walk to Dzonghla). After 45 minutes the trail swings round to enter the Dzonglha valley, offering fine views downstream towards Pheriche and Ama Dablam. Continue in the direction of Dzonglha for a few minutes to gain views of turquoise Cholatse Tsho nestling at the base of Cholatse and Arakam Tse peaks.

Before too long you'll see a trail joining from the left; follow this lower trail southeastwards back in the direction you just came from, descending the hillside and then swinging left to cross a stream just before Dughla. From Dughla you follow the main trail to Pheriche.

Day 14: Pheriche/Dingboche to Tengboche

2½ HOURS / 550M DESCENT / 70M ASCENT

Before you continue your descent along the Imja Valley, consider taking a day or three out of your itinerary for the rewarding side trip up the Imja Khola to Chhukung.

If you prefer to go directly to Tengboche, drop down the valley to Orsho, then follow the west bank of the Imja Khola to Shomare and on to Pangboche. If you haven't already visited the gompa (p79) in upper Pangboche, take the path leading uphill where the trail forks about 20 minutes below Shomare. From Pangboche, retrace your footsteps down to the Imja Khola and up through the forest to Debuche and Tengboche.

ALTERNATIVE ROUTE: PHERICHE/DINGBOCHE TO PHORTSE

5–6 HOURS / 460M/600M DESCENT / 100M ASCENT

For a bit of variety on the way downhill to Namche, consider taking a detour through Phortse, a sprawling Sherpa village on a flat-topped ridge overlooking the confluence of the Imja Khola and Dudh Kosi. The village was damaged by both the 25 April and 12 May earthquakes and much reconstruction work is underway here – if you plan to stay overnight, check ahead to make sure accommodation will be available. From Phortse, you can descend to the Dudh Kosi and cross to Phortse Thenga on the Gokyo trail, and then follow the ridge south to Namche Bazaar.

To reach Phortse, climb to upper Pangboche, then head south out of the village along the high trail that starts near the Himalayan Lodge. This is a leisurely trek through a rocky landscape dotted with scrub junipers, offering eagle-eye views over the Imja Khola Valley towards Tengboche Monastery. There are few places to replenish your water bottle so fill up at Pangboche before you set off.

The trail skirts around the ridge and eventually drops down to the potato fields of **Phortse** (p97) at 3810m.

EVEREST BOOKS & FILMS

You could fill a library with books about climbing Everest.

➡ *Everest: The Mountaineering History* (Walt Unsworth) gives a detailed one-volume history of mountaineering on the peak.

➡ *Into Thin Air* (Jon Krakauer) is the classic bestselling account of the 1996 Everest disaster. It's a powerful and gripping read.

➡ *High Adventure* (Edmund Hillary) is the classic telling of how Hillary and Tenzin 'knocked the bastard off', from the 1951 reconnoitre to the iconic 1953 summit attempt.

➡ *Boys of Everest* (Clint Willis) tells the story of a later generation of fanatical climbers led by Chris Bonington, who essentially reinvented climbing in the 1970s.

➡ *Ghosts of Everest* (Jochen Hemmleb, Larry A Johnson & Eric R Simonson) is a fascinating account of the search for Mallory and Irvine, who vanished on the north face while heading for the summit in 1924.

➡ *Touching My Father's Soul* (Jamling Tenzing Norgay) is a rousing account of a son following in his famous father's footsteps, with good background on the Sherpas.

➡ *Into the Silence: The Great War, Mallory, and the Conquest of Everest* (Wade Davis) is an acclaimed but extremely detailed history of the decades that led to the conquest of Everest.

➡ *The Climb* (Anatoli Boukreev) is another gripping description of the 1996 tragedy, by the heroic Kazakh Russian climber, and a rebuttal of criticisms made in *Into Thin Air*.

Look out also for 2015's epic 3D movie *Everest*, starring Jake Gyllenhaal, John Hawkes, and Josh Brolin, who plays Beck Weathers, the climber who spent two nights at 8000m during the 1996 climbing disaster. Some scenes were filmed on location at Everest Base Camp.

Day 15: Tengboche to Namche Bazaar

4½ HOURS / 750M DESCENT / 350M ASCENT

From Tengboche, retrace your steps down to Phunki Thenga, then climb the ridge towards Namche Bazaar. You can follow the level trail along the ridge to Chhorkung, or take the path that climbs steeply up the ridge above Sanasa to Khumjung.

Most people celebrate their return to Namche with a slap-up meal, either at their lodge or at Café Danphe, Everest Bakery or Namche Bakery Café (see p122).

Day 16: Namche Bazaar to Lukla

6 HOURS / 950M DESCENT / 250M ASCENT

Many trekkers find the descent from Namche to the Dudh Kosi to be the hardest stage of the entire trek. Although the path is all downhill, the unrelenting slope places massive impact on the knees. Using trekking poles will help, as will wearing a knee support bandage. Once you cross the high suspension bridge, the path runs mostly level to Jorsale and then climbs to Monjo, where you must show your TIMS card and your national park receipt.

It's an easy run through Benkar and Phakding to Lukla. Aim to be at the airport in Lukla around 3pm on the afternoon before your flight to reconfirm your reservation. There is usually a bit of a party atmosphere among trekkers who are finishing their trek here and several bars in Lukla offer happy-hour deals, pool tables and late-night drinking.

Gokyo Trek

Duration 12 days

Max Elevation 5360m

Difficulty Medium to hard

Season October to December & February to May

Start/Finish Lukla

Permits TIMS card, Sagarmatha National Park permit

Summary Everest too busy? Then try this fine alternative, which climbs the valley to the west of Everest to the village of Gokyo and five sacred lakes on the moraine beside the Ngozumpa Glacier.

Crowds and commercialism are driving many trekkers away from the Everest Base

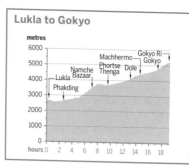

Lukla to Gokyo

Camp trek into the arms of the lovely Gokyo trek. This two-week spectacular climbs almost as high as the Everest Base Camp trek and offers similarly jaw-dropping scenery, but the trails are less crowded, the lodges quieter and the villages along the trail have a reason to exist over and above serving daal bhaat to legions of hungry trekkers.

As for the Everest Base Camp trek, there was some earthquake damage on this route, both on the lower stages before Namche Bazaar, and on the upper stages between Namche and Gokyo. Many lodges suffered minor damage, and there were more serious collapses in Machhermo and Dole. Until lodges are repaired, trekkers may need to choose alternative overnight stops. At the time of writing, it was not possible to confirm that all the lodges on this trek were open. As a sensible precaution, check locally to make sure accommodation will be available for all your overnight stops before starting your trek.

The trail follows the Everest Base Camp route as far as Sanasa, above Namche Bazaar, and then branches off the main valley to follow the Dudh Kosi to its source – a series of emerald-green lakes along the moraine of the Ngozumpa Glacier. Beside the largest of these lakes in a valley of snow peaks, Gokyo village is a more satisfying destination than Gorak Shep, not least because it is a proper Sherpa village, complete with huge herds of yaks.

From Gokyo, you can climb Gokyo Ri (5360m) for a heart-stopping view over Everest, Lhotse, Cho Oyu and Makalu, or continue north along the valley to the highest of the sacred lakes. Either way, the sense of communing with nature is more profound than on the Everest Base Camp trek.

You can also combine treks by walking to Everest Base Camp, returning to Lobuche and branching off to Dzonglha to cross

EVEREST REGION GOKYO TREK

the 5420m Cho La pass to Gokyo. See Days 12–13 (p102) of the Three Passes trek for Lobuche–Dzonglha–Gokyo details.

 ## The Trek

Days 1 & 2: Lukla to Namche Bazaar

For details of the walk between Lukla and Namche Bazaar see Days 1–2 (p68) of the Everest Base Camp trek.

Days 3 & 4: Namche Bazaar

Don't rush. The climb to Gokyo is steep and it's easy to go too high too fast and succumb to altitude sickness. Only after a minimum of three nights in the Namche-Khumjung region is it safe to begin this trek. But don't worry – there are lots of things to do. As well as exploring the village, you could make the thoroughly rewarding day or overnight hike to Thame (p73; providing conditions allow this); take a day hike through Shyangboche, Khunde and Khumjung (p76); or stroll up to the museum and visitor centre at Chhorkung (p73). Alternatively, sit back with a book and a cinnamon roll at one of the bakeries in Namche. Hiking will help acclimatisation more than the cinnamon rolls, however.

Day 5: Namche Bazaar to Phortse Thenga

2–3 HOURS / 530M ASCENT / 290M DESCENT

Heading north, you can take the easy path via Chhorkung or the steeper scenic trail via Khumjung. Whichever path you take, you will reach Sanasa, below Khumjung on the west side of the Dudh Kosi.

A signpost on the lower trail claims that you can reach Gokyo in seven hours, but you will almost certainly succumb to altitude sickness unless you spread the ascent over four days. If you come on the high path via Khumjung, there's no need to drop down to

 WARNING

It is easy to ascend faster than the recommended guidelines on the Gokyo trek, so be sure to take the recommended rest days and be alert for the symptoms of AMS.

the village – just continue level on the trail above the Sanasa junction.

As you climb up the side of the ridge, the full extent of the deforestation around Namche becomes apparent. Looking across the valley, you should be able to pick out the houses of Tengboche on the ridge below the spire of Ama Dablam (6856m) and the walled fields of Phortse sprawling across a flat-topped ridge below the snow-dusted peaks of Taboche (6542m) and Cholatse (6443m).

The track contours around the ridge to a knot of teahouses and a stupa clinging to the edge of a small pass at **Mong La** (3975m). The village is said to be the birthplace of Lama Sange Dorje, the saint who introduced Buddhism to the Khumbu.

Mountain winds curl across this exposed hillside – look out for golden eagles spiralling in the thermals. Accommodation options include the Snowland View Lodge above the stupa, the small **Hilltop Guesthouse** (www.hilltop-mongla.com) and the new View Point Guesthouse, but it's not clear if all are still operating after the disaster; ask locally to see who has rooms available. North of Mong La, the trail drops steeply on switchbacks through pine forests for one hour, with intermittent views towards Phortse.

Earthquake damage was limited at **Phortse Thenga** (3680m) and there are two places to stay here. Right on the main trail is the friendly Phortse Thenga Guesthouse, offering hot showers and outdoor seating. From the guesthouse, a side trail drops for five minutes to the Dudh Kosi, where the spacious, red-roofed River Resort offers good rooms, some with attached bathrooms, to the soothing soundtrack of the rushing river.

Day 6: Phortse Thenga to Dole

1½–2 HOURS / 410M ASCENT

It is a short, easy morning hike from Phortse Thenga to Dole, the next village along the west side of the valley, but the earthquake caused some damage here; check the status of accommodation here before leaving Phortse Tenga. With so little walking time, you might choose to spend the morning washing and drying clothes in the warmth and comfort of Phortse Thenga before you head off.

If you stayed at the Phortse Thenga Guesthouse, continue along the same main trail; if you stayed by the riverbank, take the shortcut that runs straight uphill above the River Resort. The first stage passes through a dense forest of tall, old pines and moss-covered rhododendrons, past the derelict national park checkpost at **Tongba** (3950m). The path squeezes past some enormous boulders and crosses a series of rocky cascades, rising past the stone summer houses of herders from Khumjung.

You next reach **Dole** (4090m; pronounced 'doe-lay'), set at the mouth of the Phule Khola in a wide, densely forested valley. There are good views south towards Thamserku and Khantega peaks from several high points around the village. The pastoral setting and superior lodges make Dole a good place to stop for a mandatory rest and acclimatisation day, but lodges were damaged in the earthquake so ask locally to see which currently have rooms available.

Before the quake, the preferred option for trekking groups was the **Yeti Inn** (☑ 038-540324; yetiinn@gmail.com; r without bathroom Rs 200-1000, r with bathroom US$50) on the northern side of the stream, whose stylish restaurant boasts slate tables, cream cushions and a display of antique trekking equipment belonging to the owner's father. Individual trekkers tended to prefer the relative peace and quiet of the Alpine Cottage Lodge, Himalayan Lodge, Thamserkuu View Lodge, Namaste Lodge and Trekkers Inn on the southern side of the stream.

Day 7: Dole to Machhermo

2 HOURS / 320M ASCENT

Day 7 is another short day to limit your rate of ascent. Earthquake damage was extensive in the village of Machhermo, your next overnight stop. Check locally to confirm that accommodation will be available before setting off from Dole. If no rooms are available in Machhermo, you may need to break the journey at Lhabarma or Luza instead.

From Dole, it's a steep climb out of the forest to an increasingly barren hillside, covered in tundra grasses and dotted scrub junipers. Across the valley, you can make out the high path of the east bank trail from Gokyo to Phortse.

Continue uphill past a chorten past the village of **Lhabarma** (4330m), 30 minutes from Dole; it's often marked on maps as Lhafarma or Lopharme. The agreeable Mountain View Tophill Lodge is at the bottom of the village. Below Lhabarma are the scattered stone shepherds' huts of Gyele at 4110m.

Most of the villages on the upper stages of the trek are seasonal. Families from

Gokyo Trek Day 3-7

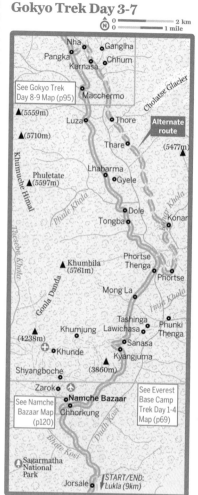

EVEREST REGION GOKYO TREK

further down the valley set up camp in the summer with their herds of yaks, cows and goats, and retreat in winter when the snow and lack of running water make it impractical to live here.

From Lhabarma, the trail climbs gently past a large chorten to **Luza**, tucked into a side valley at 4340m. There were two lodges here before the quake; the Paradise Lodge (which was probably overstating its charms) and the the large Khantega View Lodge, with good rooms and a year-round water supply.

GOKYO TREK – TIMES

The following are trekking times only; stops are not included.

DAY	SECTION	HOURS
1	Lukla to Cheplung	1:15
	Cheplung to Phakding	1:45
2	Phakding to Benkar	1:30
	Benkar to Monjo	1:00
	Monjo to Namche Bazaar	3:00
3	Rest day	
4	Rest day	
5	Namche Bazaar to Khumjung	1:00
	Khumjung to Phortse Thenga	1:30
6	Phortse Thenga to Dole	1:30
7	Dole to Lhabarma	0:30
	Lhabarma to Luza	0:30
	Luza to Machhermo	0:30
8	Machhermo to Longponga Tsho	2:30
	Longponga Tsho to Gokyo	1:00
9	Gokyo Ri	4:00
10	Gokyo to Phortse	7:00
11	Phortse to Namche Bazaar	3:00

The trail continues to climb gently along the side of the valley, over a series of sandy hummocks. You'll soon reach a chorten and fluttering prayer flags on the outskirts of Machhermo (4410m), tucked into a wide, flat-bottomed valley below the terminal moraine of the Ngozumpa Glacier. Locals claim that a yeti killed three yaks and attacked a Sherpa woman here in 1974, so keep your eyes open you if you pop to the loo after dark.

At the far northwest end of the village is the **Porter Shelter and Rescue Post** (✆ 993384007; clinic consultation US$50; ⊗ 9am-noon & 1-5pm, Mar-May & Sep-Nov), damaged but not destroyed in the earthquake. It was set up by the the International Porter Protection Group (www.ippg.net) and is staffed by international volunteer medics. As well as providing emergency treatment to trekkers and porters, the centre gives a free talk on altitude sickness at 3pm in an attempt to educate trekkers about the dangers of AMS. They also operate a shelter and clinic in Gokyo from mid-October to mid-November.

Machhermo has half a dozen lodges, all large, timber-lined and set in big, stone-walled gardens, but several were damaged in the earthquake – check locally to see where rooms are currently available. Before the quake, there were two groups of lodges.

The courtyard-style Tashi Dele Lodge, new Peaceful Lodge and the more traditional Himalayan Lodge and Snowland Lodge are on the west bank, while smaller Trekkers Lodge, Dawa Friendship Lodge and Yeti Lodge are on the eastern bank. Nearby, the impressive wi-fi-enabled **Namgyal Lodge** (✆ 038-540038; r without/with bathroom Rs 200/2500; ☎) was damaged badly in the earthquake; check locally to see if repairs are complete.

If you have time to kill, hike along the ridge above Namgyal Lodge; go far enough and you'll see the top of Everest, to the left of Cholatse.

Day 8: Machhermo to Gokyo

3½ HOURS / 350M ASCENT

On Day 8, you leave the foothills and enter the desolate tundra of the high mountains, en route to Gokyo, which saw only minor damage in the earthquake.

To start, climb steeply up a scrubby slope to a collection of chortens on the hilltop, then follow the ridge. On the way, there are good views south to Kantega (6685m) and north towards Cho Oyu (8201m), the sixth-highest mountain in the world.

After 30 minutes you come to the tiny settlement of **Pangka** (4390m), squeezed against a mound of sand and rubble at the end of the Ngozumpa Glacier.

The ridge in front of Pangka provides some welcome shelter from the wind, but not, sadly, from the snow. In 1995 an entire trekking group was killed here by an avalanche. The only lodge left, the rudimentary Fanga Viewpoint Hotel, lies well away from the old avalanche path.

Leaving Pangka, the trail climbs rapidly into a rocky cleft on stone steps beside one of the streams that feeds the Dudh Kosi. This portal releases you onto the lateral moraine of the Ngozumpa Glacier, one of the longest in Nepal, which begins 20km north on the slopes of Cho Oyu. Wedged between the mountain wall and this crumbling mound of sand and gravel are six sacred lakes, which reflect the peaks in their calm, mirrored surfaces.

You'll pass the first lake, **Longponga Tsho** (4650m), immediately after crossing the bridge. Several pairs of Brahminy ducks call the lake home.

The trail now becomes almost level as it crosses a barren landscape of lichen-encrusted boulders. You'll soon reach the second lake, **Taujung Tsho** (4730m), before continuing for 30 minutes to the village of **Gokyo** (4750m) on the shores of the third lake, known as **Dudh Pokhari** or Gokyo Tsho.

The setting is magical – the village is squeezed between a wall of moraine and the lake, which is backed by a basin of fang-like peaks. When the wind dies, the mountains are perfectly reflected in the surface of the lake. Although it isn't obvious from the shore, the lake is actually a brilliant emerald green, something that becomes apparent when you see Gokyo from above on the trek to Gokyo Ri.

There are eight lodges at Gokyo, and earthquake damage here was minor, but check locally to see whether any lodges are closed for repairs. Most of the owners divide their time between looking after trekkers and looking after huge herds of yaks. Every morning and evening, the narrow stone lanes of the village are overrun by shaggy beasts of burden as the herds are driven out onto the pastures. Many of the lodges close down in winter as the herders move their animals to lower pastures to escape the bitter cold.

The **Gokyo Resort** (☑ 993384010; r without/with bathroom Rs 200/1000) is the oldest and largest lodge here, offering a bookshop, cafe and bakery (excellent banana bread) at the top of the village. The **Fitzroy Inn** (☑ 993384009; gokyotashi@gmail.com; r without bathroom Rs 500-800, s/d with bathroom & wi-fi Rs 3000/5000; ☺ closed Dec-Mar; ☎) is a good new place with an ambitious menu, carpeted rooms, wi-fi and enthusiastic management. Asian Trekking is building a new upmarket hotel here.

You'll find the cosiest atmosphere and the best views at the Cho Oyu View Lodge and Lakeside View Lodge down on the lakeshore. Both lodges have dining rooms with

Gokyo Trek Day 8-9

big windows facing on the lake, and boxy rooms offering fine views. The other lodges have similar facilities, but less impressive views.

Day 9: Gokyo & Around

Most trekkers spend a few days in Gokyo, strolling around the lake and hiking up to some of the mountain viewpoints nearby. The most popular walk is the stiff two-hour climb to Gokyo Ri, but you can also hike north to the other lakes strung out along the moraine of the Ngozumpa Glacier. These routes were not affected by the 2015 earthquake.

SIDE TRIP: GOKYO RI

4 HOURS RETURN / 570M ASCENT / 570M DESCENT

As Gorak Shep has Kala Pattar, so Gokyo has Gokyo Ri. The 5360m-high peak on the north side of the Dudh Pokhari is an epic vantage point, offering the kind of view that is normally reserved for balloonists or mountaineers. Not affected by the quake, the path to the peak crosses the stream at the north end of the village and climbs for two hours to a cat's cradle of prayer flags at the top of the hill.

From the summit, there are panoramic views of Cho Oyu, Everest, Lhotse, Makalu, Cholatse and Taboche, with the Ngozumpa Glacier cutting across in front like a massive glacial highway. From this lofty eyrie, Gokyo is a tiny dot on the side of the moraine, and the Dudh Pokhari is a giant jade-green puddle, without a single reflection on its mirror-flat surface.

As with Kala Pattar, the most reliable weather is early morning, as clouds tend to roll in by mid-morning. The prevailing wisdom is to start up the mountain at first light, even if it looks cloudy. You'll often beat the fog to the top of the hill and have a perfect view over the top of the cloud banks. If the weather is clear, you'll get better light in the afternoon than the early morning. Some people watch sunset from the peak but you'll need to bring warm clothes and a good head torch for the twilight descent.

SIDE TRIP: THE SACRED LAKES

5 HOURS RETURN / 200M ASCENT / 200M DESCENT

The six languid pools that surround Gokyo are the source of the river you have followed since Lukla, and both Hindus and Buddhists regard them as sacred. During Janai Purnima (the Sacred Thread Festival), which usually falls in August, hundreds of lowland Nepalis make the pilgrimage to Gokyo to ritually immerse themselves in the icy waters. The route was not affected by the earthquake but watch for trail collapses along the edge of the glacier.

The first lake you will come to is **Thonak Tsho** (4835m), a steely grey pool surrounded by enormous boulders and patches of ice (one hour from Gokyo). The easiest trail from here is to follow the base of the hill to the left all the way to the fifth lake, **Ngozumba Tsho** (4980m), set beneath the icy shoulder of Cho Oyu (allow 1¼ hours). On the shore is a boulder the size of a three-bedroom house.

On the edge of the moraine to the east is a small hill, known as **Scoundrel's Viewpoint** (5000m), which offers fine views of Cho Oyu and the upper Ngozumpa Glacier. Be careful not to get too close to the crumbling moraine overhang.

Most people turn back from here. For even better views, strong and acclimatised hikers can climb **Ngozumba Ri** (5550m), the hill north of the fifth lake. It's a tough climb and the last section is a bit of a scramble but the views of Cho Oyu, the sixth lake and Everest are unsurpassed.

Die-hards can choose instead to continue for another 90 minutes to the sixth lake, **Gyazumba Tsho** (5150m), actually several lakes gripped by fingers of ice at the foot of Cho Oyu. Follow the faint trail up the valley between Ngozumba Ri and the glacier, keeping to the left and swinging left as you see Cho Oyu. A 15-minute walk due west drops you at an overlook above the lakes, with the sheer 2km high wall of Cho Oyu close enough to touch. You need to be fit and well acclimatised to make it here and back in a

---

KNOW YOUR YAKS

Everyone knows the name of those big hairy cows seen all over the Himalaya – they're yaks, right? Actually, it's not that simple. The term yak should really be reserved for the pure-blooded, long-haired bull of the species *Bos grunniens;* female animals are called *nak* by Sherpas and *dri* by Tibetans. Most of the 'yaks' seen around the Khumbu are actually *dzopkyo* (male) or *dzum* (female) – the offspring of pure-blood yaks bred with cows or Tibetan bulls, which the Sherpas call *lang* and Nepalis call *khirkoo.* The phrase 'yak cheese' is actually an oxymoron; it should be *nak* cheese.

day from Gokyo. The Fitzroy Inn in Gokyo can arrange an overnight camping trip here.

Day 10: Gokyo to Phortse

5–7 HOURS / 900M DESCENT

Rather than retrace your route, you can enjoy a change of scenery by following the east side of the Dudh Kosi Valley. Leave the trail you followed uphill at Pangka and cross the stream to a couple of *kharkas* (pastures) at **Nha** (4400m), then climb and turn south along the ridge.

The quiet trail is obvious and straightforward, with just a few awkward sections around stream crossings and landslides. There are simple lodges at **Thore** (4300m), **Thare** (4390m) and **Konar** (4000m), but facilities are more basic than elsewhere on this trek.

Eventually, the trail dips into a gully and emerges at the top of **Phortse** (3810m), just below the gompa. This village lies off the main trekking circuit and as a result it feels more like a proper Sherpa village and less like a theme park for trekkers. The slope is dotted with ancient-looking chortens and stone houses scattered among walled potato fields on a gently sloping ridge below Taboche peak, high above the confluence of the Imja Khola and Dudh Kosi. However, there was a fair bit of earthquake damage here, so check ahead to confirm that accommodation will be available before leaving Gokyo.

At the top of the village, **Phortse Gompa** (☉8-9am & 4-5pm) was built in 1996 by a team of English and Sherpa volunteers led by trekker Tony Freake. The **Khumbu Climbing Center** (www.alexlowe.org) trains Nepali climbers here and is building a new climbing centre near the village.

There were seven lodges in Phortse before the quake but it is not clear if all will be open by the time you read this; ask locally to see who has rooms. Most of the Phortse lodges are working farms, so staying here is more like a homestay than a typical trekking-lodge experience. Top picks before the disaster included the Peaceful Lodge, Thamserku Lodge, Namaste Lodge and Phortse Resort at the bottom of the village.

When you decide to move on from Phortse, there are two possible routes. You can drop down to Phortse Thenga on the trail at the southwest corner of the village by the white chorten, and continue to Namche Bazaar (as described here), or follow the high path at the northeast corner of the village to upper Pangboche (three hours) and on to Everest Base Camp (see p90).

Day 11: Phortse to Namche Bazaar

3–5 HOURS / 700M DESCENT / 300M ASCENT

A shady trail descends from Phortse through the forest to the bridge at **Phortse Thenga** and rejoins the original route from Namche Bazaar. Whether you follow the easy path via Kyangjuma or the high path via Khumjung, you should be able to reach Namche by early afternoon.

Day 12: Namche Bazaar to Lukla

6–7 HOURS / 1000M DESCENT / 300M ASCENT

For details of the walk between Namche Bazaar and Lukla (in reverse) see Days 1–2 of the Everest Base Camp trek (p68).

Three Passes Trek

Duration 20 days

Max Elevation 5535m

Difficulty Hard

Season October to November & March to May

Start/Finish Lukla

Permits TIMS card, Sagarmatha National Park permit

Summary This is the ultimate Everest circuit, rising from Lukla to Chhukung, crossing the 5535m Kongma La to Lobuche and Everest Base Camp, continuing over the 5420m Cho La to Gokyo, then crossing the 5345m Renjo La to Thame and Namche Bazaar. Only for the truly adventurous.

In the last few years, improvements on the high mountain trails have made it possible to walk a complete circuit of the Khumbu from Lukla. This is an epic journey that will take you over some of the highest mountain passes in the world. It stitches together the best of the Everest Base Camp and Gokyo treks and two of the most rewarding side treks in the lower Khumbu. It is the ultimate Everest trek.

However, several stages were affected by the earthquake, including the loop from Gokyo to Namche Bazaar via the Renjo La. It is important to check that trails are open and that food and accommodation will be available for any overnight stops before setting off;

Three Passes Trek Day 8-17

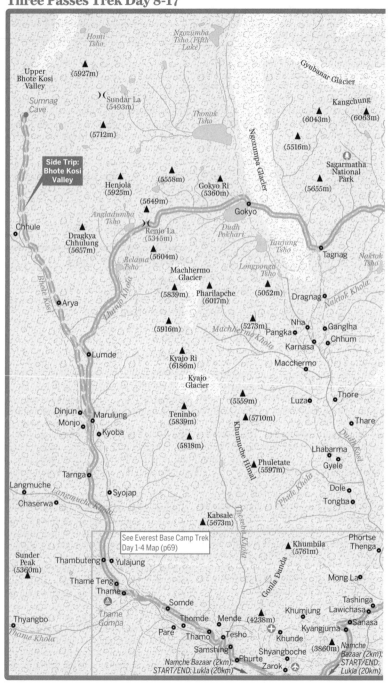

Homi Tsho

Ngozumba Tsho (Fifth Lake)

Gyubanar Glacier

Upper Bhote Kosi Valley ▲ (5927m)

Sumnag Cave

)(Sundar La (5493m)

Thonak Tsho

Kangchung

▲ (6043m) ▲ (6063m)

Ngozumpa Glacier

▲ (5712m)

▲ (5516m)

Side Trip: Bhote Kosi Valley

Sagarmatha National Park

▲ (5655m)

Henjola (5925m) ▲ (5558m) ▲ Gokyo Ri (5360m)

▲ (5649m)

Gokyo ○

Chhule ○

Angladumba Tsho

)(

Renjo La (5345m)

Dudh Pokhari

Dragkya Chhulung (5657m)

Relama Tsho

▲ (5604m)

Taujung Tsho

Tagnag ○ *Naktok Tsho*

Bhote Kosi

Lhajo Khola

Machhermo Glacier

Longponga Tsho

▲ (5839m) Pharilapche (6017m)

▲ (5052m)

Dragnag ○ *Naktok Khola*

Arya ○

▲ (5916m)

Machhermo Khola

▲ (5273m) Pangka ○

Nha ○ ○ Ganglha

Karnasa ○ ○ Chhum

Lumde ○

Kyajo Rì (6186m)

Macchermo ○

Kyajo Glacier

▲ (5559m)

Luza ○ ○ Thore

Dinjun ○ Marulung ○

Monjo ○ ○ Kyoba

Teninbo (5839m)

▲ (5710m)

○ Thare

Khumuche Himal

Dudh Kosi

▲ (5818m)

Lhabarma ○

Phuletate (5597m)

Gyele ○

Tarnga ○

Langmuche ○

Langmuche Khola

○ Syojap

Phale Khola

Dole ○

Tongba ○

Chaserwa ○

Kabsale ▲ (5673m)

Theseb Khola

Phortse Thenga ○

See Everest Base Camp Trek Day 1-4 Map (p69)

Khumbila ▲ (5761m)

Sunder Peak (5360m) ▲

Thambuteng ○ ○ Yulajung

Thame Teng ○

Thame ⌂

Thame Gompa

Somde ○

Gonla Danda

Mong La ○

Tashinga ○

Khumjung ○ Lawichasa ○

Thyangbo ○

Thame Khola

Thomde ○ Mende ○

Pare ○ Thamo ○ Tesho ○

▲ (4238m)

Khunde ○

Kyangjuma ○ ○ Sanasa

Samshing ○ ○ Phurte

Shyangboche ○ (3860m)

Namche Bazaar (2km); START/END: Lukla (20km)

Zarok ○

Namche Bazaar (2km); START/END: Lukla (20km)

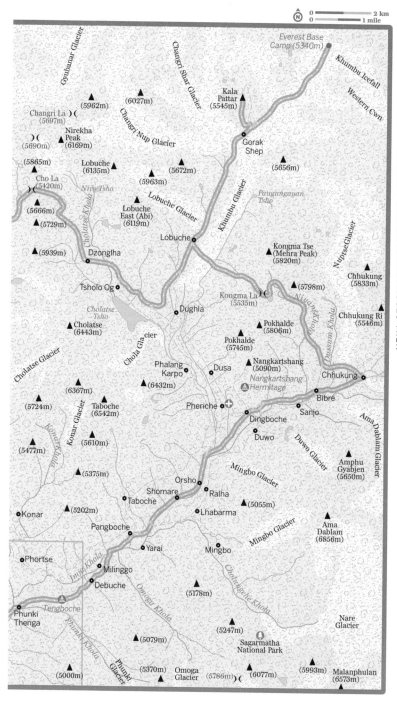

you don't want to be stuck halfway across any of these passes without shelter.

Crossing the 'three passes' is not technically difficult, but all these trails climb above 5000m, so acclimatisation is essential. If you do not take the recommended acclimatisation days, you will feel the effects of AMS on these treks. The trail passes through remote areas where there are no emergency facilities – never trek alone, and hire a guide who can communicate with local people if you get into trouble. This trek is a definite notch up in difficulty from the other treks covered here.

It is possible to walk this trek in either direction, but acclimatisation is easier if you travel from east to west, as described in this trek.

In good weather, you should be able to cross all three passes without axes, ropes or crampons, but snow and particularly ice can create difficult and potentially dangerous conditions on all of these trails. A pair of Yaktrax or Microspikes can be very useful here and are recommended.

At any time of year, down jackets and windproofs are strongly recommended. Make sure your porters are also properly equipped. All three passes can be closed by snow from December to February or after any major snowfall – check before you set off.

The Trek

Days 1–7: Lukla to Chhukung

In order to be properly acclimatised for the steep climb over the Kongma La, it is imperative to take this trek slowly. Take two days for the journey to Namche Bazaar and give yourself three nights at Namche to prepare your body for the steep ascent. Use the time to visit Chhorkung, Khumjung and Khunde to maximise your fitness for the pass.

On days five and six, you should be ready to continue to Tengboche and Dingboche. On day seven, climb to Chhukung. This section of the route forms the first part of the Everest Base Camp Trek – see p68 for a full description.

Day 8: Rest Day in Chhukung

A second night at Chhukung is strongly recommended before setting off for the pass. You can use the time to climb Chhukung Ri or make day hikes to Island Peak Base Camp or the base of Amphu Lapcha ridge. See p84 for details.

Day 9: Chhukung to Lobuche over the Kongma La

6–7 HOURS / 800M ASCENT / 620M DESCENT

To maximise your chances of clear weather on the Kongma La, you should start early from Chhukung. There are no facilities along the way and not much water, so bring a packed lunch from your lodge in Chhukung and fill your water bottle when you can. The trails are intact following the earthquake, but check locally to make sure before leaving Chukkung.

The trail climbs the hill diagonally northwest of the Chhukung Resort over the outflows of the Nuptse Glacier. The first five minutes are confusing so ask your lodge for directions to the start of the path. On the first stage of the trek, there are great views back across the valley to Island Peak and the jagged ridge of Amphu Lapcha.

The trail curves around the hillside above Bibre and then climbs along the east side of the Niyang Khola Valley, beneath a menacing wall of black rock. At the head of the valley, the path swings west, scrabbling its way up a steep slope littered with boulders. Snow often lingers on this north-facing slope, mak-

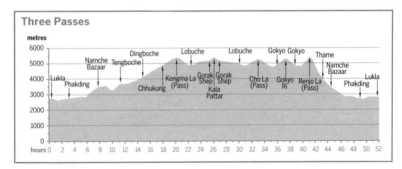

THREE PASSES TREK – TIMES

The following are trekking times only; stops are not included.

DAY	SECTION	HOURS
1	Lukla to Cheplung	1:15
	Cheplung to Phakding	1:45
2	Phakding to Benkar	1:30
	Benkar to Monjo	1:00
	Monjo to Namche Bazaar	3:00
3	Rest day	
4	Namche Bazaar to Sanasa	1:00
	Sanasa to Phunki Thenga	1:30
	Phunki Thenga to Tengboche	1:30
5	Rest day	
6	Tengboche to Pangboche	1:15
	Pangboche to Orsho	1:15
	Orsho to Pheriche/Dingboche	1:00
7	Pheriche/Dingboche to Chhukung	2:30-3:00
8	Rest day	
9	Chhukung to Kongma La	3:30
	Kongma La to Lobuche	3:00
10	Lobuche to Gorak Shep	2:30
	Gorak Shep to Base Camp (return)	5:00-6:00
11	Gorak Shep to Kala Pattar	2:00
	Kala Pattar to Lobuche	3:00
12	Lobuche to Dzonglha	3:00
13	Dzonglha to Cho La	3:00
	Cho La to Gokyo	5:00
14	Rest day	
15	Rest day	
16	Gokyo to Renjo La	3:00
	Renjo La to Lumde/Marulung	3:00
17	Lumde/Marulung to Thame	2:00-3:00
18	Thame to Namche Bazaar	3:00
19	Namche Bazaar to Monjo	3:00
	Monjo to Benkar	1:00
	Benkar to Phakding	1:30
20	Phakding to Cheplung	1:15
	Cheplung to Lukla	1:15

ing it tricky to find the icy trail. Climbing groups camp below the cliffs at the bottom of the slope before attempting the ascent of **Kongma Tse** (Mehra Peak; 5820m).

Af the top of the bluff the trail swings around past a small lake and ascends into a wide basin, dotted with small frozen lakes.

Beyond the largest lake, the trail switchbacks steeply over loose scree, gaining the **Kongma La** (5535m) around three to four hours after you left Chhukung. A cairn, mummy-wrapped in prayer flags, marks the pass. Behind you is a lunar landscape of icy lakes and frozen ridges; ahead the landscape tumbles down to the Khumbu Glacier. There are incredible views east towards giant Makalu, with peaks in Tibet visible to its left.

The final descent is the most difficult stage of the trek. Ignore the faint path running directly downhill to the tiny pool below the pass and keep to the right, dropping steeply down the scree and icy boulders for two hours to more solid ground on the edge of the moraine. Ice can make this section very slippery.

The next stage across the glacier is a final sucker punch, with lots of ups and downs – follow the stone cairns along the ever-shifting route and climb the moraine on the far side, where a clear trail runs north to Lobuche.

Days 10 & 11: Lobuche to Gorak Shep, Base Camp & Kala Pattar

After scampering over the pass, you may feel you've earned a rest, but the twin challenges of Everest Base Camp and Kala Pattar await. In the morning, head to Gorak Shep and on to Base Camp, returning to Gorak Shep to sleep. The next day, visit Kala Pattar and descend to Lobuche to rest in preparation for the scramble over the Cho La. You could push on to Dzonglha if you are feeling ambitious. For a description of this stage of the trek, see p87.

Day 12: Lobuche to Dzonglha

3 HOURS / 120M ASCENT / 220M DESCENT

Reports suggest that earthquake damage was only minor on this route, but check that accommodation will be available to Dzonghla before leaving Lobuche.

To start, head down from Lobuche for about 30 minutes before taking the lesser travelled right branch before the main trail crosses the river (the junction is at N 27°56.234', E 086°48.402'). The path skirts around the ridge, offering fine views down to Ama Dablam, Pheriche, Taboche peak and Cholatse Tsho, staying mostly level before dropping into a wide side valley used as an approach to the trekking peak of Lobuche (East). The trail then briefly climbs, decends again and then makes the final short ascent to the village of **Dzonglha** (4830m), set in a natural bowl.

Assuming all the lodges are open, the Mountain View Lodge here is a good choice and offers impressive views from its restaurant windows. The Hotel Zongla Inn and Hotel Green Valley are also good. The most

sylish option is Maison Sherpa, with its distinctive orange decor.

Five minutes' walk southwest of Dzonglha is a memorial chorten dedicated to two Korean climbers lost climbing Taboche.

Day 13: Dzonglha to Gokyo over the Cho La Pass

7–8 HOURS / 590M ASCENT / 670M DESCENT

In good weather conditions you can cross the Cho La with no specialist equipment, but warm clothing is essential. Check locally to make sure the trails are fully open before leaving Dzonghla. If the lodges at Tagnag are closed, it's a long walk to the next meal stop in Gokyo.

Start early from Dzonglha if you want to beat the clouds to the pass. The first stage is a gentle stroll as the trail runs east past a series of ominous-looking black boulders beneath the looming peak of Cholatse. At any stage on this walk, you can turn around to see **Ama Dablam** (6856m) framed perfectly at the end of the valley.

Your destination is a low point on the rock wall at the end of the valley, but the route only becomes apparent as you approach the face. After crossing several streams, the trail rises, passing to the right of two claw-shaped peaks. Make a steep, exhilarating scramble over boulders wedged against the edge of a soaring granite buttress.

As you gain the ridge, the broken face of the Cho La Glacier rises ahead. Unless there is fresh snow, you can pick out the route across the icefall using the footprints of other trekkers. Eventually, about three hours after setting off, you will reach **Cho La** (5420m), marked by a tangle of prayer flags at the edge of the glacier.

From here, there are vertigo-inducing views southeast toward Cholatse and Ama Dablam and west towards the Ngozumpa Glacier, Pharilapche (6017m) and Kyajo Ri (6186m). The descent into the Gokyo Valley is long and tedious, crossing a seemingly endless scree slope that is a minefield of loose stones and hidden ice. Look for the small stone cairns that mark the way. After what seems like an age, you'll reach the grassy hillside below the rockfall.

It's an easy walk on to **Tagnag** (Dragnag; 4700m). The landscape gets greener and the temperature warmer as you drop through a narrow gorge to the edge of the village. Assuming the lodges are open, you can thaw out your fingers with a bowl of soup at the Tashi

Friendship Lodge, Chola View Lodge or the recommended Chola Pass Lodge; these all offer decent rooms to trekkers attempting the pass in the opposite direction. Allow three hours to reach Tagnag from the pass.

The final stage to Gokyo drops over the moraine wall and crosses the groaning Ngozumpa Glacier. The trail changes every season as the ice shifts and melts, and it's not easy spotting the stone cairns that mark the way. If possible, tag along with a group or other trekkers for this section. After climbing onto the opposite moraine, you'll drop down into Gokyo village.

This trek is no harder in the opposite direction. Just stay in Tagnag on the first night and cross the pass to Dzonglha on the second day (making sure ahead of time that rooms will be available at Dzonghla).

Days 14 & 15: Gokyo

After all that climbing, you deserve a rest. Take a couple of days in Gokyo to visit Gokyo Ri for its awesome views, or hike up the valley past the Gokyo lakes for a sneaky peek at the world's highest mountain from Scoundrel's Viewpoint.

Most lodges in Gokyo can arrange a guide for either the Cho La or Renjo La for around Rs 2000 per day. See p94 for a description of Gokyo and p96 for some ideas for side trips.

Day 16: Gokyo to Lumde over the Renjo La

6–7 HOURS / 550M ASCENT / 1000M DESCENT

It takes two days to reach Thame from Gokyo and this route follows the edge of the Rolwaling region, which was badly affected by the earthquake. Even before the quake, most lodges in Lumde and Marulung remained closed over winter, and Thame village was very badly affected by the tremor, so it is essential to confirm that the trails are open and that food and accommodation will be available for all overnight stops before leaving Gokyo. Trekking in the opposite direction is generally discouraged, as the trek involves a 1000m increase in altitude over two days.

Before you set off from Gokyo, stand on the lakeshore and trace the route to the pass. The path climbs gently along the flank of Gokyo Ri and then zigzags precariously up a finger of grey scree above the northwest corner of the lake, crossing the ridge to the right of the pyramid-shaped peak.

Start off on the trail to Gokyo Ri and take the lower path that climbs gently above the north shore of the lake. The next section climbs steeply, switching back and forth like a python with indigestion, before splitting into two paths that climb up into the large mountain bowl. In general the right path is easier to follow. The two paths join at the base of the ridge wall and then follow a giant 'S' path to reach the final section of steps that leads to the pass.

About three hours after leaving Gokyo, you will gain the **Renjo La** (5345m), where an eye-popping vista awaits. If the skies are clear, you'll see the rooftops of Gokyo glinting distantly on the shore of the lake beneath the grey smear of the Ngozumpa Glacier, and the sawtooth peaks of Everest, Nuptse, Lhotse, Cholatse, Taboche, Makalu and the Cho La.

Continuing on from the pass, the trail winds down a staircase of huge stone slabs, often covered with ice, then drops steeply to the south bank of **Angladumba Tsho**, the small, serene lake below the pass that faces another razor-toothed buttress of snowy peaks. A wide and obvious dirt path drops below the lake along the north side of the valley. Arrows cut into the turf mark the route past the bow-tie-shaped **Relama Tsho**, before swinging round into the sandy valley of the Renjo Khola (two hours from the pass).

The final steep descent to **Lumde** (4350m) follows a narrow valley clogged with giant boulders. The extent of earthquake damage here is unclear; check ahead to make sure that rooms are available. Assuming all the lodges are operating, our top choices are the Renjo Pass Support Lodge (whose owner lived in Japan for some time), Kongde View Lodge and Three Passes Lodge. Lumde is marked on some maps as Lungden or Lungare.

SIDE TRIP: BHOTE KOSI VALLEY
4–5 HOURS / 750M ASCENT / 750M DESCENT

Instead of overnighting in Lumde, a popular alternative is to continue for an easy 40 minutes up the main Bhote Kosi valley to **Arya** (4360m) and use the lodges there as a base from which to explore the little-visited upper valley. The trail up the Bhote Kosi follows a route used for centuries by Tibetan traders who ferried salt and grain across the Nangpa La to and from Tibet. All along the valley you'll pass yak trails and campsites used by traders from Tingri until the pass was closed to border traffic in 2012.

However, reports suggest that landslides and rockfalls caused widespread damage here. The following route description traces the route as it was trekked before the disaster, but it is essential to check that trails are clear and that lodges are operating before attempting this route.

Assuming lodges are operating in Arya, the best overnight stop is the Arya Guesthouse. Owner Pemba Nuru is a guide and has lots of experience of arranging day hikes or camping trips up the remote upper valleys.

Most people are content just to make a day hike up the valley from Arya. The mountain views start to open up after about 40 minutes as you reach a huge trailside boulder covered with carved mantras. As you pass the empty goths of **Chhule**, the side valley opens up to offer fine views of Pangbuk (6625m), Dragnag Ri (6801m) and Singkorab (5982m) peaks.

It's another 2½ hours up the valley on a sometimes exposed trail high above the river, traversing a deeply eroded cliff with several dangerous landslide sections, to reach **Sumnag Cave**. From here you can follow the main trail for 15 minutes and then ascend the moraine to the right for fine views of the Lumsumna Glacier. From left to right are Lunag peak (6907m), Jobo Ringang (6772m) dividing the Lunag and Nangpa glaciers, the black rock of Nangpa Gotaya (5790m), the peaks of Pasanglama Chuli (7352m) and wall of Nangpa Gorsum, with Cho Oyu peeking out behind it.

Beyond here lie glacier trails to the Nangpa La, making this a good place to turn back. In 2006 Western climbers filmed Chinese border guards shooting at unarmed refugees as they attempted the crossing from Tibet, killing Kelsang Namtso, a 17-year-old nun.

Day 17: Lumde to Thame

3 HOURS / 530M DESCENT

Your destination for the day is Thame, but the village was devastated by the 2015 earthquake and many buildings collapsed. If no accommodation is available at Thame, you'll need to continue for several more hours to reach Namche Bazaar.

The first step is a 40 minute downhill walk to Marulung (4200m) on the east bank of the Bhote Kosi. Before the tremor, the stone-block Namaste Lodge and Marulung Guesthouse offered rudimentary accommodation.

Below Marulung, cross to the western side of the Bhote Kosi (there are two more lodges by the bridge) and descend for 40 minutes to **Tarnga**. Before the disaster, the Norlha Inn was offering good rooms. The trail drops into the valley of the Langmuche Khola, which drains down from Dig Tsho, the glacial lake that burst its banks in 1985, causing devastating floods along the Dudh Kosi Valley.

It's a gentle stroll down the valley to reach Thambuteng village and the 350-year-old Kyaro Kerok Gompa, before you arrive on the outskirts of Thame Teng, the upper part of Thame village. Many houses collapsed during the earthquake and it is unclear if the lodges here survived the disaster.

From the chorten at the bottom of the village it's a short ascent over the moraine to **Thame**, but most buildings here were damaged in the earthquake and lodges may be closed for reconstruction. Check ahead to make sure rooms are available. If you can't find somewhere to stay, another few hours of gentle walking along the valley will take you to Namche Bazaar.

Days 18–20: Thame to Lukla

If you stayed overnight in Thame, you can descend to Namche Bazaar in half a day. Treat yourself to a slap-up dinner and a beer – you deserve it! A long day later, you will be sitting in Lukla, ready to board your flight back to Kathmandu the next morning.

For a description of the walk between Namche Bazaar and Lukla in reverse, see Days 1–2 of the Everest Base Camp Trek (p68).

Shivalaya to Lukla Trek

Duration 6 days

Max Elevation 3530m

Difficulty Medium

Season October to May

Start Shivalaya

Finish Lukla

Permits TIMS card, Gaurishankar Conservation Area Project permit

Summary Follow in the footsteps of the early expeditions to Everest, passing through dense forests and Buddhist hill villages. This is a great acclimatisation trek to prepare for Gokyo or Everest Base Camp.

The trail to Lukla passes through classic Middle Hills country that is blissfully free from the crowds that mob the trails further north. Only 1000 trekkers walk this route a year. Views of the big peaks are in short supply but there is plenty of physical and cultural diversity. The trek is also a good option for nervous flyers who want to avoid the domestic flight to Lukla.

However, there was considerable earthquake damage at the start of this route, which passes close to the epicentre of the 12 May 2015 tremor. Both Jiri and Shivalaya saw buildings collapse and most villages along the route saw some earthquake damage.

Assuming things are open, facilities on this trek are simple but fairly comfortable. There are no internet cafes but most villages have decent lodges and menus. Beer and chhang (barley beer) are widely available; electric sockets are harder to find. Bring a spare battery for your camera just to be safe. Throughout this region, rooms cost Rs 100 person.

Even though the trek begins at just 1860m, it climbs to 3530m at the Lamjura Bhanjyang, and drops as low as 1500m at the Dudh Kosi crossing east of Nunthala. Physically speaking, this is a long, hard trek with many steep hills.The reason we grade it as 'moderate' is simply because of the convenience of teahouse accommodation and relatively low altitudes.

Small sections of this trek will likely see some changes over the coming years, as road construction advances to Kinja and between Salleri, Jubing and Surkhe. Most of the trek route should avoid the new roads.

Once you reach Lukla, most people continue to Everest Base Camp or Gokyo. Alternatively you can fly back to Kathmandu, or walk for another nine days on the little-used trail east to Tumlingtar.

🏃 The Trek

Day 1: Shivalaya to Bhandar

3–4 HOURS / 900M ASCENT / 600M DESCENT

Exactly where you start walking will depend on the state of the road from Jiri after the earthquake. Assuming it is possible to get all the way to Shivalaya, the first day of walking will start just 50m beyond the village, with an exhausting hour-long climb to **Sangbadanda** (2180m), where tea should be available at the pocket-sized Sushila Lodge. You

EARTHQUAKE DAMAGE ON THE SHIVALAYA TO LUKLA TREK

The early stages of the Shivalaya to Jiri trek pass through Dolakha District, which bore the brunt of the damage in the 12 May 2015 earthquake. Hundreds were killed and buildings collapsed throughout this area, particularly in Jiri and Shivalaya. We have described the route here as it was before the disaster, but the status of the lodges on this route will not be clear until villagers have had a chance to rebuild after the 2015 monsoon. Check locally to confirm that trails are open and accommodation is available on this route before leaving from either Shivalaya or Lukla.

cross the dirt road twice; at one point following it for 100m. If in doubt look for the painted orange circles marking the trail.

The direct route to Deurali branches off the dirt road again at a signed junction and climbs a muddy gully up the end of the spur, past the Thodung Sherpa Lodge at **Khasrubas** (2330m). For the next hour or so, the trail climbs gently towards the head of the canyon. After crossing a couple of flat wooden bridges, you'll begin the steep ascent to the Deurali pass on a winding forest trail.

The path finally emerges onto the wide saddle at **Deurali** (Deorali; 2705m), which is covered by an unusual grid of mani walls. From here on, you will see increasing evidence of Buddhist Sherpa culture. Looking east from the pass, there are grandstand views down to Bhandar and the valley of the Likhu Khola.

Before the earthquake, there were half a dozen lodges at Deurali serving lunch and offering accommodation for porters and trekkers. Assuming they are still standing, the Lama Guesthouse and Tibetan-style Highland Sherpa Guesthouse are bright and welcoming, with outdoor terraces that get lots of morning sunshine. Lodges can advise on the hour-long walk south to a hilltop that offers unobstructed views towards Gauri Shankar (7145m) and Numbur peaks.

On the far side of the pass, ignore the dirt road running south along the ridge – the correct path drops straight down into the valley on steep stone steps, passing scat-

Shivalaya to Lukla Trek Day 1-3

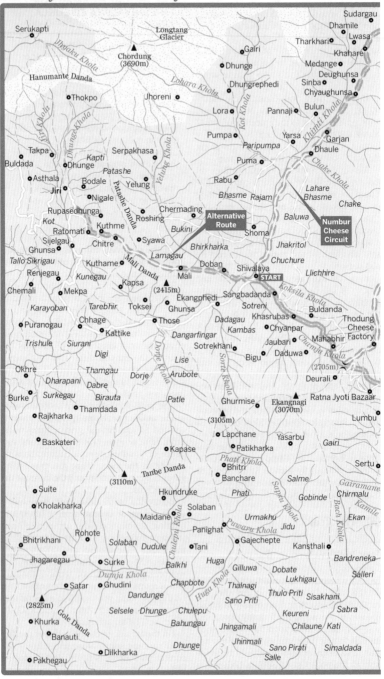

Serukapti

Longtang Glacier

Sudargau

Dhamile

Lwasa

Tharkhari

Khahare

▲ Chordung (3690m)

Gairi

Medange

Deughunsa

Hanumante Danda

Dhunge

Dhungrephedi

Sinba

Chyaughunsa

Thokpo

Jhoreni

Lora

Pannaji

Bulun

Pumpa

Paripumpa

Yarsa

Garjan

Dhaule

Takpa

Kapti

Serpakhasa

Puma

Buldada

Dhunge

Patashe

Rabu

Lahare Bhasme

Asthala

Bodale

Yelung

Bhasme

Rajam

Chake

Jiri

Nigale

Chermading

Alternative Route

Baluwa

Numbur Cheese Circuit

Rupasedhunga

Roshing

Kot

Kuthme

Bukini

Shoma

Ratomati

Syawa

Jhakritol

Sijelgau

Chitre

Lamagau

Bhirkharka

Chuchure

Ghunsa

Kuthame

Mali Danda

Doban

Shivalaya

Llichhire

Tallo Sikrigau

Kunegau

Mali

START

Renjegau

Kapsa

(2415m)

Sangbadanda

Kolesila Khola

Chemali

Mekpa

Ekangphedi

Sotreni

Buldana

Karayoban

Tarebhir

Toksei

Ghunsa

Dadagau

Khasrubas

Chyanpar

Thodung Cheese Factory

Puranogau

Chhage

Those

Dangarfingar

Kambás

Jaubari

Mahabhir

Trishule

Siurani

Kattike

Sotrekhani

Bigu

Daduwa

(2705m)

Okhre

Digi

Lise

Deurali

Dharapani

Thamgau

Arubote

Dabre

Dorje

Surke

Burke

Surkegau

Birauta

Patle

Ghurmise

Ekangnagi (3070m)

Ratna Jyoti Bazaar

Rajkharka

Thamdada

(3105m)

Lumbu

Baskateri

Lapchane

Yasarbu

Gairi

Kapase

Patikharka

Sertu

Phati Khola

Bhitri

Gairamane

(3110m)

Tanbe Danda

Banchare

Salme

Chirmalu

Suite

Hkundruke

Phati

Gobinde

Kamile

Kholakharka

Solaban

Urmakhu

Jidu

Ekan

Maidane

Panighat

Gajechepte

Kansthali

Rohote

Bhitrikhani

Solaban

Dudule

Tani

Bandreneka

Jhagaregau

Surke

Balkhi

Huga

Gilluwa

Dobate

Salleri

Dumja Khola

Chapbote

Thalnagi

Lukhigau

Satar

Ghudini

Dandunge

Thulo Priti

Sisakhani

Sabra

(2825m)

Selsele

Dhunge

Chulepu

Sano Priti

Keureni

Chilaune

Kati

Khurka

Bahungau

Jhingamali

Simaldada

Banauti

Dilkharka

Dhunge

Jhinmali

Sano Pirati

Pakhegau

Salle

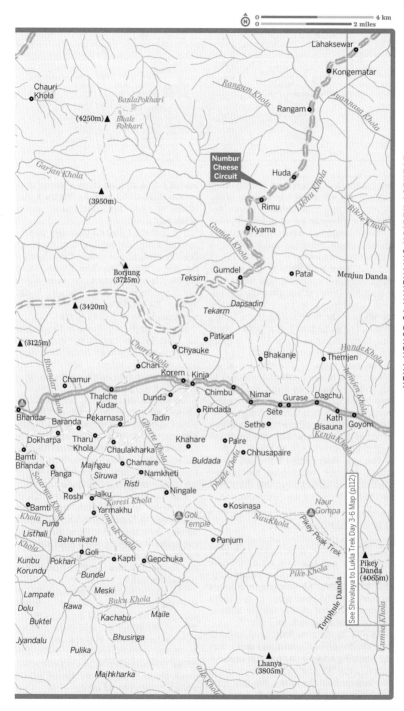

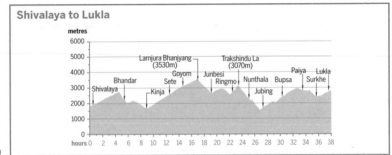

Shivalaya to Lukla

tered lodges at Changma and Bhamti. After an hour, you will reach the outskirts of old **Bhandar** (Chyangma; 2200m), known before the earthquake for its gompa, fronted by two mismatched stupas, one squat and square and the other tall and topped by a beehive-shaped tower.

The village was hit badly by the tremor so check ahead to make sure accommodation is available. Before the disaster, the best options were around the paved square below the gompa. The tasteful Ang Dawa Lodge, Shobha Lodge, Buddha Lodge (with a pharmacy) and Himalaya Lodge all offered decent rooms and good trekker food.

The new town of Bhandar lies a 10-minute walk to the south and is linked to Jiri and Kathmandu by a dirt road. If this road is still navigable following the tremor, buses should run here from Kathmandu. Before the earthquake, there was a single daily bus at 5.45am from Kathmandu's Ratna Park to Bhandar (Rs 960, 10 hours).

This is a short day, so if you are feeling strong, consider walking on for another three hours to Kinja, though this village was also badly affected by the earthquake.

Day 2: Bhandar to Sete
6–7 HOURS / 650M DESCENT / 1050M ASCENT

The main trekking trail avoids new road construction and branches left from Bhandar, staying high on the ridge, before dropping to the Likhu Khola a couple of hours further east. The road drops to the Likhu Khola earlier and climbs the far hillside, soon to reach as far as Kinja.

To pick up the new trail, head downhill from the lodges in Bhandar and veer left at the Chhiring Lodge and then the Bhandar Valley Lodge. Depending on the extent of the damage from the quake, you may need to ask directions. The path winds past farmhouses into a gully, to cross a stream on a wooden bridge and meet a 4WD track. Ask for the 'new path' to Kinja if you are unsure of the way.

The trail stays high on the valley wall for an hour before descending steeply through fields of cardamom and mandarins to cross the side stream of the Chari Khola. Fifteen minutes later you cross the main Likhu Khola and then one last suspension bridge to reach **Kinja** (1630m), at the confluence of the Likhu Khola and Kinja Khola.

Unfortunately, this bustling bazaar was hit hard by the earthquake and several buildings were destroyed. Before the tremor, there were seven lodges in Kinja, but check ahead to make sure that accommodation is available if you plan to stop here.

Before the disaster, the Sherpa Guesthouse was a good bet, with comfortable rooms, a flagstone courtyard and a restaurant serving Swiss favourites like *rösti*. Other good options were the 'best and cheaper' Sonam Lodge, and the popular New Everest Guest House, where the restaurant served yak cheese, apple cider and banana lassis.

Leaving Kinja, the trail begins a relentlessly steep ascent towards the Lamjura Bhanjyang, switchbacking up the almost vertical slope above the village. After about two hours of climbing, you'll reach **Chimbu** (2170m), and all being well, a large school, a tree-shaded chautara and the simple Hilltop Himalayan Lodge.

The trail dips into an eroded gully before the occasional mani wall indicates you are on the right track as you ascend to the friendly village of **Sete** (Seke; 2520m) with its beehive-shaped stupa and ancient *lhakhang* (Buddhist temple). Sadly, this village was also affected by the earthquake; check ahead to make sure rooms will be available when you get here.

Before the disaster, there were four farm-house-style lodges. The Sunrise Lodge and the simple Solu Khumbu Sherpa Guide Guesthouse were in the centre, while the posher Sherpa Guide lodge was at the top of the village and the New Everest Lodge benefited from a peaceful location in the fields near the stupa.

If you stayed in Kinja last night you could make it to Goyom today, though it's a long day with an elevation gain of 1570m.

Day 3: Sete to Junbesi

6–7 HOURS / 1280M ASCENT / 1220M DESCENT

Have a good breakfast before you leave Sete; the first half of the day is a long and draining climb to the 3530m Lamjura Bhanjyang pass. Check that the route is open before leaving Sete, and confirm that rooms will be availabe at Junbesi, as this village was hit badly by the earthquake.

From Sete, the trail to the pass picks its way through a dripping, moss-cloaked forest of gnarled rhododendron, magnolia, maple and birch trees. About an hour above Sete, the trail reaches **Dagchu** (2820m), a makeshift settlement of simple local lodges on a saddle near two small ponds (the better lodges are five minutes past Dagchu). From here, the route to the pass ascends a narrow spur over the roots of scrub rhododendrons, passing along a narrow, muddy chute.

The deforestation in this area is shocking. After another hour of climbing through this hacked landscape, you'll reach **Goyom** (3060m), spread over three small settlements in the forest and the last lunch spot before the pass.

Assuming the lodges here are operating after the earthquake, Goyom makes a decent overnight stop if the weather looks intimidating on the pass. Before the disaster, the Tashi Delek Lodge was a good bet for its pleasant courtyard. About 30 minutes further up the spur, the simple Lamjura Sherpa Rest House was another good choice, though rooms can be smoky; ask to try the local dried mushrooms if you eat here.

Forty minutes further, and around 25 minutes before the pass, the Hotel Numbur View Lodge and Himalayan Lodge offered better quality rooms and could arrange guides for the long day hike to Pikey Peak with its clear views towards Everest.

EVEREST REGION SHIVALAYA TO LUKLA TREK

SHIVALAYA TO LUKLA TREK – TIMES

The following are trekking times only; stops are not included.

DAY	SECTION	HOURS
1	Shivalaya to Deurali	3:00
	Deurali to Bhandar	1:00
2	Bhandar to Kinja	3:00
	Kinja to Chimbu	2:00
	Chimbu to Sete	1:30
3	Sete to Goyom	2:00
	Goyom to Lamjura Bhanjyang	2:30
	Lamjura Bhanjyang to Junbesi	2:00
4	Junbesi to Salung	1.30
	Salung to Ringmo	1:30
	Ringmo to Trakshindu La	1:00
	Trakshindu La to Nunthala	2:15
5	Nunthala to Jubing	2:15
	Jubing to Khari Khola	1:45
	Khari Khola to Bupsa	1:00
6	Bupsa to Paiya	3:15
	Paiya to Pakhepani	1.15
	Pakhepani to Surkhe	1:00
	Surkhe to Lukla	2:00

WORTH A TRIP

GOMPAS AROUND JUNBESI
....

Assuming it is possible to stay in Junbesi following the earthquake, there are some interesting side walks to Buddhist monasteries in the surrounding hills.

Twenty minutes' walk southwest of Junbesi, and easily visited en route from Sete, the Nyingma-school **Serlo Gompa** is one of the few gompas in Solu Khumbu to be founded by a Sherpa lama. Sangye Tenzing was a Solu native who studied in Tibet and fled back to Junbesi after the Chinese invasion, founding this small but attractive gompa in 1959. The gompa was damaged in the quake but still preserves some interesting murals.

The status of other gompas in this area is unclear, so ask locally before setting out to find the following places. One option close to Junbesi is the small Thumbuk Gompa, set high atop a small rocky bluff in the village of **Thumbuk** (2500m). The path starts above Junbesi, near the Apple Orchard Guesthouse, and winds south along the Junbesi Khola. You can see the monastery on the walk to Phurteng.

In the opposite direction, the valley of the Junbesi Khola runs north towards **Thubten Chholing** (3000m), a huge Tibetan Buddhist monastery founded by the revered lama Trulsik Rinpoche, who fled to Nepal from Tibet's Rongbuk Gompa (on the north side of Everest) with a large group of *ani* (nuns) and monks in the 1960s. Since then, many more refugees have fled to Thubten Chholing en route to join the Dalai Lama at Dharamsala in India. The meditation cells dotted around the hillside are used by 400 resident monks and nuns, including the occasional foreigner, but expect to see reconstruction work as some buildings were damaged by the earthquake. Relics from the original Rongbuk Gompa are preserved inside the main chapel.

The 90-minute trail to Thubten Chholing starts in front of the Junbesi gompa and follows the west bank of the Junbesi Khola upstream. Take a left at the junction marked by a chorten and eventually cross to the east bank by the huge white stupa at **Mopung**, then climb steeply up the hill to the gompa.

About 30 minutes uphill from Thubten Chholing on the west bank of the stream is the village of **Phugmocche** (3100m), which has another small gompa and a thangka art centre.

At 3530m **Lamjura Bhanjyang** is the highest point on the trek between Jiri and Namche Bazaar, marked by an untidy cairn wrapped with prayer flags and *kata* (ceremonial scarves). Assuming it is open after the quake, the Lamjura View Pass Restaurant just beyond the pass is a good place to grab tea and a snack.

Most people make the crossing at lunchtime, when the hills are blanketed by cloud. You get the best chance of clear morning views towards the white-tipped peaks above Rolwaling by overnighting at Goyom or at the pass itself. You'll often hear the rumble of planes passing low overhead on the final approach to Lukla airstrip.

From the pass, the trail makes a long, slow descent to the bottom of the valley through fragrant fir and rhododendron forests. Before the quake, there were several isolated and simple lodges surrounded by meadows on the way down the hill, including the Tashi Delek Lodge in Thagtok Kinza and the Shanti Chetra Lodge at Thagtok Bung.

The village of **Taktor** boasts boulders carved with Buddhist mantras and walls painted with Maoist slogans, as well as a small *lhakhang*. At a junction 15 minutes past the village, take the left path and keep level, rather than the downhill right trail.

Occasional mani walls and chautara mark the path onwards through fields and forests to a large chorten and a giant mani boulder topped by a prayer wheel. Continue on a mostly level path past the cliff decorated with mantras, before swinging round to see fine views of Junbesi and tomorrow's trail.

To the north, look for the looming peak of **Numbur** (6959m), which soars above the still, sacred waters of Dudh Kunda. The peak is worshipped as the guardian deity of Solu, hence its Sherpa name – Shorong Yul Lha ('God of the Solu').

A side trail here heads directly for 10 minutes to **Serlo Gompa** (see the boxed text above), damaged in the earthquake, but still containing some impressive murals.

The final stage to **Junbesi** (2680m) passes some coloured mantras carved into a rock face and drops through terraced fields. Set among scattered orchards above the Junbesi Khola, this sprawling village was noteworthy before the quake for its large white houses with carved Tibetan-style windows and overhanging eaves, but many were damaged in the disaster. Assuming it is possible to stay here, the village makes good base for short treks to Tibetan Buddhist monasteries in the surrounding valleys.

In the north of Junbesi, the **Tashi Thongmon Gompa** was founded in the 16th century, but the monastery buildings were destroyed several times by fire, and it only narrowly survived the 2015 earthquake. By a large yellow-topped stupa in the middle of the village, the Junbesi school is one of the largest set up by Edmund Hillary; there was some earthquake damage but restoration work is underway.

Before the disaster, there were nine lodges in Junbesi, all in village homes with big gardens and carved windows. Ask locally to see which are currently open. Before the disaster, good options included the venerable Ang Chhokpa's Lodge, Ang Domi Lodge and the Junbesi Guesthouse near the gompa. Set in an orchard garden beside the trail to Sete, the popular Apple Orchard Guesthouse was a good choice for its spacious rooms and wifi, while the Zambala Guest House scored points for its lovely carved wood facade and clean rooms.

In case of emergency, a 4WD road connects Junbesi with Phaplu, which has weekly flights to Kathmandu (US$154) with Tara Air. Assuming the road is navigable after the quake, a chartered jeep costs Rs 7000 one way. Salleri, near Phaplu, has daily passenger jeeps to/from Kathmandu's Chabahil suburb.

Day 4: Junbesi to Nunthala

6½–7 HOURS / 900M ASCENT / 1250M DESCENT

Before leaving Junbesi, confirm that rooms will be available at the next overnight stop, Nunthala, which was also damaged by the earthquake.

At the bottom of Junbesi, below the large chorten, the trail crosses the Junbesi Khola on a wooden bridge at 2560m, reaching an important **trail junction**. The right-hand 4WD road leads downhill to Phaplu and Salleri.

The walking trail to Khumbu leads steeply uphill into a charming forest, looping in and out of side valleys that are used for grazing by herders from Junbesi. A chautara and

prayer pole mark a viewpoint where you can look back on much of yesterday's walk. The landscape here is almost European – with all the pines and cows it could nearly be a scene from a Milka chocolate wrapper.

Make a steep, draining climb to the two lodges of **Phurteng** (Phurtyang Beni; 2900m). Compensation comes in the form of your first glimpse of Everest (if the weather is clear), tucked between the snowy crowns of Thamserku (6608m), Kantega (6685m), Kyashar (6770m), Kusum Kangru (6367m) and Mera Peak (6476m). An overnight here gives you the best chances of clear views, assuming lodges are open after the earthquake. From the white chorten just past the village there are sweeping views south towards Salleri and the Phaplu airstrip.

Before the disaster, there were three simple teahouses with OK rooms, decent food and yak cheese for sale (Rs 300 for 200g); take your pick from the Everest View Sherpa Lodge and the similarly named Everest View Lodge and Sherpa Restaurant.

Beyond Phurteng, the trail turns north and descends through meadows and copses of pines to the hamlet of **Salung** (2860m) and its simple Himalayan Lodge.

Heading to Nunthala, it's a steep descent through pines and a small landslip to a suspension bridge over the Dudhkunda Khola at 2510m.

From the river, the trail switchbacks uphill for 30 minutes to **Ringmo** (2720m), a small Sherpa village dotted with apple, peach and apricot orchards. As you might expect, the village generates lots of fruit products – jams, pickles, dried fruit, cider and delicious apple brandy – which are widely available in the village. Ringmo saw some damage in the earthquake – check which lodges have rooms when you arrive. Note that most lodges here are closed outside the high season.

In the middle of the village is a map of local attractions – a side trail to Salleri and Phaplu turns downhill to the right (south), while the Nunthala trail runs directly uphill.

There were six lodges in Ringmo before the earthquake, including the tall, imposing Apple House. Hotel Yak and Nak was another good choice for its fruit garden and valley views. Also OK were the nearby Centre Sherpa Lodge and Sherpa Guide Lodge, which were good places to buy yak cheese as well as fruity alcoholic drinks and preserves.

EVEREST REGION SHIVALAYA TO LUKLA TREK

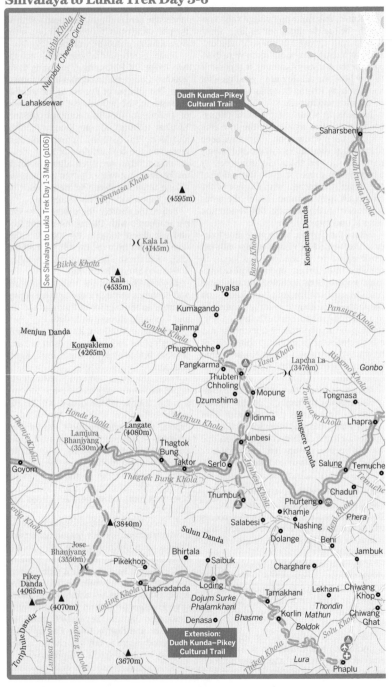

Dudh Kunda–Pikey Cultural Trail

Lahaksewar

Saharsbeni

See Shivalaya to Lukla Trek Day 1-3 Map (p106)

Likhu Khola

Numbur Cheese Circuit

Jyonnasa Khola

(4595m)

Dudhkunda Khola

Kala La (4145m)

Bilkhe Khola

Kala (4535m)

Jhyalsa

Kumagando

Basa Khola

Konglema Danda

Tajinma

Menjun Danda

Konyaklemo (4265m)

Konjok Khola

Phugmochhe

Pangkarma

Thubten Chholing

Mopung

Yasa Khola

Lapcha La (3476m)

Gonbo

Dzumshima

Idinma

Tongnasa

Pansure Khola

Ripemo Khola

Honde Khola

Menjun Khola

Junbesi

Shingsere Danda

Tongnasa Khola

Lhapra

Langate (4080m)

Lamjura Bhanjyang (3530m)

Thagtok Bung

Taktor

Serlo

Junbesi Khola

Salung

Temuche

Goyom

Thenie Khola

Thagtok Bung Khola

Thumbuk

Phurteng

Chadun

Temuche

Khamje

Phera

(3840m)

Sulun Danda

Salabesi

Nashing

Beni Khola

Jose Bhanjyang (3550m)

Dolange

Beni

Jambuk

Bhirtala

Saibuk

Pikekhop

Charghare

Pikey Danda (4065m)

Loding

Loding Khola

Thapradanda

Tamakhani

Lekhani

Chiwang Khop

(4070m)

Dojum Surke Phalamkhani

Thondin Mathun

Chiwang Ghat

Toriphule Danda

Lumsa Khola

Sadin g Khola

Denasa

Bhasme

Korlin

Boldok

Solu Khola

Extension: Dudh Kunda–Pikey Cultural Trail

(3670m)

Thiksen Khola

Lura

Phaplu

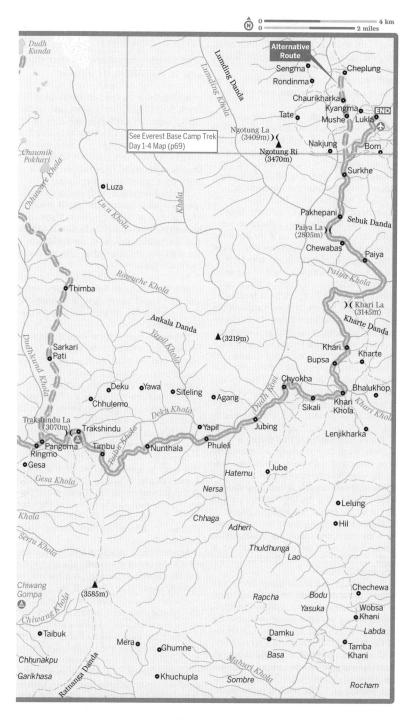

Above Ringmo, the trail climbs steeply through pine and rhododendron forest to a long mani wall in the hamlet of **Pangoma**, where a signposted side trail by the Sherpa Fast Food Lodge branches north towards **Dudh Kunda** (p116), a remote lake set at 4500m beneath the mountain wall of Numbur peak.

Above the turn-off, the trail climbs to an ancient-looking beehive-shaped stupa surrounded by mani walls, and on to a broad, flat pass marked by a white chorten and several wooden teahouses at **Trakshindu La** (3070m). Assuming it is open, the Mt Kailash Guest House here offers decent accommodation.

Fifteen minutes down from the pass, on the eastern side, the trail passes the isolated **Trakshindu Gompa**, one of the largest and most impressive monasteries in the Khumbu. The complex of monks' cells provides a home for 42 devotees, with the inner chapel featuring fine murals. Although parts of the monastery seem ancient, the gompa was actually founded in 1946 by a monk from Tengboche. Assuming the gompa is open following the earthquake, visitors can follow the clockwise pilgrim path around the large new chorten.

There were several lodges here before the quake. On the trail below the gompa, the slightly austere Mountain View Lodge was once owned by the late Babu Chhiri Sherpa, who climbed Everest 10 times, spending a record-breaking 21 hours on the summit in 1999. Other good choices were the nearby Taksindu Resort and Panorama Guesthouse.

Below Trakshindu the trail descends into a huge valley through a conifer and rhododendron forest that is alive with birds, lured here by the plentiful wild strawberries. You'll pass a few scattered *bhattis* as you drop down a long descent on a muddy, slippery path to the fields of **Timbu** (Tahi Bhug; 2590m).

Below this small village, the trail crosses a picturesque stream on a suspension bridge and then dissolves into a clutter of mule camps as it reaches **Nunthala** (Manidingma; 2220m).

The village is a single street lined with lodges, all with similar facilities, but there was a lot of earthquake damage here; ask locally to see who has rooms available. Before the quake, the Shangrila Guesthouse at the start of the village was a good choice, with a quiet side block of rooms in a large, peaceful garden. In the centre, other OK choices included the well-run Hotel Everest, the Moonlight Lodge, with a pretty flower garden, and the Himalayan Trekker Lodge across the road, with a terrace restaurant with views over the trail.

Day 5: Nunthala to Bupsa

5–6 HOURS / 800M DESCENT / 900M ASCENT

From Nunthala the descent continues to the Dudh Kosi ('Milk River'), so named for the chalky sediment carried by the river down from the Ngozumpa Glacier near Gokyo. The first stage drops steeply for an hour through mixed forest and farmland to **Phuleli**, where the Njiam Shop and Lodge should be able to rustle up a cup of *chiya* (Nepali tea).

The trail switchbacks for another 45 minutes to a mule station and small group of *bhattis* next to the 109m-long suspension bridge that crosses the Dudh Kosi at 1510m. The marigold garlands on the bridge are a sign that you are entering an area inhabited by Hindu Rais.

After crossing the Dudh Kosi, the trail climbs north through fields of barley, wheat and maize and passes several teashops to the sprawling Rai village of **Jubing** (Dorakbuk; 1680m).

Before the quake, there were a couple of lodges offering rooms – the Gorkhali Lodge was a good bet with its appealing alfresco dining area in a garden gazebo – and even a village tailor and beauty parlour. Telltale signs of Rai culture include the heavy gold earrings and glass bead necklaces worn by local women, the whitewashed, mud-covered stone houses, and the traditional bamboo pipes that bring water into the village.

Heading east, the trail climbs for a further hour to a saddle on the edge of **Khari Khola** (Khati Thenga; 2010m), which shares its name with the stream at the bottom of the next valley. Assuming they are open after the quake, the Hill Top Guest House and Kharikhola Guesthouse make good lunch spots.

Perched on a prominent ridge just one minute up above the saddle is the peaceful **Pema Namding Gompa**, constructed in 2008 by lamas from Sikkim. If the gompa is open after the quake, you may be able to view the riotously colourful statues of Guru Rinpoche, Sakyamuni and Avalokitesvara inside.

Before the quake, Khari Khola had more lodges than paying guests – a legacy of the days when this trek was the main access route to Everest. Assuming all the lodges are open, good options include the Tashi Delek Cottage Guesthouse with its private cabins, the *Han-*

sel & Gretel–style Solukhumbu Guesthouse, the Namaste Lodge, and the smart and tidy Boudha Lodge by the stupa – all strung out along the trail through the village. Above the trail is the Khare Khola hospital.

Follow the trail down through the bazaar and wheat fields to the simple, whitewashed Holiday Home, where a side trail turns east along the valley towards Pangum and the Lukla to Tumlingtar trek (p220). The Khari Khola is crossed by a drooping suspension bridge at 1930m, with several water-powered mills that grind the corn grown on both sides of the valley.

On the other side, the path makes a steep hour-long climb to **Bupsa** (Bumshing; 2360m), set among cascading wheat and maize terraces below a dense oak forest. At the bottom of the village is a tiny *lhakhang*, founded in 1892 and restored in 2006 using donations from the Ireland-based **Moving Mountains Trust** (www.movingmountainstrust.org). Locals are hard at work repairing earthquake damage to homes, lodges and the chapel.

The lodges in Bupsa are painted in a rainbow of colours but some may have earthquake damage; check locally to see who is currently offering rooms. Before the quake, there were good rooms at the Hotel Yellow Top (yellow timbers), Hotel International Trekkers (green timbers), Everest Guesthouse (lilac timbers), Hotel Sundup (pink, with good mattresses and wi-fi possible) and Kwangde View Lodge (white timbers and slate-clad walls).

Day 6: Bupsa to Lukla

6–7 HOURS / 1000M ASCENT / 650M DESCENT

Your destination today is Lukla, which saw only minor damage in the earthquake.

Above Bupsa the trail leaves the wheat fields and climbs steadily through dense forests, reaching the small settlement of **Khari** where a minor side trail branches to Pangum on the Lukla to Tumlingtar trek (p220). You'll find typical trekking-lodge rooms at the Chamling Hotel.

From Khari, the trail trawls uphill for 45 minutes, past the Sonam Lodge, to a highpoint often referred to as **Khari La** (2840m). (The real Khari La is further up the ridge on the Lukla to Tumlingtar trek.) As you climb, note the caves with soot-charred roofs – these are used as overnight stops by porters hauling goods uphill to the market in Lukla.

From the pass, the path dives into an almost primordial oak forest. Watch your footing on this section of slippery, exposed and mule-clogged trail.

Twenty-five minutes from the pass, beside an old landslide, a side trail branches off southeast towards Pangum on the Lukla to Tumlingtar trek. The main trail continues down past moss-choked branches and the rotting stumps of fallen forest giants, soon reaching a metal bridge across the Paiya Khola.

You'll soon reach **Paiya** (Puiyan, Poyan; 2770m), which saw some quake damage. Before the disaster, there were several lodges here; check locally to see who has rooms available. In the bottom part of the village, below the school, are two good options; the inviting yellow Trekkers Lodge, with its pretty flagstone terrace and thick mattresses, and the sunnier Himalayan Sherpa Lodge. For more privacy, try the cottages at the charming, terraced Beehive Lodge.

Above Paiya, you'll get your first views of the Dudh Kosi canyon, which gushes down beneath the watchful eye of Khumbila (5761m), the rocky peak above Namche Bazaar, which is worshipped as a guardian deity by Khumbu Sherpas. The path climbs steadily through patchy forest to several teahouses at **Chewabas** (Chheubas).

The views really start to shine as you climb above Chewabas to the **Paiya La** (2805m). The trail contours around the ridge and drops to **Pakhepani**, where you should be able to find a meal at the superior Khumbu View Lodge, in front of inspiring views up the Dudh Kosi to Lukla from its terrace. There is a sense that you are finally getting near the big mountains.

From Pakhepani, the trail plunges downwards on a muddy path through forest, beneath the flight path to Lukla airstrip. You'll probably be slowed down by mule trains carrying wheels of yak cheese and other goods from the villages around Lamjura.

Eventually you'll arrive at the pretty village of **Surkhe** (Surkey; 2290m), tucked into a hanging valley above the Dudh Kosi. Surkhe makes a fine tea stop; before the quake, there were several good lodges, including the chalet-like Everest Trail Lodge, set in a garden just above the stream, and the wooden Thamserku Lodge, with its potplant-filled restaurant.

From the north end of Surkhe, the trail climbs above the stream on crude stone steps for about 20 minutes to a junction by a small stream and a mani wall (N 27°40.569',

E 86°43.113'). To reach Lukla, branch right up the stone staircase and make the killer climb up the Handi Khola, gaining 550m in around 90 minutes to emerge exhausted at the bottom of the airstrip. It's a brutal end to the trek!

After the quiet villages on the trail, Lukla feels like a metropolis. At the height of the trekking season in October and November, as many as 700 new trekkers arrive in Lukla every day to start the walk north to Everest. Crack open a beer, check your emails and celebrate your trek with a well-earned pizza, steak or slice of cheesecake.

ALTERNATIVE ROUTE: BUPSA TO CHEPLUNG
6–7 HOURS / 1000M ASCENT / 650M DESCENT

If you plan to continue north to Everest Base Camp or Gokyo and can do without pizza and wi-fi for another couple of days, you can bypass Lukla and continue on a much easier, lower trail to Cheplung.

From Bupsa follow the trail to the Lukla junction just beyond Surkhe, but take the lower trail (signposted to Namche) around the hillside to a suspension bridge by a thin, sinuous waterfall pouring through a huge gorge. The path winds up between streambeds and boulders to a line of stupas and mani walls that marks the beginning of Mushe (Nangbok; 2580m). Before the earthquake, the Nawang Gyaljen Sherpa House next to the *kani* above Mushe offered good accommodation a stone's throw from the local Tashi Choeling and Kengma gompas.

This tiny village blends almost imperceptibly into Chaurikharka (Dungde; 2650m), which was severely damaged in the earthquake. Before the disaster, decent rooms were available at the Tourist Lodge, the Chaurikharka Guesthouse and the Buddha Lodge near the central white chorten, but check locally to see which lodges are currently offering rooms.

Above Chaurikharka, the path rises steadily between giant boulders to meet the main Lukla–Namche Bazaar trail at Cheplung.

OTHER TREKS

There are several interesting detours off the main trails but earthquake damage may have affected these trails – seek local advice before setting off for any of the following treks.

Numbur Cheese Circuit

This two-week trek is a good camping option far from the crowds, but it passes through an area that was badly damaged by the earthquake; check locally to make sure that trails are open. The trail heads from Shivalaya up the Khimti Khola to the sacred lakes of Jata Pokhari and Panch Pokhari, before crossing Panch Pokhari pass (4607m). The highpoint is the crossing of the Gyajo La (4880m), with a potential side trip to views of Numberchuli (6959m) at Nangpa Teng, before dropping down into the wild Likhu Khola. Expect five days of high-altitude camping, overnights in community homestays at Khahare, Lahaksewar and Kyama, and lodges at the roadhead of Gumdel. See www.numburcheese-circuit.org for more details.

September to December and March to May are the best months. You'll need a Gaurishankar Conservation Area Project permit. Nepal Maps do a useful 1:100,000 *Numbur Cheese Circuit* map.

Dudh Kunda–Pikey Cultural Trail

This remote six-day camping trek winds through the hills of Solu from the Jiri–Lukla trail to the glacial lake at Dudh Kunda (4500m), which shivers beneath the mountain wall of Numbur (6959m), but check ahead to make sure trails are clear after the earthquake. From Junbesi it takes three to five days to reach the campsite by the lake via Thubten Chholing Gompa and the Konglema Danda, then two days back to rejoin the main trail near Ringmo. It's best as an adventurous add-on to the Shivalaya to Lukla trek but is possible as a standalone trek from the airport and roadhead at Phaplu.

An extension to this six-day camping trek is to continue southwest to the Everest viewpoint at Pikey Danda (4065m) and then swing southeast back to Phaplu. There are simple *bhattis* along these routes but camping is a better option. The 1:125,000 *Jiri–Pikey–Everest* map from Nepa Maps shows the two-week loop from Phaplu airstrip to Dudh Kunda and on to Pikey Danda.

TOWNS & FACILITIES

Lukla

019 / ELEV 2800M

The main trailhead for the Khumbu region, Lukla sprawls around the steeply angled runway of Tenzing-Hillary Airport. Amazingly, considering the damage on all sides, the lodges and houses in Lukla escaped with only minor cracks and the airport reopened soon after the disaster. The single cobbled street is lined with lodges and shops selling and renting trekking gear, finally petering out at the ceremonial gateway at the north end of town that marks the start of the trail to Everest Base Camp and Gokyo.

The red and white **Kemgun Gompa** at the bottom of Lukla has a small thangka painting school. Every Thursday there's a lively **market** on the open area below the Lukla Resort.

For good mountain views, climb the hill above the airstrip to a small pavilion with a large statue of Sakyamuni (the historical Buddha).

If you have an afternoon to kill in Lukla, you could investigate the nearby Sherpa villages of **Mushe**, **Chaurikharka** and **Kyangma**; despite earthquake damage, all offer a window onto normal Sherpa life, and Kyangma has a large gompa and a school founded by Sir Edmund Hillary. See p116 for details.

🛏 Sleeping & Eating

Lukla is jam-packed with accommodation. The track running north from the airstrip is one continuous strip of lodges. Earthquake damage was limited, but with the decline in visitor numbers there is a chance some lodges may close because of lack of business. Enquire locally if any of the following lodges are locked up when you visit.

The Waves pub in Mera Lodge or the basement Irish Pub are decent spots for a celebratory, end-of-trek knees-up.

Lukla Numbur Hotel   TREKKING LODGE $
(038-550023; appa-humbur@hotmail.com; r Rs 500; 🛜) Tasteful, homey place that woos trekking groups with private bathrooms, a cosy ski-chalet-style wooden restaurant and a pretty garden. The owners have good influence with the airlines.

Hotel Sherpa   LODGE $
(r with/without toilet Rs 500/300) Conveniently located right outside the airport entrance, with a German bakery, cafe and sunny interior courtyard. Rooms with private bathroom have a toilet only.

Himalaya Lodge   TREKKING LODGE $
(s/d without bathroom Rs 200/300, s/d with bathroom from 800/1000, deluxe s 1000-4500, deluxe d Rs 2000-5000; 🛜) A wide range of rooms for every budget, a lovely dining room and lawn

EVEREST REGION LUKLA

STARTING IN JIRI

Now that buses run directly to Shivalaya, most trekkers skip the town of Jiri, though it is technically possible to start your trek from here. However, earthquake damage was severe and many buildings were destroyed. Check ahead to make sure that rooms will be available before travelling from Kathmandu. The town is home to the Jirel ethnic group, a Tibeto-Burman people with cultural links to the Sherpas and Sunwars. If you have time, visit the town's central white stupa, from where steps lead to a hillside shrine to Guru Rinpoche.

The trail to Shivalaya branches off the main road just outside Jiri and takes about three hours, weaving in and out of dirt roads to cross the ridge via the villages of Chitre and Mali.

Before the quake, Jiri was packed with comfortable places to stay but many buildings collapsed in the earthquake and it is unclear which hotels are still standing. Before the earthquake, good rooms were available at the **New Cherdung Lodge** (049-690408; r without/with bathroom Rs 200/800; 🛜), which offered wi-fi and some rooms with hot water, and the **Hotel Jirel Gabila** (049-400029; r without/with bathroom from Rs 300/700), owned by a local cheesemaker and boasting a flower-filled garden. Other good options were the concrete **Hotel Everest** (049-400030; r without/with bathroom Rs 300/500), with clean, carpeted rooms and a roof terrace, and the trekking lodge-style **New Sagarmatha Lodge** (049-690315; r Rs 200), with dark and simple wooden rooms and a cosy top-floor restaurant.

from where you can watch aeroplanes take off and land.

Khumbu Resort
LODGE **$**

(☑038-550005; www.khumburesort.com; r Rs 200; ☏) Helpful staff, a sun room, Lavazza coffee and simple wooden lodge-style rooms.

Lukla Paradise Lodge
LODGE **$**

(☑038-550029; paradise_lukla@yahoo.com; r with/without bathroom Rs 1000/300) Well-run place on the north side of the airport.

Buddha Lodge
HOTEL **$**

(☑038-550028; r with toilet/bathroom Rs 500/1000, r without bathroom Rs 300; ☏) Modern concrete place next to the airport with nice bathrooms, a fine rooftop and free wi-fi.

Mera Lodge
HOTEL **$**

(☑038-550002; r Rs 300-1000) A concrete place busy with groups but with a sunny terrace, cosy restaurant and basement Waves Bar.

La Villa Sherpani
HOTEL **$$**

(☑038-550105; www.lavillasherpani.com; r in old/new block US$20/35; @☏) On the south side of the runway is this agreeable midrange choice. The new block boasts carpeted en suite rooms, an internet cafe and pool table, set in a charming garden with its own stupa. Old block rooms in the main lodge are tired.

ℹ Information

You can usually find Diamox tablets (for AMS) at the small Gumdel Sherpa Pharmacy at the north end of the village. All hotels and cafes offer wi-fi.

Everest Clothing Bank If you have any gear you don't need at the end of your trip, donate it to this organisation, supported by Porters' Progress UK. It's diagonally opposite the Irish Pub.

Everest Cyber (per hr Rs 400; ⊙6am-9pm) Also offers per-minute rates and serves espresso coffee.

Nepal Investment Bank (⊙9am-3.30pm Mon-Thu, 9am-1pm Fri) Changes cash US dollars, UK pounds and euros at a decent rate (3% commission) and gives cash advances on Visa cards (5% commission).

Post Office (⊙10am-4pm Sun-Thu, 10am-2pm Fri) South of the airstrip near the Lukla Numbur Hotel.

Rastriya Banijya Bank (⊙10am-3pm Sun-Thu, 10am-1.30pm Fri) Changes cash, but slowly, as it's a government bank.

ℹ Getting There & Away

Set at 2800m and sloping uphill at an angle of 12 degrees, Tenzing-Hillary Airport can only accommodate tiny Twin Otter or Dornier aircraft. During the trekking season there are up to 80 flights daily to and from Kathmandu, carrying trekkers, porters, guides and cargo.

The list of airlines flying to Lukla changes yearly. **Tara Air** (☑038-50099; ⊙noon-4pm) currently has the most flights, accepts credit cards and is the most reliable, followed by Simrik Airlines, Goma Air and Nepal Airlines. Tickets from Kathmandu cost US$165 each way for foreigners, or Rs 4450/8655 for Nepalis/Indians.

Note that flights are regularly delayed or cancelled at short notice in poor visibility. If this happens at the Kathmandu end, the airline will normally find space for you on the next available flight. If aircraft are grounded at Lukla, it can lead to days of delays and rebookings. For this reason, it would be foolish to book a flight from Lukla to Kathmandu fewer than three days before your onward flight out of Kathmandu.

You should reconfirm your return flight in Lukla the day before, between 3pm and 4pm.

Changing flight dates is free of charge and rarely a problem, even for next-day travel. Expect some confusion in the morning, as you might not know which plane you are on until the last minute.

Lodge owners will often help you change dates and reconfirm.

AIR SAFETY AT LUKLA

Considering its location and the prevailing weather conditions in the Himalaya, it is remarkable that there have not been more aircraft accidents at Lukla. Nevertheless, the airport has seen a number of tragic air disasters over the years. In October 2008 a Yeti Airlines Twin Otter hit rocks below the airstrip, killing 18 passengers and crew. In September 2012 a Sita Air flight from Kathmandu to Lukla crashed, leaving 19 dead.

This record does not necessarily reflect the safety standards of the airlines involved. All the accidents at Lukla have been caused by bad weather, affecting visibility on the final approach. By the standards of short take-off and landing (STOL) airstrips around the world, Lukla has a fairly good record, but if you are a nervous flyer you might prefer to walk into Lukla from Shivalaya or Tumlingtar.

Shivalaya

ELEV 1770M

Direct buses from Kathmandu take about nine hours to get to Shivalaya, with the last unpaved section bumping along the Khimti Khola Valley. The road and town were hit hard by the earthquake, but vehicles are still limping through and collapsed buildings are being reconstructed.

Buses reach Shivalaya too late to start trekking the same day and some lodges here were badly damaged – check locally to make sure rooms will be available before heading out from Kathmandu.

Before heading off the next morning you need to register with the police station. You are also supposed to buy a Gaurishankar Conservation Area Project (GCAP) permit (Rs 2000) from the booth at the Paradise Hotel, even though you will only be trekking through the protected area for a couple of hours.

🛏 Sleeping & Eating

All the lodges in Shivalaya are wooden houses with boxy rooms for Rs 100 per person. Before the earthquake, the best choices were next to the suspension bridge over the Khimti Khola at the northwest end of the village, but where you stay will be dictated by which lodges are still standing and open for business – try the Kalopatthar Lodge, New Sherpa Guide Lodge or River Guest House.

ℹ Getting There & Away

The road to Shivalaya was damaged in the earthquake, but buses are still making it through. Before the quake, buses left daily from Kathmandu's Ratna Park bus stand at 6am and 8am for Shivalaya (Rs 740, nine hours), returning at 6am. All travel via Jiri (Rs 625 to Rs 730). There is a passport check just before arriving in Jiri.

Namche Bazaar

♪ 038 / ELEV 3420M

Set in a natural amphitheatre looking across to the jagged ridge of Kongde Ri (6187m), Namche Bazaar is the unofficial capital of the Khumbu. This tight tangle of cobbled streets is lined with cafes, trekking-gear shops, grocery stores and an ever-expanding array of lodges. Indeed, the tap-tap of stonemasons chipping rocks into neat cubes for walls and foundations is probably the main sound you'll hear as you walk around the village.

THE SATURDAY MARKET IN NAMCHE BAZAAR

Every Saturday morning, the market ground at the bottom of Namche is filled with traders for the weekly *haat* (bazaar). Most of the goods are trekked up from the lowlands, or over the border from China. For locals, the market represents a chance to socialise, drink, gamble and stock up on freshly butchered meat. Come early; things are over by noon.

Namche escaped with only minor damage in the 2015 earthquakes – astonishing considering the destruction in surrounding villages – and facilities here should be open by the time you read this.

Historically, Namche Bazaar was an important staging point for trading expeditions across the Nangpa La into Tibet, but today the village earns most of its income from the trekking industry, making it one of the richest districts in Nepal.

On one level, it's relentlessly commercial, but the spectacular setting and the handsome stone and timber buildings make it feel like a proper mountain village. Because of the steep climb from Phakding, it is essential to stay at least one extra night to adjust to the altitude, but you can fill the time with some excellent acclimatisation hikes (see p73).

There are stunning views west across the valley of the Bhote Kosi to the knife-edge ridge of Kongde Ri (Kwangde Ri; 6187m) and east across the valley of the Dudh Kosi to the snow-dusted peaks of Thamserku (6608m) and Kantega (6685m).

⊙ Sights

The best thing to do in Namche is wander around the cobbled streets. The most interesting part of the village is on the western side of the basin. At the bottom of Namche, a stream runs past water-powered prayer wheels to a large whitewashed **stupa** decorated with Buddha eyes, set among stone-walled potato fields.

Namche Gompa   BUDDHIST MONASTERY
(Map p120) Namche's main monastery enshrines a large statue of Guru Rinpoche and some fine murals painted on wooden panels. Surprisingly, it only dates from 1908. The monks here come from Tengboche; you

EVEREST REGION SHIVALAYA

Namche Bazaar

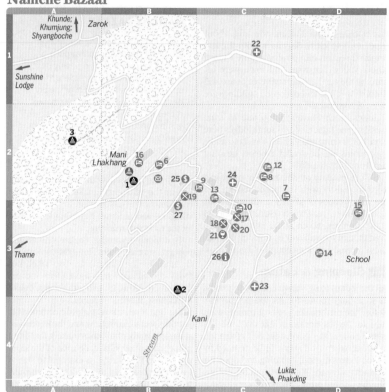

can hear them chanting mantras daily at around 8am and 5pm. Several nearby *mani lhakhang* contain enormous prayer wheels.

Nauche Gonda Visitor Centre　MUSEUM
(Map p120; admission Rs 100; ☺8am-1pm & 2-5pm Sun-Fri, Sat 1-5pm) For a brief introduction to Sherpa culture pop into this interesting museum in Namche Gompa. Nauche Gonda is the local name for Namche Gompa.

Sherpa Culture Museum　MUSEUM
(Map p120; ☏038-540005; www.sherpa-culture.com.np; Chhorkhung; admission Rs 100; ☺6am-sunset) Run by local photographer Lhakpa Sonam, this private museum in Chhorkung has an intriguing collection of Sherpa cultural objects, as well as photos and press cuttings covering all the Sherpa Everest summiteers. Look for the great photo from 1953 of Tenzing Norgay assessing his porter's loads. A new photo gallery

is under construction in the courtyard. Count on a 20-minute uphill walk from Namche's centre. The popular panoramic photos of the main Everest treks make fine souvenirs.

**Sagarmatha National
Park Visitor Centre**　MUSEUM
(Map p120; Chhorkhung; ☺8am-4pm Sun-Fri) **FREE** This park centre is worth a visit for its displays on Himalayan flora and fauna and the culture of the Khumbu Sherpas. From the flat area in front of the visitor centre, you can soak up an eye-watering panorama of Himalayan peaks, from Nuptse (7861m) and Everest (8850m) to Ama Dablam (6856m) and Thamserku (6608m). To get here, hike up to Chhorkhung saddle and then follow the signed path beside the local army barracks.

Rock Painting   BUDDHIST SHRINE

(Map p120) This sacred rock mural depicts local protector Khumbu Yul-Lha. It's a 10-minute hike above Namche Gompa, hidden in a protected grove.

🛏 Sleeping

Namche has the best selection of lodging in the Khumbu, with most places offering wi-fi, hot showers and good restaurants. Damage to lodges was minor but, it is possible that lodges may close because of the downturn in tourism; enquire locally if any of the following lodges are locked up when you arrive.

The following list is just a small selection of the best lodges – there are many more excellent places to stay. If you want to avoid the high season crowds, you could also stay in Shyangboche, Khunde or Khumjung, though you will feel the increase in altitude.

Hotel Camp de Base   TREKKING LODGE $

(Map p120; ☑ 038-540106; r with bathroom Rs 1000-2000, r without bathroom Rs 200; 🛜) European trekking groups favour this large hotel uphill from the main shopping area.

Hotel Tibet   TREKKING LODGE $

(Map p120; ☑ 038-540145; www.hoteltibetatnamche.com; r with/without bathroom US$15/Rs 200; 🛜) This busy hotel benefits from a stonefront terrace with good views.

Hotel Sherwi Khangba   TREKKING LODGE $

(Map p120; ☑ 038-540005; Chhorkung; r with/without toilet Rs 500/200; 🛜) This tranquil and inviting hotel attached to the Sherpa Culture Museum is deliciously removed from the main Namche hubbub. Rooms boast good mattresses and nice views and there's a fine library for guests.

Green Tara Resort LODGE $
(Map p120; ☑038-540079; r Rs 200; 🌐) Another good place, with pristine sinks and toilets, a fine roof terrace, a special menu of Sherpa foods and chhang by the cup. The building is a bit hemmed in so get an upper floor.

Khumbu Lodge TREKKING LODGE $$
(Map p120; ☑038-540144; www.khumbulodge.com; r with/without bathroom Rs 2500/200; 🌐) In the middle of town, this well-run place is something of an institution. The oldest lodge in Namche, former US president Jimmy Carter slept here when he trekked the Khumbu in 1985. Rooms are well kept, there's a good restaurant and Visa cards are accepted.

Hotel Namche TREKKING LODGE $$
(Map p120; ☑038-540004; r with bathroom US$20-50, r without bathroom Rs 300; 🌐) A well-established lodge with a range of deluxe rooms and a sunny dining room looking out over the valley.

Hotel Sherpaland HOTEL $$
(Map p120; ☑038-540107; www.hotelsherpaland. com; r with/without bathroom Rs 4000/500; 🌐) This well-designed hotel has good mattresses and dashes of Tibetan style that attract midrange travellers in search of a few creature comforts. Wi-fi is pricey.

Panorama Lodge HOTEL $$
(Map p120; ☑038-540159; www.panorama lodge.com.np; r without bathroom Rs 500, deluxe r US$50; ⊘closed mid-Dec–end Apr & Jun–end Sep; 🌐) High on the east side of the basin,

come here for the mountain vista and the tasteful modern rooms.

Zamling Guesthouse TREKKING LODGE $$
(Map p120; ☑038-540366; r with/without bathroom Rs 2500/200; 🌐) A good restaurant and a nice terrace are pluses here. The back block has carpeted rooms with good attached bathrooms.

Alpine Lodge TREKKING LODGE $$
(Map p120; ☑038-540300; www.alpinelodge.info; r with/without bathroom Rs 2500/350; 🌐) Tidy and carpeted rooms, woodfired pizza in the restaurant, free wi-fi and a sauna (Rs 2500 for 45 minutes).

🍴 Eating & Drinking

Your lodge owner will expect you to eat dinner where you are staying, but for lunch you can also stroll down to the **Namche Bakery Café** (Map p120; cakes from Rs 300; ⊘7am-7pm) and **Everest Bakery** (Map p120; pastries from Rs 300, pizza Rs 500-600; ⊘8am-5.30pm) at the bottom of the village. Both use gas-powered ovens to bake European-style bread and cakes, and convincing pizzas topped with yak cheese.

Several shops in town sell yak cheese for around Rs 1800 per kg.

Herman Helmers Bakery BAKERY $$
(Map p120; cakes Rs 250-400, pizzas Rs 650-900; 🌐) Good cakes, pastries, espresso coffee and pizzas, with free wi-fi and battery charging. Choose from comfy sofas or outdoor terrace.

Cafe de 8848 INTERNATIONAL $$
(Map p120; mains Rs 300-700; 🌐) A slick place serving up pork chops, bangers and mash, and traditional Sherpa-style *rgi kurr* (potato pancake with butter). Come for the

---

SAGARMATHA NATIONAL PARK

Nepal's most famous nature reserve was founded in 1976 to protect a 1148-sq-km area of forests, mountain pastures and high-altitude desert surrounding Sagarmatha (the Nepali name for Mt Everest). Since 1979 Sagarmatha National Park has been listed as a Unesco World Heritage Site, reflecting its importance as a preserve for rare Himalayan animals and plants. Himalayan tahr, musk deer and Himalayan monals (also known as danphe or impeyan pheasants) are now quite commonly seen in the forests below Namche Bazaar, but snow leopards, Himalayan bears, Himalayan wolves, red pandas and other high-altitude species still hover on the verge of extinction. The park is not a wilderness; around 6000 people live inside the boundaries, with local communities sharing in 30% to 50% of the park revenues.

Park rules prohibit trekkers from using wood as fuel, and glass bottles were banned in 1998. Sadly, the rules were not extended to plastic bottles, so discarded bottles of mineral water and soft drinks remain a depressing blot on the landscape. Do Sagarmatha a favour and pick up any litter you see and dispose of it in the next large village or back in Kathmandu.

3pm video on Sherpas, or enjoy the terrace seating for a morning Illy espresso and house-made pastry. Free wi-fi is a bonus.

Café Danphe
BAR

(Map p120; ⊙6-11pm; 🛜) The liveliest nightspot in Namche. The kitchen cooks up a tasty steak sizzler, the drinks menu (small/big cans of beer Rs 350/550) runs to imported spirits and glasses of wine, and the pool table is always in demand.

Shopping

Numerous outdoor shops sell top-end gear and some places rent equipment such as down sleeping bags (Rs 250, with US$200 deposit) and plastic climbing boots (Rs 200 to Rs 350).

Information

INTERNET ACCESS

Several cybercafes offer internet access and wi-fi and most will burn files from digital camera cards to blank DVDs for Rs 400. Almost all hotels and cafes in town offer wi-fi for around Rs 200 per hour or Rs 500 for 24 hours.

Khumbu Communications (Map p120; per 30min Rs 250; ⊙6.30am-9pm; 🛜) Offers internet access, wi-fi and internet phone calls (Rs 30 per minute).

MEDICAL SERVICES

For serious conditions, visit the **Khunde Hospital** (☑038-540053; consultations US$50; ⊙9am-5pm Sun-Fri, 9am-noon Wed) in Khunde.

Mountain Medicine Centre (Map p120; ⊙6am-7pm) Stocks iodine drops, antibiotics, sunscreen lotion and Diamox tablets, with profits going to the local community-run health centre at the top of town.

Namche Dental Clinic (Map p120; ☑038-540058; ⊙Sun-Fri) If you need an emergency filling, the Canadian-trained dentist here is your best bet.

Pure Vision Sorig Healing & Research Centre (Map p120; ☑981476771; ⊙7am-8pm) Local *amchi* (traditional doctor) Tashi Tsering Sherpa offers massage (Rs 1500 per 30 minutes) and consultations in Tibetan traditional medicine. Ask about his traditional remedies to aid acclimatisation.

MONEY

In addition to the banks, several moneychangers will change cash of all persuasions at rates slightly lower than Kathmandu.

Rastriya Banijya Bank (Map p120; ⊙10am-5pm Sun-Fri) Changes cash of most foreign currencies.

Siddhartha Bank (Map p120; ⊙10am-6pm Sun-Fri) The bank changes cash and the ATM accepts Visa, Plus and Mastercard, with a transaction limit of Rs 10,000 (five transactions allowed per day).

POST

Post Office (Map p120; ⊙10am-4pm Sun-Thu, 10am-2pm Fri) Located just below the Namche Gompa.

TOURIST INFORMATION

There are no airline offices, but any of the lodges in town can help you book or reconfirm flights out of Lukla.

Annapurna Region

Best Mountain Views

➡ Annapurna Sanctuary (p136)

➡ Upper Pisang (p151)

➡ Khopra Ridge (p133)

➡ Poon Hill (p130)

➡ Thorung La (p161)

Best of Mountain Culture

➡ Lo Manthang (p188)

➡ Manang (p156)

➡ Ghandruk (p132)

➡ Muktinath (p161)

➡ Nar-Phu (p174)

Why Go?

With well over 100,000 visitors a year, the Annapurna Himal has long been the most popular region among trekkers, and for good reason. The mountain views are exceptional, the villages you pass offer an exotic slice of Nepali and Tibetan culture, and the area is easily accessible, with excellent food and accommodation just about whenever and wherever you need it. During the 2015 earthquake, buildings collapsed in Jomsom and Mustang, but most of the region escaped without serious damage.

The city of Pokhara, with its relaxed traveller hub of Lakeside on the shore of Phewa Tal, makes an excellent base for all the treks in the Annapurna region, including the famous Circuit, the Annapurna Sanctuary and several shorter treks. The Annapurnas are also the launching pad for adventurous treks into the restricted areas of Mustang and Nar-Phu. For many of these treks, you can be on the trail within an hour or two of leaving Pokhara.

When to Go

➡ Autumn and early winter (October to December) are ideal months for trekking, with warm days and cool nights; this is the peak season. There is very little rain (although mountain weather is always unpredictable) and usually the mountain views are crystal-clear. Bear in mind that October sees twice as many trekkers in the Annapurnas than any other month.

➡ Spring (March to May) is Annapurna's second-best and second-most popular season for trekking. The days are warming up and Nepal's famous rhododendron blossoms colour the trails.

➡ The monsoon (May to September) brings rain and leeches to most trails, although not to Mustang and Nar-Phu, both sheltering in the Himalaya's rain shadow.

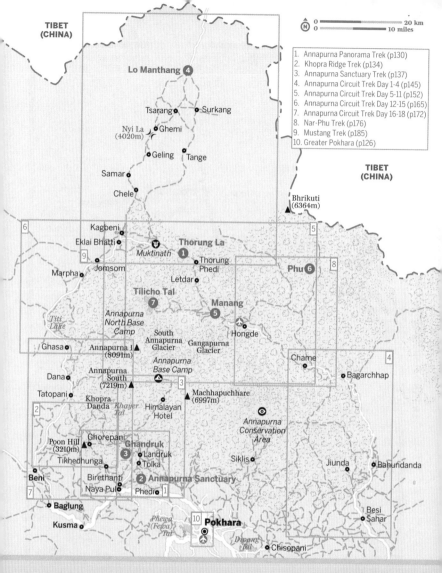

Annapurna Region Highlights

1 Trekking around the Annapurna massif, savouring perfect views and crossing the 5416m **Thorung La** (p161).

2 Watching the dawn light inch down the frozen fluted peaks from the **Annapurna Sanctuary** (p136).

3 Savouring the breakfast views of Annapurna and Machhapuchhare from the traditional Gurung village of **Ghandruk** (p132).

4 Trekking through eroded desert canyons, past ancient chortens and monasteries, to reach the fabled, walled city of **Lo Manthang** (p188).

5 Acclimatising in style on spectacular side trips to holy Milarepa's Cave or scenic Ice Lake outside **Manang** (p156).

6 Overnighting in the photogenic, medieval community of **Phu** (p177).

7 Teaming up with other trekkers for the challenging three-day excursion to high-altitude **Tilicho Tal** (p157).

Greater Pokhara

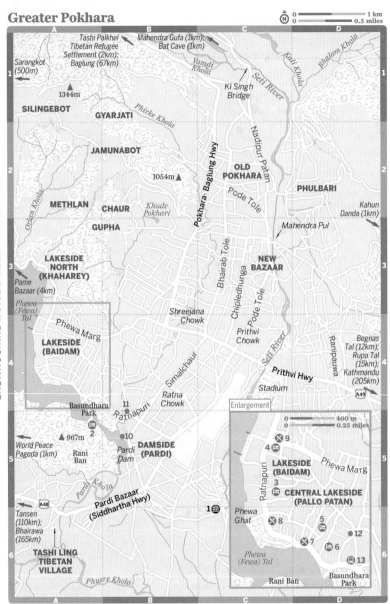

ANNAPURNA REGION ENVIRONMENT

Environment

The Annapurna Conservation Area embraces the entire Annapurna Himal. From the valley floor (below 1000m) to the summit of Annapurna (8091m), there is an amazing variety of habitats.

Trails along the lower valleys weave through terraced fields, dipping occasionally into shady broadleaf forests. Upstream, you enter spectacular rhododendron forests, the gnarled pinkish limbs festooned with epiphytic ferns and orchids. Spring brings

Greater Pokhara (see p192)

spectacular blooms, from red to pink to white. In the Annapurna Sanctuary a variety of wildflowers linger in bloom long after the monsoon, thanks to the area's high rainfall.

Keep an eye out at watercourses for a number of small but striking birds, including the white-capped river chat and the plumbeous redstart. The brown dipper may be spotted by the water's edge, and watch for a flash of turquoise as a white-breasted kingfisher takes flight. Of particular note are the large, soaring raptors that ride the thermals effortlessly for hours, such as the Himalayan griffon, golden eagle and lammergeier.

ℹ Planning

EMERGENCY

There is mobile phone reception in most villages in the Annapurna region and there are satellite phones in Thorung Phedi and Mustang. All Annapurna Conservation Area Project (ACAP) checkposts have emergency radios.

There are government hospitals at Besi Sahar, Chame and Jomsom, and health posts at Ghorepani and Muktinath. Emergency evacuation is possible from Jomsom and Manang (Hongde) airports. Pokhara has a CIWEC hospital.

MAPS

Himalayan Maphouse produces several maps of the Annapurna region, focusing on specific treks such as Around Annapurna, Annapurna Base Camp, Tilicho Lake and Ghorepani to Ghandruk. All are essentially different extents of the same map, repackaged with a different cover and name. Mandala, Nepa Maps and Shangri-La also publish several decent Around Annapurna maps. Another popular map is the National Geographic/Trails Illustrated 1:135,000 *Annapurna Adventure Map*. All these and more are readily available in Kathmandu and Pokhara.

PERMITS & REGULATIONS

No matter where you trek in the Annapurna region you come under the jurisdiction of **Annapurna Conservation Area Project** (ACAP; www.ntnc.org.np). You should buy a permit (Rs 2000) in advance at either the national parks/ACAP entry-fee office in the Tourist Service Centre at Bhrikuti Mandap in Kathmandu, at the ACAP counter in Pokhara's Lakeside district, or at the ACAP office in Besi Sahar at the start of the Annapurna Circuit. You need two photos. Your permit is valid for one entry only. If you show up without a permit at an ACAP checkpoint (including Jomsom airport), you will be charged double the entry fee.

Independent trekkers (without a guide) will need to register with the **Trekkers Information Management System** (TIMS; www.timsnepal.com), which can be done (for US$20) in Pokhara, at the Nepal Tourism Board, and Kathmandu (see p31).

ACCOMMODATION

You can safely assume you will be able to find room and board wherever you go on the main routes in the Annapurna region. The valley of the Kali Gandaki in particular boasts some of the best trekking lodges in Nepal and has sustained damage in the 2015 earthquake. During the busy October and November season, lodges are humming and bedding can get scarce. It's not essential (blankets are generally available), but it's a good idea to bring a sleeping bag on a trek to the Thorung La or Annapurna Sanctuary.

Lodge owners throughout the Annapurna region have formed local committees to fix prices, preparing printed menus for each locale. Now that everyone quotes the same rate, you can choose a hotel according to quality, not price. Prices for food increase dramatically as you go higher, especially in the Annapurna Sanctuary and near Thorung La.

ℹ Getting There & Away

Pokhara is the springboard to the Annapurna region. You will travel to Pokhara before all treks except perhaps the Annapurna Circuit, which begins in Besi Sahar, to Pokhara's east. From Pokhara, frequent public transport heads to trailheads at Phedi and Naya Pul. Buses and 4WDs ply the unpaved road as far as Jomsom, but you usually have to change transport at Beni.

SHORT TREKS NEAR POKHARA

One of the many attractions of the Pokhara region is the opportunity to make short treks ranging from a few hours to a week. If you don't have time for one of the longer treks, or don't think you are ready for one, you can cobble together an interesting walk from parts of longer treks. The following treks start less than an hour from Pokhara by bus or taxi and have teahouses or homestays for accommodation. Apart from the Panchase Trek, an ACAP permit and TIMS card is necessary.

Ghachok Trek (Two Days) This interesting two-day trek ascends the hills north of Pokhara to the traditional Gurung villages around Ghachok. It starts from Hyangja, near the Tashi Palkhel Tibetan settlement, and crosses the Mardi Khola to Lhachok before ascending to the stone-walled village of Ghachok, where you can stop overnight before turning south and returning to Pokhara via Batulechaur. With more time, you can extend this walk (beyond the reach of roads) to visit some even more remote villages in the valley leading north from Ghachok.

Ghandruk Loop (Three Days) - The trail starts at Phedi and follows Day 1 of the Annapurna Sanctuary trail to overnight at Tolka (1810m). From Tolka, trek 45 minutes to Landruk (an alternative first night halt) and then drop steeply down a stone staircase to the Modi Khola at 1315m. It's then a very steep climb up more stone stairs, thankfully via several refreshment stops, to Ghandruk (1970m). Ghandruk (p132) has numerous quality lodges with excellent mountain views. Next day descend to the road at Kimche where you can catch transport to Pokhara, or continue walking back to Birenthanti and Naya Pul.

Panchase Trek (Three to Four Days) Panchase is a region close to Pokhara boasting scenic and cultural attributes, with the added benefits of easy access from Lakeside and no ACAP/TIMS permit requirements. There are several variations of the route featuring the highpoint of Panchase Danda (2500m), and it can be done in any direction. Trails to Panchase start west of Pokhara, either at Naudanda or Khare on the Baglung Hwy or west of Phewa Tal at Ghatichhina. The trails climb through traditional villages to Panchase Bhanjyang (2030m), where you can stay overnight. Start early the next morning to trek up to the peak of Panchase Danda for a sunrise vista of the Himalaya. The trek can then conclude along any of the several routes back to Pokhara, including one where you visit the World Peace Pagoda and return to Lakeside via a boat ride on the lake.

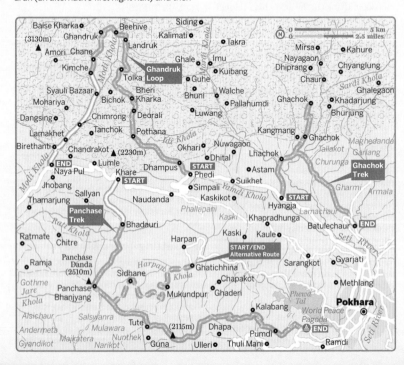

There was some damage along this road from small landslides during the 2015 earthquake but transport was operating on this route at the time of research.

There are several daily flights between Pokhara and Jomsom (US$111). All Jomsom flights operate from Pokhara in the early morning, requiring an overnight in Pokhara (though you can make it to Kathmandu the same day, changing planes in Pokhara). Airlines include Nepal Airlines (www.nepalairlines.com.np), Simrik Airlines (www.simrikairlines.com) and Tara Air (www.taraair.com).

The Jomsom runway is sealed and flights operate year-round, though weather can disrupt service. Flights usually operate full in high season; if you arrive without a reservation you may have to wait a day or more.

Manang airport is in the village of Hongde (3420m) near the upper end of the Marsyangdi Valley. There is a severe risk of altitude sickness if you fly to Manang and attempt to cross Thorung La within a couple of days. You should view Manang only as an emergency or exit airport; it is not a sensible starting point for an Annapurna trek unless you have a week or more to acclimatise.

ANNAPURNA HIMAL

The longer treks around, and into, the Annapurna Himal rank among Nepal's classic routes. You can walk around the range, jeep up the western flank to Jomsom and Muktinath, or trek into its icy heart inside the Annapurna Sanctuary.

The entire Annapurna Circuit from Besi Sahar to Naya Pul can be done in 17 days, but it's usually worth adding on a few extra days to explore the viewpoints around Manang. Experienced trekkers can add on spectacular side trips to Tilicho Tal (three days) and the Dhaulagiri Icefall (two days), as well as excellent day hikes from Manang, Muktinath and Kagbeni. Increasing numbers of trekkers are forsaking the road down the Kali Gandaki and finishing their circuit at Jomsom, taking a jeep or flight back to Pokhara. For the ultimate Annapurna experience, continue from Ghorepani to Khopra Ridge and/or the Annapurna Sanctuary for a total of 25 or more days.

There are plenty of shorter combinations: catch a jeep to Jomsom and spend a few days visiting Marpha, Kagbeni and Muktinath, before walking down the valley to Ghasa and Tatopani (seven days); combine the Annapurna Sanctuary with a visit to Ghorepani and Poon Hill (12 to 13 days); or do one of the short treks from Pokhara, ranging from three to six days.

🛈 Towns & Facilities

Naya Pul and Birethanti (p193) are the trailheads for several treks into the Annapurna foothills.

Annapurna Panorama Trek

Duration 5–6 days

Max Elevation 3210m

Difficulty Easy to medium

Season October to May

Start Naya Pul

Finish Phedi

Permits ACAP permit, TIMS card

Summary After a stiff climb to Ghorepani and great views of Dhaulagiri and the Annapurnas, this trek returns through the large Gurung village of Ghandruk, past wonderful views of Machhapuchhare.

🏃 The Trek

Day 1: Naya Pul/Birethanti to Tikhedhunga

3–4 HOURS / 540M ASCENT

A small sign in Naya Pul directs you to a steep trail leading down to a bridge over a stream. Cross the bridge and follow the road along the east bank of the Modi Khola for 25 minutes to another bridge crossing to Birethanti (1000m), a large and prosperous village. Alternatively, catch a taxi to Birethanti from either Pokhara or Naya Pul. The TIMS checkpost is on the east side of the flag-festooned bridge. Cross the bridge to show your ACAP permit at the ACAP checkpost. The trail branches left passing through the village. The right-hand trail/road leads up the Modi Khola to Ghandruk.

Birethanti has numerous lodges, but it's better to break the 1750m climb to Ghorepani into two stages by continuing to Hille or Tikhedhunga for the night. (If you are returning from Jomsom, then Ghorepani to Birethanti is an easy, although long and knee-cracking, descent.) The trail to Ghorepani winds through bamboo forests and past a large waterfall and swimming hole. The trail stays on the north bank of the Bhurungdi Khola.

Beyond Sudami, the trail climbs steadily up the side of the valley to reach **Hille** (1510m). The Annapurna and See You lodges are among the several hotels alongside the wide stone trail. There are more lodges, including the Riverside and Tikhedhunga guesthouses (s/d Rs 300/500), in **Tikhedhunga** (1540m), about 15 minutes above Hille. If you arrive early, you can trek on up the endless stone staircase to Ulleri.

Day 2: Tikhedhunga to Ghorepani

4–6 HOURS / 1360M ASCENT

The trail crosses the Tikhedhunga Khola on a suspension bridge, then drops to cross the Bhurungdi Khola on a large bridge at 1520m. The trail climbs very steeply on a stone staircase that is said to have more than 3300 steps. There is a lodge and several *bhattis* (teashops) serving tea and cold drinks beyond the bridge. As you reach the Annapurna View Guest House, the tops of Annapurna South (7219m) and Hiunchuli come into view.

The unrelenting staircase continues to the large Magar village of **Ulleri** (2080m). There are a dozen lodges spread along the trail, which continues to climb through cultivated fields. The fields soon give way to

deep forests as the trail climbs to Banthanti, a settlement of hotels at 2250m.

Beyond Banthanti, the trail enters magnificent oak and rhododendron forests and crosses sparkling clear streams before making a short, final climb to **Nangathanti** (2460m), with a hotel in a forest clearing. *Thanti* is a Magar word meaning 'rest house' or *dharamsala*.

Ghorepani (2750m) is about an hour past Nangathanti. In the winter the trail can be covered with snow and sloppy mud, so some short detours might be necessary. Ghorepani means 'horse water', and was a watering stop for the mule caravans that carried goods between Pokhara and Jomsom. There are several hotels in lower Ghorepani, but most people continue 10 minutes up to **Upper Ghorepani** (2870m), or Deorali, where more than two dozen lodges and shops cram the saddle to make the most of the view. You'll have to register with the police post to the south of town. The hillsides below Ghorepani are swathed in eight different species of rhododendron, including the crimson-red flowering *lali gurans,* Nepal's national flower.

A signboard map in the village shows the location of the lodges (r Rs 300 to 600). The Annapurna View, Snow View and **Nice View Point Lodge** (✆9847655568) are among the

Annapurna Panorama Trek

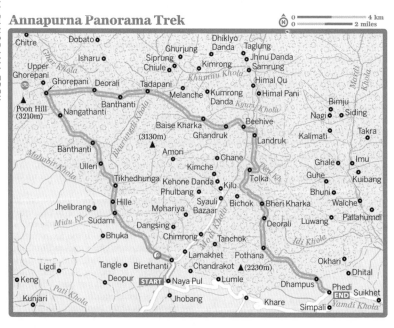

TADAPANI TO CHHOMRONG & THE SANCTUARY

To add on a trek to the Annapurna Sanctuary to your Annapurna Circuit or Annapurna Panorama trek, head off to Chhomrong from Tadapani (three to 4½ hours, 780m descent, 280m ascent). Descend from the Grand View Lodge on a narrow trail through forests to a pasture. The **Mountain Discovery Lodge** (r Rs 350) here lacks the mountain views of Tadapani but makes up for it with a peaceful location (2280m). Ten minutes later pass the farm-like Hillside Lodge at Chiule (one hour) and drop down on steep steps to Siprung, passing through the courtyard of the British Gurkha Lodge (1980m). A further 10 minutes' descent will bring you to a suspension bridge over the Khumnu Khola (1930m), making a total descent of almost 800m in 90 minutes.

The trail starts climbing immediately to the spread-out village of Ghurjung (2010m), passing the school and then the Namobuddha Guest House. The trail passes through several properties, crossing a wooden bridge near the Hotel Green Hill. It's then a 30-minute walk in and out of side valleys to Dhiklyo Danda (2½ hours), where the Ghandruk–Chhomrong trail joins the route. Climb steeply to crest a ridge, gaining views of Machhapuchhare. Forty minutes later you pass Taglung and the signed trail from Jhinu Danda and swing round the ridge for views of Chhomrong (2210m) just beyond.

There is a shorter alternative trail, but it involves more climbing. Start near the Fishtail View Top Lodge in Tadapani and descend through rhododendron forests to the Brahman village of Melanche (2050m). Below Melanche the trail descends steeply. It's not easy to find the correct trail; ask the people in the village for directions to Kimrong. As it nears the river, the route becomes less distinct, but just keep heading downhill, aiming for the only settlement you can see on the river. Cross the Khumnu Khola and join the Ghandruk–Chhomrong route, making the steep climb to Dhiklyo Danda and on to Taglung and Chhomrong.

largest. The Super View and other 'view' lodges are further up the hill. A small group of lodges huddled on the north side of the pass is popular for lunch.

Most people rise before dawn the following day to make the early-morning excursion to **Poon Hill** (3210m), about an hour's climb from the pass. The spectacular panorama stretches from Dhaulagiri I (8167m) and Tukuche (6920m) to Nilgiri (6940m), Annapurna South, Annapurna I (8091m), Hiunchuli (6441m) and Tarke Kang (formerly known as Glacier Dome; 7193m). Watching the sun rise over the unobstructed Himalaya is a defining moment, but don't expect much serenity – this is a popular trip. The early-morning sky above Ghorepani buzzes with planes on their way to Jomsom.

Day 3: Ghorepani to Tadapani

5–6 HOURS / 550M ASCENT / 710M DESCENT

Two trails head east from Ghorepani, from either the Sunny Guest House or Dhaulagiri Hotel. They join after 15 minutes at a *chautara* (resting place for porters) on a grassy knoll that offers mountain views similar to those from Poon Hill, and a panorama all the way south to the plains. Keep climbing past a teahouse to meander along the ridge in pine and rhododendron forests, reaching a crest at 3210m. Descend on the north side of the ridge along a slippery trail interlaced with tree roots to two lodges and a collection of hat and sock shops in a clearing called Deorali (3090m), 1¼ hours from Ghorepani.

The trail descends through rhododendron forest to the small Hotel Lali Guras Lodge, where a side trail climbs for 10 minutes to a ridge-top viewing tower known as 'Gurung Hill'. A ridge hides the mountains as the trail makes a steep descent on a narrow path alongside the stream.

The descent becomes more gentle as the route reaches **Banthanti** (2606m; 2¼ hours), several lodges in the shadow of a huge rock face. (Note that this is not the same Banthanti that is between Ulleri and Ghorepani.) After crossing to the north side of the stream the trail starts climbing, leaving the moist forests and entering a field of cane, making some ups and downs to the Tranquillity Guest House. Ten minutes beyond is the simple Trekkers Sanctuary Lodge, offering great views over the gorge to Ulleri. A rocky trail descends steeply for 20 minutes to the Bhurungdi Khola before climbing through forest for a further 20 minutes to **Tadapani** (2710m), a jumble of hotels and souvenir stands. The views of Annapurna South, Hiunchuli and Machhapuchhare are spectacular from here, especially at sunset and from the Shiva Temple just above the village.

Tadapani's most popular lodge is probably the **Hotel Panorama Point** (☑9746046394; s/d Rs 300/400), but it's often booked with groups. In fact the whole village can fill up, so book ahead or arrive early to avoid disappointment. The Grand View, Super View and Himalaya Tourist Guest House are all good.

Tadapani means 'far water' and the water supply is a long distance below the village. Before the water pipe was constructed it took porters more than 30 minutes to fetch each load of water.

Day 4: Tadapani to Ghandruk

2–3 HOURS / 720M DESCENT

The Ghandruk trail descends steeply from the Himalaya Tourist Guest House through forests to Baise Kharka (Buffalo Pasture), a clearing with hotels. There are two trails from here, both of which lead to Ghandruk. The left-hand trail follows the Kyuri Khola to join the Chhomrong–Ghandruk route. The right-hand trail makes a short, steep descent among rocks to a stream crossing, then leads out on a ridge towards the top of Ghandruk village.

There's plenty to see, do and eat in the charming village of Ghandruk. But if you choose to end the trek here, it is a simple descent to Kimche (1640m) along the mule trail from where jeeps and buses can be caught to Birenthanti, Naya Pul and Pokhara.

GHANDRUK

Ghandruk is the second-largest Gurung settlement in Nepal (the largest is Siklis). It's surrounded by neatly terraced fields and framed by outstanding views of Annapurna South and Machhapuchhare. Older maps spell the village 'Ghandrung', but Ghandruk is the accepted Nepali spelling. The village's Gurung name is Kond.

It is wonderfully easy to get lost in the network of narrow alleyways. The dozen or so lodges scattered throughout the village are quite far apart, both in distance and elevation. There are little signboards at most trail junctions directing you to various hotels that are '1 minute away' – times that are very optimistic. All hotels in Ghandruk charge Rs 250/350 for a single/double, or Rs 400/650 with a private bathroom.

The charming **Gurung Cottage** (☑9746 009682) is in a lovely secluded location with a patio of flowers. The owner, Kishan Gurung ,is a fine host and connoisseur of local coffee. The large **Trekkers Inn** (☑061-522448), in the busier far south of the village, has won three 'lodge of the year' awards from ACAP and has a good restaurant. Its neighbour, the well-run Milan, is comfortable and like most lodges in Ghandruk uses kerosene and gas exclusively, provides safe drinking water, and has a septic tank to handle toilet waste. There is plenty of accommodation in Ghandruk: both the Ghandruk Guest House and the Excellent View have views of the village and Annapurnas.

If you arrive early, there's plenty to do. Not one but two museums duel for your attention. Best is the **Gurung Traditional Museum** (admission Rs 75; ⊙7am-7pm), an Aladdin's Cave of hidden treasures. Highlights include a shield made from elephant skin and a bow string made from nettle fibre. The other, **Old Gurung Museum** (admission Rs 75; ⊙7am-7pm), is also worth a visit and offers a small selection of local cuisine to sample.

EARTHQUAKE DAMAGE AT ANNAPURNA

Most of the Annapurna region saw only minor damage in the 2015 earthquakes, but a number of traditional buildings collapsed in Jomsom and Mustang and landslides briefly blocked the Kali Gandaki river. The good news is that all trails in this region are expected to be open as usual following the 2015 monsoon season. A post-quake survey by earthquake specialists Miyamoto International found that only a 500m stretch of the Annapurna Circuit trek was affected, and the trail to Annapurna Base Camp was trekkable within days of the disaster.

The treks in this region were researched shortly before the earthquake struck and we have updated since the disaster using local sources, but the full scale of damage to rural areas is only slowly becoming apparent, and there is still an increased risk of landslides, so seek local advice before setting off and check the status of all accommodation and food stops along the route before leaving the trailhead.

The **ACAP Visitor Centre** (☺10am-5pm Sun-Thu, to 3pm Fri) below town provides information about its activities and screens daily video shows. If your backpack isn't quite heavy enough, invest in one of the local carpets or visit the handicraft shop in the Local Youth Eco Trekking Centre, which also provides local guides and offers cultural and nature tours.

Day 5: Ghandruk to Tolka

2–3 HOURS / 670M DESCENT / 480M ASCENT

Directly after leaving through the entry/exit arch, the trail forks. Turn left at the sign to Landruk (straight ahead leads to Birenthanti) and descend steeply to the Modi Khola, climbing first to Landruk and then on to Tolka (p138).

Day 6: Tolka to Phedi

3–4 HOURS / 370M ASCENT / 1030M DESCENT

Follow Day 1 of the Annapurna Sanctuary trek (p138) in reverse.

Khopra Ridge Trek

Duration 5–6 days

Max Elevation 3660m (side trip 4600m)

Difficulty Medium

Season October to November, March to April

Start Ghorepani

Finish Tadapani

Permits ACAP permit, TIMS card

Summary Trek away from the popular trails to the panoramic viewpoint of Khopra Ridge on the flanks of Annapurna South, with the option of climbing to a high-altitude lake for even more magnificent views.

Khopra Ridge, also known as Khopra Danda, is the prime objective and viewpoint of several treks that take advantage of a network of old trails in the Annapurna-Dhaulagiri region. This description is of a loop from the Annapurna Circuit/Annapurna Panorama trails. See the boxed text (p135) for more on exploring the less-frequented trails of this region.

ⓘ Planning

This trek can be done in either direction; for options on how to get to Ghorepani and Tadapani see the Annapurna Panorama trek (p129).

There is now regular road transport as far as Kimche (just below Ghandruk). Also, there are lodges along the route to help you break the journey into different segments to those described here.

There is limited accommodation in the community lodges – to avoid disappointment when planning to stay at the community lodges at Bayeli, Dhan Kharka (Chistibang) and Khopra Ridge call Mr Chitra Pun (☎ 9857622028) beforehand to ensure there is a room and food available.

🏃 The Trek

Day 1: Ghorepani to Swanta

3–4 HOURS / 310M ASCENT / 900M DESCENT

Descend from the ridge-top cluster of lodges at Ghorepani Deurali, on the Annapurna Circuit trail, through rhododendron forests towards the spread-out settlement of **Chitre** (2390m). Lodges in Chitre include the New Annapurna View at the top of the village and, further down, the large New Dhaulagiri View Hotel, with a pleasant garden.

The village of Chitre merges with that of the smaller **Phalate** (2280m). Near the school and a couple of trail-side teashops look out for the ACAP black-and-yellow sign pointing down a steep staircase towards Swanta and Khopra Ridge. The trail drops quickly to the Ghar Khola and passes stone houses, many retaining traditional rock-slab shingles – a nice change from the ubiquitous blue corrugated iron of Ghorepani. Cross the suspension bridge and climb for 20 minutes to reach the Magar settlement of **Swanta** (2270m).

The increasing popularity of Khopra Ridge is evident here with the number of new lodges recently built or under construction. A good place to stay that has hot showers is the original **Swanta Guesthouse** (r Rs 300), though there are other choices nearby, such as the Hotel Trekkers Sanctuary.

Day 2: Swanta to Dhan Kharka

4–5 HOURS / 810M ASCENT / 120M DESCENT

Walk through the school yard in Swanta, skirting fields to enter a forest and begin a gradual ascent beside the Dhoske Khore Khola. After two hours the trail drops to a bridge beside a lovely waterfall and bamboo grove. The trail immediately starts to climb up the other side of the valley, and in 15 minutes emerges at **Ahl Kharka** (2540m) and the Evergreen Rest Cottage. **Evergreen** (daal bhaat Rs 430) is a delightful thatch-roofed restaurant with a sunny patio that demands patronage due to its neat and tidy

ANNAPURNA REGION KHOPRA RIDGE TREK

appearance and friendly host. It is also the only place to fuel up before the climb ahead.

It's a fairly straightforward climb through forests to the clearing with a rustic stone shelter and a sign announcing this place as 'Dobato' (two ways). There is also a sign to Khopra and some blue-and-white blazes to help you find the correct trail. Two hours after leaving Ahl Kharkha you will approach the two lodges at **Dhan Kharka** (aka Chisti-bang; 3020m). The first lodge is the privately owned Hotel Rockland. Above this is the community-owned **Dhan Kharka Community Lodge** (r Rs 400), which is a joint venture of the Sikha Higher Secondary School and the Kindu Primary School. The lodge provides clean bedding, daal bhaat (Rs 430) and a hot bucket shower (Rs150).

Day 3: Dhan Kharka to Khopra Danda

3–4 HOURS / 640M ASCENT

Today's trail is short and steep, providing views to the east of the buildings of Bayeli Community Lodge across the valley. To the north, the Khopra Ridge itself blocks the views of the Annapurna peaks. When you reach a rocky clearing of several ruined stone buildings, stunted trees and thorny barberry bushes, look for the painted signs to 'Khop-

ra'. The trail heads up towards a large rocky outcrop visible just below the ridgeline. After 40 minutes you skirt behind this outcrop to arrive at a sheltered area with a prayer-flag-adorned rhododendron tree. This is the junction of the high trail to/from Bayeli. This high trail is highly seasonal and should not be used if there is any snow. The alternative is to return to Dhan Kharka and take a lower trail to Bayeli (see Day 4).

Soon you are above the treeline. Khopra Ridge feels ever so close though you still have to negotiate several spurs coming off the ridge. The exposed trail offers spectacular views towards Dhaulagiri, but it can be quite challenging if covered in snow, either early or late in the season. Eventually you come around a corner to see the Khopra Community Lodge perched magnificently on a spur with the block-face of Dhaulagiri directly ahead. Above and behind the lodge the ridge climbs and steepens in an unbroken arc towards the peak of Annapurna South (7219m), and then around to Bharha Chuli (aka Fang; 7647m). It's visually, if not technically, very close to a mountain-climbing experience, especially when everywhere around you is covered in snow.

The community-owned **Khopra Community Lodge** (r Rs 400) is a joint venture of the Paudwar High School and Nangi's

Khopra Ridge Trek

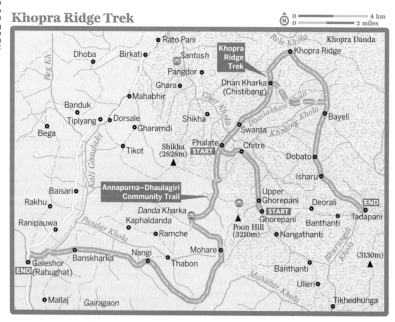

COMMUNITY TREKKING TO KHOPRA RIDGE

Investment in community lodges and homestays has opened up this popular camping-trek destination to teahouse trekkers and promoted the development of local trails into trekking routes. Several trekking companies promote the **Annapurna– Dhaulagiri Community Trail** and they use local guides and porters to maximise the positive impacts. The region serviced by these old trails is mostly in the Myagdi district, running from the Kali Gandaki River, between Beni and Tatopani, east towards the peaks of the Annapurnas. The area is predominantly peopled by Magars, and it was to help the local population that several homestays, community lodges and dining halls were developed, along with handicraft industries such as weaving and paper making.

The powerhouse behind these community trails is Mahabir Pun, who has also brought wi-fi communication and other technologies to remote villages. The best way to find out about the amazing Mr Pun and his projects, including this trek, is to visit Mahabir Dai's Restaurant at the **Centre for Nepal Connection** (www.nepalconnection.org.np; Mandala St, Thamel) in Kathmandu.

In addition to getting off the beaten track, spreading the trekking dollar and diluting trekking's environmental footprint, a significant feature of this trek is the strong community involvement. You will stay in friendly homes, eat in community dining halls, meet local teachers and community organisers, and visit village industries such as weaving and paper making. The community lodges have also adopted ecofriendly practices such as safe-drinking-water stations and solar and micro-hydro electricity.

The Community Eco-trek, as it has also been dubbed, usually starts in **Galeshor (Galeshwar)** on the west bank of the Kali Gandaki about 5km north of Beni. You then trek to the orange-growing village of **Banskharka** with homestay accommodation. Next is the community hub of **Nangi**, where there is a lodge, secondary school and handmade paper enterprise. From Nangi it is a steep climb to **Mohare Danda** (3320m) for awesome views of the Annapurna range and Dhaulagiri. Then the trail heads towards **Khopra Ridge**, crossing the Annapurna Circuit at Phalate to **Swanta**. See p133 for more description of this trek. The community trail organisers have several trails available for the return leg to the Kali Gandaki River and the Beni–Jomsom Rd. You can head to Narchayang or the hot springs of Tatopani, go back through Swanta, or head over to the Annapurna Sanctuary trek via Tadapani.

Himanchal High School. The lodge provides clean bedding, daal bhat (Rs 430), hot bucket shower (Rs 150), wi-fi and a cosy fire.

SIDE TRIP: KHAYER LAKE

There is an ambitious but rewarding day trip from Khopra to a beautiful alpine lake, Khayer Lake, perched at 4600m directly beneath the peaks. That's a 1000m ascent and descent from Khopra! It can be done in a day (nine to 10 hours) if you start early, are fit and acclimatised, and have a knowledgable guide. It would be better, however, to take a tent and camp in the high-altitude summer pasture just before the sacred lake.

Day 4: Khopra Danda to Bayeli

6–7 HOURS / 900M ASCENT / 1100M DESCENT

Retrace your steps back to the trail junction where the high trail to Bayeli peels off. If the caretaker at Khopra and/or your guide is

happy with the state of the trail (ie there's been no land slides or snow), this is the quickest way to Bayeli. It also avoids most of the descent and ascent to be endured on the alternative route. However, it is a narrow and exposed trail in places and you will soon appreciate why it would be dangerous if there is snow.

The alternative is to retrace your steps down to Dhan Kharka for refreshments before taking the low trail to Bayeli. This trail drops through oak and rhododendron forest from Dhan Kharka to cross a clear stream, and then another, as it skirts the bowl-shaped valley. You then start ascending through bamboo and daphne, with giant fir trees towering overhead.

A trail junction is reached at **Thabla Kharka** (3085m; two hours from Dhan Kharka). A sign here points the way down to Swanta or up along the ridge to Bayeli. The latter trail follows the ridge shaded by stately moss-adorned oaks and firs to reach a steep grassland. The lodge is visible above, and so is the steep valley you must now skirt around to reach it. Pass a small shrine with Shiva tridents and then the junction with the high trail coming from Khopra. Around 2½ hours from Thabla Kharka you should arrive at the cosy Bayeli Guest House (r Rs 400), a joint community/private lodge. As well as tidy lodgings there is a warming fireplace, bucket hot water (Rs 150) and good daal bhaat (Rs 450). The views from the lodge take in the lodges at Dhan Kharka and Khopra Ridge, and stretch to Dhauligiri.

Day 5: Bayeli to Tadapani

7–8 HOURS / 300M ASCENT / 960M DESCENT

From the lodge at Bayeli the trail soon climbs to a ridge. Upon reaching the apex the ground suddenly drops away to the east providing spectacular views of the Annapurna range. The trail follows this narrow ridge through rhododendrons, heading south to the three lodges that make up the locality of Dobato (3450m; two hours). This is a recommended night stop if you are doing this trek in the other direction and have departed that morning from Tadapani. Hotel Mt Lucky (s/d Rs 300/400) has hot meals and a hot shower. From Dobato local guides can be hired to take you to Mulde viewpoint (3630m; six to seven hours return) for more Annapurna views.

From Dobato the trail contours around to the east through pine and rhododendron for one hour before reaching a small prayer-flag-adorned shrine at (3300m). The trail passes through the shrine to drop down an eroded gully into a valley of grassland and pine. Half an hour from the shrine, the lodges of Isharu (3235m) come into view. Hotel Green Hill Point (☑ 9816127074; r Rs 400) has basic rooms and a fire-warmed restaurant with valley views. Isharu is a good lunch stop

if you are trekking in either direction. The trail zigzags steeply down a stone staircase into bamboo and rhododendron forests, and after 40 minutes reaches the basic Heaven View Top lodge at Meshar Danda (2970m). Continue to descend through verdant forests, keeping an eye out for blue-and-white trail blazes and signs for Tadapani (two hours from Meshar Danda). The cluster of half a dozen lodges in Tadapani (2710m; p131) can become a bit of a bottleneck, with trekkers coming from all directions, so try to call ahead to book a room before you arrive, or grab a room as soon as possible.

Annapurna Sanctuary Trek

Duration 10 days

Max Elevation 4130m

Difficulty Medium

Season October to November, March to April

Start Phedi

Finish Naya Pul

Permits ACAP permit, TIMS card

Summary Trek through Gurung villages and climb through the Modi Gorge into the Annapurna Sanctuary, an amphitheatre of huge Himalayan peaks. This trek offers fine close-up mountain views without the acclimatisation problems of the Everest region.

The route to the Annapurna Sanctuary (Annapurna Deuthali in Nepali) and Annapurna south-face Base Camp is a spectacular short trek. Although it has some long steep climbs and descents, primarily on stone steps, the trek is not difficult if you take your time.

The trail to the Annapurna Sanctuary traverses a huge variety of terrain, from

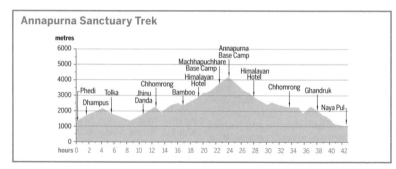

Annapurna Sanctuary Trek

Annapurna Sanctuary Trek

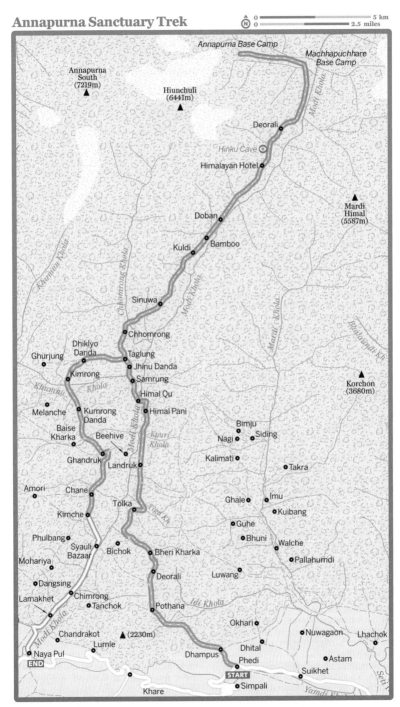

ⓘ WARNING

Between Doban and Machhapuchhare Base Camp there are several places where avalanches from unseen slopes of Hiunchuli come crashing onto the trail. It is the only major trekking route in Nepal with significant avalanche danger, and you must enquire locally about whether the trail is safe. In March 2002 three German trekkers were killed between Deorali and Machhapuchhare Base Camp, and other trekkers have been stranded in the sanctuary for days. Remember that most avalanches occur after 9am. Be especially wary if there has been recent heavy rainfall in the lowlands. The best source of reliable information about avalanche danger is the ACAP checkpost at Chhomrong. Be sure to always ask about trail conditions in the sanctuary at lodges en route.

Be watchful for symptoms of altitude sickness as you reach Machhapuchhare Base Camp. Do not continue to Annapurna Base Camp if you are not well acclimatised.

rice terraces to glacial moraine, and offers outstanding high mountain views. You can make the trek from Pokhara to Annapurna Base Camp and back in fewer than 10 days, but it is best to allow a little longer to appreciate the high-altitude scenery.

A diversion to Ghorepani on the return route provides the added bonus of a view of Dhaulagiri from Poon Hill, and is particularly spectacular in spring, when the rhododendrons are in full bloom.

The first few days of the Annapurna Sanctuary trek are actually the hardest because of all the climbs and descents into side valleys, and are much tougher than a glance at the map might suggest. The second half of the trek is a more gradual ascent up the Modi Khola.

ⓘ Planning

WHEN TO TREK

The major danger with this trek is that it can become impassable because of snow and avalanches in winter and early spring. If there is snow, it's possible you won't get beyond Doban.

EMERGENCY FACILITIES

There are landlines and mobile phone reception as far as Chhomrong, and limited (but improving) mobile reception further up the sanctuary. In an emergency you can send a message asking for evacuation from a helipad in Kuldi or Machhapuchhare Base Camp.

ACCOMMODATION

You will rarely walk longer than an hour on this trek without finding some source of refreshment or accommodation. Lodges extend all the way into the sanctuary, though in winter some are closed.

Beyond Ghandruk most of the hotels in winter serve meals on a large communal table with a heater under it. You may be charged a small 'heater fee' for this. In the sanctuary the heaters are often kerosene pressure stoves – they're noisy, smelly and can consume all the oxygen in the room. Open doors or windows to ensure sufficient ventilation in the dining room.

Due to the funnel shape of the trek and the fact that ACAP has limited the size of hotels above Chhomrong, you might find the lodges full in high season, especially if you arrive in the late afternoon. You may have to continue an hour or more or bunk down in a dining room, in which case you'll be more comfortable if you have your own sleeping bag.

ⓘ Getting To/From the Trek

Take a taxi or a frequent Baglung-bound bus from Pokhara's Baglung bus station to the roadside shacks of Phedi (Rs 57, 1½ hours). The start of the trail heads up the hill on a steep set of steps across the road.

🥾 The Trek

Day 1: Phedi to Tolka

5–6 HOURS / 1030M ASCENT / 370M DESCENT

The entire region from Phedi, on the valley floor, to the top of the hill is commonly known as Dhampus, but the main part of Dhampus village is on the top of the ridge, more than 500m above. Starting at an elevation of 1130m, the trail climbs steeply for about 45 minutes. It becomes less steep as it follows a stone staircase and climbs over a wall to a small temple. Here, a sign directs you to the steep uphill trail to Dhampus. Trek past the Evergreen Restaurant to another trail junction, where a steep uphill trail leads to the main part of **Dhampus** (one hour), on top of the ridge at 1700m.

You are rewarded with great mountain views as you continue along the ridge. There are a few hotels at this end of Dhampus, including the pleasant Moonlight and Lali

Gurans, making this a decent place to overnight if you started late from Pokhara (the dawn Himalayan views are excellent). Follow the dirt road past the Hotel Orchid and drop below the road to a collection of lodges, a camping area and the large **Dhaulagiri View Hotel** (☑ 061-690626; s/d from Rs 700/800). Ten minutes later you'll have to register your TIMS permit at a checkpost (90 minutes).

The trail climbs to a rhododendron forest and passes a sign bidding you farewell to Dhampus as you climb to **Pothana** (1990m), a charming collection of hotels, ideal lunch stop, and an ACAP checkpoint (you'll need your ACAP permit), 2½ hours from Phedi. From Pothana there's an excellent view of Machhapuchhare (6997m), the 'fishtail' mountain (*machha* means 'fish' and *puchhare* means 'tail'). You can spend the night in the Annapurna Lodge, **Heaven's Gate Guesthouse** (s/d Rs 150/300, d with bathroom Rs 600) or one of Pothana's other hotels. Most hotels from here on boast large billboard-style maps of the region that portray the route to the sanctuary and estimated walking times with varying degrees of accuracy.

The trail takes a couple of right branches and climbs through forests to a pass with views of the Mardi Khola far below, before descending to two lodges at **Deorali** (2150m). Order a cup of tea and savour the fine views of Annapurna South and Hiunchuli to the north, and Pokhara and Phewa Tal to the southeast. Make a steep descent through forests that are alive with birds, ferns and orchids into a huge side canyon of the Modi Khola. Descend past the Archana Guest House and down a steep stone trail to the Sundara Guest House at **Bheri Kharka**.

Descend to the head of the valley on the upper trail, cross a stream and climb gently out of the side canyon on the road. The Sunlight Tourist Guest House marks the spot where the trail emerges into the main Modi Khola valley. A short distance below is the Namaste Tourist Guest House and Sapna Lodge, the first of several clusters of hotels that comprise the spread-out settlement of **Tolka** (1790m). The trail/road descends through the village, passing the basic Hilltop Ram Lodge, the school and then down to the recommended **Sunny Guest House** (s/d Rs 200/350) and the popular International Guest House.

If you have the energy, continue 45 minutes to the better choice of accommodation at Landruk.

Day 2: Tolka to Chhomrong
5–6 HOURS / 450M DESCENT / 870M ASCENT

The trail descends a long stone staircase to a suspension bridge across the Tigu Khola at 1720m, then climbs through forests to meet a road. It's then an easy walk past streams, fields and thatched stone buildings. You can see the Modi Khola far below and the houses of Jhinu Danda halfway up the hill far ahead. Make a long traverse to the school, cross the Ghora Khola on a suspension bridge and you will arrive at the top of **Landruk** (1620m), a Gurung village with a good choice of accommodation. You can see Ghandruk, high above you across the valley. The best lodges are above the village and include the Captain Lali Gurans, popular with camping groups, and the well-run Hungry Eye, with a cosy dining hall. The Maya Guest House, 10 minutes further down the village, is a quieter option with a nice garden.

Five minutes below the Maya Guest House is a signed junction: left down the hill and then up to Ghandruk or right to Chhomrong. Take the right path over a wooden bridge and past a hydroelectricity pipe, then cross a second wooden suspension bridge beside a waterfall. The jungly trail descends through ferns to fine views of Annapurna South, high above the jade river, and continues to the Himalpani Guest House. A short walk leads across the bridge to **Himal Qu** (1410m), also known as Naya Pul (New Bridge), where there are simple lodges. The trail climbs steeply to Samrung, then crosses a stream on a cement bridge. This is the lower part of the Khumnu/Kimrong Khola, which is known here as the Kladi Khola.

Heading north, a stiff climb leads to **Jhinu Danda** (1750m), where there are several

THE END OF THE ROAD?

The Annapurna region is changing fast. Roads are inching up both sides of the circuit and into the foothills around Pokhara, is having a visible effect on trekking routes. Avoiding the roads altogether is usually not possible, but don't worry, the scenery is still magnificent, and there are plenty of trails that avoid the roads. ACAP is busily opening alternative trails and lodges away from the roads. In many cases the new detours are even better than the original trails.

lodges on a ridge. There is a hot spring with cement bathing pools about 15 minutes downhill (and 30 minutes back up) on a side trail; ask a lodge owner about it. The houses on the top of the ridge far above you are your next destination.

It is a long, steep climb, broken only by a few teahouses, to a cluster of teashops at Taglung (2190m), atop the treeless ridge. A this point the trek joins the main Ghandruk–Chhomrong route.

A short distance from Taglung are the Panorama Point and Himalayan View lodges, as well as an ACAP office and a safe drinking water station. This is the upper part of Chhomrong (2210m), where there are several lodges (s/d Rs 150/300). The recommended Excellent View, International and Kalpana lodges at the top of Chhomrong are some of the nicest lodges on the trek, offering slate patios and dining rooms overlooking a spectacular panorama of peaks. A little further down is the excellent Chhomrong Cottage, famed for its pizza and chocolate cake, and there are other options nearby.

Descend on a long staircase for 10 minutes to the fixed-price Chhomrong Wholesale Shop, the last place to stock up on reasonably priced supplies.

Beyond Chhomrong, camping is restricted to ACAP-designated campsites and hotel construction is strictly controlled. ACAP regulations prohibit the use of firewood, so all campers and hotels must cook with gas or kerosene.

This is the highest permanent settlement in the valley, but herders take sheep and goats to upper pastures in the sanctuary during the summer. There is a tremendous view of Annapurna South and Hiunchuli, which tower above the village, and there are good views of Machhapuchhare across the valley. In 1957 Wilfred Noyce and David Cox climbed Machhapuchhare to within 50m of its summit. After this attempt, the government prohibited further climbing on the mountain, so technically it remains unclimbed.

Day 3: Chhomrong to Bamboo

3–4 HOURS / 610M ASCENT / 510M DESCENT

Leaving Chhomrong, the trail descends 150m on a stone staircase and crosses the Chhomrong Khola on a swaying suspension bridge at 1860m, then climbs out of the side valley via the tiny settlement of Tilche, through forests of bamboo, rhododendron and oak. Climbing further on a rocky trail you reach Bhanuwa and the Sherpa Guest House (one hour). A further climb of about 45 minutes will take you to Sinuwa (2340m), where there are two hotels on a ridge. The Sunwa Guest House (s/d Rs 150/300), just below the ridge, is a more peaceful place to overnight, with clean rooms and a hot shower.

Climb for about an hour in a forest of rhododendrons, festooned with orchids and ferns, to a stone-paved trail that passes Kuldi (2470m). The ruins here once housed an ACAP visitor centre. The trek now enters the upper Modi Valley and you can see the lodges of Bamboo and Doban below.

Descend a long, steep, slippery stone staircase into a dense bamboo and rhododendron forest, before arriving at Bamboo (2310m), a collection of five hotels crammed into the narrow valley. These lodges fill quickly in high season so aim to get here early in the day. In early autumn and late spring, this part of the trail is crawling with leeches. In winter, it's common to find snow anywhere from this point on.

Day 4: Bamboo to Himalayan Hotel

2–3 HOURS / 530M ASCENT

The trail climbs steeply through stands of bamboo, then through rhododendron forest up the side of the canyon. Occasionally the trail drops slightly to cross tributary streams, but ascent is the order of the day. Keep an eye out for troops of black-faced langur monkeys. When there is snow, this stretch of trail is particularly difficult because the bamboo lying on the trail, hidden beneath the snow, provides an excellent start to a slide downhill. Local people harvest the dense bamboo forests beyond Kuldi to make mats for floors and roofs, and for dokos, the baskets that porters carry.

After traversing several avalanche chutes you'll reach a small hydro plant and the Hotel Tiptop, Annapurna Approach Lodge and Dovan Guest House alongside the stone-paved trail of Doban (2500m), 45 minutes from Bamboo.

Beyond Doban the trail crosses a stream and avalanche chute, then climbs across a landslide. In the forest is a small temple where local people leave offerings of flowers, cloth or leaves. There's a sign in Nepali saying that one should not carry eggs or meat beyond this point, out of respect for the local

TREKKING PEAKS

Hiunchuli (6441m) Forms part of the mountain chain surrounding the Annapurna Sanctuary. Not an easy climb, requiring traverses of snow, ice and rock.

Mardi Himal (5587m) Five-day slog up the Mardi Khola to approach the peak. It is the southern outlier of Machhapuchhure.

Singu Chuli (6501m) Reached from the Annapurna Sanctuary. Its original name was Fluted Peak, due to the steep ice slopes that make it difficult to climb.

Tharpu Chuli (5663m) Originally named Tent Peak, it's in the Annapurna Sanctuary. The climb involves glaciers and crevasses; most people climb the easier Rakshi Peak to the south.

Chulu East (6584m) The ascent starts after a long approach from Manang; the climb needs one or two high camps.

Chulu West (6419m) The route circles Gusang Peak to climb Chulu West from the north, requiring at least two high camps.

Pisang Peak (6091m) Long slog above Pisang village through snow, with steep snow at the top.

deity, Baraha Than. Climb past a cascade over a rock platform and pass a trailside temple decorated with Shiva tridents and flowers. Twenty minutes later you'll reach two lodges that are both named Himalaya in a deep gorge at **Himalayan Hotel** (2840m). If you arrive early, it's worth trekking on for an hour to Deorali to make the following day easier.

Day 5: Himalayan Hotel to Machhapuchhare Base Camp

3–4 HOURS / 860M ASCENT

From Himalayan Hotel it's about 40 minutes' walk, first on a rocky trail through forests, then up a steep ravine, to **Hinku Cave** (3100m), named after the huge overhanging rock that used to house a small hotel. High cascades tumble off the high rock walls in all directions.

The trail crosses the remnants of a glacier (a major avalanche track) just beyond Hinko, then climbs through large boulders to **Deorali** (3140m), where the best of the hotels are the Panorama Guest House and the Dream Lodge. Above Deorali, the valley widens and becomes less steep, and you can see the 'gates' to the sanctuary as the mountains really start to make their presence felt. After heavy snowfall, avalanches from Hiunchuli and Annapurna South, peaks that are above this point but not visible, come crashing into the valley with frightening speed and frequency. The lodge owners in Deorali can tell you whether there have been any avalanches recently.

The trail diverts to the east side of the valley to avoid a dangerous avalanche area and climbs through an unusual mix of bamboo and birch. Cairns point you across a bridge to the west side and rejoin the old trail just before Bagar, a meadow and some abandoned hotels at 3270m.

From Bagar, climb across more avalanche paths, then through a sparse birch forest. Cross a moraine and descend to a stream. A stone staircase leads to the Cosy Lodge, a helipad and a nearby German meteorological office. If you stay on the lower trail you'll soon climb to the cluster of four hotels that are known as **Machhapuchhare Base Camp** (MBC; 3700m). The hotels are cosy and comfortable, especially the Gurung Co-operative and the Sanker, and there's good camping below the Fishtail Lodge. One or two of the hotels in the sanctuary generally stay open during the winter. All are operated by people from Ghandruk or Chhomrong, so you can find out in advance which are operating. There's technically no such thing as 'Machhapuchhare Base Camp', since ascents of the mountain are prohibited.

The mountain views are stupendous; the panorama includes Hiunchuli, Annapurna South, Annapurna I, Annapurna III (7555m), Gangapurna (7454m) and the ever-changing Machhapuchhare, whose sheer triangular face takes on yet another aspect here.

You are now at an elevation where altitude problems can occur. It's another 430m of elevation gain to Annapurna Base Camp, so the best plan is to spend the night here to acclimatise and go higher the following day.

Many trekkers avoid an overnight stay at Annapurna Base Camp by leaving at around 4.30am to catch the dawn light, returning to MBC by lunchtime and then continuing down the valley to Himalayan Hotel or Doban by the afternoon.

Day 6: Machhapuchhare Base Camp to Annapurna Base Camp

1½–2 HOURS / 430M ASCENT

The climb to **Annapurna Base Camp** (ABC; 4130m) – four large lodges on a knoll beside a huge glacial moraine – takes under two hours. It's a pleasant walk, but the route can be hard to find if there's fresh snow. The trail follows a stream, then climbs to a few shepherds' huts. Before long you can see the hotels of base camp, but the view is deceptive and it takes quite a while to reach them as the trail sticks close to the foot of a large lateral moraine.

In the high season the lodges here can be packed with trekkers. All the lodges have private rooms and decent loos and serve sur-prisingly good food, including high-altitude apple pie. There's little to differentiate the four lodges, which are all well run. The area is cold, windy and often snowbound. In spring the snow reaches the hotel roofs.

There are tremendous views of the near-vertical south face of Annapurna towering above the sanctuary to the northwest. The ascent of this face in 1970 by an expedition led by Chris Bonington remains one of the most spectacular climbs of an 8000m peak. Mornings are usually clear, clouds often roll in to obscure the peaks by noon, and then clear in the late afternoon.

Walk west past the porter shelter and volleyball court to a prayer-flag-draped viewpoint on the moraine for a spectacular view over the glacier. Nearby is a memorial chorten (stone Buddhist monument) to the well-known climber Anatoli Boukreev, who was killed in 1997 by an avalanche. Climb the moraine behind the hotels for a fine valley overview.

Several peaks accessible from the sanctuary are on the government's official list of 'trekking peaks'. Tharpu Chuli (formerly Tent Peak; 5663m) offers a commanding 360-

ANNAPURNA PEAK

The 50km-long Annapurna massif encompasses a swath of spectacular peaks, including four summits named Annapurna. The mountain is named after the female Hindu god of harvest, fertility and abundance.

The main summit is to the west of the Annapurna Sanctuary and is hardly visible at all from the Annapurna Circuit trek. Gangapurna (7454m) towers above Manang, and Annapurna II (7937m) is above Chame, about 24km to the east. Annapurna South (7219m) is clearly visible from the trekking routes leading up to the Annapurna Sanctuary.

Annapurna (8091m) was first climbed by a French expedition led by Maurice Herzog in 1950. Equipped with 150 porters, the team became the first Westerners to ascend the Kali Gandaki Valley, initially basing themselves at Tukuche. After deciding Dhaulagiri was too difficult, they turned their attention to climbing Annapurna, the world's 10th-highest peak. Hampered by inaccurate maps (it took the team weeks just to find the mountain), they eventually ascended via the Miristi Khola to the north face and made what was the first ascent of any 8000m peak on 3 June, just days before the start of the monsoon. The summiteers suffered severe frostbite on the descent (as depicted in Herzog's classic *Annapurna*) and were finally evacuated back to the road head in India.

Annapurna was not climbed again until 1970, when a British Army expedition followed essentially the same route as Herzog. At the same time Chris Bonington led a successful British expedition to the very steep and difficult south face. An all-woman team marked the first American ascent in 1978. Annapurna II was first climbed in 1960 by a team under Jimmy Roberts that included a younger Chris Bonington.

Annapurna is considered one of the hardest and most dangerous peaks in the Himalaya, with an ascent rate half (and a death rate triple) that of Everest, largely due to the avalanches that regularly rip down the mountain. Famed mountain guide Anatoli Boukreev (one of the climbers involved in the Everest disaster of 1996, depicted in *Into Thin Air*) was killed by an avalanche while attempting a winter ascent on Christmas Day in 1997, and you can visit his memorial chorten at Annapurna Base Camp.

ROUTE OPTIONS BACK TO POKHARA

You can return from Chhomrong to Pokhara by a variety of routes. The quickest way is to descend steeply to Jhinu Danda and Himal Qu and then follow trails down the west side of the Modi Khola, past a couple of lodges at Beehive (where a trail branches right uphill to Ghandruk), and continue all the way to Syauli Bazaar to join the main Ghandruk–Birethanti trail/road. A more interesting option is to trek south to Ghandruk and then descend to catch transport from Kimche or follow the Modi Khola to Birethanti. Alternatively, extend your trek by a day or two and trek to Ghorepani to get the views from Poon Hill, as described in reverse in the Annapurna Panorama trek. From Ghorepani you can either head north to Jomsom and Muktinath, or head back to Pokhara via Birethanti in a long day.

degree view of the entire sanctuary. Its higher neighbour to the north is Singu Chuli (Fluted Peak; 6501m), while to the south is Hiunchuli. All three of these peaks present significant mountaineering challenges and require skill, equipment and advance planning.

Day 7: Annapurna Base Camp to Himalayan Hotel

3½–4½ HOURS / 1320M DESCENT

Heading back down the valley is much easier. Even if you do some exploring in the morning, you should have no problem reaching Himalayan Hotel or even Doban or Bamboo in a single day from Annapurna Base Camp.

Day 8: Himalayan Hotel to Chhomrong

5–7 HOURS / 1140M DESCENT / 510M ASCENT

Retrace your steps to Doban and back down to apple-pie country, making a long, steep climb back to the top of Chhomrong.

Day 9: Chhomrong to Ghandruk

3–4½ HOURS / 700M DESCENT / 480M ASCENT

To reach Ghandruk from Chhomrong, return to the trail junction near the teashops at Taglung and swing right to stay west above the fields. Climb to the top of a landslide (40 minutes) and 10 minutes later turn left at the trail junction (the right trail continues to Ghurjung and Tadapani). Look south straight across the valley (that's your destination), then look straight down to the valley floor 470m below you (that's where you are headed now). It's a heartbreaking sight.

Descend steeply through forests and switchbacks for 40 minutes, past the simple Kimrung Lunch Centre to the village of **Kimrong** (Khumnu; 1810m), just above the

Khumnu Khola (90 minutes). The Kimrong Guest House and Navina Hotel here are a decent place for a break, as is the teashop near the bridge.

At Kimrong, cross the bridge and stay on the left-hand trail as it climbs out of the Khumnu Valley. The trail makes a steep 430m climb through forest on an interminable set of switchbacks to a cluster of ridge-top lodges at **Kumrong Danda** (2220m), where you can take a well-earned rest.

If you want to beat the madding crowd, follow the side trail northeast from Kumrong along the ridge for 20 minutes to the Little Paradise Lodge, run by local doctor Man Prasad Gurung.

From Kumrong Danda it's an easy descent to a bridge over the Kyuri Khola at 2010m. Ten minutes from here the route is joined by a fork of the Ghorepani–Ghandruk trail. Turn east and climb to the northeast end of Ghandruk (1990m; p132). Continue through the village for 10 minutes to the centre.

Day 10: Ghandruk to Kimche, Birenthanti or Naya Pul

1½–4½ HOURS / 1000M DESCENT

As you leave town, descend to a stream and water-driven mill and trek to an entrance/exit arch where the trail to Landruk exits left and downhill on a steep stone staircase. The main trail to Birethanti leads ahead and south from here, dropping at first on a staircase, then traversing high above the river on a wide stone-paved trail. Cross a stream at Chane (1690m) and continue to **Kimche** (1640m), where there are a couple of teashops and restaurants. At the time of research this was the road head, and buses and jeeps bound for Naya Pul and Pokhara are available. The bus/share jeep/reserved jeep to Pokhara costs Rs 300/600/5000. If you prefer to walk, the trail

ANNAPURNA REGION ANNAPURNA SANCTUARY TREK

continues downhill through fields and crosses the zigzagging road several times. Follow the ridge downhill to join the Modi Khola at Syauli Bazaar (1140m). If you're walking the other direction from Birethanti to Ghandruk, this is the start of a tough 850m climb; you can arrange a guide and porter here.

From Syauli Bazaar the walking is flat, often along the road. The route follows the river valley to Chimrong, then Lamakhet and finally Birethanti (1000m).

You can stay in Birethanti or head into Pokhara. Taxis (Rs 2000) are available across the bridge. Alternatively it's a 30-minute walk to Naya Pul, where buses and taxis to Pokhara are available well into the night.

Annapurna Circuit Trek

Duration 12–18 days

Max Elevation 5416m

Difficulty Medium to hard

Season October to November, March to April

Start Besi Sahar or Bhulebule

Finish Jomsom or Naya Pul

Permits ACAP permit, TIMS card

Summary Nepal's classic teahouse trek takes you past a wide range of spectacular mountain scenery to cross Thorung La (5416m) – probably the highest you'll get without putting on crampons.

The Annapurna Circuit has long been considered one of the world's great treks. Like all the best journeys, the trek reveals itself gradually, as it climbs through subtropical jungle to a Tibetan-influenced valley and then over the high Thorung La to the Kali Gandaki Valley, a desert-like Trans-Himalayan region that was once a vital trade corridor to Tibet. Although road construction has affected the trek (see the boxed text, p167), the side trips that line the circuit rank among Nepal's most spectacular. There is a road from Beni to Jomsom (and beyond); however, ACAP have introduced numerous detours to minimise the amount of time spent walking on the road.

The real appeal of this trek lies in its variety. The trail winds through rice paddies and climbs through the deep gorge of the Marsyangdi, before swinging west into the arid Manang region, with its awesome views of the north side of the Annapurnas. The cultural mix takes in Gurung, Manangi and Thakali communities and their traditional stone-walled villages, Tibetan-style monasteries and animist totems.

Almost everyone treks the circuit anti-clockwise to avoid the difficult and dangerous ascent of Thorung La from the west side. Also, if you go against the flow in an effort to avoid the crowds, you'll actually meet many more trekkers because you'll be passing an endless stream of them en route.

 Planning

CLOTHING & EQUIPMENT

Proper gear for porters must be a prime consideration if you are taking them over Thorung La. Many lowland porters have suffered frostbite or snow blindness on this pass because trekkers (and/or their guides) have not provided the proper footwear, clothing and sunglasses. Porters from near-tropical villages like Besi Sahar don't necessarily know what to expect on a snow-covered pass, or they hope that the pass crossing will be in warm weather, and may join a trekking party clad only in flip-flops and cotton clothing. If you employ porters for a crossing of Thorung La, you incur both a moral and a legal obligation for their safety and wellbeing.

ACCOMMODATION

There are teashops and lodges every couple of hours along the Annapurna Circuit. ACAP has standardised prices for food and accommodation in each village and ensures reasonable minimum standards. Food and lodging become increasingly expensive as you trek further from the road. A daal bhaat that costs Rs 250 in Bhulbule will cost almost double this in Thorung Phedi.

 Towns & Facilities

The traditional starting point for the Annapurna Circuit Trek is Besi Sahar (p194), and the finishing point is Naya Pul (p193). However, some trekkers now finish in Jomsom (p194), and fly or bus back to Pokhara from there.

The Trek

Day 1: Besi Sahar to Bhulbule
2¾ HOURS / 50M ASCENT

Today's trek either follows the dirt road to Bhulbule or the alternative trail on the east bank of the Marsyangdi River. If you arrive in Besi Sahar at lunchtime, it's possible to take the bus or hike along the road to Bhulbule or even Ngadi that same day.

At the northern end of the Besi Sahar bazaar, the road drops down to continue to Khudi (830m; two hours), the first Gurung

Annapurna Circuit Trek Day 1-4

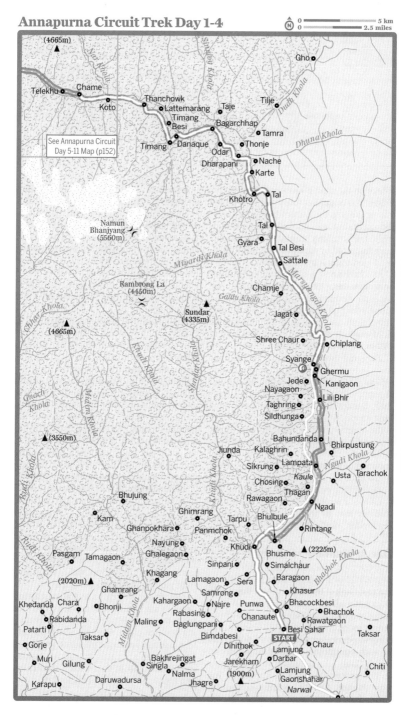

0 ———— 5 km
0 ———— 2.5 miles

▲ (4665m)

Gho

Telekhu
Chame
Koto
Thanchowk
Lattemarang
Taje
Tilje
Timang
Besi
Bagarchhap
Tamra
Danaque
Timang
Thonje
Odar
Nache
Dharapani
Karte
Khotro
Tal

See Annapurna Circuit
Day 5-11 Map (p152)

Namun
Bhanjyang
(5560m)

Tal
Gyara
Tal Besi
Sattale

Rambrong La
(4450m)

Galdu Khola

Chamje

Sundar
(4335m)

Jagat

▲ (4665m)

Shree Chaur

Chiplang

Syange

Ghermu

Jede
Kanigaon
Nayagaon
Lili Bhir
Taghring
Sildhunga

▲ (3550m)

Bahundanda

Bhirpustung

Jiunda
Kalaghrin

Sikrung
Lampata

Chosing
Kaule
Usta
Tarachok

Bhujung
Thagan
Rawagaon
Ngadi

Ghimrang
Tarpu
Bhulbule

Kam
Ghanpokhara
Panmchok
Rintang

Nayung
Khudi
Bhusme

Pasgam
Ghalegaon
Simalchaur
▲ (2225m)

Tamagaon
Sinpani
Baragaon

Khagang
Lamagaon
Sera
Khasur

(2020m) ▲
Samrong
Bhacockbesi

Ghamrang
Kahargaon
Najre
Punwa
Bhachok

Khedanda
Chara
Bhonji
Rabasing
Chanaute
Rawatgaon

Rabidanda
Maling
Baglungpani
Besi Sahar
Taksar

Patarti
Bimdabesi
START

Gorje
Dihithok
Chaur

Taksar
Lamjung
Darbar

Muri
Gilung
Bakhrejingat
Jarekham
Lamjung
Chiti

Karapu
Daruwadursa
Singla
Nalma
(1900m) ▲
Gaonshahar

Jhagre
Narwal

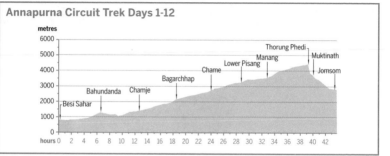

Annapurna Circuit Trek Days 1-12

village on the trek; it has a couple of simple lodges. You can either follow the road all the way or cross to the eastern bank and follow the alternative trail marked by the red-and-white trail markers – although this too has been impacted by road building and the Upper Marsyangdi A hydro project.

At Khudi cross a sidestream and continue to **Bhulbule** (840m). You enter the Annapurna Conservation Area in Bhulbule, though the first checkpoint is in Dharapani. Himalchuli and Ngadi Chuli (also known as Manaslu II and formerly as Peak 29), at 7879m, dominate the horizon.

The trail leaves the road at Bhulbule and descends past the **Thorung-la Guest House** (☑ 9846249243), popular for its restaurant, and the small Everest Guest House, then crosses the Marsyangdi Khola on a long suspension bridge. Across the bridge is the traditional and rickety **Heaven Guest House** (☑ 9846074178), with balconies overlooking the river and very basic rooms. Accommodation rates in Bhulbule are fixed at Rs 200/300 for singles/doubles.

Depending on time, you might be able to continue to Ngadi, 90 minutes away. Remember that by the end of October you'll start to lose sunlight by 5pm.

Day 2: Bhulbule to Ghermu

5–6 HOURS / 480M ASCENT / 180M DESCENT

Beyond Bhulbule the trail/road travels up the east bank of the river, past an impressive 60m waterfall surrounded by palm-like trees called pandanus (or screw pine). Watch for langur monkeys playing in the treetops. The road wanders through extensive rice terraces with continuing views of Manaslu and Ngadi Chuli.

The mountain views disappear as you near **Ngadi** (900m). Accommodation is divided into two sections, which are 10 minutes apart. The best of several options south of the village is the **Hiker's Lodge** (☑ 9856045940; r Rs 350), run by a local school teacher, with tidy rooms, garden sitting areas and a small bookshop. Further along, the old flagstoned bazaar still exists but is easy to miss; it's as though the new road has simply shunted it aside. Inside you will find the atmospheric but lonely Kamala, Annapurna, Marsayangdi and Mina lodges.

Cross the Sisne Khola for a good look at the Upper Marsyangdi A hydro project, before crossing the Ngadi Khola. On the hills above the Ngadi Khola is the village of Usta, on an old disused trekking route.

Eventually the trail leaves the road, briefly, to meet it again at Lampata. As you curve around the hillside you can see Bahundanda to the right of the conical hill. Take the left turn at the end of Lampata into a bowl of terraced rice fields. The trail winds around to the small but friendly Manaslu Guest House and makes a steep 15-minute climb through groves of bamboo to **Bahundanda** (1270m).

Bahundanda ('Hill of the Brahmans') is the northernmost Brahman settlement in the Marsyangdi Valley. The strategically placed Anjana Restaurant offers hot and cold beverages beside the police post where you will be asked to register. The Hotel Mountain View and Hotel Superb View tempt you to climb even higher to witness their panoramic views.

Descend on a steep, rocky trail past an impressive amphitheatre of terraces. Look for noisy flocks of slaty-headed parakeets raiding the rice crops. Contour across terraces to a teashop under a spreading pipal tree. Drop to cross a stream with enticing-looking cascades and pools, then make a short climb to a couple of restaurants at Lili Bhir.

ANNAPURNA CIRCUIT TREK DAYS 1–12 – TREKKING TIMES ONLY

DAY	SECTION	HOURS
1	Besi Sahar to Khudi	2:00
	Khudi to Bhulbule	0:45
2	Bhulbule to Ngadi	1:15
	Ngadi to Bahundanda	1:45
	Bahundanda to Kanigaon	1:30
	Kanigaon to Ghermu	0:15
3	Ghermu to Syange	0:15
	Syange to Jagat	1:30
	Jagat to Chamje	1:00
	Chamje to Tal	2:00
4	Tal to Karte	1:30
	Karte to Dharapani	0:40
	Dharapani to Bagarchhap	0:45
	Bagarchhap to Danaque	0:30
	Danaque to Timang	1:10
	Timang to Thanchowk	1:10
	Thanchowk to Koto	0:35
	Koto to Chame	0:25
5	Chame to Telekhu	0:25
	Telekhu to Bhratang	1:10
	Bhratang to Dhukur Pokhari	1:20
	Dhukur Pokhari to Pisang	0:50
	Pisang to Upper Pisang	0:20
6	Upper Pisang to Ghyaru	2:00
	Ghyaru to Ngawal	1:30
	Ngawal to Bragha	2:30
	Bragha to Manang	0:30
7	Manang	
8	Manang to Tengi	0:30
	Tengi to Gunsang	0:45
	Gunsang to Yak Kharka	1:30
	Yak Kharka to Letdar	0:55
9	Letdar to Thorung Phedi	2:00
10	Thorung Phedi to High Camp	1:00
	High Camp to Yakawa Thorung Ri teashop	0:45
	Yakawa Thorung Ri teashop to Thorung La	1:30
	Thorung La to Chabarbu	2:45
	Chabarbu to Muktinath	1:00
	Muktinath to Ranipauwa	0:15
11	Ranipauwa to Jharkot	0:25
	Jharkot to Khingar	0:35
	Khingar to Kagbeni	1:00
12	Kagbeni to Eklai Bhatti	0:40
	Eklai Bhatti to Jomsom	1:30

MIX IT UP

How your first few days' itinerary works out depends on several variables: what time your bus arrives in Besi Sahar, whether you take the bus or jeep to Bhulbule or Chame, and whether jeep transport pushes further along the circuit over the coming years. Consider the first few days of this trek a sample itinerary only.

Beyond Manang you need to stick to our itineraries for proper acclimatisation, but below Manang you can simply consult the tables of times (p147 & p169) for each stage to devise your own itinerary.

To avoid the crowds, try overnighting in smaller villages like Timang, Trichyungalta, Koto, Thanchowk, Karte, Dhukur Pokhari and Ghyaru. All offer good accommodation and you'll likely be the only guest there.

The trail then traverses high above the river on an exposed trail where some railings have been installed. A climb over a ridge leads to the pleasant village of **Kanigaon** (1170m), named after the small *kani* (chorten-shaped arches over trails) that mark the entrance and exit to the town. Many of the old villages from here to Kagbeni have entrance *kanis*, though these are usually bypassed by the new road. The Peaceful Guest House offers a good, offbeat place to lunch or overnight.

Ten minutes later the large **Crystal Guest House** (☑ 9846181865; s/d Rs 200/300, dal bhaat Rs 330) boasts the region's most impressive menu, serving Indian and Italian dishes, and marks the beginning of **Ghermu** (1140m). Pass several more guesthouses and shops, including a pharmacy, before reaching the Rainbow Restaurant and Lodge, which offers the best views of the huge waterfall on the other side of the Marsyangdi Valley. Ghermu is a quieter and nicer place to overnight than the older roadside lodges at Syange.

Day 3: Ghermu to Tal

5–6 HOURS / 640M ASCENT / 80M DESCENT

From Ghermu the trail drops quickly past the Summit Restaurant to cross the Marsyangdi on a long, rattling suspension bridge at **Syange** (1080m). The riverside lodges in the cobblestone village include the New Thakuri Guest House (☑ 9936 60053; s/d Rs 200/300) and the Sonam Tibetan Guest House, both of which get busy at lunchtime.

Beyond Syange the valley closes in to become a steep canyon. Follow the road until it starts to switchback up the hillside and then switch to the steep uphill short cuts. The trail climbs to a cold-drinks stop at the Marco Polo Hotel (1265m) and then crosses a high exposed trail (now road) blasted out of the nearly vertical cliffs. When Tilman

walked this section in 1950 the trail followed a series of wooden galleries tied to the face of the rock cliffs.

It's a short descent past a small waterfall to **Jagat** (1330m), inhabited, as are most villages in this region, by people of Tibetan heritage. Jagat means 'toll station'; this was once the site of a tax-collection post for the Tibetan salt trade. The tightly packed stone village has a medieval feel and boasts a dozen lodges. The Hotel Mont Blanc at the southern end of town has a lovely garden area for lunch. Other good places include the **Tibet Pemba Hotel** (s/d Rs 200/300) and the similar Eco Home, Paradise Hotel and North Face River View Guest House. All offer a couple of rooms with private bathroom in addition to basic rooms with shared facilities. There is a small hot spring located 15 minutes below the village.

From Jagat, the trail/road descends to the Ghatta Khola. The **Nepali Kitchen Guest House** (☑ 9856045319; s/d Rs 200/300) has rooms beside the ever-restless river and a cheery restaurant. The owner is interested in local wildlife (goral frequent the area), and he can arrange fishing trips and visits to a hot spring. It's then a stiff climb to fantastic views of a series of explosive cascades opposite the Super Rainbow View Guest House. Five minutes further is **Chamje** (1410m), under towering cliffs. Past the venerable Tibetan Hotel are half a dozen other lodges (s/d Rs 200/300). Descend past a big overhanging rock to the Tibet Lhasa Guest House and the Hotel Chymche.

Cross to the east bank of the Marsyangdi and follow the trail along the river embankment. The trail passes under a house-sized boulder, then climbs a rocky trail and a steep stone staircase to a couple of simple teashops in Sattale (1480m).

Climb past fields, then through bamboo and rhododendron to an exposed trail that traverses high above the steep riverbank. The trail makes a short descent to a single *bhatti* at **Tal Besi** (1590m), then climbs steeply beside the Marsyangdi, which has become an underground waterfall beneath huge boulders. The trail crests a ridge topped by a razor-wired army base to enter Manang district and the valley opens into a fertile plain. In this dramatic setting, at the foot of a large waterfall, is **Tal** (1700m), a string of lodges and trading posts reminiscent of an old American pony-express outpost. The town gets its name from the lake *(tal)* that once filled the flat-bottomed valley.

With over 25 lodges, Tal is an excellent place to overnight. Rooms here cost Rs 150/250 for singles/doubles, and a daal bhaat is Rs 400. From south to north you pass the Father and Son Guest House, Peaceland Guest House, Dragon Hotel, Hotel Mona Lisa and the Manaslu Guest House. All are good options, as is the Himalayan Hotel, north over the bridge. The **Hotel Paradise** (☎9846229760), in a secluded garden at the far northern end of town, is the most popular lodge in Tal, partly because of its superb potato, bean and pumpkin house special (Rs 400).

Tal's shops sell everything from biscuits to sunscreen, though for water go to the **safe drinking water station** (per litre Rs 40). For a short stroll, follow the trail behind the Hotel Paradise to a picturesque chorten at the base of the waterfall.

The region around Tal and Bagarchhap is called Gyasumdo (meaning 'three trails'), one of three distinct divisions within Manang. Gyasumdo was once highly dependent on trade with Tibet, including the sale of local musk, though since the disruption of cross-border trade in 1959, herding and agriculture have assumed greater importance.

Day 4: Tal to Chame

6½–7½ HOURS / 1100M ASCENT / 90M DESCENT

Today's walk is a relatively long one, but you can shorten it by overnighting at Timang or Koto. From Tal the trail heads north past the Hotel Paradise, over a wooden bridge, and then makes its way along the riverbed to Sirantal. Follow the riverside trail to a 60m-long suspension bridge across the Marsyangdi.

Trek past several *bhattis,* cross a bridge over a side cascade and pass by the Manaslu Lodge at **Khotro** (1860m). Descend to a long, high suspension bridge that leads to the east bank of the river and the sunny courtyards of the 3-Sister, New World and Dorchester hotels at **Karte** (1850m). Perched on a ledge, Karte makes a good overnight stop.

The main trail heads left from Karte and climbs over a ridge, entering the churning river gorge before dropping to a suspension

---

ⓘ SAFETY ON THORUNG LA

The 5416m Thorung La is one of Nepal's highest passes and crossing it is potentially dangerous. In terms of altitude acclimatisation it is safest to cross it from east to west. The trek up to the pass from Manang is not difficult but it is a long way at high elevation, which can cause problems. Be sure to read up on acute mountain sickness (AMS) before you go, so that you can be aware of the symptoms. Be prepared to return all the way to Besi Sahar if it is impossible or dangerous to cross the Thorung La. Trekkers have died on Thorung La because of altitude sickness, exposure, cold and avalanches. All trekkers, including porters, must be adequately equipped for severe cold and snow.

Thorung La is usually snowbound and closed from mid-December to March, although it is impossible to give exact closure dates. The trail to the pass can be extremely hard to find in fresh snow and you should be prepared to turn back or stay put in a lodge in bad weather. At any time local storms or cyclones generated in the Arabian Sea or Bay of Bengal can close the trail with sudden and massive snowfalls. In such conditions and at these altitudes, simply sitting out bad weather in a lodge can be life saving.

Tragically this was made all too clear in October 2014 when almost 1.8m of snow fell in 12 hours. In the ensuing days over 500 people were rescued in the vicinity of Thorung La and Muktinath, and 43 lives were lost. Those who died were caught outdoors by avalanches, extreme cold and white-out conditions.

Be certain you are prepared for this long trek. Once you start, the only ways out are to retreat back to Besi Sahar (walking and share jeep), fly from Hongde airport near Manang or cross the pass to Jomsom and fly from there.

SAFE DRINKING WATER STATIONS

An estimated one million unrecyclable and unbiodegradable plastic bottles are carried into the Annapurna Conservation Area each year. In an attempt to halt this flood of plastic, ACAP (with the assistance of the New Zealand government) operates the Safe Drinking Water Scheme – 16 outlets selling purified water to trekkers. The outlets are found in Tal, Bagarchhap, Chame, Pisang, Hongde, Manang, Letdar, Thorung Phedi, Muktinath, Kagbeni, Jomsom, Marpha, Tukuche, Khobang, Larjung, Lete and Ghasa.

Prices range from Rs 40 to Rs 60 per litre, which is around a third of the price of bottled mineral water, and stations are generally open from 6am to 6pm.

bridge that takes you back to the west side of the Marsyangdi. A side trail branching right from Karte offers an excursion, climbing steeply for an hour, to the little-visited town of Nache (2500m), before dropping back to rejoin the main trail just before the suspension bridge. ACAP is promoting a three-day camping trek from Nache up to Dhuna Lake (4700m), but the altitude gain is much too rapid to be considered advisable.

The main trail continues from the bridge up to the Tashi Delek, Eco Himalaya and Lhasa hotels, the first two of which offer a taste of the trail's first 'German bakeries'. A mini-hydro plant harnesses the impressive cascades to provide 24-hour electricity. A stone *kani* marks the formal entrance to **Dharapani** (1960m), which has a post office, police post and a couple of basic lodges. Just beyond the town are several better lodges: the recommended Hotel The Seven, Green Park, and **New Tibet Guest House** (☑ 994660000; s/d Rs 400/500, without bathroom Rs 200/300), the last of which has a free solar hot shower and gas-heated shower (Rs 100). Both the New Tibet and the Eco Himalaya offer good camping for Manaslu trekkers.

About 10 minutes further on is an ACAP checkpost, where you'll need to register and show your ACAP permit. This upper section of Dharapani marks the junction of the Marsyangdi and Dudh Khola. The Tibetan Hotel and Kangaroo Guest House offer good opportunities to break for tea. The latter has a campsite.

Beyond Dharapani, the wide trail climbs gradually over a spur. (Hard-core hikers could detour up the stone staircase here to the remote village of Odar – *odar* means cave – which is said to offer fine views of Manaslu.) Stick with the dull main road for the 30-minute walk to Bagarchhap, through a forest of blue pine, spruce, hemlock, maple and oak. As the trail curves around the ridge to enter Bagarchhap, you are rewarded with your first Annapurna views.

Bagarchhap (2160m) is a village of closely spaced stone houses. In November 1995 a landslide destroyed much of the village, including two lodges. A memorial chorten in the centre of the village commemorates those killed. The well-maintained Diki Gompa is a couple of minutes above the village. The Marsyangdi Hotel, Pasang Guest House and Eco Holiday Home still offer accommodation (singles/doubles Rs 250/400) and a daal bhaat lunch, but many hoteliers have rebuilt their lodges in Danaque, 30 minutes up the valley.

The trek now enters the Manang Valley and continues west up the valley, offering views of the Himalayan peaks to the south. There are occasional glimpses of Lamjung Himal (6986m) and Annapurna II (7937m) to the west and the peaks of Manaslu Himal to the east. The trail stays on the south bank of the river, climbing through pine and fir forests to **Danaque** (2210m), also called Syal Khola ('the river of jackals').

In lower Danaque you'll find the family-run Snowland Hotel and the Hotel Tibetan, both popular lunch spots. Opposite the Hotel Tibetan is a public phone booth and a safe drinking water station (Rs 40 per litre). Five minutes later you'll pass a *mani dungkhor* (chapel with large prayer wheel) beside a mani wall, and then a trio of good lodges – the Mt Kailash, Lotus Guest House and Potala Guest House. These lodges are your last chance to get food or accommodation before the long climb to Timang. Danaque is surrounded by orchards, and apples and peaches are available during autumn.

Beyond Danaque the route crosses a stream and starts to climb steeply, criss-crossing sections of road through rhododendron forest to eventually gain 500m in elevation. Cross a stream on a concrete bridge by the Syalque mini-hydro project and then climb again, to eventually arrive at the Shanta Restaurant at 2545m.

After a further climb you'll reach the muddy road and scruffy settlement of **Timang** (2630m), perched high over the valley with several lodges. Very few trekkers overnight in Timang but the Prasanna Hotel and Hotel Royal Garden both offer decent rooms, rewarding you with early-morning views of Manaslu.

Follow the trail as it climbs a ridge at 2720m and then descends through pine forest, leaving the road behind. Several lodges prematurely signal the upcoming village of Thanchowk. A trio of chortens reveal the heartbreaking sight of the trail descending steeply into a side valley, only to climb straight back up the other side. The stone-walled village of **Thanchowk** is eventually reached. It is one of the most traditional villages on the circuit, with typical Tibetan architecture of closely packed stone houses with flat roofs piled high with firewood. The comfortable Himalayan Hotel offers a quiet place to overnight, or continue through apple orchards at the end of the village to the simple Hotel Cho-Yoo. Stacks of pine needles mark the end of the village as you follow the easy wide trail down past the fields of Chhetipu to the entrance *kani* of **Koto** (2640m). You'll need to stop and register at the police checkpost opposite the *gompa*.

There are several places to stay in Koto (also known as Kyupar), including the good Hotel Super View, Snowland Hotel and Hotel Petunia, though most trekkers continue to better facilities at Chame. Koto is the turn-off point for the spectacular but restricted Nar-Phu Valley (p174) to the north.

It's an easy 25-minute stroll on to the large village of **Chame** (2710m), the administrative headquarters for the Manang district and, at the time of research, the end of the road for jeeps from Besi Sahar. En route you'll find more good accommodation at the Peaceful and Nurpu Linga Guest Houses in Trichyungalta. At the entrance to Chame is a mani wall with many prayer wheels. Be sure to walk to the left and spin the wheels clockwise. The southern section of Chame is lined with guesthouses: Tibet Guest House, Trekking Holiday Hotel, Manaslu View and **Hotel New Shangri-La** (☑066-440191; r with bathroom Rs 350, s/d without bathroom Rs 150/250; daal bhaat Rs 375).

Cross a stream and pass the safe drinking water station and police station to the closely spaced stone buildings of the town centre. The shops here are some of the best stocked

on the circuit, offering everything from novels to trekking supplies. The **Nepal Bank** (☺10am-3pm Sun-Thu, to noon Fri) changes cash and the nearby Danfe Hotel offers internet access (Rs 5 per minute).

Other lodges in the centre include the **Marsyangdi Mandala Hotel** (☑066-440146), whose detached chalets offer more privacy than standard lodge rooms. Alternatively, continue across the Marsyangdi on the suspension bridge or new road bridge to several more lodges, including the bright Sangso Guest House and New Tibet Hotel and, behind the latter, the secluded Hotel Mountain Lodge. And a short walk from Hotel Mountain Lodge is a **hot spring** where there's a tiny cement plunge pool. There are fine views of Lamjung Himal, Annapurna II and Annapurna IV (7525m) from here. If you have time on your hands, pop into the large, central *mani dungkhor* or visit the small gompa at the northern end of town.

Day 5: Chame to Upper Pisang

4–5 HOURS / 600M ASCENT

Trekking west from the bridge you pass an older part of Chame and the impressive *kani* that marks the entrance to the village. Climb past mani walls, looking back for impressive but fleeting views of Manaslu, to the New Mountain View Hotel in tiny **Telekhu** (2840m). There's a long, mostly level walk through forests to a large apple orchard surrounded by a stone wall. Ninety minutes from Chame are the rough stone houses of **Bhratang** (2950m), where the simple Bhratang Teahouse offers a welcome tea stop.

Just beyond this collection of lodges is a bridge leading to the old part of Bhratang, an abandoned Khampa settlement and guerrilla camp dating from the 1960s. Across the bridge there is a small stone memorial to a Japanese climber who died in an avalanche while trekking across the Thorung La – a sobering reminder to wait several days after any heavy snowstorm before trying to cross the pass. Check with the teahouse in Bhratang to see if this short alternative trail is open, otherwise don't cross the bridge; stay on the northern side of the river and follow the dramatic trail (now road) that has been blasted out of the side of the cliff.

The trail/road rounds a bend to reveal the first views of the dramatic **Paungda Danda** rock face, a tremendous curved slab of rock rising more than 1500m from the river. Locals call it the Swarga Dwar (Gateway

Annapurna Circuit Trek Day 5-11

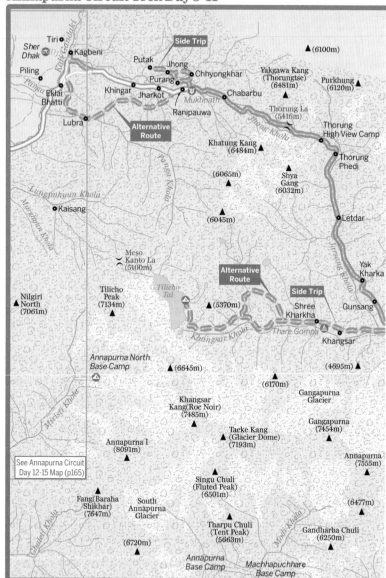

to Heaven) and believe the spirits of the deceased must ascend this wall after leaving their bodies. There are awesome views of Annapurna II to the south, Pisang Peak (6091m) to the northeast and Himalchuli and Ngadi Chuli, down valley to the east.

Cross to the south bank of the Marsyangdi on a suspension bridge (3080m), make a short steep climb past a porters' stop through forests of blue pine (and 20 minutes of road), then descend to the first of half-a-dozen lodges at **Dhukur Pokhari** (3200m), named after

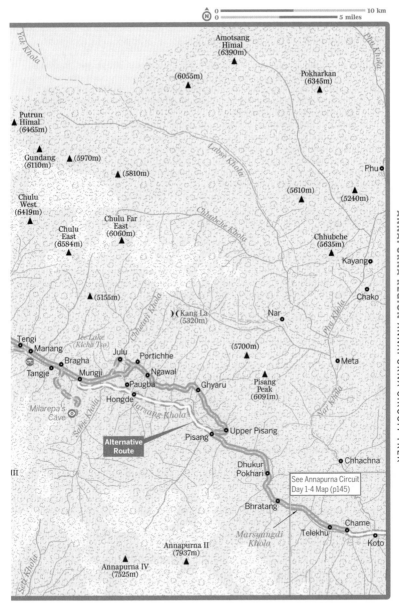

the tiny lake you pass just after the village. This is a fine place to break for lunch.

You can follow the road out of Dhukur Pokhari to Lower Pisang, but ACAP have marked (with red-and-white blazes) an alternative trail to Upper Pisang. Take the trail that heads across a bridge to the north bank of the Marsyangdi.

Lower Pisang, a cluster of lodges and a long mani wall with prayer wheels, is at an elevation of 3240m. Facilities include a safe drinking water station and a post

ANNAPURNA CONSERVATION AREA PROJECT (ACAP)

ACAP (www.ntnc.org.np) was established in 1986 as part of an innovative approach to environmental protection. The project encompasses the entire Annapurna range, an area of 7683 sq km, but also a population of some 40,000 people in 300 villages. Traditional national park practices at that time dictated that few, if any, people could reside within park boundaries, so a new model, a 'conservation area', had to be charted to include the participation of local people and emphasise environmental education and environmentally sustainable economic development.

Projects include the training of lodge owners, the introduction of alternative fuels and technologies such as solar panels and back-boiler stoves to reduce deforestation, cultural re-enforcement programs and the implementation of a system of fixed prices for food and accommodation to decrease competition and undercutting. ACAP encourages the use of kerosene for cooking throughout the region, and requires its use in hotels above Chhomrong in the Annapurna Sanctuary.

ACAP is supported by the 'conservation fee' of Rs 2000 that it collects from all trekkers in the Annapurna Conservation Area. There are ACAP checkposts and visitor centres throughout the region where you can learn more about the project.

office. There are some fine lodges here, but with most trekkers now taking the upper trail several owners have opened second lodges in the old village of **Upper Pisang** (3310m). The traditional upper village offers bags of atmosphere and infinitely better mountain views than Lower Pisang. Accommodation (s/d Rs 250/400) includes the simple but friendly Manang Marsyangdi, Yak and Yeti, Tukuche and Annapurna hotels. The higher the hotel, the better the views. Even if you don't stay in Upper Pisang, it's worth exploring the village's two gompas and then continuing up to the chortens and ruins of an old *dzong* (fort; 3443m) for fabulous views.

Pisang marks the beginning of the region known as Nyesyang, the upper portion of the Manang district. The people of Nyesyang raise wheat, barley, buckwheat, potatoes and beans; the cold, almost arid climate limits them to a single crop annually. Horses are the traditional means of transport, and you'll see locals riding them with great élan up and down the valley.

Day 6: Upper Pisang to Manang via Ngawal

6–7 HOURS / 540M ASCENT / 310M DESCENT

There are two routes to Manang. The easier low route follows the valley floor road via Hongde, while the more strenuous but far more scenically impressive high route climbs above the river on the north side of the valley. The high route takes about three hours longer but is absolutely worth it and so is described here as the main route. The views of Annapurna II and III are simply superb and a night in Ghyaru or Ngawal will aid acclimatisation as you head towards the Thorung La.

From Upper Pisang the high trail enters pine groves to reveal views of the small turquoise lake of Mring Tso below you, just before a connector trail joins from Lower Pisang. The trail passes a line of 'eight plus one' chortens and stays on the ridge to cross a bridge and ascend steeply on switchbacks to **Ghyaru** (3670m). The **Yak Ru Mount View Lodge** (s/d Rs 150/300) has a traditional caravanserai-style design, with rooms arranged around a central courtyard. The Gorkhali and Annapurna hotels also offer decent accommodation. Ghyaru is believed to be a corruption of the original name Yak Ru (Yak Horn). There is a gleaming white **Jhunju Chorten** and an interesting gompa in the village, which is also the start of climbing routes to Pisang Peak, Chulu East (6584m) and Chulu West (6419m), all of which are visible from the trail.

The trail stays high after passing a restored *kani* with a protector deity inside, and 30 minutes later traverses above a ruined *dzong* once used by the local Ghale dynasty. Pass a chorten, then the Nice View Café by a collection of more chortens, to descend for 30 minutes to **Ngawal** (3660m). The trail does a dog-leg through the charming village, passing underneath a fine *kani* (look up to see the painted mandalas). A white chorten with a water-driven mani wheel and dragon-mouth spouts marks a trail junction; left to Manang or straight uphill to the Ney Guru Sang Phuk and restricted area of Nar-Phu. Ngawal is a fine place to overnight. The pleasant Peaceful Hotel at the entrance to the village offers good food and thick mattresses. The Kailash Guest House, a little further on, is most notable for its spectacular rooftop dining (order in the restaurant opposite); it's just beside an ancient juniper tree and mani wall. If you have some time, you could follow the prayer flags above town up to the chorten for more views. A harder hike continues up the hillside for a further 45 minutes to the **Ney Guru Sang Phuk**, a cave said to contain a 'self-arisen' (ie not human-made) image of the Himalayan sage Guru Rinpoche. Back in town the Sanga Dedul Pelgye Ling Gompa dates from 1990.

From Ngawal the trail traverses the hillside down to Portichhe village and the monastery-like Lophelling Boarding School. The direct trail heads south and descends down the southern side of the hill. A more interesting option, involving some route-finding, is to descend west from the school straight down the slippery switchbacks and over a bridge to **Julu** (Chullu) village. Swing left down the valley, past some marshy hot springs and then bear right, past eroded cliffs to join the main route, above a boarding school. From here it's 25 minutes along the valley floor to **Mungji** (3500m), where three teahouses offer seabuckthorn juice, yak meat and cheese, but not accommodation. Just above the village is Sher Gompa, actually a nunnery used for retreats that last three years, three months and three days. The snowy peak at the head of the valley is Tilicho Peak.

The route continues through fields for 20 minutes to **Bragha** (3470m), one of the most picturesque villages in the Annapurnas. The *kani* that marks the entrance to the village is particularly impressive. The **Bragha Gompa** (admission Rs 100; ◷ 8-11am & 2-5pm), perched on a high crag overlooking the medieval village, is the largest in the district and has an outstanding collection of statues, thangkas (Tibetan religious paintings) and manuscripts estimated to be 500 years old. Take a torch to visit the gallery that runs behind the main altar. Most of the village's 200 houses are stacked one atop the other, each with an open verandah formed by a neighbour's rooftop.

The **Hotel New Yak** (☎ 9843172248; s/d Rs 150/200, r with bathroom 400) and the next-door Hotel Buddha and Himalayan Lodge all get excellent reviews, making Bragha a great alternative to staying in the busier and more commercialised Manang. All three places have good bakeries and filter coffee, while the New Yak offers local Nyesyang specials such as *potey kein* (rice with buckwheat daal).

The valley around Bragha is very arid, dominated by dramatic eroded cliffs and the towering heights of the Annapurnas. It is only a short walk, past chortens and mani walls, to a stream where several mills grind wheat and barley. A short climb leads to the plateau and village of **Manang** (3540m). The eastern half of town is lined with lodges, trekking shops and video cafes, while the medieval western old town is a compact collection of 500 flat-roofed houses separated by narrow alleyways. The setting of the village is most dramatic, with the summits of Annapurna and Gangapurna less than 8km away, and a huge icefall rumbling and crashing on the flanks of the peaks.

The large **Hotel Yeti** (☎ 9846229885; www.yetihotelmanang.com; s/d Rs 300/500, r without bathroom Rs 200) is a bit of a hub, with a popular bakery and internet cafe. The US doctors at the Himalayan Rescue Association recommend the restaurant's quesadillas and sizzling vegie fajitas, and so do we. The next-door Tilicho Hotel is almost identical. The wooden Yak Hotel is the village's biggest and one of the oldest lodges. Other places include the Himalayan Singi, set back from the main road, and the Hotel Mountain Lake, which boasts a cosy sunroom but somewhat dark rooms.

Mavis' Kitchen (mains Rs 150-300) is a popular place for lunch, serving up ambitious dishes like julienne salad and yak steak. The Hotel Nilgiri Bakery & Restaurant offers a wide choice of burgers and pastries plus filter coffee. And if you like the food, you can also stay here.

Manang's shopkeepers know exactly what you dream about in your sleeping bag at night, and the shops are almost as well stocked as those in Pokhara. If you or your porters do not have warm socks, hats, gloves or sunglasses, this is the time and place to buy them. Other facilities in town include a pharmacy, a safe drinking water station, shoe repair and a post office. ACAP has a **visitor** centre (⊙10am-1.30pm & 2-5pm Sun-Thu, Friday to 3pm) with information on local excursions.

During the trekking season, the **Himalayan Rescue Association** (HRA; ☑ 993665055; www.himalayanrescue.org; ⊙9-10am & 1.30-5pm Mar–mid-May & Oct–mid-Dec) operates an aid post behind the Hotel Nilgiri Bakery & Restaurant. The free daily lectures (at 3pm) on altitude sickness are worth attending; the organisation proudly claims that no one who has been to one of these lectures has ever died of AMS. The foreign doctors are available for advice and treatment (consultation US$35).

If you're ill or injured, hotels can arrange horse hire to the airport, Thorung La or even Muktinath, although you still have to walk some steep downhill sections.

SIDE TRIP: MILAREPA'S CAVE
4–5 HOURS / 800M ASCENT / 800M DESCENT

A worthwhile side trip from Bragha is to Milarepa's Cave, a pilgrimage site that celebrates a famous story involving the Tibetan poet and singer Milarepa. Milarepa was meditating in a cave above Bragha when a Gurung hunter, Khyira Gonpo Dorje, and his dog stalked a deer into the ascetic's cave, only to be persuaded by the saint to relinquish his bow and become Milarepa's disciple. The story is celebrated in literature, songs and dances across the Tibetan world.

To get to the site from Bragha, cross the bridge to the south side of the valley and head southwest to where a trail ascends the hillside to the left of an eroded crag. At some herders' huts (45 minutes) a sign points you left, into a gully, and then up switchbacks to a white chorten draped in prayer flags. The small **gompa** (4100m; N 28°38.271', E 84°02.303') is often locked. The statue of Milarepa was flown here in 2004 by helicopter – the sight of a Tibetan sage flying through the air was probably enough to double attendance at the local gompas! Hundreds of pilgrims set up camp in the meadows here during a festival in June.

A further 45 minutes up the gully, following the chortens, gets you to a 4320m ridge with views of the nearby glacier. As you descend back towards the cliff, look up to see the bow left behind by Gonpo Dorje. The old ladders that once accessed the cave have been destroyed by rockfalls. Pilgrims also visit the saint's footprints, which are carved into the rock face. Figure on half a day for the excursion.

ALTERNATIVE ROUTE: VIA HONGDE
4–5 HOURS / 350M ASCENT

To take the lower route to Manang, head out of Pisang along the south side of the Marsyangdi, cross a stream and climb past mani walls and a memorial to a group of German climbers who died attempting Pisang Peak. The road makes a long climb over a forested ridge (3440m) that offers an excellent view of the Manang Valley, with Tilicho Peak (7134m) at its head. After a short descent, the trail reaches the broad valley floor.

The trail/road follows the valley floor to Manang's airstrip at **Hongde** (Ongre; 3420m), 90 minutes from Pisang. The Airport Bakery Hotel at the southern end of town churns out hot croissants and cinnamon rolls. Stay to the left of the town's long central mani wall, past well-stocked shops and a large *mani dungkhor*.

The airport is at the northern end of town, near the incongruous bandstand, though Nepal Airlines has its office at the southern end of town in the New Himalayan Hotel. At the far end of town is a police checkpost.

Thirty minutes beyond the airport is the huge Sabje Valley, with Annapurna III and IV at the head. Just south of the trail, in this spectacular setting, is a mountaineering school operated by the Nepal Mountaineering Association.

The trail crosses to the north bank of the Marsyangdi on a wooden bridge near Mungji. See the main trek description for the route from Mungji onwards.

Day 7: Acclimatisation Day in Manang

You should spend a second night in the Manang region (not necessarily Manang itself – consider Khangsar, Shree Kharka and Bragha) to acclimatise to the higher elevations you will encounter towards Thorung La (in fact, the Himalayan Rescue Association recommends a minimum of three nights). Climbing high during the day will speed up acclimatisation, and you could easily spend three days exploring the stunning scenery around Manang.

One of the easier trips is to descend from the village to the bridge and up the spine of the glacial moraine to the **Chongar viewpoint**, atop a hill decorated in prayer flags (40 minutes). There are fine views of the milky-blue glacial lake at the foot of the spectacular Gangapurna Icefall. You can even get a cup of tea here at the Chonkhor Viewpoint Restaurant.

A more strenuous day hike is the climb south of Manang to 'point 4695' on the Schneider map (sometimes referred to as Papuchong). Take the path below Manang, crossing a bridge to the right of Gangapurna Lake, then climb the ridge to the right of the Gangapurna Glacier, headed towards Tarke Kang and Gangapurna, for close-up glacier views (four hours).

One popular excursion is to **Praken Gompa** (3945m), a *tsamkhang* (meditation retreat) high on the hillside above Manang. For a donation, the resident Lama will bless your impending crossing of the Thorung La by tying a sacred thread around your neck. The views of Annapurna IV, Annapurna II, Gangapurna and Tarke Kang are fantastic. The path ascends the hillside from the eastern end of town and the climb takes about 1¼ hours.

After a visit to Praken you can descend to Manang and branch left into the floodplain to visit the 400-year-old **Karki Gompa**, surrounded by ancient juniper trees. You could then cross the stream and climb the bluff to **Bocho Gompa**, situated just below a ruined fort and deserted village. Also worth a visit is the **Kagyud Gompa** at the western end of Manang village. Your best chance of finding the gompas open is between 10am and 11am, or from 4pm to 6pm.

The toughest and most spectacular excursion from Manang is the day hike up to **Ice Lake** (Kicho Tso; 4620m), a relentless four-hour climb that gains over 1000m to reveal staggering Annapurna views. Because of the significant altitude gain, it is better to leave this trip to the second day of a three-night acclimatisation halt in Manang. The clearest trail leads diagonally up the hillside behind Bragha, zigzagging up to the top of a ridge. A quicker but steeper alternative trail leads from Manang. The Ice Lake is actually the second of two lakes. A viewpoint to the side of the lake offers superb scenery. This is a long day hike so make sure you set off early and carry enough food and water.

For something less strenuous, the town's **Manang Cultural Museum** (☏019-442009; admission Rs 100; ☉10am-5pm, closed Jan & Feb) is worth a visit for its insights into traditional Manangi life. The museum also offers local guides for an hour-long guided walk through Manang's old town.

A half-day option is to head south to Bragha and up to Milarepa's Cave (see p156).

SIDE TRIP: KHANGSAR & TILICHO TAL
3½ DAYS

The side trip to Tilicho Tal is an adventurous add-on to the Annapurna Circuit and will certainly aid your acclimatisation process, but it's a challenging trip. Your rewards are superb high-altitude views of both the lake and its 'Great Barrier', a name given by Maurice Herzog to the high snowbound ridge between Khangsar Kang (7485m) and Nilgiri North (7061m).

MANANG TO KHANGSAR
1½–2 HOURS / 200M ASCENT

A sign just before an archway in old Manang directs you to either the Thorung La or Khangsar. The Khangsar trail descends to a chorten, then turns northwest and heads down towards the river. Don't cross the suspension bridge. Stay on the north bank and head west, following the river. You'll soon come to a bridge (3560m, 40 minutes) just above the confluence of the Marsyangdi and the Jarsang Khola. Cross the Jarsang Khola on the suspension bridge and climb steeply onto a ridge where the eroded ruins of an old *dzong* offer a view back to the villages of Manang and Pisang.

Follow the power lines along the ridge on a wide trail, then traverse along the south side of the ridge through a blue pine forest and then wheat fields, climbing to the entrance *kani* in **Khangsar** (3745m).

Khangsar is a collection of traditional stone buildings surrounding a village square. Four hotels, the Mountain Yak, the simple family-style red-painted Himalchuli Laxmi, Hotel on Height and the friendly

ANNAPURNA REGION ANNAPURNA CIRCUIT TREK

SEABUCKTHORN JUICE

In the upper Manang Valley you'll find seabuckthorn juice on many menus. The juice is made from the orange berries of a hardy, multipurpose shrub with large thorns. The berries are harvested, crushed and mixed with water and a bit of sugar to produce a tasty drink (like a combination of honey and fruit juice) with a vitamin content said to be higher than any other fruit or vegetable. Seabuckthorn berries have been used in traditional Chinese medicine since the Tang dynasty and contain more than 100 different kinds of nutrients and bioactive substances.

Maya Hotel (☎9846229728), offer decent accommodation (singles/doubles Rs 300/500). Near the top of the village is a small Sakyapa-school monastery. The hotels can provide horses, porters and guides and can organise a day hike up to Dawa Tal (Moon Lake; 4910m).

KHANGSAR TO TILICHO BASE CAMP HOTEL
4–6 HOURS / 570M ASCENT / 190M DESCENT
From Khangsar the trail climbs steeply past the gompa to a small chorten, then climbs more gently through juniper and wild rose. Cross a small stream and traverse to the isolated Thare Gompa (3930m; 45 minutes). There is no permanent monk body here, but the caretaker should let you in if she's around.

Ten minutes later the trail joins the main track to/from Yak Kharka. A further 10 minutes brings you to Shree Kharka (4045m), and the Blue Sheep Hotel, Himalayan Guest House and the Hotel Tilicho Peak (☎9849584446; dm Rs 100, s/d with bathroom Rs 250), a possible place to break the return trip. Traverse into a side valley and climb steeply up the other side to some herders' huts and a trail junction. The high trail to Tilicho Base Camp branches to the right. This high route avoids the most dangerous section of the trail to Tilicho Base Camp, but it involves a long climb to 4700m, followed by a steep (and initially very exposed) 650m descent on scree to the Tilicho Base Camp Hotel, and takes an hour longer than the low route. This trail was closed at the time of research. Ask locals for the current conditions of this trail.

The more popular lower trail makes a steep descent to a wooden bridge, then climbs past several *goths* (shepherds' huts) to a ridge at 4230m. A short descent leads to a stream, then the trail makes a long, difficult traverse across a huge, steep and unstable scree slope that is subject to frequent rockfall from above. There are a couple of very hairy sections of trail here so follow the advice of local people before setting off. The scary trail eventually rounds a ridge and makes a long traverse to the simple Tilicho Base Camp Hotel, at the foot of the moraine beside a stream at 4140m. There are two other lodges in the vicinity: Hotel Kangsar Kang and New Tilicho Base Camp Hotel (☎9849584446; dm Rs 100, r Rs 300). Overcrowding is not so much an issue now, but there's not much to do here, so try not to arrive too early in the day. With no electricity or heat, you can expect a long, cold night here.

TILICHO BASE CAMP HOTEL TO TILICHO TAL
5–6 HOURS / 870M ASCENT
The trail to Tilicho Tal starts up a side valley then traverses onto a moraine, making a long climb to 4710m. There are outstanding views of Tarke Kang, Gangapurna and the claw-like black face of Khangsar Kang (Roc Noir; 7485m), as well as views down the valley to Manang and upper Pisang. The trail then makes a series of steep switchbacks, climbing for an hour to a chorten marking a false summit and on to a crest at 5010m. Expect the next 45 minutes to be on snow from November until at least May. Passing two tarns, the trail crests at a prayer-flag-draped cairn (5005m; N 28°40.661', E 83°51.871'), where you'll get your first view of the lake, which is 4km long and 2.5km wide. If you're making a day walk from the Tilicho Base Camp Hotel, this is the spot to turn around.

Tilicho Tal (4920m) presents a particularly dramatic spectacle. Sometimes its turquoise waters reflect the surrounding peaks, but more often (between October and May), it's frozen over. Herzog's maps depicted Tilicho as the 'great ice lake' and his team walked across it. The lake sits at the foot of the extensive glacier system of the Great Barrier, the highest point of which is Tilicho Peak (7134m). The glaciers terminate in a vertical wall of ice 70m high that forms the west shore of the lake. When it's warm, small icebergs calve off and crash into the lake.

From the viewpoint, a long traverse leads you around the east side of the lake to a good campsite near a large rock at 4930m. There is no shelter of any kind near the lake. At night you'll be kept awake in your tent by the roar of avalanches tumbling from the glaciers above. Bear in mind that the lakeshore trails depicted on most maps are just figments of a cartographer's overactive imagination.

From Tilicho Tal most people spend a second night at Tilicho Base Camp. You could push through to Shree Kharka or Khangsar in a long eight- or nine-hour day, but the scree slopes are not something to be attempted on tired legs.

You can avoid backtracking to Manang by cutting across from Shree Kharka towards the (virtually) abandoned settlement of Up-

ⓘ WARNING – UNSTABLE SCREE SLOPES

The narrow and scary trail to the Tilicho Base Camp Hotel crosses some extremely unstable scree slopes. It is easily the most dangerous section of trail on the Annapurna Circuit and we do not recommend this side trip for inexperienced trekkers. If there is snow or rain, the route can be treacherous. We have included the description here to help you understand that the trip to Tilicho is more difficult than the brochure and signboards of the Tilicho Base Camp Hotel suggest. It's a spectacular side trip, but don't approach it without sufficient preparation and definitely don't walk it alone. If you do attempt the crossing, leave some space between team members in case of rockfall, bring trekking poles for stability and avoid a crossing in the rain.

per Khangsar, then to a viewpoint on a spur overlooking the junction of the Marsyangdi and the Jarsang Khola (keep an eye out for blue sheep). The trail then drops down through groves of birch to a bridge across the Jarsang (aka Thorung Khola) and then climbs to the main trail from Manang. Ask for advice at the ACAP office in Manang and again in Khangsar and Shree Kharka before you commit to this short cut.

Day 8: Manang to Letdar

3½–4½ HOURS / 720M ASCENT

The trek now begins its ascent of almost 2000m to the Thorung La. Local traders ride horses from Manang to Muktinath in a single day, but the large elevation gain, the need for acclimatisation and the high altitudes all make it imperative to take at least three days to do the trip on foot. It's possible to reach Thorung Phedi in a single day from Manang, but you must spend a night at either Yak Kharka or Letdar in order to acclimatise. If you have any altitude sickness symptoms, you should descend to Manang, or lower, to recover.

From Manang village, the trail climbs to a chorten and then continues to Tengi (3690m), 30 minutes from Manang and the last permanently inhabited village in the valley. The simple, traditional Tanki Guest House offers a quiet alternative to the bustle of Manang and is authentic enough to have a yak's head nailed to the wall.

The trail continues to climb out of the Marsyangdi Valley, then turns northwest up the valley of the Jarsang Khola, losing sight of the Manang Valley behind you. The trail follows this valley north, passing a few goths as it steadily gains elevation. You have left the large trees below; the vegetation now consists of scrub juniper and alpine grasses. The trail climbs to the small village of Gunsang (3920m). With good accommodation and fine views of Annapurna II and IV, Gunsang makes an ideal tea break, either on the rooftop of the simple Chullu West Hotel or in the garden of the fancier Marsyangi Lodge.

The route enters pastures and miniature forests of juniper, rose and barberry. Swing into a side valley to see yaks grazing below the peaks of Chulu West and Gundang (6110m), then cross the suspension bridge to a teashop and an ancient mani wall at 3990m. A few minutes later the short-cut route from Khangsar joins from the left.

Beyond is Yak Kharka (4020m), also known as Koche. The six lodges here are much better than those in Letdar; try the rustic Yak Hotel & Restaurant or the rightly popular Gangapurna Lodge (☑ 994660008; r Rs 400, s/d without bathroom Rs 150/300), which offers cottages and rooms with private bathroom. A little further is the simpler and cheaper Hotel Nyeshang. About 10 minutes above Yak Kharka is the New Himalayan View, offering good rooms (some with Western toilet) and ambitious dishes like pizza and moussaka. A large herd of yaks grazes in the fields nearby (yak kharka translates as 'yak pastures'), and it's worth visiting the yak herders' camp in the late afternoon when the animals are herded down from high pastures. The views of Annapurna III are excellent.

An hour further is Letdar (4230m; sometimes spelt as Lathar), the penultimate shelter before the pass. The first hotel, the Snowland Lodge, is probably the best; others include the cosy Churi Lattar and the simpler Jimi Lodge, but all are pretty basic. The Churi Lattar houses the safe drinking water station (Rs 50 per litre). The HRA doctors suggest that you spend two nights at Letdar, which is a pretty grim prospect.

ANNAPURNA REGION ANNAPURNA CIRCUIT TREK

CROSSING TO JOMSOM

Beyond Tilicho Tal, two passes lead into the Kali Gandaki Valley: Meso Kanto La (5100m) and another, unnamed, 5230m pass a little further north. This is a full-on alpine expedition rather than a trekking route and we do not recommend it. Even experienced trekkers will need expert professional support, including a local guide, as both trails are difficult and hard to find. This is certainly not a place to bring ill-equipped and inexperienced porters.

The route starts by heading northeast up a gully behind the campsite, then traverses around the north side of a ridge at 5380m. It's then cross-country to one of the passes. Meso Kanto is the more difficult of the two. The Kali Gandaki side is so steep that you'll likely have to fix a rope. The unnamed pass to the north is less difficult, but it's a messy descent through loose shale and mud. Both passes are extremely treacherous when there's snow. Once across the pass you need to make your way north across the head of the Lungpuhyun Valley and descend the ridge that forms its north side. Do not follow the trail along the southern ridge as this leads past a shooting range to the Army Mountain Warfare Camp at Kaisang. Campsites are very limited on this side of the pass and there is no shelter at all except for a few stone huts (no water available) at 3040m, about six hours below the pass.

The High Route to Tilicho – the Hidden Lake, a 1:50,000 map, is published by Nepa Maps but it's essentially just a detail of its Annapurna map.

If you've been up to Tilicho Tal and spent a couple of nights at Tilicho Base Camp then you should be acclimatised enough to continue to Thorung Phedi today.

Day 9: Letdar to Thorung Phedi

2 HOURS / 240M ASCENT

From Letdar the trail continues to climb along the east bank of the Jarsang Khola, then descends and crosses the stream on either the new suspension bridge or the wooden bridge at 4310m. The two trails make a short ascent to a collection of prayer flags and join near the Deurali Teahouse, a welcome tea stop. The route then follows a narrow trail across an exposed slope and climbs to **Thorung Phedi** (4540m), a desolate rock-strewn meadow surrounded by cliffs. The higher trail on the east side of the valley is currently not in use.

There are two lodges at Thorung Phedi (and one under construction at the time of research). The large **Thorung Base Camp Lodge** (☑ 993664535; r Rs 200-300; 🛜) offers a bakery, a range of rooms (some with private toilet) and even wi-fi internet access. The next-door **Hotel New Phedi** (☑ 993664557; r Rs 200) is smaller and quieter. Thanks to a nearby mini-hydro plant, Thorung Phedi has electricity, although this dries up (along with the electric heating) when water levels are low.

Both lodges can be very crowded in high season, especially if snow has backed up traffic over the pass. Somehow they can accommodate and feed up to 200 trekkers in a maze of double rooms, dormitories and outhouses.

Nights can be miserable because of the altitude and the early-morning departure. Some trekkers set off at 4am, but there's really no reason to depart this early. A more reasonable departure time is daybreak, around 6am. Because people leave early in the morning, the hotels insist that you settle your bill at night. If you are not feeling well, there is sometimes a horse available to ride over the pass (US$150). When there are no horses or the snow is very deep, yak herders circle the camp like sharks in search of sick-looking trekkers whom they can hit for a US$200 yak ride over the pass. If weather conditions deteriorate and it looks like snowing, gather as much local advice as possible and heed any warnings. Do not underestimate the difficulty of this crossing in poor weather and mistakenly push on to perceived safety on the other side of the pass (see the boxed text, p149).

Blue sheep and even snow leopards sometimes magically appear in this valley; the crow-like birds are choughs, and the large birds that circle overhead are lammergeiers and Himalayan griffons.

Be sure to boil or treat water here; the sanitation in Thorung Phedi and Letdar is poor, and giardiasis can be rampant. The Base Camp Lodge has a satellite phone you can use in an emergency.

There is another lodge, **Thorung High Camp Hotel** (☑ 993664505; r Rs 350, dm/r without bathroom Rs 100/150), popularly known as High Camp, an hour above Thorung Phedi at 4850m, but it is cramped and cold and a night here can be dangerous because of the altitude. It's common to see restless trekkers climbing up beyond Thorung Phedi after lunch, only to return in the late afternoon with a splitting headache or worse.

Day 10: Thorung Phedi to Muktinath & Ranipauwa

6–8 HOURS / 1040M ASCENT / 1620M DESCENT

Phedi, which means 'foot of the hill', is a common Nepali name for any settlement at the bottom of a long climb. The trail becomes steep immediately after leaving Thorung Phedi, switchbacking up moraines and following rocky ridges as it ascends to the pass. Local people have long used this trail to bring herds of sheep and yaks in and out of Manang, so while the trail is often steep, it is well defined and easy to follow.

The main complications to the crossing are the high elevation and the chance of snow. The pass is usually snowbound from mid-December to late February, but snow can block the pass at any time of year. During the main trekking months you can expect to walk for several hours on a snowy trail that has been packed down by hundreds of boots. When there is deep new snow, the crossing becomes difficult – often impossible. It then becomes necessary to retreat back to Manang, or to wait a day or two until the snow has consolidated and the yaks have forged a trail. Should the weather suddenly deteriorate on your way up to the pass, it may be better to retreat back to Phedi and wait for conditions to improve rather than risk the crossing.

From High Camp the trail climbs and climbs, traversing in and out of canyons formed by a maze of moraines. Poles mark the trail when it's under snow. About 45 minutes above High Camp you pass the tiny seasonal Yakawa Thorung Ri teashop at 5030m. It takes three to five hours to climb from Thorung Phedi to the pass, but the altitude and the many false summits mean the climb seems to go on forever. A set of prayer flags indicates you are 15 minutes from the pass.

The wide **Thorung La** (N 28°47.614', E 83°56.336'), with its traditional chorten, prayer flags and stone cairn, is at an elevation of 5416m. The views from the trail, and from the pass itself, are outstanding. You can see the long Great Barrier ridge, which separates the drier, Tibet-like region of Manang from the rest of Nepal, as well as (to the south) the Annapurnas, Gangapurna and the heavily glaciated peak of Khatung Kang (6484m). The barren Kali Gandaki Valley is far below you to the west, and the 6481m rock peak of Yakgawa Kang (also known as Thorungtse) lies to the north. A sign congratulates you for making it to one of the world's highest trekking passes and the creaking and crashing of glaciers makes for an eerie soundtrack. Amazingly, there's a teashop here, the **Thorung Top Teashop** (with equally amazing prices – Rs 130 for black tea), on what feels like the roof of the world.

In many ways the descent (more than 1600m in about four hours) from the pass is harder than the ascent, especially if you have bad knees. The first section of trail can be over melting snow and some of the traverses can be very slippery, as can the later switchbacks. Sometimes the correct route is not obvious; just remember that you are headed downhill and that Muktinath is on the south side of the valley. During the descent there are excellent views of Dhaulagiri across the valley. Eventually the moraines yield to grassy slopes and the final descent to Muktinath is a pleasant walk along the Jhong Valley.

There are six simple lodges at **Chabarbu** (4190m), about 2¾ hours from the pass. You're only an hour from Muktinath so it's better to rely on these lodges for refreshment rather than accommodation, although you could stay here if you are crossing the pass in the opposite direction. If you are following this route in reverse, it's about 3½ hours from Chabarbu to the pass.

The trail crosses meadows, drops into a deep ravine that marks the start of the Jhong Khola, climbs out and follows a wide trail into **Muktinath** (3800m) and its large walled temple complex. There is no accommodation at the temple; for that you'll have to continue for 10 minutes to **Ranipauwa** (3710m). There's plenty to explore in Muktinath, so it's a good place to rest up after today's exertions!

Ranipauwa is the site of a large rest house for pilgrims (Ranipauwa means 'Queen's Hostel') and a host of hotels and *bhattis* that are often crowded with Indian pilgrims and foreign tourists. The Shree Muktinath Hotel, Hotel Mona Lisa and

ANNAPURNA REGION ANNAPURNA CIRCUIT TREK

MUKTINATH SHRINES & PILGRIMS

The temple and the religious shrines of **Muktinath** are a 15-minute walk above Ranipau-wa. For both Hindus and Buddhists the compound constitutes the Nepal Himalaya's most important pilgrimage site (see www.muktinath.org for more information on the shrines).

As you enter the walled complex, lined by Tibetan-style prayer wheels, you pass the Gompa Sambha (First Monastery) on the left and then a Shiva Temple ringed by four shrines. The focal point of the complex is the pool and its 108 brass waterspouts (108 is a sacred number in Tibetan Buddhism), cast in the shape of cows' heads, which pour forth sacred water. Hindu pilgrims bathe in the frigid waters and visit the attached Vishnu Temple, which houses images of Vishnu and Lakshmi to the right and Saraswati (Soosti or Bumi) to the left. Vishnu is worshipped here as Muktinath, the Lord of Salvation, while Buddhists associate the deity with Chenresig, the Tibetan bodhisattva of compassion (yes, it's complicated).

To the left is the Buddhist Marme Lhakhang, whose central image is of Guru Rinpoche (Padmasambhava), here holding a Hindu-style trident instead of his normal staff. Buddhists believe that the guru visited Muktinath in the 8th century. Hindus associate the Bön-influenced deity Sengye Droma (to the left) with their demon god Narsingha.

A short walk past a collection of chortens is the Dhola Mebar Gompa, or Jwalamai (Goddess of Fire) Temple, where a holy flame of natural gas burns behind a grill just above a spring, whose sacred water pours through a cow's head spout. This auspicious combination of earth, fire and water is responsible for the religious importance of Muktinath. Take your shoes off before entering the temple. For a Rs 10 donation the nun will light a butter lamp for your safe return trek.

You will encounter many Nepali and Indian pilgrims on the trail from Jomsom, on foot, horseback or, increasingly, in planes, jeeps and motorcycles. The most colourful pilgrims are the ascetic sadhus who make the trek carrying little more than a blanket and a trident (a symbol of Shiva). A small donation to these holy men is not out of place. They are Shaivite mystics on a pilgrimage that, more often than not, began thousands of kilometres away in the steamy jungles of India.

friendly **Hotel North Pole** (☑ 9847670336; r with/without bathroom Rs 300/200) are all recommended. The funky **Hotel Bob Marley** (☑ 9857650097; r Rs 200) in the east of town is an oasis of good food and dub reggae, where the share bathrooms feature solar hot water and soothing pebble-floor showers.

In the middle of town there's a police checkpost (you'll need to register) and an **ACAP visitor centre** (⊘ 6am-noon & 2-6pm summer; 8am-noon & 2-5pm winter), the latter with a safe drinking water station (Rs 50 per litre). Local women sell excellent yak-hair scarves and blankets on the main street.

It's easy to walk from Ranipauwa to Jomsom (or even Marpha) in a day, but it's well worth taking some time to enjoy the area around Muktinath, before descending to overnight in the medieval village of Kagbeni. Another option is to catch one of the crammed-to-full 'pilgrimage' jeeps down to Jomsom from the Ranipauwa jeep stand.

SIDE TRIP: JHONG
3 HOURS / 190M ASCENT / 190M DESCENT

From Ranipauwa you can make a fine half-day hike to the little-visited villages and monasteries on the north bank of the Jhong Khola. Traditionally part of Mustang and long off-limits, these charming villages can be visited without a permit.

From the red-walled gate at the eastern end of Ranipauwa, follow the signed trail leading down past the red-walled Gargen Chhyoling Nunnery (you'll see a second nunnery below you to the left). Descend to cross a bridge to join a trail that winds down from the Thorung La. Take the left path to **Chhyonkhar Gompa** (Chhokor; 3680m), an atmospheric 200-year-old Tantric monastery. At the end of the lovely village, branch right towards three chortens, descend to cross the bridge over the Jhong Chanba Khola and continue along the ridge to **Jhong** (Dzong; 3580m), the former capital of the region. The views over the village to Muktinath, Dhaulagiri and the top of Nilgiri peak are superb. Drop down to the village past mani walls and climb the hilltop to the ruined 14th-century Rabgyel Tse fort, which names the village (*jhong* means 'fortress'). The 16th-century Sakyapa-school Chode Shedrup Choephel Ling Monastery here is worth a look if it's open. If you want to stay in Jhong, the Milan Guest House offers a simple alternative to staying in busy Ranipauwa.

It's possible to continue down the north side of the valley as far as Putak but to continue further along this trail to Kagbeni (three hours) you need a restricted-area permit (check with the ACAP office in Ranipauwa to see if this has changed). Return to Muktinath from Jhong by heading southeast to the top of town and dropping steeply past fields to cross the river on two wooden bridges. The trail isn't always clear so you'll have to ask for directions. Climb to the lovely village of **Purang** and then follow the red dots that lead through the village, past three chortens en route to Muktinath. An alternative trail descends from Jhong directly to Jharkot, across the Jhong Khola.

Day 11: Ranipauwa to Kagbeni

2½–3 HOURS / 870M DESCENT

From Ranipauwa follow the road down the steep, barren hillside. You soon get spectacular views down onto **Jharkot** (3500m), perched on a bluff 20 minutes from Ranipauwa. With its picturesque *kani*, large **gompa** (admission Rs 100) and attached Tibetan medical institute, the impressive fortress-like village (*kot* means 'fort' in Nepali) is well worth exploring, and many trekkers suggest staying here instead of busy Ranipauwa. The two life-sized clay guardians just below the gompa are a reminder that the region's pre-Buddhist animist past is far from dead. You can follow the kora (pilgrim path) around the monastery for views across the valley to the abandoned Buddhist caves of **Myabrak**. The comfortable New Hotel Plaza and the simple, friendly Hotel Sonam are in the centre of town. The Prakash Hotel cooks with solar energy, while the Himali Hotel, just above the village, offers solar-heated rooms. Across the valley to the east you can see the villages of Jhong, Purang and Chhyonkhar.

The walk from Jharkot down to **Khingar** (3400m) is a delightful stroll among meadows and fruit trees, though road traffic is increasingly taking its toll. If you're coming from Jomsom or Kagbeni, Khingar has several roadside teahouses where you can take a break from the stiff climb.

Eventually the trail makes a descent down the Jhong Valley, short-cutting the winding loops made by the road. Along this section you'll see hundreds of cairns erected by pilgrims to honour their departed ancestors, while across the valley you can see the ruins of Phudzeling, a settlement that dates back three millennia.

Below you is the green oasis of **Kagbeni** (2840m), at the junction of the Jhong Khola and the Kali Gandaki. This upper section of the Kali Gandaki Valley is the traditional home of the Baragaunle – the people of the '12 villages'. They are of Tibetan ancestry and practise a kind of Tibetan Buddhism that has been influenced by ancient animistic and pre-Buddhist Bönpo rituals.

KAGBENI

Kagbeni (or Kag) still feels like a medieval village, with its closely packed mud houses, dark tunnels and alleys, imposing chortens and a large, ochre-coloured gompa perched above the town. Situated at an auspicious river confluence, it is also the gateway to upper Mustang. This is the furthest north you can venture without a restricted-area permit.

The large but rather bland Hotel Dragon sits on the Muktinath trail above town and boasts splendid views. The trail enters Kagbeni proper at the Nilgiri View Lodge at the southern end of town. Follow the flagstone path to the large 17th-century Tibetan-style chorten, with its fine interior mandalas. Stay on the flagstones past the oddly familiar red-and-yellow trim of YacDonalds Restaurant and cross the footbridge across the Jhong Khola. The flagstones continue to the Dancing Yak and venerable Red House, then lead through two tunnels to a row of prayer wheels, the simple Hotel Star and the **ACAP office** (⊘7am-5pm) that administers upper Mustang. Gaze wistfully into Mustang with a cold beer or espresso coffee in the incongruous Cafe Applebees opposite ACAP. As you head back to the chorten, look for the clay 'Meme' (Grandfather), the town's pre-Buddhist protector, complete with erect phallus. The spirit traps and goat heads that adorn the nearby doorways certainly add to the spooky animist feel.

Kagbeni has over a dozen lodges. All offer wi-fi but it is painfully slow. The **New Asia Trekkers Home** (📞9847680504; r with/without bathroom Rs 300/150) has fine views from the back rooms. Another good choice is the **Hotel Shangrila** (r with/without bathroom Rs 400/200), where you can join your porters in the cosy kitchen (the 'potatoes fried in sesame seeds with sauce and veg' is recommended). Both places are by the central chorten.

With its private 350-year-old chapel and Buddhist murals in the dining room, the **Red House** (📞993694011; r Rs 300-500) is probably the most interesting accommodation option, though the rooms themselves vary. The **New Annapurna Lodge** (📞993691019; s/d Rs 150/300) at the far southern end of town has comfortable rooms with pine furniture, decent mattresses and Western toilets, plus Indian food and real coffee.

If you arrive early enough, pay a visit to the impressive red-walled **Kagchode Thubten Sampheling Gompa** (admission Rs 100; ⊙6am-6pm), a Sakyapa-school monastery founded in 1429. The main hall holds some fine festival masks and *kangling* (trumpets), as well as a 500-year-old text written in gold ink.

For a taste of forbidden Mustang, cross the Kali Gandaki over the bridge in the southwest of town (follow the trail from the Hotel Himalaya) and hike an hour north out to the village of **Tiri** on the west bank of the valley. Above Tiri is the Sumdu Choeden Gompa (David Snellgrove's 'Tingri Gompa'), whose entrance is guarded by fine slate carvings of the Four Guardian Kings. The central statue is of Guru Rinpoche flanked by three turbaned kings. No restricted-area permits are required on this side of the valley as far as Tiri.

For a much more strenuous day hike, take the scary-looking, almost vertical trail that zigzags straight up the cliff west of Kagbeni to the Sher Dhak viewpoint. The views of Yakgawa Kang, Tilicho Peak and others are awesome, but it's a very strenuous hike.

For details of the trek from Kagbeni to Lo Manthang, see the Mustang trek (p184).

ALTERNATIVE ROUTE: RANIPAUWA TO JOMSOM VIA LUBRA

5 HOURS / 150M ASCENT / 1190M DESCENT

If you are headed directly from Muktinath back to Jomsom along the road, it's an easy three-to-four-hour downhill walk that can become tedious if there is a strong headwind.

An interesting and challenging alternative route is via the traditional village of **Lubra**, hidden in the side valley of the Panga Khola. Lubra has managed to preserve a pocket of Bön religion since the 12th century and still boasts two Bön monasteries, one in the centre and the other 15 minutes above town. The trail to Lubra (two to three hours) branches off the main road just below Ranipauwa, near the Hotel Dream House and beside the jeep stand. Go through the rock quarry following blue-and-white blazes and signs to Lubra. The trail climbs over a couple of ridges to a prayer-flagged highpoint, **Dhangladanda** (3830m) before dropping into the Panga Khola. You cross the river on a suspension bridge and then the trail descends to the river bed for the final walk into Lubra. The **Yung Drung Phuntsokling (Bön) monastery** (admission Rs 100) in the centre of town is worth a look. The Dakar Lodge & Restaurant can provide basic lodging and daal bhaat.

High river levels often close this route in May and June. The exact route depends on river levels and can be hard to discern, so it's a good idea to take a guide or get advice from locals. From Lubra the trail continues down the valley, crossing back to the north bank on a suspension bridge, before dropping to the river bed. After 90 minutes the trail joins the Jomsom road near Eklai Bhatti.

Day 12: Kagbeni to Jomsom

2½–3½ HOURS / 180M DESCENT / 50M ASCENT

Get an early start from Kagbeni to avoid the winds that whistle up the valley after about 11am. An interesting alternative to the road between Jomsom and Syang is the scenic detour via the east bank. It's also possible to continue through Jomsom to stay in the atmospheric village of Marpha.

From Kagbeni the trail quickly joins the road from Muktinath and continues through desert scenery to Chhancha Lhumba, better known as Eklai Bhatti ('alone

---

ⓘ WARNING

If you bus or fly directly to Jomsom, you are better off overnighting first in Marpha and then Kagbeni, as a minimum, to help acclimatisation before ascending to Muktinath. Don't even consider flying in to Jomsom and then tackling the Thorung La.

Annapurna Circuit Trek Day 12-15

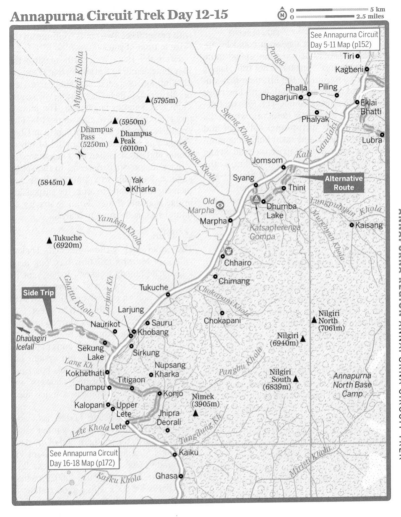

hotel'), at 2830m. Despite its name, several lodges offer lunch and a chance to get out of the wind. A rough alternative west-bank route from Kagbeni via Piling/Pagling joins the road here on a suspension bridge.

Just past a walled tree plantation, the trail crosses the Panga Khola, where there's a side trail leading to the Bön village of Lubra. The trail continues to follow the road through the stony river valley, eventually short-cutting along the river-bed to reach the entrance to Jomsom. The village sustained a fair amount of damage in the 2015 earthquake, but most infrastructure is intact.

The trail passes the school to enter the narrow main street of **Old Jomsom**. Continue past local inns and shops to the now restored bridge across the Kali Gandaki, where you'll find the side trail to Thini, Thak Khola Lodge and the post office.

The trail continues south down the west bank, past the hospital and the compound of the Army School of Mountain Warfare. The camouflaged soldiers jogging in the mornings are a surreal sight in this remote location. Pass the bank to enter the main drag of new Jomsom. See p194 for further details of Jomson.

Day 13: Jomsom to Marpha

1–1½ HOURS / 80M ASCENT / 160M DESCENT

This is a very short day, so it could be appended to Day 12 or you could spend more time exploring Marpha. The trail leaves southern Jomsom by the Mustang Eco Museum and follows the road over a low ridge to cross the Syang Khola. The foot trail detours right to **Syang** (2800m), where the interesting and picturesque old town and large Dechenling and Tashi Lhakhang monasteries are on a ridge above the road. Syang is one of the Panch Gaon ('five villages'; the others are Marpha, Chhairo, Chimang and Thini) that give the region its name.

At the southern end of Syang, rejoin the road and follow it all the way to **Marpha**, crossing the Pankya Khola to enter at the northern end of town.

ALTERNATIVE ROUTE: JOMSOM TO MARPHA VIA THE EAST BANK

2–3 HOURS / 190M ASCENT / 250M DESCENT

The interesting east-bank footpath from Jomsom to Syang, via Katsapterenga Gompa and Thini, requires a bit more time and effort than the direct west-bank route (figure on an extra two hours' walking), but it avoids the road and offers some excellent, little-seen views.

From the bridge dividing old and new Jomsom, take the signed trail southwest to **Thini** (2860m), a 30-minute walk past barley fields (both the high and low trail lead to the village). Thini is the oldest village in the valley and boasts an old gompa above the town's archery ground. Take a right opposite the archery ground (the trail directly ahead leads to Tilicho) and drop down to cross the Lungpuhyun Khola, climb the other side and pass by the hilltop ruins of Gharab Dzong, built by local King Thing Migchen as the region's original settlement.

Contour around the hillside past a house to **Dhumba Lake** (2830m; one hour) lined with prayer flags. Two paths continue up the ridge in front of you.

From the ridge it's worth making the 15-minute detour to **Katsapterenga Gompa** (2920m) for its spectacular 360-degree view of Nilgiri peak, Tilicho Pass, Syang village and Thini and Jomsom below you. The monastery is named after five clay statues (the Five Treasures) brought here from Samye in Tibet. The gompa is home to a handful of novice monks and can be visited for a donation.

Back at the ridge, descend to the south, angling diagonally to Dhumba village and then curving around to cross the suspension bridge opposite Syang. From Syang it's 30 minutes along the road to Marpha.

MARPHA

The large and well-maintained Thakali village of **Marpha** (2680m) has long been a favourite among trekkers. It has kept its traditional narrow paved alleys and passageways and an extensive drainage system flows under the flagstone-paved street. Fortunately the road bypasses Marpha and has not destroyed the atmosphere of the town. Impressive *kanis* mark both ends of town.

In Marpha, the Thakali inn system has reached its apex and most hotels boast private bathrooms, gas-heated showers and extensive menus. Marpha is a much nicer place to stay than Jomsom.

The central Dhaulagiri Lodge has elaborately carved windows and cosy inner courtyards. Towards the southern end of town are the Hotel Marpha Palace, Hotel Mount Villa, Paradise Guest House, and the excellent **Neeru Guest House** (☑069-400029; r without bathroom Rs 300-500), with a good restaurant and decent rooms in the lower courtyard.

Other facilities in Marpha include bookshops, a shoe-repair facility, a safe drinking

VISHNU IN STONE

Traders the length of the Kali Gandaki Valley will offer to sell you saligrams. These are black stones that, when broken open, reveal the fossilised remains of prehistoric ammonites that lived here more than 140 million years ago, when the ancient Tethys Sea covered the region. You might find some saligrams yourself along the riverbed near Jomsom, although you can always buy them from the traders – and then curse yourself all the way back to Pokhara for carrying a backpack full of rocks. Hindu pilgrims purchase these ammonites because they believe them to be manifestations of the god Vishnu, who was turned to stone by the beautiful and virtuous Vrinda after he tried to seduce her. Devotees believe that saligrams bestow wealth, forgiveness, health and happiness. If nothing else, it's pretty cool to hold something that was alive before the Himalaya even existed.

ANNAPURNA CIRCUIT – THE KALI GANDAKI SECTION

The trek down the Kali Gandaki from Jomsom to Tatopani is currently in a state of flux owing to the road. Jeeps and buses now shuttle up and down the valley, causing some trekkers to dismiss this section of the trek as 'over'. Certainly far fewer trekkers walk *up* the valley compared to a few years back. Some trekkers end their trek in Jomsom and fly, jeep or bus back to Pokhara.

However, there are still many reasons to trek down the Kali Gandaki. The network of alternative trails described in this section takes you away from the road and in fact the new routes via Katsapterenga Gompa, Chimang village and Titi Lake offer some of the prettiest landscapes in the valley. The superlative mountain views are still here, of course, as are the region's excellent lodges and picturesque villages.

An alternative to walking this trek as the second part of an Annapurna Circuit is to catch transport up to Jomsom and spend a few days visiting Marpha, Kagbeni and Muktinath, before walking down the valley to Ghasa and Tatopani. From Tatopani you can continue up to Ghorepani for the impressive dawn views from Poon Hill. From there, descend to Naya Pul or continue into the Annapurna Sanctuary. There's no reason why you can't follow this section of the circuit trek (as far as Muktinath) in the opposite direction.

water station (inside the Yak bookshop) and a moneychanger. Pop into the central Bhakti Shop for a taste of the local apple cider, dried fruit and good conversation, courtesy of the owner Bhakti Hirachan. Locally produced apple cider and fruit preserves are available in both Marpha and Tukuche, along with apple, apricot and peach *rakshi* (fortified rice wine).

Marpha's large, Nyingma **Samtenling Gompa (Tashi Lhakhang)** was renovated and enlarged in 1996; as in Tengboche (in the Everest region), the Mani Rimdu festival is celebrated here in the autumn.

In 1899 the Japanese explorer Ekai Kawaguchi (the first outsider to visit Marpha) stayed for three months in the house of the local *subba* (customs/tax officer), which still boasts its original woodcarvings, at the southern end of town. For an excellent account of Kawaguchi's amazing travels through Nepal and Tibet read Scott Berry's book *A Stranger in Tibet*.

You can take in the views of the town from the natural stone chorten on the hillside to the north, or continue over the ridge to the original settlement of Old Marpha. Lodge owners can advise on the day hike to Yak Kharka, which is also the route taken by expeditions headed to Dhaulagiri and the Hidden Valley, via the 5250m Dhampus Pass.

Day 14: Marpha to Larjung

3–4 HOURS / 200M ASCENT / 310M DESCENT

Head south through Marpha's entrance *kani,* past a long whitewashed mani wall

and a blacksmith settlement to Om's Home Marpha, a clean hotel with excellent food and a range of accommodation.

Five minutes past the Shangrila Hotel is the turn-off and bridge to Chhairo and Chimang. The road continues south for 90 minutes directly to Tukuche but it's well worth taking the alternative east-bank trail via Chhairo and Chimang (two hours). You'll avoid the road traffic and get great views of Dhaulagiri en route.

Across the bridge on the east side of the river, **Chhairo** is a Tibetan refugee settlement of around 40 houses. The 300-year-old Chhairo Gompa is being restored under the auspices of Restoration Works International (www.restorationworksinternational.org/nepal.php). The Guru Rinpoche Lhakhang ,in particular, has some fine old statues, thangkas and murals.

Continue past mani walls and pine groves to Chhairo village, with its school and lovely old chorten. Follow the signs left to Chimang, climb to a meadow and a small waterfall and continue uphill, curving around fields to the traditional village of **Chimang** (2870m; 1¼ hours), perched on a ridge. The little-visited village offers some of the best views you'll get of Dhaulagiri.

Descend steps on the far side of the ridge and keep to the right of the Chimang Khola, crossing a bridge to rejoin the main lower trail. Pass a small village to arrive at a bridge over the Kali Gandaki. With some extra time, you could explore the village of Chokapani, high on the east bank and accessible on a

ANNAPURNA REGION ANNAPURNA CIRCUIT TREK

ⓘ WINDY TRAILS

The flow of air between the peaks of Annapurna and Dhaulagiri creates strong winds that howl up the Kali Gandaki Valley. The breezes blow gently from the north during the early hours of the day, then shift to powerful gusts from the south throughout the late morning and afternoon. If you are headed south anywhere between Kagbeni and Tukuche, make sure you set off early and wear a bandana, a scarf and sunglasses to avoid the dust and sand that kicks up at around 11am.

trail from the bridge. For Tukuche, cross the bridge and walk down the road for 25 minutes. It's possible to continue south down the east bank to the villages of Sauru (two hours) and Sirkung (one hour), crossing the Kali Gandaki on a seasonal bridge (mid-October to mid-April) to Larjung or Tukuche. It will take at least five hours to reach the lodges in Kokhethati. Ask in Chimang or at the ACAP checkpost in Jomsom about the state of this trail.

TUKUCHE

Back on the main road, cross the Thapa Khola and enter the large village of **Tukuche** (2580m), once the valley's most important Thakali village. Tukuche (*tuk* means grain and *che* means flat place) was the meeting place where traders laden with salt and wool from Tibet bartered with traders carrying grain from the south. Many of the town's stone houses once served as salt and grain storehouses.

It's worth spending some time wandering around the town, taking in the fine facades and gompas or paying a visit to the 200-year old complex of the **Tukuche Distillery**, a former customs post, in the south of town. Nuns will let you into the lovely nearby Mahakala Gompa, though the other gompas, including the nearby Rani (Tashi Choling) Gompa are usually locked. Internet (Rs 200 per hour) is available in the Thak Library in the south of town.

Tukuche's dozen hotels are mostly in beautiful old Thakali homes with carved wooden windows, doorways and balconies. The Nepali-Dutch **High Plains Inn** (✆9756703091; www.highplainsinn.com; r with/without bathroom Rs 500/200) at the northern end has everything you want from a

lodge: clean bathrooms, a fireplace, a bakery and real Dutch coffee. The nearby **Yak Hotel** (✆9847638078; s/d without bathroom Rs 100/200) is also good value, offering evening song and dance performances if there are enough guests. Further along, Sherpa Guest House is a cheaper option. The demanding half-day hiking trail to the Yak Kharka pastures branches off from near here.

In the stone-walled village itself the whitewashed **Tukuche Guest House** (✆9741170035; r with/without bathroom Rs 500/400) has an explanation of local history on the wall and a cosy Tibetan-style dining room, with clean rooms around a central courtyard. The nearby **Sunil Guest House** (s/d without bathroom Rs 100/200) has simple rooms around a lovely courtyard of flowers and claims the best apple pie in town.

TUKUCHE TO LARJUNG

From Tukuche the road makes numerous ups and downs to Larjung. It's possible to avoid the road by making short cuts across the riverside gravel bars if the water is low. In 1972 the French adventurer Michel Peissel travelled up the Kali Gandaki in a hovercraft and managed to get this far before he was forced to admit that, yes, it was a silly plan after all.

There are good views of Dhaulagiri and Nilgiri North along this section of the Kali Gandaki Valley, which some claim is the world's deepest, the rationale being that in the 38km between the peaks of Annapurna I and Dhaulagiri I (both above 8000m) the valley floor drops over 5000m.

The three villages of Kanti, Khobang and **Larjung** (2560m) blur into one. Pass the chalet-style **Musk Deer Valley Resort** (r Rs 300-500). To the left of the trail, on a rise overlooking the Kali Gandaki, is a small but charming nunnery, the Makhi Lhakhang, which is the southernmost Tibetan Buddhist temple in the valley. Pass the Sunrise Guest House and Peaceful Lodge, cross the Larjung Khola and branch left to the Himalayan, River Side and Mt Ice View lodges in Larjung village.

The **Larjung Lodge** (✆9847788640; r Rs 300-400, without bathroom 200), at the southern end, is a good choice and may be able to offer information about the trip to the Dhaulagiri Icefall. A safe drinking water station is also here. The most luxurious place in town is the **Lodge Thasang Village** (✆019-446514; www.lodgethasangvillage.com; s/d US$215/250), high on the ridge above Larjung. It accepts walk-ins, but it's best to have a reservation.

There's plenty to explore around Larjung. On the cliffs behind the village are a series of crumbling retreat caves, at the base of which you might see locals practising their archery. You could hike up the hill to the west of Larjung, via the red and green temples of Gau-chan and Taluchan, to Naurikot village, with its Bön monastery and fine views of Dhaulagiri. Lodge owners can give information on the day hike to the Guru Sangpo Cave (associated with Guru Rinpoche) further up the hillside.

ANNAPURNA CIRCUIT TREK DAY 13–18 (KALI GANDAKI) – TIMES

The following are trekking times only; stops are not included.

DAY	SECTION	HOURS
13	Jomsom to Syang	0:40
	Syang to Marpha	1:00
14	Marpha to Tukuche via Chimang	2:30
	Tukuche to Khobang	0:50
	Khobang to Larjung	0:15
15	Larjung to Kokhethati	0:45
	Kokhethati to Titigaon	1:00
	Titigaon to Konjo	0:45
	Konjo to Lete	1:00
	Lete to Ghasa	1:30
16	Ghasa to Eagle's Nest Guest House	0:15
	Eagle's Nest Guest House to Kopchepani	1:50
	Kopchepani to Rupse Chhahara	0:10
	Rupse Chhahara to Dana	1:00
	Dana to Tatopani	1:40
17	Tatopani to Ghar Khola	0:30
	Ghar Khola to Durbin Danda	0:50
	Durbin Danda to Shikha	1:50
	Shikha to Chitre	1:30
	Chitre to Ghorepani	1:00
18	Ghorepani to Ulleri	2:00
	Ulleri to Tikhedhunga	1:15
	Tikhedhunga to Hille	0:15
	Hille to Birethanti	1:40
	Birethanti to Naya Pul	0:30

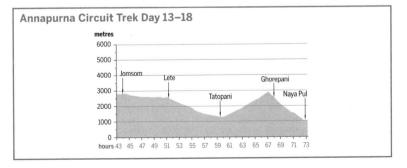

Annapurna Circuit Trek Day 13–18

SIDE TRIP: DHAULAGIRI ICEFALL
8–9 HOURS / 1200M ASCENT / 1200M DESCENT

A two-day side trip up the side of the Kali Gandaki Valley will take you to the foot of the Dhaulagiri Icefall and provide great views of Dhaulagiri I and the Annapurna range. It's a 1200m climb, so it's a bit tough to climb up and back in a single day, but it's still worth going part-way on a day trip. There is no accommodation on this route, so you'd need a tent in order to spend the night.

There are a few potential dangers to this trip: if it's cloudy, route-finding is a problem; there is a danger of altitude sickness, especially if you've taken the bus here; and there are avalanches in, and sometimes near, the icefall itself. The mountaineering route up the icefall is a particularly hazardous climb. In 1969 an avalanche in the icefall killed seven members of the US Dhaulagiri expedition.

The route starts just south of Larjung village, a couple of hundred metres past the suspension bridge on the south side of the wide Ghatta Khola. A small trail signed to the 'Icefall' leads up steeply through the forest then descends through pasture to some herders' huts, with the icefall straight ahead. Take the left path up through pine and rhododendron to a field (take the right branch for Sekung Lake). The trail continues steeply for another hour to a signposted hut that offers fine views (two hours).

The path, in grasslands, is now well defined but extremely steep. You should reach a cairn in another hour and a small basin with yak pastures in a further 30 minutes. There are great views of the Kali Gandaki from Larjung to Lete, the Nilgiris and Annapurna I across the valley and the route up to North Annapurna Base Camp. Cross the basin, keep slightly to the right and climb up to reach some large boulders in a further 45 minutes. The glacier is now immediately below with the icefall beyond.

The return route is the same, although there are a few short cuts. When you get back to the lower huts, cut to the left (north) towards **Sekung Lake** (2725m) for sublime views of the Annapurnas reflected in the calm water. The lake alone is worth a fine short day hike from Larjung.

You can descend to the Ghatta Khola the way you came. Alternatively, head northwest to the head of the stream above Sekung Lake (avoiding the gorge), cross it and swing down the north side of the river valley to the small Bhuturcho Lake, hidden in forests, 40 minutes from Sekung Lake. A trail at the far end of the lake drops down to the Ghatta Khola where you started.

Day 15: Larjung to Ghasa
5–6 HOURS / 200M ASCENT / 760M DESCENT

From Larjung, join the road as it swings into the wide mouth of the Ghatta Khola. The road bridge is a long distance upstream so most locals cut straight across the river on temporary bridges. When the road returns to

---

THE WHITE MOUNTAIN

Dhaulagiri (8167m), the 'White Mountain', was sighted by British surveyors in India in the early 1800s and was mapped by secret Indian surveyors in 1873, but the region remained largely unknown until a Swiss aerial survey in 1949.

The French Annapurna expedition in 1950 had permission to climb either Annapurna or Dhaulagiri but opted for Annapurna after a discouraging reconnaissance of Dhaulagiri. A Swiss party failed in 1953 as did an Argentine group one year later.

After four more expeditions had failed, eight members of a Swiss expedition first reached the summit in 1960. The climb followed a circuitous route around the mountain from Tukuche, over Dhampus Pass and French Col (named after the French Annapurna expedition), to approach the summit from the Northeast Col. The expedition was supplied by a Swiss Pilatus Porter aircraft, the 'Yeti', which landed on the Northeast Col at 5977m after skis were fixed to the undercarriage. Near the end of the expedition the plane crashed near Dhampus Pass and the pilots, including the famous Emil Wick, walked down the mountain to Tukuche.

The peak was climbed again by the Japanese in 1970, the Americans in 1973 and the Italians in 1976. Captain Emil Wick airdropped supplies to the US expedition. Among the delicacies he dropped were two bottles of wine and a live chicken. The sherpas would not allow the chicken to be killed on the mountain, so it became the expedition pet. It was carried, snow-blind and crippled with frostbitten feet, to Marpha, where it finally ended up in the cooking pot.

TRANS-HIMALAYAN TRADE

For centuries, hardy caravans of yaks or goats, led by Tibetans clad in *chubas* (Tibetan woollen cloaks), have criss-crossed the high Himalaya, bringing salt harvested from Tibet's great salt lakes to swap for rice and barley carried up from the Middle Hills of Nepal. Wool, livestock and butter were also exchanged for sugar, tea, spices, tobacco and manufactured goods from India, but the salt-for-grain trade dominated the economy. Twelve major passes link Nepal and Tibet, of which the four easiest are in Mustang, so Tukuche in the Kali Gandaki Valley soon became the main entrepôt for transferring, storing and taxing the trade. The salt trade also took place in Dolpo, filtering south via the villages of Tarakot and Tibrikot. The bulk of the trade in Tibetan wool funnelled through Sikkim's Chumbi Valley to Kalimpong and British India.

This colourful Himalayan trade has almost disappeared over the last half-century, largely because of the effect of political and economic changes in Tibet, but also because Indian salt is now available throughout Nepal at a much lower price than Tibetan salt. Many people in Nepal once suffered from goitres because of the total absence of iodine in their diet. Indian aid programs distributed Indian sea salt (which contains iodine) in a successful effort to prevent goitres, but the Tibetan salt trade suffered because of the artificially low price of Indian salt. The Thakali middlemen of the Kali Gandaki Valley, in particular, grew rich from their monopoly of the salt trade. Over the last 40 years most have turned to agriculture, tourism and other forms of business as the salt trade has dried up.

the bank of the Kali Gandaki, the trail crosses the river on a high suspension footbridge and climbs through fir, juniper and cypress trees to descend to the Earth Home and **Dhaulagiri Icefall Lodge** (☑ 9756703028; s/d Rs 200/300) in **Kokhethati** (45 minutes).

To avoid this section of road altogether, ask in Larjung whether it's possible to cross the Kali Gandaki on seasonal bridges (October to March only) to the east bank and continue downstream through forest to Kokhethati.

A little-used road continues south to Dhampu, crossing the Kali Gandaki to arrive in Kalopani and upper Lete. Far more interesting is the east-bank detour on foot via Titi Lake and Taglung, which is described here.

Ten minutes past Kokhethati, branch left on a tractor path signposted for Titi Lake. A 45-minute gradual climb brings you to Titigaon village, offering fine views ahead to Nilgiri and Annapurna, and back to Dhaulagiri and Tukuche peaks. There is a simple lodge here. Just past Titi a trail branches left to Nupsang Kharka, a high summer pasture that offers fine Dhaulagiri views. Just a minute further on the main trail you pass pretty **Titi Lake** (2670m). Climb for 15 minutes to the crest of a ridge marked by three chortens and offering more fabulous views.

The tractor road makes a large curve below the ridge, so take the footpath that drops to the left, short-cutting to the lovely traditional village of **Konjo** (2590m), 1¾ hours from Kokhethati. The views of Nilgiri peak towering above the village's emerald-green terraces is one to remember. Villagers report sighting Himalayan bears here in September. A short detour leads to the red-roofed Taglung Gompa, on a hillside beside a huge sacred tree. Strange stories of human sacrifice swirl around Konjo village. Villagers tell stories about an ancient custom of releasing a chicken into a cave high above the village. The cave allegedly led to the Manang side and when a Manangi found and ate the chicken, he was then promptly taken to Konjo to be sacrificed. A sheep is allegedly still sacrificed in the cave every July. Luckily chicken isn't on the menu of the village's only teahouse, just daal bhaat... Ask in the village about the steep trail that leads directly up the hillside to Nupsang Kharka and the impressive Poonging ('Lemon Tree' in Thakali) Dhara viewpoint.

From Konjo follow the signs to **Chhayo** (Chhoyo) by descending into the huge floodplain of the Pangbu Khola. A junction here leads south to Jhipra Deorali, but landslides currently block this trail so cross the suspension bridge over the Kali Gandaki to the west bank. Take the right fork for 20 minutes to arrive in Lete, or branch left to join the main road south to Ghasa.

Annapurna Circuit Trek Day 16-18

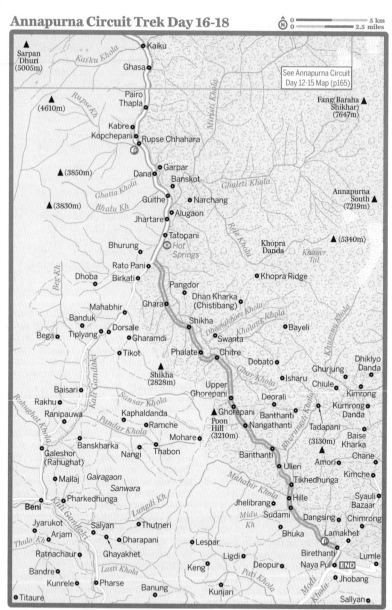

There are well over a dozen roadside lodges in spread-out **Lete** (2480m), including the Lete Eco Guest House and Old Namaste Guest House in the south of town. The upper/northern part of Lete merges into **Ka-**lopani (2530m), which is the village you will come to first if you didn't take the Titi Lake detour. The excellent **Kalopani Guest House** (☏ 019-446518; r Rs 500-1000; @) offers internet access and great food and coffee.

Also in Kalopani are the small Kasturee Cottage and the upmarket See You Lodge.

In Kalopani a signed trail heads 25 minutes up to Dhulu Danda, a 360-degree viewpoint that offers a panorama of peaks: Dhaulagiri, Tukuche Peak, the three Nilgiris, Fang and Annapurna I. If you have some time to kill in Kalopani, check to see if the **Cultural Thakali Museum** (admission Rs 50; ⊙ 6am-6pm) is open.

Heading south from Lete, drop past the Namaste Lodge to cross the Lete Khola. Follow the red-and-white blazed trail to avoid much of the road. The trail drops to the road near the neglected Green Forest Rest House in Ghumaune, passes the Bimala Hotel in Kaiku at 2180m, to continue through forests to Ghasa, 1½ hours from Lete.

The village of **Ghasa** (2000m) marks a cultural and ecological milestone. Not only is it the last Thakali village on the trek and the southernmost limit of Tibetan Buddhism, but from here on the mountain pine and birch of the middle valley start to give way to subtropical trees and shrubs. Ghasa has three separate settlements. At the northern end you'll find the Florida Guest House, National Guest House, the ACAP checkpost and bus station. Lodges in middle Ghasa include the Kali Gandaki Guest House, which doubles as the safe drinking water station. This part of the village has some lovely traditional touches, including thatched dovecotes and cow's-head waterspouts. The **Eagle's Nest Guest House** (☑ 9857650101; dm Rs 100, r Rs 700, without bathroom Rs 200-300), 15 minutes south of the main village, has the nicest location in Ghasa, with bright en suite rooms and a pleasant garden.

Day 16: Ghasa to Tatopani

4½–5½ HOURS / 90M ASCENT / 900M DESCENT

From Ghasa you can avoid the road by crossing the suspension footbridge just south of the Eagle's Nest Guest House and follow the trail down the eastern side of the valley. This mule trail climbs the rocky cliffside to a ridge, leaving Mustang district, to make a long descent on steps past a few neglected teahouses at Pairo Thapala to a bridge at Kopchepani (90 minutes). Don't cross the bridge over the Kali Gandaki to the road; instead follow the trail as it zigzags uphill to a plateau of fields with views across the valley to the large Rupse Chhahara ('Beautiful Waterfall'). The trail then descends down a staircase to a bridge across to Dana (for good

accommodation), or you can continue on the east bank through Garpar, passing the hydro station, climbing to Banskot and descending to Narchyang Besi to cross the bridge just before Tatopani (four to five hours).

Tatopani (1190m) means 'hot water' in Nepali and the village gains its name from the **hot springs** (Rs 100; ⊙ 5am-9pm) below the village. There are two stone pools, alternately filled and cleaned, and a bar and restaurant. The water is surprisingly hot at around 37°C! Be sure to bring a bathing costume (there's little privacy) and don't pollute these pools by using soap in them. The village sits on a shelf above the hot springs and road.

Tatopani has long been a favourite stop with weary trekkers and the new road has brought many more road travellers. The food at **Dhaulagiri Lodge** (☑ 9741194872; r Rs 500, without bathroom Rs 200-250) deservedly gets rave reviews and the rooms are in a lush garden of banana and orange trees. The nearby concrete **Himalaya Lodge** (☑ 993695006; s/d Rs 200/250, r without bathroom Rs 100) is another good bet, with a bakery. It can even change money and take credit cards. Other options include the Old Kamala and the Trekkers Lodge at the northern end of town. There's a TIMS checkpost at the southern end.

Day 17: Tatopani to Ghorepani

6–7 HOURS / 1750M ASCENT / 140M DESCENT

From Tatopani you may want to take a bus down to Beni and Pokhara. Alternatively, make the big ascent (the biggest of the Annapurna Circuit!) to Ghorepani, and possibly continue to Khopra Ridge or the Annapurna Sanctuary.

Head south for 30 minutes, leaving the road to cross the Kali Gandaki. Just before the bridge across the Ghar Khola a trail veers left for Paudwar and Khopra Ridge. This long, steep route is best done in the reverse direction: descending from Khopra Ridge to overnight in a homestay in Paudwar and finally soak in the spring at Tatopani. Follow the trail to Ghorepani and cross the Ghar Khola. The peak to the north is Nilgiri South (6839m). At Ghar Khola village the trail branches left up a series of stairs.

A steep ascent of 380m, criss-crossing a road, leads to the Shantosh Top Hill Lodge, atop a rocky spur called **Durbin Danda** (1555m). From here on the valley opens up and you ascend through terraced fields, on and off the road, to the Nice Breeze Restaurant at the top of **Ghara** (1780m; 2¼ hours). The trail makes a gentle ascent across a landslide area to the first houses of **Shikha** (3¼ hours), a large and prosperous Magar village that marks the halfway stage, if you can't face the full climb today. Cross a stream and climb to Shikha's stone-paved main street. The **Moonlight Guesthouse** (☏ 9746702345; r with/without bathroom Rs 500/200) is a great choice in Sikha, with hot showers and good views. Keep climbing for 15 minutes past the See You Lodge and an ACAP checkpoint to the **Serendipity Guest House** (r Rs 200), in a quiet location with a pleasant garden and helpful owners. From here it's another 2½ hours to Ghorepani.

Keep climbing to **Phalate** (2390m), where the trail to Swanta and Khopra Ridge (p133) heads north, and then to **Chitre** (2420m; 4½ hours). There are several trail junctions, but the correct trail almost invariably leads uphill. Lodges in Chitre include the large New Dhaulagiri View Hotel with sunny garden seating and the New Annapurna View at the top of the village.

From Chitre the trail makes a steep ascent for an hour through lovely rhododendron and magnolia forests, interspersed with a few shepherds' huts and pastures, to reach the first lodges of Ghorepani (p130).

Day 18: Ghorepani to Naya Pul

6–7 HOURS / 1900M DESCENT

After an early-morning visit to Poon Hill (p130), you can make the long descent on endless stone staircases to Naya Pul (follow Day 1 and 2 of the Annapurna Panorama trek in reverse; see p129), or you can cut across to Tadapani to link up with the Annapurna Sanctuary trek (see Day 3 and Day 4 of the Annapurna Panorama trek, p131).

NAR-PHU

Closed to tourism until 2002, the Nar and Phu Valleys are far removed in both time and space from the neighbouring Annapurna Circuit. As you branch north up the Nar Valley, the flood of trekkers passing through Manang turns to a tiny trickle. Yak herding and agriculture remain the mainstays of the economy, rather than tourism, and the traditional stone-walled villages seem to have maintained a lifestyle untouched for centuries.

The Nar and Phu Valleys were briefly cut off from the outside world again following the 2015 earthquake, when landslides blocked the main trails. Access has now been restored but we researched this trek shortly before the disaster and the full extent of damage in this remote region is still not clear. It's important to seek local advice on the trails before you set off. Make sure that food and accommodation will be available at your planned overnight stops unless you are on a completely self-sufficient camping trek.

The trek takes you up narrow gorges to medieval villages, past impressive chortens, herds of blue sheep and spectacular cliffside trails and over one of the region's highest trekking passes. You'll pass abandoned settlements once used by Khampa rebels and teams of mountaineers headed to the popular peaks of Himlung, Kang Guru and Ratna Chuli.

The trek is an excellent adventurous add-on to a visit to the Manang region or the Manaslu trek. After Nar-Phu you could even continue to Jomsom, either over the Thorung La or, if you are properly equipped, via Tilicho Lake and Meso Kanto La, making full use of your camping crew.

ⓘ Planning

WHEN TO TREK

September and October are the best months for this trek. The Kang La pass is normally closed in January and February, and crossing this pass is not advisable in spring due to the risk of avalanches. You can expect heavy snow on the pass any time between November and May.

Nar and Phu are in the Himalayan rain shadow so a monsoon trek is feasible, though not completely rain-free. You'll lose some mountain views at this time and the approach routes from Besi Sahar will be full of leeches, but you could catch the horse-riding and archery festivals that bring a festive air to the valleys in June and July.

MAPS

Nepa Maps' 1:60,000 *Naar-Phu*, by Robin Boustead, covers the region well. General Annapurna maps such as the National Geographic Annapurna map (1:135,000) show the region in less detail.

BOOKS

Cloud Dwellers of the Himalayas (Time Life, 1982) by Windsor Chorten, with contributions from famed anthropologist Christoph von Fürer-Haimendorf, is a well-written portrait of Nar-Phu with fine photos, in the manner of an extended *National Geographic* article. You'll have to track the book down as it's out of print.

David Snellgrove's *Himalayan Pilgrimage* and Tilman's *Nepal Himalaya* also touch briefly on Nar and Phu.

ACCOMMODATION & SHOPPING

There are simple lodges and homestays at Meta, Nar and Phu where you can get a bed and daal bhaat. ACAP has established camp sites and bare wooden shelters (used by porters and cooking crews) at Dharamsala, Khyang, Phu, Nar Phedi and Kang La Phedi. You may have to be self-sufficient for food in Khyang and Nar Phedi and between Nar and Ngawal.

If you don't mind long days, it's just about feasible to do the trek without a tent and a stove but it's risky if the beds in Meta or Phu fill up. You are better off being self-sufficient with tents and a cooking crew.

RESOURCES

ACAP (www.ntnc.org.np) administers tourism and community development programs in the two valleys and may be able to help with information. **Destination Manang** (www.destination-manang.com) also has some information.

PERMITS & REGULATIONS

You need a restricted-area trekking permit to trek in Nar-Phu. This costs US$90 for a week during the peak season of September to November, or US$75 between December and August. The permit must be arranged through a registered trekking company and the trek must comprise at least two trekkers (not counting support staff). The police check at Koto is the only place you'll need to produce this permit.

You need to buy an ACAP permit (Rs 2000) in Kathmandu, Pokhara or Besi Sahar to get to and from the trailheads along the Annapurna Circuit.

ℹ Getting There & Away

See Days 1 to 4 of the Annapurna Circuit (p144) trek for details of trekking from Besi Sahar to Koto. Walking from Ngawal back to Besi Sahar takes from four days, via Chame and Tal. For details of the trail follow Days 1 to 6 of the Annapurna Circuit trek in reverse. A return trip from Kathmandu takes around 14 days.

Nepal Airlines schedules Pokhara to Hongde flights (US$115) in the trekking season, though the airline is notoriously unreliable and flights usually operate when full rather than to schedule. Hongde is at 3420m, so it makes sense to hike down to Chame (2710m) on your first day to acclimatise.

Nar-Phu Trek

Duration 7 days

Max Elevation 5320m

Difficulty Medium to hard

Season May to October

Start Koto

Finish Ngawal

Permits ACAP, TIMS, restricted-area permit

Summary This excellent add-on to the Annapurna Circuit offers medieval villages, gorges and 7000m peaks in a spectacular Tibetan enclave, opened only since 2002.

🏃 The Trek

Day 1: Koto to Dharamsala

4½ HOURS / 700M ASCENT / 20M DESCENT

Nar-Phu has long been considered a *baeyul,* or 'hidden land', and even these days most Annapurna trekkers stride straight past the entrance to the valley without even realising it. The trek branches off the Annapurna Circuit at Koto (Qupar). After registering and showing your trekking permit to the police station by the town's exit *kani,* drop steeply down to a suspension bridge and head up on the true right side of the Nar Phu Khola. Much of today's walk is spent in the shade of this deep gorge, which only opens up around Meta. The dense gnarled forests here could form the backdrop to one of Grimm's fairy tales.

The trail makes a short descent to a section chiselled out of the cliff and then hugs the river, until crossing a suspension bridge to the east side (1½ hours). Remember to look back occasionally for views of the Annapurna wall behind you. Cross the side stream of the Seti (Suti) Khola and pass by an **ACAP campsite** that boasts a public toilet. The trail climbs steeply above the river through silent forest into a vertical world of cliffs, pine and bamboo.

As the gorge narrows, the trail hugs the cliff face once more. Cross a side stream and then a second suspension bridge back to the west bank. Five minutes later fill up your water bottle before passing a small cave signposted as the **Hulaki Odar** (Postman Cave; 3060m). After crossing the Phu

Nar-Phu Trek

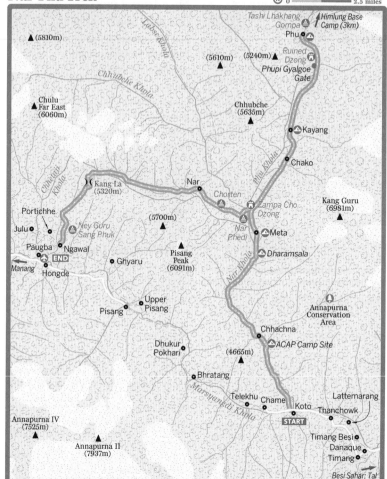

Khola one final time to the eastern bank, consider a one-minute detour downstream to a small but charming riverside hot spring that bubbles from a sulphurous fault line. Thirty minutes later the trail ducks dramatically under a waterfall to arrive at the scrappy ACAP campsite of **Dharamsala** (3220m), 4½ hours from Koto.

Dharamsala is not the nicest of spots and serves as something of a bottleneck for groups heading up and down the valley, so if you're acclimatised after visits to Manang or Manaslu, it's tempting to continue for another 90 minutes to **Meta** (3610m), which offers

far nicer camping. (It's then possible to make it as far as Phu the next day, but again, only if you are acclimatised to elevations of 4000m.) If you've come straight from Besi Sahar, then the elevation gain of almost 1100m in one day is too much to be considered safe, so overnight in Dharamsala.

Day 2: Dharamsala to Khyang

5½ HOURS / 800M ASCENT / 180M DESCENT

From Dharamsala climb past a landslip and a goth to cross a side stream. The trail then veers right, up a side valley, and climbs steeply on switchbacks for 30 minutes, gaining 400m until reaching a white chorten at 3540m. Continue into a wide bowl, past abandoned barley fields to the winter settlement of **Meta** (3610m; N 28°39.329', E 84°14.308'), 90 minutes from Dharamsala.

The spacious campsites here are often used as base camp for climbers tackling 6981m Kang Guru, accessed up the gorge behind Meta. Up among the stone houses of the empty village stands the simple **Kang Garu Hotel** (dm Rs 200, daal bhaat Rs 300), but there are only three simple rooms here and hygiene is not a priority in the kitchen so you might want to consider camping. Villagers from Nar use Meta as a winter settlement and the village remains deserted for the rest of the year.

The next section of trail from Meta to Khyang is far more tortuous than a glance at the map would suggest. Much of your energy is spent crossing a roller-coaster maze of glacial moraines, ascending and descending to cross streams that spill from hidden glaciers high above the cliffs.

Traverse the Meta bowl to reach a chorten on the northern side. You soon come to a trail junction (25 minutes), whose left branch leads to Nar (the monastery and chorten of Nar Phedi are visible below you). Continue right up the main valley and 15 minutes later, by some goths, you'll pass a second junction to Nar; this is the route you'll take on the way back (Day 4). Climb to a chorten at **Jhunam**, a former Khampa settlement at 3640m.

Armed Khampa rebels settled in the Nar-Phu region in the late 1960s after fleeing a failed uprising in Tibet. Their presence created considerable tension, both with the Chinese authorities and also the local residents, and by the 1970s the government had then moved on to camps at Pokhara, Dhorpatan and Kathmandu. The guns they left behind were later confiscated by Maoist rebels.

From Jhunam, descend into a side khola (stream) and climb the glacial moraine on the far side to a chorten (two hours). Listen for the occasional crash of the glacier that tumbles off Kang Guru to the east. A row of chortens guides you past more deserted fields to **Chyakhu** (3800m), another former Khampa settlement. Climb above the village and descend into a small khola; the path splits but both trails meet after a few hundred metres. Descend past birch trees, cross the wooden bridge and grind up another moraine to yet another chorten. The

river marks the border between Nar and Phu. Another drop and then a climb over a moraine gets you to a small pass marked by prayer flags. The Annapurna views behind you are superb and just seem to get bigger the further away you move.

After nearly four hours from Meta, drop down to **Khyang** (3840m), a winter settlement occupied for three months of the year by villagers from Phu. An ACAP campsite and shelter here boast superb mountain views of Pisang Peak (6091m), Annapurna II (7937m), Gyaji Kang (7030m) and Tilje Peak (6530m).

Day 3: Khyang to Phu

3 HOURS / 230M ASCENT

From Khyang you swing into the dry, desert-like gorge of the Phu Khola, inching along on a hair-raising section of trail carved out of the cliff face. Continue along the east side of valley, passing (but not crossing) a wooden bridge below you and then ascending a short staircase past a smooth eroded rock. Keep an eye out for blue sheep grazing on the khaki hillsides. Eventually the S-shaped valley swings to the left, past eroded spires. Two hours from Khyang, the trail switchbacks steeply on a tenuous trail alongside a huge rock spire, crossing one particularly heart-stopping 'bridge' to pass through the **Phupi Gyalgoe gate** and enter the Phu region – surely one of the most spectacular approaches to any Himalayan village. The trail edges along the eroded hillside, past a **ruined dzong** to descend to a collection of chortens beside a bridge. Continue past a mani wall and some caves high on the far cliff, to reach the suspension bridge and campsite just across from the village of **Phu** (4070m).

Phu is an extraordinary village of around 40 households piled up on a bluff at the junction of a side valley. Camp in the stony **ACAP campsite** (per person Rs 100) or on the roof of an unmarked inn at the bottom of town (it's the first house after crossing the bridge). An unmarked homestay in the upper village offers four beds in a simple mud-walled room, with meals eaten in the traditional kitchen. You may have to ask around for the owner Tashi Khandru; look for the multicoloured windows. There are no formal shops in Phu but you can buy supplies like milk powder, jam and biscuits at Tashi's, and will be well fed on porridge, soup and daal bhaat. All supplies are carried here by mule caravans from Koto.

NAR-PHU TREK – TIMES

The following are trekking times only; stops are not included.

SECTION	HOURS
Koto to Dharamsala	4:30
Dharamsala to Meta	1:30
Meta to Khyang	3:45
Khyang to Phu	2:45-3:00
Phu to Nar Phedi	5:30
Nar Phedi to Nar	2:30-3:00
Nar to Kang La Phedi	1:30
Kang La Phedi to Kang La	2:30
Kang La to Ngawal	3:00

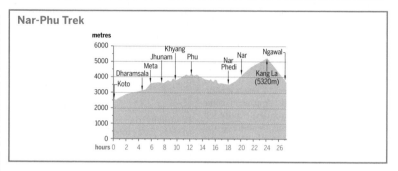

Nar-Phu Trek

Devote some time to exploring the fascinating village. The deserted and crumbling uppermost section is home to the original fortified residence. Phu means 'Head of the Valley' and the 6364m pyramid-shaped peak to the north is named Bhrikuti after the Nepali wife of Tibetan King Songtsen Gampo; beyond is Tibet. Phu village is snowbound and almost completely deserted in winter (December to March).

Nar-Phu's most important monastery is the **Tashi Lhakhang Gompa** (4150m), crowning a hillside cut by two rivers to the north of town. One of the resident *ani* (nuns) will show you around the main prayer hall; it's adorned with some fine ceremonial trumpets and photos of the current Karmapa (the monastery was founded by the 10th Karmapa). Look for the festival mask of the god Dorje Drolo. There's no entry fee so leave a donation. Other rooms include the quarters of lama Karma Sonam Rinpoche, a famous *amchi* (traditional healer) who fled Tibet with the Dalai Lama and who now lives in Kathmandu. Also here is a library, protector chapel and a *menkhang*

(apothecary), lined with jars of herbs, potions and antibiotics. A fine kora leads up past blue painted mani stones and back down to the lama's helipad, offering excellent views of Phu.

The smaller Samtenling Gompa above the village is normally closed. There are more good village views from the bluff to the south of the village, up the steep goat track that leads to Ubi village.

If you have budgeted an extra day in Phu (highly recommended), consider a hike up to either the summer pastures of Ngoru Kharka or to Himlung Base Camp. For views of Himlung (7125m) you can follow the yak trail onto the moraine but for base camp itself (three hours) follow the streamside trail that squeezes between the hillside and the moraine.

Day 4: Phu to Nar Phedi

5½ HOURS / 250M ASCENT / 770M DESCENT
From Phu retrace your steps past Khyang, Chyarkha and Jhunam to the **junction**, 45 minutes past Jhunam, where the trail branches right to Nar.

The trail then drops past fantastically eroded hoodoos, over sandy gullies connected by bridge-like platforms. The entire mountainside feels like it's about to collapse at any moment. Look for the ruined Zampa Cho Dzong (*zampa* is Tibetan for 'bridge') on the hill to the right. Just below are the twin bridges that cross the 80m-deep slot canyon of the Dho Khola. Many maps use the modern name Mahendra Pul (*pul* means 'bridge' in Nepali) for these bridges.

The ACAP campsite across the bridge suffers from a chronic lack of water so it's best to continue up the main trail, climbing for 10 minutes and then descending on a side trail to **Nar Phedi** (3550m), traditionally known as Yunggar. There's good camping in front of the Narsadak Changu Tashi Choling Gompa or you may be lucky enough to score the spare room in the monastery annexe.

A short walk to the north offers views down to the 400-year-old **Sadik Chorten**, also known variously as the Yunkar Lhacho Chorten (Snellgrove) or Gyalbu Kumbum. The attached Satte Gompa is empty.

Day 5: Nar Phedi to Nar

2½–3 HOURS / 700M ASCENT

Today's climb starts immediately with a steep burst up to the main trail and it doesn't ease up for an hour or more. Walk through the Nar gate and continue climbing. The trail curves around a ridge, offering fantastic views of Pisang Peak, and passes a wall and gate that pens in Nar's yaks. Climb over the wall to an elaborate eight-sided and multitiered **chorten** (4140m), 1¾ hours from Nar Phedi.

Turn a corner and you'll see **Nar** (4180m) curving around barley fields in a natural bowl. Branch right at the village *kani* to reach the main lodges.

The large village has four lodges, though the only one that is reliably open is the Shanti Lodge, a friendly but simple place with six rooms, a toilet and a shop selling supplies. The camping ground is above the lodges near a school.

Nar (Place of the Blue Sheep) is larger than Phu, with around 65 houses stacked in tiers around a smattering of prayer wheels and small chapels. The village's four Kagyud gompas are worth a visit, though tracking down the keys from the four different caretakers can eat up a large chunk of the day.

If you are not able to cross the Kang La, or decide not to, it's possible to hike back down to Koto in a long day.

Day 6: Nar to Kang La Phedi

1½ HOURS / 440M ASCENT

Today's stage is less than two hours so you can either spend most of the day exploring Nar before departing for Kang La Phedi, or set off very early from Nar and push through all the way to Ngawal in one long day.

Leave Nar through the village *kani* and take the gradual path up through the valley, with Pisang Peak and its razorback ridge to your left. Traverse yak pastures after one hour, then contour around a hill and descend to the head of the valley. There's a small ACAP campsite here at Jhambu Kharka, also known as **Kang La Phedi** (4620m) or Kang La 'Base Camp'.

Day 7: Kang La Phedi to Ngawal

5½ HOURS / 680M ASCENT / 1700M DESCENT

The ascent to the Kang La isn't all that difficult in good conditions, though it can be treacherous in bad weather or if there's a lot of snow. You can expect snow and ice as late as September, but the trail is generally kept clear by convoys of yaks and trekking groups. It's best to tackle the pass early in the morning, before the ice becomes slippery.

Cross a stream on a log bridge and climb steeply to a chorten, before curving into the ridge ahead. Cross the river to its true right side and ascend the switchbacks up to a cairn. The climb begins in earnest here, up a steep but well-graded trail on a mix of snow, ice and yak dung with fine views. The final half-hour push zigzags to the top of a razor-sharp ridge at the **Kang La** (5320m), marked by a large cairn.

If you arrive early enough you may be rewarded with incredible views over the Annapurnas. The incredibly steep initial descent can prove tricky if there's snow, but it should be clear in September and October. The trail switchbacks down scree slopes as the valley starts to open up. As long as your knees hold up, the rest of the day is a lovely downhill stroll offering awesome views of the Annapurna II, Gangapurna and Tilicho peaks and Hongde airstrip below.

Ninety minutes from the pass there's a metal-roofed *bhatti* that can provide accommodation in an emergency. As the trail curves around a bend look, for the two icy waterfalls in the far right distance towards Chulu peak. Just past a goth at 4220m the trail splits. Branch left to detour to the Ney Guru Sang Phuk, a sacred cave marked by prayer flags and said to contain a 'self-arisen' statue of Guru Rinpoche. Alternatively, continue down for 40 minutes to the chortens and prayer flags that stand sentinel above the charming medieval town of **Ngawal** (3615m), about three hours from the pass.

You're now firmly back on the Annapurna trail, so celebrate your arrival with a beer and a slice of apple pie. Looking back up towards the pass it's hard to believe you ever made it up there. It also quickly becomes clear that you don't ever want to consider doing this climb in the opposite direction!

If you are flying back to Pokhara, Hongde (Manang) airport is less than an hour's walk downhill. The trail branches off by the Hotel Gangal in the centre of the village.

MUSTANG

The former Himalayan kingdom of Mustang is a starkly beautiful land. Its allure has come from a history of relative inaccessibility and a reputation as a bastion of traditional Tibetan culture. For centuries the kingdom channelled the wealth it amassed as a conduit for trade with Tibet into its monasteries, creating some of the finest remaining frescos in the Tibetan world. There are reports of damage to historic monuments in Mustang from the 2015 earthquakes, but the trails are open and trekking companies are planning to return to the region following the 2015 monsoon.

Regulations to limit tourists have been quietly ignored in recent years and now over 3000 trekkers a year visit the region. Even with the high permit fees, the trails, lodges and campsites of Mustang can be noticeably crowded during the months of September and October. Add to this the continued upgrading of the road through the kingdom and it's clear that Mustang is witnessing great change.

In common usage, the name Mustang refers to the arid, Tibet-like region (known to its inhabitants as Lo) at the northern end of the Kali Gandaki. Mustang is probably a Nepali mispronunciation of the town of Manthang, the capital of Lo. The name is pronounced 'Moo-stang' and has nothing to do with either the automobile or wild horse. Officially Mustang is the name of the entire district along the Kali Gandaki from the Tibetan border south to Ghasa on the Annapurna Circuit. The restricted area of Tibetan influence lies north of Kagbeni, and Nepalis refer to this as upper Mustang.

Upper Mustang consists of two distinct regions: the southern part, with five villages inhabited by people related to the Manangis; and the northern area (the ancient kingdom of Lo) where the language, culture and traditions are almost purely Tibetan. The capital of Lo is Manthang, which translates from the Tibetan as 'plain *(thang)* of aspiration *(mon)*'. Many texts refer to the capital as Lo Manthang, but this is not strictly correct. Other texts spell the name of the kingdom as Lho, but this is a transliteration of the Tibetan word for 'south' and is also incorrect. Thus the portion of the upper Mustang district north of Samar is Lo and its capital is Manthang. The king of Lo is the Lo Gyelbu, although the Nepali term *raja* is also used. To avoid total confusion with existing maps and texts, in this guide 'Lo' refers to upper Mustang and the capital of Lo is called 'Lo Manthang'.

History

Mustang has a long, rich and complex history that makes it one of the most fascinating corners of the Himalaya. The early history of Lo is shrouded in myth and mystery. For example, very little is known about the cave dwellings dotted throughout Mustang; they may be thousands of years old. For centuries the economic lynchpin of the region was the transborder exchange of Tibetan salt and wool for Nepali grain and spices, ferried down the Kali Gandaki from the high passes of the Kore La, Phutu La and Sherpa La.

There are official records of events in Lo dating back to the 8th century. It is quite likely that the Tibetan poet Milarepa visited Lo in the 11th century. Upper Mustang was once part of Ngari, a name for far-western Tibet. Ngari was not a true political entity, but rather a loose collection of feudal domains that also included parts of Dolpo. By the 14th century much of Ngari, as well as most of what today is western Nepal, was part of the Malla empire governed from the capital at Sinja, near Jumla.

It is generally believed that Ame Pal (A-ma-dpal in Tibetan) founded the kingdom of Lo in 1380; indeed, the last king of

Mustang, Jigme Palbar Bista, can trace his family back 25 generations to this founding father. Ame Pal, or perhaps his father, conquered a large part of the territory in the upper Kali Gandaki and was responsible for the development of the walled town of Lo Manthang and the construction of many gompas throughout the region.

To the west, the Malla empire declined and split into numerous petty hill states. By the 18th century, Jumla had consolidated and reasserted its power. In an effort to develop their domain as a trading centre and to obtain Tibetan goods, the rulers of Jumla turned their attention eastward and assumed control over Lo, from which they exacted an annual tribute.

Prithvi Narayan Shah's Gorkha armies never entered Lo and recognised the rule of the Mustang *raja*. Although Mustang became part of Nepal, the *raja* retained his title and a certain amount of autonomy. In the 1850s the *raja* directed peace talks between Nepal and China, for which he was awarded a ceremonial hat with three feathers donated by the Dalai Lama, the Manchu emperor and the king of Nepal.

Lo maintained its status as a separate principality until 1951. After the Rana rulers were overthrown and King Tribhuvan re-established the rule of the Shah monarchs in Nepal on 15 February 1951, Lo was more closely consolidated into Nepal. The *raja* was given the honorary rank of colonel in the Nepal army.

During the 1960s, after the Dalai Lama had fled to India and Chinese armies established control over Tibet, Mustang was a centre for guerrilla operations against the Chinese. The soldiers were the Khampas, Tibet's most fearsome warriors, who were backed by the CIA (some Khampas were secretly trained in the USA). At the height of the fighting there were at least 6000 Khampas in Mustang and neighbouring border areas. The CIA's support ended in the early 1970s when the United States, under Kissinger and Nixon, initiated new and better relations with China. The government of Nepal was pressed to take action against the guerrillas and, making use of internal divisions within the Khampa leadership and the Dalai Lama's taped plea for his citizens to lay down their arms, it managed to disband the resistance without using the 10,000 Nepali troops that had been sent to the area.

THE TRANS-HIMALAYAN HIGHWAY

In 1999 upper Mustang's local village development committees (VDCs) began construction of a road from the Kore La on the Tibetan border to Lo Manthang, allowing Chinese trucks to drive to Lo Manthang bringing supplies of rice, timber, concrete, kerosene, electrical goods and tractors. A gravel road now continues south of Lo Manthang to Jomsom. Although it is now possible to drive from Kathmandu to Lo Manthang: a once unimaginable prospect, the journey is not straightforward. Bridges remain missing and vehicle changes are required at several points. Road blockages from snowfall, landslides and rising rivers are seasonal and common.

Although Mustang remained closed to foreigners, the government allowed a few researchers into the area. Toni Hagen included Mustang in his survey of the entire kingdom of Nepal, and Giuseppe Tucci visited in the autumn of 1952. Professor David Snellgrove surveyed Buddhist gompas throughout Dolpo, Mustang and Nupri, describing them in his book *Himalayan Pilgrimage*, though he wasn't allowed as far as Lo Manthang. Dr Harka Bahadur Gurung also visited and wrote about upper Mustang in October 1973. Other than a few royal guests, the first legal trekkers weren't allowed until March 1992.

In 2008, Nepal's newly formed republic abolished the Mustang monarchy's official status. Nevertheless the 'king' of Mustang and his family retain a powerful influence in the region.

Geography

Mustang has been described as a thumb-like part of Nepal extending into Tibet. Yet on the map it is hardly a bump in Nepal's northern border. This is not the result of an inaccurate description by early writers, but rather that the map changed. In 1960 there was a controversy between Nepal and China over the ownership of Mt Everest. This resulted in extended negotiations and the China–Nepal Boundary Treaty of 1963 that completely redefined Nepal's northern frontier. Nepal gained a considerable amount of territory to the east and west of the old

ANNAPURNA REGION MUSTANG

boundaries in Mustang, so the protrusion of Mustang into Tibet became much less pronounced. To make matters more confusing, most official maps were not updated until about 1985.

The trek to Lo is through a virtually treeless, barren landscape. Strong winds usually howl up the valley in the afternoon, generally subsiding at night. Being in the Himalaya's rain shadow, Lo has much less rain than the rest of Nepal. During the monsoon the skies are cloudy and there is some rain. In winter there is usually snow; sometimes as much as 40cm accumulates on the ground.

In Lo itself the countryside is similar to the Tibetan plateau with its endless expanses of yellow and grey rolling hills eroded by wind. There is more rain in the lower part of upper Mustang where the red hills have been eroded into fluted cliffs. Villages are several hours apart and appear in the distance almost as mirages; during summer, after the crops are planted, they are green oases in the desert-like landscape.

TREKKING IN MUSTANG AFTER THE 2015 EARTHQUAKE

The Mustang Trek is a Himalayan classic that offers a window back in time to the days before Nepal opened up to the outside world, but the 2015 earthquake caused some damage to traditional buildings in this region, including to some of Mustang's most famous monasteries and palaces. Adding to Mustang's problems, visitor numbers have declined massively following the 2015 earthquake amd many local residents have deserted the area seeking work elsewhere. This trek was walked by our author shortly before the earthquake and we have updated our coverage using local sources, but no formal audit of damaged monuments had been carried out at the time of writing and it may be some time before the full extent of the damage in Mustang becomes clear. Be prepared to seek local advice if any features of these routes have changed since the disaster, and check the status of all the accommodation and food stops along the route before setting off from Kagbeni.

People & Culture

The 7000 people of upper Mustang call themselves Lobas. To be strictly correct, this word would be spelled 'Lopa', meaning 'Lo people', in the same way as Sherpa means 'east people' and Khampa 'Kham people'. The people of Lo, probably because of regional dialect, pronounce the word with a definite 'b' sound instead of the 'p' sound the Sherpas and Khampas use. So here we follow Lo tradition and spell the word as it is pronounced ('Loba') although most anthropological texts disagree with this.

Due to the lack of rain, Lobas build houses and temples with rammed earth or sun-baked bricks of mud on a stone foundation. Astonishing edifices, such as the city wall and the four-storey palace in Lo Manthang, are built in this manner. It is said that there were once large forests in Lo, but now wood for construction is hauled all the way from Jomsom or pruned from poplar trees that are carefully planted in every village. In the 1990s much of the wood, including the timbers used in the restoration of Thubchen Gompa, was brought from Tibet.

The people herd yaks, raise goats and sheep, and farm buckwheat, barley, wheat and mustard. The harsh conditions allow only one crop a year, except in the villages below Chhuksang where two crops are grown. Planting is in April and May, and during September the entire region is busy with the harvest. Many residents leave Mustang between November and March to sell sweaters in southern Nepal or India or work in Kathmandu. In general Mustang's population is in decline.

Religion

Although there are Gelug- and Nmuyingma-school gompas in Mustang, the primary form of Tibetan Buddhism practised in Mustang is that of the Sakya lineage. Lama Ngorchen Kunga Sangpo introduced the Sakya tradition to Lo during three visits between 1427 and 1447. He was the head of the Ngor sub-school of Sakya Buddhism, and this is the tradition followed in Mustang today. The Sakya school is more worldly and practical in outlook, and less concerned with metaphysics, than the more predominant Nyingma and Gelug schools.

Sakya followers paint their religious structures in stripes of grey (protection), white (compassion) and yellow (wisdom), a pattern that is repeated throughout the Mustang region, alongside ochre and white chortens and red-walled gompa buildings.

ⓘ Planning

WHEN TO TREK

Most of the population departs from Lo on trading expeditions during the winter to avoid the cold and snow. The trekking season, therefore, is possible from March until early November, with the most popular months being May to October. The trek does not go to extremely high elevations, but the cold, dust and unrelenting afternoon winds can make it less pleasant than other treks in Nepal.

The 10-day permit allows ample time to get to Lo Manthang, do some exploring and make a leisurely return. A 13-day permit will allow you to make trips on horseback to villages north of Lo Manthang, as well as visit the fascinating cave complex of Luri Gompa. It's possible to hurry from Kagbeni to Lo Manthang and back within seven days, but this is not a region to race through. Because of the wind and the lack of water, groups generally camp in a village, but these are not conveniently spaced, so some days are too short and others too long.

EMERGENCY FACILITIES

There is sporadic cell phone reception in most towns but the coverage is spreading fast. Other telephones (landline and satellite) are available in Jomsom, Ghemi and Kagbeni and the police in Lo Manthang have a radio. Rich tourists sometimes chopper in or out of Lo Manthang. In an emergency situation it's worth asking the ACAP office if a flight is expected. If you are injured or ill, you can return to Jomsom by jeep or bus but it wont be reliable, speedy or comfortable.

MAPS

Maps of the area include Nepa Maps' 1:60,000 *Mustang* and 1:80,000 *Upper Mustang*, both by Paolo Gondoni. Nepal Map Publisher has a 1:90,000 *Upper & Lower Mustang Pocket Map*, which is accurate and a convenient size. The Nepal Survey series 1:50,000 *Mustang* maps are also good.

BOOKS & FILMS

Mustang – A Lost Tibetan Kingdom, by Michel Peissel, was the first contemporary description of Mustang, published after Peissel spent several months in the area in spring 1964. It provides great background reading and, surprisingly, many of the descriptions still ring true.

Peter Matthiessen's *East of Lo Monthang* describes his trek to Mustang and contains many excellent photographs by Thomas Laird.

The Last Forbidden Kingdom: Mustang, Land of Tibetan Buddhism, by Clara Marullo and Vanessa Boeye, describes their visit to Mustang with some outstanding photos.

Earth Door Sky Door by Robert Powell is a spectacular collection of paintings of Mustang, with an introduction by Tibetologist Roberto Vitali.

Other useful but hard-to-find books include *Journey to Mustang*, by Giuseppe Tucci, *Mustang Bhot in Fragments* by Manjushree Thapa, and David P Jackson's *The Mollas of Mustang*.

The PBS documentary *Lost Treasures of Tibet* (2003) follows architect John Sanday and art restorer Rodolfo Lujan as they attempt to renovate Thubchen Gompa in Lo Manthang. You can watch the program online and get information on the restoration process at www.pbs.org/wgbh/nova/tibet.

PERMITS & REGULATIONS

Trekking permits for Mustang were previously set by the government at a painful US$500 per person for 10 days, with extra days charged at US$50 per person. However, following the earthquake in 2015, the fee has been temporarily lowered to US$100 per person for 10 days, though it is likely to rise again as tourism to Nepal recovers following the disaster.

Under the terms of the permit, trekkers are admitted for 10 days, not 10 nights, starting and ending at Kagbeni. The permit specifies the date of entry to and exit from the restricted area above Kagbeni. Because of possible delays in Jomsom flights, the entry date is supposed to have a three-day leeway, although some bureaucrats are not aware of this. Once you start from Kagbeni, you must return within the period of your permit, but you need not start on a precise date. The rules require that you trek in a group of at least two.

There are no permits required to trek from Pokhara to Jomsom and Kagbeni, but you must pay the additional Rs 2000 ACAP conservation fee, even if you fly in to Jomsom. The US$50-per-day permit is required only north of Kagbeni.

The ACAP administers trekking in upper Mustang and its signposts line the main trail. Although the majority of the permit fee goes into the government general fund, ACAP receives a small portion of Mustang trek royalties, which it channels into local development projects. Mustang is in fact the only restricted area for which any part of the permit fee goes into a special fund.

You must register with the police post and ACAP office in Jomsom and Kagbeni, where they will check your permit, equipment, stoves, food and fuel. You should have several lists of group members and equipment available for this purpose.

At the conclusion of the trek you are required to register again with the ACAP office and show all your rubbish to prove you have carried it out for disposal in Jomsom.

ACCOMMODATION

It's possible to visit Mustang as a teahouse trek. There are basic lodges at Chhuksang, Chele, Samar, Shyangmochen, Geling, Jaite, Ghemi, Tsarang, Lo Manthang, Dhi and Tange, but these are limited in the number of beds and fill up quickly when more than one group arrives, so it's still best to bring a tent and camping supplies, especially as this gives you greater flexibility over where to stay.

Note that lodges and food stops may not be open if there are not sufficient visitor numbers to persuade operators to stay in the mountains. Many villagers have left the area to seek work elsewhere following the 2015 earthquake so check the situation locally before starting your trek.

HORSES

Groups should consider hiring horses from upper Mustang at Jomsom or Kagbeni. Horses cost much the same as porters but carry twice the load, so are economically competitive. Horses are more reliable and environmentally friendly, plus by hiring horses from Mustang, you are benefiting the local economy. This is one of the few opportunities you have to contribute to the economy of upper Mustang. A major advantage of using Mustang horses is that you also gain the services of a local horseman who can serve as a guide and expediter.

FESTIVALS

The spring festival of Tiji (Tenche) at the end of the third Tibetan month (around May) is a three-day ritual re-enacting the battle of Dorje Jono against his demon father to save Mustang from drought. Highlights include the unfurling of a giant *thong-drol* (large festival thangka) of Guru Rinpoche and lots of colourful *chaam* dancing. Monks create an effigy of the demon from barley grain, butter and yak hair, which is then stabbed and burned, exorcising the town's evil spirits. An explosion of musket fire concludes the celebrations, which marks the end of the dry winter and the beginning of the wetter growing season. The festival is popular with tour groups so expect accommodation and camping spots to be tight at this time.

Mustang also celebrates the Yartung festival in late August with horse races, religious parades and plenty of *chhang* (barley beer).

❶ Getting There & Away

The trek described here begins and ends in Kagbeni, about two hours' walk north of Jomsom. There are daily flights to Jomsom (US$111) from Pokhara; flights are in the early morning, so you must spend a night in Pokhara en route to Jomsom.

Buses and jeeps also run between Pokhara and Jomsom, though you may have to change transport somewhere, depending on the quality of the road.

Mustang Trek

Duration 10 days

Max Elevation 4325m

Difficulty Medium to hard

Season May to October

Start/Finish Kagbeni

Summary A challenging trek through arid desert canyons to the walled city of Lo Manthang. A pocket of lost Tibet that boasts spectacular gompas, walled villages and remote cave shrines.

 The Trek

Day 1: Kagbeni to Chele

5–6 HOURS / 430M ASCENT

At the police checkpost at the northern end of Kagbeni is a sign saying: 'Restricted Area, tourists please do not go beyond this point'. If you have the correct permit for upper Mustang, you will complete formalities here and step into this long-forbidden region. There are two routes up the Kali Gandaki. Get local advice and then stick to either the high trail or the riverbed route, depending on the height of the river. It's hard to get back to the high trail if you reach a dead end along the river.

RIVERBED ROUTE

In the dry season, it is possible to trek the entire route up the river along the sand and gravel of the riverbed. This will require at least two, and perhaps many, fords of the several channels of the meandering Kali Gandaki. When Lo people bring their horses to Kagbeni, they travel straight down the centre of the river valley, jumping onto the backs of their horses whenever it is necessary to cross the river. If you don't have a horse to ride, you'll have to wade the river. Sandals with straps are essential for this undertaking. Much of the trek up the riverbed is on rounded river boulders that make walking difficult.

HIGH ROUTE

The high route takes a bit longer and involves a fair amount of climbing, but it offers a visit to the picturesque village of Tangbe. From Kagbeni the trail climbs immediately to a ridge marked by a small stone chorten, then descends and climbs over an-

Mustang Trek

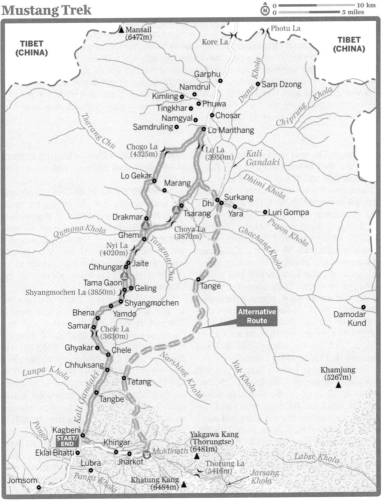

Mustang Trek

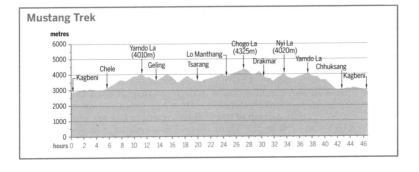

CHUNGSI CAVES

An alternative trail leads from Samar to Shyangmochen via the Chungsi Caves. If you take this spectacular canyon trail, it makes sense to overnight at Samar. After exiting Samar via a chorten, climb the right fork to the **Chungsi La** at 3810m, contouring through amazing canyons for about 2½ hours. It's a short 10-minute climb to the **Chungsi Caves**, whose large stalactites resemble *rangjung* ('self-arisen', ie not human-made) chortens. The Buddhist saint Guru Rinpoche is said to have meditated here. Himalayan griffons nest in the surrounding cliffs. After visiting the caves, climb gradually past pastures to Shyangmochen.

other ridge. The trail mostly follows a road above the river along a steep slope. After a few more ups and downs the trail climbs to a plateau at 3040m, where there is an apple orchard protected by an earthen wall. The trail then drops steeply into a dry riverbed. It's then a short climb to **Tangbe** (Tangwe; 3060m), where you'll find a teahouse on the road above the town. The town is a labyrinth of narrow alleys among whitewashed houses, fields of buckwheat, barley and wheat, and apple orchards. Walk below the village to see the picturesque chorten decorated with stucco reliefs of elephants, horses, peacocks and *garuda* (half-human, half-bird) figures. Nearby are the ruins of an ancient *dzong*. Look for the black, white and red chortens that typify upper Mustang.

About one hour beyond Tangbe you will reach the village of **Chhuksang** (2980m) at the confluence of the Narshing Khola and the Kali Gandaki. Soon after you leave Tangbe you can see Gompa Kang and some caves on the west bank of the river. This Nyingma gompa is associated with Chhuksang, but is usually deserted because it is inaccessible from the town when the water level in the Kali Gandaki is high. Nilgiri peak, which dominates the southern skyline at Kagbeni, continues to loom at the foot of the valley.

Chhuksang consists of three clumps of whitewashed stone houses and narrow alleyways. The **Mentsun Khang cave gompa** (admission Rs 130) is above the southernmost settlement. If you can find the man with the key, you can clamber up the rickety ladders to see the centuries old, sooty and unrestored statues, including Maitreya. A trail up the south bank of the Narshing Khola leads to Tetang (also known as Te), where there is a gompa, a small salt mine and a trail that leads over a high pass to Muktinath. There is a campsite at the south end of Chhuksang, just past the archery ground, and another

near the Narshing Khola where the Bhrikuti Hotel offers both camping and basic hotel facilities.

Across the Kali Gandaki from Chhuksang are some spectacular red organ-pipe eroded cliffs above the mouths of inaccessible caves. The five villages in this area – Chele, Ghyakar, Chhuksang, Tangbe and Tetang – are a culturally unified group of people who call themselves Gurungs and are more closely related to the Manangis than to the Thakalis or Lobas.

Cross the Narshing Khola and continue north, making several ups and downs. Descend to the riverbank near a huge red chunk of cliff that has cleaved off, forming a tunnel through which the Kali Gandaki flows. A steel foot bridge spans the river just in front of the tunnel. North of here, the Kali Gandaki becomes impassable for those on foot, although locals sometimes travel this route on horseback through a steep narrow canyon made dangerous by falling rocks. There are many ancient caves high on the fluted red bluffs above the eastern bank of the river. Some of these now-inaccessible caves were used as living quarters and others were burial places. They were probably reached by ladders or by trails that eroded long ago.

The trek now leaves the Kali Gandaki Valley and climbs steeply up a rocky gully to **Chele** (Tsele; 3100m). The small village boasts several lodges and teashops among the extensive fields of wheat and barley, including the Mina Coffee Shop, with a couple of rooms, and the cheerful Mustang Gate Guest House. Higher up the cobbled street is the Bishal Guest House, with a campsite.

From here the culture changes from the Manangi culture of the five 'Gurung' villages to the Tibetan culture of Lo. Most Lo houses have sheep horns above their doorways and you will see many twigs in the shape of a cross with threads in five colours woven in a diamond-shaped pattern. These spirit traps are called *zor* and are supposed to capture evil spirits.

Trading patterns also change from here on. Packaged Chinese food becomes more common than Nepali or Indian food and several houses have Chinese stoves, porcelain and other articles. Much of the decoration for the gompas comes from Tibet.

Day 2: Chele to Geling

7–8 HOURS / 1060M ASCENT / 590M DESCENT

The rest of the trek to Lo Manthang is through high-altitude desert country, climbing in and out of immense side valleys of the Kali Gandaki. The climb from Chele leads up a steep spur to a cairn and a view of Ghyakar across a huge canyon (linked by a high suspension bridge). A long wall of packed earth encircles Ghyakar and its fields. The climb continues – a long, steep, treeless, waterless slog – switchbacking up the side of a spectacular steep canyon, then traversing to a cairn marking the **Chele La** (Dajori La; 3630m). After crossing the ridge the trail enters a large side valley and makes a long gradual descent to **Samar** (3620m), surrounded by a grove of poplar trees. This is a key stop for horse caravans and there are many horse stables. Lodges include the cosy Himali Hotel and the Hotel Annapurna, which has an excellent campsite, a bright dining room and clean rooms. Samar used to be one of the major Khampa camps and several of the hotels that used to cater to them still operate. The Annapurna Himal, still dominated by Nilgiri, is visible far to the south.

The trail climbs above Samar to a ridge, descends steeply to a stream, then climbs back to a chorten painted in red, yellow, black and white – all pigments made from local minerals. The trail goes into another valley filled with stumps of juniper trees that have been harvested for firewood, crosses a stream and climbs up to the Bhena La at 3830m and drops gently to the three houses of **Bhena** (3860m). The route skirts a gorge, crosses a stream and climbs slightly to **Yamdo**: two houses at 3920m. Climb to yet another pass, the Yamdo La at 4010m, descend steeply and then follow a ridge as it descends to **Shyangmochen** (Syangboche; 3800m), with good campsites and three teahouses, including the Nigiri Green, Anita Green and Hotel Dhaulagiri & Garden Camping.

It's a short gentle climb to the **Shyangmochen La** at 3850m, where the route enters another huge east–west valley. A road now runs from here all the way to Lo. Descend past a large painted square chorten and a view of Geling to a trail junction. The left trail is the direct route to the Nyi La via Tama Gaon and Chhungar, bypassing Geling. Take the right fork and descend to the picturesque village of **Geling** (3570m), with its poplar trees and extensive fields of barley. A large red gompa overlooks the whitewashed houses scattered around the valley. As you enter the green edge of town you'll find the New Kunga Hotel on your left, which also has a camping ground.

Day 3: Geling to Tsarang

6–7 HOURS / 890M ASCENT / 870M DESCENT

The trail from Geling turns westward and climbs gently through fields in a broad valley, passing below Chhungar and its imposing chorten. Turning north, it rejoins the road and becomes an unrelenting climb across the head of the valley to the **Nyi La** (4020m). The Nyi La is the southern boundary of Lo; people who live south of the pass call it the Jaite La. The descent from the pass is gentle for about 45 minutes to the Ghemi La, a cairn on a ridge top about 45 minutes below the pass. The trail then drops steeply to the whitewashed buildings of **Ghemi** (3510m).

Ghemi is the third-largest village in Lo and is surrounded by extensive fields, about half of which are barren because of irrigation problems. Ghemi has a police post and a couple of guesthouses, including the Hotel Royal Mustang, a traditional old building in the centre of the village operated by a grand-nephew of the King of Lo. The hotel offers camping in its peaceful walled orchard. At the southern edge of the village is the Lo-Ghami Guest House, which has a satellite phone (Rs 150 per minute). A small red nunnery dominates a crag at the far end of the village. The trail to Drakmar and Lo Gekar (your return route from Lo Manthang) leads to the west from the upper part of the village.

The Tsarang track descends below the blue, grey and red cliffs across the valley to a steel bridge that crosses the Tangmar Chu, then climbs past what is perhaps the longest and most spectacular **mani wall** in Nepal. The large building to the east of the mani wall is a hospital built by a Japanese project. Beyond the mani wall the route climbs a rocky gully, then traverses to the **Choya La** (3870m). Once over the pass the route (a dusty road) makes a long gentle descent past a big prayer flag and across fields to **Tsarang** (Charang; 3575m), the second-largest town in Lo and the former capital.

Tsarang is a maze of fields, willow trees and houses separated by stone walls at the top of the large Tsarang Chu canyon. The village sustained some damage in the 2015 earthquake and a number of its historic buildings need repairs, including the huge five-storey white **dzong** and ochre gompa, perched on the edge of the Tsarang Khola gorge at the eastern end of the village. The former palace was built in 1378 and once boasted the greatest library in Mustang. The library is a shadow of its former self, but it still houses a famous gold-leafed prayer book. In the *gonkhang* (protector chapel) you'll find a cache of old weapons and the mummified severed hand of a thief clasped in the talons of 'Garuda'! The hand belonged to a pious monk or the architect who built the *dzong*, depending on who's telling the story. The remarkable Japanese traveller Ekai Kawaguchi stayed in Tsarang for almost a year in 1899.

The 14th-century **gompa** houses a collection of statues and thangkas, as well as many large paintings of seated Buddhas and a sorry looking stuffed snow leopard, but the building took some damage in the 2015 earthquake. Below the gompa is the house of the king's niece, Maya Bista, which doubles as Maya's Inn, the town's main hotel and restaurant. There is a camping ground behind the hotel and at two others nearby. The village has a fine entrance chorten, as well as its own electricity supply; you cross under the pipes of the hydro plant just beyond the village.

Day 4: Tsarang to Lo Manthang

4–5 HOURS / 450M ASCENT / 200M DESCENT

The trail descends about 125m from Tsarang, crosses the Tsarang Chu and follows the road to a cairn on a ridge opposite the village at 3580m, then enters the Tholung Valley. The dirt road turns north and climbs gently to the large isolated **Sungda chorten** that marks the boundary between Tsarang and Lo. The road crosses a stream, then becomes a wide thoroughfare travelling across a desert-like landscape painted in hues of grey and yellow. Finally, from **Lo La** (3950m), there is a view of the walled city of Lo Manthang.

A short descent leads onto the Plain of Aspiration, then the trail crosses a stream and climbs up onto the plateau of Lo Manthang (3840m), crossing an irrigation canal at the southern wall of the city of Lo Manthang.

LO MANTHANG

The only entrance to the city is at the northeastern corner, so circumambulate the wall to the gate where you are sure to find a group of adults and children playing, spinning prayer wheels and gossiping. The city walls are 750m long, 9m high and have 14 towers. Just inside the wooden gate you are confronted by the palace wall and a statue of Chenresig protected behind a wire screen.

The whitewashed wall around Lo Manthang resembles a misshapen 'L'. The closely packed houses of the city itself, along with the palace and temples, are in the bottom portion; the vertical part of the 'L' houses the monastic community and two gompas (this portion of the city wall is painted red).

The school and health post and several important chortens are outside the walls to the north of the gate and east of the monastic part of the city. Peissel wrote in 1962 that the population of the city consisted of 'twelve dukes, 60 monks, 152 families and eight practising witches'. Today there are about 150 houses (plus numerous monastic residences), with a population of around 1000. The number of witches is unknown. The only agricultural land inside the walls is a field owned by the monastery near the city centre.

The wall of Lo Manthang was once more imposing than it is now. In the mid-1980s the *raja* sold much of the land surrounding the city. As a result, numerous stables, houses and stone-walled fields now adjoin the wall. Nothing will grow in this arid land without irrigation. A small canal flows around the city providing sustenance for a few willow trees and another canal flows under the wall and through the city itself. The entire plain surrounding the town is covered with walled irrigated fields that provide one crop a year of wheat, buckwheat, barley, peas or mustard.

There are several lodging options in Lo Manthang. The basic **Lomanthang Guest House** (☑9746708281; r with/without bathroom Rs 600/400) has an entrance on the outside of the city wall and it continues through the wall; its other entrance is above the post office in the square across from the palace. The Lotus Holiday Inn is outside the city

LIFE BEHIND THE WALLS OF LO MANTHANG

Despite the apparent squalor of Lo Manthang, the city is prosperous and maintains a strong sense of community. Although the people call themselves Lobas (people from Lo), they are very much Tibetan and have a sophisticated culture and economy. Before trade with Tibet was disrupted, all the salt and wool trade on the Kali Gandaki passed through Lo Manthang, and this brought a sizeable amount of money to the city. Wealth is now primarily measured in land, horses and social standing.

The doors of most houses open onto a two-storey open central courtyard. The ground floor is used for storage of food, horse trappings, a pile of dung for fuel, and farm implements. A wooden staircase leads to the first storey, which typically has a balcony overlooking the courtyard and doors leading off to living rooms and the kitchen. A notched log leads to the roof, which is surrounded by huge stacks of juniper twigs and firewood. The roof is an important part of the house, used for relaxing or working in the sun. Adorning the roofs of most houses are the horns of sheep and yak and, on the palace, horns of *shou* (an extinct species also known as Sikkim stag) that are over 100 years old.

Virtually every house has an indoor toilet on the upper floor that drops into a ground-floor chamber. Ashes from the hearth are dumped into the toilet to eliminate the smell, and the resulting product is a nutritive, not-unpleasant fertiliser. The stoves used in Lo Manthang are of a special design. They are a three-armed affair with a 30cm-high burning chamber that roars like a volcano when fed with yak dung and goat droppings. People rarely burn the wood on the roof for cooking; it is there largely as a show of wealth and for ceremonial occasions.

walls; it has 14 rooms, a good restaurant and a camping ground. Other options include The Tashi Delek, Himalayan and Mona Lisa. A large new hotel is being built by the royal family northest of the walled city.

Days 5–6: In Lo Manthang

With a handful of temples and the raja's palace in town, plus some noteworthy sites in the surrounding area, there's enough in and around Lo Manthang to keep you occupied for a couple of days. Lo Manthang is the highlight of this trek, so don't scrimp on your time here.

TEMPLES & MUSEUM

There are four major temples within the city walls, each of which is locked. The caretaker and the key are available only at certain times. You need to purchase a combined entry ticket (US$10), which will gain you entry to the four temples and the Monastic Museum. The monks prohibit taking photographs inside the gompas in an effort to limit interest in the statues and paintings among collectors of stolen art.

The three-storey **Jampa (Champa) Lhakhang** (*lha khang* means 'house of the gods') was built in 1447–48 under the inspiration of Ngorchen Kunga Sangpo (although local tradition dates it to 1387). The central courtyard with its carved wooden pillars has fallen into disrepair. Inside the temple is a huge 15m-tall painted clay statue of Jampa (Maitreya), the future Buddha, sitting on a pedestal that occupies the entire ground floor. Unlike most statues of Jampa, which are seated on a chair, this statue is seated in a meditative cross-legged (lotus) position. The 1.6m-thick walls are painted with elaborate mandalas that rank as some of the finest in the Tibetan world. The view from the roof is superb.

The red 15th-century **Thubchen Gompa** near the centre of the city consists of a massive assembly hall supported by 35 huge wooden columns. It was built by the third king of Mustang and dates from the same period as the Jampa Lhakhang. (Tucci observed that the same artists had painted frescos in both temples.) There are statues of Sakyamuni Buddha surrounded by Chenresig (Avalokitesvara), Vaisravana (the god of wealth) and Guru Rinpoche (Padmasambhava).

One wall of the temple is completely destroyed; on the other walls are intricate frescos in various stages of restoration/repainting. The entrance hall contains huge scowling statues of the four Lokapala: the

ANNAPURNA REGION MUSTANG TREK

protectors of the cardinal points of the compass. The structure of the gompa has been restored, while the cleaning and repainting of the frescos is currently ongoing.

The other two temples are within the monastic quarter. The main temple is the **Chöde Gompa**, which was founded in 1710. Its major image is a painting of the fearsome protective deity Mahakala, and it contains dozens of beautifully crafted bronze, brass and copper statues, many said to have been cast in Lo Manthang itself.

Nearby is the newer assembly hall, **Choprang Gompa**, which is generally known by the name 'new gompa'. The student monks use this gompa for prayers every morning and evening. Inside are pictures of His Holiness Sakya Trichhen Rinpoche, the head of the primary Sakya lineage, and the heads of the two secondary Sakya lineages: Ngor Sakya and Tsar Sakya. The masks used in the annual Tiji festival are stored here.

Near the entrance to the monastic quarter is the **Monastic Museum**, part of the **Tsechhen Shedrubling Monastic School**, which was established in 1994 to train monks from Lo Manthang, Chosar and Nyanul, the three patron villages of Chöde Gompa. The museum contains many interesting artefacts from everyday and monastic life, including ancient texts recovered from nearby caves.

RAJA'S PALACE

The raja's (or king's) palace is an imposing four-storey building in the centre of the city. It is the home of the present raja, Jigme Parbal Bista, and the queen *(rani)*, who is from an aristocratic family of Lhasa. Although his duties are largely ceremonial, the raja is respected by the people and consulted about many issues by villagers throughout Lo. The *durbar* (palace) sustained some damage in the 2015 earthquake but repairs are underway.

The raja's family name was originally Tandul. It was changed in accordance with a recent tradition in which many people of Tibetan descent Nepalised their surnames. This practice is similar to the custom of the 'Matwali Chhetris' of Dolpo in which Khampas adopted Hindu surnames. It is also similar to the practice of many Manangis who call themselves Gurungs. Many Lobas use their original Tibetan name, but almost all have a second Nepali name that was assigned when they enrolled in school.

EXPLORING THE TOWN

Take a walk through the narrow alleyways. Visit the ACAP office in the square in front of the palace. There are numerous shops selling Tibetan-style handicrafts, although virtually all are made in Kathmandu. Pricey Chinese-made carpets and Tibetan carpets are often available. In the late afternoon pay a visit to Tarchun Gurung's souvenir shop and climb up to the roof for a view of the town and a short walk along the flagstone-topped wall.

AROUND LO MANTHANG

After visiting the temples in the city, consider hiring a horse to visit some of the other villages in the area.

There are two valleys above Lo Manthang. In the western valley are **Tingkar** (the site of the raja's summer palace, Kimling Gompa), Phuwa Gompa and Namgyal Gompa ('the monastery of victory'). **Namgyal**, situated in a spectacular setting atop a desolate ridge, is of the Gelug tradition and is the newest and most active gompa in Lo. As long as you have time on your permit you may visit these villages, but you must return to Lo Manthang for the night.

In the valley east of Lo Manthang is **Chosar**, the site of Garphu and Nyphu gompas and some fascinating cave dwellings. This is the main trading route to Lhasa, a route Tucci describes as 'used over the centuries by pilgrims and apostles, robbers and invaders'. The ruins of numerous forts along the trail lend credence to this observation.

On the two hills to the north of town are the ruins of castles. The castle on the higher hill was the palace of Ame Pal, the founder king of Mustang. On the lower hill are the ruins of the round castle of the queen. This is now a sky burial site.

Day 7: Lo Manthang to Drakmar

5–6½ HOURS / 710M ASCENT / 730M DESCENT

There is an opportunity to vary the return route, visiting two villages that you didn't see on the trek northward. Instead of following the trail south to Tsarang, turn southwest along an indistinct trail that passes the irrigated fields of the city, generally following the irrigation canal. (Alternatively, cut west from Tsarang to Lo Gekar via Marang.)

The trail to Lo Gekar is not a main trading route and the area is criss-crossed with herders' trails, so a local guide is particular-

CREATION OF GHAR GHOMPA

Ghar Gompa is related to Samye monastery, which is in Tibet near the Lhasa airport. During Samye's construction, it is said, demons destroyed the monastery several times. Construction was stopped and Ghar Gompa was built to appease the demons, after which the construction of Samye proceeded without incident. This story corroborates a legend that the great magician and saint Guru Rinpoche visited Ghar Gompa and hid some texts called *terma* for later discovery by the right teachers. Since Guru Rinpoche is also recognised as a founder of Samye, which was built between 775 and 787, this suggests that Ghar Gompa is one of the oldest active gompas in Nepal.

ly useful here. The trail climbs steadily to a cairn on a pass at 4000m, offering a last glimpse of Lo Manthang. The trail climbs to a ridge at 4070m where a large cairn marks a pass into a side valley. Climb to the head of this valley and cross the **Chogo La**, at 4325m the highest point on the trek. The trail traverses above a big grassy valley, crosses a ridge at 4270m, then makes a long rough descent in a gully beside a stream to a large chorten at 4030m. The trail makes a short, steep descent to a wooden bridge across the Tsarang Khola, then climbs past an unpainted stone chorten and across a swampy meadow to **Lo Gekar** (which means 'pure virtue of Lo'). Ghar Gompa is a small monastery in a grove of large trees.

Ghar Gompa means 'house temple' and is so-named because the structure is built like a house with small separate rooms. The gompa is affiliated with the Nyingma lineage and is one of the oldest in Mustang. The primary figures are Guru Rinpoche and his consorts Yeshe Tsogyel and Mandarava, placed above a brass altar inside a dark alcove; on one wall of the alcove there is a self-emanating (ie naturally occurring) statue. In another alcove is a large statue of the protective deity Palden Lhamo on a horse. The real treasures of Ghar Gompa are the hundreds of painted carved stones in wooden frames displayed on the walls of the main chapel and three other upstairs rooms. David Snellgrove stayed at the monastery, writing that 'of all the places we have seen in this whole area, it is here we would stay most readily'.

There is no village nearby, but near the gompa there are a series of quarters for monks and pilgrims that provide protection from the wind. The gompa is supplied with electricity via a long transmission line from Marang village. You can see Marang, and below that Tsarang, in the valley below.

Climb to a ridge, then across a valley to a cairn and a pass at 4170m. The route crosses some alpine meadows to a crest, then drops down a steep eroded gully overshadowed by red rock towers to the upper part of **Drakmar** ('red crag') at 3820m. The colour of the cliffs is said to be from the blood of an ogress who was vanquished by Guru Rinpoche. A large stream meanders through the village, making this a particularly pretty valley, with several pleasant grassy campsites. The New Tenjin Hotel & Guest House is the best of the small selection of lodges.

ALTERNATIVE ROUTE: LO MANTHANG TO KAGBENI

An interesting return option is to take the eastern winter route from Lo Manthang to Dhi, Tange and Tetang villages, detouring en route to Yara and Luri gompas. This high route takes you across some dramatic canyon ridges.

After crossing the Lo La outside Lo, a well-signposted route leads east through narrow canyons to the banks for the Kali Gandaki and the green oasis of Dhi. There are a couple of campsites in Dhi, and a nicer one in Yara, a couple of hours' walk to the east via the village of Surkang. Not far from Yara is the Tashi Kumbum, a collection of six cave dwellings.

Most impressive are the caves at **Luri Gompa** (4000m), across the Puyon Khola, whose Newari-style Buddhist frescos and 14th-century chortens are hidden in a fantastical landscape of fluted and eroded cliffs. Ascend to a lower cave, climb a notched log to the gompa and an outer chamber and then visit the inner cave to make a kora of the central chorten. In these caves are one of several discoveries of cave paintings dating

ANNAPURNA REGION MUSTANG TREK

from the 12th century, revealing Indian and Kashmiri influences that lead back to India's Ajanta Caves.

From Luri or Dhi you can head back across the Kali Gandaki to Tsarang or Ghemi. Alternatively you can continue south to Tange, and then the next day to the fortified village of Tetang. Villages are far apart on this route and there is limited water and no shelter, except possibly caves, between them. If you attempt this route, be prepared for at least one long 10-hour day of more than 30km. From Tetang it's three hours to the 4300m Gyu La, before dropping down to Muktinath.

Day 8: Drakmar to Shyangmochen

5–6 HOURS / 645M ASCENT / 671M DESCENT

The trail descends alongside a stream passing the stone walls and fields of the extensive village of Drakmar, then climbs to a ridge chorten and onto a ridge at 3710m. It then descends to another stream and makes a short climb to the upper part of Ghemi.

Descend to the lower part of Ghemi, then follow the upward route, climbing to a cairn on the Ghemi La and contouring upwards to the **Nyi La** (4020m). Descend steeply into the Geling Valley, but stay high and follow the trail that bypasses Geling. Pass an isolated teahouse and campsite at **Jaite** (3820m) and descend gently to **Chhungar**, a large chorten, house and campsite beside an apple orchard at 3750m. The trail then makes a long traverse past a mani wall to the three houses of **Tama Gaon** (3710m). A steep set of switchbacks down a rocky canyon leads to a stream, then the trail climbs to a huge painted chorten before rejoining the Geling trail near the ridge, just below the Shyangmochen La. Cross the pass and descend to the teahouses at **Shyangmochen** (see Day 2 on p187).

Day 9: Shyangmochen to Chhuksang

6–7 HOURS / 1100M DESCENT

Retrace the upward trail through Yamdo and Bhena to Samar and descend through Chele to the Kali Gandaki. Trek downstream to Chhuksang.

Day 10: Chhuksang to Kagbeni

3½–4½ HOURS / 70M DESCENT

Trek back to Kagbeni before your permit expires. You can easily continue another three hours or so to Jomsom to be ready to catch a flight the following day.

TOWNS & FACILITIES

Pokhara

061 / ELEV 884M

No matter where you trek in the Annapurna region, you'll pass through Pokhara, the largest and most laid-back town in central Nepal. Plan to spend a day or two here paddling in the lake, paragliding and enjoying the excellent restaurants, bustling nightclubs and comfortable hotels. Most tourist facilities are in Lakeside, next to Phewa Tal (*tal* means lake). There was very little damage here from the 2015 earthquake.

A spectacular panorama of the Annapurnas, Machhapuchhare and Manaslu dominates the skyline, especially from the viewpoints of Sarangkot and the World Peace Pagoda. Pokhara is at a lower elevation and warmer than Kathmandu.

Sights

International Mountain Museum MUSEUM (Map p125; 061-460742; www.international mountainmuseum.org; foreigner/SAARC Rs 400/200; 9am-5pm) This expansive museum is devoted to the mountains of Nepal, the mountaineers who climbed them and the people who call them home. Inside, you can see original gear from many of the first Himalayan ascents, as well as displays on the history, culture, geology, and flora and fauna of the Himalaya.

Sleeping

There are dozens of cheap guesthouses in the lanes that run off Lakeside.

Luxury resorts include the **Fish Tail Lodge** (Map p125; 061-465201; www.fish-tail-lodge.com.np; r from US$170;), in a dramatic setting on the shore of Phewa Tal, and the spectacular **Tiger Mountain Pokhara Lodge** (061-691887, in Kathmandu 01-4426427; www.tigermountainpokhara.com; cottages per person US$250;), set on a lofty ridge 10km east of town.

Little Tibetan Guest House   GUESTHOUSE $
(Map p125; 061-461898; littletibgh@yahoo.com; s/d from US$9/18;) This Tibetan-run lodge east of Camping (Hallan) Chowk is rightly popular for its calm and relaxed atmosphere. Rooms are elegantly decorated with Tibetan wall hangings and bedspreads. Balconies overlook a serene garden and while there's no restaurant, bed- and breakfast-packages are available.

Peace Eye Guest House   HOTEL $
(Map p125; 061-461699; www.peaceeye-guest house.com; s/d Rs 600/800, without bathroom Rs 450/600, deluxe r Rs 1200;) Established in 1977, the chilled-out Peace Eye retains all the qualities that attracted the original visitors to Pokhara 30 years ago. Inexpensive, laid-back and friendly, its brightly decorated rooms are well-kept and clean. Budget rooms are smallish but the others are spacious. It also has a vegetarian restaurant and small German bakery.

Hotel Travel Inn   HOTEL $
(Map p125; 061-462631; www.hoteltravelin.com; s/d incl breakfast & taxes US$10/22, r with air-con US$35-50;) Although it caters for all budgets, even the cheapest rooms here are spotless. It's worth the step up to deluxe for the comfy beds and bathtubs. The owner here claims tourists want three things: cleanliness, friendliness and quietness, and this modern hotel delivers on all fronts. It's the UN's choice of hotel when it's in town.

★**Temple Tree**
Resort & Spa   LUXURY HOTEL $$$
(Map p125; 061-465819; www.templetreenepal. com; s/d from US$160/180;) Tricked-out Temple Tree raises the bar in Lakeside. Plenty of timber and slate and straw-coloured render add delightful earthy tones. The standard rooms aren't huge, but they are exceptionally comfortable and most sport a bathtub and private balcony. There are two restaurants, a health spa, and a bar beside the lovely pool.

✗ Eating & Drinking

Lakeside is lined with dozens of good cafes and restaurants, including the popular **Moondance Restaurant** (Map p125; www. moondancepokhara.com; mains Rs 240-1400; 7am-10.30pm;) for excellent Thai and Indian curries, and the smart **Caffe Concerto** (Map p125; 061-463529; mains Rs 350-800; 7am-10.30pm;), known for its pizza,

pasta and gelato. For a post-trek meat-fest try the **New Everest Steak House** (Map p125; 061-466828; Phewa Marg; mains Rs 400-1400; 9am-10pm). For beers, everyone ends up at either Club Amsterdam or the Busy Bee Café sometime during the evening.

ⓘ Information

Lakeside is lined with travel agencies, internet cafes, trekking-gear shops and ATMs.

Get your ACAP permit and TIMS permit at the **ACAP office** (Map p125; 061-463376; 10am-5pm Sun-Fri, to 4pm Sat, to 4pm winter) in Damside. The **immigration office** (Map p125; 465167; Sahid Chowk; 10am-4pm Sun-Thu, 10am-3pm Fri), for visa extensions, is also located in Damside.

ⓘ Getting There & Away

All domestic airlines run several flights each day from Kathmandu (US$120). Sit on the right-hand side of the plane for a view of the Himalayan peaks, including Ganesh Himal, Himalchuli, the Annapurnas and Manaslu. Airlines currently operating flights to Jomsom (US$111) include Nepal Airlines, Tara Air and Simrik Airlines.

Most people take the tourist buses to/from Kathmandu (Rs 800, seven hours). Buses leave Pokhara at 7.30am from the tourist bus stand (Mustang bus stand) at Mustang Chowk, a short taxi ride from Lakeside. Any agent or hotel can book a ticket. Slightly more comfortable air-con buses are run by **Greenline** (Map p125; 061-464472; www.greenline.com.np) and **Golden Travels** (061-460120). Greenline leaves from an office in east Lakeside, whereas Golden Travels buses leave from the tourist bus stand.

Buses to trailheads for most Annapurna treks (except Besi Sahar) leave from the Baglung bus station, about 2km north of the centre on the main highway. Buses leave every hour or so. Buses to Besi Sahar leave from the main bus station. See the relevant treks for more details.

Taxi fares from Lakeside are around Rs 200 to the tourist bus stand, and Rs 300 to the main bus station and the airport.

Naya Pul & Birethanti

061 / ELEV 1070M (NAYA PUL); 1025M (BIRETHANTI)

Naya Pul, the traditional start and end of several treks into the Annapurna foothills, including the Annapurna Sanctuary, is little more than a roadside bazaar. There was some earthquake damage here, and also at Birethani, a more appealing village 30-minutes' trek upstream, where most travellers prefer to base themselves. Many taxis

ANNAPURNA REGION NAYA PUL & BIRETHANTI

(and probably buses by the time you read this) can now take you directly to Birenthanti. It boasts numerous trekkers lodges (rooms from Rs 400 to 800), restaurants, an art gallery, an ACAP checkpost (right beside the bridge) and a TIMS checkpost (east of the bridge), where you will need to present your ACAP permit and TIMS card, respectively.

ⓘ Getting There & Away

Naya Pul is on the Pokhara–Baglung road at Km42, at the foot of the hill below Khare. Take one of the numerous daily Baglung buses from the bus station near Bhairab Tole in the northwestern part of Pokhara and get off in Naya Pul (Rs 180, 90 minutes), or splurge on a faster, comfier taxi to Birenthanti (Rs 2000).

Besi Sahar

📑 066 / ELEV 800M

Besi Sahar, the headquarters of Lamjung district, has long been the starting point for the Annapurna Circuit trek, though road construction means you can now continue the same day by bus up to Bhulbule or by jeep to Chame.

The town is strung out for over 1km. Buses stop to let off passengers at the Hotel Tukuche Peak, but if you're headed for the trail, stay on the bus until its terminus at the northern end of town. If you arrive too late to start trekking, it makes sense to stay in the northern end of town.

If you did not get your ACAP permit in Kathmandu or Pokhara, you can purchase one here (Rs 2000) at the ACAP Entry Fee Office, about 200m south of the TIMS office and opposite the Gateway Himalaya Resort. If you get all the way to the Dharapani ACAP checkpoint without a permit you will have to pay Rs 4000 for a permit. The TIMS office is about 200m up the road, near the Hotel Super View.

There are ATMs in Besi Sahar and several hotels, including the **Hotel Tukuche Peak** (📑 066-520162; r with/without bathroom Rs 800/400), which boasts solar hot water, clean bathrooms and a decent restaurant. Options at the northern end of town include the large **Hotel Gangapurna** (📑 066-520342; hotelgangapurna@gmail.com; r Rs 500) and, more upmarket, the plush **Gateway Himalaya Resort** (📑 066-521301; www.gatewayhimalaya.com.np; r Rs 1400-2000; ❄).

ⓘ Getting There & Away

Minibuses leave Kathmandu's Gongabu bus park between 6.30am and noon to Besi Sahar (Rs 400, six hours). Buses also run daily from the Gongabu bus stand to Bhulbule (Rs 475) at 6.45am and 8.30am. Return minibuses leave from both ends of Besi Sahar. If you'd prefer to travel in slightly more comfort, you could take a tourist bus to Pokhara (Rs 450), jump off at Dumre and continue the 43km on a minibus to Besi Sahar (Rs 100), though it's hard to see how this is much of an improvement. A taxi from Kathmandu to Besi Sahar costs around Rs 6000.

From Pokhara (Rs 450, five hours), there is a tourist bus leaving at 6.30am from the tourist bus park, or you can take any bus or microbus bound for Kathmandu and change at Dumre. Many minibuses leave from the main road, outside the main bus station.

Minibuses run every hour or so beyond Besi Sahar to Bhulbule (Rs 200, 45 minutes) and Ngadi. However, it's such an uncomfortable ride that you're probably better off walking anyway. Share jeeps ply the same route (Rs 250) and continue all the way to Chame (Rs 1600) if the road hasn't been destroyed by monsoon rains. By the time you read this, the jeeps may well be running all the way to Manang.

Jomsom

📑 069 / ELEV 2760M

Straddling the Kali Gandaki, **Jomsom**, or more correctly Dzongsam (New Fort), is the region's administrative headquarters, home to a busy regional airport, banks, bureaucrats, military personnel, merchants and jeep owners. Many buildings here were damaged in the 2015 earthquake, including the historic wooden bridge across the Kali Gandaki, which warped dramatically, but restoration work is underway and the town is open to trekkers.

At the southern end of town a concrete stairway leads to the **Mustang Eco Museum** (admission Rs 100; ⊘10am-5pm Tue-Thu, Sat & Sun, to 3pm Fri, to 4pm in winter), worth a visit for its displays on herbal medicine and a re-created chapel. This southern fringe of Jomsom is properly known as Puthang. Just northeast of here is the airport, where you'll find the main hotels, restaurants, shops and airline offices.

Xanadu Guesthouse (📑 069-440060; chandramohangauchan@yahoo.com; r from Rs 700, without bathroom Rs 300; ☎) is popular for its clean rooms, excellent restaurant (yak steaks and hot chocolate apple pie!) and laundry service. Other good places on the main drag include the Trekkers Inn, Majesty, Moonlight and Tilicho hotels, all with en suite rooms for around Rs 800, as well as cheaper options. Most have a central courtyard surrounded by rooms, and meals are often served at a *kotatsu* – a Japanese-style table covered with a blanket to warm your legs with the heat from a charcoal brazier.

Slightly upmarket options include rambling **Om's Home** (☑069-440042; info@ omshomejomsom.com; s/d Rs 1750/2200, with breakfast Rs 2100/2900; ☎), with tiled hot-water bathrooms, a sunny courtyard and a cafe, and the **Alka Marco Polo** (☑069-440007; r with/without bathroom from Rs 700/300; @☎), which boasts a sauna (Rs 500) and internet access.

Jomsom has numerous well-stocked shops, including the Round Annapurna Trekking Equipment Shop, which can arrange porters.

You must register at the **TIMS checkpost** (⊙10am-5pm) near the Trekkers Inn, and across the road at the **ACAP visitor centre** **and checkpost** (⊙6am-6pm summer, 7am-5pm winter), where there's also a safe drinking water station (Rs 40 per litre). The nearby **Machhapuchhare Bank** (⊙9am-2.30pm Sun-Thu, 9am-12.30pm Fri) changes cash and travellers cheques and even boasts an ATM (Visa only), whenever there's electricity!

ℹ Getting There & Away

The arrival of the morning flight from Pokhara is the highlight of the Jomsom day. **Tara Air** (☑069-440069; www.taraair.com), **Simrik Airlines** (☑069-440167; www.simrikairlines. com) and **Nepal Airlines** (☑069-440081; www. nepalairlines.com.np) operate flights (US$111) to Pokhara and have offices where you can book and reconfirm tickets. Flights depart between 7am and 9am. Jeeps and buses operate on the new road to/from Ghasa (Rs 830, five daily) for connections to Beni. En route destinations include Marpha (Rs 180), Tukuche (Rs 305), and Larjung (Rs 415). Enquire at the ticket office by the Alka Marco Polo. For Muktinath (Rs 710, 1½ hours) visit the office at the northern edge of Old Jomsom.

Langtang, Helambu & Manaslu

Why Go?

The first trekkers in Nepal started on the outskirts of Kathmandu, and the mountains north of the capital have long been the favoured choice of trekkers with limited time in the world's highest mountains.

Unfortunately, Langtang, Helambu and Manaslu were the three areas hardest hit by the 2015 earthquakes. Entire villages were destroyed by landslides in the Langtang Valley, and lodges collapsed like children's building blocks along all the main trekking routes in these areas.

It is likely that the Langtang Valley and associated treks to Gosainkund and the Ganja La will be off-limits to trekkers until at least mid- to late 2016, and even then, these treks may only be possible as camping treks until trails and infrastructure are restored.

North of the earthquake epicenter at Gorkha, Manaslu was also devastated, with collapsed lodges and small landslides all along the Around Manaslu trail. Many villages in Helambu – the closest trekking area to Kathmandu – were also destroyed, though the Tamang Heritage Trail escaped with less damage.

At the time of writing, only the Tamang Heritage Trail was officially open to trekkers. It is essential to seek local information on the current status of trails and lodges before attempting any trek in this region.

When to Go

➡ In the past, October and November have been seen as the prime months for hiking this region. April, when the hillsides are aflame with colourful rhododendron flowers, is another popular time to trek.

➡ Trekkers have tended to avoid December to March, when the Laurebina La, Ganja La and higher parts of Manaslu trek are closed by snow, and lodges close at higher elevations.

➡ Mid-winter trekking is possible, though, on the much lower Helambu Circuit and the Tamang Heritage Trail.

Langtang, Helambu & Manaslu

1. Langtang Valley Trek (p200)
2. Tamang Heritage Trail (p202)
3. Ganja La Trek (p204)
4. Gosainkund Trek (p206)
5. Helambu Circuit Trek (p209)
6. Around Manaslu Trek (p212)

25 km
15 miles

TIBET (CHINA)

Longtang Glacier
Lomnang
Chilankha
Dolkha
Charikot
Shalbachum Glacier
Barabise
Bansangu
Kodari
Ghunthang
Syaule
Chautaara
Chang Samarphu (3913m)
Balephi Khola
Jhumri Khola
Penthang Ri (6830m)
Langshisha Kharka
Langtang National Park
Langshisha Glacier
Kyungka Ri (6979m)
Langshisha Ri
Kyanjin
Kyanjin Gompa
Tarke Ghyang
Kakani
Thimbu
Chipling
Chisopani
Sundarijal
KATHMANDU

Bhote Kosi
LANGTANG
Langtang
Thulo Syabru
Tharepati
HELAMBU
Shivapuri Nagarjun National Park
Kakan
Naubise

Rasuwagadhi
Syabrubesi
Dhunche
Gotlang
Betrawati
Trisuli Bazar
Ratmate
Bhaireni
Malekhu
Benighat
Hugdi

Tatopani
Paldor (5928m)
Great Himalayan Trail
Arughat Khola
Dhading
Trisuli
Trisuli

TIBET (CHINA)
Ngu La
Shar Khola
Sringi Himal (7187m)
Ganesh II (7118m)
Ganesh Himal
Ganesh IV (7140m)
Namrung
Ghap
Deng
Chuling Khola
Baudha (6674m)
Jagat
Dudh Pokhari
Mimi Pokhari
Tharo Khola
Machha Khola
Machha Khola
Soti Khola
Khanchowk
Arughat
Soti Khola
Chepe Khola
Gorkha
Cheres
Mugling
Abu
Khaireni
Dumre
Turture
Besi Sahar
Damauli
Madi Khola

Kang Guru (6981m)
Pisang Peak (6091m)
Annapurna II (7937m)
Dharamsala (Larkye Phedi)
Laiyang La (5098m)
Larkya La (5100m)
Samdo
Bimtang
Soti Khola
Phungi (6328m)
Manaslu (8156m)
Dharapani
Gho
Sama
Lho
Manaslu Conservation Area
Himalchuli (7893m)
Chame
Annapurna Conservation Area
Sundar (4335m)
Lamjung Himal (6986m)
Taunja Danda
Telbrung Danda
Bahundanda
Jagat
Baro Pokhari
Krapa Danda
Chisopani
Rupa Khola
Begnas Tal
Khaireni
Prithvi Hwy
Seti River
Shaktikhor

Nar Khola
Dudh Khola
Marsyangdi Khola
Kali Gandaki

TIBET (CHINA)

TREKKING AFTER THE 2015 EARTHQUAKES

The 2015 earthquakes caused devastation to trekking routes in central Nepal. Here is an overview of the status of treks in this region.

Langtang Valley Trek Landslides destroyed paths and entire villages; trails are unlikely to reopen until late 2016 and routes may change.

Tamang Heritage Trail Some earthquake damage but the route was declared open in July 2015.

Ganja La Trek Widespread damage to trails and increased risk of avalanches at the pass, but may reopen before other treks because already a camping route.

Gosainkund Trek Widespread damage to trails and villages but trails anticipated to reopen earlier than other routes as this is an important pilgrimage route.

Helambu Circuit Trek Massive damage to villages, trails and roads to trailheads; may revert to being a camping trek.

Around Manaslu Trek Widespread damage to lodges, villages and trails – was still being assessed at the time of writing; may revert to being a camping trek.

ⓘ Planning

PERMITS & REGULATIONS

Assuming trekking is permitted, the Langtang, Gosainkund and Helambu treks enter Langtang National Park and trekkers must pay an Rs 3000 entry fee, payable at the Tourist Service Centre (p59) in Kathmandu.

Treks starting or ending at Sundarijal enter Shivapuri National Park and are subject to an Rs 500 entry fee, payable at Chisopani or Sundarijal.

For Manaslu, a restricted area permit is required. In the past, these have been easy enough to get through a trekking agency. Trekking this area means entering the Manaslu Conservation Area, which levies an Rs 2000 MCAP fee.

Use of firewood is officially prohibited throughout all protected areas, even though most lodges use it, and you must carry stoves and fuel if you are camping.

ACCOMMODATION

Before the earthquake, most treks through Langtang, Gosainkund, Helambu and Manaslu were teahouse treks, with lodges dotted all along the main trails. The exception was the remote and challenging Ganja La trek, which required camping equipment and mountaineering gear. Today, with so many lodges damaged or destroyed, all treks in these areas are likely to be camping-only in the short term, if they are open at all.

Before the disaster, the abundance of lodges had forced down prices in this region, with many places charging only a nominal amount for accommodation (from around Rs 300 on the Langtang trail, and from Rs 250 on other trails), on the understanding that trekkers eat on site. Facilities were not quite as developed as those on the Everest and Annapurna trek routes but adequate, with (normally free) hot solar showers, though these were rarely hot enough to encourage use.

Where lodges are open after the disaster, you should expect things to be a little less comfortable than before, as lodge owners will be putting all their efforts into rebuilding. Prices are also hard to predict. It is essential to confirm that accommodation and meals will be available for all overnight stops before attempting any route in this area.

GETTING THERE & AWAY

Unlike other trekking areas in Nepal, there are no reliable flight options into the Langtang or Manaslu regions. Before the earthquakes, it was possible to reach Kyanjin Gompa by chartered helicopter in the peak season (budget on US$300 per person for a group of four or five).

The main route to the trailheads in this area is by bus or taxi from Kathmandu, though the Helambu trek can be started on foot from the outskirts of Kathmandu, and it was previously possible to start the Manaslu trek on foot from Gorkha.

Road transport to the trailheads is slowly being restored as part of the post-earthquake rescue effort, but depending on the condition of trails, it may be necessary to follow alternative routes – check ahead before leaving Kathmandu.

FILMS

The fascinating documentary *Unmistaken Child* (www.unmistakenchild.com) records the search to find the reincarnation of respected teacher Lama Konchog. It was filmed in the Tsum Valley.

Mani, the Hidden Valley of Happiness at a Crossroads is a 2013 film exploring the challenges facing the Tsum Valley as it builds its first ever road to China.

LANGTANG VALLEY

Langtang is a narrow valley sandwiched between the main Himalayan range to the north, bordering Tibet, and a slightly lower range of snowy peaks to the south. Mighty Langtang Lirung (7246m) dominates the valley to the north; Gang Chhenpo (6388m) and the trekking peak of Naya Kangri (5846m) lie to the south; and Dorje Lakpa (6966m) protects the east end of the valley. The appeal of Langtang has always been the chance to explore Nepali villages, snow-capped peaks and imposing glaciers at a comfortably low elevation, but the region has always been much less visited than Everest or Annapurna, despite its proximity to Kathmandu.

Everything changed in April and May 2015. The earthquakes shook apart hundreds of homes and trekking lodges all along the valley, and Langtang village itself was utterly destroyed by landslides, with just a few houses left standing. International aid agencies are engaged in a massive program of reconstruction in the valley, but at the time of writing this was still an emergency relief effort, and the Langtang valley was expected to be closed to trekkers for some time. Even when it reopens, this route may only be accessible as a camping trek until trails and infrastructure are restored.

The trek description below explains the trek as it was walked before the disaster, but the damage to trails and villages is so severe that some sections may need to be abandoned and new routes found.

Langtang Valley Trek

One of Nepal's 'big three' treks, the week-long walk up and down the Langtang Valley traces a narrow forested valley, tight against the icy-cold Langtang Khola (River Langtang), emerging in the shadow of the mighty Langtang mountains. Reaching a maximum elevation of 3870m, the trails climb through ever-changing forests, which start out sub-tropical, turn deciduous and then, higher up, morph into pine and rhododendron forest. From the end point, Kyanjin Gompa, the views are even more spectacular, and trails climb further into the hills, opening up some memorable day and overnight detours.

However, this route was severely affected by the 2015 earthquakes. Few settlements in the valley escaped without some collapsed buildings, and Langtang itself was completely destroyed by a deadly landslide that killed hundreds of local people and trekkers. Trails and bridges were also badly damaged all along the route, with many sections blocked by small landslides. Trekking agencies are predicting that even if the trek reopens, the route may need to change to avoid areas that are vulnerable to further landslides and rockfalls because of the destabilising effects of the earthquake.

At the time of writing, all three possible trailheads for the trek – Syabrubesi, Dhunche and Thulo Bhakrhu – and most villages along the route were active disaster zones, with aid organisations engaged in a massive program of reconstruction. If the trails do reopen, it may only be possible to

EARTHQUAKE DAMAGE IN LANGTANG, HELAMBU AND MANASLU

Before the 2015 earthquakes, the trails through Langtang, Helambu and Manaslu were favourite options for trekkers looking for a short, sharp dose of Himalayan trekking without the hassle of flying to distant trailheads. Unfortunately, the disaster has redrawn the trekking map in this region. Parts of the Langtang Valley were all but destroyed, and more than 200 people lost their lives, including many foreign trekkers, as buildings collapsed and landslides engulfed whole villages along the route to Kyanjin Gompa. There were more landslides, more building collapses and more deaths throughout Helambu and Manaslu. It will be some time before trekking is possible on most routes in this area, and it may be years before all the trails are fully open again as teahouse treks.

At the time of writing, only the Tamang Heritage Trail was open to trekkers. The Langtang Valley was expected to be closed completely to trekkers until the main trails could be repaired, and Helambu and Manaslu were also off-limits pending assessments of the trails and surveys of earthquake-damaged buildings. In all of these areas, routes may need to change, and villages may need to be moved or abandoned because of the ongoing risk of landslides after the disaster.

Langtang Valley Trek

Ganesh Himal;
Paldor;
Saljung Himal

Rasuwagadhi

Timure

Langtang II
(Ghenge Liru)
(6571m)

Khaidi

Phentnng Khola

Bhote Kosi

Ghote Khola

L A N G T A N G

P a n g s a n g   L e k h

Tharuche

Dal

Phyasing

Ghumba

Tatopani
Hot Springs

Nagthali
Ghyang

Thuman

Lingling

Thangshyap

Langtang

Chilime Khola

Gonggang

Brindang

Pelko

Briddim Khola

Ghora Tabela

Cherka

Patjhung

Briddim

Gumanchok
(Riverside)

Chilime

Brajam

Pajun

Bahun Danda
(2180m)

Wangal

L a n g t a n g

Thambuchet

Khangjung

Lama Hotel
(Changtang)

LANGTANG

Goljung

Bhanjyanggaon

Rongga
Bhanjyang
(2190m)

Syabrubesi

Syarpagaon

Rimche

START/
END

Bamboo

C h i m i s e d a n g   L e k h

Sano
Bharkhu

Doman

Pairo

Brabal

Thulo
Syabru

U Kyang

Thulo
Bharkhu

**Alternative
Route**

*Ganesh
Kund*

Dhunche

Chalang

Ghopcha Khola

Sing Gompa
(Chandan Bari)

Trisuli

Pati

Trisuli

visit the valley on a camping trek until lodges are rebuilt, and it may be years before the area is fully open to trekkers. It is vital to seek local advice on the status of trails and lodges before attempting to trek in this area.

ⓘ Planning

There have traditionally been three approaches to Kyanjin Gompa, beginning in either Syabrubesi, Thulo Bharkhu or Dhunche, but most trekkers avoided the steeper and less interesting direct approach from Dhunche via Sing Gompa. However, all three villages were devastated by the earthquakes and transport to the trailheads was still affected at the time of writing. From Kyanjin Gompa, trekkers could either return via the same route, or continue over the challenging Ganja La into Helambu, though this trek requires basic mountaineering skills, camping equipment and an ex-

perienced guide, and is only possible in good weather. A third option was to trek back to Thulo Syabru from Langtang, then cross into Helambu via Gosainkund. Whether any of these routes are open when you visit will depend on the progress of the reconstruction effort.

Before the earthquakes, there were national park radios at Ghora Tabela, Langtang and Magin Goth, and mobile phone reception for users of the Namaste network and its spin-off services. Satellite phones were available at Kyanjin Gompa to summon a chopper in an emergency, and medical treatment was available at the hospital at Dhunche and the health post at Syabrubesi. The best map for this region is the Nepa Maps/Himalayan Maphouse 1:120,000 *Langtang Gosainkund & Helambu* (2010), which also covers the Tamang Heritage Trail.

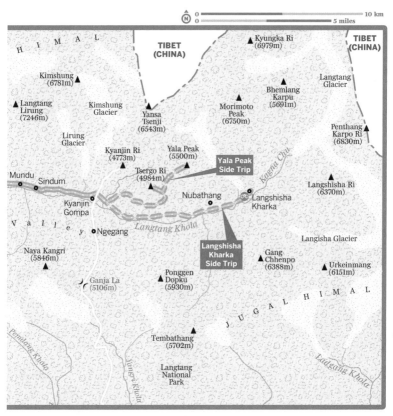

Duration 7–9 days

Max Elevation 3870m

Difficulty Medium

Season September to May

Start Syabrubesi (or Thulo Bharkhu)

Finish Syabrubesi (or Dhunche)

Permits TIMS permit required and entry ticket to Langtang National Park (Rs3000)

Before the disaster, the trek was broken down into the following stages, but some of these steps are impassable after the disaster because of landslides. If the trek reopens in future, it may follow a quite different route.

DAY 1: SYABRUBESI TO LAMA HOTEL
(5–6 HOURS, 1070M ASCENT)

After registering and showing permits at Syabrubesi, and crossing the Bhote Kosi riv-er, the first day involves a climb through scenic forests to Changtang, popularly known as **Lama Hotel** (2480m), via the villages of Doman, Pairo, Bamboo and Renche. However, all villages higher than Bamboo were badly affected by the earthquake, and the lodges at Lama Hotel were also severely damaged.

ALTERNATIVE DAY 1: THULO BHARKHU TO LAMA HOTEL
(7 HOURS, 340M ASCENT)

From earthquake-damaged Thulo Bharkhu on the Syabrubesi road, a stone staircase climbs through pine and Rhododendron forests to villages at **Brabal** (2200m) and **Thulo Syabru** (2260m). The path to Langtang continues through forest to **U Kyang** (2040m), descending to meet the Langtang Valley trail just east of Doman. An alternative trail climbs directly to Thulo Syabru from Syabrubesi.

Tamang Heritage Trail

DAY 2: LAMA HOTEL TO LANGTANG
(4–5 HOURS, 980M ASCENT)

The trail from Lama Hotel rises past small villages in the forest, before emerging into a classic U-shaped glacial valley. Before the quake, permits were checked at the army post just before Thangshyap, but all the settlements between Lama Hotel and Thangshyap were badly damaged by the tremors, and the section of trail beyond was obliterated by a vast landslide, which flattened the villages of Tsarding, Chamki, Gumba and **Langtang**, formerly the overnight stop for Day 2. A new route will need to be found to bypass this damaged section of the trail.

DAY 3: LANGTANG TO KYANJIN GOMPA
(2–3 HOURS, 460M ASCENT)

The trail onwards from Langtang climbs through increasingly rugged country through the small yak-herding villages of Mundu, Sindum and Yampha, eventually tracing the path of the Langtang Khola to **Kyanjin Gompa** (3870m). However, landslides blocked many sections of the trail and most lodges in all villages on this section of the trail were badly damaged, though the damage was not as severe as at Langtang village.

DAYS 4–5: LANGTANG VALLEY (LOCAL TREKS)

Having reached Kyanjin Gompa, most travellers take a few days to explore the surrounding valleys. One popular trail follows the **Lirung Valley**, which cuts a dramatic track to the north, framed by a line of peaks along the Tibetan border. Northeast of Kyanjin Gompa, the viewpoint at **Kyanjin Ri** (4600m) is still spectacular despite the disaster, as is the viewpoint at **Tsergo Ri** (4984m), a longer day trip to the east. The two-hour trip to **Tsona Lakes** is a less energetic alternative. Depending on the state of trails, these detours may feature on new trekking itineraries in the future.

TAMANG HERITAGE TRAIL

As part of its Tourism for Rural Poverty Alleviation Programme (TRPAP), the Nepal Tourism Board established the Tamang Heritage Trail, a village tourism project in the Tibetan-influenced Rasuwa district bordering Langtang. The aim of the initiative is to bring tourism money to communities off the main tourist routes. Profits from homestay accommodation, food sales, handicrafts and Tamang cultural performances are split between the individuals concerned and village social funds. The route provides an interesting add-on to the more commercialised Langtang area, and the trails saw only limited damage from the 2015 earthquakes, thanks in part to the use of timber rather than stone to build houses in this area. The route was declared open to trekkers in July 2015, but check locally to make sure that the trails are operating and food and accommodation are available before setting off from Kathmandu.

A five- or six-day loop of the region from Syabrubesi is the most popular option. Day one takes you up steep switchbacks, gaining 720m to the Rongga Bhanjyang. Head up the hill for a detour to Goljung or continue along the dirt road to Gotlang, the largest, and most beautiful, Tamang village in the area, from where you can make the short detour to Parvati Kund lake. Day two takes you to the community-run hot spring pools at Tatopani, via Chilime and Gonggang (an ascent of 840m). Day three climbs 560m to the ridge of Nagthali Ghyang for fine mountain views into Tibet and descends 820m to Thuman. On day four follow the ridge, then descend another 640m to cross the Bhote Kosi and hike south to Briddim (a 400m ascent from the river) via Lingling. Briddim (2229m) has masses of simple homestays. From here it's all downhill (770m descent) to Syabrubesi via Wangal, or you can link up with the Langtang trek by taking the high northern alternative route via Syarpagaon. Many maps and route descriptions talk about walking from Thuman to Timure and then onward to the Tibet border, but recent, and ongoing, road construction and some huge hydro-electric projects have made this part of the walk rather unpleasant.

Accommodation is available in homestays in Gotlang, Thumen and Briddim, which offer a more intimate experience than the large-scale trekking lodges. There are also teahouses and lodges in all three of these villages, as well as every other village along the route, but check before you set off in case any have been affected by the earthquake. Standards are generally lower than on most established routes, and costs are around Rs 200 to Rs 500 per person per night. You should be able to find a licensed guide in Syabrubesi for around Rs 1500 per day, which includes their food and accommodation.

SIDE TRIP: LANGSHISHA KHARKA
(6½–7½ HOURS, 500M ASCENT, 500M DESCENT)

A more challenging add-on from Kyanjin Gompa is the long day, or overnight' camping trek to Langshisha Kharka, a remote summer pasture with eye-popping views of Doje Lakpa (6966m) and Penthang Karpo Ri (6830m). The trail follows the Langtang Khola east up the valley.

SIDE TRIP: YALA PEAK
(2 DAYS; 1630M ASCENT, 1630M DESCENT)

Another challenging bolt-on is the two-day return trip to Yala Peak (5500m), a decommissioned trekking peak to the east, accessible as a camping trek from Kyanjin Gompa. No extra permits are required, but you will need camping equipment, basic mountaineering gear (ice-axes, ropes and crampons) and an experienced guide. The route traces the trail to Tsergo Ri before climbing the southern slope of the peak.

DAYS 6–7: RETURN TO SYABRUBESI OR THULO BHARKHU
(2 DAYS, 2510M DESCENT)

For the return trip, you can go back the way you came, to Syabrubesi or Thulo Bharkhu, over two days, or continue over the Ganja La, or via Gosainkund, to Helambu. There is also a high trail back to Syabrubesi via Syarpagaon (2600m), taking around five hours.

TREKKING PEAKS

There's only one frequently climbed trekking peak in the Langtang region: **Naya Kangri** (5846m), visible to the south of Kyanjin Gompa. The ascent requires a snow and rock climb from a base camp north or south of Ganja La.

LANGTANG, HELAMBU & MANASLU LANGTANG VALLEY TREK

Ganja La Trek

The most challenging, and dangerous, trekking trail in the Langtang area is the short, sharp crossing of the 5106m Ganja La from Kyanjin Gompa in Langtang to Tarke Ghyang in Helambu. However, this is a challenging crossing, requiring camping equipment, cold weather gear and an experienced guide who knows the route. Crossing the Ganja La allows for a neat 14-day loop that combines the Langtang Valley and Gosainkund lakes, without the need for backtracking. However, the parents of a trekker who died on this route have asked we emphasise that under no circumstances should you attempt to cross the pass alone or without sufficient equipment.

Unfortunately, as with all treks in this chapter, the route has been badly affected by the earthquakes, with massive destruction to both the approach trek via the Langtang Valley, and to Tarke Ghyang and other villages on the far side of the pass. Before the quakes, lodges in Kyanjin Gompa could arrange guides and porters for the crossing; today, arrangements may need to be made in Kathmandu, assuming that the trail is open. The pass is usually closed from late November to May and may be closed at other times because of snow at the pass. Note that the trek may be even more avalanche- and landslide-prone following the disaster.

Duration 5 days

Max Elevation 5106m

Difficulty Hard

Season October to November, March to May

Start Kyanjin Gompa

Finish Tarke Ghyang

Permits TIMS permit required and entry ticket to Langtang National Park (Rs3000) and, if you walk all the way back to Kathmandu on the Helambu circuit, an entry ticket to Shivapuri National Park (Rs500)

Before the disaster, the trek was broken down into the following stages, beginning at Kyanjin Gompa at the end of the Langtang Valley trek. At the time of writing, this approach route was closed, and the end destination, Tarke Gyang, had been devastated by the earthquake. As this is a camping trek, it may be possible to walk the route again once the trails are surveyed, but it is not possible to say if the same route will be followed in future. The trek is not walked in the opposite direction because of the large altitude gain.

DAY 1: KYANJIN GOMPA (REST DAY)

The altitude gain requires an extra rest day in Kyanjin Gompa, but this is an opportunity for some rewarding side treks.

DAY 2: KYANJIN GOMPA TO NGEGANG
(5 HOURS, 130M ASCENT)

The first day is a short climb from Kyanjin Gompa, crossing the Langtang Khola and ascending through forest to the yak pasture at **Ngegang** (approx 4000m).

DAY 3: NGEGANG TO KELDANG
(7 HOURS; 1106M ASCENT, 836M DESCENT)

The actual crossing of the pass involves a steep climb through an avalanche-prone valley and this stage can be covered by deep snow. From the pass itself, the views to the north from the pass, of Langtang Lirung and the peaks in Tibet, including Shisha Pangma at 8013m, are outstanding. The trail then makes a dangerous and precarious descent to the Yangri Khola on an indistinct trail (an experienced guide is essential here) before reaching a pasture and scattered goths at **Keldang** (approximately 4270m).

DAY 4: KELDANG TO DUKPU
(7 HOURS, 190M DESCENT)

The total altitude change is deceptive on this leg, as there are hours of ups and downs as you follow the ridge to the summer pasture at **Dukpu** (4080m).

DAY 5: DUKPU TO TARKE GHYANG
(6 HOURS, 1490M DESCENT)

There's one more pass to climb, with spectacular views towards the Khumbu region, before the trail descends rapidly though rhododendron forest to the monastic retreat at **Gekye Gompa** (3020m). The final stage is a steep plummet towards the Sherpa village of **Tarke Ghyang** (2590m), which was badly damaged in the earthquake, with many buildings destroyed. From here, it is possible to follow the Helambu Circuit trek in either direction, or you could return directly to Kathmandu.

Gosainkund Trek

Rather than returning directly to Kathmandu at the end of the Langtang Valley trek, a popular alternative is the eight-day crossing to Helambu, via holy lakes of Gosainkund, which makes for a highly underrated trek in its own right. Upper stages of the route offer stunning views and the sacred lakes are a popular pilgrimage site, drawing up to 20,000

Hindu pilgrims during the August full-moon festival of Janai Purnima. The lake is also sacred to Buddhists, who have lined the shore with hundreds of cairns. At Tharepati, the trek connects with the Helambu Circuit Trek (p208), offering three potential routes back towards Kathmandu, the most rewarding emerging right on the outskirts of the capital.

However, once again, earthquake damage is extensive on this route. At the time of writing, trails were yet to be properly surveyed, but many buildings had been destroyed on both the Langtang and Helambu side, and there were reports of landslides and rockfalls along the route. Trekking agencies are predicting that this trek may reopen ahead of other treks in the area to accommodate the needs of pilgrims, but it may only be possible as a camping trek until infrastructure is restored and it is not possible to say if the same route will be followed. Note that teahouses on this route have traditionally closed during winter (early December to early March), when the higher stages are snowbound. Trekking to Gosainkund directly from Helambu is not recommended because of the steep altitude gain; we've met many people suffering pulmonary oedema on the trails between Tharepati and Gosainkund.

There is a strict ban on the use of firewood in Gosainkund; if you are camping, be sure to bring kerosene for fuel.

Duration 8 days

Max Elevation 4610m

Difficulty Medium to hard

Season October to November, March to April

Start Thulo Syabru, Syabrubesi or Dhunche

Finish Sundarijal

Permits TIMS card, Langtang National Park permit (Rs3000) and, if you join up with the Helambu circuit, a ticket to Shivapuri National Park will be required (Rs500)

Before the disaster, the trek was broken down into the following stages, beginning at Thulo Syabru, Syabrusei or Dhunche at the start of the Langtang Valley Trek (p199). However, all these trailheads were badly damaged by the earthquake, as was the road from Kathmandu. The trek is not usually walked in the opposite direction because of the large altitude gain - we've seen

Gosainkund Trek

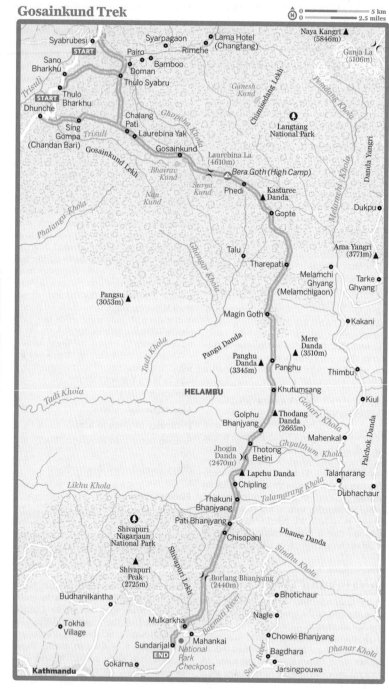

firsthand the effects on trekkers who have ignored this advice.

DAY 1: THULO SYABRU TO SING GOMPA
(3–4 HOURS, 1040M ASCENT)

From the earthquake-damaged village of Thulo Syabru (2260m), close to the trailhead at Thulo Bhakhu, the easiest route to follow climbs to the village of Dursagang (2735), then goes steeply uphill through hemlock and rhododendron forest to the top of the ridge at Phoprang Danda (3190m). The trail then crosses the ridge and climbs through forest to the cluster of lodges at Chandan Bari, also known as **Sing Gompa** (3330m). It is also possible to start this trek from Dhunche, climbing to Sing Gompa via the villages of Deorali and Dimsa.

DAY 2: SING GOMPA TO LAUREBINA YAK
(2–3 HOURS, 590M ASCENT)

After a climb through forests, the second day enters the Gosainkund protected area, and the views get better and better. The trail continues to climb though Chalang Pati (3550m) to **Laurebina Yak** (3920m), where the reward is a vista spanning the Annapurnas, Manaslu (8156m), the four peaks of the Ganesh Himal (with Paldor Peak), some enticing unnamed peaks in Tibet and finally Langtang Lirung. It's possible to continue to Gosainkund, and many people do, but it makes more sense to stay here to aid acclimatisation before ascending another 500m.

A warning: many maps show a trail from Laurebina Yak to Ghora Tabela, but it does not exist and trekkers have become lost and have even died trying to find it. If you need to return to Langtang, go the long way round via Thulo Syabru.

DAY 3: LAUREBINA YAK TO GOSAINKUND
(2–3 HOURS, 540M ASCENT)

The climb to the lakes enters alpine country above the treeline. Your first sight of the lakes is the waterfall descending from Saraswati Kund, but it's a tricky and exposed climb to actually reach the lakes, on a trail that can be dangerous if snowbound. If conditions look bad, it's wise to return to Laurebina Yak. After passing some stone Ganesh carvings, you'll reach **Bhairav Kund**, and finally **Gosainkund** (4400m), said to have been created by Shiva piercing a glacier with his trident (*trisul*) to obtain water to quench his thirst after consuming poison gathered from the churning of the oceans. It is said that the water from this lake disappears underground

via a subterranean channel and surfaces in Kumbeshwar pool, next to the five-storey Shiva Temple in Patan, more than 60km away.

Before the quake, the pilgrim village had lodges, a Shiva shrine and a helipad, but the condition of these after the earthquake is unknown. Pilgrims circumambulate the lake in a clockwise direction, passing hundreds of small cairns. For the best views of the lake climb the ridge behind the lodges to two viewpoints (4640m; 25 minutes) decorated with prayer flags. Hundreds of people come here to worship and bathe during the full-moon festival each August.

For a longer half-day exploration it's possible to follow faint trails south from the southeast corner of the lake to a series of smaller half-frozen lakes: Dudh Kund (Milk Lake), Chandra Kund (Moon Lake), Ragat Kund (Blood Lake) and finally Ama Kund (Mother Lake; 4540m).

DAY 4: GOSAINKUND TO GOPTE
(6–7½ HOURS, 300M ASCENT, 1320M DESCENT)

The trail traverses the northern side of Gosainkund Lake and climbs past rock cairns to **Laurebina La** (4610m), with more dramatic views over this mountain lakeland. Beyond the pass, the trail drops to 'High Camp', a collection of seasonal lodges at **Bera Goth** (4230m). Two trails run on to Tharepati – the upper trail is steep, and dangerous after snow, with no accommodation or shelter until Tharepati; stick to the lower, safer trail that descends for an hour down the middle of the valley to **Phedi** (3740m), three hours from Gosainkund. The trail onwards climbs through bamboo forest to Kasturee Danda (Musk Deer Ridge), then drops below the towering cliffs of Thare Danda to **Gopte** (3440m).

DAY 5: GOPTE TO THAREPATI
(1½ HOURS, 330M ASCENT)

Ups and downs and a long descent through ravines will take you to **Tharepati** (3640m), an exposed collection of lodges on a windy ridge that marks the high point of the Helambu Circuit trek. It is not clear if the lodges here survived the earthquake.

DAY 6: THAREPATI TO GOLPHU BHANJYANG
(5–6 HOURS, 210M ASCENT, 1650M DESCENT)

It takes two days to reach Sundarijal on the Helambu Circuit trail. The first day drops off the ridge and descends to Magin Goth (3285m) and the Langtang National Park office at Khutumsang (2450m). There is one more pass to cross before the trail drops to **Golphu Bhanjyang** (2140m).

DAY 7: GOLPHU BHANJYANG TO CHISOPANI
(5–6 HOURS, 970M ASCENT, 790M DESCENT)

Walk on through rhododendron forest through the villages of Thotong, Lapchu Danda and **Chipling** (2170m). Continue south past Sherpa and Chhetri villages to reach the comparatively modern settlement of **Chisopani** (2251m) at the end of a 4WD track.

DAY 8: CHISOPANI TO SUNDARIJAL
(5–6 HOURS, 150M ASCENT, 1150M DESCENT)

To reach Sundarijal (1350m) and a bus back to Kathmandu, continue to descend through the villages of Borlang Bhanjyang and Mulkharka to reach a Shivapuri National Park checkpoint, then drop down to the Sundarijal bus stand.

HELAMBU

Circling the valley of the Melamchi Khola, just 75km north of Kathmandu, the Helambu area offers classic Himalayan foothill landscapes, with plenty of dramatic rises and plummeting descents. However trails are rarely crowded and there are no overbooked flights to worry about at the end of the trek – you can just hop on the bus or jump into a taxi back to Kathmandu. In just one week, you can loop around from Sundarijal to Thimbu, passing mountain viewpoints, alpine meadows and Buddhist villages. Alternatively, you can tack Helambu onto the end of the Langtang or Gosainkund trek, crossing into Helambu via the high-altitude passes at Laurebina La (4610m) or Ganja La (5106m). Both routes involve steep gains in altitude, so AMS is a serious risk and the passes are snow-covered and dangerous in winter.

Earthquake damage was severe on Helambu and buildings collapsed in most villages in the region. Trails and roads were affected by landslides and the status of villages along the Helambu Circuit trek had, at the time of writing, yet to be formally assessed. If the trails do reopen, it may only be possible to visit the valley on a camping trek until lodges are rebuilt, and it may be years before the area is fully open to trekkers. It is vital to seek local advice on the status of trails and lodges before attempting to trek in this area.

Helambu Circuit Trek

The closest trek to Kathmandu, this week-long hike passes cascading terraces, Sherpa villages, alpine meadows, rhododendron forests and mountain viewpoints. Although road construction is eating away at parts of the route (you're never more than a day and half walk from a road and a bus back to Kathmandu), it offers a sampler for what the rest of Nepal has to offer.

Unfortunately, Helambu was ravaged by the 2015 earthquakes; many settlements have been almost entirely destroyed and road transport into this region has also been disrupted. Before the earthquake, the most popular place to begin the trek was the village of Sundarijal, but it was also possible to start from Thimbu in the valley of the Melamchi Khola; whether this is still true will depend on the condition of the roads after the disaster. Check the status of trails and lodges before coming out from Kathmandu.

Because the elevation rarely exceeds 3500m, it is possible to trek in Helambu from October to May, but be prepared for snow at Tharepati in winter. Before the quakes, lodges were charging Rs 100 to Rs 200 per person; shared bathrooms are usually outside the main building – keep your coat, shoes and torch handy for night-time toilet trips.

Duration 6 days

Max Elevation 3640m

Difficulty Easy to medium

THE SHERPAS OF HELAMBU

The tribal people of upper Helambu are often described as Sherpas, but they call themselves Yolmo, after the original name for the Helambu Valley. Like the Sherpas of the Khumbu region, the Yolmo came to Nepal from the Tibetan plateau in the 15th century, settling in Tarke Ghyang and other villages around the Melamchi Khola. The Yolmo use the cursive Umescript, which is still used for handwritten texts in Tibet, and speak their own language, Yolmo, which is quite different to the Sherpa language of Khumbu.

Helambu Circuit Trek

Season October to April

Start/Finish Sundarijal or Thimbu

Permits TIMS permit required and ticket for Shivapuri National Park (Rs500)

Before the disaster, the trek was broken down into the following stages, beginning at the bus stand in Sundarijal, a short bus or taxi ride away from Kathmandu. However, the trails were badly affected by the quake and, until reconstruction work is complete, it is not possible to say if the same route will be followed. Check that accommodation will be available for all stops before attempting to trek in this region.

DAY 1: SUNDARIJAL TO CHISOPANI
(3½–4½ HOURS, 1150M ASCENT, 150M DESCENT)

The first day starts with a steep climb from the Sundarijal bus stand to a Shivapuri National Park checkpoint and dam. A dirt track leads first to Mulkharka (1800m) then crosses the pass at **Borlang Bhanjyang** (2440m). It's then a peaceful descent through forest to the comparatively modern village of **Chisopani** (2140m).

IN THE FOOTSTEPS OF GURU RINPOCHE

Also known as Padmasambhava, the Indian mystic Guru Rinpoche is credited with introducing Buddhism to Tibet and Bhutan in the 8th century on an epic grand tour of the Himalaya. The exact route he followed is hotly debated, but residents of Helambu believe that the Guru was a frequent visitor to Melamchi Ghyang, leaving his mark at several locations around the village.

As well as sitting in a stone throne near the path to Tharepati, the saint is believed to have meditated in the small cave at the top of Melamchi Ghyang, taken tea near the cliff wall below the village, and washed his clothes in a stream behind the village school. Locals still venerate the Guru by leaving offerings of prayer flags at all these locations.

There are many other sites in Helambu linked to Padmasambhava, who can easily be recognised by the three human heads impaled on his spear, representing the three *kayas* or metaphysical states of the Buddha.

Melamchi is also linked to the Tibetan poet and yogi Milarepa, who is said to have meditated in a cave on the east bank of the Melamchi River in the 11th century, composing the uplifting poem 'Song of a Yogi's Joy'. A new gompa has been built on the site by lamas from Bodhnath – you can get here from Melamchi Ghyang in around two hours, but you'll need to ask for directions to find the trail.

DAY 2: CHISOPANI TO GOLPHU BHANJYANG
(5–6 HOURS, 890M ASCENT, 970M DESCENT)

The trail onwards follows a 4WD track then drops off the ridge towards Pati Bhanjyang and **Chipling** (2170m). Meander on through fields and forests to the villages of Lapchu Danda, Thotong and finally **Golphu Bhanjyang** (2140m), where a road runs towards Kathmandu.

DAY 3: GOLPHU BHANJYANG TO THAREPATI
(6–7 HOURS, 1650M ASCENT, 210M DESCENT)

Views get increasingly impressive as you climb past streams and cow meadows to the village of **Khutumsang** (2450m), where officials collect the Langtang National Park entry fee. Continue north, climbing steeply through Panghu and Mere Danda to **Magin Goth** (3285m). There's one more steep climb to reach the ridge and **Tharepati** (3640m), where the trail to Gosainkund branches off to the northwest. Be wary of attempting the Gosainkund trek in this direction – many have succumbed to AMS on this route because of the steep climb to Laurebina La.

DAY 4: THAREPATI TO MELAMCHI GHYANG
(3–4 HOURS, 1160M DESCENT, 100M ASCENT)

Drop down from the ridge at Tharepati through forests and meadows full of ruined goths, before descending rapidly to the large village of **Melamchi Ghyang** (2530m), where many buildings collapsed in the quake. If there is no accommodation available here, you may need to continue walking down into the valley.

DAY 5: MELAMCHI GHYANG TO TARKE GHYANG
(5–6 HOURS, 610M ASCENT, 670M DESCENT)

Both the start and end point of this stage were devastated by the earthquake. Depending on the state of trails and lodges, it may be necessary to descend directly to Thimbu, connected by bus to Kathmandu. If it is possible to trek onwards, the trail winds past chortens and over a suspension bridge to Nakote, Dozum, Chiri and, eventually, **Tarke Ghyang** (2590m). From Tarke Ghyang, the Ganja La trail climbs to the southeast, but this route should only be attempted with an experienced guide and proper camping and mountaineering equipment.

DAY 6: TARKE GHYANG TO THIMBU
(3 HOURS, 1310M DESCENT)

The old Helambu trail continues to Sermathang, also damaged badly by the earthquake, but most trekkers descend to **Thimbu** (1580m) via the village of Kakani. Before the earthquake, there were daily buses from Thimbu to Kathmandu, but it was possible to hitch a lift down the valley to Melamchi Pul Bazaar, also devastated by the earthquake, which had more frequent transport. Whether any transport runs to Kathmandu will depend on the condition of the roads.

MANASLU HIMAL

The trek around 8156m Manaslu, the world's eighth-highest mountain, was only opened to tourists in 1991, and for years it was only possible as a camping trek, following trails beaten by mountaineering pioneers like HW Tilman and Jimmy Roberts as far back as the 1950s. Before the 2015 earthquakes, the circuit around the Manaslu massif was gaining prominence as the best new teahouse trek in Nepal, challenging more famous routes in the Annapurna and Everest regions. Indeed, with its high pass and staggering views, many considered this to be Nepal's best trek.

So it is all the more disheartening to see the destruction caused by the earthquakes on this spectacular trekking route. Starting just northeast of Gorkha, the Around Manaslu trek passes close to the epicentre of the 25 April earthquake, and damage has been extensive, with trails blocked by landslides and collapsed houses and lodges all along the trails, including on the side trek to the Tsum Valley.

While relief workers have reported from many villages, the route has yet to be formally surveyed and trails were closed to trekkers at the time of writing. Even when the trails reopen, it may only be possible to visit the valley on a camping trek until lodges are rebuilt. It is vital to seek local advice on the status of trails and lodges before attempting to trek in this area.

ℹ Planning

ACCOMMODATION & SUPPLIES

Before the earthquake, there were lodges all along the Around Manaslu route, offering simple but comfortable rooms for around Rs 200 per bed, with a daal bhaat ranging from Rs 300 to Rs 600. There were also shops in Lho and Namrung, and telephones in most villages, but no health facilities along the route. Many of the lodges have been damaged in the earthquake, and at the time of writing, it was not clear which villages had accommodation available. In time, lodges will be rebuilt, but in the immediate future the Around Manaslu circuit may only be possible as a camping trek.

The trek traverses a large elevation range, from the unpleasantly hot and humid lower valleys (even in October and November) to snow on the pass, so you and your porters will need an appropriate range of clothing.

MAPS

Nepa Maps produces a 1:110,000 *The High Route Around Manaslu* map and a useful pocket-sized 1:175,000 *Manaslu & Tsum Valley* map. The more

detailed 1:60,000 *Manaslu Base Camp* map covers the upper three-quarters of the trek and its most interesting detours.

The 1:85,000 *Ganesh Himal Tsum Valley* offers the best detail on Tsum, but doesn't cover Manaslu.

PERMITS & REGULATIONS

You need a restricted-area permit to trek the Manaslu Circuit, which can only be arranged through a trekking company. You must trek with a registered guide in a party of two or more.

The permit fee is US$70 for the first week (then US$10 per day) from September to November, and only US$50 per week (then US$7 per day) during the remainder of the year. The permit date starts from the day you leave Jagat.

The Manaslu Conservation Area Project (MCAP) is under the administration of Annapurna Conservation Area Project (ACAP), which levies a Rs 2000 MCAP fee.

You'll also need to pay in advance an additional Rs 2000 ACAP fee for the section from Dharapani to Besi Sahar. The ACAP checkpost is in upper Dharapani, just after you join the Annapurna trail.

As with other treks we cover, you now also need to arrange a TIMS card.

You also need a restricted-area permit for the Tsum Valley. The fee is lower than Manaslu, at US$35 per week from September to November, and only US$25 per week during the remainder of the year.

ℹ Towns & Facilities

Arughat (p217) and Besi Sahar (p194) are the main trailheads for the Manaslu region, though it's also possible to start the trek from Gorkha (p217). Note that Gorkha and Arughat were particularly badly hit by the 2015 earthquakes.

Around Manaslu Trek

Regarded by many as Nepal's best trek, the Manaslu Circuit offers an Annapurna-like package of spectacular views, increasingly rugged scenery and a high pass crossing at Larkya La (5100m), but without the crowds and apple pies. However, this is no walk in the park. In many places the walls of the Buri Gandaki Valley are perpendicular, so there is a huge amount of extra climbing as you hike up and down over ridges or across cliffside shelves. The trail is rough and steep and in a couple of places literally hangs on a bluff high above the river.

The trek is both geographically spectacular and culturally fascinating. The inhabitants of the upper Buri Gandaki, a region

Around Manaslu Trek

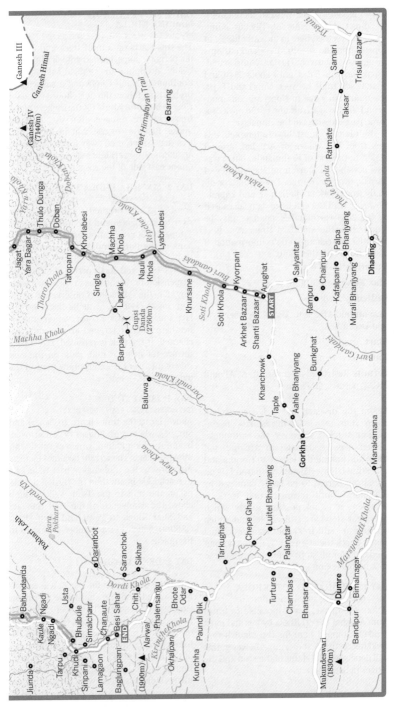

known as Nupri ('the western mountains'), are direct descendants of Tibetan immigrants who settled here in the early 1600s. In upper Nupri the speech, dress and customs are almost exclusively Tibetan. Nupri actually paid taxes to Tibet until about 1840 and there is still trade between Nupri and Tibet. The mountain views in Nupri are sensational, and the Larkya La is one of the most dramatic pass crossings in the Himalaya.

Traditionally, most have attempted this trek from the village of Arughat, around 125km northwest of Kathmandu, but it was also possible to start from the villages of Barpak, over the Rupina La (4720m), or directly from Gorkha via Barpak and Laprak. However, with the extensive damage caused by the 2015 earthquakes, changes may be required to the standard itinerary - it is essential to seek up-to-date information if planning to trek this route.

Duration 16–18 days

Max Elevation 5100m

Difficulty Medium

Season mid-March to May & October to mid-December

Start Arughat

Finish Besi Sahar

Permits Restricted-area permit, ACAP and MCAP permit, TIMS card

Before the disaster, the trek was broken down into the following stages, beginning at Arughat. However, the earthquake caused massive damage to Arughat and the roads linking the village to Gorkha and the Prithvi Hwy. The stages beyond Jagat are also reported to be badly damaged by landslides. Until reconstruction work is complete, it is not possible to say which overnight stops are still viable, and which sections are still trekkable via the original route. Check the status of trails and accommodation for all stops before attempting to trek in this region.

DAY 1: ARUGHAT TO SOTI KHOLA
(3½–4 HOURS, 220M ASCENT, 110M DESCENT)

Before the quake, it was possible to travel from Arughat to Soti Khola by bus and most trekkers stopped here for the night before trekking on the next morning; however, this will depend on the status of the road and the lodges in Soti Khola.

DAY 2: SOTI KHOLA TO MACHHA KHOLA
(5 HOURS, 300M ASCENT, 100M DESCENT)

The trek starts on a mule track and climbs on perilous steps blasted into a cliff face, before dropping to **Lyabrubesi** (880m). Continue to Nauli Khola and a suspension bridge, then follow the Buri (Budh) Gandaki river to **Machha Khola** (900m), where many trekkers were rescued after the 25 April quake. Reports suggest that in future, the trek may be rerouted away from the river to an alternative overnight stop in Kashi Gaun on the east side of the river.

DAY 3: MACHHA KHOLA TO JAGAT
(6–7 HOURS, 730M ASCENT, 100M DESCENT)

For Day 3, the original route follows the river to Khorlabesi and the warm spring at Tatopani (930m), continuing on the eastern bank of the Buri Gandaki to Doban, Thulo Dunga and **Yara Bagar** (1370m). The trail crosses back and forth across the river on suspension bridges to reach the entry gateway for the Manaslu Conservation Area and **Jagat** (1410m), with its flagstone village square. There's a conservation area office here where restricted area permits are checked. If the trek is rerouted, Day 3 may involve following a high path on the east side of the river before dropping to meet the old trail near Doban.

DAY 4: JAGAT TO DENG
(6–7 HOURS, 550M ASCENT, 80M DESCENT)

Above Jagat, the trail climbs to Salleri and Sirdibas, where most houses were destroyed, before reaching Philim, which escaped with minor damage. The terrain becomes increasingly arid as the trail snakes past waterfalls to reach Ekle Bhatti then the turnoff to Lokpa on the trail to the Tsum Valley. Climb above the confluence of the Buri Gandaki and Shar Khola to Pewa and then **Deng** (1860m), which lost a number of houses to the quake.

DAY 5: DENG TO GHAP
(3–4 HOURS, 420M ASCENT, 120M DESCENT)

Ghap, the destination for Day 5, was severely damaged and an alternative overnight stop may be required. From Deng, the trail passes a sidetrail to the stone-carving village of Bhi, sadly ravaged by the earthquake, before reaching Bhijam, still tracing the route of the Buri Gandaki. A side trail runs from Bhijam to the Buddhist village of Prok, but many buildings here were destroyed, including the monastery. Eventually, the trail drops into **Ghap** (2110m), but many lodges were damaged here and there were landslides around the village, damaging paths.

DAY 6: GHAP TO NAMRUNG
(2½–3 HOURS, 680M ASCENT, 120M DESCENT)

Day 6 climbs above the Tom (Tum) Khola to Longa Chuta and then enters an enchanting forest of fir and rhododendron full of birds and langur monkeys on the north bank of the Buri Gandaki. Cross back to the southern bank to reach **Namrung** (2660m), a former customs post in the days of the salt route to Tibet. Many buildings here were badly damaged by the earthquake and it is not clear which lodges have survived.

DAY 7: NAMRUNG TO LHO
(3½–4½ HOURS, 610M ASCENT, 90M DESCENT)

Beyond Namrung the trek enters upper Nupri where the dialect changes to a form of Tibetan and most people dress in *chubas*, the Tibetan-style wraparound cloak. Climb past barley fields with watchtowers for bears, through Barsam and Lihi, where most houses were severely damaged. Above Lihi, the trail passes turn-offs to a series of local gompas and to the base camp for ascents of Himalchuli (7893m), before reaching, **Sho** (2960m), also damaged by the quake. Views become increasingly epic as Manaslu, Manaslu North (7157m) and Naike Peak (5515m) appear at the head of the valley. It's a short walk on to Shrip and finally **Lho** (3180m), which saw damage to its large and busy Ribum Gompa, as well as to lodges and houses.

DAY 8: LHO TO SAMA
(3–4 HOURS, 570M ASCENT, 220M DESCENT)

Destruction follows the trail to **Shyaula** (3520m), where most buildings were damaged, including the gompa. Continue across a series of valleys, passing trails to more rural gompas, to reach **Sama** (3530m) also known as Samagaon. Many buildings collapsed here and it was not clear at the time of writing which lodges, if any, were still operational. There are several interesting monasteries in and around the village, showing varying levels of damage from the earthquake.

DAY 9: ACCLIMATISATION DAY IN SAMA

The altitude gain requires one or even two rest days in Sama. Most spend the time exploring the gompa at **Pungyen** (4070m), a day hike via a side trail branching off halfway between Shyaula and Sama. It is possible to continue up this valley to the moraine of the Pungyen Glacier. Other options include trips to the lake at **Birendra Tal** (3450m) and the challenging climb onwards to **Manaslu Base Camp** (4900m). North of Birendra Tal, **Milarepa's Cave** was said to have been used as a meditation retreat by the Buddhist saint, but you'll need a guide to find it.

DAY 10: SAMA TO SAMDO
(2–3 HOURS, 340M ASCENT)

The trail onwards drops back to the Buri Gandaki, passing the turn-off to Birendra Tal and Manaslu Base Camp. The valley widens as you reach Kermo Kharka, but it's a long walk to reach the white *kani* (gateway) marking the entrance to **Samdo** (3860m). Many buildings here were badly damaged; assuming it is possible to stop here, you'll have time to walk to the peak above the village for grandstand views of Manaslu. If you feel like another acclimatisation day, a rewarding six to seven hour hike climbs 640m to the moraine of the **Fukang Glacier**, with sweeping views towards the passes used by locals to cross into Tibet (closed to foreigners).

DAY 11: SAMDO TO DHARAMSALA
(2½ HOURS, 630M ASCENT)

This short day descends through fields before starting the climb towards the Larkya La. There are stunning views of the Manaslu and the Syacha Glacier, and a chance of spotting blue sheep, as you climb to reach **Dharamsala** (4480m), as high as you can go for the day without risking acclimatisation problems. This is the only shelter before the pass and it is not known if the lone teahouse survived the quake. This section of the trek is prone to snowfall and the Samdo Lodge is usually closed from mid-December to mid-March, when snow blocks the Larkya La. Check in advance before trekking up from Samdo.

DAY 12: DHARAMSALA TO BIMTANG
(7-9 HOURS, 810M ASCENT, 1570M DESCENT)

It takes three to five hours to cross the **Lakya La** (5100m), the high point on this trek. The ascent is cold and windy and the crossing can be dangerous if there is snow on the pass. Check the status of the crossing before leaving Samdo. The trail to the pass is marked by cairns but is indistinct and hard to follow after snow. Follow the moraine to four frozen lakes, then ascend to the pass itself for a show-stopping line-up of peaks: Himlung Himal (7126m), Cheo Himal (6820m), Gyaji Kung (7030m), Kang Guru (6981m) and Annapurna II (7937m).

LANGTANG, HELAMBU & MANASLU AROUND MANASLU TREK

Descend to the west over treacherously slippery scree to reach Taubuche, where the trail becomes easier. As the valley widens, the trail drops into **Bimtang** (3720m), once a major trading post on the Tibetan salt route, where many trekkers gathered for safety after the 25 April earthquake. An interesting side trek follows a trail above Bimtang to the crystal-clear glacial lake of **Pungkar Tal** (4110m).

DAY 13: BIMTANG TO GHO
(4–5 HOURS, 1160M DESCENT)

The descent begins in earnest on Day 13, so make the most of the scenery in the morning before heading down to the Dudh Khola and on to **Soti Khola** (2700m), also known as Khare, beneath the looming mass of Phungi Peak (6258m). Follow a sweeping arc off the ridge down to the river bank and the village of **Gho** (2560m).

DAY 14: GHO TO DHARAPANI
(3-4 HOURS, 640M DESCENT)

The landscape gets greener as you drop through fields and forests to follow the north bank of the Dudh Khola to **Tilje** (2300m), the first real village after Samdo. This flagstone-paved village is home to many Gurung people. Leave Tilje via the *kani* at the end of the village, then cross the stream to reach Thonje. Continue to **Dharapani** (1920m) by crossing a suspension bridge over the Marsyangdi. You have now connected with the Annapurna Circuit trek (p144), and can enjoy creature comforts for the final descent to Besi Sahar and on to Pokhara.

DAYS 15-16: DHARAPANI TO BESI SAHAR
(390M ASCENT, 1530M DESCENT)

Dharapani has jeep connections to Besi Sahar, but the ride is such a bone-shaker that many continue on foot to pick up a bus in Chame or Bhulbule.

TOWNS & FACILITIES

Dhunche
ELEV 1950M

With the road extending as far as Syabrubesi, fewer people start the Langtang Valley Trek from Dhunche (pronounced 'doon-chay'), 117km from Kathmandu, though the direct (steep) trail to Sing Gompa and Gosainkund begins here. However, like Syabrubesi, Dhunche was hit badly by the 2015 earthquakes, with damage to many buildings and to the road in both directions. Before the disaster, trekkers were required to pay the Langtang National Park entry fee (or show that they had already paid in Kathmandu) at the checkpoint 1km before Dhunche.

Work is underway to fix the road and restore buildings damaged in the quake, but at the time of writing, it was not clear which hotels had survived the disaster. Before the tremor, there were several decent, if rustic, choices, including the **Hotel Langtang View** (☑ 010-540141; r with/without bathroom Rs 500/300 ; ☎) and **Hotel Himalaya Legend** (☑ 010-540112; d with/without bathroom Rs 400/200; ☎), but check ahead to make sure that rooms are available.

Road transport from Kathmandu was always a gruelling experience, and it is likely to be even more challenging following the earthquakes. Before the disaster, tourist class (Rs 500, 7am, eight hours) and local buses (Rs 340, 6.20am, 6.50am and 7.30am, eight to 10 hours) to Dhunche left from Machha Pokhari (Fish Pond), diagonally across the Ring Rd from Gongabu bus station. Contact Pasang Lhamo Transport (p60) to see if buses are running.

Jeep-taxis charged Rs 500 per seat on the same route; hotels can arrange tickets. Renting a private jeep for the journey to Kathmandu cost between Rs 9,000 and Rs 12,000, depending on jeep type.

Syabrubesi
ELEV 1470M

Before the earthquakes, Syabrubesi was the main trailhead for treks into the narrow Langtang Valley, with a string of well-stocked roadside shops and lodges and a camp site linked to the old part of the village by a bridge over the Bhote Kosi river. Sadly, both the new and old towns were devastated by the earthquakes, with damage to the road from Dhunche, and to many buildings in town.

Reconstruction is underway, but at the time of writing, it was not clear which hotels in Syabrubesi survived the disaster. Before the tremor, the **Hotel Namaste** (☑ 01-0670223; r Rs 500; ☎), **Hotel Peaceful** (☑ 01-0541009; r Rs 500; ☎) and **Hotel Tibet** (☑ 01-0670102; r Rs 100; ☎) were good choices, but check ahead to make sure that rooms are available.

Road transport from Kathmandu was also disrupted. Before the earthquakes, tourist class (Rs 500, 7am, eight hours) and local buses (Rs 340, 6.20am, 6.50am and 7.30am) left from Machha Pokhari (Fish Pond), diagonally across the Ring Rd from Gongabu bus station. Contact Pasang Lhamo Transport (%01-4356342) to see if buses are running. Jeep-taxis charge Rs 600 per seat on the same route; hotels can arrange tickets. Renting a private jeep for the journey to Kathmandu will cost between Rs 10,000 and Rs 13,000 depending on jeep type.

Thulo Bharkhu

ELEV 2140M

Thulo Bharkhu offers an offbeat start to the Gosainkund or Langtang treks, but the town was badly damaged in the earthquake and transport here will depend on the progress of reconstruction of the road from Kathmandu. Before the quake, there were two rustic lodges, but it is not known if these survived the disaster. If it is possible to trek from here, it's a steep ascent to Thulo Syabru.

Sundarijal

ELEV 1350M

The main starting point for the Helambu trek, Sundarijal is just a short bus or taxi ride from Kathmandu, but there was severe earthquake damage here, including the collapse of some hotels. If transport is running from Kathmandu, most people start walking the same day and there is no pressing need to stay over. Before the quake, there were regular buses to Sundarijal from Kathmandu's Ratna Park bus stand (Rs 35, one hour). Taxis charge Rs 1500 for the trip. If you feel like walking from Kathmandu, it's only 7km from Bodhnath along a level, partly surfaced road.

Thimbu

Before the earthquakes, Thimbu was the end point of the Helambu trail, with a couple of average places to stay, and bus connections to Kathmandu (Rs 225, five hours). However, many buildings collapsed along this route and it is not clear if the road is open, or if any of the basic hotels in Thimbu survived the disaster.

Arughat

☑ 010 / ELEV 600M

The market town of Arughat straddles the Buri Gandaki River, but the earthquake caused massive damage here and it was not clear at the time of writing if the roads from Kathmandu and Gorkha were open as far as Arughat. There were several hotels here before the quake, but around 90% of buildings were damaged, and the status of the hotels was also unclear. Check locally to find out the current situation before coming out from Kathmandu. Previously, trekkers were required to register trekking permits with the district police station in the west of town.

If buses are running, the bus station to Kathmandu is on the east bank, while the main town and bus stands for Gorkha and Soti Khola are on the western side. Coming from Kathmandu, buses to Arughat Arughat (Rs 385, seven hours) previously left from the green Buddha Mahal (p60) office on the ring road, 100m west of Gongabu bus station. It was also possible to reach Arughat via Dhading, Soti Khola or Gorkha (Rs 110, three hours).

Gorkha

☑ 064

The historic town of Gorkha is an alternative transit point for treks up the Buri Gandaki, but many buildings were damaged this close to the epicentre, including the fort, palace and temple complex of **Gorkha Durbar** (admission Rs 50, camera Rs 200; ⊙6am-6pm Feb-Oct, 7am-5pm Nov-Jan), the former palace of the Shah kings, which is now closed for reconstruction.

Most hotels saw some earthquake damage but repairs are underway. Decent choices include the inexpensive but rustic **New Hotel Gorkha Prince** (Prince Hotel; ☑064-420030; r without bathroom Rs 500) near the bus station and the more comfortable **Hotel Gorkha Bisauni** (☑064-420107; gh_bisauni@hotmail.com; r Rs 800-1500, r without bathroom from Rs 500; 🛜) and **Gurkha Inn** (☑064-420206; bishnurg@yahoo.com; r US$30; @🛜).

Gorkha has daily microbuses to Pokhara (Rs 240, five hours) and 10 daily buses to Kathmandu (Rs 300, five hours). An unpaved road connects Gorkha to Arughat, but transport will depend on the condition of the road after the earthquake.

Eastern Nepal

Most Beautiful Places to Sleep

➡ Mamanke village (p242)

➡ Khambachen (p239)

➡ Sele La (p240)

➡ Yangle Kharka (p231)

➡ Ramche (p243)

Best Views

➡ Ridge near Makalu Base Camp (p229)

➡ Drohmo Ri (p241)

➡ Sele La (p240)

➡ Boktoh Viewpoint (p244)

Why Go?

Far from the epicentre of the 2015 earthquake, Eastern Nepal is an untamed frontier rising upwards to a sheer mountain wall that includes two of the world's tallest peaks. In the far east, Kanchenjunga clocks in as the planet's third-highest mountain (8586m), while a few valleys to the west, mighty Makalu (8463m) comes in at number five. Earthquake damage here was limited and the foothills of these Himalayan giants offer some of the most exciting trekking in Nepal, passing through remote country that provides a flashback to what the whole country must have been like in the 1970s when the first foreign trekkers took to Nepal's trails.

Hiking trails in eastern Nepal pass by terraced rice fields, dense rhododendron forests, alpine meadows and the desolate landscapes of the high Himalaya. The beautiful villages along the way are home to a diverse range of tribal people, but infrastructure is limited and many areas are only open to organised trekking groups.

When to Go

➡ As with most treks in Nepal, mid-September to November are the prime times to hike. April, when spring flowers are blooming, is also a fine time to trek.

➡ The upper stages of the Makalu Base Camp and Kanchenjunga treks are closed by snows from December to February.

➡ Due to the direction of the monsoon winds, eastern Nepal experiences higher rainfall than many other parts of the country.

➡ In spring and autumn, you can expect clouds and rain in the Arun Valley, even when the weather is fine in the rest of the country.

➡ Throughout the region the forested lower slopes are often draped in a thick fog, which gives a surreal, spooky light, but also obscures the mountain views.

ℹ Planning

MAPS

The trail from Lukla to Tumlingtar is covered in limited detail on Shangri-La Maps' 1:225,000 *Kangchenjunga Makalu*. The first and last stages of the route are better covered by Nepa Maps' 1:100,000 *Jiri to Everest* and 1:80,000 *Makalu Base Camp*, which also covers the trails to Makalu. The Himalayan Map House produces the decent 1:100,000 *Kangchenjunga Region* map and Nepa Maps' 1:100,000 *Kangchenjunga*. Both cover the north and south trails to Kangchenjunga from Taplejung and the Pathibhara and Limbu cultural trails. The first map also covers the Great Himalayan Trail high and cultural routes. The trails to Kanchenjunga from Basantpur are only covered on the low-detail Shangri-La Maps' 1:225,000 *Kangchenjunga Makalu*.

1. Lukla To Tumlingtar & Makalu Base Camp Treks Map (p222)
2. Kanchenjunga Map (p236)

EASTERN NEPAL

Eastern Nepal Highlights

❶ Reliving the glory days of trekking on the peaceful exit route from **Lukla to Tumlingtar** (p220).

❷ Visiting the mountain villages of **Tashigaon** (p230), **Pangum** (p221) and **Mamanke** (p242), home to Sherpas, Rais, Limbus and Walungs – ancient peoples who can trace their history to medieval Tibet.

❸ Camping your way up to 'the throne of the gods' – mighty **Makalu** (p229), the fifth-highest peak on earth.

❹ Getting up close and personal with Kanchenjunga, the world's third-highest peak, on the **Kanchenjunga North** (p234) trek.

❺ Keeping an eye out for goblins in the moss-covered, mist-draped fantasy forests on the trail to **Kanchenjunga South** (p241).

❻ Linking the Kanchenjunga North trail with Kanchenjunga South trail by huffing and puffing over the spectacular **Mirgin La** or **Lapsang La** passes (p240).

TREKKING PEAKS

There's only one official trekking peak in this far eastern end of Nepal and that's the newly opened Mt Bokta (6143m), which can be climbed in a couple of days from Ramche on the Kanchenjunga South trek. A permit for seven people costs US$500. There are a number of lower peaks and ridges that can be climbed in a few hours and for which permits aren't required (including a short hike up the lower slopes of Bokta).

BOOKS

The Ancestral Forest: Memory, Space and Ritual Among the Kulunge Rai of Eastern Nepal, by Nicoletti Martino, is a serious anthropological examination of the Rai people. There are several rousing tomes devoted to early expeditions to Kanchenjunga – most are out of print, but copies can be ordered from specialist bookshops. Definitive titles include *Round Kangchenjunga*, by Douglas W Freshfield (first published in 1903, but republished in paperback in 2012); *The Kangchenjunga Adventure*, by FS Smythe (published in 1930, but with a couple of reprints since; in 2013 a Kindle edition was released in the UK only); and Charles Evans' *Kangchenjunga: The Untrodden Peak*, covering the first ascent in 1955.

PERMITS & REGULATIONS

As well as obtaining a TIMS (Trekking Information Management System) card, you must pay a Rs 3000 national park fee to enter the Makalu-Barun National Park or the Kanchenjunga Conservation Area. To trek in the Kanchenjunga area, you must also obtain a permit through a recognised trekking agency.

GETTING THERE & AWAY

By far the most convenient way to reach eastern Nepal is to fly. There are airstrips at Tumlingtar, Taplejung (Suketar), Bhojpur and Lamidanda, with regular flights from Kathmandu (either direct or via Biratnagar). People trekking east from Solu Khumbu usually fly into the airstrip at Lukla.

Travelling to eastern Nepal by bus will add days to your journey. The main gateway town is Dharan Bazaar, which has regular buses north to Basantpur (for the Kanchenjunga North trek) and Hile, where you can change for a jeep to the Sabha Khola crossing near Tumlingtar (for treks to Lukla and Makalu Base Camp). The recently upgraded road to Taplejung for the Kanchenjunga South trek starts from the tea town of Ilam.

At the time of research the airstrip at Taplejung (Suketar) was closed for renovations until late 2015.

ARUN VALLEY & MAKALU

The valley of the mighty Arun Kosi forms the approach route for treks to the base camp of Makalu (8463m), the fifth-highest mountain in the world, as well as the culturally interesting exit trek from the Khumbu region to Tumlingtar.

Both treks are at the upper end of difficulty and attract just a handful of trekkers a year, but if you are experienced and want an off-the-beaten-track teahouse experience, the region offers plenty of scope for adventure and a challenging alternative to more commercialised regions of Everest and Annapurna.

The 2015 earthquakes caused some serious damage in the area south of Makalu-Barun National Park, and also to villages close to Lukla, but most places visited by trekkers escaped serious destruction and all trails are expected to be open following the 2015 monsoon season.

Lukla to Tumlingtar Trek

Duration 9 days

Max Elevation 3350m

Difficulty Medium

Season October to April

Start Lukla

Finish Tumlingtar

Permits TIMS card, Makalu-Barun National Park permit

Summary Follow in the footsteps of Bill Tilman and the first Everest explorers on this little-walked exit trek from the Khumbu to eastern Nepal, passing through the lush green landscape of the Middle Hills.

Most trekkers to the Everest Region finish their treks at Lukla, but an interesting alternative is to punch east from Solu Khumbu across three passes to the valley of the Arun Kosi. Most of the trekkers on this little-used route are climbing groups bound for Mera Peak, so independent trekkers can enjoy a level of seclusion unheard of on the Khumbu trails. We didn't meet a single other trekker here on our shoulder-season trip in February.

HW Tilman followed this trek from Hile to Lukla as part of his ground-breaking trek to Everest Base Camp in 1950, described in his book *Nepal Himalaya*. The trek works equally well in either direction, but it is particularly satisfying as an exit route from the Everest region. There was some earthquake damage to villages on the early stages of this trek, but most stops escaped with only minor damage.

Be warned: this is a physically tough trek with lots of ups and downs and only the simplest teahouse infrastructure to support you. If you are at all squeamish about local-style accommodation, you are better off doing this as a camping trek.

ℹ Planning

PERMITS & REGULATIONS

Much of this trek passes through the Makalu-Barun National Park – you can pay the Rs 3000 national park fee in Kathmandu or on arrival at the checkpoint in Bung.

ACCOMMODATION

There are simple trekking lodges in many villages along the trail between Lukla and Tumlingtar, and many more *bhattis* (teashops) offer rough wooden rooms upstairs. Facilities are more basic than most treks we've covered so be prepared for smoky rooms, thin mattresses and blankets of dubious origin. Unless otherwise stated, rooms at the lodges on this trek cost Rs 100 to Rs 200 per person, with a daal bhaat around Rs 300.

🏃 The Trek

See Map p222.

Day 1: Lukla to Paiya

4 HOURS / 310M DESCENT / 240M ASCENT

Today is a short day, giving you time to enjoy the morning in Lukla. You may notice the odd cracked wall marking the passage of the earthquake as you wander around the village. Alternatively, you could continue straight to Kharte in around six hours from Lukla.

The first day of the trail plummets downhill along the Shivalaya path, starting from the bottom of the Lukla airstrip. There was some earthquake damage in Paiya but it still makes a good overnight stop. A more enjoyable but slightly longer alternative is to head north from Lukla for 10 minutes, drop down on the side trail to Mushe and continue to Surkhe on the lower route. See p115 for accommodation options in Paiya.

Day 2: Paiya to Pangum

5 HOURS / 770M ASCENT / 650M DESCENT

The trail to Pangum branches off the main Shivalaya–Lukla trail 40 minutes south of

Paiya, below an area of dense and damp primordial forest. Look for the signposted path ('Arun Valley Treak') climbing steeply up an old landslide to the left (N 27°38.103', E 86°43.512').

The steep trail climbs above the landslide to the **Khari La** (3145m), with its fine views and single teashop, and then traverses the hillside, weaving in and out of gullies through a forest silence broken only by birdsong.

Just over an hour from the pass you'll meet the Sherpa Guest House at **Kharte**, offering food and simple dorm accommodation. Side trails run from here down to Khari on the main Shivalaya–Lukla trail.

From here, the path runs southeast through forested gullies, crossing two side streams, first over a stone bridge and then over a broken wooden bridge. As you crest the ridge you'll see the yellow-roofed Namdroling Gompa across the valley. At a junction just past here take the right branch. From the wooden bridge over the headwaters of the Khari Khola you climb for just less than an hour past a collection of mani walls to arrive in **Pangum** (2850m), hanging below the pass.

EARTHQUAKE DAMAGE IN EASTERN NEPAL

Most of the trekking routes through Eastern Nepal escaped serious damage in the April and May 2015 earthquakes, though some destruction was reported in villages close to the Everest region and in Sankhuwasabha district to the south of Makalu-Barun National Park. The good news is that the trails to the Arun Valley, Makalu and Kangchenjunga are open to trekkers, though you may see signs of earthquake damage on the early stages of these treks. These routes were researched shortly before the earthquake struck and we have updated our coverage since the disaster using local sources, but it will be some time before the full extent of the damage becomes clear. Be ready to seek local advice if any features of these routes have changed since the disaster, and check the status of all food and accommodation stops before setting off on your trek.

Lukla to Tumlingtar & Makalu Base Camp Treks

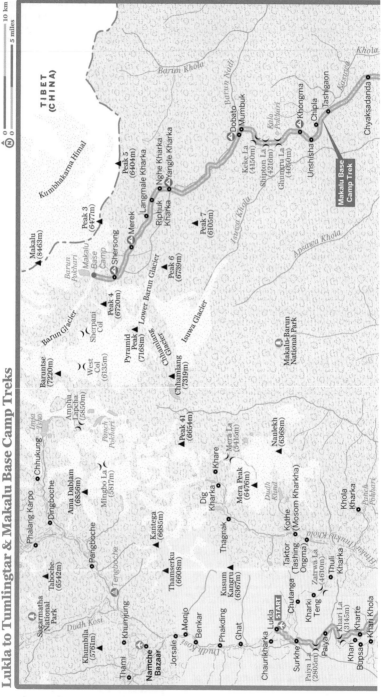

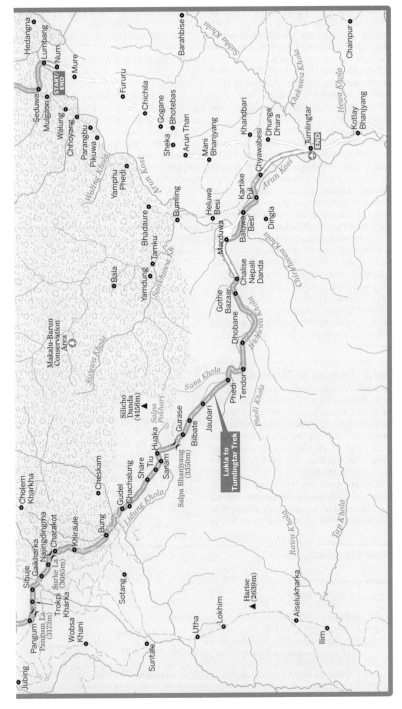

The houses of Pangum are scattered across the hillside around a white chorten and a tree covered in fluttering prayer flags. The village is famous for its *lokta* (Daphne bark paper), which is transported to Kathmandu to be used for official Nepali government transactions. Pangum is often pronounced 'pan-ko-ma' on this side of the valley. Some minor earthquake damage was reported here.

At the start of the village is the cosy Himalayan Trekkers Lodge, the best accommodation option, with a newly constructed block of 12 rooms. If you follow the side path to the chorten, you'll reach the farmhouse-style Numbur Lodge, with an ancient *mani lhakhang* (prayer-wheel shrine) built into its walls. At the top of the village is the more rustic New Panorama Lodge.

Just above the New Panorama, a side trail branches left for 10 minutes to **Pangum Gompa**, also called Trulo Gompa, which has a cluster of stone monks' cells and a dinner bell made from a mountaineer's oxygen cylinder. If you are continuing towards the pass from the gompa, a short cut runs across the hillside, rejoining the main Najingdingma trail at a large mani stone, 15 minutes below the pass.

Day 3: Pangum to Najingdingma

5½–6 HOURS / 1120M ASCENT / 1320M DESCENT

From Pangum it's a 45-minute climb to the **Pangum La** (Satu La; 3173m), which divides the Dudh Kosi and Hinku (Inkhu) valleys. If there is no cloud at the pass, enjoy grandstand views of the Khumbu Himalaya and Mera Peak (6476m), one of Nepal's most popular trekking peaks.

From the pass, the trail contours to the north and descends for 30 minutes through a patchy forest of straggly rhododendrons to an unnamed lodge run by a friendly family

at **Trokpi Kharka**. This makes an excellent alternative end to day two.

The path continues its descent past a giant boulder carved with Tibetan mantras to the small Sherpa village of **Sibuje** (Shibuche; 2500m), also known as Basme and Chatuk.

At the top of the village is the Namaste Lodge, which offers simple rooms and contains the village shop. Further downhill, on a side path, you'll see the pocket-sized village **gompa**, maintained by the owners of the lodge. In fact, this is actually a *lhakhang* (Buddhist chapel or temple) as there are no resident monks.

From Sibuje, the trail runs steeply down the spur. The landscape soars to the tops of snow peaks on one side and plunges to rows of diminishing hills on the other. Before long, the path begins an almost vertical descent of the valley, switching back on itself like a broken slinky, before reaching a teashop, balanced on a spur of land between two sparkling waterfalls, about two hours after leaving Sibuje. Our condolences to anyone headed up this hill in the opposite direction!

The trail continues across the Hinku Khola on the left of two steel-cable bridges. The next stage climbs for 45 minutes through humid, ferny forest, emerging among the grassy terraces, scattered farmhouses and two teashops of **Gaikharka** ('cow pasture') at about 2300m. Another 1½ hours of climbing through soggy forests will take you to a clear area of grassland, used as summer grazing by people from the surrounding valleys.

Beyond the meadows, the crude wooden houses of **Najingdingma** (2650m) are set against a curtain wall of bamboo-covered cliffs. The village has a strangely temporary feel as many villagers move downhill to warmer pastures in winter. The best place to stay is the cheerful wood-slatted Namaste

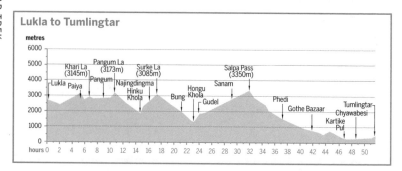

Lukla to Tumlingtar

ALTERNATIVE DAY BREAKDOWN

Fit trekkers who have come from Shivalaya or Everest Base Camp may find they can cover this trek faster than described in the main trek description. If this is you, consider the following alternative schedule:

Day 1 Lukla to Paiya (four hours)

Day 2 Paiya to Trokpi Kharka (6½ hours)

Day 3 Trokpi Kharka to Khiraule Gompa (six hours)

Day 4 Khiraule Gompa to Gudel (4½ hours) or Sanam (eight hours)

Day 5 Sanam to Phedi (seven hours)

Day 6 Phedi to Marduwa (seven hours) or Chyawabesi (nine hours)

Day 7 Chyawabesi to Tumlingtar (2½ hours)

Lodge, which serves up tasty food and has simple stone rooms. Just behind the lodge is an unfinished village *lhakhang*. Further along the trail is the less gastronomically exciting Hotel New Mera View.

Day 4: Najingdingma to Bung

6–7 HOURS / 430M ASCENT / 1680M DESCENT

Leaving Najingdingma, the trail ascends steeply towards a notch in the cliff wall, branching right at a signed junction. An hour's climb, increasingly steep, deposits you at the **Surke La** (Sipki La; 3085m), emerging through a tiny crack into the Hongu Valley.

At the pass, a steep stone stairway climbs to a viewpoint with epic vistas across the hilltops towards Numbur, Karyolung and Khatang peaks. All of the land north of here lies inside the Makalu-Barun National Park. Heading downhill towards Bung, the main trail makes a gentle, 20-minute descent to the village of **Charakot**, with two basic, local lodges.

At the bottom of the village is an important trail junction. The trail leading uphill to the north runs along the ridge to the Panch Pokhari lakes and Mera Peak (6476m). The trail to Bung drops below the last shop in the village, then turns immediately right (south) through a towering moss-drenched rhododendron forest, emerging onto a clear hillside with soaring views over the surrounding valleys. Mani walls mark the descent to a large moss-covered stupa, one hour from Charakot.

In the valley below, a perfect circle of tall juniper trees marks the location of the **Khiraule Gompa**, also known as Baskam Gompa The gompa was once highly revered by Sherpas, but the surrounding land is now occupied by Hindu Rais, and the monastery has fallen out of use. An unsigned path branches left off the main trail beside a mani wall and drops to the gompa and the agreeably rustic Khiraule Himalayan Lodge, whose owners have taken on the task of restoring the gompa. This is a good alternative place to spend the night on day three.

Continuing on the main trail, you'll enjoy glorious views over the wide, fertile Hongu Valley, which produces much of the rice consumed in Solu Khumbu. You can pick out your route across the hillside by the scattered mani walls, built by Buddhists when the area was dominated by Sherpas.

As you drop down the hillside, you'll see the farmland becoming richer and more varied, and racks of beans, maize and other crops drying on the wooden balconies of whitewashed Rai houses. You'll pass another turn-off to Khiraule Gompa and another stupa before dropping down to **Bung**, which tumbles down the steep hillside from around 1900m. The final approach to the village follows a stream along a narrow, shaded gully. Allow 3½ hours from the Surke La.

You must show your national park receipt or pay the Rs 3000 fee at the Makalu-Barun National Park checkpost just before the main village square. By the square is the simple Pumori Lodge, whose Rai owners cook up a feast – in autumn, ask to sample their fiery tree-tomato chutney.

Rai food can be a real treat after the bland meals of the high mountains, with lots of meat and hot spices. The dark-leaved plant with red flowers that you see in every garden is a kind of flowering ginger – its roots are used as a flavouring in Rai curries.

If you have the energy, continue the extra 2½ hours to Gudel.

MERA PEAK & THE HINKU VALLEY

Hidden in the remote upper Hinku Valley inside the Makalu-Barun National Park, Mera Peak (6476m) is the highest trekking peak in Nepal that can be climbed without previous mountaineering experience. It's no walk in the park; several steep sections require ropes, ice axes and crampons.

There are several possible approach routes. Most groups trek from Lukla over the Zatrwa (Chatrwa) Pass, but alternative approaches from the Pangum La and Surke La on the Lukla-to-Tumlingtar trail offer a safer rate of acclimatisation.

The ascent involves trekking up to the Mera La (5415m) and nearby base camp, from where you ascend to High Camp to begin climbing. Good acclimatisation is the key to summitting this peak. Two-week trips from Kathmandu cost around US$2000, though you may find teahouse trekking options for US$1500. Climbs run in November, April and May. Don't confuse Mera Peak with Mehra Peak (Kongma Tse), further north.

The opening of teahouses along the approach route means that experienced and adventurous trekkers can now also consider the route as a nonclimbing trek. Again, good acclimatisation is essential, so this is perhaps best done after an Everest trek. A guide is very useful as the trails are not well marked. Lodges are only reliably open from April to May and from September to November. It's a good idea to bring a tent as a backup, as lodges are not plentiful and can be full in high season or closed in the shoulder season.

There are three main routes into the Hinku Valley.

➡ From the Pangum La on the Lukla–Tumlingtar trek a side trail heads to Nyingsor for an overnight at a lodge, the next day continuing to a basic lodge at Chettre Bakula. The next day continue up the Hinku Valley to Taktor (Tashing Ongma) before overnighting at Kothe (Mosom Kharkha).

➡ Another approach option is from the Surkhe La, up the ridgeline to a lodge at Cholem Kharka (3560m), continuing the next day to the Panch Pokhari lakes (4330m) and nearby Khola Kharka. The following day you'll reach Kothe.

➡ For the direct and very steep approach from Lukla there are teahouses for overnight stops in Chutanga (3350m to 3535m) and at Kharki Teng (4080m) and Thuli Kharka (4230m) on either side of the Zatrwa Pass (4610m). An acclimatisation day at Chutanga and/or Kharki Teng is essential. From here you descend into the Hingku valley to lodges at Thaktor (3640m) and Kothe.

Kothe (3600m) has four lodges and offers the option of a side trip to the Milarepa Cave and gompa. From here it's about five hours of hiking to Thagnak (4300m), which has four lodges. You should spend at least one extra day acclimatising here, perhaps on a day hike to nearby Sabai Tsho. Another five-hour hike brings you via a teashop at Dig Kharkha (4660m) to Khare (5000m), which has five lodges. There are currently no lodges beyond Khare, though guides report that there is a very basic wooden porters' shelter at Mera La, just after the pass.

Day 5: Bung to Sanam

6–7 HOURS / 200M DESCENT / 1530M ASCENT

Moving on from Bung, the main trail drops through a patchwork of rice, millet and soybean terraces, then bears right at the bottom of the fields into groves of bamboo and cardamom. The Hongu Khola is crossed by a suspension bridge at about 1320m. A sign welcomes you to the 'open defecation free area of Gudel'. On the other side, a rough *bhatti* marks the start of a gruelling 90-minute climb up a never-ending gully to the Rai village of **Gudel** at 1900m.

The early explorer HW Tilman wrote a short poem to capture his frustration with the long descent and climb between these two villages:

For dreadfulness, naught can excel
The prospect of Bung from Gudel;
And words die away on the tongue
When we look back on Gudel from Bung.

Gudel is another pleasant Rai village of white-washed houses and kitchen gardens, almost a mirror image of Bung across the valley, and it's a good place to spend some time. The friendly and excellent-value Namaste Lodge is set in a small, flowery garden, while the Kopil Guest House 100m further is also good.

The trail to Sanam runs uphill beside the lodge to a junction by a cluster of mani stones. Take the path that climbs gradually along the ridge – the trail leading straight uphill is used by woodcutters whose handiwork has resulted in several large landslides. Below the path, you'll see the village of Chachalung.

The rest of the day is a leisurely but sustained ascent into a forest of rhododendrons, brown oaks and chir pines. With each step, more of the lush, forested valley ahead is exposed. There are a couple of trail junctions here; if in doubt, stay on the level path, don't descend down the hillside.

About two hours from Gudel is the village of **Share**, with a paper factory, a teashop and an old gompa. You are now back in Sherpa country and many houses have finely carved wooden balconies. The trail doglegs around the large white chorten.

Above Share, the trail passes an enormous rock carved with Buddhist mantras – it's a magical spot to rest and soak in the views. Continue past the schoolhouse and a thundering waterfall to a covered wooden bridge. Another half-hour will get you to the village of **Tiu** (Tiyu; 2470m), which has the simple Arun Valley Lodge.

Finally, cut back into the forest for one last 45-minute climb to **Sanam** (2850m), passing the huge, hollow stumps of vanished oaks and pines. The village consists of a single row of houses; one serves as the village gompa and another is the Gumba Lodge – authentic and atmospheric or just dark and dirty, depending on your frame of mind. The inhabitants of Sanam keep large herds of cattle, so ask about the availability of curd, *serkum* (cottage cheese) or *churpi* (dry cheese). Sanam is 3½ hours from Gudel.

Day 6: Sanam to Phedi

7–8 HOURS / 600M ASCENT / 1770M DESCENT

Moving on from Sanam, the path runs across the hillside and into a damp forest full of moss and lichen, eventually passing a collection of herders' huts at **Hwaka**.

The trail follows the main stream in the valley and then turns southeast, rising steeply up stone steps. It's a gruelling climb of an hour or more to reach the open area of loose stones and dwarf rhododendrons below the **Salpa Pass** (3350m), dividing the Hongu and Irkhuwa valleys.

From here, you can gaze back across the forest to a line of distant peaks before you take your leave of Solu-Khumbu district. Chilly winds blow over the pass, so duck inside the low stone *bhatti* at the top for a warming bowl of noodle soup. The pass is sometimes temporarily covered by snow in winter, so check conditions in Sanam.

An overgrown stupa marks the high point of the pass and the junction with a side trail to **Salpa Pokhari**, a wish-fulfilling sacred pool set at 3414m, surrounded by hemlock and fir forests that abound with bird and animal life. It takes about 30 minutes to reach the lake, with good views en route, and you can continue downhill to rejoin the main trail in Bilbate, a total journey of around two hours.

The trail to Phedi drops straight into the valley, passing through a rhododendron forest dotted with overgrown mani walls and stupas, a sign of declining Sherpa influence on this side of the pass. An hour below the pass are the herders' huts of **Gurase** (2880m), with the simple Salpa Pass Hotel offering accommodation another 10 minutes further. About 20 minutes further on is **Bilbate** (2800m), set on a saddle by a shallow pond, where a signposted junction marks the other end of the Salpa Pokhari trail.

The Phedi trail climbs over the top of the spur and then drops down towards a forest of oak, birch and rhododendron, offering giddying views of the plunging valley to the south. It's a pleasant descent through the forest, with lots of sunny clearings for rest stops.

The stone path gets steeper as you approach the sprawling village of **Thulo Phokte** (2140m), but you'll have to descend another 100m to reach **Jaubari**, with its tiny one-room gompa, and the Everest Sherpa Hotel and Sonam Hotel, both of which serve lunch on outdoor dining tables.

The final 90-minute descent to Phedi is perilously steep, dropping along the spur that divides the Irkhuwa Khola and the Sanu Khola. Anyone with dodgy knees will suffer during today's cartilage-crushing 1700m descent.

The path emerges at the top of **Phedi** (1680m) – continue through the cobbled village square to a pair of basic lodges by the river. Irkhowa Lodge has the better food, but rooms are slightly better at the next-door Sherpa Lodge. Both have pleasant gazebos.

Day 7: Phedi to Gothe Bazaar

5 HOURS / 120M ASCENT / 1230M DESCENT

From the Sherpa Lodge head down steps to a bamboo bridge over the Sanu Khola; at times of high water, use the steel-cable bridge just upstream. The trail passes frames for drying traditional paper and follows the north bank of the Irkhuwa Valley for 15 minutes before crossing the river.

For the next stage the trail follows the south bank, passing the huge sail-like nets of giant orb spiders. The lush terrain alternates between damp patches of forest (with abundant leeches in the monsoon season) and open rice terraces divided by trickling irrigation channels full of frogs. The Arun Valley is a lepidopterist's paradise – keep an eye out for giant swallowtails and fluttering groups of grass yellow butterflies.

Pass through the sprawling villages of **Tendor** and **Tallo Phedi**, with their thatched-roofed houses, cutting in and out of the forest. Eventually the trail drops down a spur to two busy *bhattis* at **Dhobane** (920m), where a side stream meets the Irkhuwa Khola. Dhobane means 'where the river divides'.

Continuing downriver, ignore the large suspension bridge running north across the Irkhuwa Khola towards Limkim and continue east via a second suspension bridge, cutting back into the forest on the low riverside trail.

Before long, you'll cross to the north bank, continuing through rice terraces on a path that follows the irrigation channels. Note the granaries, raised on stilts to keep the drying rice safe from rats. In autumn, villagers wait by the path selling piles of *suntala* (Nepali oranges).

About two hours past Dhobane you'll reach the village of **Gothe Bazaar** (775m), at the mouth of the Benkhuwa Khola. At the far end of the suspension bridge is the *bhatti*-style Kirat Hotel & Lodge, the only accommodation in town. The name Kirat comes from the original name for the Rai people. According to legend, the Kirati were the indigenous inhabitants of Nepal.

Day 8: Gothe Bazaar to Chyawabesi

5–6 HOURS / 700M ASCENT / 1150M DESCENT

From Gothe, the trail continues along the north bank of the Irkhuwa Khola, climbing a ridge along a road-sized section of trail.

The path crosses back to the south bank on a suspension bridge and turns into a fledgling road as it climbs for 90 minutes to the village of **Marduwa** atop the headland that divides the Irkhuwa Khola and the Arun Kosi.

After crossing the ridge you'll get your first glimpse of the verdant Arun Valley. The Arun rises in Tibet and snakes down to the Terai, merging with the Tamur Kosi and the Sun Kosi to form the mighty Sapt Kosi ('Seven Rivers'), which flows into the Ganges at Kursela in India. Elevated flow on this river caused by above-average rainfall led to devastating floods in August 2008 that displaced more than a million people.

After crossing the ridge, the road drops to the Sagarmatha Hotel, where a friendly family offers very simple accommodation. From here a footpath largely avoids the switchbacking road, crossing it a couple of times as it drops past a fine viewpoint and several local snack stalls to roll into the tiny village of **Balawa Besi** (320m) on the banks of the Arun Kosi.

Cross the rusty blue metal bridge and walk through the fields for 15 minutes to reach **Kartike Pul** (300m). As well as shops and *bhattis*, this lively village has numerous tailor's shops, staffed by members of the Damai caste. Local shops have phones where you can call ahead to reconfirm your flight out of Tumlingtar.

The trail crosses the Arun on a suspension bridge and continues for 25 minutes along the beach to **Chyawabesi** (250m) on the east bank of the Arun. Chyawabesi has several local-style wooden lodges but you'll get better rooms 10 minutes further, near the school, at the bamboo-walled *bhatti* of Bimala Rai (there's no sign, so ask).

Day 9: Chyawabesi to Tumlingtar

2½–3 HOURS / 210M ASCENT

You may find jeep taxis running from Chyawabesi to Tumlingtar for Rs 150 per seat, or you can get someone to call one from Tumlingtar for Rs 4000.

The trail continues south along the east bank of the Arun through a series of small Rai, Chhetri and Brahman villages. Houses in this area are raised above the ground on stilts or a plinth of stones and mud, with woven-bamboo walls to aid ventilation in the sticky heat.

Twenty-five minutes from Chyawabesi the footpath branches off the dirt road, making a short cut as it alternates between sandy river bank and rice paddies. Follow the other foot travellers rather than the road, which makes a large detour.

About an hour from Chyawabesi, the village of **Bheteni** has a cluster of hotels selling plates of *channa masala* (chickpea curry) and chow mein. Continue on the east bank, passing a cantilevered metal bridge across the Arun, then branch left away from the road up onto the broad plateau between the Arun Kosi and Sabha Khola.

From here it's a 30-minute walk on the dirt road into **Tumlingtar** (460m).

Makalu Base Camp Trek

Duration 13 days

Max Elevation 4950m

Difficulty Hard

Season October to November, mid-March to May

Start/Finish Num

Permits TIMS card, Makalu-Barun National Park Permit

Summary A rugged and remote route through the wild country of the Arun and Barun Valleys into some of the most impressive high-altitude scenery in Nepal.

The fifth-highest mountain in the world, Makalu (8463m) is considered one of the hardest 8000m peaks to climb because of its steep, exposed ridges. Edmund Hillary failed twice, leaving it to a French expedition to make the first ascent in 1955. Even the mighty Reinhold Messner only succeeded on his third attempt. You won't face quite so many obstacles getting to the base camp of the mountain, through this is a challenging and difficult trek through one of the most remote and undeveloped parts of Nepal.

The reward for this hardship is the chance to trek through an unspoiled Himalayan landscape far from the trappings of the modern age. En route, you will pass some epic viewpoints that will put you face to face with the 'the throne of the gods', along with Baruntse (7220m) and the eastern slope of the Everest range.

The gateway town for this trek is Tumlingtar (p245), accessible by air or a very long bus/jeep combo from Kathmandu, followed by a half-day jeep ride to the trailhead at Num.

Note that some villages along the early stages of this walk sustained damage in the 2015 earthquake, particularly Seduwa, where a number of houses collapsed. It is essential to confirm that food and accommodation is available at all your planned stops before you set off.

🛈 Planning

PERMITS & REGULATIONS

Most of this trek passes through the Makalu-Barun National Park – you can pay the Rs 3000 national park fee in Kathmandu or on arrival at the checkpoint in Seduwa.

Trekkers are not permitted to collect or burn firewood inside the Makalu-Barun National Park.

RESOURCES

The Khandbari-based agency **Makalu Arun Social Trek** (MAST; ☑ 029-560716; www.social-treknepal.com) can arrange insured local porters (US$20 a day per porter, plus food) and teahouse treks in the region and is a good source of information on the Makalu trek. The agency uses profits to support an orphanage and can place short-stay vounteers and homestays in Naya Bazaar and Sekaha; contact Tejanath Pokharel.

The website www.trekkingmakalu.blogspot.co.uk gives a useful daily description of the trek.

MAKALU-BARUN NATIONAL PARK

The high mountains north of Tumlingtar are protected by the Makalu-Barun National Park, which was established in 1992 as a joint venture between Nepal's Department of National Parks and Wildlife Conservation and the Mountain Institute (www.mountain.org).

Bordered by the Arun Valley to the east and Sagarmatha National Park to the west, the 2330-sq-km reserve includes the towering peaks of Makalu (8463m), Chhamlang (7319m) and the many numbered peaks surrounding the Barun Glacier, giving the park an amazing 8000m vertical spread of elevation.

Most of the park is true wilderness, providing a home for more than 3000 species of flowering plants and hundreds of varieties of orchid. Notable fauna includes snow leopards, red pandas, musk deer and *bharals* (blue sheep).

ACCOMMODATION & SUPPLIES

There are rustic teahouses along the trek now, all the way up to base camp, but these are only reliably open during the trekking high season (October, November, April and May). Most lodge owners are from Tashigaon so this is a good place to enquire as to which lodges are open; the owners may even follow you up the trail to open the lodge. There was earthquake damage along this trail so check that accommodation is available for all your planned overnight stops before you set off. Lodges generally charge up to Rs 300 per bed, with a daal bhaat peaking at around Rs 500.

Lodges are basic on this trek, with limited menu options, and you should bring supplies with you, especially for lunches. There's always the chance that lodges will be closed, especially at the beginning or end of the season. If you are trekking at these times it's a useful backup to have a tent.

National park regulations mean you should stick to designated campsites, though in reality most groups simply camp next to the teahouses. Be sure not to leave litter, and bury toilet waste behind when you move on.

At higher elevations, you will have to draw water from muddy streams, so carry a water filter as well as purification tablets.

Stock up on supplies in Tumlingtar or Khandbari as there's almost nothing available along the trek.

🏃 The Trek

See Map p222.

Day 1: Num to Seduwa

4–5 HOURS / 880M DESCENT / 920M ASCENT

Jeeps run regularly from Tumlingtar to Khandbari and on from Khandbari and Mani Bhanjyang to Num, so most people now start their trek here instead of walking for two days from Khandbari.

Num is set on a promontory above the Arun Kosi, giving you good views over the valley towards Seduwa, your destination today. It will soon become clear that you have a long descent, followed by an equally long climb. On a clear day, you can see as far as the peaks flanking the Shipton La.

To reach Seduwa, follow the obvious trail north along the ridge, then drop steeply down through almost impossibly green, terraced fields to **Lumbang**. The final descent to the river is steep and vertiginous, but after about an hour you'll reach a dubious-looking suspension bridge, crossing the Arun Kosi at 620m.

The north side of the valley is a patchwork of tiny, terraced fields and exposed rocks, where locals grow rice, maize, barley and buckwheat. You must now climb for nearly 1000m, and the only place to find refreshments is a lone teashop at 820m. Eventually, after several hours, you'll reach **Seduwa** (Murmidanda; 1540m) and the entry checkpoint for the Makalu-Barun National Park. There was a fair amount of damage here from the 2015 earthquake, and a number of buildings were destroyed, but villagers are slowly rebuilding. You must register your TIMS card at the police post.

There is a large, flat camping ground below the national park office, or try the New Makalu Restaurant and Lodge run by Ngawang Pemba Sherpa.

Day 2: Seduwa to Tashigaon

4–5 HOURS / 620M ASCENT

The trail from Seduwa climbs the ridge, passing a national park forestry project. As you climb gently northwards through rice terraces to the village of **Manigaon**, look back to see Num on the far side of the valley. On the way, you must cross several streams on stones or temporary, bamboo bridges.

From Manigaon the trail turns west and makes a gradual climb high above the Kasuwa Khola to a mani wall at **Chyaksadanda** (1890m), marked as Narbugaon on the Nepa Maps *Makalu Base Camp* map. Look out for locals using back-strap looms on the porches of village houses. The plants with red flowers and vivid green and purple leaves are a form of ginger.

It's a gentle walk past farms, meadows and forested glades to the school at the bottom of **Tashigaon** (2070m) the last permanent settlement in the valley and the best place to check which lodges are open further up the trail.

There are half a dozen Sherpa-run lodges in Tashigaon, including the Mount Summit Hotel, Makalu Hotel and Sagamartha Hotel and these rank as the best on the trek, with hot showers and full menus. The village also has a kerosene depot and a helipad for emergency evacuations.

Day 3: Tashigaon to Khongma

4–6 HOURS / 1420M ASCENT

The daily schedule above Tashigaon is dictated by the availability of open lodges and designated national park campsites. This

Num to Makalu Base Camp

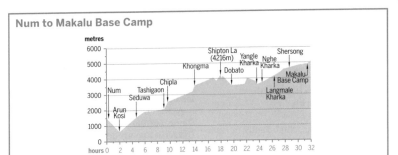

stage of the trek involves a 1400m climb on a very steep trail – this will take you to an elevation where you may experience the first signs of altitude mountain sickness (AMS), so be alert for the symptoms.

Starting from Tashigaon, climb over the ridge and ascend through forests to a stream. The path levels out at the next ridge before climbing to a shepherds' hut atop another ridge at **Chipla** (2520m). Here the trail becomes even steeper, struggling up past streams and a huge overhanging rock to a small *kharka* (communal pasture) in the forest. Continue over rocks and tree roots to reach **Unshisha**, a tiny soggy meadow at 3180m.

The last stage to **Khongma** (Kauma; 3560m) is a draining climb through forest along the ridge that separates the Isuwa Khola and Kasuwa Khola. After about 1½ hours, you'll reach the national park and a Sherpa-run lodge. The water supply here is limited to a muddy spring so many people continue to nearby **Danda Kharka**, which also has a lodge.

If you have time to kill, climb the ridge above Khongma for a distant view towards Kanchenjunga far to the east.

Day 4: Khongma to Dobato
5–7 HOURS / 1170M ASCENT / 1180M DESCENT
From Khongma, climb the ridge on steep switchbacks to a stone chorten at 3840m and feast your eyes on views of Chhamlang, Peak 6 (6739m) and Peak 7 (6105m). Scrubby rhododendrons and mossy boulders line the trail as you climb a stone staircase over several false ridges towards the small pass known as **Ghungru La** (Tutu La; 4050m).

Drop down beside the Kalo Pokhari, a still, mysterious lake at 3840m, then climb steeply up a rocky gully to **Shipton La** (4216m),

named after Eric Shipton, who followed this route with Edmund Hillary during the 1952 Everest reconnaissance expedition. The pass is regularly blocked by snow in winter and you can expect a dusting of flakes here at any time of year.

On the far side of the pass is another small basin and a quiet, eerie lake of Tulo Pokhari (Big Lake), where you might find a teashop in season. The path skirts the lake and climbs to the obvious dip in the hills on the far side. This is the **Keke La** (4150m), the last steep climb for the day. Beyond the pass, the trail dips into a pretty valley filled with rhododendrons that becomes a carpet of brilliant flowers in spring.

It's an hour or so through the forest before you reach **Mumbuk** (3550m), in a clearing near a small, trickling stream. The only accommodation is a single basic teahouse at nearby **Dobato** (Dobate).

Day 5: Dobato to Yangle Kharka
4–5 HOURS / 700M DESCENT / 750M ASCENT
From Mumbuk, the trail drops down a scree-covered slope into the long, curving Barun Valley, which forms a natural highway towards your destination. Walk down towards the streambed then turn west along the south side of the valley. You must watch your footing as you dodge tree roots, scramble over landslides, squeeze between boulders and leap over small streams.

Beyond the landslides, the valley widens and the forest gives way to rolling alpine meadows with good views of Peak 7. The trail crosses the Barun on a wooden bridge and rises to two lodges at **Yangle Kharka** (3600m). Chopal Sherpa's Lodge or Dawa Sherpa Lodge have similar rooms, but there may be some rebuilding going on here following the earthquake.

This is also a fine flat area for camping, with a reliable water source of the gushing Barun Khola. The surrounding meadows are covered in fluttering prayer flags tied to wooden stakes.

Day 6: Yangle Kharka to Langmale Kharka

3–4 HOURS / 800M ASCENT

From Yangle Kharka, climb gently to Nghe Kharka (3750m), another cluster of herders' huts and prayer flags on the opposite side of the Barun Khola. The landscape here could be something from the Rocky Mountains and the snowline seems almost close enough to touch.

Beyond Nghe Kharka, the river makes a huge S-shaped curve between curtain walls of cliffs that tower on either side of the river. From the meadow at Riphuk Kharka (3930m), climb past a waterfall and up over swampy ground to a lonely stone hut at Jhak Kharka (4210m).

Another gentle climb past a mani wall will bring you to Langmale Kharka (Yak Kharka; 4400m), where Riji Sherpa's Lodge offers a decent overnight stop.

If for some reason the lodges are shut, you'll have to camp at the rather bleak campsite at Merek (4570m), passing through a dizzying landscape of Himalayan giants – lean back to gaze up at the summits of Peak 4 (6720m), Chhamlang, Peak 3 (6477m) and Peak 5 (6404m).

Day 7: Langmale Kharka to Makalu Base Camp

4–5 HOURS / 450M ASCENT

Today's elevation is right at the upper end of the recommended maximum. Most trekking companies follow the itinerary laid out here, largely because there is no lodge at Shershong. Until one is built, it's not a bad idea to add in an extra day's acclimatisation at Langmale Kharkha, making a day hike up to Shershong and detours to several high points around the valley.

From Langmale Kharka the landscape here is an arid mass of sand and gravel – follow the trail west beside a small stream on the north side of the moraine, with the pyramid peak of Hongku Chuli (6833m) rising ahead.

As the path turns northwards into a side valley, Makalu finally soars into view. There are trails on both sides of this rocky valley, but stick to the faint, flat trail that follows the east bank of the stream for another hour. Shersong (4660m) is little more than a small stone hut and a flat area where you can set up a tent among the yak pastures. A low ridge provides some shelter from the wind, but this is still a bleak and lonely spot.

As with Everest Base Camp, Makalu Base Camp (4870m), on the side of the Barun Glacier, is a poorly defined patch of rubble. A number of mountaineers were trapped here following the 2015 earthquake but there were no casualties. Different expeditions have camped in different places at different times and unless there is a group attempting the ascent while you're there, there is little to see apart from rocks and sand. However, the views on the way are inspiring.

There are four cramped lodges at base camp, including Rinjin Sherpa's Makalu Hotel and Lodge.

Day 8: Day Trip from Makalu Base Camp

4–7 HOURS / 400M ASCENT

It's possible to make a long, draining day trip to the Hillary Base Camp (used by Edmund Hillary in 1952, sometimes called advanced base camp) or the French Base Camp (used by the French expedition for the first successful ascent in 1955). Both sit beyond the still, silent Barun Pokhari (4950m) at the north end of the valley. Views up the Barun Glacier towards Lhotse, Baruntse and Everest are superb.

Another great day hike is to return to Shershong and climb the 5250m ridge to its northeast on the lower slopes of Peak 3. There is no fixed trail – just climb north along the grassy slope to be greeted by a 'drop to your knees in praise' view of the world's fifth-highest peak.

From this lofty vantage point, there are also views northwest to Lhotse, Lhotse Shar and Everest, with the Kangshung Face and South Col clearly in view. When you tire of having your awe inspired, return the same way or drop down the eastern slopes to return to base camp for the night.

Day 9: Makalu Base Camp to Yangle Kharka

7–8 HOURS / 1250M DESCENT

Retrace your steps down the Barun Valley to the lodges and campsite at Yangle Kharka.

Day 10: Yangle Kharka to Dobato

3–4½ HOURS / 520M DESCENT / 420M ASCENT

Continue descending through the rockfall and then climb the rocky gully to the shelter of Dobato.

Day 11: Dobato to Khongma

5–6 HOURS / 870M ASCENT / 820M DESCENT

Trek across Shipton La and descend to Khongma. It is also possible to continue all the way down to Tashigaon in one extremely long and hard day.

Day 12: Khongma to Tashigaon

3–4 HOURS / 1270M DESCENT

Make a long, steep descent back to civilisation at Tashigaon.

Day 13: Tashigaon to Num

6–7 HOURS / 1590M DESCENT / 900M ASCENT

Retrace your approach route, following the trek descriptions for Days 1 and 2 (p230). The following day you can take a jeep down to Tumlingtar. Try to reconfirm your flight by phone en route.

KANCHENJUNGA

Only Everest and K2 are taller than Kanchenjunga (8586m), the massive block of rock and ice that straddles the border between Nepal and Sikkim in India. There have been relatively few attempts to climb this mighty mountain, partly because Kanchenjunga is worshipped as a tutelary spirit by the Sikkimese. The first serious attempt to conquer the peak was the 1905 expedition led by the occultist Aleister Crowley, but a British team finally gained the summit in 1955. Even today, most expeditions stop just below the summit as a gesture of respect.

The foothills of Kanchenjunga have been open to trekkers since 1988, but permit restrictions mean that it's only possible to walk here as part of an organised trek arranged through an agency. This is an inconvenience, but it does mean that the trails are blissfully free from the crowds found around Everest and Annapurna (when we walked here while updating this information we only encountered two other trekkers in the whole time). If talk of organised tours puts you off, then fear not because 'groups' can be as little as two people with a guide/porter.

When it comes to logistics, earthquake damage was limited this far from the epicenter, but some landslides were reported; seek local advice on the current best routes to follow to avoid these obstacles. There are two main approach routes to Kanchenjunga. The trek to south base camp starts from the airstrip at Suketar (near Taplejung), taking two weeks to climb to the Yalung Glacier and return. The difficult 18-day trek to north base camp can be started from Basantpur (near Hile) or, on a shorter route, from Suketar. For the ultimate in Kanchenjunga experiences it's possible to combine these two treks by crossing the Mirgin La (4663m) or the Lapsang La (5160m) in order to make a neat three-week-plus loop.

The Kanchenjunga area is the homeland of the Limbu people, who speak a language related to Tibetan and follow a mixture of Buddhist, Hindu and animist beliefs.

ⓘ Planning

PERMITS & REGULATIONS

Trekking permits for Kanchenjunga are not expensive, but they are only issued to groups of two or more trekkers who apply through a recognised trekking agency. The trekking permit fee is US$10 per week per person.

You must also pay the Rs 3000 fee to enter the Kanchenjunga Conservation Area – this is best paid in Kathmandu at the Department of National Parks and Wildlife Conservation (p67).

ACCOMMODATION

There are scattered lodges on the early stages of the Kanchenjunga North trek and along the

---

TONGBA

While the Sherpas of Khumbu are enthusiastic consumers of *rakshi* (fortified rice wine) and *chhang* (rice beer), the Limbu of eastern Nepal prefer the warm millet beer known as *tongba*. Traditionally served in a lathe-turned, wooden pot, this intoxicating beverage is prepared using hot water, poured over a mash of fermented millet seeds. A long, bamboo straw filters out the seeds, allowing you to slurp up the warming, alcoholic liquid. If you order *tongba* in a lodge, the owners will keep refilling your pot with hot water until you say enough. The alcohol content of *tongba* falls somewhere between beer and wine, but be wary of drinking too much at altitude.

entire route of the Kanchenjunga South trek. However, once you leave the last village behind these lodges can only really be counted on to be open between about March to late October. Beyond that period some might be open, but equally they might all be closed. For safety's sake it's best to come prepared to camp and be self-sufficient. Where rooms are available, the going rate is Rs 200 per person; meals cost around Rs 150 to Rs 250. Throughout this region lodges are very simple affairs aimed more at local herders than foreign trekkers. Don't expect hot showers and apple pie!

SUPPLIES & EQUIPMENT

The trekking agency should provide tents, stoves and porters, but you will need to bring clothing for extreme cold weather and a four-season sleeping bag. Most villages now have some kind of electric current – sometimes it's proper mains electricity, at other times via solar power. Even so, it's best to carry spare batteries for electronic devices. Packet noodles and other supplies can be purchased on arrival in Suketar or Basantpur as well as, for increasingly high prices, in many of the villages and teashops on the trail.

Ice axes and crampons are usually not necessary, though they might be useful for crossing the Lapsang La.

Note that the main source of income in these parts comes from harvesting cardamom and very few people are interested in working as a porter. This means you really need to bring all your porters with you from Kathmandu, which adds significantly to the cost of trekking here.

Kanchenjunga North Trek

Duration 18 to 20 days

Maximum Elevation 5140m

Difficulty Hard

Season October to November, March to May

Start Basantpur or Suketar (Taplejung)

Finish Suketar (Taplejung)

Permits US$10 per week per person, available to groups of two or more trekking through a recognised agency

Summary The most spectacular route to Kanchenjunga, climbing from Basantpur through rising country to the rugged north face, hidden away in remote alpine country.

This exciting trek, which offers a bit of everything, climbs slowly along valleys of rushing rivers to the snow-packed north face

of Kanchenjunga and culminates, after several dramatic days in the high mountains, among the glaciers at Pang Pema (5140m). As with all the hikes in eastern Nepal you can walk out here for days without running into another foreign hiker. There was little earthquake damage on this route, but check locally in case any trails have been affected by landslides.

Facilities for trekkers are limited. Most overnight stops are at remote *kharkas* (pastures), though between March and late October there are many informal teahouses ,which can provide plate meals, hot pots of tea and *tongba* and often a bed for the night. Bring warm clothes – the upper stages of the trek pass through a desolate valley, scoured by icy mountain winds.

There are two ways to begin the trek to Pang Pema. You can set off from Basantpur, on the road east from Hile, or, for a shorter walk, you can fly or bus into Suketar/Taplejung, descending for two days to meet the main trail at Chirwa (see Day 6). Above Ghunsa, be alert for the symptoms of AMS.

🏃 The Trek

See Map p236

Day 1: Basantpur to Chauki

5–6 HOURS / 580M ASCENT / 100M DESCENT

From the dusty roadhead at Basantpur, the trail climbs up through mossy rhododendron forests, with superb views over the valleys of the Arun Kosi and Tamur Kosi. This is a major trade route so you will travel in the company of droves of porters, most of whom will soon turn off on a side trail to Chainpur.

The first stage is a steady climb along the ridge through several small settlements to **Door Pani** (2780m). The trail then dips down to Tinjure Phedi and rises to the appealing village of **Chauki** (2680m), which sits on a grassy hilltop with plenty of space for camping. Several teahouses offer mountain meals and austere wooden beds.

From the ridge, there are views north towards a line of snow peaks that seem to float in the cloud – on a clear day, you can see Chhamlang (7319m), Makalu and even the east face of the Everest range.

Day 2: Chauki to Gupa Pokhari

4–5 HOURS / 320M ASCENT / 110M DESCENT

Most of the day's hike follows Milke Danda ridge, through pretty meadows with views of

THE KANCHENJUNGA CIRCUIT

Because Kanchenjunga forms the border between India and Nepal, it is not possible to complete a circuit around the mountain. However, you can visit both the north and south base camps on the Nepali side on a long and arduous, 25- to 28-day trek that crosses the 4663m Mirgin La. It is also possible to link these two treks via the 5160m Lapsang La, a tortuous high route that is frequently blocked by snow until late in the season. Unlike the high passes around Everest and Annapurna, this route sees little traffic and groups may need to forge a new trail every season. Although it only takes two days to cross either pass, it's best to allow up to four weeks to complete this trek so that you can take it nice and slow and enjoy the scenery and the villages.

the snowy mountain ranges that form your final destination. The trail dips up and down for several hours before reaching two small lakes at **Lamo Pokhari** (2940m). The second half of the day is generally downhill to another collection of mountain pools at **Gupa Pokhari** (2890m). This village has a large Tibetan population and some run-down and gloomy teahouses. There is a small Buddhist shrine on one of the lakes behind the village.

Day 3: Gupa Pokhari to Nesum

6–7 HOURS / 310M ASCENT / 1580M DESCENT

This is a long day, and you will probably only have time to reach Nesum. Follow the trail uphill from the Milke Danda ridge to a second ridge running northeast towards the Tamur Kosi. Enjoy the shade of rhododendrons until **Akhar Deorali** (3200m), and then follow an undulating path through mixed deciduous forests to **Gurja** (Gurja Gaon; 2000m), where you'll find meals and rooms at a couple of teahouses.

The latter part of the day is a long, at times tedious, descent though cultivated country to the village of **Chatrapati**, where there are local teashops. Finally, drop down a rocky trail to **Nesum** (1620m) and set up camp for the night.

Day 4: Nesum to Thumma

5–5½ HOURS / 120M ASCENT / 980M DESCENT

Below Nesum, the trail continues its descent to the Tamur Kosi, zigzagging down past scattered farms to a suspension bridge over the small Maiwa Khola. You will need to present your TIMS card and permit before you cross into **Dobhan** (640m), about three hours after leaving Nesum.

Dobhan is a small, grubby bazaar town with a health post and an assortment of shops. There are several unpolished lodges

and a good campsite below the village on the riverbank.

The trail to Thumma follows the substantial Tamur Kosi northeast towards Sakathum. There are tracks on both sides of the valley and the trail cuts back and forth over the river on a series of bridges in varying states of repair.

On either side of the river, the trail picks its way through tropical forest passing occasional farmhouses. The trails are badly eroded, but after about two hours you'll reach a bridge across the Tamur Kosi at **Thumma** (760m). Most groups camp in the main part of the village on the west bank.

SIDE TRIP: TO TAPLEJUNG/SUKETAR

5 HOURS / 1200–1700M ASCENT

At Dobhan you can cross the Tamur Kosi and make the steep, testing ascent to Taplejung or Suketar. This is a useful exit route if any member of your party becomes ill, but there is no particular reason to visit otherwise.

If you are starting the Kanchenjunga North trek at Suketar, you can save time by following a second trail that runs north along the ridge through Phurumbu and Linkhim, dropping to meet the Sakathum trail at Chirwa.

Day 5: Thumma to Chirwa

6–8 HOURS / 430M ASCENT

Follow the east bank of the Tamur as the trail dips and rises along the riverside, skirting rocky fields and landslides, to the Chhetri bazaar at **Mitlung** (880m), where a few wooden teahouses offer meals. Continue along the east bank to **Sinwa** (980m), which has more teahouses.

The valley narrows and the trail deteriorates as it picks a route between landslides and boulder-strewn alluvial deposits. Descend to a wooden bridge across the Thiwa Khola at 1140m, then wind up and down along the riverbank to **Chirwa** (1190m), a cheerful bazaar

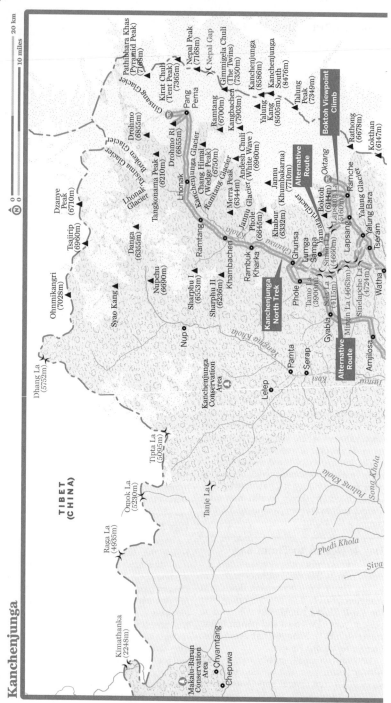

EASTERN NEPAL

Kanchenjunga

TIBET (CHINA)

Kimathanka (2248m)
Makalu-Barun Conservation Area
Chyamtang
Chepuwa

Raga La (4935m)
Omok La (5280m)
Tanje La
Tipta La (5095m)
Dhang La (5752m)

Ohmikangri (7028m)
Syao Kang
Nup
Kanchenjunga Conservation Area
Lelep
Serap
Pamta

Tsajirip (6960m)
Danga (6355m)
Nupchu (6690m)
Dzanye Peak (6710m)

Tangkonama Peak (6210m)
Tsisima Glacier
Broken Glacier
Lhonak Glacier
Sharphu I (6533m)
Sharphu II (6236m)
Khambachen
Rambuk Kharka

Pathibhara Khas (Pyramid Peak) (7165m)
Kirat Chuli (Tent Peak) (7365m)
Drohmo (6855m)
Ginsang Glacier
Pang Pema
Drohmo Ri (6855m)
Lhonak
Ramtang
Kanchenjunga Glacier
Chang Himal (Wedge Peak) (6750m)
Ramtang Glacier
Merra Peak (6344m)
Andesh Chuli (White Wave) (6960m)
Jannu Phole (6645m)

Nepal Peak (7168m)
Nepal Gap
Ramtang (6700m)
Gimmigela Chuli (The Twins) (7350m)
Kangbachen (7903m)
Yalung Kang (8505m)
Jannu (Khumbakarna) (7710m)
Khabur (6332m)

Kanchenjunga (8586m)
Kanchenjunga South (8476m)
Yalung Kang
Yalung Peak (7349m)

Boktoh Viewpoint Climb

Rathong (6678m)
Kokthan (6147m)

Ghunsa Khola
Ghunsa
Lumga
Sampa
Tamo La (3900m)
Phole
Gyabla
Amjilosa
Watha

Alternative Route
Oktang
Boktoh (6114m)
Yamatari Glacier
Simbu La
Yamar La
Sinion La (4660m)
Sele La (4115m)
Mirgin La (4663m)
Sinelapche La (4724m)

Lapsang La (5160m)
Ramche
Lapsang
Yalung Glacier
Yalung Bara
Tseram

Kanchenjunga North Trek

Ghunsa Khola
Tamur Khola
Ramtang
Ramche

Alternative Route

Tamur Khola
Yamphu Khola
Kosi
Simu

Song Khola
Phumu Khola
Phedi Khola
Siva

Rantang
Lhonak
Khambachen

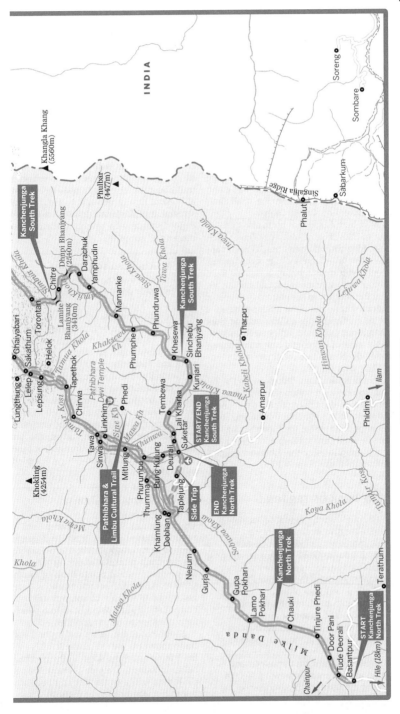

EASTERN NEPAL

village with a few *bhattis* and shops and some porter-style lodges. There is a good campsite about 15 minutes past the village.

Day 6: Chirwa to Sakathum
5–5½ HOURS / 450M ASCENT
Day 6 follows the Tamur to the confluence with the Ghunsa Khola. Stroll north along the east bank of the river on a rolling trail to the Chhetri village of **Tapethok** (Taplethok; 1320m). There's a teashop and you must present your permit, TIMS card and national park receipt at the Kanchenjunga Conservation Area checkpoint. Take the bridge across the Tamur to the west bank and climb high above the river through the small Sherpa village of **Lepsung** to **Lelep**.

From here, a trail runs north along the Tamur to the village of **Lelep** (3220m), which is studded with chortens, stupas and mani walls. This is the largest village of the Walung people, who speak a language derived from Tibetan and share many cultural similarities with the Sherpas. In the past this has been a restricted area, but some trekking agencies are now offering trips to Walunchung Gola (Olangchun Gola), the valley stretching directly north of Lelep, and continuing across the 4776m Nango La to rejoin the main trail at Phole near Ghunsa.

To reach Sakathum, drop down to the Tamur and cross on a suspension bridge. On the east side of the river, you'll see the village of Helok, on the old trail to Ghunsa. From the suspension bridge, it's a short walk along the steep and narrow Ghunsa Valley to a riverside campsite near the Tibetan village of **Sakathum** (Sukethum; 1640m).

THE PEAK OF TERROR...
It is not always the highest peaks that make the hardest climbs. Just west of Kanchenjunga, Jannu (7710m) was not conquered until 1962, nearly a decade after the first Himalayan ascents. Early expeditions called the mountain 'Mystery Peak' and 'Peak of Terror' because of the perilous nature of the ascent – a sheer climb up an almost vertical rock face to a knife-edge ridge less than 1m across. The Nepalis renamed the mountain Khumbakarna in 1984 when a committee 'Nepalised' the names of many peaks. There are great views of Jannu all along the Kanchenjunga North trek.

The village has a helipad and a tiny teashop. If the weather is clear, you will get your first close-up views of the spire of Jannu (7710m) at the end of the Ghunsa Valley.

Day 7: Sakathum to Amjilosa
4–5 HOURS / 890M ASCENT
Start on the narrow trail that winds along the north bank. After a few ups and downs beside the river, you'll reach some stone steps that scramble high above the river to a waterfall and the tiny hamlet of **Ghaiyabari** (2150m). Here, the incline becomes gentler, as you follow an exposed and precarious trail above steep grassy slopes to a crest at 2530m. Finally, descend to the Tibetan settlement of **Amjilosa** (2490m), a loosely defined village with several scattered teahouses and campsites.

Day 8: Amjilosa to Gyabla
4–4½ HOURS / 240M ASCENT
This relatively short day continues to climb along the Ghunsa Valley. You'll definitely feel the mountains are getting closer as you climb to a flat ridge and meander through a forest of bamboo, rhododendrons and gnarled brown oaks, passing scattered pastures and waterfalls.

Eventually, you'll come to a large cascade on the Ghunsa Khola. Here the trail begins a grinding climb to the Sherpa village of **Gyabla** (2730m), also called Chapla or Kyapra. The village has a good campsite and some teahouses with rooms. The far side of the valley is densely forested, but the slopes around Gyabla have been denuded by woodcutters.

Day 9: Gyabla to Ghunsa
6–7 HOURS / 680M ASCENT
The day begins with a steep drop into a ravine, followed by an easy level stage through fir and rhododendron forests along the riverbank. It takes all morning to trek to the yak pastures and potato fields of **Phole** (3210m). There are several teashops here and the small wooden gompa contains several old statues and *thangkas* (cloth paintings) transported here from Tibet.

Above Phole, the valley widens and the trail improves as you trek through fields and larch forests, dipping down to the riverbed before crossing to **Ghunsa** (3410m). This is the largest village on the trek and Buddhist prayer flags flutter over the rooftops.

THE GREAT HIMALAYAN TRAIL

If the month-long circuit of Kanchenjunga isn't enough of a challenge for you, then how about conquering the Great Himalayan Trail? Eventually this trail will, it's hoped, stretch 4500km from Nanga Parbat in Pakistan to Namche Barwa in Tibet and pass through the mountains of Pakistan, India, Nepal, Bhutan and Tibet. For the moment the Nepali section, which alone covers 1700km and takes around 150 days to walk, is the best established, although only one group has so far walked the trail in its entirety (most people are expected to walk sections of it and then return at a later date to walk another section). The route starts at Kanchenjunga north base camp and finishes in the Darchula district in the far west of Nepal. Along the way the high route takes in all the main trekking areas plus numerous very remote regions. There's also a second, lower, trans-Nepal trail called the Great Himalayan Trail Cultural Trail. This route, which takes around 100 days, sticks to the Middle Hills of Nepal and passes through endless villages, reaching a maximum height of 4519m. For more information on both trails see http://thegreathimalayatrail.org.

Beyond the square chorten at the start of the village are several lodges and a few shops with a fair stock of trekking supplies.

Two trails lead on from Ghunsa. The trail to Pang Pema continues north along the river, while the path to Lapsang La and Mirgin La runs south towards the small Yamatari Khola.

Day 10: Acclimatisation Day at Ghunsa

You have now entered serious mountain country. An acclimatisation day at Ghunsa is mandatory to reduce the risk of AMS on later stages of the trek.

Ghunsa is an attractive place to kick back for a day – many people use this rest day to stroll up to the fading gompa above the village, but you can also take a rewarding day hike along the trail to Lapsang La, following the Yamatari Khola to a lake at the terminal moraine of the Yamatari Glacier.

Day 11: Ghunsa to Khambachen

5–6 HOURS / 740M ASCENT

Heading north from Ghunsa, the trail makes a gradual ascent through a forest of larch and juniper along the east bank of the river. After crossing a sandy, boulder-strewn floodplain, the path crosses a rickety, wood-and-stone bridge to the west side of the river at **Rambuk Kharka** (3720m). The hillsides become increasingly barren as you climb along the valley.

Continue north past a waterfall then make a short, steep ascent over a very unstable scree slope.

Beyond the landslide, the trail climbs gradually then drops down to **Khambachen** (4150m), a Tibetan outpost of about a dozen shingle-roofed stone houses, wedged into a side valley at the confluence with the Nupchu Khola. There are flat areas for camping on both sides of the stream and a few teahouses, including the excellent Kanchenjunga White House, which has pristine white sheets on the beds and good food.

Day 12: Acclimatisation Day in Khambachen

After a steep ascent on Day 11, you must take another rest day. The views from Khambachen are superb – the peaks of Khabur (6332m), Phole (6645m) and Jannu (7710m) are lined up at the end of the valley to the east, while the snowcapped ridges beyond the Kanchenjunga Glacier loom dramatically to the north.

For the best views, climb the ridge north of the village – from here, the Khabur, Phole and Jannu peaks rise over the valley like three frozen giants.

Day 13: Khambachen to Lhonak

4–5 HOURS / 640M ASCENT

Above Khambachen, the trail enters a desolate landscape gouged by the icy fingers of glaciers. The path climbs gradually across the scree slopes of recent landslides and up and down hillsides to another area of pasture at **Ramtang** (4350m). Prepare for serious cold.

Above Ramtang, the trail runs along the lateral moraine of the Kanchenjunga Glacier, following the north bank of the river to a wooden bridge at the mouth of the Lhonak Glacier. On the east side of the valley is the crown-shaped ridge of **Merra Peak** (6344m), not to be confused with the famous Mera Peak east of Lukla or Kongma Tse (Mehra Peak) near Lobuche.

The village of **Lhonak** (4790m) sits beside a wide, often-dry lakebed, on an open, sandy plain. Water is scarce here but some large boulders provide shelter for tents.

The views from here are stupendous in every direction. Across the Kanchenjunga Glacier, the door-wedge summit of Chang Himal (Wedge Peak; 6750m) dominates the valley.

Day 14: Lhonak to Pang Pema

3–4 HOURS / 360M ASCENT

The end point for the trek is the base camp for ascents to the north face of Kanchenjunga at **Pang Pema** (5140m). It would be possible to make an arduous day trip from Lhonak, but clouds often obscure the views by mid-morning, so most people set up a high camp on the exposed, sandy plain at Pang Pema. As soon as the sun leaves the valley, the mercury crashes – be prepared for a cold, restless night.

To reach Pang Pema from Lhonak, ascend gradually across the plain and follow the line of the moraine. The most stable trail climbs onto the ridge before dropping to a pair of lonely-looking huts at Pang Pema. If you are lucky, the clouds will part just before sunset for a view of the cascading ridges of the third-largest mountain mass in the world.

Day 15: Pang Pema to Khambachen

6–7 HOURS / 1000M DESCENT

Rise at dawn to hike up the ridge north of Pang Pema for the kind of views that inspire religions. From a vantage point about 300m up the slope, you will have a panorama of Kanchenjunga, Taple Shikhar (6510m) and Gimmigela Chuli (The Twins; 7350m). To the east, the iconic summits of Pathibhara Khas (Pyramid Peak; 7168m) and Kirat Chuli (Tent Peak; 7365m) rise like sentries over the border with Sikkim. To the west, the knife-edge ridge of Chang Himal towers above the Kanchenjunga Glacier.

As usual, the descent is faster, so you can get back to Khambachen in a single day.

Day 16: Khambachen to Ghunsa

4–4½ HOURS / 740M DESCENT

Retrace the approach route to Ghunsa, following the description for Day 11.

ALTERNATIVE ROUTE: KANCHENJUNGA NORTH TO KANCHENJUNGA SOUTH

It is possible, and highly recommended, to link the Kanchenjunga North and Kanchenjunga South treks by crossing the Mirgin La (4663m) or the Lapsang La (5160m). The two trails split just south of Ghunsa, near the bridge over the Yamatari Khola.

The trail to Mirgin La crosses the stream and climbs the ridge to the south. This is the safest and easiest route but you must still haul yourself over five passes. The trail climbs the Tamo La (3900m), the Sele La (4115m), the Sinion La (4660m), the Mirgin La and finally the Sinelapche La (4724m). Most groups stop to camp for the first night by a hut and meandering stream at enchanting Sele La. On day two carry on to meet the Kanchenjunga South trail at Tseram or Yalung Bara.

Crossing the Lapsang La is a much more serious proposition. There is no regular traffic on this route, so you may have to forge a new trail, following a broken line of snow markers. The Lapsang La is frequently blocked by snow between November and May – enquire locally about conditions on the pass before leaving Ghunsa.

To reach the Lapsang La, follow the hillside to the north of the Yamatari Khola, and cross the moraine of the Yamatari Glacier to a camping area at Lumga Sampa (4206m). On day two, make the steep climb over the Lapsang La and drop down to meet the Kanchenjunga South trail at Lapsang (4430m). You should be able to reach Ramche (4620m) by nightfall.

Day 17: Ghunsa to Amjilosa

6–7½ HOURS / 920M DESCENT

Retrace the approach route back to Amjilosa, described on Day 8 and Day 9.

Day 18: Amjilosa to Chirwa

7–8 HOURS / 1340M DESCENT

Follow the approach trek back to Sakathum, then meander back along the Tamur Kosi to Chirwa (see Days 6 and 7).

CLIMBING DROHMO RI

Pang Pema is a remote and magical spot. Most people only stay one night but, if time allows (or the bitter cold doesn't scare you away), it's well worth spending a second night up here. If you do, dedicate your second day here to climbing **Drohmo Ri** (5915m and not be confused with the much more daunting 6855m Drohmo). The peak rises up roughly 800m above Pang Pema and offers superb views. Kanchenjunga views are at their best from about halfway up, but from the top you can admire a frozen lake and a spread of massive peaks. This is a serious gain in altitude and the risk of AMS is high. The route, which is fairly well marked with rock cairns, starts from a dip just to the east of the huts and climbs steeply up through scree fields. The last half-hour is spent clambering over big boulders. Allow at least four to five hours for a return trip.

Day 19: Chirwa to Linkhim

6–7 HOURS / 330M ASCENT

To reach Basantpur, you can follow the first five days of the Kanchenjunga North trek in reverse. However, most groups choose to finish the trek in Suketar, connecting to Kathmandu by air.

From Chirwa, follow the trail that climbs on the east bank of the Tamur Kosi to **Diwa**, then skirt above the houses of **Tawa** (1170m). The trail drops into a side canyon, then climbs back to the ridge, eventually reaching **Linkhim** (1520m), where you can set up camp for the night.

Day 20: Linkhim to Suketar

6–7 HOURS / 900M ASCENT / 120M DESCENT

From Linkhim, trek in and out of side canyons through small Limbu villages to **Phurumbu** and a ridge overlooking a vast landslide. The final stage is a three- to four-hour climb through the Sherpa villages of Bung Kulung and Lakchun to the airstrip at Suketar.

Kanchenjunga South Trek

Duration 14 days

Maximum Elevation 4800m

Difficulty Hard

Season October to November, March to May

Start/Finish Suketar (Taplejung)

Permits US$10 per week per person, available to groups of two or more trekking through a recognised agency

Summary The shorter, lower Kanchenjunga trek, climbing through stunning forests and high mountain country to the moraine of the Yalung Glacier, below the soaring south face of Kanchenjunga.

The trail to south base camp cuts straight to the heart of the Kanchenjunga massif, climbing over vertiginous ridges and plunging into seemingly bottomless valleys. In the space of two weeks, you will cover more than 15,000m of altitude change, gaining a maximum elevation of 4800m, on a par with the summit of Mont Blanc.

The rewards for this effort are enormous – the trail passes by remote, and very beautiful, Limbu villages that see few outsiders, through ancient forests festooned in dangling Spanish mosses, before finally climbing to the foot of Kanchenjunga, for the kind of views normally reserved for mountaineers. However, the one big drawback with this trek is that you spend an awful lot of time walking to the high mountains, but only really one night in amongst them before spinning around and walking all the way back again.

You *could* do this trek pretty much all the way as a 'teahouse' trek, but because there is no permanent habitation beyond day five and there's a chance that the lodges further up the trail might be closed (a certainty between November and early March) you really should carry tents and food. As for the Kanchenjunga North Trek, there was little earthquake damage on this route, but check locally in case any trails have been affected by landslides.

The trek to south base camp normally starts from the airstrip at Suketar (Taplejung), reached via a one-hour flight from Biratnagar. At the time of research, though, the airport was closed for renovations (due to reopen late 2015). Therefore most people were travelling by jeep from Ilam to Taplejung and either starting their trek there (a very steep two-hour climb up endless steps to Suketar) or getting a ride in one of the frequent jeeps from Taplejung to Suketar.

The Trek

See Map p236

Day 1: Suketar to Tembewa

3-4 HOURS / 180M ASCENT / 700M DESCENT

Suketar is a cold and wind-exposed gathering of stone houses spread along a small ridge. The first stage of the journey partly follows the unfinished dirt road (work was taking place on this during research, so it will probably be surfaced by the time you get there) along a rhododendron-covered ridge known as **Surke Danda** (2580m). At the highest point of the ridge, a side trail branches north towards the revered Hindu Pathibhara Devi Temple.

The trail on to Kanchenjunga winds down through forests filled with huge tropical trees, often crossing and re-crossing the dirt road, to a collection of basic teashop lodges in the village of **Lali Kharka** (2220m), and then drops amongst terraced fields to the substantial Limbu village of **Tembewa** (1880m), where groups set up camp for the night on the school playing field. The village is full of neat whitewashed houses, and a few teashops provide meals.

Day 2: Tembewa to Khesewa

4-5 HOURS / 810M ASCENT / 730M DESCENT

From Tembewa, the trail drops steeply down stone steps through fields of millet and rice to a suspension bridge across the Phawa Khola at 1430m. Climb steeply up the east side of the valley to the Limbu village of **Kunjari** (1700m).

Turn left just beyond the Kunjari school and climb through wheat fields to a level saddle, then make a long, looping traverse to **Sinchebu Bhanjyang** (2240m), marked Kande Bhanjyang on the Nepa Maps *Kangchenjunga* map. This small Gurung settlement has several teahouses and you will catch your first views of the snowy caps of Kanchenjunga and Kyabru (7412m). Look out for the peg-like summit of Jannu (Khumbakarna; 7710m) to the west of the main ridge.

Most people continue over the pass into the valley of the Kabeli Khola, then turn left (north) and make a winding 25-minute descent below the ridge to the scattered village of **Khesewa** (1960m), which has camping areas and teahouses.

Day 3: Khesewa to Mamanke

5-6 HOURS / 520M DESCENT / 370M ASCENT

From Khesewa, it's an easy descent past a series of small waterfalls and streams to a crude bridge over the Nadewa Khola. Just beyond is **Phundruwa**, which is shown on some maps with the fanciful spelling 'Phun Phun'. Cross the saddle and turn north towards **Yangpang**, where you may be able to find some lunch. There's a small Hindu temple here as well as stunning views of Mt Jannu.

The path climbs through forests past a large waterfall, and then descends across a series of gullies to a ridge at 1850m. Another 30 minutes will take you to tiny **Phumphe** (1780m), where there's camping and a teahouse. Continue to descend past rice terraces to a sinuous suspension bridge over the Khakseno Khola at 1540m.

The last stage of the day is a tiring 45-minute climb past the dotted houses of Pauwa to **Mamanke** (1780m). This prosperous Limbu village is one of the most attractive on the whole trek with several *bhattis* serving hot meals, a couple of simple homestay-style lodges and several flat areas for camping.

Day 4: Mamanke to Yamphudin

2-3 HOURS / 140M DESCENT / 50M ASCENT

This is a short day, heading north along the Kabeli Khola. Start by climbing the ridge, then drop gradually down to a gushing stream, crossing on a fragile-looking wooden bridge that's replacing a sturdier (though not sturdy enough) suspension bridge that collapsed during a landslide. Follow switchbacks up the far side of the valley, then descend beneath rocky cliffs on the rubble of past landslides. Drop down to the Kabeli Khola and follow the west bank upstream through pretty forest to **Yamphudin** (1690m).

Set at the confluence with the Amji Khola this is an appealing village of Sherpas, Limbus, Rais and Gurungs, with some basic lodges.

Day 5: Yamphudin to Amji Khola

4-5 HOURS / 850M ASCENT / 200M DESCENT

There are few facilities for trekkers above Yamphudin, so it's best to be self-sufficient for the rest of the trek. Start the day by following the faint track heading up the side-river crossing to the east bank on the suspension bridge, and begin the steep climb up the ridge between the Amji Khola and Kabeli Khola.

The path zigzags up through fields of corn and barley to a handful of houses at Darachuk. Just above the first house (and a short way before the hamlet itself) the trail splits. The most obvious path heads straight on to Darachuk while the other path veers sharply right and climbs very steeply uphill. Take this path and climb through meadows to a pass at **Dhupi Bhanjyang** (2540m; 2½ to three hours). That's the hard work over – the final stage of the day is a gradual descent through ferns and gorgeous rhododendron forests to the river. Cross a new suspension bridge and after five minutes you reach the small terraced clearing of **Amji Khola** (2340m), with its seasonal lodge and beautiful camping area.

Day 6: Amji Khola to Torontan

6–7 HOURS / 1180M ASCENT / 530M DESCENT

Brace yourself for a long day of ups and downs. From the campsite at Amji Khola, it's a steep hour-long climb through forests to a *kharka* at **Chitre** (2920m), which often resounds to the chiming of yak bells. The final stage up to the **Lamite Bhanjyang** (3410m) is less strenuous, passing through rhododendron and pine forest in which every tree seems to wear a cloak of long, draping Spanish moss. It's real fantasy forest and it would be hard for even the most scentifically minded not to think of goblins racing up and down the path under the moonlight! At the pass there's a cold, soggy area for camping as well as a rustic teahouse. On a clear day the ridge provides grandstand views of Jannu, sticking out like a rocky thumbs-up on the skyline.

Beyond the pass the trail skirts the vertigo-inspiring edge of a massive landslide, which has literally taken out half the mountainside. The trail across this rockfall is hazardous, poorly defined and changes after each monsoon when more of the mountain slides away. Hitting more stable ground, the path then zigzags very steeply downhill through damp fairy-tale forests filled with creatures of a vivid imagination, crossing streams and isolated clearings used by herders and woodcutters.

The trail finally emerges into the open above the churning Simbua Khola; follow it upstream to a bouncy suspension bridge, turn right after the bridge and head gently uphill to **Torontan** (2990m), where a handful of teahouses offer meals, rudimentary rooms and a fine camping area.

Day 7: Torontan to Tseram

3½–4½ HOURS / 880M ASCENT

Despite a steady climb, today is one of the easier days on this trek. The hike starts in forests of mixed rhododendrons and climbs over the scars of old landslides to an isolated *goth* (hut) at **Tsento Kang** (3360m; 1½ hours). Continue through an atmospheric forest dripping with Spanish moss, with glimpses of the snow peaks between the trees.

After passing a creaky old seasonal teahouse in a flat clearing at **Watha** (3370m), continue for an hour to a cave shrine decorated with rock cairns, prayer flags and three-pronged iron *trisuls* (the trident weapon of Shiva). Inside is a streak of dark stone which resembles a snake, revered by Hindus and Buddhists.

Many maps show a trail to the Mirgin La turning west just above Watha, but most trekkers approach the pass from the north, coming back down the valley on a trail that branches off near Yalung Bara, or via a second trail above Tseram. This is a two-day crossing over a series of ridges that peaks at 4663m before dropping down to Ghunsa.

The snow peaks become more imposing as you follow a gravel streambed towards **Tseram** (3870m), a grassy meadow beside a jumble of mossy boulders at the edge of the tree line. There are several seasonal lodges serving local yak herders and passing trekking and climbing groups. Campers can pitch tents just in front.

Tseram is nearly 900m above Torontan, and the climb takes you to an elevation where you may feel the first effects of altitude sickness.

Day 8: Tseram to Ramche

3–3½ HOURS / 750M ASCENT

Above Tseram, the trail climbs to the treeline, passing the junction with another small trail to the Mirgin La. Above a mani wall at 4040m, alpine meadows slope up the valley towards the peaks of Rathong (6678m), Kabru Dome (6700m) and Kabru IV (7318m). You are now in serious mountain country and there is little shelter from the icy winds that blow off the glacier.

The trail climbs alongside the terminal moraine of the Yalung Glacier to a yak pasture at **Yalung Bara** (4260m). Many groups

BOKTOH VIEWPOINTS

A worthwhile half-day scramble from the lodge at Ramche will take you up towards (but not actually to) the base of Mt Boktoh (6114m). It's a bit of a DIY adventure, but it does provide memorable views of Kanchenjunga's south face and a packed grandstand of other massive peaks. From the lodge at Ramche walk 100m up the valley to where faint tracks (used more by animals than people) lead up the side of the steep, grassy slope on your left. There's no discernible start or end to this walk. Just climb as high as you feel comfortable going. A good bet, though, is to aim for the jagged rocky pinnacles on the eastern edge of the ridge (reaching these involves some clambering over boulders). From these pinnacles you'll be rewarded with extraordinary views up the valley towards Kanchenjunga. Afterwards cross the obvious grassy ridge for a stunning view back down the valley you've just spent the past few days walking up, then head straight back down to the lodge. This suggested route takes about two to three hours return and will take you to around 5100m, so be very aware of altitude sickness.

headed for the Mirgin La turn off here and climb west for four to five hours to a campsite below the pass. For south base camp, continue along the north side of the valley to a small, often-frozen lake at **Lapsang** (4430m).

Just beyond Lapsang, a smaller trail turns west along a side valley towards the Lapsang La (5160m), the high pass leading to Ghunsa.

To finish Day 8, keep climbing to another lake and a meadow in a broad, flat valley at **Ramche** (4620m). There are basic facilities here, including a ramshackle lodge that mainly caters to porters, and there's plenty of space for campers. The view is dominated by the spectacular peak of Rathong, straddling the Nepal–India border to the east.

You'll probably arrive here before lunch, in which case make the quick 15-minute scramble up to the viewpoint, which is the low ridge immediately southeast of the lodge.

Day 9: Day Trip to Oktang & the Yalung Glacier; Return to Tseram

6–7 HOURS / 200M ASCENT / 950M DESCENT

The actual base camp for mountaineering ascents of Kanchenjunga is a one- or two-day walk along the Yalung Glacier and essentially impossible for 'normal' hikers to reach. Therefore the end point of this walk for most trekkers is at Oktang, a stone chorten and viewpoint on top of the moraine and overlooking the glacier.

From the campsite at Ramche, follow the stream and then climb up onto the top of the moraine to the cairn-like chorten (1½ hours) of Oktang stuck with prayer flags and tridents, for a heart-stopping view of the south face of Kanchenjunga, which from here seems to occupy the entire skyline.

This is a good place to turn around and retrace your steps. Return to Ramche and descend to Tseram for the night.

If you are heading on to Ghunsa, you can turn west at Yalung Bara or Tseram and camp on the east side of the Mirgin La.

Day 10: Tseram to Lamite Bhanjyang

6–7 HOURS / 530M ASCENT / 990M DESCENT

Retrace the route along the Simbua Khola (Days 6 and 7), climbing back to an overnight camp at Lamite Bhanjyang (carry extra water).

Day 11: Lamite Bhanjyang to Yamphudin

4½–5½ HOURS / 200M ASCENT / 1920M DESCENT

Descend from Lamite Bhanjyang to the Amji Khola, then scoot over the Dhupi Bhanjyang and descend to Yamphudin for the night, using the description from Days 5 and 6.

Day 12: Yamphudin to Phumphe

5–6 HOURS / 380M ASCENT / 290M DESCENT

Follow the Kabeli Khola back to Phumphe, using the description from Days 3 and 4.

Day 13: Phumphe to Kunjari

6–7 HOURS / 940M ASCENT / 930M DESCENT

Return to Kunjari, following the route from Day 2 and 3.

Day 14: Kunjari to Suketar

7–8 HOURS / 1150M ASCENT / 450M DESCENT

The last day is a long climb and a short descent to Suketar or Taplejung.

OTHER TREKS

Pathibhara & Limbu Cultural Trail

The government is promoting several new itineraries in the foothills of Kanchenjunga, starting from Suketar airstrip near Taplejung. These treks visit Limbu villages that have so far seen few foreign trekkers. The most interesting trip loops around through Deurali and Phedi to the wish-fulfilling Pathibhara Devi Temple, which attracts large numbers of Hindu and Buddhist pilgrims during the annual *mela* (festival) in March.

Another, longer route, links Suketar with Thumbeding via Kande Bhanjyang and Tellok; allow four days. There's transport from Thumbeding back out of the mountains.

TOWNS & FACILITIES

Tumlingtar

☑ 029 / ELEV 460M

The main gateway to the Makalu region, Tumlingtar sprawls across a broad plateau near the confluence of the Arun River and the Sabha Khola. The town airstrip receives flights from Kathmandu and Biratnagar, and road transport runs to Khandbari and Hile. It's a pleasant, laid-back village, especially during Friday's colourful market, and there was little earthquake damage here.

🛏 Sleeping & Eating

Hotel Arun & Lodge GUESTHOUSE $
(☑ 029-575107, 9742011182; r Rs 300-600) About 500m from the airstrip, in front of the Friday market, this charming wooden building has spacious and clean rooms with a shared bathroom (hot water in buckets) and small garden gazebos, which offer a perfect place to kick back with a post-trek beer. The helpful manager can assist with making phone calls or booking flights, and there's a noticeboard full of information about the Makalu-Barun National Park.

Hotel Buddha HOTEL $
(☑ 029-575080; r without bathroom Rs 300-500, r with bathroom Rs 400-800; 🖥) Rooms are clean at this concrete hotel, though there's not much natural light. The ground-floor restau-

rant offers good food including some excellent thalis. The free wi-fi sometimes works.

Urubashi Resort HOTEL $$
(☑ 029-575033; r with bathroom Rs 500-800, deluxe Rs 1000-5000; 🖥) New in 2015, this lime-green concrete mess has the best rooms in town, as well as a restaurant and a planned internet cafe. Rooms vary but all are spacious. It's in front of the noisy jeep/bus stand.

❶ Getting There & Away

Buddha Air (☑ 029-575115; www.buddhaair.com) and **Yeti Airlines** (☑ 029-575120; www.yetiairlines.com) offer daily flights to/from Kathmandu (US$139); Nepalis are charged Rs 5500. Buddha Air also flies to Biratnagar (US$97) three times a week. Changing the date of your flight is rarely a problem, even for next-day travel.

Buses run to Dharan (Rs 650, 10 hours) via Hile between 4am and 7am but it's quicker to take a jeep to Hile (Rs 600, four hours) and then change for another to Dharan (Rs 200, two hours). From Dharan there are overnight buses to Kathmandu, making for an exhausting 24-hour journey.

Headed north towards Makalu, jeeps run when full on the paved road to Khandbari (Rs 100, 30 hours). One jeep runs daily if full to Num (Rs 600, four hours), though it's often easier to find one in Khandbari or Mani Bhanjyang. A reserve (chartered) jeep costs Rs 1000 to Khandbari and Rs 10,000 to Num, and seats up to 10 pasengers.

Khandbari

☑ 029 / ELEV 1020M

Khandbari (Khadbari) is the headquarters of Sankhuwasabha District and a more substantial village than Tumlingtar, and also escaped serious damage in the quake. You may be stuck here if you can't find a direct jeep from Tumlingtar to Num.

There are plenty of shops and restaurants, a Saturday market and several simple hotels close to the main square. Trekkers favour the funky **Hotel Aarti** (☑ 029-560017; s/d Rs 600/750), which has simple rooms but can help arrange porters and flight tickets. The nearby **Hotel Barun** (☑ 029-560582; r without bathroom Rs 400, s/d with bathroom Rs 600/700) has some good-value rooms at the back.

The bus stand below town has early morning buses and jeeps to Hile and Dharan, as well as jeeps to Num.

Biratnagar

ELEV 72M

Tucked up snug against the Indian border, and unaffected by the earthquake, Biratnagar is Nepal's second-largest city and the main industrial centre in the Terai. Most trekkers only come here to change flights or buses. With the vagaries of air travel in Nepal it's easy to get stuck here overnight, but there are a handful of decent hotels and good road links to other towns in the Terai.

🛏 Sleeping & Eating

There are several local restaurants around Traffic Chowk.

★ **Hotel Eastern Star** HOTEL $$
(☑ 021-471626; easternstar_brt@wlink.com.np; Road Cess Chowk; s/d with fan Rs 1500/1900, s/d with AC from Rs 1850/2150; P❄🛜) The best-value place in town, it has a wonderful location in a quiet area south of the bus park. Rooms, which have a certain faded charm, are massive and well furnished, and have comfortable beds, satellite TV and clean bathrooms. Staff are friendly, and there's a good Indian restaurant and well-stocked bar.

ℹ Getting There & Away

Buddha Air (☑ Kathmandu 01-5542494; www. buddhaair.com) and **Yeti Airlines** (☑ Kathmandu 01-4465888; www.yetiairlines.com) both have numerous daily flights between Biratnagar and Kathmandu (around US$150 to US$190, 35 minutes).

The bus stand is a rickshaw ride (Rs 30) southwest from Traffic Chowk in the city centre. There are regular buses to Kathmandu (normal/deluxe/air-con Rs 920/1120/1420, 14 hours).

Local buses run to Dharan (Rs 80, 1½ hours) throughout the day. There are also early-morning buses to Dhankuta (Rs 250, three hours) and Hile (Rs 300, 3½ hours).

Dharan

ELEV 366M

Just north of the Mahendra Hwy at the start of the winding road to the hill towns of Dhankuta, Hile, Basantpur and Tumlingtar, Dharan is a busy bazaar town with an agreeably industrious atmosphere. There's nothing much to see but you may have to stop here overnight on the way to or from the hills. The town was only lightly affected by the earthquake.

🛏 Sleeping & Eating

For meals, there are lots of cheap places near the clock tower.

New Dreamland Hotel & Lodge HOTEL $
(☑ 021-525024; r with/without bathroom Rs 1200/700, with AC Rs 2300; P❄🛜) If you can cope with the near-incessant traffic noise, Dreamland, with its large, carpeted rooms, exceptionally helpful staff and attractive garden restaurant, is an excellent choice. To get there from Bhanu Chowk (the clock-tower square in the town centre) head west three blocks.

ℹ Getting There & Away

Several buses a day leave from Bhanu Chowk for Kathmandu (normal/deluxe Rs 800/1000, 14 hours), with the first at 4.30am and the last at 5pm. There are also buses to Biratnagar (Rs 80, 1½ hours). Heading north, local buses run regularly from 4am to 4pm to Bhedetar (Rs 55, 45 minutes), Dhankuta (Rs 175, two hours) and Hile (Rs 215, three hours).

Hile

ELEV 1850M

Now that the road has advanced along the valley towards Tumlingtar and Khandbari, Hile is no longer the busy trekking hub it once was. Nevertheless, the village has a bustling bazaar feel, particularly during the weekly Thursday market, and there are several gompas founded by Tibetan refugees. There's a good mountain viewpoint about 30 minutes' walk above town (follow the Basantapur road to the army post, then turn north along the trail to Hattikharka). Little earthquake damage was reported here.

🛏 Sleeping & Eating

A handful of simple lodges line the main road through the village. At the time of research a huge new hotel complex was under construction on the hill above the town.

Kanjirowa Makalu Hotel HOTEL $
(☑ 026-540509; r from Rs 1200; 🛜) A smart red-brick hotel on the outskirts of town, its large rooms are by far the most comfortable in Hile. It has a good international menu and a bar with an impressive cocktail list.

ℹ Getting There & Away

Frequent local buses run from Dharan to Hile (Rs 215, two hours), with the last bus at 4.30pm. A few continue up the Arun Valley as far as

Leguwa (Rs120, three hours). Some buses from Dharan continue to Basantapur (Rs 100 from Hile, 1½ hours).

Taplejung

ELEV 1820M

Hovering above the Tamor Nadi, Taplejung is a bustling, scrappy small town well stocked with shops. Most trekkers, however, fly into the airstrip at Suketar, about two hours' climb above the village. There's no need to come into Taplejung unless the airstrip is closed by bad weather and you need to travel south by road or you came up by bus from Ilam. The town was hit badly by a tremor in 2011 but escaped damage in the 2015 quake.

🛏 Sleeping & Eating

Taplejung Guest House   HOTEL $
(Taplejung; s/tw Rs 500/600) After a long, cold hike there's probably nothing you'd like more than a delicious luxury hotel. Well, this isn't it. But it does at least have windows between your bathroom and your neighbour's bathroom, which is certainly an unusual touch. Camping is possible in the car park.

ℹ Getting There & Away

Nepal Airlines normally flies between Biratnagar and Suketar, but at the time of research the airport was closed for major renovations. Flights were expected to have recommenced by the end of 2015.

The road between Taplejung and Ilam has improved enormously in recent years. Jeeps leave fairly frequently throughout the morning to/from Ilam (Rs 700, seven hours). If you were to rent a jeep privately, in one long day you could get all the way down to the lowlands to Kakar-bhitta on the Indian border or Bhadrapur, from where there are daily flights to Kathmandu.

Basantpur

ELEV 2200M

An alternative trailhead for treks to Kanchenjunga is Basantpur, a small hill village on the road from Hile to Terathum. Set on a ridge above the Tanmaya Khola, the village has well-stocked shops and a scattering of teahouse lodges, and there was no earthquake damage, but the dust and noise deter most people from staying longer than it takes to find the trail to Chauki.

🛏 Sleeping & Eating

Basantpur has a scattering of crude lodges, but none are exactly salubrious. If you are camping, there is a flat meadow about 1km uphill from Basantpur on the trail to Chauki.

ℹ Getting There & Away

Basantpur is 37km from Hile. Buses run downhill to Hile (Rs 100, 1½ hours) and Dharan Bazaar (Rs 315, 4½ hours) every few hours throughout the day.

Western Nepal

Why Go?

The allure of Western Nepal is the immense scale of the landscape; extensive forests and alpine meadows give way to wave after wave of stark, khaki ridges that spread through the rain shadow of the Himalaya, all framed by snowcapped peaks. Touched lightly by the 2015 earthquakes, this remote expanse hides some of the country's best trekking secrets, including spectacular turquoise lakes, timeless Tibetan monasteries and breathtaking high passes. With language and traditions quite different from the rest of the country, western Nepal feels very much like the frontier it is.

All treks in Nepal's Wild West are seriously off the beaten track – these aren't teahouse-and-apple-pie treks. If you're not put off by the logistical difficulties of securing flights, fuel, permits and food, or the relatively higher costs of trekking far from Kathmandu, then the west is the place for you. This is one corner of Nepal where you need a reliable trekking agency on your side.

Best Views & Viewpoints

➡ Phoksumdo Lake (p263)

➡ Jaljala La (p272)

➡ Rara Lake (p254)

➡ Kagmara Phedi (p261)

➡ Numa La (p268)

Best Architecture & Culture

➡ Shey Gompa (p276)

➡ Thasung Chholing Gompa (p264)

➡ Bön monasteries of Do Tarap (p267)

When to Go

➡ Most of western Nepal is either outside the monsoon's influence or in the rain shadow of the Dhaulagiri Himal.

➡ Summers (June to August) tend to be drier here than in the rest of Nepal, and there are few leeches, although one problem with summer treks in the west is the inordinate number of flies.

➡ The trekking season, therefore, is from late spring and throughout summer until late October, though the best time to visit the high valleys is from late August to September, when the wildflowers are in bloom.

➡ Snow blocks passes in winters and many higher villages are deserted.

History

Much of western Nepal was part of the ancient Tibetan Zhang Zhung kingdom, an empire that extended north into Ngari (western Tibet) and west to Kumaon (India), and this legacy is visible in the region's scattering of Bön monasteries. Tibetan peoples migrated into Dolpo and Humla during the 6th and 8th centuries when Zhang Zhung was conquered by central Tibet. Until Jumla was conquered by the army of Bahadur Shah in 1788, the people of western Nepal had very little to do with Kathmandu.

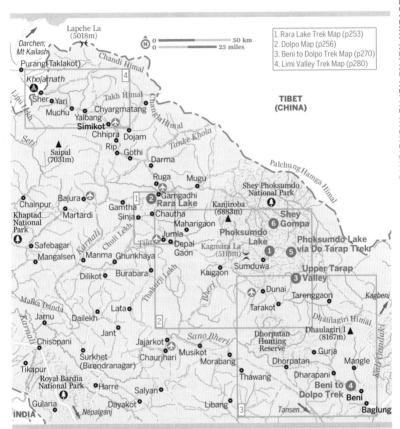

1. Rara Lake Trek Map (p253)
2. Dolpo Map (p256)
3. Beni to Dolpo Trek Map (p270)
4. Limi Valley Trek Map (p280)

Western Nepal Highlights

1 Camping by the meditative turquoise waters of **Phoksumdo Lake** (p263), Nepal's deepest and most beautiful lake.

2 Trekking through verdant, bird-filled forests to the tranquil shores of **Rara Lake** (p254) for a rare taste of picture-postcard wilderness.

3 Walking with yak caravans and exploring the stone villages and Bön monasteries of the **upper Tarap Valley** (p267).

4 Making your own inner journey in the footsteps of Matthiessen's *The Snow Leopard* on the **Beni to Dolpo trek** (p269), the enchanting approach trek to legendary Dolpo.

5 Pitching your tent in the starkly beautiful wilderness between the Baga La and Numa La on the **Phoksumdo Lake via Do Tarap trek** (p264).

6 Discovering remote monasteries and sacred peaks in the snow leopard country surrounding the fabled Crystal Mountain and **Shey Gompa** (p276).

TREKKING IN WESTERN NEPAL AFTER THE EARTHQUAKES

The west of Nepal saw only slight damage from the massive earthquakes that struck the centre of the country on 25 April and 12 May 2015. At the time of writing, all trails in the west of the country are expected to be open as normal in 2016. However, there are reports of damage to traditional stone-walled buildings in Humla and Inner Dolpo areas and the region is still vulnerable to landslides following the disaster. The drop in the number of tourists visiting Nepal may also have a knock-on effect on tourist infrastructure in this less visited quarter. Flights may be cancelled because of reduced demand, and lodge owners may decide that it is not worth their time opening up for small numbers of visitors.

The trek descriptions in this chapter were researched shortly before the disaster and we have since updated using local sources, but this is a remote area and it will be some time before the full scale of the damage from the earthquake becomes apparent. Before starting any trek in this region, seek local information to make sure that trails are open and that food and accommodation are available for overnight stops, unless you plan to be completely self-sufficient.

Sandwiched between the more powerful kingdoms of Lo and Jumla, Dolpo has always been too rugged, remote and sparsely populated to be a major player. The Tibetan kingdom of Purang nominally controlled Dolpo between the 9th and 14th centuries, followed by Mustang, to which it was forced to pay an annual tribute. When Mustang became part of the Gorkha kingdom in 1789, Dolpo followed it by default into the Nepal political sphere. A greater change came to Dolpo in the 1960s, when the Chinese closure of the Tibetan border cut the region's traditional trading and herding routes.

In contrast to the Tibetan Buddhist borderlands, the lowlands of western Nepal are predominantly Hindu. The major legacy of western Nepal's Malla kingdom, based at capitals at Sinja and Dulla, is its language Khasa, which remains the basis of modern Nepali.

Environment

Western Nepal, particularly the Dolpo area, is reminiscent of Kashmir in its rich variety of flora. To witness the full spectrum of wildflowers, visit in July and August. From Jumla eastwards one may recognise ground orchids, edelweiss, corydalis, campanulas, anemones, forget-me-nots, impatiens and roses. Higher up in the alpine areas, larkspurs, geraniums, poppies, sedums and saxifrages proliferate.

Look for flocks of swift-flying snow pigeons and gliding pairs of Himalayan griffons. Within the forests along the trek to Rara Lake it is entirely possible to catch sight of Nepal's national bird, the impeyan pheasant.

Excellent places to spot blue sheep include the Kagmara La trek, the Tarap Valley and the high ground between Dhorpatan and Dunai. Your chance of sighting a snow leopard is best in sparsely populated upper Dolpo, for example around Shey Gompa, though realistically, you are about as likely to spot a snow leopard as you are a yeti.

ℹ Planning

EMERGENCY FACILITIES

Western Nepal is remote and lacking in both communication and medical facilities. There are telephones and mobile phone reception in the district headquarters towns of Simikot, Dunai and Jumla, and satellite phone links in Ringmo (Phoksumdo Lake).

MAPS

Most trekkers will be happy with the Nepal Map Publisher's 1:125,000 *Upper and Lower Dolpa*, which covers everything from Kagmara La to Kagbeni. Himalayan Maphouse (Nepa Maps) produces 1:125,000 *Dolpo Circuit*, 1:125,000 *Dhorpatan Hunting Reserve* (Beni to Dolpo), and 1:15,000 *Dunai to Rara Jumla* maps. In collaboration with the Great Himalaya Trail (GHT) they also produce 1:150,000 *Dolpo and Mugu* and 1:150,000 *Far West Nepal* maps.

An excellent and detailed map for the Rara Lake trek is the Nelles/Schneider 1:100,000 *Jumla-Rara Lake*, or try the hard-to-find Nepa Maps 1:135,000 *Rara Lake and Jumla* map.

Place Names

The people of western Nepal speak their own version of Nepali, which Kathmandu Nepalis barely understand. People may say the hike to the next village is an easy one by saying the trail is *sasto*, which translates as 'inexpensive'. Similarly a trail can be *ek bhat* shorter than another; this translates as 'one rice' or 'one meal' – a charming way to say half a day. This charm, of course, can lead to complications.

West Nepali lingo also pervades place names. The name for a river is *gaad*, a high meadow is a *patan*, a pasture or campsite is a *chaur* and a pass is a *lagna*.

BOOKS

Peter Matthiessen's *The Snow Leopard* is the classic account of a trek from Beni to Shey Gompa in inner Dolpo. It's a must-read for anyone headed on the Beni–Dolpo trek or to inner Dolpo. *Stones of Silence*, by George B Schaller, offers a more prosaic view of the same trip from the famous naturalist.

David Snellgrove's classic 1958 *Himalayan Pilgrimage* has a lot of background on the area, including the Tarakot, Tarap Valley and Phoksumdo Lake regions.

High Frontiers, by Kenneth M Bauer, is an academic overview of the region's history and changing trading patterns, touching on everything from the history of trade with Tibet to the cultural impact of the film *Caravan*, plus everything you ever wanted to know (and more) about yak husbandry.

Tales of the Turquoise: A Pilgrimage in Dolpo, by Corneille Jest, is a collection of legends and stories compiled by an authority on Dolpo.

MOVIES

Dolpo was the setting for Eric Valli's movie *Caravan* (also released as *Himalaya*), which was nominated for a Best Foreign Film Oscar in 1999. The movie was filmed at Phoksumdo Lake, Tsakang Monastery and in the Tarap and Charka (Tsarkha) valleys and presents a stunning view of Dolpo and the region's yak caravans.

ACCOMMODATION

One of the largest ethnic groups in the region is the Thakuris, the Chhetri caste with the highest social, political and ritual status. Westerners, who are considered low caste by high-caste Hindus, are traditionally not welcome in Thakuri homes. For this reason teashops are scarce and cater mainly to locals. Consequently, it is quite difficult to trek in much of lower western Nepal using teahouses solely for food and accommodation.

PORTERS

Porters are available in Jumla and Dunai but they won't necessarily have much experience in working with foreigners and probably won't speak English. Some groups use pack animals (mules, horses and even yaks), which can be arranged in Jumla and Dunai.

❶ Getting There & Away

The main entry points for treks in western Nepal are Jumla and Dunai, both accessible by air from Kathmandu via Nepalganj (see p287). An alternative to Dunai airport when wind or snow delay flights is Chaurjhari, three days' walk south of Dunai on the Thulo Bheri.

RARA NATIONAL PARK

Rara Lake (2980m) is the focal point of Rara National Park and if you are looking for wilderness and solitude, this is a great destination. The route is well off the beaten track and affords glimpses of cultures and scenery very different from those in the rest of Nepal. There was no serious earthquake damage reported in this area.

❶ Towns & Facilities

Gamgadhi is the regional headquarters for the Mugu district and has an airport nearby at Talcha. Nepal Airlines and Tara Air fly Nepalganj to Talcha (US$187). However, most people trekking to Rara Lake start and finish at Jumla, as Gamgadhi is only a few hours' walk from the lake. For details on getting to/from Jumla see p287.

Rara Lake Trek

Duration 9 days

Max Elevation 3710m

Difficulty Medium

Start/Finish Jumla

Permits TIMS card, restricted-area trekking permit, Rara National Park permit

Summary Lots of up-and-down walking through forests and isolated villages leads to Rara Lake, perfect for birdwatchers and wilderness lovers.

Rara Lake is a clear, high-altitude lake ringed with pine, spruce and juniper forests and snowcapped Himalayan peaks. In winter there is often snow on the ridges surrounding the lake. Designated a national park in 1975,

---

❶ WARNING

There is an amazing amount of marijuana in western Nepal, both wild and cultivated. The locals do sometimes smoke it, but it is cultivated for its fibres and for the seeds, which are processed into cooking oil. The police and national park officials have been known to arrest trekkers who transport marijuana in their luggage. In many places, you may walk through, or camp in, fields of cannabis. If you've done so, it's worth giving your boots and gear a scrubbing before you head home so your luggage doesn't attract the attention of airport sniffer dogs.

this trek offers remoteness and a wilderness experience unlike any other in Nepal. Except for the army personnel assigned to the park, nobody lives at the lake because the government resettled all the people of Rara and Chapra villages when the area was declared a national park. At the time of writing, there were no reports of serious damage from the 2015 earthquake, but as a sensible precaution, seek local advice on the status of trails and infrastructure before starting a trek in this area.

ⓘ Planning

SUPPLIES

The trek to Rara is quite strenuous, and tends to be expensive because both food and labour are scarce in this part of Nepal.

It is difficult to purchase enough food for a trek in Jumla Bazaar, despite extensive cultivation of red rice near Jumla, and the Nepalganj–Jumla shuttle flights carrying in white rice and other staples to supply the army and government officials. It is better to carry all your food from Kathmandu – if you can get it onto the plane. Park regulations prohibit the use of firewood so you must stock up on adequate supplies of kerosene.

Merchants fly white rice to Jumla and then transport it to more remote regions using trains of horses, mules, sheep and goats. The goat 'trucks' of western Nepal are a fascinating and disappearing sight. Traders equip herds of 100 or more sheep and goats with tiny woollen panniers that carry 10kg of rice, then herd the animals through the countryside.

FEES & PERMITS

The Mugu district restricted-area trekking permit costs US$70 for one week plus US$15 per day thereafter. To enter Rara National Park you must pay the park entrance fee of Rs 3000. You will also need a TIMS card.

🏃 The Trek

Day 1: Jumla to Danphe Lagna Camp

5–6 HOURS / 1230M ASCENT / 250M DESCENT

Most trekkers will arrive in Jumla by air from Nepalganj. In Jumla there are shops, pharmacies, a bank and a few restaurants along the stone-paved main street. There are two routes from Jumla to Danphe Lagna. The more popular trail crosses a high pass that is closed when there is heavy snow; to reach this trail, follow the main street of Jumla north up the Jugad Valley past the hospital. The wide, level trail leads past college buildings to a settlement known as Campus. As

the trail slowly gains elevation it passes the residences of staff from the Karnali Technical Institute, a vocational school at Ghumurti (2550m), a short distance above.

After a long climb past the school, the trail passes through Sisnamul (2830m), then enters a forest that soon gives way to meadows. Chere (3010m) is a large horse and sheep pasture with a few open herders' huts. Beyond Chere the trail becomes steeper and climbs through meadows to Danphe Lagna, a pass at 3720m offering views of Patrasi Himal (6860m) and Jagdula Himal (5785m) to the east. The trail descends gently through forests of spruces, birches and rhododendrons to a camp the locals call Danphe Lagna Camp (3500m) in an attractive meadow beside a clear stream. It is often possible to spot the Himalayan monal (or impeyan pheasant), the colourful national bird of Nepal, in the nearby forests.

ALTERNATIVE ROUTE: LOW TRAIL

If the pass at Danphe Lagna is closed by snow, you will have to take the longer, lower route from Jumla, which follows the north bank of the Tila Khola, before turning north up the Chaudhabise Khola. The Jumla Valley disappears behind a ridge as the trail follows the river, keeping fairly level and passing through fields and pine forests. The trek heads in the direction of Uthugaon (2530m), then begins an ascent up the Padmara Valley, beginning gently but becoming steeper as the climb continues. There is a good campsite near the school, across the river from Uthugaon.

Along the Padmara Valley, the trail ascends through a forest of pines, spruces and firs, squeezing between cliffs as the canyon narrows. The large Chhetri town of Padmara (2900m) is the last village in the valley. The climb continues through forests, over the Khali Lagna at 3550m, and down to Danphe Lagna Camp on the opposite side. This route takes half a day longer than the high trail.

Day 2: Danphe Lagna Camp to Chautha

5–6 HOURS / 410M ASCENT / 770M DESCENT

The trail descends gently alongside the stream to two *bhattis* (teashops) at Tharamara (3280m). The descent becomes steep, through forests of fir, walnut and bamboo, to Hiran Duski (2840m). After a short level stretch the trail zigzags down to the Sinja Khola, crossing it on a suspension bridge at 2680m. Follow

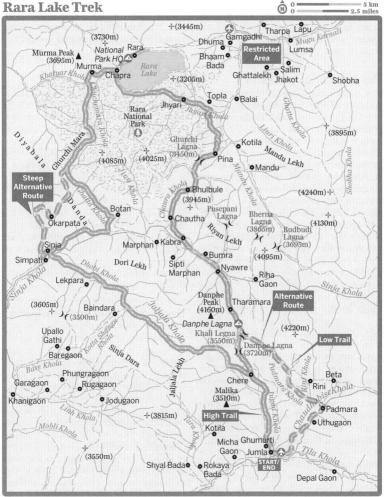

the river downstream to **Nyawre** (2660m), then through fields near the riverbed. The trail that climbs steeply up the ridge is longer and more difficult than the riverbed route.

The trail leaves the river and starts a serious climb, passing through fields below Bumra village, then over a ridge into a side valley, dropping to cross a stream near some water-driven mills. A steep set of switchbacks leads to **Kabra** where, crammed under a huge overhanging rock, there is a scruffy hotel and health post, specialising in ayurvedic medicines. The rock is a source of *shilajit*, a mineral claimed to have such amazing cu-

rative properties it is carried to Jumla, then flown to Nepalganj and exported to India.

The steep climb continues, then levels out before **Bhara** (2920m), also known as Bhadgaon. It is a classic Tibetan-style village surrounded by fields of wheat. Beyond this large village the trail makes a turn into a valley then descends to the Chaura Khola. Just across this stream is the tiny village of **Chautha** (2770m). The Bhandari Hotel here offers rough accommodation. If you are camping, try the fields before the village or else continue an hour or more up the valley and camp alongside the stream. The trail exiting the village to the south follows the Sinja Khola to Sinja. The Rara Lake trail heads north up the Chaura Khola. Local folklore says that Chautha is the halfway point between Jumla and Rara Lake.

Day 3: Chautha to Dhotu

4–5½ HOURS / 780M ASCENT / 1050M DESCENT

A rocky trail follows the stream uphill, crossing it as the wooded valley closes in. About 30 minutes beyond Chautha the valley widens, and there is a house and fields at Chante Chaur (2940m). The climb continues to the Rara National Park entrance station at **Bhulbule** (3130m). Show (or buy) your entry ticket and then have a cup of tea at a *bhatti* five minutes beyond the entrance station. Above Bhulbule the trail emerges into a vast meadow, and climbs gently but steadily to an assortment of chortens, cairns and prayer flags atop the **Ghurchi Lagna**, a 3450m pass. From here, there are views of the Mugu Karnali River and snowy peaks bordering Tibet.

The trail now follows the trade route to Mugu through the Mandu Valley. From the pass the route descends gently on a broad path before dropping precipitously down a rough trail through spruce forests. The trail levels out at around 2900m, 45 minutes below the pass. Watch for a trail junction. It may still be marked with a wooden post with 'Rara' painted in red. The inconspicuous trail to the left (north) is the direct route to Rara Lake. The broad trail that goes straight on is the trade route leading to Pina (2400m), and then on to the restricted area of Mugu. Follow the direct trail to Rara Lake, which stays more or less level through pine forests, then descends to the Jhyari Khola at 2400m. Another stretch of easy walking leads to the small settlement of **Dhotu**, an army camp and helipad. Stay level and left; do not descend and cross the river.

Day 4: Dhotu to Rara Lake

3–4 HOURS / 550M ASCENT / 70M DESCENT

Cross a stream and make a steep climb to the Thakuri village of Jhyari at 2630m, in a picturesque grove of giant cedars. Continue climbing through cedar forests to a huge meadow atop a 3050m ridge with a great view of Rara Lake. Don't follow any of the trails leading along the top of the ridge; descend a short distance to **Rara Lake**. There are no campsites along the southern shore.

The national park headquarters and camping ground are on the northern side of the lake. It will take two hours or more to walk around the lake to the camping ground.

Day 5: Rara Lake

4–5 HOURS

Rara Lake (2980m) is the largest lake in Nepal. It is almost 13km around the lake, and a day devoted to making this circuit is well spent. There are a few park wardens' houses, and the remnants of the now-deserted villages of Rara and Chapra on the northern side of the lake, but otherwise it is an isolated region where birds, flowers and wildlife thrive. Among the mammals in the region are Himalayan bears, Himalayan tahrs, serows, gorals, musk deer, red pandas and both rhesus and langur monkeys. Swimming in the 170m-deep lake are otters and fish and the lake and associated wetlands are an internationally important Ramsar (www.ramsar.org) site for migrating waterfowl.

Day 6: Rara Lake to Gorosingha

4–5 HOURS / 770M ASCENT / 830M DESCENT

Although you can return to Jumla via the same route, it is more rewarding to make a circuit via a different trail. From the bridge at the western end of Rara Lake the trail follows the Khatyar Khola (called the Nisa Khola in its upper reaches) to Majhghatta, about 15 minutes from the bridge. A trail ascends from here to Murma, but you do not have to go through Murma. Take a lower trail that descends gradually to the river, cross the river on a log bridge, and then cross another stream beside a decrepit mill. A small trail leads straight up the hill, climbing through pine, then spruce and rhododendron forests.

The ascent becomes less steep through forests of pines and birches, crossing meadows to a ridge at 3660m. There are views of Rara Lake far below as the trail skirts the head of a huge valley to the crest of the **Ghurchi Mara** at 3710m. If the weather is clear, there is an excellent view of the western Himalaya from this ridge.

There are two choices of route to Sinja: the long route or the short, steep route. Both allow you to reach Sinja the next day.

To go by the longer route, follow the main trail as it drops into the Ghatta Valley, then heads towards **Gorosingha**. The local people call Gorosingha 'the poster', referring to the army post there. From above, the post looks like a classic Hollywood Western ranch in a beautiful grassy vale. There are several excellent campsites along the Ghatta Khola, both above and below Gorosingha.

To go the shorter, steeper way to Sinja, watch for an inconspicuous trail junction at 3000m, about an hour below the crest of the Ghurchi Mara and just before the main trail reaches the Ghatta Khola. Don't descend into the valley towards Gorosingha. Stay high on the side of the treeless Ghatta Valley and follow the trail until it descends to a small campsite by a stream.

Day 7: Gorosingha to Sinja
4–5 HOURS / 450M ASCENT / 1010M DESCENT

After working your way down the Ghatta Khola past Botan you will meet the Sinja Khola. It is then a short walk down this fertile valley, through a heavily populated region, to the Brahman and Chhetri village of Sinja (2440m).

If you have come the short, steeper way, the trail climbs a big gully from the stream to a ridge at 3450m. It's easy to get lost between here and Sinja, so you'll be much better off with a local guide. From the ridge, follow the left trail and stay as high as possible on the ridge, before descending gradually to Okarpata (3070m), then steeply down the ridge on a rough, rocky trail to Sinja.

From the 12th to the 14th centuries, Sinja was the capital of the Malla dynasty that ruled western Nepal. The ruins of the palace can be seen across the river.

Day 8: Sinja to Jaljala Chaur
5–6 HOURS / 830M ASCENT

It is very difficult to reach Jumla in a single day from Sinja, so it's best to break the trek with a night in the high meadows. From Sinja, the trail crosses the Sinja Khola on a wooden cantilever bridge, then begins a long trip up the Dhobi Khola. After passing a few small villages and a trail to the temple, the trail crosses back and forth across the river on a series of log bridges. Most of the trek is through forests although there are a few scattered houses and barley fields. From Chala Chaur, a meadow with a few herders' huts at 2900m, the trail climbs steeply to Jaljala Chaur, a broad meadow with grazing horses at 3270m.

Day 9: Jaljala Chaur to Jumla
3–4 HOURS / 240M ASCENT / 1140M DESCENT

Keep climbing through forests to another meadow, just below the ridge at 3510m, then descend to a few houses at Chauri Khola (3090m). Cross a stream and contour around the head of the valley, staying high, eventually crossing another ridge to rejoin the upward 'high trail' at Chere (3010m). The final descent to Jumla is the reverse of Day 1, through Sisnamul, past the school at Ghumurti, then from Campus to Jumla.

DOLPO

Dolpo is a remote and spectacular corner of the Himalaya, bound to the east and south by the huge Dhaulagiri and Churen Himal ranges, to the west by Jumla district and isolated from the rest of Nepal by high passes to the south. It is vast, occupying 15% of the country and forms Nepal's largest district, Dolpa. (Dolpo is the local name for the region; Dolpa is the government spelling.)

Dolpo has long been bypassed by development and, until recently, by tourism. Although a few anthropologists and geographers explored the region, the entire district was closed to trekkers until 1989, when the southern part of Dolpo was opened to organised trekking groups. This region was not untouched by the 2015 earthquake – there are

DOLPO CHARITIES

The following nongovernmental organisations (NGOs) work with mountain communities in the region.

➡ **Action Dolpo** (www.actiondolpo. com) French NGO that founded the Crystal Mountain School.

➡ **Drokpa** (www.drokpa.org) Funds a range of projects involving alternative energy, traditional medicine and schools in Charka and Tinje.

➡ **Friends of Dolpa** (www. friendsofdolpa.org) US-based community development project that funds schools in Tapriza and Dunai.

➡ **Tapriza Project** (www.tapriza.org) Swiss organisation behind the Tapriza school, as well as monastery restoration in Ringmo and Hurikot.

Dolpo

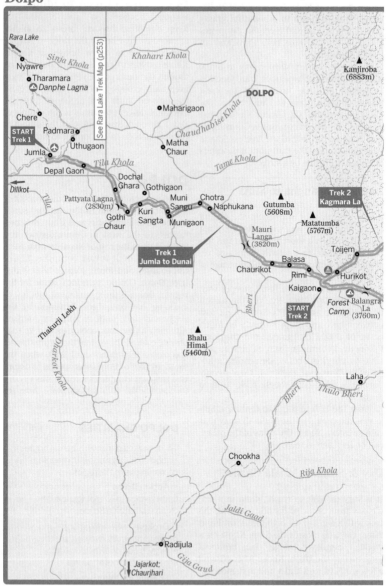

reports of damage to traditional stone-walled buildings, particularly in inner Dolpo – but no fatalities were reported and groups were able to trek in this region within weeks of disaster.

Much of the region is protected by 3555-sq-km Shey Phoksumdo National Park,

Nepal's largest protected area. Dolpo is also known to Tibetan Buddhists as a *bae-yul*, or 'hidden land'. Peter Matthiessen's *The Snow Leopard* and David Snellgrove's *Himalayan Pilgrimage* have crystallised Dolpo's mystique in many Western minds.

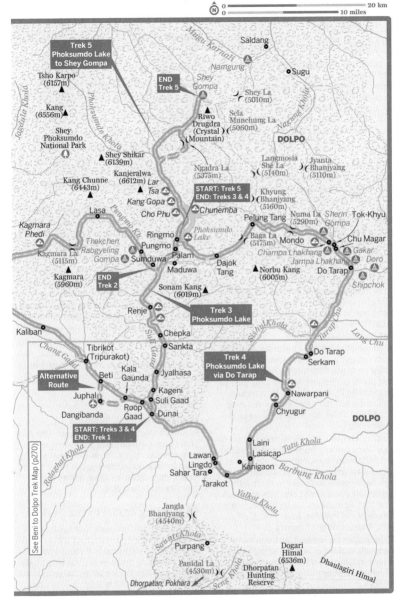

The Tibetan-style villages of Tarap and Phoksumdo Lake boast impressive gompas and Bön monasteries, and yak caravans remain the main form of transportation. While much of the region remains culturally and religiously linked with Tibet, and the people continue to trade with Tibet on the ancient 'grain for salt' trade routes, the southern part of Dolpo is a region of Hindu influence.

❶ Planning

FEES & PERMITS

For all treks in this section you require a TIMS card in addition to the trekking permits. Lower/outer Dolpo treks (ie to the Do Tarap Valley and Phoksumdo Lake) require a US$10-per-week trekking permit. This is easy to obtain through a trekking agency. Inner Dolpo is subject to high restricted-area permit fees of US$500 per 10 days (US$50 per day thereafter). No trekking permits are necessary for the Beni to Dolpo, Jumla to Dunai or Kagmara La treks.

You must pay the park entrance fees of Rs 3000 each to enter Shey Phoksumdo National Park and/or Dhorpatan Hunting Reserve (the latter on the Beni to Dolpo trek).

ROUTE OPTIONS

You can reach Dolpo on foot from Jumla (six days), Beni (12 days), Surkhet (nine days) and Jomsom (11 days, but subject to a US$700 permit fee). The Dolpo airport in Juphal is half a day from the district headquarters in Dunai.

The following sections describe the treks from Jumla to Dunai, visits to Phoksumdo Lake and Tarap, and an alternative high route over Kagmara La. There is also a description of the trek from Beni, near Pokhara, to Dolpo.

You can combine these treks into various permutations; a 24-day trek from Beni to Dunai via Do Tarap and Phoksumdo Lake; or 18 days from Jumla to Phoksumdo via the Kagmara La and on to Do Tarap and Dunai. Most popular is the superb 12-day loop from Dunai, taking in the Tarap Valley, the Numa La, Baga La and Phoksumdo.

Inner and outer Dolpo combinations that visit Shey Gompa include from Phoksumdo to Shey and Saldang and then south over the Jyanta La to Do Tarap, continuing back to Dunai (18 days). A 16-day itinerary could take you from Dunai to Kagbeni via Phoksumdo Lake, Shey and Charka (Tsarkha). Adventurers can try the amazingly remote 21-day trek from Jumla to Kagbeni via Shey, Phoksumdo and Kagmara La.

The options are limitless but these routes are tough, wild and extremely remote and you really need the support of a reliable agency and a Tibetan-speaking guide with a knowledge of the area.

For more on tourism in Dolpo, follow the links to specific regions on www.welcomenepal.com.

❶ Towns & Facilities

The gateways for this region are Dunai (p287; and Juphal airstrip; p287), Jumla (p287) and Beni (p288).

Jumla to Dunai Trek

Duration 6 days

Max Elevation 3820m

Difficulty Medium

Season March to October

Start Jumla

Finish Dunai

Permits TIMS card

Summary Walk through Nepal's 'Wild West' with its eclectic mixture of ethnic groups. There are no high Himalayan peaks, but lots of grand high-altitude scenery.

This trail connects two important gateways in the West, and should either one of the airstrips (Jumla or Juphal) be closed you may have to trek to the other. There are lots of ups and downs, and a few challenging gradients, though altitude shouldn't be a problem as the trail threads its way through valleys, wildflower meadows and thick forests. A cultural highlight of the journey is the carved wooden effigies (*dokpa*) that adorn local buildings.

At the time of writing, there were no reports of serious damage from the 2015 earthquake, but as a sensible precaution, seek local advice on the status of trails and infrastructure before starting a trek in this area.

❶ Planning

ACCOMMODATION & SUPPLIES

Facilities on this route are very sparse. There are a few shops and teahouses, but nothing resembling a trekkers lodge. You would do well to bring a tent for your porters so they don't have to hunt for accommodation in Thakuri homes where they may not be welcome.

❶ Getting to/from the Trek

It's best to fly into Jumla and then spend the rest of the day hiring porters, buying last-minute provisions and sorting loads. If you fly into Jumla and start walking the same day, you will probably have to alter the stopping places suggested here, because it takes a full day to reach Gothi Chaur.

The Trek

See Map p256

Day 1: Jumla to Gothi Chaur

6–7 HOURS / 610M ASCENT / 250M DESCENT

From Jumla (2370m) the trail leads past the airport to the eastern end of the runway, past several water-driven mills, then drops to the confluence of the Tila Khola and the Chaudhabise Khola (also known locally as the Juwa Nadi) at 2330m. Cross both rivers on cantilever bridges.

The trail climbs gently in a fertile valley of rice terraces along the southern side of the Tila to Depal Gaon. It criss-crosses irrigation canals as it approaches Jharjwala, then leaves the Tila Khola and climbs a ridge to the small villages of Bhajkati, Dugri Lagnu and finally **Dochal Ghara** (2530m). Do not follow the steep trail that leads uphill here. Instead, take the lower trail following a stream through a forest of maples and walnuts to a meadow.

Beyond the meadow the trail climbs to a rock cairn at **Pattyata Lagna** (2830m), then descends into a magnificent alpine amphitheatre. The trail descends past the government sheep-breeding-research buildings at **Gothi Chaur** to a stream at the bottom of the valley. There are some 13th-century Malla dynasty stone carvings at the spring here.

Day 2: Gothi Chaur to Naphukana

5–6 HOURS / 420M ASCENT / 70M DESCENT

There is another trail junction at Gothi Chaur. Do not take the trail that leads uphill out of the Gothi Chaur Valley. Instead, walk downstream through forests to a series of mills at Kuri Sangta. There is a good campsite a short distance beyond where the Kuri Sangta Khola joins the Tila Khola.

The route has now re-entered the Tila Valley and over the next day you will follow the river to its source. Here the Tila is known as the Bapila Khola. The villages of Gothigaon and Khudigaon are visible high on the other side of the river. The trail crosses to the northern side of the Tila and then climbs through fields of buckwheat and barley.

The river forks at Munigaon, a village with a complex mixture of Chhetri, Thakali and Tibetan inhabitants. There are several houses and a rudimentary hotel at the trail junction, **Muni Sangu**. Look both above and behind the houses for some peculiar carved wooden faces. You will see these effigies throughout Dolpo. They are called *dokpa*, and are supposed to offer protection from evil. The police at the Muni Sangu checkpost will probably want to see your passport.

The route follows the left fork of the Tila Khola, which has again changed its name and is now the Churta Khola. The valley narrows and the trail stays on the southern side of the river, so don't cross any of the several bridges you pass. A short distance beyond Changrikot (several houses on the opposite side of the river; 2900m) the trail finally crosses the river and climbs to the stone houses of **Chotra** (3010m). The inhabitants of Chotra are Khampas, people from eastern Tibet who are Buddhists by tradition. Despite their background, these villagers long ago adopted Hindu names, dress and traditions in an effort to integrate themselves into Nepali society.

A short distance beyond Chotra is the Tibetan settlement of **Naphukana** (3080m). The large gompa above the village is Urgen Sanga Chholing. The villagers of Naphukana keep yaks and horses. There are campsites near the village, but there are better spots an hour further on, in a meadow at 3200m.

Day 3: Naphukana to Balasa

6–7 HOURS / 740M ASCENT / 710M DESCENT

The trail becomes steeper as it climbs past the rocky fields of Rapati Chaur to forests of oak and birch. After crossing a side stream, the trail crosses the Churta/Bapila/Tila Khola and starts a serious climb to **Mauri Lagna** ('Honey Pass') at 3820m. When trekking in spring, the final approach to the pass is through meadows alive with blue lilies and stands of blooming azaleas and rhododendrons. In winter the trail is hidden under deep snow. From the pass there are views of the snowy peaks of Gutumba (5608m) and Matatumba (5767m) to the northeast and Bhalu Himal (5460m) to the south.

From the pass the trail descends, then makes a long traverse across a steep and potentially dangerous area. At the end of the traverse, marked by cairns of stones, the trail starts a descent into a forest of pines and oaks, passing a few herders' huts before reaching a stream at 3110m. Staying in forests, the trail makes a few ups and downs, then climbs again to a ridge at 3140m. The trail turns into the Bheri Valley, keeping high on the side of the ridge, and making short excursions in and out of side valleys to **Chaurikot** (3060m).

From Chaurikot the trail drops to a stream at 2940m then climbs to a notch on the ridge at 3080m. This would be an excellent campsite, except there is no water. About 30 minutes beyond the ridge is **Balasa**. There are several possible campsites alongside the trail, and others further on in the fields of Jyakot or Rimi. You can see Kagmara peak on the horizon and Balangra La, the next obstacle on the route to Dolpo.

Day 4: Balasa to Forest Camp

6–7 HOURS / 610M ASCENT / 430M DESCENT

The trail descends to a stream, then climbs to the ridge in a forest of walnut trees. Walnuts will be constant companions throughout the rest of the trek to Dunai. Although the local people occasionally eat them, their primary value is as a source of cooking oil.

The trail contours past the corn and potato fields and apple orchards of Jyakot then descends to Rimi (2890m). The trail descends, steeply in places, through walnut groves to the closely spaced stone houses of Majagaon, then down a rocky trail to the Bheri River. A police checkpost and a large school dominate the bank of the Bheri at 2610m.

Just across the bridge is Kaigaon, which boasts a veterinary station, a *bhatti* and the first real shop since Jumla. Kaigaon is the departure point for a crossing of Kagmara La (see p261).

From Kaigaon the route climbs through pasture, then into a forest of birches and wild roses. Near the top of the ridge the climb becomes very steep and there are no stone steps.

The trail crests at an elevation of 3230m, then levels out in a forest of rhododendrons. A trail heads south from the pass and this is a route to Jajarkot and Chaurjhari. The Dunai trail continues east, and descends gently along the side of a large valley to a few small campsites in the forest.

Day 5: Forest Camp to Tibrikot

7–8 HOURS / 470M ASCENT / 1660M DESCENT

The trail makes many ups and downs as it contours out onto a ridge before a long climb to a false summit at 3660m. There is yet another false summit before Balangra La (3760m) itself, marked with cairns and prayer flags. If it's clear, you'll see Dhaulagiri Himal to the east. You will also probably see herds of yaks grazing high on the grassy slopes above the pass.

There are two trails off the pass. The old trail heads straight down into forests while a new trail contours around the ridge to the left. Both end at a government yak farm in a forest at 3160m. From the yak farm, the trail heads out onto a ridge high above the Chang Gaad. There are a few campsites along the route and there is even a *bhatti* at Ghora Khola. Stay on the upper trail and be aware of steep drop-offs on the edge of the trail. Beyond Bungtari, cross a stream and climb to Kaliban. Drop to a stream in a large side valley, then climb again to Dagin (2930m). After passing Para and a few other small villages, the route reaches a treeless, waterless, uninhabited ridge, then makes a miserable 500m descent on a clutter of loose rocks to a stream just below Tibrikot (2100m). You can make a good camp by the stream.

Day 6: Tibrikot to Dunai

4–5 HOURS / 80M ASCENT / 50M DESCENT

From the stream, the trail climbs slightly to Tibrikot (Tripurakot), a picturesque village

DUNAI TO JUPHAL (DOLPO) AIRPORT

Dolpo flights always arrive and depart early in the morning to avoid the high winds that blow through the Thulo Bheri from 10am. As it takes at least three hours to walk from Dunai to the airport in Juphal village (the ascent is 480m), the only reasonable solution is to spend a night at the airport.

To get to the airport, head back along the south bank of the Thulo Bheri past the Suli Gaad confluence and on to Roop Gaad. Continue along the riverbank to Kala Gaunda (2030m). Take the trail leading uphill and climb steeply to a large house. The trail then traverses through meadows to the many houses of Dangibanda. Stay high and climb less steeply around the head of the valley towards Juphal. As the village comes into view take the left-hand trail to traverse above the village and climb to the large school. There is a maze of trails, but keep heading up and eventually you will emerge at Juphal (2490m), a collection of houses, offices and crummy hotels. Above the village are some basic shops in a complex of flat-roofed, mud buildings beside the airport. The Jharana Hotel has basic accommodation and camping and there is a popular campsite at Hotel Putha just below the settlement.

You should reconfirm your seats in person with the airline station manager the day before the flight. The best way to find the airline station manager is to ask the police near the control tower. Baggage weight limits are strictly enforced and excess baggage is expensive.

on a promontory overlooking the Thulo Bheri ('Big Bheri') Valley. This is an old fortress town and the police checkpost commands a view up and down the river. The houses have carved wooden windows, and a large shrine and temple are dedicated to the goddess Tripura Sundari Devi. From the shrine, the trail descends past rice terraces to a long suspension bridge at 2050m.

For the rest of the day, you will follow the large, fast-flowing, dark-grey Thulo Bheri, through arid country on a trail that follows the Bheri all the way from Chaurjhari. Passing the tiny settlement of Su Pani, the route passes over a low ridge and drops to **Beti**, beside a small stream.

The direct trail to Dolpo airport, above Juphal village, starts at Beti. If you want to confirm a flight, take the upper route, which climbs 450m to the airport and rejoins the river trail at Kala Gaunda. The lower trail passes far below the airport.

After more desolate country you will reach Kala Gaunda, where the airport trail rejoins the route. The trail climbs over two ridges, then drops to a large side stream, three small *bhattis* and a campsite at **Roop Gaad** (2050m). This is an excellent place to camp if you want to avoid staying in Dunai village. You can see the start of the trail to Phoksumdo Lake on the opposite riverbank.

From Roop Gaad the trail remains level, passing the national park and army offices on the opposite side of the river at the confluence of the Suli Gaad and the Thulo Bheri. A few twists and turns of the trail lead to a view of Dunai. The trail enters **Dunai** through a fancy gate near the health post, then passes through the old bazaar along a stone pavement.

Kagmara La Trek

Duration 4 days

Max Elevation 5115m

Difficulty Medium to hard

Season March to October

Start Kaigaon

Finish Sumduwa

Permits TIMS card, Shey Phoksumdo National Park permit

Summary A high pass crossing offering a variation on the route from Jumla to Dolpo and a short cut to Phoksumdo Lake.

This challenging detour across Kagmara La encompasses long days and significant altitude gains. Be aware of signs for AMS and be prepared for sudden weather changes. The rewards are magnificent mountain views and opportunities to spot blue sheep and perhaps a snow leopard.

While the pass is open following the 2015 earthquake, little information has emerged from this region, so seek local advice on the current status of trails and infrastructure before trekking the Kagmara La.

ℹ️ Planning

A high route to Dolpo leads across the 5115m Kagmara La. It is not a difficult crossing, but you may have trouble finding porters willing to make the trip. From November to early May the pass is snowbound, and potentially dangerous or impassable. A reasonable crossing takes four days from Kaigaon to Sumduwa. Kagmara translates as 'crow killer'; the high pass on the eastern edge of Dolpo is Cheelmara, 'eagle killer'.

ℹ️ Getting to/from the Trek

To get to Kaigaon, follow Days 1 to 4 of the Jumla to Dunai trek (see p258).

🏃 The Trek

See Map p256

Day 1: Kaigaon to Toijem

5–6 HOURS / 310M ASCENT

From the school at Kaigaon, stay on the west bank of the Bheri, passing Hurikot and its Bönpo gompa, to a sign proclaiming the entrance to Shey Phoksumdo National Park. The trail stays high above the river to the confluence where the Jagdula Khola and Garpung Khola join to form the Bheri. Drop to the Jagdula Khola, crossing it on stones, and camp near the army post at **Toijem** (2920m).

Day 2: Toijem to Kagmara Phedi

7–8 HOURS / 1080M ASCENT

Follow the trail up the western side of the Garpung Khola to about 3650m, then cross to the eastern side and continue upstream. The valley narrows and the river becomes a series of waterfalls as the trail climbs to a moraine at 3900m. Make a high camp at **Kagmara Phedi**, at about 4000m. The panoramic views of the peaks are sensational. This is an excellent place to sight blue sheep.

Day 3: Kagmara Phedi to Lasa

8–9 HOURS / 1110M ASCENT / 1050M DESCENT

Start early and climb alongside the Kagmara Glacier to the **Kagmara La** at 5115m (the last 90 minutes might be in snow), then descend about 900m along a stream to a campsite on pastures in the Pungmo Valley. On this side of the pass there are sweeping scree slopes and massive rock formations in stacked layers. Descend to **Lasa**, a shepherds' camp at about 4060m.

Day 4: Lasa to Sumduwa

6–7 HOURS / 900M DESCENT

The trail stays high above the stream, which eventually becomes the Pungmo Khola. The route enters birch and juniper forests, which give way to blue pines as the trail crosses the river on a wooden bridge. There are views up side valleys of Kanjeralwa (6612m) in the stretch before the barley fields of **Pungmo**, a fortress-like village with an atmospheric Bönpo monastery. If you have a special interest in Bön monasteries, consider a half-day detour to **Thekchen Rabgyeling Gompa**, an hour-long trek high up the Kunasa Khola from just below Pungmo. Continue downstream to the river junction at **Sumduwa** and descend to a camp on the banks of the Phoksumdo Khola.

The next day, follow the trail up the Phoksumdo Khola to Phoksumdo Lake (see Day 3 of the Phoksumdo Lake trek).

Phoksumdo Lake Trek

Duration 3 days

Max Elevation 3730m

Difficulty Medium

Season May to October

Start Dunai

Finish Phoksumdo Lake

Permits TIMS card, Lower Dolpo restricted-area trekking permit, Shey Phoksumdo National Park permit (Kathmandu/Suli Gaad)

Summary A clear trail provides easy access to Nepal's highest waterfall and the dramatically clear waters of Phoksumdo Lake.

The trek to Phoksumdo Lake up the Suli Gaad is a short one but boasts a lot of variety, with some lovely forested sections, dramatic Phoksumdo Lake and a pocket of the unusual Bönpo culture. There were no reports of serious damage to Lower Dolpo during the 2015 earthquake, and trekkers returned to the trails within weeks of the disaster, but as a sensible precaution, seek local advice on the current status of trails and infrastructure before starting a trek in this area.

The lake is within Shey Phoksumdo National Park, which was established in 1981. The national park literature uses the spelling Phoksundo, but local informants believe the correct transliteration is *Phok, sum* (three), *do* (stones), relating to the three arms of the lake. The park is said to abound in wildlife, although the most spectacular inhabitants – snow leopards and herds of blue sheep – are found primarily in the northern restricted regions of the park near Shey Gompa. The lake and trail are snowbound from mid-November to mid-May. Almost all the inhabitants of Ringmo village move to lower elevations at this time.

From Phoksumdo Lake you can return to Dunai by the same route or make a loop via the Baga La and Numa La to Tarap, following the Phoksumdo Lake via Do Tarap trek (p264) in reverse. If you are prepared to pay for a restricted-area permit, you can also trek over the mountains north of the lake to Shey Gompa and remote inner Dolpo.

ℹ Planning

FUEL

National park restrictions prohibit the use of firewood, so you must carry kerosene in addition to food. This requires planning because kerosene supplies in Jumla aren't always reliable. There is often kerosene in Dunai, however.

ACCOMMODATION & SUPPLIES

Campsites are somewhat limited in the gorge between Dunai and Renji. It's just about possible to do this trek without a tent, staying in lodges and homestays in Chepka, Jharana Hotel and Ringmo, but the Chepka lodges in particular are very simple. Basic food supplies are available in Chepka and Ringmo.

ℹ Getting to/from the Trek

There are numerous ways to get to Dunai. You can fly to Juphal and walk the three hours down to Dunai (p260) or walk from Jumla (p258). A much longer but rewarding alternative is the 12-day Beni to Dolpo trek (p269).

The Trek

See Map p256

Day 1: Dunai to Chepka

4½–5½ HOURS / 770M ASCENT

From the bazaar in Dunai (2030m), cross the suspension bridge and turn west, following the trail past the hospital, and continue along the bank of the Thulo Bheri to its confluence with the Suli Gaad at 2070m. Follow the trail north up the east bank to the mule depot and teashops of **Suli Gaad**. Stop at the Shey Phoksundo National Park office to register and pay your entry fee (Rs 3000). If you are headed downstream directly to the airport, the suspension bridge across the river offers a direct route to Juphal.

Another hour of walking takes you to Kala Rupi and then on to **Kageni** (2260m), where there is a good campsite just south of the bridge over the Suli Gaad.

Cross to the west bank and the abandoned settlement of Raktang and trek past goths (herders' huts) and horse pastures over a ridge to the rough stone houses of Jyalhasa, a wintering spot for the people of Ringmo.

Keep walking upstream to a bridge attached to a huge boulder, cross it to the east bank, and make your way past deserted teashops at **Sankta** (2460m) to a house, campsite and bridge over the Ankhe Khola. A sign declares the beginning of the Shey Phoksumdo National Park. The trail makes some ups and downs through grass and ferns to a trail junction. Take the left fork.

The right fork leads to the villages of Parela, Rahagaon and Ankhe high on the ridge above. These three villages – Parela (*parela* means eyelash), Rahagaon (*raha* means eyebrow) and Ankhe (*ankha* is eye) – have a strange name connection. This region produces a lotus-like plant called *chuk*, which is used to make vinegar and medicines. It is dried and flown from Dolpo to Nepalganj and exported to India.

The Phoksundo Lake trail climbs over a ridge at 2710m, then descends on a rocky path to **Chepka** (2670m), a string of crummy lodges – La Lee Gurans Hotel and Lodge, Yak Hotel & Lodge (with its colourful wooden carvings) and Hotel Jharana. All offer daal bhaat and basic rooms, but little in the way of bedding. You can camp here or at another good spot beside a huge rock in a walnut grove about 20 minutes beyond Chepka.

Day 2: Chepka to Renje

3–4 HOURS / 500M ASCENT / 320M DESCENT

The trail stays near the river, climbing over a small ridge, then crossing to the west side to avoid a steep ridge and returning to the east side an hour later near a pleasant riverside campsite. The wooden bridge is carved with phallus motifs that recall the mountain deity Masta. The trail becomes a collection of rocks and sticks forming a dyke along the riverbank. If the water is high and covers the trail, this can be a treacherous, or impossible, place to traverse. The trail makes several more ups and downs through forests of firs and larches as it continues upstream to a bridge that leads to the village of **Renje** (3010m) on the opposite side of the river. There is a simple lodge and a muddy campsite here beside the trail.

Day 3: Renje to Phoksundo Lake

6 HOURS / 880M ASCENT / 90M DESCENT

The Suli Gaad Valley turns eastward and becomes even steeper and narrower. The trail climbs over a ridge and descends to a wooden bridge then continues its ups and downs along the valley floor for an hour to the confluence of the Suli Gaad and Pungmo Khola. North of this point the Suli Gaad is known as the Phoksundo Khola. A wooden bridge past the confluence leads up the Pungmo Khola towards the Kagmara La (p261), while the trail to Phoksundo Lake and Tarap continues along the eastern bank of the river. The name of the all-but-deserted village (there's one basic lodge) that overlooks the confluence, **Sumduwa**, reflects this. In Tibetan, *sum* means 'three' and *duwa* is 'trail'.

After 15 minutes you'll come to a yellow-roofed building that looks like a gompa. It's actually the **Tapriza Cultural School**, a nongovernmental organisation (NGO) project that teaches the Tibetan language, English, the Bön religion and traditional arts, in addition to the standard Nepali curriculum.

After crossing to the north side of the river you pass the **Jharana Hotel** (3130m), which offers food, supplies and decent rooms (from Rs 350). Nearby is the Gangchhen Menkhang, a traditional clinic run by a local *amchi* (traditional healer).

The Phoksundo trail climbs through a forest of big cedars, past fading Maoist slogans, to **Palam** (3280m), a winter settlement used by the people of Ringmo village. The route switchbacks steeply on a sandy trail through open country, then starts up an even steeper set of dusty switchbacks, gaining over 400m to a ridge at 3730m. Just before the ridge, prayer flags mark a close-up view of a spectacular 200m-high **waterfall**, the highest in Nepal. Shortly afterwards you get your first views of Phoksumdo Lake.

The trail makes a descent through a forest of birch and chir pine to the upper reaches of the brilliantly clear, rushing waters of the Phoksumdo Khola, then climbs gently to the charming village of **Ringmo** (3640m), a picturesque, medieval-looking settlement of flat-roofed stone houses, carved mani walls and ancient chortens. Locals also call the village Tsowa, which means 'beside the lake'. A couple of shops sell supplies like instant coffee, packet soups and jam at expectedly high prices, alongside locally made yak-hair blankets and belts.

The village **Sherpa Hotel & Lodge** (r from Rs 250) is a friendly refuge, where you can order such luxuries as muesli, milk tea, French fries and pancakes in the traditional Tibetan-style kitchen. The owner Phurba Tenzin speaks good English. The nearby satellite telephone office offers phone calls to Kathmandu, but connections are hit-and-miss.

Just below Ringmo, cross a bridge and follow a trail north to the perennially closed park-ranger station at **Phoksumdo Lake** (3620m). Continue to the lakeshore near the point where the Phoksumdo Khola flows out of the lake. There are national park **campsites** (tent Rs 100) on both sides of the river and park rules prohibit camping in other places. Phoksumdo is a crossroads for treks throughout Dolpo and there are normally three or four groups camped here during the trekking season. The wind picks up after noon, causing temperatures to feel much colder than they are.

A dramatic cliffside trail along the lake's western side leads to inner Dolpo and Shey Gompa. Access to this route is restricted to those with a special US$500 permit, but at the time of research the lack of any checkpost meant you could make a short walk along the trail to a hidden beach spectacularly positioned at the base of glaciers tumbling off Kanjeralwa (Kanchen Ruwa) peak. From here the trail to Shey climbs almost vertically up the mountainside. This section of trail featured prominently in Eric Valli's movie *Caravan* (when the yak falls off the trail into the lake).

The lake is surreally spectacular. It is 4.8km long, 1.8km wide and estimated to be 650m deep, making it Nepal's deepest lake. It's famed for its intense aquamarine colour – a miraculous greenish blue likened to *yü*, or Tibetan turquoise. The lack of aquatic life in the lake helps keep the waters brilliantly clear.

Ringmo is Bönpo country, where people practise a shamanistic-influenced religion that predates Tibetan Buddhism. Much of Bönpo symbolism is the opposite of Buddhist practice. You should walk to the right of the ancient mud chortens, which are inscribed with swastikas with their arms pointing in the opposite direction to the Buddhist version. Instead of the Buddhist chant of '*om mani padme hum*', the Bönpos chant '*om ma tri mu ye sa le du*'.

A trail leads through juniper trees to the eastern shore of the lake and the white **Thasung Chholing Gompa** (admission Rs 200, Nepalis Rs 80), a ramshackle Bönpo gompa said to have been built 60 generations ago. The fine interior murals depicting Bön deities are painted not on the walls but on wooden boards. Several houses in the small monastic community have atmospheric private chapels but these are normally locked.

It's worth hiking up to the hilltop south of the lake for views of Ringmo and the snowcapped peak of Sonam Kang (5916m) behind.

Phoksumdo Lake via Do Tarap Trek

Duration 9 days

Max Elevation 5290m

Difficulty Hard

Season May to October

Start Dunai

Finish Phoksumdo Lake

Permits TIMS card, Lower Dolpo restricted-area trekking permit, Shey Phoksumdo National Park permit

Summary A long walk to an isolated enclave of rich Tibetan culture, then over two high passes, through remote yak-herding country to spectacular Phoksumdo Lake.

Tarap is a remote valley of pure Tibetan influence east of Phoksumdo Lake and south of Shey Gompa. You can visit Tarap by making a loop from Dunai up the Thulo Bheri to the Tarap Chu, across two high passes to Phoksumdo Lake and back to Dunai. You can also make the trek in the reverse direction, starting from Dunai or even from Jumla. At the time of writing, there were no reports of serious damage from the 2015 earthquake, but as a sensible precaution, seek local advice on the current status of trails and infrastructure before starting a trek in this area.

The highlights of this excellent trek include the wild gorge of the Tarap Chu, a remote valley dotted with Tibetan monasteries, and some of Nepal's most beautiful alpine scenery between Do Tarap and Phoksumdo. The crossing of Numa La and Baga La is a reasonably difficult undertaking, which takes you through some wild, high country without rescue or communications facilities.

Planning

It's possible to combine a trek up the Do Tarap Valley with a trek to inner Dolpo. A remote route to Shey Gompa starts between Numa La and Baga La. A more-frequented alternative route to inner Dolpo crosses the river at Tok-khyu and follows a trail along the north branch of the Tarap Chu to Saldang. It is a high, difficult and remote route over the 5110m Jengla/Jyanta Bhanjyang. These restricted-area treks require a US$500 permit fee.

The Numa La and Baga La are generally open until at least late October. This itinerary is possible as a monsoon trek, though flights are subject to delays during these months.

ACCOMMODATION & SUPPLIES

You need your own tent, a stove and food for this trek. It's possible to get simple daal bhaat at Laisicap and simple rooms and supplies (rice, noodles, biscuits etc) at Do Tarap. There are tent teahouses at Nawarpani, Laisicap and Laini, where you can get basic food. Kerosene is available in Dunai only.

Getting to/from the Trek

Start from Dunai, or follow the Beni to Dolpo route (p269) and join the Tarap trek just below Tarakot.

The Trek

See Map p256

Day 1: Dunai to Tarakot

5 HOURS / 430M ASCENT

Follow the trail eastward out of Dunai along the south bank of the Thulo Bheri. A short distance beyond Dunai the route crosses to the north bank and near the end of the day crosses back to the south bank at **Lawan**. There is a police checkpost near this bridge, then the trail passes below the fields of **Tarakot** to a campsite near the Chyada Khola at 2450m, just below the fortress of Tarakot village. It's worth the short climb to look around the village, which was built as a fortress (*kot* is 'fort' in Nepali) of the Tichurong kingdom.

Day 2: Tarakot to Laini

6–7 HOURS / 810M ASCENT / 100M DESCENT

From the school cross the river and climb gently through pink fields of flowering buckwheat. Detour south into a side valley with views of Putha Himal, cross the Yalkot Khola and climb to a trail that hugs the south side of the Thulo Bheri. Above Tarakot the Thulo Bheri is known as the Barbung Khola.

The trail stays mostly high above the river, climbing to 2670m before descending past cypress trees and a white chorten to a 120m-long, high suspension bridge at **Laisicap** (2600m), three hours from Tarakot. Just before the bridge you'll need to register and show your Dolpo permit to the police post. There is fine camping on the east bank of the Barbung Khola in a lovely cedar grove just north of the police post, where the Tarap Chu

WESTERN NEPAL PHOKSUMDO LAKE VIA DO TARAP TREK

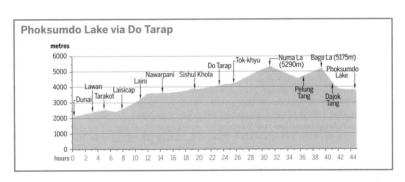

Phoksumdo Lake via Do Tarap

metres

(*chu* is Tibetan for river) joins the Barbung Khola. This lovely valley continues along a remote route to Jomsom. Cross the bridge to a tented teahouse that offers daal bhaat and a water pipe for washing. High above the trail is the village of **Kanigaon**. Be sure to look for white-breasted dippers, birds only found in western Nepal, along the river.

After lunch it's worth making the short detour to **Chhandul (Sandul) Gompa**, on the far side of the Tarap Chu. The 15-minute climb to the monastery is lined with chortens and mani walls, while the monastery has a very atmospheric hidden back chapel.

Back on the main trail, continue through cedar forest as the valley walls close in. Three-sided tunnels are blasted out of the rock through the steepest part of the gorge, as the river drops steeply (600m in only 3km) alongside the trail. The gorge finally starts to widen near **Laini**, a small meadow at 3160m, but just when you think the day's trek is almost over, the trail ends at a sheer cliff face. If this section hasn't been repaired, you face a strenuous 45-minute detour up the steep hillside, gaining an extra 200m on a rough path, only to then drop down another 200m to rejoin the main trail just before Laini.

Laini is a former trail construction camp; a couple of seasonal tent teahouses still cater to traders, trekkers and mule caravans. You can buy tea, noodles and Chinese beer. There's a quieter alternative campsite at the foot of a small waterfall, five minutes further on.

Day 3: Laini to Nawarpani
5 HOURS / 500M ASCENT / 60M DESCENT

After five minutes to warm up, you face a stiff 50-minute climb on switchbacks to a mini-pass marked with prayer flags at 3540m. The trail then makes a dramatic and very enjoyable high traverse through a gorge so steep that you can't even see the river below you. The trail eventually descends to cross the cascades of the Tilba Khola (3570m), before ascending again on some gravity-defying steps. Climb one more ridge and descend to the **Chyugur Khola**, a small campsite beside a stream at 3520m.

Cross the suspension bridge to the river's true left and after 20 minutes pass a side stream, the Chaya Khola, to another potential camp spot beside a cave. Continue to Tazam where a couple of huts offer food and supplies between May and November. Cross the suspension bridge to the true right bank. When there are no monsoon flows you can

avoid a climb here by following the riverside trail, before arriving at **Nawarpani**, a mule-caravan stop at 3545m.

It's worth continuing another 40 minutes, past honey-coloured rock walls that resemble Tajikistan or Chitral, to a long, flat stretch of pristine meadow that forms a perfect **campsite** (3590m; N 28°59.849', E 083°05.144').

Day 4: Nawarpani to Do Tarap
6½ HOURS / 630M ASCENT / 140M DESCENT

As the gorge narrows, cross to the true left bank over an ancient-looking bridge and pass a small cave and campsite to climb a thrilling section of trail chiselled out of the sheer rock face. The trail then recrosses the Tarap Chu on a wooden cantilever bridge at **Tal Tole** (3680m). The barren canyon walls of this section glow like amber, creating the feel of a Middle Eastern wadi.

The route crosses the Tarap Chu on a very short bridge after passing a narrow slot canyon. Climb on the east bank through an eroded landscape to a chorten on a ridge (2½ hours). This is **Serkam** (3870m), an abandoned border post that was the checkpoint between Nepal and Tibet in the 19th century. Only traces of the chorten's original coloured stucco remain.

Descend from Serkam and cross back to the west bank on a crooked wooden bridge high above the Tarap Chu. A kilometre or so further and you swing into the **Sishul Khola** (three hours), where there is a dirty campsite at 3840m. A better option is to climb gently to two weatherworn chortens and a mani wall atop a ridge, then descend past impressive views to campsites (3870m, 3½ hours) on the flat valley floor.

It's only about three hours to Do Tarap from here, so you could quite easily push on if your porters are game.

The rocky trail traverses beneath cliffs to a bridge at 3920m. Cross to the east bank where a side valley leads up the Lang Chu to the remote village of Lang. The Tarap trail instead heads north up the Tarap Chu, climbing slowly alongside the river past mani walls and eroded cliffs; keep an eye out for blue sheep along this section. Climb to a line of ancient chortens at 4040m; from here it's an easy 20-minute walk to **Do Tarap** (4080m). Choose between a couple of basic lodges or campsites in grassy meadows to the south or west of the village, near the confluence of the Tarap Chu and the Doro Chu, but bear in mind that the wind blows fiercely in Tarap from noon to sunset. A shop/teahouse stocks a few supplies. Climb up to the chorten on the ridge to the south for views over the village.

Day 5: Do Tarap

Tarap is worth exploring, so don't hurry through this region. You could easily fill a day in Do Tarap, visiting the surrounding monasteries, exploring the village or even bagging the peak to the south of the village.

The name Tarap refers to the entire region. The correct name of this village is Do, meaning 'lower end of the valley' in Tibetan, but most local people refer to the village as Do Tarap. It consists of several clusters of closely packed stone houses and corrals, surrounded by fields of 'naked' barley *(uwa)*. In October everyone is busy threshing and winnowing the barley crop to make *tsampa* (roasted barley meal) for the upcoming winter. The animals used for ploughing and carrying loads here are huge shaggy yaks, not the more docile crossbreeds found in the Khumbu.

The **Ribo Bhumpa Gompa** above the village was rebuilt in 1955; beside it is the unique 'chorten in a chorten' containing the supposed remains of a demon killed by Guru Rinpoche. The paintings inside the chorten represent both Bönpo and Nyingma traditions, although the gompa itself is Nyingma. The views over the valley are superb.

For a leisurely half-day excursion, head east up the valley of the Doro Chu for about half an hour to Doro and Shipchok monasteries. Atmospheric **Doro Gompa** is on the north side of the river and has an unusual side entrance. The lama's house is next door in case it's locked. Across the river is the Bönpo-school **Shipchok Gompa**, recognisable by the dozen chortens that arc away from the monastery. Look for the wonderfully carved door and finely painted prayer wheel in the atrium. A remote trekking route continues up the valley and over several high passes to Charka and eventually Jomsom.

Day 6: Do Tarap to Numa La 'Base Camp'

3–4 HOURS / 360M ASCENT

There's not much walking today but expect to make lots of detours to explore the various villages and gompas. Head west out of Do Tarap, leaving the village through its impressive *kani*. After about 20 minutes a side footpath climbs for 30 minutes to the century-old

CREATION STORY

According to legend, Phoksumdo Lake was formed by a spiteful female demon. In *Buddhist Himalaya,* David Snellgrove recounts how the demon was fleeing from the saint Guru Rinpoche (Padmasambhava) and gave the village people a turquoise after they promised not to tell that she had passed by. The Guru turned the turquoise into a lump of dung, which upset the local people so much they revealed the demon's whereabouts. She, in return, caused the flood. It is said you can see the remains of the village below the lake's surface.

Mekyem Gompa, which features a large statue of Jampa (Maitreya Buddha).

Back on the main trail you'll soon pass the **Crystal Mountain School**, a private facility established in 1994 and funded through an NGO in Dunai. This is the first serious attempt to bring education to this remote region. Polite and well-dressed children will wish you a *'namaste'* or *'tashi delek'* as you pass. If you brought pens or school books with you, the school is the place to donate them.

The trail continues uphill to **Gakar** ('white mountain') village and the Dorje Phurba Gompa. The gompa was probably built to house a red mask of Guru Dragpo (a terrible form of Guru Rinpoche), brought here a long time ago by a lama from Kham. The place is richly decorated and has a collection of ancient weapons in the chapel.

A bit further on is Chu Magar (1¼ hours), which means 'don't cross the river'. Just afterwards is an unmarked trailside **teahouse** that offers tea (Rs 30), food and simple lodging (bed Rs 100). Soon the trail crosses the Tarap Chu (known here as the Thakchio Khola) on a wooden bridge that leads to Mondo (4170m). Here the valley divides; the route to the Numa La follows the southern branch, passing the white-walled **Jampa Lhakhang** to Tok-khyu village at 4180m. The north branch heads to Saldang in restricted upper Dolpo.

You can camp at **Tok-khyu**, but if you are going to cross the pass the following day, it's worth continuing on to **Numa La 'Base Camp'** (4440m; N 29°10.313', E 083°08.026'), sometimes called Tok-khyu High Camp, which is tucked in a side valley by a stream just before a steep climb, little more than an hour beyond Tok-khyu.

The large white building across the valley to the north is **Sherin Gompa**, rebuilt in 1965 using stones from the original building. Nearby in a side valley is the largely ruined Draglung (Joglung) Gompa, whose chapel and library have been there for at least six generations. Both gompas are normally locked but the superb views alone justify the hour-long diversion.

Day 7: Numa La 'Base Camp' to Pelung Tang

6–7 HOURS / 540M ASCENT / 960M DESCENT

It's a long pull over the Numa La, so start early. The pass is often snowbound as late as May, and new snow can make the trek a tough climb. If there is snow you may have to make an additional, higher camp in order to cross the pass in the early morning when the snow is still hard. Under normal conditions, however, the pass crossing is reasonably straightforward – just long and high. Note that the trail to the pass is marked incorrectly on almost all maps; the real trail and pass is actually further south.

From Numa La 'Base Camp', cross the stream on rocks and climb steeply on yak trails up to a ridge where there are several mani walls and a chorten at 4580m. In this desolate, improbable location a large *puja* (prayer) is celebrated in July. It is said a hermit monk lives in a cave below the chorten and spends his life carving mani stones. Continue up the ridge to a grassy knoll and a tiny stream at 4700m; this is a possible 'high base camp' site.

The route is fairly obvious, dipping into a glacial bowl (4960m) before crossing a small stream and making the long climb up a moraine to the 5290m **Numa La**, about three hours from the base camp (or 1½ hours from the high camp). From the pass you can see Shey Shikar (6139m) and Kanjeralwa to the northwest, and the tip of Dhaulagiri I (8167m) to the southeast. Climb 20m higher to the crest on the right (east) for the best views of the trek.

Descend from the pass into a U-shaped valley. The trail swings sharply left, where you can see, far across the valley, the Baga La, the next obstacle on the trek. Along this section of trail you may well pass yak caravans hauling timber. Watch for blue sheep and snow leopards in this remote valley. Follow the rocky, but spectacularly scenic, valley as it drops steeply, crossing a stream and scree slopes.

The valley is joined by another from the east, the Gyambo Khola, to form the Poyon Chu. This is a good place to break for lunch (five hours; 4540m). Follow the river downstream past dramatically eroded cliffs for half an hour, then cross it on a combination of rocks and logs and climb again up the south (river left) bank. The trail along the left bank climbs gently, and the river drops steeply, so you are soon high above the river.

Shortly the trail makes a U-turn to the left, swinging into a side valley. The river you see disappearing into a gorge below you is headed for Phoksumdo Lake.

Walk round the ridge into the valley and climb gently to a good **campsite** (N 29°10.510', E 083°03.121') in pastures at 4465m. This spot is known as **Pelung Tang** (*tang* in Tibetan means 'meadow') and is marked on some maps as Danigar. The spectacular glaciated peak at the head of the valley is Norbu Kang (6005m). And, yes, that steeply switchbacking trail in front of you is your route tomorrow morning.

Day 8: Pelung Tang to Dajok Tang

6 HOURS / 670M ASCENT / 1330M DESCENT

Today will be a tough day if the pass is covered in snow, but it's not difficult when the route is clear. The trail crosses a stream, then switchbacks up a slope to a meadow known as **high camp** (4740m). The trail then hits the snowline and climbs a ridge to offer views of Norbu Kang, before ascending a moraine into a large bowl marked by a chorten (two hours). The trail arcs gently around the bowl on a scree slope to several rough cairns atop **Baga La** (5175m), three hours from Pelung Tang.

Descend from the pass, steeply at first, then more gently, staying high above the right bank of the stream. The trail is well defined in most places, although it sometimes disappears into loose scree and crosses two large side streams that present a rock-hopping challenge.

At 4390m the trail turns a corner and enters a huge valley, making a final descent on steep switchbacks to **Dajok Tang** ('Prayer-flag Meadow') at 4080m (5½ hours). The stream drops beside the trail in an impressive series of cascades. This is truly a spectacular valley, our favourite of the trek and one of the most scenic in western Nepal, with a large moraine at its head and numerous waterfalls shooting off the striped valley walls. Several snowy peaks, including Kagmara (5960m), crowd the horizon at the end of the valley.

If you have energy, you can push on down the Maduwa Valley to good campsites 15 minutes (3930m), 40 minutes (3830m) or an hour (3820m) below Dajok Tang. The last site nestles in meadows five minutes before you catch sight of the snowy peak of Sonam Kang (6019m), up a side valley to the south. After two nights sleeping above 4400m, there's a real sense of relief to be sleeping at lower, warmer elevations.

Day 9: Dajok Tang to Phoksumdo Lake

3–4 HOURS / 70M ASCENT / 270M DESCENT

Follow a trail down past views of Sonam Kang and a national park building to a collection of five sod-covered herders' huts (20 minutes). Traverse high above the river through groves of thorny shrubs, juniper and blue pine (the first trees for five days) into a valley headed by the distant snowy range of Kagmara Lekh. After an initial descent the trail climbs on an exposed, built-up cliffside trail. You can see the village of Rilke below to the left and the blue river and trail descending from Phoksumdo straight ahead. Contour around to a ridge decorated in prayer flags (3750m), climb for 10 minutes and you'll first hear, and then see, the waterfall across the valley.

The trail descends gently to the chortens and barley fields of **Ringmo** village at 3640m. From here it's a 10-minute walk to the shores of stunning **Phoksumdo Lake** (3620m). There are national park campsites by the park building or, better, across the lake outlet. For more on Ringmo and the lake see p263.

To continue the loop trek to Dunai follow the Phoksumdo Lake trek (p262) in reverse. Trekking downhill in this direction it's possible to reach Dunai in two days from Phoksumdo, overnighting in Chepka. Alternatively, enjoy an extra morning at the lake, overnight at Renje (four hours from Phoksumdo) and make a long day's hike to Dunai the next day.

Beni to Dolpo Trek

Duration 12 days

Max Elevation 4540m

Difficulty Medium to hard

Season May to October

Start Beni, Babiyachour or Darbang

Finish Dunai or Kanigaon

Permits TIMS Card, Dhorpatan Hunting Reserve permit

Summary A long, high and difficult trek over six passes, with terrain ranging from rice fields to alpine tundra.

This route is described in detail by George B Schaller in *Stones of Silence* and by Peter Matthiessen in *The Snow Leopard*. For anyone who's read the latter, this trek feels like nothing short of a pilgrimage. March and April bring lovely rhododendron blooms to the lower hills, but the high passes will have snow at this time. At the time of writing, there were no reports of serious damage from the 2015 earthquake, but as a sensible precaution, seek local advice on the current status of trails and infrastructure before starting a trek in this area.

If you add a circuit through Tarap and Phoksumdo Lake, you can make an outstanding 23-day trek that offers a real sense of journey, from one region of Nepal to another. One hiker commented that you'll see more blue sheep than people on this trek.

HIMALAYAN VIAGRA

Yartse gumpa (Cordyceps) is one of the Himalaya's oddest exports. Known as the 'summer-grass, winter-worm' in Tibetan, the 'herb' is a fusion of a caterpillar larvae and the parasitic fungus that digests it from the inside. Its reputation in traditional medicine as a tonic for vigour, endurance and a booming libido has led to it being dubbed 'Himalayan Viagra'. Customers in China pay as much as US$20,000 per kilogram, and it is the region's only significant cash crop and the main reason you'll see bottles of Lhasa Beer littering even the remotest valleys.

Since harvesting of the worm was legalised in 2000, thousands of people have flocked to Dolpo's high-altitude pastures each June, living in seasonal camps that recall America's gold rush. The camps cause great stress on the fragile high-altitude environment and tensions between rival valleys over harvesting rights often erupt into violence. On the Beni–Dolpo trek you'll pass the litter of several harvesting camps and in the prime months of June and July you'll find it noticeably harder to find porters in Dolpo.

Beni to Dolpo Trek

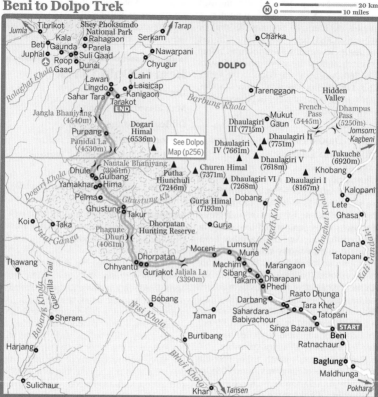

ℹ Planning

ACCOMMODATION & SUPPLIES

You need to bring a tent and stove for this trek. Simple lodges, seasonal tent hotels and meals of daal bhaat are available as far as Dhorpatan, but you are better off camping.

Food supplies such as rice, vegetables and noodles are available at most settlements en route, though you need to be fully self-sufficient for the six-day section between Dhorpatan and Tarakot.

🥾 The Trek

Day 1: Beni to Babiyachour

4–5 HOURS / 160M ASCENT

The trek starts in Beni (p288). Today's walk is along the road and so it is feasible to take a vehicle from Beni to Babiyachour or to Darbang. Buses to Darbang leave from the west end of town.

The trail to Dolpo heads west along the river from the western end of town, passing a series of five high cascades, before starting to climb. An hour's walk brings you to Kotsangu (also known as Chutrini), where the foot trail joins the new dirt road. A further 45 minutes along the road is Singa Bazaar, with a collection of shops and teahouses.

Continue through Rakshe and on to **Tatopani** ('hot water'), named after the small riverside hot-springs complex below the village. Past the springs in the main bazaar, Milan Guest House and Himalayan Guest House both offer simple rooms and daal bhaat.

Continue along the road for 40 minutes to Simalchaur. Continue a further hour to **Tara Khet** and then climb over a small ridge to **Babiyachour** (990m), named after a local grass, *babiyo*, which is woven into ropes. A derelict government agricultural project offers a convenient campsite, with a toilet and water supply. The upper part of the village is a substantial bazaar, which boasts the simple Sherchan Guest House, Riverside Restaurant, and a medical dispensary.

Day 2: Babiyachour to Dharapani

4½–5½ HOURS / 630M ASCENT / 80M DESCENT

Head out of Babiyachour along the road. An hour into the walk it's worth detouring through the traditional stone houses of **Sahardara**. From the rickety suspension bridge at the end of town, it's 20 minutes on to **Raato Dhunga**, a small bazaar at 1020m.

The road climbs above the river and then drops down to Dar Kharka, the first village on the trek to sport prayer flags, marking the beginning of Buddhist influence. Take the left branch through the village and climb across a rocky slope where slate is mined for roof shingles. On the opposite bank are the faint remains of the landslide that destroyed old Darbang in 1983.

New **Darbang** (2½ hours) has a large, well-stocked bazaar that is flourishing in its status as the roadhead and mule-caravan terminus. You need to register your passport with the police post. There are several lodges including the friendly Rainbow Thakali Guesthouse with four simple rooms.

On the suspension bridge cross the Myagdi Khola and branch right to follow it for 45 minutes past stone houses to **Phedi** (1095m), at the foot of a steep series of switchbacks.

Cross the Danyga Khola on a big suspension bridge and grind up a series of steep switchbacks. After about 250m of climbing, pine trees and a chautara (porters' rest stop) offer welcome shade and you'll get your first glimpse of the massive white wall of Dhaulagiri. After another 100m of ascent, the trail becomes more gentle; turn a corner for a good view of Dhaulagiri IV and V and the Gurja Himal. Traverse a bit, then climb to **Dharapani** (1550m). There are grassy camp-sites at the schools located at either end of the village. Alternatively, the **Roka Hotel** (r Rs 100), one of two lodges, offers very basic rooms but decent food.

Day 3: Dharapani to Lumsum

6–7 HOURS / 720M ASCENT / 110M DESCENT

The trail contours up above the village to a crest at 1630m (one hour). The mountain views are glorious as you traverse past the Dhaulagiri Boarding School to the Hotel Rajan. Keep climbing along the side of the hill to **Sibang** (1610m; two hours). Just past the village the pleasant **Hotel Namaste and Restaurant** (bed Rs 100) offers beds under a ceiling of dried corn cobs.

Climb over a ridge at 1840m and you'll get good views of the steep and jungly main Myagdi Valley to the north. The Dhaulagiri Circuit trail branches right from the trail 20 minutes further on to climb this valley. Thirty minutes later a pleasant *bhatti* at **Machim** offers a good lunch spot (three hours).

After lunch, crest a second ridge and descend a steep stone stairway to cross the Ghatta Khola at the small village of the same name. The main trail stays level as it traverses via a schoolhouse on a ridge at Paliya Gaon to the small settlement of **Muna** (four hours). Porters may take the high route that stays above Muna, before rejoining the main trail and dropping to a bridge across the Dhara Khola (4½ hours).

The trail climbs gently alongside the Dhara Khola's true left bank to a suspension bridge in front of an impressive waterfall. The next 1½ hours are a long climb to the Magar village of **Lumsum** (2150m). Red pandas (*malchaura* in Nepali) are occasionally spotted in this region.

Lumsum is noticeably poorer than other villages you passed today. The basic Hotel Himalayan, at the beginning of the village,

WESTERN NEPAL BENI TO DOLPO TREK

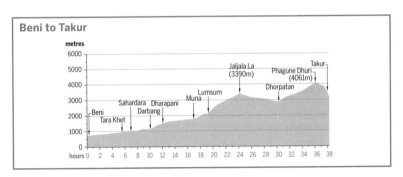

Beni to Takur

metres

6000
5000 — Jaljala La (3390m), Phagune Dhuri (4061m), Takur
4000 — Dhorpatan
3000 — Sahardara, Dharapani, Muna, Lumsum
2000 — Beni, Tara Khet, Darbang
1000
0
hours 0 2 4 6 8 10 12 14 16 18 20 22 24 26 28 30 32 34 36 38

offers food and a simple room in the rafters but you're better off camping at the Village Development Committee (VDC) camping ground in the centre of town. You'll likely be asked for a school donation here.

Day 4: Lumsum to Jaljala La

4½ HOURS / 1230M ASCENT

About 30 minutes beyond Lumsum the route crosses the Dhara Khola on a suspension bridge before starting the long climb to Jaljala La. The route towards the pass climbs steeply to scattered houses and a teahouse at **Moreni** (2670m). The peak visible over the ridge to the north is Churen Himal (7371m).

Climb through a burned forest to a herders' goth at 2770m (three hours), then continue up the ridge through a forest of rhododendrons. It's a long, unrelenting climb to a notch at 3350m. The trail climbs to a crest, then contours to the right, under prayer flags, to the large meadow at **Jaljala La** (3390m), fringed by rhododendron forests, some goths and a seasonal tea hut, making the meadow an excellent campsite. The only water available during the spring season is a tiny spring near the notch on the crest of the ridge. The sunset views from the meadow are some of the best in Nepal, stretching across the entire Dhaulagiri massif from 7246m Putha Hiunchuli to 7061m Nilgiri Peak and the Annapurna Himal.

Day 5: Jaljala La to Dhorpatan

6–7 HOURS / 530M DESCENT

The trail continues across the plateau, featuring great Dhaulagiri views, to a second meadow (30 minutes) and alternative campsite. From here the trail descends past three wooden bridges to the junction of two streams, about 1½ hours from the camp. Follow the stream past herders' huts and another bridge through a forest of pines to the open valley junction at **Gurjakot** (3010m; three hours). People from Dhorpatan bring their horses here to graze. The house at the far end of the village offers daal bhaat if you have time to wait for it to cook.

Just over 30 minutes from Gurjakot, past a couple of riverside camping spots, the trail suddenly veers right for 10 minutes up a side valley to cross the Simudar Khola on a suspension bridge. There are lots of swampy areas to dodge and small streams to cross on precarious logs.

The first village in the Dhorpatan Valley is **Chhyantu** (2990m). Just before you ar-

rive at Chhyantu look for the red walls of Tashi Gedye Tarke Ling Gompa to the right, surrounded by a village of Tibetan refugees. Chhyantu (4¾ hours) has a couple of basic hotels amid the apple orchards but none are signed. A trail up the canyon to the north leads to a high short-cut route to Dolpo.

Continue past the scattered houses of Bagatar and Baglung to the village of **Dhorpatan** (2860m) and the office of the **Dhorpatan Hunting Reserve** (admission Rs 3000). Unsurprisingly, many travellers baulk at paying an entry fee to a reserve that caters mainly to rich hunters who want to kill blue sheep. A few hundred metres south of the office, beside an unmarked teahouse and the abandoned Dhorpatan airstrip, is the Dhorpatan Community Lodge and a camping area.

The Dhorpatan Valley is inhabited by Tibetan refugees and there are also several Magar settlements around the edge of the basin. *Patan* means 'flat place' in the local dialect, and the Dhorpatan Valley is one of the largest flat places in the hills of Nepal.

If for some reason you need to abandon your trek, the nearest road is a two-day walk south via Bobang to the roadhead at Omitaksa.

Day 6: Dhorpatan to Takur

7–8 HOURS / 1280M ASCENT / 920M DESCENT

From Dhorpatan you begin the second phase of the trek and venture north into largely uninhabited wilderness. From the reserve office pass a mani wall and follow the trail as it climbs, branching right after 25 minutes up to a collection of houses. Continue uphill, aiming to the right of a round hill towards a notch (one hour), where you'll get your last look back at the Dhorpatan Valley. You'll see Salje village below you. From the crest the trail descends into the boggy Phagune Valley through rhododendron forests, crossing several streams. At Jaunde Bisauni pass a teahouse to a false summit and continue climbing to a crest and goths at 3510m (3½ hours). From the crest there are views of the Phagune Dhuri pass far ahead.

The trail keeps climbing alongside a stream, passing a goth at the valley junction (continue up the main valley) and shortly afterwards climbs steeply up a series of switchbacks on the left side of the valley. Eventually the trail angles left up a steep eroded gully, crossing a stream and scree slopes, before emerging at a chorten atop **Phagune Dhuri** (4061m; five hours). From here, there are

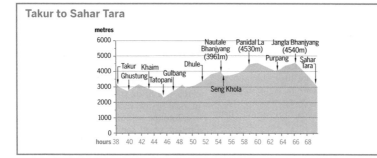

Takur to Sahar Tara

great views of Churen Himal and of Putha Hiunchuli (7246m), the 'butterfly' mountain.

From the pass the route descends gently to a stream and small campsite at 4000m. The trail makes a long traverse before starting steeply down. After a few ups and downs the trail reaches Dupi Neta, a meadow atop a hill at 3810m that offers a possible campsite with mountain views. Below Dupi Neta the route re-enters forests and makes a slippery descent over tree roots and down switchbacks to the hidden valley of **Takur** (3190m). Camp near the smoky local-style *bhatti* in a meadow.

Day 7: Takur to Tatopani
6½–7½ HOURS / 470M ASCENT / 1260M DESCENT

The route now heads west, past a mill and down the Ghustung Valley, through a forest of fir and oak and past an easily-missed holy pond at 2980m. After 30 minutes you'll cross a wooden bridge decorated with ribbon-like 'spirit traps' (the intricate threads are supposed to catch troublesome spirits). The trail turns to the consistency of toffee as you make your way down alongside the raging river to a bridge at 2710m (1½ hours).

Cross a bridge and climb steeply to the two houses of **Ghustung** village, where you may be able to buy some sugar cane *(uku)* or roasted corn on the cob *(makai)*. The trail climbs above the hillside, finally emerging on a ridge at 3140m. Follow this ridge, known as the Selep Danda (marked on some maps as Phorsadeur Danda), for a long distance, making ups and downs to **Khaim** (2890m), a convenient tea stop straddling a notch (four hours).

The *bhatti* marks a junction; the main left trail switchbacks down to Pelma (2540m) along the old trail to Dhule. Most trekkers these days take the steeper but shorter route to the right, down through deep forest to Tatopani; this is the trail described here.

The trail drops steeply over roots and through thick forest – a difficult ordeal if it's been raining. Eventually the path becomes clearer and makes a long descent for 1½ to two hours, through patches of forest and past two villages of just three houses each.

Eventually, you'll cross the Jatlung Khola on a bridge and 10 minutes later arrive at the valley junction at **Tatopani** (2400m; not to be confused with the Tatopani you pass on Day 1). Camp in the small field just above the river junction, which you'll have to share with local cows. A tiny hot spring beside the river gives the junction its name (Tatopani means 'hot water').

Day 8: Tatopani to Dhule
4 HOURS / 940M ASCENT

Today's walk is relatively short so take your time in the villages en route or enjoy a late start. The trail crosses the Pelma Khola on a bridge, climbs steeply for 20 minutes and then winds northwest around the hillside. Eventually you pass the fields of maize and marijuana that surround **Hima** village (one hour). From here, it's another hour following the valley contours in and out of side valleys to arrive at the larger village of **Gulbang** (2680m; two hours).

At Gulbang the trail swings left and climbs out of the Pelma Khola Valley. It's a long grind up through fields, over a side stream and into a steep rutted gully of rhododendrons. Finally you crest a pass and make the short descent to **Dhule**, half a dozen houses in a small bowl at 3340m.

This settlement is the last until Tarakot so you or your porters may want to try to rustle up some extra supplies, including vegetables and biscuits. You can get a cup of tea and daal bhaat at the Hotel Copila, the lowest house in the village.

Day 9: Dhule to Seng Khola

5–6 HOURS / 790M ASCENT / 290M DESCENT

The trail climbs steeply through the moss-draped forests above Dhule to the top of a ridge (15 minutes) and then continues to climb along the ridge to a chautara (1½ hours). Continue along the ridge above the treeline through scenery reminiscent of the Scottish Highlands to a second chautara (3790m) where there are outstanding views of the Dhaulagiri Himal. The trail cuts across the bare hillside to the northwest, climbing gradually to what looks like two stone chortens (actually the remains of a *kani*-style gate) atop **Nautale Bhanjyang** (3961m). Nautale (Nine Steps) is a reference to Bön belief, a sign that the religious landscape is changing along with the physical.

Descend steeply for 30 minutes, then contour above the **Seng Khola**, a tributary of the Pelma Khola. The trail continues along the west bank of the river, climbing gradually past a small cave, pastures and a goth at the entrance of a side valley (four hours). There are messy campsites here near the river at 3820m or continue for 50 minutes to a better campsite.

Day 10: Seng Khola to Purpang

5½–6½ HOURS / 720M ASCENT / 510M DESCENT

About 30 minutes from the goth you branch left, away from the main valley, up the steep grassy slope to a **campsite** (4030m; N 28°44.848', E 082°58.822') near a small stream (50 minutes).

It's along this next part of the trail that Matthiessen and Schaller got lost and climbed the wrong ridge during their trek to Dolpo. To avoid their error, don't climb the hill to the north-northwest; instead, head generally west to a ridge crest at 4260m. The trail crosses into another side valley and traverses above a small lake. The route climbs gradually towards the **Panidal La** (4530m; 2¾ hours) and drops into another basin. Descend past a summer-time *yartse gumpa* harvesting camp and head down to the Saunre Khola at 4020m (3½ hours). There's no bridge but you should be able to rock-hop across the river. A single goth marks the location of **Purpang**. There are some damp campsites on an island in the river.

If you have the energy it's a good idea to get a jump on tomorrow's climb by climbing steeply for an hour past the ruined building and a chorten up to **meadows** (4270m; N 28°48.260', E 82°56.611') in a high bowl. High,

wild and remote, this a beautiful spot. Look for blue sheep on the crags and remote Sirma Daha lake in a high bowl far to the east.

Day 11: Purpang to Sahar Tara

5½–7 HOURS / 570M ASCENT / 1610M DESCENT

The morning's immediate steep 20-minute climb will bring you to the first mini-pass, marked by two rock cairns at 4340m. Traverse into the next valley, where people from Tarakot graze their horses, and follow a stream for about 30 minutes to the foot of the pass. The trail climbs a sandy, rocky ravine to five rock cairns atop **Jangla Bhanjyang** at 4540m (1¾ hours). Here, there are epic 360-degree views over the grey ranges of Dolpo towards 6612m Kanjeralwa, a peak near Phoksumdo Lake.

The trail descends steeply from the pass for the first 400m, then it levels out and makes a high traverse. The forested valley below you offers the short, steep route down the Jangla Valley to Dunai; you can see the town far below to the northwest. The Tarakot trail stays high and keeps to the right as it heads northeast to a ridge at 4056m (3¼ hours). Round the ridge into the next valley for fine views of sacred Putha Himal and descend, steeply at first and then more gradually. After passing through a forest draped with Spanish moss, the trail eventually skirts a field beside a good campsite to enter the village of upper **Sahar Tara** (3010m; 5½ hours). There are more good campsites in nearby pastures. The village's **Tanti Gompa** is worth a visit for its murals.

This region of the upper Bheri is known as Tichurong in Tibetan. Many people refer to the entire region as Tarakot, although this name correctly applies only to the fortress-like village perched on a ridge a further 1½ hours downhill near the river. The people are Magars, but they practise many Tibetan traditions and have their own language, Kaike, which is spoken only in this region.

If your knees haven't completely given up the ghost, it's possible to continue downhill for 45 minutes to **lower Sahar Tara** (2760m; six hours), or another hour to Tarakot (2550m; seven hours).

Day 12: Sahar Tara to Tarakot

2 HOURS / 560M DESCENT

From the campsite in upper Sahar Tara, descend for 45 minutes through fields past a *kani* to the main part of **Sahar Tara** at 2760m. The people of Tichurong believe if ghosts have to bend over they cannot enter a house, so all the houses of the traditional village have low ceilings. You may be able to recruit local porters here, although the main focus of this village's trade is running horse caravans south along the Thulo Bheri to the roadhead at Chaurjhari, five days away. James Fisher's 1986 book, *Trans-Himalayan Traders*, describes this region in detail.

Descend steeply to the village water supply, then contour above fields to **Tarakot** proper, perched on a spine-like ridge at 2550m. From the ridge the trail drops steeply to a school and a good campsite beside the Chhyada Khola (2450m).

From here trails continue east to the Tarap Valley or northwest to Dunai, a long day's walk away. If you're trekking to Dunai follow Day 1 of the Phoksumdo Lake via Do Tarap trek (p265) in reverse. If continuing through Do Tarap to Phoksumdo Lake, head for Kanigaon, following Day 2 of the Phoksumdo Lake via Do Tarap trek (p265).

INNER DOLPO

The northern part of Dolpo is usually called inner Dolpo and has long had an aura of mysticism about it. The goal of most trekkers to inner Dolpo is Shey Gompa, largely because of the metaphysical discussions of the region in Peter Matthiessen's book *The Snow Leopard*. Shey was closed to foreigners until 1992. One story cites the reason for closure as the large-scale theft of statues from monasteries. Despite the mysticism surrounding Shey and the 'Crystal Mountain', this is not a popular region for trekking. The harsh terrain, the tough physical challenge and high fees deter many. All trekkers will need to do this walk as part of an organised trek (minimum two persons), so our best advice is to go with an experienced company that knows the route well. While the trails in this area remained open through the 2015 earthquakes, there are some reports of damage to traditional buildings in this region. As a sensible precaution, seek local advice on the status of trails and infrastructure before starting a trek in this area.

ⓘ Planning

MAPS
Nepal Map Publisher has a 1:125,000 *Upper & Lower Dolpa* map and Himalayan Maphouse (Nepa Maps) publishes a similarly scaled *Dolpo Circuit* map. Both maps cover Jomsom, Shey Gompa and Dunai routes.

FEES & PERMITS
The restricted-area permit for inner Dolpo is US$500 for the first 10 days and US$50 per day thereafter. If you are only going to Shey, the daily rate is especially expensive because the trek takes only six to eight days to complete. You will also need a TIMS card and a Shey Phoksumdo National Park permit (Rs 3000)

The 'restricted' part of this trek starts from Ringmo village at the southern end of Phoksumdo Lake. To visit Shey you need to trek from Dolpo airport in Juphal or make a longer trek from Jumla. Once you are at Shey, you can continue to Saldang and trek into Tarap via either of two passes. If you have lots of time, you can keep trekking north, then turn east and spend another two weeks (at US$50 per day) in astoundingly remote desert-like country, eventually ending up in Jomsom.

ⓘ Getting There & Away

Phoksumdo Lake, the start of this trek, can only be reached by trekking (see the Phoksumdo Lake Trek, p262).

Phoksumdo Lake to Shey Gompa Trek

Duration 7 days or more

Max Elevation 5160m

Difficulty Medium to hard

Season May to October

Start Phoksumdo Lake

Finish Dunai, Tarap or Jomsom

Permits TIMS card, restricted-area trekking permit, Shey Phoksumdo National Park permit

Summary Cross high passes from Phoksumdo Lake to the legendary Crystal Mountain and Shey Gompa. There are several options for the return trek to Dolpo.

This is a challenging and truly adventurous trek into the heart of inner Dolpo. Altitude gains are significant, so be alert for signs of AMS and be prepared to spend an extra day acclimatising at Phoksumdo Lake before heading off. The panoramic views from these altitudes are vast and humbling, and your chances of seeing herds of blue sheep are excellent. Inner Dolpo remained open to trekkers throughout the 2015 earthquakes. but as a sensible precaution, seek local advice on the status of trails and infrastructure before starting a trek in this area.

🚶 The Trek

Day 1: Phoksumdo Lake to Chunemba

5–6 HOURS / 570M ASCENT / 560M DESCENT

From the campsite at 3620m on the southern end of Phoksumdo Lake, the trail contours on a rocky ledge as it skirts the western shore of the lake. As you cross a stream, look up at the glacier descending from the upper slopes of Kanjeralwa (6612m). Climb to a crest at 4060m for a spectacular view of the lake with the snowy peak of Sonam Kang (6019m) in the background. The trail makes a steep descent through birches and blue pines to the westernmost edge of the lake at 3630m, where the Phoksumdo Khola enters it. There's a campsite here in a lush meadow known as **Cho Phu**. The route now heads northwest up a long, wide valley. Follow an indistinct trail through thorn bushes and scrub, criss-crossing boggy marshes and tributaries of the Phoksumdo Khola. Camp in a forest of blue pines at **Chunemba**, an undeveloped national park camping ground at 3630m.

Day 2: Chunemba to Lar Tsa

4–5½ HOURS / 570M ASCENT / 80M DESCENT

Continue along the level path that heads north through a glacial valley. Cross to the east bank of the Phoksumdo Khola about 30 minutes from Chunemba. Soon the valley narrows and a mountain stream flows from a steep valley to the north. This is the difficult high route to Shey via the Ngadra La, which is described as an alternative route.

The best route to Shey follows the main valley for another hour to **Kang Gopa**, a pretty campsite in a grove of birch trees at 3710m. Climb steeply from Kang Gopa and stay on the grassy ridge. Don't follow the level trail that heads northwest; it leads only to some herders' huts. It's a long climb up the ridge past a few groves of birch trees. There are spectacular mountain views with Shey Shikar (6139m) and Kang Chunne (6443m) dominating the skyline to the west. After cresting at 4200m the route descends gently on a rocky trail to **Lar Tsa**, a campsite beside the river at 4120m.

It's possible to continue walking, but you have now ascended more than 500m in a day and should spend the night at Lar Tsa for acclimatisation.

Day 3: Lar Tsa to Mendok Ding

2–3 HOURS / 520M ASCENT / 130M DESCENT

Cross a new bridge and climb to the top of a scree slope at 4490m, then make your way up a grassy ridge to a crest at 4640m. Contour and then drop gently into **Mendok Ding** ('Flower Valley'). Climb alongside a stream to a campsite at 4610m. You are almost certain to spot herds of blue sheep on the slopes above the camp.

Day 4: Mendok Ding to Shey Gompa

7–8½ HOURS / 1040M ASCENT / 1240M DESCENT

The route follows the upper reaches of the Phoksumdo Khola, then turns north towards the peak of Riwo Drugdra (Crystal Mountain). There is a choice of trails here. The easier and shorter route, which is also the route for pack animals, crosses the Dolma La to the east of the mountain and descends on a steep narrow trail to Shey. The more scenic pilgrim route crosses the Sehu La to the west of Crystal Mountain, making a kora (circumambulation) of this sacred peak. The Dolma La trail turns north soon after camp while the pilgrim trail starts up a steep scree slope on the opposite side of a stream that flows from the north.

After a long pull to **Sehu La** (5160m), also known as Mendok Ding La, the trail descends a scree slope to meadows beside a stream at 4620m. The trail climbs out of the valley and begins a series of long ascents and descents in and out of side valleys as it traverses around Crystal Mountain. After a steep climb to a crest at 5010m and another at 4860m, the trail begins the descent to the Tar Valley. Soon after the route reaches grassy slopes a side trail leads to **Tsakang**, a gompa said to be 800 years old perched dramatically on the side of a cliff. You can visit Tsakang and reach Shey via a lower route. The direct route to Shey traverses past goths and yak pastures, where you are likely to spot blue sheep. The

Phoksumdo Lake to Shey Gompa

final descent is on a wide trail to a campsite in a large meadow near a few nomads' huts at 4310m, just below Shey Gompa.

Cross the river on a log bridge and climb past a big chorten and a field of mani stones to **Shey Gompa** (4390m). The gompa itself is not large, and there are no artefacts or paintings of note inside. Although the building is apparently 800 years old, the wall paintings are relatively recent, probably done in the 1970s. The statues on the altar are of Guru Rinpoche, Sakyamuni and Milarepa. The gompa also houses an ancient Tibetan scroll that describes the myth of Crystal Mountain and Shey Gompa. According to the inscription, there is a holy lake in a crater among the mountains that surround Shey. When a pilgrim makes nine circumambulations of this lake the water turns into milk. A sip of this milk, and the pilgrim can see Mt Kailash in the distance.

A caretaker lives in one of the houses adjacent to Shey Gompa. To the east of the gompa is the trail that leads to Saldang village, and eventually to Jomsom or south to Tarap.

ALTERNATIVE ROUTE: VIA NGADRA LA

The route ascends a narrow valley that heads north from the Phoksumdo Valley east of Chunemba. The trail is indistinct as it climbs over rocks and boulders and fords a stream. A long climb brings you to a meadow where the trail veers up a steep ravine. A hard climb to the top brings you to yet another valley where you can see the Ngadra La, the pass leading to Shey Gompa. If you are in good shape and the porters agree, you might make it on to Shey Gompa on the same day, or you can camp before the pass in the place that Peter Matthiessen christened 'Snowfields Camp'.

Climb up the steep hill littered with slate towards the pass. The climb is physically demanding, especially when you slip on the loose slate. From the top of the 5375m **Ngadra La** (which Matthiessen called the Kanga La), you can look down upon a large valley that leads to Shey. Descend steeply into the valley floor and make a long, meandering trek along the banks of the river, crossing and recrossing it several times. A red chorten heralds the gate to Shey Gompa.

RETURN ROUTES

You can return to Phoksumdo along the approach route or you can make a three-day trek across four high passes to Tarap.

To do this, follow the trail east from Shey and turn onto a route leading south.

Climb to the Sela Munchung La at 5060m and descend across numerous side valleys to a campsite. Traverse the 5140m Langmosia She La and then the 5160m Khyung Bhanj-yang. Descend alongside a stream to the junction of the route over the Numa La. Refer to Days 6–7 of the Phoksumdo Lake via Do Tarap route (p267) in reverse to get to Tok-khyu and on to Do Tarap.

Alternatively, follow the Shey Gompa to Jomsom trek (p285).

HUMLA

Humla has traditionally been treated as the region to trek through on the way to Mt Kailash and Manasarovar. Reducing the fees to visit the Limi Valley has opened up this incredible region to those who want to experience an adventurous, culturally and scenically rewarding trek in the most remote corner of Nepal. Humla offers a rich tapestry of geography and culture, previously off-limits to trekkers. However, the region saw landslides and damage to buildings from the aftershocks that hit Nepal in the weeks following the 12 May tremor. As a sensible precaution, seek local advice on the status of trails and infrastructure before starting a trek in this area.

In this impoverished far northwestern corner of the country centuries-old migration paths have shaped a way of life cut off from the rest of Nepal. Nowhere in the Himalaya have Buddhists and Hindus lived together for so long without giving up the essence of their beliefs, values and codes of behaviour. In the lower reaches near the district capital Simikot, the Hindu Thakuris and Chhetris eke a living from the thin soil that provides barely one crop a year. White-turbaned *dhamis* (local sorcerers or soothsayers) share the narrow trails of Humla with men whose *tarchok* (topknot of hair) is one of the last visible signs of the fading Bön tradition. Upper Humla is home to Bhotias, clever and boisterous traders who have used the proximity to Tibet to their best advantage.

History

Humla was once part of the western Tibet region known as Ngari. Present day Ngari includes the Chinese village of Purang (better known by its Nepali name, Taklakot), Guge and the 'lost' villages of Toling (Zanda) and Tsaparang on the banks of the Sutlej River, but it once extended eastward to upper Mustang. Much of Ngari was annexed by the great Malla empire administered from Sinja near Jumla. By 1789 the Gorkha armies of Prithvi Narayan Shah had seized control of much of the Ngari region, including Humla.

Taklakot in present-day Tibet was once part of Nepal; on a map you can see the chunk taken out of the northwest corner of Nepal like a bite. It is said that in 1959 the Chinese offered the people of Limi – settled by Tibetans over 800 years – 1000 silver coins to become part of Chinese Tibet. The villagers prayed to their protective goddess Alchi whose oracle told them to refuse the Chinese offer.

Trade via Taklakot remains an important focus for Humli traders, who have special trading passes that allow them to cross into Tibet without a passport. The kinds of goods being bought and sold have changed significantly over the years. The traditional salt-for-grain trade is being gradually replaced by the movement of mass-produced and manufactured food and consumer goods.

ⓘ Planning

WHEN TO TREK

Trekking here is possible only in the late spring and summer months from mid-May to October. Much of the region is snowbound in the winter and passes are closed. You should check with locals in Simikot before deciding in which direction to do this trek as the Nyalu Lagna remains snowbound longer and is used less than the Nara La.

EMERGENCY FACILITIES

It is worthwhile bringing a satellite phone if you are trekking in Limi. There are telephones in Simikot, and NTS and CDMA mobile phones will work in the district capital, but not much beyond. There are sometimes radios in the police posts at Dharapuri, Muchu, Hilsa and Halji, but these are not reliable. Satellite phones with a Nepal SIM card may not work in Hilsa.

There is helicopter landing pad just outside Til and helicopters regularly land in Hilsa to deliver Indian tourists en route to Kailash during the pilgrimage season. There is an excellent, well-stocked 24-hour hospital in Simikot run by **Citta Nepal** (www.citta.org). An English-speaking, India-trained doctor is usually in residence during the summer months and the well-trained staff are experienced in dealing with most medical emergencies. The hospital is run through overseas donations.

MAPS

The best trekking map is the hard-to-get Map Point's 1:175,000 *Kailash & Lake Manasarovar*. Himalayan Maphouse (Nepa Maps) produces a 1:200,000 *Kailas-Manasarovar* map

BOOKS

Vignettes of Nepal, by the late Dr Harka Gurung, is an excellent geographic and ethnographic narrative of travels through Humla in 1977 by one of Nepal's most respected scholars.

Hidden Himalayas, by Thomas Kelly and Carroll Dunham, is a beautiful pictographic account of Humla through its four seasons, accompanied by evocative text describing life in Humla.

To the Navel of the World by Peter Somerville-Large is an account of travels to Kailash and a trek into Nepal.

Himalayan Traders by Christoph von Fürer-Haimendorf provides good background reading for this area.

Spy on the Roof of the World by Sydney Wignall is a fascinating account of the 1955 Welsh expedition to Gurla Mandata, just over the border from Humla, which doubled as a spy mission for Indian military intelligence.

PERMITS & REGULATIONS

Trekking in Humla requires a TIMS card and a restricted-area permit (US$50 per week per person and then US$7 per day thereafter).

ACCOMMODATION

The Limi Valley trek is camping only. There are no guesthouses along the trail and there are long stretches with no habitation whatsoever. The number of organised campsites with a cooking shelter has increased, but it is still essential to bring a cooking tent.

SHEEP CARAVANS

In many parts of northwestern Nepal you may still see herds of sheep carrying small backpacks made of rough woven fabric. The animals are perfectly suited to the narrow and treacherous trails typical of this region and are a lot cheaper than a horse or a yak. Each sheep can carry up to 12kg of rice or salt, though these days it's more common to see the little backpacks stuffed full of cheap Chinese booze.

Though the *changla* sheep is known for its superior long-fibre wool, it is the native *ronglu* sheep that lead the caravans because they are better at navigating the tricky paths and handling the heat of the Middle Hills. Raised at altitudes above 3000m, the *changla* sheep produce some of the longest woollen fibres in the world – coarse, incredibly strong and perfect for Tibetan carpets.

FOOD & FUEL

Humla is barely able to feed its own population, so you must be self-sufficient in terms of food. You must cook with kerosene, and careful planning is needed because it cannot be carried on the plane. Arrange to send food by plane with your trekking crew and phone someone in Simikot ahead of time to arrange for kerosene to be available.

 Towns & Facilities

The town of Simikot (p288), which has an airstrip, is the main town and gateway to Humla.

Limi Valley Trek

Duration 17 days

Max Elevation 4990m

Difficulty Medium to hard

Season Mid-May to early October

Start/Finish Simikot

Permits TIMS card, restricted-area trekking permit

Summary A scenically and culturally diverse trek over two high passes into the most remote region of Nepal. The ancient gompas and fortress-like stone villages of Jang, Halji and Til are unquestionably the highlight of this trek.

This lengthy trek takes you deep into a little-visited corner of Nepal where the resilient peoples of the Limi Valley continue to practice age-old Tibetan traditions. Seasonally isolated by snow and ice and surrounded by Himalayan peaks, this trek follows ancient trade routes featuring timeless monasteries and villages, yak meadows and glacial streams.

This trek description was researched shortly before the 2015 earthquakes, and there are reports of damage to several villages in this region from the aftershocks that followed the 12 May 2015 tremor. As a precaution, seek local advice on the status of trails and infrastructure before starting a trek in this area.

 The Trek

Day 1: Simikot

Flights arrive into Simikot early in the morning. Take it easy because the town is at an elevation of 2960m. If your trekking crew arrived the day before and has organised pack animals, you could leave straight away for the first day's trekking. Even so it's not a bad idea to spend the night in Simikot. Your *sirdar* (head sherpa) will need to register trekkers with the military police and you may also be asked to pay a small local tax by the VDC on arrival. There are several places to camp, including near the Nepal Trust guesthouse and the Citta hospital.

Day 2: Simikot to Dharapuri

4–6 HOURS / 270M ASCENT / 980M DESCENT

Start climbing from the Simikot airstrip on a rough rocky trail bordered with cannabis and nettles. Trek past the stone houses of upper Simikot and the community water supply to a large rock cairn and a small teashop at the top of a forested ridge overlooking the town. Here the track splits into two. Following the well-graded right-hand path heading to Yakba affords tremendous views down the Humla Karnali Valley.

The more commonly used left-hand path drops steeply in a knee-crunching 800m descent to the town of **Masigaon** (Tuling; 2270m) where your crew can cook lunch in a small teahouse. As you descend do not follow paths heading to the cluster of flat-topped houses on your left (Dandaphoya) but keep heading north. Following the Humla Karnali River flowing about 400m below, you eventually reach a metal bridge crossing the Hepka (Yakba) Khola into **Dharapuri** (2270m), where there are clearly marked camping spots and a cooking shelter next to some superb swimming holes. Check in with the police post about five minutes up the trail.

ALTERNATIVE ROUTE: SIMIKOT TO DHARAMSALA

An alternative route to the Nyalu Lagna follows the high route out of Simikot through Yakba, Lekh Dhinga and over the Sechi La (Landok Lagna; 4550m) and Kuki La (4900m), but is a much more serious (and dangerous) undertaking for trekkers and animals. The route gets less sun, so snow remains later into the season and makes the trail treacherous.

This route takes about one hour longer than the usual path and you eventually drop steeply to the Hepka Khola and a small bridge that takes you to the campsites at Dharapuri. Take a packed lunch and a Nepali-speaking staff member if you use this route and send your trekking crew on the lower trail on which you will return just over two weeks later.

Limi Valley Trek

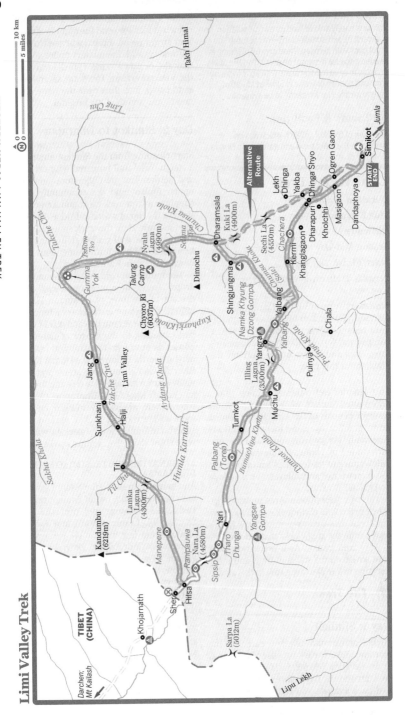

Day 3: Dharapuri to Kermi

4–5 HOURS / 440M ASCENT / 100M DESCENT

After checking in with the police, stay on the north side of the river. The trail snakes up and down to **Chachera** (2350m), a shepherds' camp near a series of three waterfalls. The trail climbs so steeply that horses and yaks have to be unloaded so they can scramble up the slope. Climb beside the waterfall and follow the narrow trail that has been blasted out of the cliff to reach Dhara Kermi (*dhara* means 'washing place') in about five hours. The best place to camp in **Kermi** (2690m) is before the village and you should arrive in time for a late lunch. About 40 minutes above Kermi are some hot springs that are well worth the visit. The main trail bypasses Kermi village itself.

Day 4: Kermi to Chumsa Khola Valley

5 HOURS / 700M ASCENT / 60M DESCENT

If you didn't spend time in Kermi village yesterday, take a small detour and head up through the town before dropping back onto the main trail. It's then a long climb over a ridge into a valley with potato and buckwheat fields. The trail levels as it makes a long traverse through a sparse pine forest and after about two hours you will come to a mani wall and rock cairn on a **ridge** at 2990m. People travelling to Kailash will follow the path down to the Chumsa Khola (also known as the Sale Khola), but instead you turn right into a stunning pine-filled valley.

After two hours dropping through forest you come to a small bridge crossing the river. After three hours you cross another bridge before reaching a wide open field and **stone shelters** at around 3400m. There is a great camping spot next to the river; it's also possible to camp about 90 minutes further up the valley at **Shingjungma** (3600m).

Day 5: Chumsa Khola Valley to Dharamsala

4 HOURS / 600M ASCENT

It is not a long day to reach the base camp of the Nyalu Lagna, so you can leave as late as 11am if you have a packed lunch. The trail climbs steadily through moss-covered birch and pine forests. After about two hours the trail climbs briefly onto benign glacial moraine before turning left into the sweeping expanse that marks the confluence of several small streams and the Chumsa Khola.

The best place for bigger groups to camp is on a flat area located at about 4000m. Smaller groups can camp about 200m higher at **Dharamsala** where there are some stone huts and a small stream. This day involves a steep gain in altitude so watch for symptoms of altitude sickness at this elevation.

Day 6: Dharamsala to Talung Camp

7–8 HOURS / 1000M ASCENT / 600M DESCENT

Leave camp before 5am for the long grind over the 4990m Nyalu Lagna (Nyu La). This also makes it easier for your animals to cross any snow patches you are likely to encounter along the way. The path climbs initially up grassy slopes before turning onto moraine and a trail that skirts above the western shore of **Selima Tso** (4600m). The trail then sweeps west into a wide, often snow-filled valley that can be difficult for animals to navigate. If there is snow and it is firm, veer right and sidle along the eastern then northern wall of the valley to reach the pass after about five hours.

The **Nyalu Lagna** (4990m) is marked with cairns and prayer flags. You can head to a point about 20 minutes northeast above the pass for great views across the Tibetan plateau. On a very clear day it is possible to see Kailash and Gurla Mandata. From the pass the trail drops steeply to a flat expanse dotted with hundreds of stone markers. It is said that each marker represents a sighting of Mt Kailash by local traders.

From here there are two options. If it is snow-free enter the steep gully to the right and make a careful descent to the Talung Valley floor at 4400m. If there is snow you can glissade down the gently angled slopes directly below you, although the animals will have to follow the generally snow-free slopes on the right-hand skyline. The bottom of the valley to the **Talung camp** (4380m) is a three-hour walk.

Day 7: Talung Camp to Jang

6–7 HOURS / 450M DESCENT

The wide Talung Valley is confined by steep scree slopes and falls in a series of steps carved out by ancient glaciers. From the camp the trail follows high above the shoreline of the 1200m-long **Tshom Tso**. Dammed at the confluence of the Talung Chu and Ling Chu, the head of the lake is dominated by giant white sand dunes (three hours). You need

LIMI VALLEY

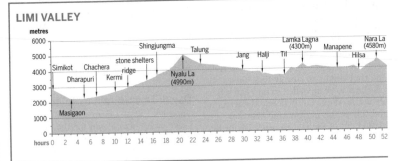

to cross the Ling Chu before climbing out of the Talung Valley and into the Takche Valley.

At the top of the sand dunes you can see the 24km trail leading into Tibet via the Lapche La (5018m). Below is **Gumma Yok** (4170m), once the most important village of Limi, but now abandoned. Stay above the river until you cross a suspension bridge to the north side of the Takche Chu. After four hours the trail levels off and wanders through the Takche Valley. A riverside **camp** (4070m) has been established by locals near a small hot spring, about 40 minutes before you reach the village of **Jang**.

Day 8: Jang

It is worth spending a rest day here to wash your clothes and explore Jang. Leaving the camp, jump across a small stream and pass a series of distinctly burnt-orange and white chortens. After exiting the upper portion of the Takche Chu Valley the trail becomes rocky; about 20 minutes later you crest a small rise marked with prayer flags that offers views down to the impressive stone houses of Jang (3930m). A steep gorge turns the river into a thunderous cascade that runs alongside the trail, and a series of irrigated barley fields marks the beginning of the village.

Jang Village is divided into three sections – two above the trail and one below. The main monastery is right in the middle of town.

Day 9: Jang to Halji

3–4 HOURS / 400M DESCENT

Follow the trail back to Jang and exit the village through a *kani* with an ornately painted roof. Halji is just 9km (three hours) west of Jang so leaving early will give you enough time to visit the Rinzin Ling Gompa, said

to be the most important in Limi. The rocky undulating trail has some steep minor ascents and descents until you eventually crest the top of a small ridge that protects Halji from the winds. Take a moment to admire the view of barley and wheat fields spilling out below you and the town of **Halji** (3670m). A giant chorten and an exceptionally long prayer wall *(mendong)* mark the southeastern entrance to the village. The best camp is located near a small willow grove on the river flats below. Walk past the stone Nepal Trust health post to reach the camp.

The **Rinzin Ling Gompa** has a courtyard with monks' quarters on three sides and a temple precinct to the north. The ground-floor chapel to the north is the oldest part of the Sakyapa-school gompa. A steep staircase leads to the main shrine, featuring a metal statue of Sakyamuni in the centre of the room. The rest of the gompa is filled with paintings, statues, texts, hats and masks of various characters used during festivals.

Day 10: Halji to Til

5–6 HOURS / 150M ASCENT / 50M DESCENT

It is 10km from Halji to Til so you should arrive in time to spend several hours exploring this last village in the Limi Valley.

From the campsite, climb back to the main trail and walk past fields that line the western entry to Halji. The trail then drops back to the Takche Chu and crosses a bridge at 3710m and brings you to the south side of the river.

After about two hours you reach a suspension bridge and return to the north side of the river. After another hour you reach a large flat area almost directly opposite the village gompa, which is spectacularly perched on the other side of the narrow valley. You can camp here, savouring the outstanding views south to the Phupharka Hi-

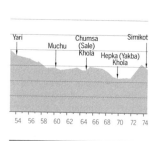

mal and northwards to a 6300m spike peak that dominates the backdrop of Til.

To reach the village of Til (3700m), climb about 20 minutes above the campsite, passing the trail to Hilsa on your left until you cross a small wooden bridge. The gompa is located about another 30 minutes northeast of the village along a narrow trail.

Day 11: Til to Manepene

8 HOURS / 870M ASCENT / 580M DESCENT

On the map the distance between Til and Manepene looks pitifully short, but on the ground the convoluted trail weaves its way through ravines and up and down trails etched into steep slopes. Give yourself plenty of time today and stock up on water and food before you leave Til.

Leaving the camp, the trail climbs steadily and after half an hour you can see on the left a helicopter pad. Three hours from Til is a tiny stream and a collection of small flat platforms that can be used as a campsite. Note that there is another water source about four hours from Til and again in Manepene.

From the small perched campsite a stiff 200m climb up a stark hillside gets you to the 4300m **Lamka Lagna**. From here you plunge down a steep stone pinnacle on a well-formed track. Soon afterwards you climb again to just over 4000m for views southeast of the Humla Karnali River carving its way towards Muchu.

The campsite of **Manepene** (3970m) is named after a giant stone that is carved (now rather faintly) with the mantra *'om mani padme hum'*. It is not an ideal site because the only flat spaces are deep in animal droppings.

Day 12: Manepene to Hilsa

4 HOURS / 300M ASCENT / 400M DESCENT

The trail continues through ravines, staying above a major landslide, from where you will catch your first views of the imposing Nara La trail on your left. The northern reaches of the Simikot–Hilsa road can be seen snaking their way up the stark hillside. The expanse of the Tibetan plateau stretches out to the north and a tiny pocket of barley fields identifies Sher (on the Tibetan side) and the Tibetan border far below.

The village of **Hilsa** (3720m) is a depressing collection of grey buildings located on windy flats across the suspension bridge spanning the Humla Karnali River that flows into Nepal from Tibet. As you round the final ridge do not stay on the main trail unless you are heading for Kailash. Drop instead onto a rough trail down to the bridge. A couple of white road markers to the right mark the official Chinese border. Be careful because sometimes Hilsa porters insist that you unload your animals and carry your gear across the bridge for an exorbitant price. Insist you have not come from Tibet and have been trekking solely within Nepal's borders using Humla locals to transport your goods.

Hilsa has a few shops stocked with Chinese goods. There are a couple of small lodges and flat spaces to camp. There is a

---

LIMI BOWLS

The people of Limi make wooden bowls (*phuru*) from pine, birch and maple trees that grow on the south side of the river. The bowls are made using simple foot-powered lathes made from wood and drive belts made out of leather. Ever-resourceful, many bowl makers still use sand and small stones glued to leather instead of commercial sandpaper to smooth the wooden surfaces. You will probably see piles of these bowls drying in the sun.

Surprisingly, Limi dominates the supply of wooden bowls to Tibet. High-quality bowls are made from the burls of maple trees. The scarcity of these burls in Limi has required people to find alternative sources of supply from Kumaon in northern India, yet the bowls are still manufactured in Limi. Even in Lhasa, wooden bowls from Limi are prized over those made elsewhere. Locals are happy to sell their bowls, which can range from Rs 500 to Rs 5000 depending on what wood is used and whether or not it is adorned with silver.

cooking shelter for hire, but for the most part this is a miserable, windy place littered with glass. As a border town, Hilsa sees a steady stream of Humli people bringing wood into Tibet and returning with alcohol, clothing, consumer goods, cement and fuel. It is also the last police post in Nepal and you must have your permits checked here. If you are not carrying your passport with you, you'll need at least a photocopy of the photo and visa pages to show here.

Day 13: Hilsa to Palbang

7–8 HOURS / 800M ASCENT / 1200M DESCENT

Leaving Hilsa, avoid the road by taking a trail that follows the river and then climbs steeply up on loose stones towards **Ranipa-uwa** (4370m), another flattish area littered with broken glass. This is a great spot to look back towards Tibet and catch your breath. Follow the gently angled road or brace yourself for a nail-biting ascent of some of the narrowest paths in Nepal, as the trail follows the face of this mountainside. The best route changes regularly so follow the lead of locals. Be watchful for yaks coming towards you carrying wood, and plan for a route to get out of their way in good time.

The **Nara La** (4580m) takes about four to five hours to summit. Past the small lake on the top is a giant cairn often blasted by a strong wind that signals your return to the fertile Humla Karnali Valley. The road continues down the other side of the pass and offers an uninspired hour-long descent to **Sipsip** (4330m) where there is water.

To your right is **Yari** (3670m), a compact settlement of stone houses below the trail. **Yangser Gompa** is 6km west of Yari, though most people just keep going at this point. From Sipsip it takes about two hours to reach an often-windy camp above the tea-shop at **Palbang** (Torea; 3380m).

Day 14: Palbang to Muchu

4 HOURS / 50M ASCENT / 480M DESCENT

This is an easy day of mostly downhill that finishes at a pleasant camp next to the Humla Karnali River. You will start meeting trekking groups travelling to Tibet via Hilsa, although this itinerary is designed to avoid – for the most part – camping in the same places used on a standard Kailash trek.

From Palbang the trail climbs gently through juniper trees to a cairn at 3310m and then drops gradually to the top of a steep rock-filled gully (3270m). This trail delivers you into **Tumkot** (3000m) after about four hours. It's a regular camping spot for Kailash-bound groups and enterprising locals will usually place a bucket of river-water-cooled beer and soft drinks in front of you for temptation. The trail leads through orchards until about two hours later you eventually spot **Muchu** (2920m), a village with a police post and government hospital. Check in with the police and continue through the village. Around 15 minutes later you will spot a large flat area on the south side of the river below you: a perfect campsite at 2800m.

Day 15: Muchu to Chumsa Khola

5–6 HOURS / 200M ASCENT / 260M DESCENT

This is one of the most beautiful days on the trail, following the brilliant blue waters of the Humla Karnali. From the campsite, cross the bridge and follow a lower trail dropping back to the river. The higher trail will take you over the **Illing Lagna** (3500m) – a lookout towards Yari. The lower trail is easier and clearly marked. After 2½ hours you reach a

MT KAILASH EXTENSION

A pilgrimage to sacred Mt Kailash in western Tibet's Ngari region is an interesting add-on to a Limi Valley trek. Opened to foreign trekkers since 1993, the cross-border trip is essentially a seven-day extension from Hilsa. The normal itinerary is to drive from Sher to Darchen via Khojarnath and an overnight in the trading town of Purang (Taklakot). The actual kora (circumambulation) is a three- or four-day trek, crossing the 5630m Drolma La. It's a day's drive back to Sher. It's also worth adding some time to take in sacred Lake Manasarovar.

You'll need a reliable Nepali agent with good Chinese connections to arrange transport from the Chinese border to Darchen, as well as a specially endorsed Chinese visa. Your Nepali trekking agent will arrange two Nepali trekking permits with dates a week apart, one for the trip to the border and the other for the return. You will also need a double-entry Nepali visa. It's a complicated and expensive add-on, so it makes sense to join an organised group for this trip of a lifetime.

FAR WESTERN NEPAL

The Tourism Development Society, based in Dhangadhi, has worked with local people in Nepal's far west to develop several trekking and cultural itineraries. For more information on the region and the following treks see their website www.farwestnepal.org.

A six- to seven-day trek into **Khaptad National Park** (entry permit Rs 1000) starts from the town of Silgadhi, an eight-hour drive from Dhangadhi airport (daily flights from Kathmandu are US$216). The park features swaths of oak and pine forests, undulating grasslands and wildflower-carpeted meadows. The national park was declared in 1984 and was named after a Hindu holy man, Khaptad Baba. Khaptad Baba Ashram, near the park headquarters, is a focal point of the park, attracting Shiva-worshipping pilgrims. Another option sure to gain popularity is the trek from Rara Lake to Khaptad National Park (also possible in the reverse direction) over eight to 10 days. Nepa Maps produces a 1:50,000 *Rara to Khaptad* map of the trail, which is available in Kathmandu's numerous map shops.

Even more remote is the **Api Nampa Conservation Area** (entry permit Rs 1000, established 2010) where the treks, linked to ancient pilgrimage routes to Mt Kailash in Tibet, are relatively undeveloped. You will need to employ local guides and be self-sufficient in supplies and camping equipment.

fast-flowing stream just before **Yangar**, a settlement surrounded by sprawling fields. The trail winds its way through the town and locals will point you in the right direction if you take a wrong turn. About 40 minutes and a few minor ups and downs later you reach **Yalbang** (2890m), a beautifully situated village.

Yalbang shares a hydroelectric power supply with its neighbour Yangar. For an interesting side trip, follow the signs to the **Namka Khyung Dzong Gompa**, a 20-minute climb above the trail. This Nyingma gompa is about 60 years old and has an active monastic community.

After 1½ hours descending from Yalbang through the forest you'll get to a suspension bridge (2830m) across the Chumsa (Sale) Khola and a large flat expanse that you cross before climbing to a beautiful campsite.

Day 16: Chumsa Khola to Dharapuri

5–6 HOURS / 230M ASCENT / 740M DESCENT

You have come full circle. A short haul to 2990m returns you to the trail junction and pass where you turned to head towards the Nyalu Lagna two weeks ago. You are back in familiar territory trekking through the fields below Kermi and down to Dharapuri and the familiar riverside campsite.

Day 17: Dharapuri to Simikot

6 HOURS / 980M ASCENT / 270M DESCENT

Take the low main route to Masigaon and take a deep breath before tackling the 900m

grind to the top of the hill overlooking Simikot. Drop 300m into town and check in with the airline office as soon as you arrive to reconfirm your flight to Nepalganj and onward connection to Kathmandu.

OTHER TREKS

The following routes are expected to be open as normal following the 2015 earthquakes, but as a precaution, seek local advice on the status of trails and infrastructure before starting a trek in these areas.

Shey Gompa to Jomsom

It's a long (12 days), hard, remote trek from Shey Gompa to Jomsom, across the roof of Nepal. There are few villages, no lodges or telephones and almost no food available. You will need to go with an experienced trekking company and a Tibetan-speaking guide is recommended. Note that you'll be spending 15 days in the restricted area at a permit cost of US$750 (this include three days minimum from Phoksumdo to Shey Gompa).

The trek starts by trekking east from Shey Gompa. Turn north (straight ahead goes to Do Tarap) and cross the gentle 5010m Shey La (Se La or Ge La). Much of the trek over the next 11 days is over 4000m in extremely remote and sparsely populated country. On the penultimate day you descend into the Kali Gandaki Valley, with fine views of Mustang, to the large village of Dhagarjun (3290m), three hours from Jomsom (2670m). A steep alternative trail leads down to Kagbeni.

Around Dhaulagiri

The long (16 days), difficult trek around Dhaulagiri (8167m) starts from Beni on the Kali Gandaki. The first few days follow the Beni to Dolpo trek (p269) along the Myagdi Khola, before swinging north on a tiny trail through dense forests into the high country at Italian Camp at around 3650m. Much of the next week is on snow and glaciers above 4500m and subject to avalanches as it crosses the Chhonbarang Glacier to French Col (5240m), traverses the head of Hidden Valley and crosses the 5250m Dhampus pass. The views of the Dhaulagiri peaks are awesome, from the glacier and from Dhampus Pass. You and your porters need to be well acclimatised and very well equipped to deal with several nights above 5000m.

The trek ends with a steep descent to Marpha and a return to Pokhara, either via the Kali Gandaki Valley or a flight from Jomsom. Permits required for this trek include the Rs 2000 ACAP permit and a TIMS card.

Guerrilla Trek

An interesting addition to the list of trekking possibilities is this trail through erstwhile Maoist strongholds promoted by the communist-led government using terms such as 'war tourism'. The trail starts in Beni and follows the first seven days of the Beni to Dolpo trek (p269). Beyond Tatopani the trail makes a tight turn to the left before meandering through villages that were the backbone of the rebellion – Maikot, Taka and Thawang – and finishing at the roadhead of Sulichaur. Accommodation is in homestays, lodges and/or camping. You will need a TIMS card and you will have to pay the Rs 3000 fee to enter the Dhorpatan Hunting Reserve. Nepa Maps produces the 1:150,000 *Guerrilla Trek* map; it's available in Kathmandu map shops.

Saipal Base Camp Trek

This is an adventurous but extremely rewarding off-the-beaten-track trek to the base camp of western Nepal's second-highest mountain, stunning Mt Saipal (7031m). It is best trekked between mid-October and November, after the harvest has cleared fields to camp on.

It's logistically complex: you need to bring your own porters on this trek as locals in this rarely visited region are unfamiliar with foreign trekking routines. A 24-day itinerary runs from Silgadhi (a sealed road reaches Silgadhi from Dhangadhi) through Khaptad National Park to reach the Seti River Valley and the Bajhang district capital of Chainpur, from where you continue on to Saipal Base Camp. There are flights out of Chainpur at the end of the trek. If you are flying in and out of Chainpur, budget three weeks. You should send your porters ahead by bus; the fair-weather road stops at Tamail Bazaar, about two hours from Chainpur.

TOWNS & FACILITIES

Most trailheads for treks in Western Nepal ecaped serious damage in the earthquakes in 2015.

Nepalganj

☎ 081 / ELEV 160M

Nepalganj is the largest town in western Nepal and a transport hub for flights and buses throughout western Nepal. It is in the Terai just 6km from the Indian border, and so is oppressively hot for much of the year. If you are flying to one of the remote airstrips in western Nepal, you'll have to spend a night in Nepalganj.

Nabil Bank (⊙10am-4.30pm Sun-Thu, 10am-2.30pm Fri) offers foreign exchange and a 24-hour ATM.

🛏 Sleeping

Traveller's Village GUESTHOUSE $$
(✆081-550329; travil@wlink.com.np; Surkhet Rd; s/d US$25/35; ✳@🛜) The hotel of choice for UN and NGO workers, Traveller's Village is run by a welcoming American lady (Candy) who's lived here for more than 20 years. Rooms are cosy and spotless, with air-con, hot water and TV. Reservations are absolutely essential.

Kitchen Hut HOTEL $$
(✆081-551231; www.kitchenhut.com.np; Surkhet Rd; s/d Rs 2000/2500; ✳@🛜) This modern business hotel, situated about 3km northeast of Birendra Chowk, boasts spacious tiled rooms with flat-screen TVs. Tasty meals are served in the Tripti restaurant. Free pick-up from airport and bus station is on offer.

Hotel Sneha
HOTEL **$$**

(✆ 081-520119; hotel@sneha.wlink.com.np; Surkhet Rd; s/d/ste US$40/50/60; ❄ 🛜 🏊) This old-fashioned conference hotel is set in sprawling grounds. The spacious rooms are set around a courtyard of royal palms and boast soft mattresses and modern amenities. The attached casino doesn't improve the atmosphere.

ℹ️ Getting There & Away

Buddha Air (✆ 081-525745; www.buddhaair. com) and **Yeti Airlines** (✆ 081-526556; www. yetiairlines.com) operate two or three daily flights each between Kathmandu and Nepalganj (US$183). **Nepal Airlines** (www.nepalairlines. com.np) and **Tara Air** (www.taraair.com; a division of Yeti Airlines) have flights to Jumla (US$90) and offer flights to Juphal/Dolpo (US$167). Nepal Airlines offers scheduled flights to Simikot (US$150) and there are sometimes flights with Tara. Booking priority on these feeder flights is given to clients flying from Kathmandu. Delays and cancellations are common due to poor weather, especially in the monsoon.

Jumla, Dolpo and Simikot flights are scheduled to depart at dawn. Make sure you book your taxi the night before. Beware of baggage charges on Jumla and Dolpo flights. The free allowance is a slim 15kg, plus 5kg hand luggage. The rate for excess baggage from Nepalganj to Jumla is Rs 90 per kilogram. Many cargo charter flights are operated by businesspeople sending rice and other goods; if you have trouble sending all your gear, you may be able to ship it as freight on one of these flights.

Nepalganj can also be reached by road. Day/night buses from Kathmandu charge Rs 1000/1200 (12 hours). Buses back to Kathmandu (and Pokhara) leave early in the morning or in the afternoon.

Jumla

✆ 087 / ELEV 2370M

Jumla, on the banks of the Tila Khola, is the gateway to the wild northwest and one of the highest rice-growing areas in the world. The unique local red rice is more tasty than white rice but scorned by most Nepalis.

Jumla Bazaar has a small supply of canned goods, jam and other packaged items, but you probably will not find speciality foods such as muesli.

🛏️ Sleeping

Kanjirowa Hotel
HOTEL **$**

(✆ 9741111733; r Rs 1500-2000; 🛜) This recently constructed stone hotel near the airport

has comfortable, Tibetan-decorated rooms and an excellent restaurant.

Hotel Snowland
HOTEL **$**

(✆ 087-520188; r from Rs 800; 🛜) A good choice near the bazaar is this rickety wooden hotel, a 15-minute walk from the airport. Look out for the sign in the bazaar directing you down a small side street.

ℹ️ Information

Rural Community Development Service (RCDS; ✆ 087-520227) This group is involved in promoting tourism and can often find a guide and porters, along with information on the area.

ℹ️ Getting There & Away

As with most destinations in western Nepal, to get to Jumla you must fly to Nepalganj (US$183), spend a night and then take a 35-minute flight to Jumla (US$90). Jumla Bazaar is a 10-minute walk from the airport.

Dunai

✆ 087 / ELEV 2030M

As the capital of Dolpa district, Dunai is the logistical base for treks to the Tarap Valley, Phoksumdo Lake and inner Dolpo. It's a pleasant town with well-stocked shops. The main facilities are at the eastern end of the village. The small gompa is across the river from the Blue Sheep Trekkers Inn.

The **Dolpa Tourism Festival** (www.dolpafestival.org) takes place in September, bringing cultural shows and lots of traditional dance and food. Flights and accommodation can be tight at this time.

CG Trekking Store
TREKKING

(✆ 087-550165; www.cgtrekkingstore.com) Sells trekking foods and can put you in touch with a porter or guide.

🛏️ Sleeping

Blue Sheep Trekkers Inn
HOTEL **$**

(✆ 087-550119, 9848 303676; r from Rs 600; @) This friendly place at the southeastern end of town is your best bet, with private rooms, clean bathrooms, a camping area and intermittent internet access.

ℹ️ Getting There & Away

The airport for the Dolpo region is in Juphal village, on a hill about three hours' walk from the main town of Dunai. Tara Air and Nepal Airlines run scheduled flights from Nepalganj (US$167) and charter flights by both plane and helicopter carry food into the region. Helicopters land at the western end of Dunai town, whereas all planes arrive at Juphal airport.

Catching a flight to Juphal at short notice can be difficult because of heavy passenger and cargo traffic, but flying out is much easier, even without advance planning, because the empty cargo charters carry passengers on the return trip. It's best to build in a buffer of a couple of days at the end of any Dolpo trek.

Cargo helicopters arrive at short notice and fly to either Surkhet or Pokhara (from US$180 for foreigners). From Surkhet it's a four-hour drive to Nepalganj.

Beni

✈ 069 / ELEV 830M

Beni is a bustling market town on a plateau above the junction of the Kali Gandaki and Myagdi rivers. Long an important staging post, the village has lost much of its importance with the arrival of the new road. There was some damage here in the 2015 earthquakes but reconstruction is underway.

The **Machhapuchare Bank** (✆069-520964; ⊙10am-3pm Sun-Thu, 10am-1pm Fri) changes cash and travellers cheques for a Rs 200 commission.

Opposite the police post at the south end of town is a lovely temple overgrown by a tree, like the temples of Angkor Wat in Cambodia.

🛏 Sleeping & Eating

If the better Hotel Yeti is full, try the **Hotel Namaste** (✆069-520093; r with/without bathroom Rs 500/400) or **Hotel Dolphin** (✆069-520107; r from Rs 500), both of which have restaurants.

Hotel Yeti   HOTEL **$**
(✆069-520142; www.hotelyeti.com; r with/without bathroom Rs 800/500; 🕸) This is the best place to stay and is down an alley by the Machhapuchare Bank. It offers a pleasant restaurant and owner Bimala Gauchan can help arrange a guide and/or porter.

ⓘ Getting There & Away

Buses and minibuses run every hour or so to Pokhara's Baglung bus station (Rs 250, four hours). A taxi to/from Pokhara costs around Rs 4000 and takes three hours. There are also buses north to Tatopani (Rs 600) and Jomsom (Rs 1600). Buses and taxis depart from the north end of town.

Simikot

✈ 087 / ELEV 2960M

Simikot is the headquarters of Nepal's most remote district, Humla. It's spectacularly situated on a ridge high above the Humla Karnali and encircled by snow-covered ridges.

The main bazaar is just north of the gravel airstrip and boasts shops with basic supplies that are either flown in or carried by animals from Tibet. Government offices, shops and airline offices line the trail that leads from the bazaar to the airport terminal. The older and newer parts of Simikot are clearly distinguishable from a southern vantage point near the Citta hospital.

There was some earthquake damage in Humla so check the current status of trails and infrastructure before trekking on from Simikot.

🛏 Sleeping & Eating

The **Nepal Trust** (✆in Kathmandu 01-4372354; www.nepaltrust.org) has a guesthouse close to the airport.

Sun Valley Resort   HOTEL **$$$**
(✆087-680171, in Kathmandiu 01-4432190; www.sunvalleyresort.net; r US$123) An impressive stone building houses this upmarket resort spectacularly located on the hillside below the trail leaving Simikot.

🔒 Shopping

Kerosene can be purchased in Simikot, but arrange this in advance as there are often shortages. Bring all your own food, especially fresh produce and rice, because there is a chronic shortage in Humla. A few small shops in the bazaar sell biscuits, instant noodles and basic staples.

ⓘ Getting There & Away

There is no direct air service from Kathmandu to Simikot. You must first fly to Nepalganj (US$183) on the southern border of Nepal, spend the night and take an early-morning flight to Simikot (US$150). Allow at least three days in your itinerary for weather-related flight delays in and out of Simikot.

Simikot is serviced by Tara Air and Nepal Airlines. The 50-minute, 218km flight traverses almost the entire width of western Nepal, affording views of 7031m Saipal Himal just before you touch down on the spectacularly situated airstrip.

Understand Nepal

Nepal Today

Over the last few decades, Nepal has endured economic hardship, a Maoist uprising that turned into a civil war, the collapse of a centuries-old monarchy, and the creation of a democratic federal republic. However, Nepal's greatest crisis of modern times was a result of geology rather than politics; the massive earthquakes that hit Nepal on 25 April and 12 May 2015 killed more than 8500 people, causing devastation across central parts of the country.

Best in Print

Arresting God in Kathmandu (Samrat Upadhyay) Nine short stories from the first Nepali writer to be published in English.

Snake Lake (Jeff Greenwald) Memoir of family loss set against Nepal's political revolution.

Little Princes (Conor Grennan) Moving and inspiring account of volunteering in a Nepali orphanage.

While the Gods Were Sleeping (Elizabeth Enslin) Part memoir, part-anthropological account of the author's time living as a wife in a Brahman family in western Nepal.

Kathmandu (Thomas Bell) Impressionistic historical portrait of Kathmandu from the British journalist, published in India and available in Kathmandu.

Best in Film

Himalaya (1999; Eric Valli) Stunningly shot in Dolpo; also released as *Caravan*.

Everest (1998; David Breashears) Imax film shot during the disastrous 1997 climbing season.

Destruction and Reconstruction

The tremors that shook the Kathmandu Valley in April and May 2015 saw destruction on a level that had not been seen for almost a century. Temples and palaces crumbled to dust, houses toppled, roads buckled and landslides and avalanches wiped whole villages off the map. The economic cost of the disaster has been estimated at US$10 billion, nearly half of Nepal's gross domestic product, but the human cost is even more tragic; thousands of families lost loved ones and hundreds of thousands were left homeless.

Nepal's greatest challenge over the coming years will be to rebuild lives and livelihoods. Across the country, thousands of homes and businesses need to be stabilised and repaired, and many more homes need to be built to accommodate the homeless. The tourist industry, which employs 4% of the population but indirectly supports millions more, was particularly badly hit following the disaster and bookings have collapsed in many areas. With tourism contributing nearly 10% of GDP, this is income that Nepal can ill afford to lose.

Money has flooded into Nepal from international donors since the disaster, but the country has a long way to go to raise the estimated US$6.7 billion needed for reconstruction. Nepal's recovery will depend on the resilience of its people through lean years to come, as well as the goodwill of foreign governments and the willingness of foreign travellers to look beyond the tragedy and return to Nepal's hotels, restaurants and trekking lodges.

Recovering From War

Against this backdrop, the ordinary struggles of day to day politics seem somehow less important, but Nepal is still struggling with the legacy of a decade of armed conflict. Inflation is rampant, and crumbling infrastructure, held back by years of under-investment, makes daily life a struggle for most Nepalis. Kathmandu's population, in particular, boomed during the civil war and the city is now close to breaking point, with daily electricity shortages a crippling fact of life.

Politically speaking, disappointingly little has been achieved since the end of the war. Years of deadlock and wrangling between Communist and Congress parties has resulted in the fall of six governments in six years. The political infighting has repeatedly delayed the writing of a new constitution, to the growing frustration of many Nepalis.

Since the end of the civil war the Maoists have seen a spectacular fall from grace, from winning the national election in 2008 to coming a dismal third in 2013. As former fighters start to lose political influence and contentious issues such as immunity from crimes committed during the civil war come to a head, there is always the danger that Nepali politics will return to the days of strikes and political violence.

The wounds of the People's War will doubtless take a long time to heal. Over 1000 Nepalis remain unaccounted for, victims of political 'disappearance' or simple murder, and finding justice for these crimes may prove elusive.

Economic Ups And Downs

Despite the political impasse there are signs of life in Nepal's economy. A recent spate of multibillion dollar contracts with both China and India should see some huge hydroelectric and road building projects over the coming years. India's role in developing Nepal's rivers and China's influence on Nepal's Tibetan refugee community remain hot topics as Nepal tries to juggle influences from its giant neighbours.

The Chinese presence in Nepal in particular is becoming pronounced. As road, air and eventually even train links bridge the Himalaya, Chinese tourists are becoming an essential part of the Nepali economy. Large swathes of Thamel are now devoted exclusively to Chinese tourists and Nepal's ever-adaptable guides and touts are rapidly learning the new language.

Tourism remains essential to Nepal's economy, employing around one million people directly or indirectly, and things are once again booming. Hotels and restaurants are crammed to capacity and funds are being poured into infrastructure and hotel construction.

Twin tragedies shook the tourism industry in 2014. In April 16 Sherpas were killed on the Khumbu icefall, shutting down Everest climbing for a season as Sherpa families sought compensation in a labour dispute with the government. Just six months later a blizzard in central Nepal killed 43 trekkers and guides in the Annapurna region, turning a spotlight on mountain safety and renewing calls for tighter controls on Nepal's trekking industry.

A long-term problem for Nepal is the large numbers of Nepalis heading abroad every year in the search for work and opportunities. Remittances remain the number one source of foreign currency for Nepal, dwarfing tourism, but halting the brain drain is essential to the country's future.

POPULATION: 31 MILLION (2014 ESTIMATE)

AREA: **147,181 SQ KM**

LIFE EXPECTANCY: **67 YEARS**

ADULT LITERACY RATE: **57%**

GROSS NATIONAL INCOME: **US$730 PER CAPITA**

AVERAGE AGE: **23 YEARS**

if Nepal were 100 people

16 would be Chhetri   7 would be Tharu
13 would be Brahman-Hill   57 Tamang, Newar
7 would be Magar   & Other Groups

belief systems
(% of population)

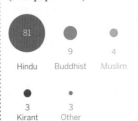

| 81 | 9 | 4 |
| Hindu | Buddhist | Muslim |

| 3 | 3 |
| Kirant | Other |

population per sq km

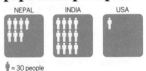

NEPAL   INDIA   USA

≈ 30 people

History of Trekking

Nepal's trekking trails have evolved from a dense network of Himalayan trade routes, pilgrim paths and herder's tracks, trod for generations by traders, porters, government officials and pilgrims, as well as countless pioneering trekkers and mountaineers. Walking paths are central to the cultural history of the Himalaya and they remain vital today, as mountain people travel on foot for weddings, funerals, festivals, school or medical care. Trek in Nepal and you are walking in the footprints of the past.

Early Explorers

Nepal's mountain trails have been used for centuries by Himalayan traders, porters, migrating peoples and herders. Salt traders would crisscross the high passes from Tibet to swap their wool and yak butter for rice and other goods from lowland India, while in their tracks would come dreadlocked Hindu pilgrims headed to sacred mountain lakes or Buddhists walking to the holy sights of Kailash or Lhasa.

Nepal was largely closed to the outside world until the 1950s, so the only foreigners who visited the hills of the country were illegal visitors such as Japanese explorer Ekai Kawaguchi and secret map makers, called 'pundits', who were sent into Nepal by the Survey of India.

The Age of Conquest

In 1949 Nepal opened its frontiers to the outside world. Within eight years, 10 of the 14 peaks over 8000m had been climbed, largely by huge military-style Swiss, British and French expeditions, in what is considered the golden age of Himalayan climbing.

Annapurna (8091m) was the first to be climbed in 1950, followed by Tenzing Norgay and Edmund Hillary's iconic conquest of Everest (8848m) in 1953. Soon afterwards came Cho Oyu in 1954, Kangchenjun-

---

TREKKING LITERATURE

The Snow Leopard (Peter Matthiessen) Classic and profound account of a trek to Dolpo; as much an inner journey as an external trek.

Annapurna (Maurice Herzog) Best-selling mountaineering classic from 1950, describing the first ever ascent of an 8000m peak and the harrowing descent.

Into Thin Air (Jon Krakauer) Emotionally gripping story of the 1996 Everest disaster.

The Ascent of Rum Doodle (WE Bowman) Highly enjoyable spoof of all those serious mountaineering tomes. The cast of characters includes Pong, the expedition's disastrous 'Yogistani' cook.

Nepal Himalaya (WH Tilman) Delightful British wit from the 1950s trekking pioneer, touching on Langtang, the Annapurna Circuit and the Everest region.

Himalayan Pilgrimage (David Snellgrove) Timeless account of the Tibetan scholar's epic 1956 exploration of the Tibetan areas between Dolpo and Manaslu, including Mustang, Nar-Phu and Manang.

293

ga and Makalu in 1955, Manslu and Lhotse in 1956, and Dhaulagiri in 1959. By 1964 all the major Himalayan giants had been climbed.

Trekking in Nepal really took off with the first expeditions to the base of Mt Everest: an American led expedition in 1950 and a British one in 1951. Several of today's trekking routes still follow the trails pioneered by these tweed-clad expeditions.

The Birth of the Trekking Industry

The first trekker in Nepal was Bill Tilman, who wrangled permission from the king in 1949 to make several treks, including around the Kali Gandaki, Helambu and Everest.

The godfather of Nepal tourism was Boris Lissannivich, an emigre Russian ballet dancer and club owner, who accepted King Tribuhvan's invitation to set up Nepal's first ever hotel. The Royal Hotel and its famous Yak & Yeti bar became the meeting place for climbers and trekkers from the 1950s until 1971, when the hotel was closed.

Colonel James OM Roberts was the first person to realise that trekking would appeal to tourists. 'Jimmy' Roberts had spent years in Nepal attached to the British residency and accompanied Tilman on his first trek. In 1965 he took a group of ladies to the Khumbu region and founded Mountain Travel, the first of Nepal's trekking companies and the inspiration for the adventure travel industry. The rest is history.

Trekking Today

With over 650 registered trekking companies, trekking has become a vital part of Nepal's economy. The Khumbu region around Everest is the richest district in Nepal, with locals enjoying twice the average income of Kathmandu. Change has come quickly since the first airstrips were built in the region in the 1960s. As lodge owners have become wealthy, many families have moved from the mountains to the cities.

The Maoist uprising in the 2000s affected trekking, as large parts of remoter Nepal became off-limits to trekkers. Maoist groups often forced trekkers to make 'donations'. Today the 'Guerilla Trek' through central-western Nepal gets its inspiration from this dark period in Nepal's recent history.

Nepal's catastrophic earthquake of 2015 topped off a terrible year, in which fatal blizzards killed trekkers in the Annapurna region and a record number of Sherpas died on Everest. The quake was felt especially keenly in the Langtang, Helambu and lower Manaslu regions, where many trekking lodges and even entire villages were destroyed. It will take time for the Langtang region in particular to recover from the disaster.

The longest-lasting change to trek routes comes from road construction, from both inside Nepal and neighbouring Tibet. As roads inch further into the Mustang, Tsum and Humla regions some trek routes will die and new ones will appear. As they have done for the last 50 years.

History of Nepal

Squeezed between the Tibetan plateau and the plains of the subcontinent – the modern-day giants of China and India – Nepal has long prospered from its location as a resting place for mountain traders, travellers and pilgrims. An ethnic melting pot, it has bridged cultures and absorbed elements of its neighbours, yet has retained a unique character. Despite ancient roots, the modern state of Nepal emerged only in the 18th century and is still forging itself as a modern nation state.

The Kiratis & Buddhist Beginnings

Nepal's recorded history emerges from the fog of antiquity with the Hindu Kiratis. Arriving from the east around the 7th or 8th century BC, these Mongoloid people are the earliest known rulers of the Kathmandu Valley. King Yalambar, the first of their 29 kings, is mentioned in the Mahabharata, the Hindu epic, but little more is known about the Kiratis.

References for most things in Nepal are notoriously inconsistent. Spellings, statistics, historical dates and temple names always have several variants. We use the most commonly agreed options, with alternative names in brackets.

In the 6th century BC, Prince Siddhartha Gautama was born into the Sakya royal family of Kapilavastu, near Lumbini, later embarking on a path of meditation and thought that led him to enlightenment as the Buddha, or 'Enlightened One'. The religion that grew up around him continues to shape the face of Asia.

Around the 3rd century BC, the great Indian Buddhist emperor Ashoka visited Lumbini and erected a pillar at the birthplace of the Buddha. Popular legend recounts how he then visited the Kathmandu Valley and erected four stupas around Patan (these still exist), but there is no evidence that he actually made it there in person. Either way, his Mauryan empire (321–184 BC) played a major role in popularising Buddhism in the region, a role continued by the north Indian Buddhist Kushan empire, which spanned the 1st to 3rd centuries AD.

Over the centuries the resurgent faith of Hinduism came to eclipse Buddhism across the entire subcontinent. By the time the Chinese Buddhist pilgrims Fa Xian (Fa Hsien) and Xuan Zang (Hsuan Tsang) passed through the region in the 5th and 7th centuries the site of Lumbini was already in ruins.

TIMELINE	60 million BC	100,000 BC	c 563 BC
	The Himalaya rise as the Indo-Australian tectonic plate crashes into the Eurasian plate. The Tethys Sea is pushed up, resulting in sea shells atop Mt Everest and fossilised ammonites in the Kali Gandaki Valley.	Kathmandu Valley is created as a former lake bed dries. Legend relates how the Buddhist Bodhisattva Manjushri created the valley by cutting the Chobar Gorge and draining the lake's waters.	Siddhartha Gautama is born in Lumbini into royalty and lives as both prince and ascetic in Nepal before gaining enlightenment, as the Buddha, under a Bodhi (pipal) tree.

Licchavis, Thakuris, then Darkness

Hinduism reasserted itself in Nepal with the arrival from northern India of the Licchavis. In AD 300 they overthrew the Kiratis, who resettled in the east to become the ancestors of today's Rai and Limbu people.

Between the 4th and 9th centuries the Licchavis ushered in a golden age of cultural brilliance. Their strategic position allowed them to prosper from trade between India and China. The chaitya (a style of stupa) and monuments of this era can still be seen at the Changu Narayan Temple, north of Bhaktapur, and in the backstreets of Kathmandu's old town. It's believed that the original stupas at Chabahil, Bodhnath and Swayambhunath date from the Licchavi era.

Amsuvarman, the first Thakuri king, came to power in 602, succeeding his Licchavi father-in-law. He consolidated his power to the north and south by marrying his sister to an Indian prince and his daughter Bhrikuti to the great Tibetan king Songsten Gampo. Together with the Tibetan king's Chinese wife Wencheng, Bhrikuti managed to convert the Tibetan king to Buddhism around 640, profoundly changing the face of both Tibet and the Himalaya. As Buddhism lost ground in India, Buddhism's key texts and concepts would eventually return to Nepal from Tibet across the high Himalayan passes.

From the late 7th century until the 13th century, Nepal slipped into its 'dark ages', of which little is known. Tibet invaded in 705 and Kashmir invaded in 782. The Kathmandu Valley's strategic location and fertile soil, however, ensured the kingdom's growth and survival. King Gunakamadeva is credited with founding Kantipur, today's Kathmandu, around the 10th century.

The Golden Age of the Mallas

The first of the Malla (literally 'wrestlers' in Sanskrit) kings came to power in the Kathmandu Valley around 1200, after being exiled from India. This period was a golden one that stretched over 550 years, though it was peppered with fighting over the valuable trade routes to Tibet.

The first Malla rulers had to cope with several disasters. A huge earthquake in 1255 killed around one-third of Nepal's population. A devastating Muslim invasion by Sultan Shams-ud-din of Bengal less than a century later left hundreds of smouldering and plundered Hindu and Buddhist shrines in its wake, though the invasion did not leave a lasting cultural effect (unlike the invasion of the Kashmir Valley, which remains Muslim to this day). In India the damage was more widespread and many Hindus were driven into the hills and mountains of Nepal, where they established small Rajput principalities.

Travellers can visit the archaeological site of Kapilavastu, at Tilaurakot, where Siddhartha Gautama (the Buddha) lived for the first 29 years of his life.

In 2013 archaeologists unearthed a sixth-century BC shrine underneath Lumbini's Maya Devi shrine, making this the earliest Buddhist shrine ever uncovered. Within the shrine were the remains of a tree, possibly the tree that Maya held onto when giving birth to Siddhartha (the Buddha).

c 250 BC	57 BC	AD 464	629
Mauryan Emperor Ashoka (r 268–231 BC) visits Lumbini, embraces Buddhism and reputedly builds four stupas on the outskirts of Patan, ushering in a golden age for Buddhism.	Nepal's official Vikram (Bikram) Samwat calendar starts, in spring. Thus to Nepalis the year 2016 is 2073.	Nepal's earliest surviving inscription is carved into the beautiful Changu Narayan Temple in the Kathmandu Valley on the orders of King Manadeva.	The Chinese Buddhist pilgrim Xuan Zang (Hsuan Tsang) visits Lumbini and describes the Ashoka pillar marking the Buddha's birthplace. His text helps archaeologists relocate and excavate the lost site in 1895.

Apart from this, the earlier Malla years (1220–1482) were largely stable, reaching a high point under the third Malla dynasty of Jayasthithi Malla (r 1382–95), who united the valley and codified its laws, including the caste system.

After the death of Jayasthithi Malla's grandson Yaksha Malla in 1482, the Kathmandu Valley was divided up among his sons into the three kingdoms of Bhaktapur (Bhadgaon), Kathmandu (Kantipur) and Patan (Lalitpur). The rest of what we today call Nepal consisted of a fragmented patchwork of almost 50 independent states, stretching from Palpa and Jumla in the west to the semi-independent states of Banepa and Pharping, most of them minting their own coins and maintaining standing armies.

The rivalry between the three kingdoms of the Kathmandu Valley expressed itself not only through warfare but also through the patronage of architecture and culture, which flourished in the climate of jealous one-upmanship. The outstanding collections of exquisite temples and buildings in each city's Durbar Sq are testament to the fortunes spent by the kings in their attempts to outdo each other.

The building boom was financed by trade, in everything from musk and wool to salt and Chinese silk. The Kathmandu Valley stood at the departure point for two separate routes into Tibet, via Banepa to the northeast and via Rasuwa and the Kyirong Valley near Langtang to the northwest. Traders would cross the jungle-infested Terai during winter to avoid the virulent malaria and then wait in Kathmandu for the mountain passes to open later that summer. Kathmandu grew rich, and its rulers converted their wealth into gilded pagodas and ornately carved royal palaces. In the mid-17th century Nepal gained the right to mint Tibet's coins using Tibetan silver, further enriching the kingdom's coffers.

In Kathmandu, King Pratap Malla (1641–74) oversaw that city's cultural high point with the construction of the Hanuman Dhoka palace and the Rani Pokhari pond. He also built the first of several subsequent pillars that featured a statue of the king facing the protective temple of Taleju, who the Mallas had by that point adopted as their protective deity. The mid-17th century also saw a high point of building in Patan.

The Malla era shaped the religious as well as the artistic landscape, introducing the dramatic annual chariot festivals of Indra Jatra and Machhendranath. The Malla kings shored up their divine right to rule by claiming to be reincarnations of the Hindu god Vishnu and by establishing the cult of the Kumari, a living goddess whose role it was to bless the Malla's rule during an annual celebration.

The cosmopolitan Mallas also absorbed foreign influences. The Indian Mughal court influenced Malla dress and painting, introduced the Nep-

A History of Nepal by John Whelpton is one of the few available titles on the subject. It focuses on the last 250 years and explains not only political events but also the changes in people's lives. It's for sale in Nepal at a discounted local price.

The mid-14th century saw the de facto rule of Malla Queen Devaladevi, the most powerful woman in Nepal's history.

879	c 1260	1200–1500	1349
The Newari lunar calendar, the Nepal Samvat, is introduced as the national calendar and used officially until the late 18th century. It is still used for Newari festivals in the Kathmandu Valley.	Nepali architect Arniko travels to Lhasa and Kublai Khan's capital Dadu (Beijing), bringing with him the design of the pagoda and changing the face of religious temples across Asia.	The Khasa empire of the western Mallas reaches its peak in the far western Karnali basin around Jumla. Its lasting contribution is Nepali – the national language spoken today.	Muslim armies of Sultan Shams-ud-din plunder the Kathmandu Valley, destroying the stupa at Swayambhunath and carrying off cartloads of booty.

alis to firearms and exported the system of land grants in return for military service, a system that would have a profound effect in later years.

But change didn't only come from abroad. A storm was brewing inside Nepal, just 100km to the east of Kathmandu.

Unification under the Shahs

In 1768 Prithvi Narayan Shah, ruler of the tiny hilltop kingdom of Gorkha (halfway between Pokhara and Kathmandu), stood poised on the edge of the Kathmandu Valley, ready to realise his dream of a unified Nepal. It had taken more than a quarter of a century of conquest and consolidation to get here but Shah was about to redraw the political landscape of the Himalaya.

Shah had taken the strategic hilltop fort of Nuwakot in 1744, after fighting off reinforcements from the British East India Company, but it took him another 24 years to take Kathmandu, finally sneaking in while everyone was drunk during the Indra Jatra festival. A year later he eventually took Kirtipur, after three lengthy failed attempts. In terrible retribution his troops hacked over 50kg of noses and lips off Kirtipur's residents; unsurprisingly, resistance melted away in the wake of the atrocity. In 1769 he advanced on the three cowering Malla kings and ended the Malla rule, thus unifying Nepal.

Shah moved his capital from Gorkha to Kathmandu, establishing the Shah dynasty, whose line continued right up until 2008. Shah himself, however, did not live long after his conquest; he died in Nuwakot in 1775, just six years after unification, but is still revered as the founder of the nation.

Shah had built his empire on conquest, and his insatiable army needed ever more booty and land to keep it satisfied. Within six years the Gurkhas had conquered eastern Nepal and Sikkim. The expansion then turned westwards into Kumaon and Garhwal, only halted on the borders of the Punjab by the armies of the powerful one-eyed ruler Ranjit Singh.

The expanding boundaries of 'Greater Nepal' by this time stretched from Kashmir to Sikkim, eventually putting it on a collision course with the world's most powerful empire, the British Raj. Despite early treaties with the British, disputes over the Terai led to the first Anglo-Nepali War, which the British won after a two-year fight. The British were so impressed by their enemy that they decided to incorporate Gurkha mercenaries into their own army, a practice that continues to this day (Gurkha troops served recently in Iraq and Afghanistan).

The 1816 Sugauli treaty called a screeching halt to Nepal's expansion and laid down its modern boundaries. Nepal lost Sikkim, Kumaon, Garhwal and much of the Terai, though some of this land was restored to Nepal in 1858 in return for support given to the British during the Indian

Nepal's flag is like no other, consisting of two overlapping red triangles, bearing a white moon and a white 12-pointed sun (the first mythological kings of Nepal are said to be descendants of the sun and moon).

Nepal's founding father, Prithvi Narayan Shah, referred to Nepal as 'a yam between two boulders' – namely China and India – a metaphor that is as true geologically as it is historically.

1380	1428–82	1531–34	1641–74
Ame Pal founds the kingdom of Lo (Mustang). The present king of Mustang, Jigme Palbar Bista, traces his family back 25 generations to this king. Mustang remains an independent kingdom until 1951.	The rule of Yaksha Malla, the high point of the Malla reign, ends in the fracture of the Kathmandu Valley into the three rival kingdoms of Kathmandu, Patan and Bhaktapur.	Sherpas (literally 'easterners') settle in the Solu-Khumbu region near Mt Everest. The Nangpa La remains the most important Sherpa trade route with Tibet.	Rule of Malla king Pratap Malla, a dancer, poet and great supporter of arts, who shapes the face of Kathmandu, building large parts of Hanuman Dhoka palace.

Mutiny (Indian War of Independence). A British resident was sent to Kathmandu to keep an eye on things but the British knew that it would be too difficult to colonise the impossible hill terrain and were content to keep Nepal as a buffer state. Nepalis to this day are proud that their country was never colonised by the British, unlike the neighbouring hill states of India.

Following its humiliating defeat, Nepal cut itself off from all foreign contact from 1816 until 1951. The British residents in Kathmandu were the only Westerners to set eyes on Nepal for more than a century.

On the cultural front, temple construction continued apace, though perhaps of more import to ordinary people was the revolutionary introduction, via India, of chillies, potatoes, tobacco and other New World crops.

The Shah rulers, meanwhile, swung from ineffectual to sadistic. At one point the kingdom was governed by a 12-year-old female regent, in charge of a nine-year-old king, while Crown Prince Surendra (r 1847–81) expanded the horizons of human suffering by ordering subjects to jump down wells or ride off cliffs, just to see whether they would survive.

The Ranocracy

The death of Prithvi Narayan Shah in 1775 set in motion a string of succession struggles, infighting, assassinations, backstabbing and intrigue that culminated in the Kot Massacre in 1846. This blood-stained night was engineered by the young Chhetri noble Jung Bahadur and it catapulted his family into power, just as it sidelined the Shah dynasty.

Ambitious and ruthless, Jung Bahadur organised (with the queen's consent) for his soldiers to massacre 55 of the most important noblemen in the kingdom in one night, while they were assembled in the Kot courtyard adjoining Kathmandu's Durbar Sq. He then exiled 6000 members of their families to prevent revenge attacks.

Jung Bahadur took the title of prime minister and changed his family name to the more prestigious 'Rana'. He later extended his title to *maharajah* (king) and decreed it hereditary. The Ranas became a parallel 'royal family' within the kingdom and held the reins of power, as the Shah kings were relegated to listless, irrelevant figureheads, requiring permission even to leave their palace.

The family line of Rana prime ministers held power for more than a century, eventually intermarrying with the Shahs. Development in Nepal stagnated, although the country did at least manage to preserve its independence.

Jung Bahadur Rana travelled to Europe in 1850, attending the opera and the races at Epsom, and brought back a taste for neoclassical architecture that can be seen in Kathmandu today. Under the Ranas, *sati* (the

The first cars were transported to the Kathmandu Valley in parts, on the backs of porters, before there were even any roads or petrol in the kingdom. You can see one of these, an early Hudson, at Kathmandu's National Museum.

For a impressionistic historical portrait of Kathmandu check out journalist Thomas Bell's kaleidoscopic *Kathmandu*, published in India and available in Kathmandu.

18th century	1729	1750	1768–69
Capuchin missionaries pass through Nepal to Tibet, later supplying the West with its first descriptions of exotic Kathmandu.	The three kingdoms of the Kathmandu Valley send presents to the Qing court in Beijing, which from then on views Nepal as a tributary state.	King Jaya Prakash Malla builds Kathmandu's Kumari Temple, followed by the Nyatapola Temple in Bhaktapur, the literal high point of stupa-style architecture in Nepal.	Nepal is unified under Prithvi Narayan Shah (1723–75), known as the father of the Nepali nation, to form the Shah dynasty. Kathmandu becomes the capital.

Hindu practice of casting a widow on her husband's funeral pyre) was abolished, 60,000 slaves were released from bondage, and a school and college were established in the capital. Despite the advances, the peasants in the hills were locked in a medieval existence, while the Ranas and their relatives lived lives of opulent luxury.

Modernisation began to dawn on Kathmandu with the opening of the Bir Hospital, Nepal's first, in 1889. Over the next 15 years Kathmandu saw its first piped water system, the introduction of limited electricity and the construction of the Singh Durbar, considered at one time the largest palace in Asia. The 29-year reign (1901–29) of Prime Minister Chandra Shumsher in particular brought sweeping changes, including the introduction of electricity and the outlawing of slavery. In 1923 Britain formally acknowledged Nepal's independence and in 1930 the kingdom of Gorkha was renamed the kingdom of Nepal, reflecting a growing sense of national consciousness.

Elsewhere in the region dramatic changes were taking place. The Nepalis supplied logistical help during Britain's invasion of Tibet in 1903, and over 300,000 Nepalis fought in WWI and WWII, garnering a total of 13 Victoria Crosses – Britain's highest military honour – for their efforts.

After WWII, India gained its independence and the communist revolution took place in China. Tibetan refugees fled into Nepal in the first of several waves when the new People's Republic of China tightened its grip on Tibet, and Nepal became a buffer zone between the two rival Asian giants. Meanwhile King Tribhuvan, forgotten in his palace, was being primed to overthrow the Ranas.

You can visit the birthplace and launching pad of Nepal's unifier, Prithvi Narayan Shah, at Gorkha, and see his second royal palace at Nuwakot.

Restoration of the Shahs

In late 1950 King Tribhuvan was driving himself to a hunting trip at Nagarjun when he suddenly swerved James Bond–style into the Indian embassy, where he then claimed political immunity and jumped into an Indian Air Force jet to Delhi. At the same time, the recently formed Nepali Congress Party, led by BP Koirala, managed to take most of the Terai by force from the Ranas and established a provisional government that ruled from the border town of Birganj. India exerted its considerable influence and negotiated a solution to Nepal's turmoil, and King Tribhuvan returned in glory to Nepal in 1951 to set up a new government composed of demoted Ranas and members of the Nepali Congress Party.

Although Nepal gradually reopened its long-closed doors and established relations with other nations, dreams of a new democratic system never quite got off the ground. Tribhuvan died in 1955 and was succeeded by his cautious son Mahendra. A new constitution provided for a parliamentary system of government, resulting in Nepal's first ever general election in 1959. The Nepali Congress Party won a clear victory and BP

1790–92	1814–16	1815	1846
Nepal invades Tibet and sacks Shigatse. Avenging Chinese troops advance down the Kyirong Valley as far as Nuwakot. As part of the ensuing treaty the Nepalis pay tribute to the Chinese emperor until 1912.	Anglo-Nepali War ends in victory for Britain. The ensuing Treaty of Sugauli establishes Nepal's boundaries and gives Britain the right to recruit Gurkha soldiers and maintain a residency in Kathmandu.	5000 Nepali soldiers begin serving as troops in the East India Company after impressing the British with their valour and loyalty.	The Kot Massacre ends in the killing of the cream of the court aristocracy, ushering in the Rana era (1846–1951) and sidelining the Shah kings to puppet status.

Koirala became the new prime minister. In late 1960, however, the king decided the government wasn't to his taste after all, had the cabinet arrested and swapped his ceremonial role for direct control (much as King Gyanendra would do 46 years later).

In 1962 Mahendra decided that a partyless, indirect *panchayat* (council) system of government was more appropriate to Nepal. The real power remained with the king, who chose 16 members out of the 35-member National Panchayat, and appointed both the prime minister and his cabinet. Political parties were banned.

Mahendra died in 1972 and was succeeded by his 27-year-old British-educated son Birendra. Nepal's hippie community was unceremoniously booted out of the country when visa laws were tightened in the run-up to Birendra's spectacular coronation in 1975. Simmering discontent with corruption, the slow rate of development and the rising cost of living erupted into violent riots in Kathmandu in 1979. King Birendra announced a referendum to choose between the *panchayat* system and one that would permit political parties to operate. The result was 55% to 45% in favour of the *panchayat* system; democracy had been outvoted.

Nepal's military and police apparatus were among the least publicly accountable in the world and strict censorship was enforced. Mass arrests, torture and beatings of suspected activists were well documented, and the leaders of the main opposition, the Nepali Congress, spent the years between 1960 and 1990 in and out of prison.

During this time over one million hill people moved to the Terai in search of land and several million crossed the border to seek work in India (Nepalis are able to cross the border and work freely in India), creating a major demographic shift in favour of the now malaria-free Terai.

People Power

In 1989, as communist states across Europe crumbled and pro-democracy demonstrations occupied China's Tiananmen Sq, Nepali opposition parties formed a coalition to fight for a multiparty democracy with the king as constitutional head; the upsurge of protest was called the Jana Andolan, or People's Movement.

In early 1990 the government responded to a nonviolent gathering of over 200,000 people with bullets, tear gas and thousands of arrests. After several months of intermittent rioting, curfews, a successful strike and pressure from various foreign-aid donors, the government was forced to back down. On 9 April King Birendra announced he was lifting the ban on political parties and was ready to accept the role of constitutional monarch. Nepal had become a democracy.

In May 1991 the Nepali Congress Party won the general election and two years later a midterm election resulted in a coalition government led

For some interesting historical snippets check out the blog www.historylessonsnepal.blogspot.co.uk.

1850	1854	1856	1911
Jung Bahadur Rana travels to Europe, becoming the first Nepali ruler to cross the *kalo pani* (black water, or ocean) and thus temporarily losing his caste.	The Muluki Ain legal code formalises the Nepali caste system, defining diet, legal and sexual codes and enshrining state discrimination against lower castes. The law is revised only in 1963.	Peak XV is declared the world's highest peak. It is later renamed Everest after the head of Trigonometric Survey, George Everest (who actually pronounced his name eve-rest).	King George V visits the Terai on a hunting trip as a guest of the maharajah of Nepal, bagging 39 tigers and 18 rhinos, travelling with a small army of beaters.

by the Communist Party. This was one of the few times in the world that a communist government had come to power by popular vote.

Political stability did not last long, and the late 1990s were littered with dozens of broken coalitions, dissolved governments and sacked politicians. After a decade of democracy it seemed an increasing number of people, particularly young Nepalis and those living in the countryside, were utterly disillusioned.

The People's War

In 1996 the Maoists, a Communist-party splinter group, angered by government corruption, the dissolution of the communist government and the failure of democracy to deliver improvements to the people, declared a 'people's war'. The Maoists presented the then prime minister with a 40-point charter of demands that ranged from preferential state policies towards backward communities to an assertive Nepali identity, an end to privately funded schools and better governance.

The insurgency began in the Rolpa district of midwestern Nepal and gathered momentum, but it was initially ignored by Kathmandu's politicians. The repercussions of this nonchalance finally came to a head in November 2001 when the Maoists broke their ceasefire and attacked an army barracks west of Kathmandu. The initial Maoist forces were armed with little more than ancient muskets and *khukuris* (Gurkha knives) but

> For background on the Maoist rebellion read *Himalayan People's War: Nepal's Maoist Rebellion*, edited by Michael Hutt.

TRANS-HIMALAYAN TRADE

For centuries, hardy caravans of yaks and goats criss-crossed the high Himalaya, bringing salt harvested from Tibet's great inland lakes to exchange for rice and barley carried up from the Middle Hills of Nepal. Wool, livestock and butter from Tibet were exchanged for sugar, tea, spices, tobacco and Indian manufactured goods. Twelve major passes linked Nepal and Tibet, the easiest of which were in Mustang, ensuring that the Kali Gandaki Valley became the main entrepôt for transferring, storing and taxing the trade.

Over the last half-century much of the traditional border trade has dried up. The arrival of the Indian railway line at the Nepali border greatly aided the transportation of cheap Indian salt, sounding a death knell for the caravan trade. The real nail in the coffin came in the 1960s, when the Chinese closed the borders to local trade.

Ironically, the Chinese are currently leading a resurgence of trade and road construction. Chinese truckers now drive over the passes to Lo Manthang in Mustang and in 2012 another road border crossing opened at Rasuwaghadi, linking the Tibetan Kyirong Valley with Nepal's Langtang region along a route long used for trade and invasion. You'll see the occasional yak caravan headed for the Tibetan border laden with timber and the medicinal root *yartse gumba*, as well as telltale cans of Lhasa Beer littering trekking routes in the Manaslu, Everest and Mustang regions.

1914–18	1934	1949	1951
Around 100,000 Nepalis fight and 10,000 lose their lives in WWI. Thirty years later 200,000 Gurkha and army forces serve in WWII, mostly in Myanmar (Burma).	A massive earthquake destroys much of the Kathmandu Valley, killing over 8000 people in under a minute, injuring 16,000 and destroying a quarter of all homes in Nepal.	Bill Tilman gets permission from King Tribhuvan to trek in Nepal, including around the Kali Gandaki, Helambu and Solu-Khumbu regions. He is the first foreigner to trek to Everest Base Camp.	King Tribhuvan and the Nepali Congress Party, with Indian support, overthrow the Rana regime and establish a new coalition government. Nepal opens its doors to the outside world.

they quickly obtained guns looted from police stations, homemade explosives and automatic weapons, all bankrolled by robbery and extortion (in September 2000 Maoists stole Rs 50 million from a bank in Dolpo) and aided by an open border with India.

Initial police heavy-handedness fuelled a cycle of violence and retribution that only succeeded in alienating the local people. Political disenfranchisement, rural poverty, resentment against the caste system, issues of land reform and a lack of faith in the squabbling, self-interested politicians of distant Kathmandu swelled the ranks of the Maoists, who at their peak numbered 15,000 fighters, with a further militia of 50,000. Attacks spread to almost every one of Nepal's 75 districts, including Kathmandu. At their peak Maoists effectively controlled around 40% of the country, including two protected areas in the far west and several of Nepal's main trekking routes.

The political temperature reached boiling point when the king brought in the army and armed militias loyal to the government in 2001. The USA labelled Nepal's Maoists a terrorist group and handed over millions of dollars to help fight Nepal's own 'war on terror'. Although they were self-declared Maoists, the group owed more to Peru's Sendero Luminoso (Shining Path) than to any Chinese connection. Ironically the 'people's' armed struggle was led by two high-caste intellectuals: Pushpa Kamal Dahal (known by his *nom de guerre* Prachanda, which means 'the fierce') and Baburam Bhattarai, both of whom would later serve as Nepal's prime minister.

One early victim of the war was the freedom of the Nepali press. Between 2002 and 2005 more journalists were arrested in Nepal than in any other country and in 2005 Reporters Sans Frontiers described Nepal's media as the world's most censored.

Several Maoist truces, notably in 2003 and 2005, offered some respite, though these reflected as much a need to regroup and rearm as they did any move towards a lasting peace. By 2005 nearly 13,000 people, including many civilians, had been killed in the insurgency. Amnesty International accused both sides of horrific human-rights abuses, including summary executions, abductions, torture and child conscription. Dark days had come to Nepal.

Forget Kathmandu: An Elegy for Democracy, by Manjushree Thapa, starts with Nepal's royal massacre, moves to a political history of the last 200 years, then ends with a description of a trek through Maoist-held areas in 2003.

Nepal is said to get its name from Nepa, the name given to the Newari kingdom of the Kathmandu Valley; the word Nepa is derived from the name of a mythological Hindu sage, Ne, who once lived in the valley.

Stalled Development & the Failure of Aid

During the second half of the 20th century Nepal saw impressive movements towards development, namely in education and road construction, with the number of schools increasing from 300 in 1950 to over 40,000 by 2000. Since then relentless population growth (Nepal's population grew from 8.4 million in 1954 to 26 million in 2004) has simply

1953	1954	1955–72	1959
Everest is summited for the first time by New Zealander Edmund Hillary and Tibetan Sherpa Tenzing Norgay on 29 May, just in time for the coronation of Queen Elizabeth II.	Boris Lissanevitch establishes Nepal's first hotel, the Royal, in the Bahadur Bhawan palace. Its Yak and Yeti Bar becomes the expat hub for mountaineers and diplomats until its closure in 1971.	The rule of King Mahendra sees the introduction of elections, which are then voided as the king seizes direct power, introducing the *panchayat* system of government.	Nepal's first general election is held. The Dalai Lama flees Tibet and China closes the Tibet–Nepal border, seriously affecting the trade of salt for grain and creating great social change in the Himalaya.

cancelled out many of these advances, turning Nepal from a food exporter to a net importer within a generation.

The Maoist insurgency only worsened the plight of the rural poor by bombing bridges and telephone lines, halting road construction, diverting much-needed government funds away from development and causing aid programs to suspend activity due to security concerns. It is estimated that during the decade-long conflict the Maoists destroyed Rs 30 billion of government infrastructure, while the government blew US$108 billion on military spending. Caught in the middle, an entire generation of rural Nepali children missed out on their education.

After a half-century of outside assistance and more than US$4 billion in aid (60% of its development budget), Nepal remains one of the world's 10 poorest countries, with the highest income disparity in Asia and one of its lowest health-spending levels. Seven million Nepalis lack adequate food or basic health care and education.

Royal Troubles & Political Change

On 1 June 2001 the Nepali psyche was dealt a huge blow when Crown Prince Dipendra gunned down almost every member of the royal family during a get-together in Kathmandu. Ironically Dipendra did not die straight away and was pronounced the king of Nepal, despite being in a coma. His rule ended two days later, when he too was declared dead. King Birendra's brother Gyanendra was then crowned in what may for him have been a moment of déjà vu – he had already been crowned once before, aged three, and ruled as king for three months, after his grandfather Tribhuvan fled to India in 1950.

In the days that followed the massacre, a tide of emotions washed over the Nepali people – shock, grief, horror, disbelief and denial. A 13-day period of mourning was declared and in Kathmandu impromptu shrines were set up for people to pray for their king and queen. About 400 shaven-headed men roamed the streets around the palace on motorbikes, carrying pictures of the monarch. Half a million stunned Nepalis lined the streets during the funeral procession. When the shock of this loss subsided the uncertainty of what lay ahead hit home.

The beginning of the 21st century saw the political situation in the country turn from bad to worse. Prime ministers were sacked and replaced six times between 2000 and 2005, marking a total of nine governments in 10 years. The fragile position of Nepali politicians is well illustrated by Sher Bahadur Deuba, who was appointed prime minister for the second time in 2001, before being dismissed in 2002, reinstated in 2004, sacked again in 2005, thrown in jail on corruption charges and then released.

Confusingly, three Koirala brothers have all served as prime ministers of Nepal; BP Koirala in 1959, MP Koirala in 1951 and 1953 and GP Koirala, four times, most recently in 2006. Their cousin Sushil Koirala was prime minister in 2015.

Massacre at the Palace: The Doomed Royal Dynasty of Nepal, by Jonathan Gregson, takes a wider look at Nepal's royal family and reveals that assassination and murder have been part of royal life for centuries; it also examines the recent massacre. Also published as *Blood Against the Snows.*

1960	1965	1975	1990
Eradication of malaria opens the Terai to rapid population growth. Today the Terai contains around half of Nepal's population and most of its industry and agricultural land.	Colonel James 'Jimmy' Roberts founds Mountain Travel, Nepal's first trekking company, and leads a group of women up the Kali Gandaki Valley, laying the path for Nepal's trekking industry.	Birendra is crowned king in Kathmandu's Hanuman Dhoka, three years after the death of his father Mahendra. The king wears the traditional jewel-encrusted and feathered headdress of the Shah kings.	The mass demonstrations of the People's Movement force King Birendra to accept a new constitution, restoring democracy and relegating the king to the role of constitutional Hindu monarch.

Nepal's disappointing experiment with democracy faced a major setback in February 2005 when King Gyanendra dissolved the government amid a state of emergency, promising a return to democracy within three years. Freedom of the press was curtailed and telephone lines were cut periodically to prevent demonstrations. Tourism levels slumped and a mood of pessimism descended over the country.

Everything changed in April 2006, when days of mass demonstrations, curfews and the deaths of 16 protestors forced the king to restore parliamentary democracy. The following month the newly restored parliament voted to reduce the king to a figurehead, ending powers that the royal Shah lineage had enjoyed for over 200 years. The removal of the king was the price required to bring the Maoists to the negotiating table,

THE ROYAL MASSACRE

The night of 1 June 2001 has entered the annals of history as one of Nepal's greatest tragedies, a bloodbath that could have been lifted straight from the pages of Shakespeare.

That night, in a hail of bullets, 10 members of Nepal's royal family, including King Birendra and Queen Aishwarya, were gunned down during a gathering at the Narayanhiti Palace by a deranged, drunken Crown Prince Dipendra, who eventually turned a weapon on himself. The real motive behind the massacre will never be known, but many believe Dipendra's rage was prompted by his parents' disapproval of the woman he wanted to marry.

The initial disbelief and shock gave way to suspicion and a host of conspiracy theories, many concerning the new king, Gyanendra (who was in Pokhara at the time of the massacre), and his son Paras (who emerged unscathed from the attack). None of this was helped by an official inquiry that initially suggested the automatic weapon had been discharged by accident, or the fact that the victims were quickly cremated without full post-mortems and the palace building then razed to the ground. Other theories included that old chestnut – a CIA or Indian secret-service plot.

A surreal royal exorcism followed on the 11th day of mourning, as a high-caste priest, dressed in the gold suit, shoes and black-rimmed glasses of King Birendra and donning a paper crown, climbed onto an elephant and slowly lumbered out of the valley, taking with him the ghost of the dead king. The same scapegoat ritual (known as a *katto* ceremony) was performed for Dipendra, except that a pregnant woman dashed underneath the elephant en route, believing this would ensure she give birth to a boy. She was trampled by the elephant and died, adding a further twist to the tragedy.

Doubtless, the truth of what really happened that night will never be known. In the words of Nepali journalist Manjushree Thapa: 'We lost the truth; we lost our history. We are left to recount anecdotes and stories, to content ourselves with myth.'

1996–2006	May 1996	June 2001	Feb 2005
A decade-long Maoist insurgency brings the country to its knees and results in the death of 13,000 Nepalis. Development projects stall and tourism levels plummet.	Eight climbers die on a single day, May 11, on Everest, making this the single worst year for Everest fatalities. An Imax film and Jon Krakauer's book *Into Thin Air* chronicle the disaster.	Prince Dipendra massacres 10 members of the royal family in the Narayanhiti Palace, including his father, King Birendra, before shooting himself. The king's brother, Gyanendra, is crowned king of Nepal.	King Gyanendra dismisses the government and assumes direct control of the country in a state of emergency, citing the need to crush the Maoist rebels.

and a peace accord was signed later that year, drawing a close to the bloody decade-long insurgency.

The ensuing pace of political change in Nepal was head-spinning. One month after the Maoists achieved a majority in the April 2008 elections parliament abolished the monarchy completely by a margin of 560 votes to four, ending 240 years of royal rule. The new government saw former guerrilla leader Pushpa Kamal Dahal as prime minister and Dr Baburam Bhattarai as finance minister. In 2009 Pushpa Kamal Dahal resigned due to infighting, hinting at political turmoil to come.

Former Maoist 'terrorists' became cabinet ministers, members of the People's Liberation Army joined the national army and a new constitution was commissioned (though close to a decade later it has still to be written), all as part of a process to bind the former guerrillas into the political mainstream. After a decade of darkness, violence and social upheaval, a renewed optimism in the political process was palpable throughout Nepal. It remains to be seen whether this spirit of optimism can survive the ongoing political wrangles and the economic uncertainty that Nepal now faces after the worst earthquake in nearly a century (see p8).

Following the 2008 abolition of the monarchy, the king's face was removed from the Rs 10 note, the prefix 'Royal' disappeared from the name of the national airline as well as national parks, and the king's birthday was dumped as a national holiday.

HISTORY OF NEPAL ROYAL TROUBLES & POLITICAL CHANGE

2006	May 2008	2014	April 2015
After weeks of protests, King Gyanendra reinstates parliament, which votes to curtail his emergency powers. Maoists and government officials sign a peace agreement and the Maoist rebels enter an interim government.	Parliament abolishes the Nepali monarchy, ending 240 years of royal rule.	Twin disasters hit Nepal's mountains. On April 16 Sherpa guides are killed on the Khumbu icefall in Everest's single deadliest disaster. In October 43 trekkers and porters die after heavy snowfall in the Annapurna region.	A massive 7.8-magnitude earthquake strikes central Nepal, killing 8500 and causing devastation across the Kathmandu Valley.

People & Culture

Trekking in Nepal is not wilderness walking. You'll share the trail with Sherpas, Gurungs, Rai and Thakalis and pass by monasteries, temples and sacred sites, all the time experiencing the friendliness, outgoing nature and good humour that characterises almost all Nepalis. Visitors are unanimous in praising the gentle and hospitable nature of the hardy people that inhabit this spectacular and physically challenging country.

The National Psyche

Namaste is the universal greeting in Nepal, accompanied by placing the hands in a prayer-like position. To show added respect, use the formal version, *namaskar*.

Nepal's location between India and Tibet, the diversity of its 60 or more ethnic and caste groups, its isolating geography and myriad (up to 123) languages have resulted in a complex mosaic of customs and beliefs that make it hard to generalise about a 'Nepali people'.

Perhaps the dominant Nepali cultural concepts are those of caste and status, both of which contribute to a strictly defined system of hierarchy and deference. Caste determines not only a person's status, but also their career and marriage partner, how that person interacts with other Nepalis and how others react back. This system of hierarchy extends even to the family, where everyone has a clearly defined rank. The Nepali language has half a dozen words for 'you', each of which conveys varying shades of respect.

When it comes to their religious beliefs, Nepalis are admirably flexible, pragmatic and, above all, tolerant – there is almost no religious or ethnic tension in Nepal. Nepalis are generally good humoured and patient, quick to smile and slow to anger, though they also have a reputation as fierce fighters.

Do as locals do by addressing strangers roughly your age as *dai* (elder brother) or *didi* (elder sister).

The Nepali view of the world is dominated by prayer and ritual and a knowledge that the gods are not remote, abstract concepts but living, present beings who can influence human affairs in very direct ways. Nepalis perceive the divine everywhere, from the greeting *namaste,* which literally means 'I greet the divine inside of you', to the spirits and gods present in trees, passes, sacred river confluences and mountain peaks.

The notions of karma and caste, when combined with a tangled bureaucracy and deep-rooted corruption, tend to create an endemic sense of fatalism in Nepal. Confronted with problems, many Nepalis will simply respond with a shrug of the shoulders and the phrase *khe garne?,* or 'what is there to do?', which Westerners often find frustrating yet oddly addictive.

MOVING TIGERS

Nepal's national board game is *bagh chal,* which literally means 'move the tigers'. The game is played on a lined board with 25 intersecting points. One player has four tigers, the other has 20 goats, and the aim is for the tiger player to 'eat' five goats by jumping over them before the goat player can encircle the tigers and prevent them moving. You can buy attractive brass *bagh chal* sets in Kathmandu and Patan.

Nepal's other popular game is *carom,* which looks like finger snooker. Players use discs that glide over a chalked-up board to pot other discs into the corner pockets.

Traditional Lifestyle

The cornerstones of Nepali life are the demands (as well as the rewards) of one's family, ethnic group and caste. To break these time-honoured traditions is to risk being ostracised from family and community.

In most ethnic groups, joint and extended families live in the same house. In some smaller villages extended clans make up the entire community. Traditional family life has been dislocated by the large number of Nepali men forced to seek work away from home, whether in Kathmandu, the Terai or abroad.

Arranged marriages remain the norm in Nepali Hindu society and are generally between members of the same caste or ethnic group, although there is a growing number of 'love marriages'. The family connections generated by a marriage are as much a social contract as a personal affair, and most families consult matchmakers, lamas or astrologers when making such an important decision.

To decide not to have children is almost unheard of and Nepali women will often pity you if you are don't have children. Having a son is important, especially for Hindu families, as some religious rites (such as lighting the funeral pyre to ensure a peaceful passage into the next life) can only be performed by the eldest son. Girls are regarded by many groups as a financial burden whose honour needs to be protected until she is married.

Children stay at school for up to 12 years; 70% of children will begin school but only 15% reach their 10th school year, when they sit their School Leaving Certificate (SLC) board examination. Many villages only have a primary school, which means children either have to walk long distances each day or board in a bigger town to attend secondary school. The ratio of boys to girls at secondary schools can be almost 2:1 in favour of boys.

Find an interesting collection of interviews with Nepali mountain folk on a wide variety of topics at www.mountain voices.org/nepal. asp.html.

CULTURAL DOS & DON'TS

➡ Most Nepalis eat with their hands. If you follow suit, use only your right hand and wash it before and after eating.

➡ Don't touch food or eating utensils that local people will use. Any food that a (non-Hindu) foreigner has touched becomes *jutho* ('polluted') and cannot be eaten by a Hindu. This practice does not apply to Sherpas.

➡ Don't let your mouth touch a water jug or your water bottle if you are sharing it with others.

➡ Don't throw anything into the fire in any house – Buddhist or Hindu. In most cultures the household gods live in the hearth.

➡ A Nepali person will not step over your feet or legs. If your outstretched legs are across a doorway or path, pull them in when someone wants to pass. Similarly, do not step over the legs of a Nepali.

➡ The place of honour in a Sherpa home is the seat closest to the fire. Do not sit in this seat unless you are specifically invited to do so.

➡ Don't point the soles of your feet at people.

➡ When giving or receiving money, use your right hand and touch your left hand to your elbow as a mark of respect.

➡ Do not enter a Hindu temple if you are wearing leather shoes or a leather belt (cows are sacred to Hindus).

➡ Generally you should remove your shoes and hat when entering a Buddhist *gompa*. Leave an offering in the monastery donation box or on the altar.

➡ Always ask permission before photographing religious festivals, cremation grounds and the inside of temples.

NEPALI NAMES

You can tell a lot about a Nepali person from their name, including often their caste, profession, ethnic group and where they live. Gurung and Sherpa are ethnic groups as well as surnames. The surname Bista or Pant indicates that the person is a Brahman, originally from western Nepal; Devkota indicates an eastern origin. Thapa, Pande and Bhasnet are names related to the former Rana ruling family. Shrestha is a high-caste Newari name. The initials KC often stand for Khatri Chhetri, a mixed-caste name. The surname Kami is the Nepali equivalent of Smith.

Sherpa names even reveal which day of the week the person was born: Dawa (Monday), Mingmar (Tuesday), Lhakpa (Wednesday), Phurba (Thursday), Pasang (Friday), Pemba (Saturday) and Nyima (Sunday). The one thing you can't tell from a Sherpa name is their sex – Lhakpa Sherpa could be a man or a woman!

Older people are respected members of the community and are cared for by their children. Old age is a time for relaxation, prayer and meditation. The dead are generally cremated and the deceased's sons will shave their heads and wear white for an entire year following the death.

> Nepal currently has a population of around 31 million (2014 estimate), a number that is increasing at the rate of 1.2% annually. Over 2.5 million people live in the Kathmandu Valley. Four million Nepalis reside in India.

Rural Life

Despite what you may see in Kathmandu and Pokhara, Nepal is overwhelmingly rural and poor – 83% of people live in the countryside. Farming is still the main occupation and debt is a factor in most people's lives. Large areas of land are still owned by *zamindar* (absent landlords) and up to 50% of a landless farmer's production will go to the landowner as rent.

Most rural Nepali families are remarkably self-sufficient in their food supply, selling any excess in the nearest town, where they'll stock up on things such as sugar, soap, cigarettes, tea, salt, cloth and jewellery. Throughout Nepal this exchange of goods has created a dense network of trails trodden by everyone from traders and porters to mule caravans and trekking groups.

The rhythms of village life are determined by the seasons and marked by festivals – New Year, harvest and religious festivals being the most important. Dasain remains the biggest event of the calendar in the Middle Hills and is a time when most Nepali families get together.

People

The human geography of Nepal is a remarkable cultural mosaic of peoples who have not so much assimilated as learned to coexist. The ethnic divisions are complex and numerous; you'll have to do your homework to be able to differentiate between a Limbu, Lepcha, Lhopa and Lhomi – and that's just the Ls!

> Both Magars and Gurungs have made up large numbers of Gurkha regiments, and army incomes have contributed greatly to the economy of their regions.

Nepal is the meeting place of the Indo-Aryan people of India and the Mongoloid peoples of the Himalaya. Thanks largely to Nepal's tortured topography, Nepal's ethnic groups have largely retained their own traditions. Social taboos, especially among caste Hindus, have limited further assimilation between groups.

Nepal's diverse ethnic groups speak somewhere between 24 and 123 different languages and dialects, depending on how finely the distinctions are made. Nepali functions as the unifying language, though less than half of Nepal's people speak Nepali as their first language.

People of the High Himalaya

The hardy Tibetan peoples who inhabit the high Himalaya are known in Nepal as Bhotias (Bhotiyas), a slightly derogatory term among caste Hindus. Each group remains distinct but their languages are all Tibetan-based and, with a few exceptions, they are Tibetan Buddhists.

The Bhotiyas' names combine the region they came from with the suffix 'pa' and include the Sherpas (literally 'easterners') of the Everest region, the Dolpopas of the west and the Lopas, or Lobas (literally 'southerners'), of the Mustang region.

The withering of Trans-Himalayan trade routes and the difficulty of farming and herding at high altitude drive these people to lower elevations during winter, either to graze their animals or to trade in India and the Terai. Yak herding and the barley harvest remain the economic bedrocks of the high Himalaya.

Contrary to perceptions in the West, Sherpas actually do very little portering, focusing mostly on high-altitude expedition work. Most of the porters you meet on the trails are Tamang or Rai, or from other groups.

PEOPLE & CULTURE PEOPLE

Thakalis

Originating along the Kali Gandaki Valley in central Nepal, the Thakalis have emerged as the entrepreneurs of the Nepal Himalaya. They once played an important part in the salt trade between the subcontinent and Tibet, and travellers will meet them most frequently in their adopted roles as hoteliers and lodge owners, especially on the Annapurna Circuit. Originally Buddhist, many pragmatic Thakalis have now adopted Hinduism.

Tamangs

The Tamangs make up one of the largest groups in the country. They live mainly in the hills north of Kathmandu and have a noticeably strong Tibetan influence, from their monasteries, known as *ghyang*, to the mani (stone carved with the Tibetan Buddhist chant 'om mani padme hum') walls that mark the entrance to their villages. You can stay in traditional Tamang villages along the Tamang Heritage Trail.

According to some accounts, ancestors of the Tamang were horse traders and cavalrymen from an invading Tibetan army who settled in Nepal. They are well known for their independence and suspicion of authority, probably caused by the fact that in the 19th century they were relegated to a low status, with much of their land distributed to Bahuns and Chhetris. As bonded labourers they were dependent upon menial work such as portering. Many of the 'Tibetan' souvenirs, carpets and thangkas (religious paintings) you see in Kathmandu are made by Tamangs.

Tibetans

About 20,000 of the 128,000 Tibetans in exile around the world live in Nepal. Although their numbers are small, Tibetans have a high profile, partly because of the important roles they play in tourism and the Tibetan carpet industry.

CHORTENS

You'll pass chorten (stupas) on every trek in Nepal. The very first chorten were built to hold the remains of Buddha and many chorten still hold religious relics or the ashes of lamas inside them.

Each of the elements of a chorten has a symbolic meaning, from the square base (earth) and the hemispherical dome (water) to the tapering spire (fire), whose 13 step-like segments symbolise the steps leading to Buddhahood. On top of the 13 steps is an ornament shaped like a crescent moon (air), and a vertical spike, which symbolises ether or the sacred light of Buddha. The central rectangular tower is painted with the all-seeing eyes of Buddha. What appears to be a nose is actually the Sanskrit character for the number one, symbolising the absoluteness of Buddha.

A special type of chorten is a *kani*, which is an arch-like monument erected at the entrance to villages.

Tibetans are devout Buddhists and their arrival in the valley has rejuvenated a number of important religious sites, most notably the stupas at Swayambhunath and Bodhnath.

Up to 2.1 million Nepalis work overseas; over 40% in India and 38% in the Gulf States, and smaller numbers in Malaysia. Workers overseas send home US$4 billion a year, or about 25% of Nepal's GDP, making this Nepal's largest single source of foreign currency.

Sherpas

The Sherpas who live high in the mountains of eastern and central Nepal are probably the best-known Nepali ethnic group. These nomadic Tibetan herders moved to the Solu Khumbu region of Nepal 500 years ago from eastern Tibet, bringing with them their Tibetan Buddhist religion. Sherpas are associated with the Mt Everest region, although only a small percentage of Sherpas actually live in the Khumbu; the rest live in the lower valleys of the Solu region. The Sherpas of the Helambu region call themselves Yomlo and speak a distinct dialect. Potatoes were introduced to the region in the late 19th century and are now the main Sherpa crop.

Tourism stepped in after the collapse of trade over the Nangpa La pass in 1959, when the Chinese sent thousands of troops to enforce their claim on Tibet. These days the Sherpa name is synonymous with mountaineering and trekking, and Sherpas can be found working as high-altitude mountain guides as well as owners of travel agencies and trekking lodges.

People of the Middle Hills

The Middle Hills of Nepal are the best places to witness village life at its most traditional. In the east are the Kirati, who are divided into the Rai and Limbu groups. The Newari people dominate the central hills around the Kathmandu Valley, while the Magars and Gurungs inhabit the hills of the Kali Gandaki northwest of Pokhara.

Moving west, the Bahun and Chhetri are the dominant groups, although the lines between castes have become blurred over time.

Rais & Limbus

The Rais and Limbus are thought to have ruled the Kathmandu Valley in the 7th century BC until they were defeated around AD 300. They then moved into the steep hill country of eastern Nepal, from the Arun Valley to the Sikkim border, where many remain today.

PRAYER FLAGS & WHEELS

Wherever you trek in highland Nepal, strings of coloured prayer flags and walls of carved mani stones indicate you're getting close to the Tibetan world.

Prayer flags are strung across passes, streams and houses to sanctify the air, pacify the gods and bring merit to the owners. There are several types of prayer flags, but in all the colours are highly symbolic and arranged in a specific order: white (representing air), red (fire), green (water), yellow (earth) and blue (space or ether). Flags can be horizontal (called *darding*) or vertical (*darchok* or *chatdar*), but all are printed with an image of the wind horse *(lungta)*, which carries the prayers to the four corners.

Large piles of *mani* stones mark the entrance to most villages and monasteries in highland Nepal. They are normally inscribed with the Tibetan Buddhist mantra 'om mani padme hum', which is often simply translated as 'hail to the jewel in the lotus' (though its true meaning is far more complex).

Mani walls are joined by long lines of prayer wheels, which pilgrims spin to activate the thousands of prayers wrapped inside. On a trek you'll see everything from personal-sized, hand-spun prayer wheels to huge house-sized wheels called *mani dungkhor,* which come with their own private chapels *(mani lhakhang)*.

Remember, always walk to the left of mani walls and chorten (Tibetan stupas) and spin your prayer wheels in a clockwise direction.

VISITING A GOMPA

From Lhasa to the Langtang Valley, Tibetan-style gompa (monasteries) share a striking continuity of design. Most are located on a hillside with a fine view, demonstrating their strategic importance, while others are in villages, at the heart of the local community.

Most small monasteries in remote communities have only one room, the *dukhang* (assembly hall), while others also have side chapels. The vestibule features colourful painted representations of the Wheel of Life alongside the Four Guardian Kings, while the ceilings of both monasteries and *kani* (entry-gate chorten) are decorated with kaleidoscopic mandalas, a kind of geometric visual aid to meditation.

The main altar will have photos of important lineage holders, such as the Karmapa or Dalai Lama, plus bowls of water, butter lamps and some plastic flowers. Hanging in the semi-darkness are demonic festival masks and sometimes ceremonial trumpets.

The main statues are likely to include Sakyamuni, the historical Buddha; Jampa (Maitreya in Sanskrit), the future Buddha; and the 'lotus born' saint Guru Rinpoche. Bodhisattvas include Chenresig (Avalokitesvara), representing compassion; Jampelyang (Manjushri), representing wisdom; and Drolma (Tara), a female deity symbolising purity and fertility. Fierce protector gods such as Channa Dorje (Vajrapani) and Nagpo Chenpo (Mahakala), the Great Black One, guard the entries.

Another common figure is the popular 11th-century magician and poet Milarepa, who is said to have travelled widely throughout the Himalayan borderlands, including to Shey Gompa, the Manang Valley and Nupri.

Describing themselves as Kirati, these tribes are easily distinguishable by their Mongolian features. They are of Tibeto-Burmese descent and their traditional religion is distinct from Buddhism and Hinduism, although the latter is exerting a growing influence. Himalayan hunter-warriors, they are still excellent soldiers and are well represented in the Gurkha regiments.

Many of the men still carry a large *khukuri* (traditional curved knife) tucked into their belt and wear a *topi* (traditional Nepali cap). Some communities in upper Arun live in bamboo houses.

Changes in trading patterns and traditional culture among Nepal's Himalayan people are examined in *Himalayan Traders*, by Christoph von Fürer-Haimendorf.

Newars

The Newars of the Kathmandu Valley number about 1.3 million and make up 5% of the population. Their language, Newari, is distinct from Tibetan, Nepali or Hindi, and is reputed to be one of the world's most difficult languages to learn. The Newars are excellent farmers and merchants, as well as skilled artists, famed across Asia. The Kathmandu Valley is filled with spectacular examples of their artistic work, and their aesthetic influence was felt as far away as Lhasa.

Gurungs

The Gurungs, a Tibeto-Burmese people, live mainly in the central midlands, from Gorkha and Baglung up to Manang and the southern slopes of the Annapurnas, around Pokhara. One of the biggest Gurung settlements is Ghandruk, with its sweeping views of the Annapurnas and Machhapuchhare. Gurung women wear nose rings, known as *phuli,* and coral necklaces.

Sherpas: Reflections on Change in Himalayan Nepal, by James F Fisher, offers an anthropological snapshot of how tourism and modernisation have affected Sherpa religious and cultural life.

The Gurungs (who call themselves Tamu, or highlanders) originally migrated from western Tibet, bringing with them their animist Bön faith. One distinctive aspect of village life is the *rodi* (a cross between a town hall and a youth centre), where cooperative village tasks are planned. In the 1970s photographs portraying the alarmingly brave honey-collecting antics of Gurung men became world famous. The harvesting of hives continues, but only in remote areas.

Magars

The Magars, a large group (around 8% of the total population), are a Tibeto-Burmese people who live in the midlands zone of western and central Nepal. With such a large physical spread there are considerable regional variations.

The Magars are excellent soldiers and fought with Prithvi Narayan Shah to help unify Nepal. The Magars generally live in two-storey, rectangular or square thatched houses washed in red clay. They have been heavily influenced by Hinduism, and in terms of religion, farming practices, housing and dress, they are hard to distinguish from Chhetris.

Bahuns & Chhetris

The Hindu caste groups of Bahuns and Chhetris are dominant in the Middle Hills, making up 30% of the country's population.

Even though the caste system was formally abolished in 1963, these two groups remain the top cats of the caste hierarchy. Although there is no formal relationship in Hinduism between caste and ethnicity, Nepal's Bahuns and Chhetris (Brahmin priests and Kshatriya warriors, respectively) are considered ethnic groups as well as the two highest castes.

Bahuns and Chhetris played an important role in the court and armies of Prithvi Narayan Shah and after unification they were rewarded with tracts of land. Their language, Khas Kura, then became the national language of Nepal and their high-caste position was religiously, culturally and legally enforced. Ever since, Bahuns and Chhetris have dominated the government in Kathmandu, making up over 80% of the civil service.

The Bahuns tend to be more caste-conscious and orthodox than other Nepali Hindus, which sometimes leads to difficulties in relationships with 'untouchable' Westerners. Many are vegetarians and do not drink alcohol; marriages are arranged within the caste.

Bahun and Chhetri men can be recognised by their sacred thread – the *janai*, worn over the right shoulder and under the right arm – which is changed once a year during the Janai Purnima festival.

Women in Nepal

Women have a hard time of it in Nepal. Female mortality rates are higher than men's, literacy rates are lower, and women generally work harder and longer than men, for less reward. Women only truly gain status in traditional society when they bear their husband a son. Bearing children is so important that a man can legally take a second wife if the first has not had a child after 10 years.

In the far western hills, a system of polyandry (one woman married to two brothers) developed over time in response to limited amounts of land and the annual trading trips that required husbands to leave their families for months at a time. The system continues in remoter Tibetan communities.

Traditional prejudice against daughters is reflected in the bitter Nepali proverb: 'Raising a girl is like watering your neighbour's garden.'

HUMAN TRAFFICKING IN NEPAL

Trafficking of girls is a major problem in Nepal's most impoverished rural areas. Some 10,000 to 15,000 girls are tricked or sold every year into servitude, either as domestic, factory or sex workers. Brokers called *dalals* sell Nepali girls into the brothels of Mumbai. It is believed that over 100,000 Nepali women work in Indian brothels, often in conditions resembling slavery, and around half of these women are thought to be HIV positive. When obvious AIDS symptoms force these women out of work, some manage to return to Nepal. However, they are shunned by their families and there is virtually no assistance available for them or their children.

CHAUTARA

As you trek through Nepal you'll pass dozens of convenient stone resting spots. These are *chautaara,* built by locals as an act of piety, often in the name of a deceased relative, for porters to rest their loads upon as they pause during the hot, steep climbs. In the lowlands *chautaara* are normally built under the shade of a large banyan or pipal tree. It was under a pipal tree that Buddha attained enlightenment over 2000 years ago.

Nepal has a strongly patriarchal society, though this is less the case among Himalayan communities such as the Sherpa, where women often run the show (and the lodge). Boys are strongly favoured over girls, who are often the last to eat and the first to be pulled from school during financial difficulties. Nepal has a national literacy rate of 66%, with the rate among women at 57%.

Environment & Wildlife

Nepal is both blessed and burdened by its incredible environment. Its economy, history, resources and culture are all intrinsically tied to the string of magnificent mountains that represent a continental collision zone. As the human population continues to rise, and technology aids development of once-remote ecosystems, the Nepal Himalaya is faced with enormous environmental threats.

The Lay of the Land

Around 64% of Nepal is mountainous. The flat strip of the Terai accounts for just 17% of its Nepal's total area but half of its population and 70% of its agricultural land!

Nepal is a small, landlocked strip of land, 800km long and 200km wide. However, it fits a lot of terrain into just 147,181 sq km. Heading north from the Indian border, the landscape rises from just 70m above sea level to 8848m at the tip of Mt Everest. This dramatic landscape provides an outstanding variety of habitats for an incredible array of plants and animals.

Colliding Continents

Perched atop a geological collision zone of continental proportions, it is not surprising that Nepal is still an active seismic zone. A huge 8.2 magnitude earthquake caused devastation around the country in 1934, while an earthquake in 1255 is thought to have killed 30% of the local population. Most recently, in April 2015, at least 8000 people were killed following a 6.9 magnitude earthquake centred on the Lamjung/Gorkha region. There was no advance warning of the earthquake but it was hardly unexpected.

Around 60 million years ago the space currently occupied by Nepal was an open expanse of water, with the Tibetan plateau as its northern coast. As the Indo-Australian plate collided with the Eurasian continent, it bucked the earth's crust up into mighty concertina ridges, forming the mountains we now call the Himalaya.

The upheaval of mountains caused the temporary obstruction of rivers that once flowed unimpeded from Eurasia to the sea. Simultaneously, new rivers arose on the southern slopes of these young mountains as moist winds from the tropical seas to the south rose and precipitated. For the next 60 million years, the mountains moved up, and rivers and glaciers cut downwards, creating the four mountain systems and north-south valleys seen across Nepal today.

Saligrams (fossilised ammonites) are found throughout the Himalaya and are regarded as symbols of Vishnu – they also provide proof that the Himalaya used to lie beneath the ancient Tethys Sea.

The process is far from over. The Indo-Australian plate is still sliding under the Eurasian Himalaya at a rate of 27mm per year and pushing the Himalaya even higher. Occasionally the plates slip, releasing pent-up tension like a spring, and this is what happened during the April 2015 earthquake, as a block of the earth's crust 120km long and 40km wide slipped some 3m to the south. As a result of the quake Kathmandu rose by 1m and Mount Everest shifted southwest by 3cm.

Because the quake was shallow the surface movement was relatively severe, resulting in widespread damage across central Nepal. That's not the end of the bad news. Seismologists warn that the tension between the two plates was not fully released and that another significant earthquake is possible in the coming years.

Valley Low & Mountain High

Nepal's concertina topography consists of several physiographic regions, or natural zones: the southern plains, the four mountain ranges, and the valleys and hills in between. Most people live in the fertile lowlands or on the sunny southern slopes of mountains. Above 4000m the only residents are yak herders, who retreat into the valleys with the onset of winter.

The Kali Gandaki Valley between the Annapurna and Dhaulagiri massifs is considered the world's deepest gorge, with a vertical gain of 7km.

The Terai & Chure Hills

The only truly flat land in Nepal is the Terai (or Tarai), a patchwork of paddy fields, sal and riverine forests, tiny thatched villages and sprawling industrial cities. The vast expanse of the Gangetic plain extends for 40km into Nepal before the land rises to create the Chure Hills.

Mahabharat Range

North of the flat inner Terai, the land rises to form the Mahabharat Range, or the 'Middle Hills'. These vary between 1500m and 2700m in height and form the heartland of the inhabited highlands of Nepal. Locals cultivate rice, barley, millet, wheat, maize and other crops on spectacular terraced fields set among patches of subtropical and temperate forest. These hills are cut by three major river systems: the Karnali, the Narayani and the Sapt Kosi.

Pahar Zone

Between the Mahabharat Range and the Himalaya lies a broad, extensively cultivated belt called the Pahar zone. This includes the fertile valleys of Kathmandu, Banepa and Pokhara, which were once the beds of lakes, formed by trapped rivers. After the Terai this is the most inhabited part of Nepal, and the expanding human population is putting a massive strain on natural resources.

The Himalaya

One-third of the total length of the Himalaya lies inside Nepal's borders, and the country claims 10 of the world's 14 tallest mountains. Because of the southerly latitude (similar to that of Florida), along with the reliable rainfall, the mountains are cloaked in vegetation to a height of 3500m to 4000m. People mainly inhabit the areas below 2700m.

The Himalaya does not form an unbroken wall of peaks. Instead, the range is broken up into groups of snowy massifs (*himal*) divided by glaciers and rivers draining down from the Tibetan plateau.

CLIMATE CHANGE IN THE HIMALAYA

The Himalaya is on the front line of climate change. Rising global temperatures are melting the glaciers that snake down from the Himalaya, swelling glacial lakes to dangerous levels. The Khumbu Glacier in the Everest region has retreated 5km since 1953, increasing the flow of the Dudh Kosi and Imj Kosi.

In 1985 a natural dam collapsed in the Thame Valley, releasing the trapped waters of the Dig Tsho lake and sending devastating floods roaring along the Dudh Kosi Valley.

Scientists are now watching the Imja Tsho in the Chhukung Valley with alarm. Since 1960 the lake has grown by over 34 million cu metres – when it ruptures, experts are predicting a 'vertical tsunami' that will affect one of the most heavily populated and trekked parts of the Himalaya.

ENVIRONMENT & WILDLIFE THE LAY OF THE LAND

The Trans-Himalaya

North of the first ridge of the Himalaya is a high-altitude desert, similar to the Tibetan plateau. This area encompasses the arid valleys of Mustang, Manang and Dolpo. The moisture-laden clouds of the monsoon drop all their rain on the south side of the mountains, leaving the Trans-Himalaya in permanent rain shadow. Surreal crags, spires and badlands eroded by the scouring action of the wind are characteristic of this starkly beautiful landscape.

Wildlife

Nepal is a region of exceptional biodiversity, with a rare concentration of varied landscapes and climatic conditions. If you're a nature buff, it's worth bringing a spotters' guide.

Mammals & Birds

The diverse environments of the Himalaya and the Middle Hills provide a home for a remarkable array of birds, reptiles, amphibians and mammals. However, poaching, hunting and population pressure threaten many mammal and bird species. Your best chances for spotting wildlife are in national parks and conservation areas, or high in the mountains far away from human habitation.

Predators

Nepal's iconic 'signature species' largely reside in jungle and grasslands near the Indian border. For a glimpse of a royal Bengal tiger, one-horned rhinoceros, Asian elephant or crocodile you'll have to visit Chitwan or Bardia National Parks or Sukla Phanta Wildlife Reserve, all in the Terai.

The spotted leopard *(chituwa)* is more common than the tiger and is a significant threat to livestock. Like the tiger, this nocturnal creature has been known to target humans when it is unable, through old age or illness, to hunt its usual prey.

The endangered snow leopard *(heung chituwa)* is so rare and shy that it is seldom seen, but there are thought to be 350 to 500 snow leopards surviving in the high Himalaya, particularly around Dolpo. It hunts blue sheep and other ungulates on the edge of the treeline or in the rocky cliffs where its thick silver-grey coat blends superbly with the snow and rock. Snow leopards are so elusive that many locals believe the animals have the power to vanish at will.

The predator most commonly seen in mountain areas is the Himalayan black bear. This large omnivore frequently raids crops on the edge of mountain villages. Nepal's bears are known to roam in winter instead of hibernating.

Himalayan wolves are known to roam to heights of around 6000m, preying on game birds and grazing herds, but packs will also prey on domestic livestock. There are believed to be just a few hundred wolves left in the wild because of conflict with humans.

Several members of the mustelid family prey on smaller mammals, birds and insects in the Himalaya. The yellow-throated marten is found in temperate forests, while the Himalayan weasel roams above the treeline – it can often be spotted rearing up on its hind legs for a view over the tundra.

The endangered red panda survives on a diet of bamboo shoots, but it belongs to the same family as the racoon and it is not a true bear like the giant panda. These rare animals are occasionally spotted in remote bamboo groves in Makalu-Barun National Park and the Kanchenjunga Conservation Area.

The Sanskrit word Himalaya means abode *(alaya)* of the snows *(himal)*, meaning it's technically incorrect to refer to the region as the Himalayas. To pronounce it correctly, as they do in the corridors of the Royal Geographical Society, emphasise the second syllable – him-*aaar*-liya, old chap...

The word 'trek' is derived from the Boer language (spoken by the Dutch settlers in South Africa), meaning a long, hard journey. The root of the word is Dutch 'trekken', which means to pull or haul.

MONKEY MAYHEM

Because of Hanuman, the monkey god from the Ramayana, monkeys are considered holy and are well protected, if not pampered, in Nepal. You will often see troops of muscular red-rumped rhesus macaques harassing tourists and pilgrims for food scraps at Kathmandu's monuments and temples. These monkeys can be openly aggressive and they carry rabies, so appreciate them from a distance (and if that doesn't work, carry a stick).

You may also spot the slender common langur, with its short grey fur and black face, in forested areas up to 3700m. This species is more gentle than the thuggish macaque, but again, keep your bananas out of sight and out of reach.

Smaller Mammals

Deer are abundant in the lowland national parks, but a handful of species has adapted to life in the mountains. In forests up to 2400m, you may hear the uncannily dog-like call of the barking deer *(muntjac)*. At higher altitudes, look for the pocked-sized musk deer, which stands just 50cm high at the shoulder. Unfortunately these animals have been severely depleted by hunting to obtain the musk gland found in the abdomen of male deer.

At high altitudes, look out for the Himalayan tahr (a shaggy mountain goat) and the blue sheep *(naur* in Tibetan, *bharal* in Nepali), which is genetically positioned somewhere between goats and sheep. Tahr are easily spotted on precipitous cliffs throughout the Everest region, while blue sheep can be seen on scree slopes and high pastures around Kanchenjunga, Dolpo and Mustang.

The boulder fields and stunted forests of the high Himalaya also provide shelter for several small rodents. The mouse-hare *(pika)* is commonly spotted scurrying nervously between rocks on trekking trails. You must climb even higher to the Trans-Himalayan zone in western Nepal to see the Himalayan marmot, related to the American groundhog. Marmots live in large social groups and sentry animals keep watch for predators by standing on their hind legs, issuing a shrill whistle in the event of danger.

Birds

More than 850 bird species are known in Nepal and almost half of these can be spotted in the Kathmandu Valley. The main breeding season and the best time to spot birds is March to May. Resident bird numbers are augmented by migratory species, which arrive in the Terai from November to March overwintering from Tibet and Siberia. The best places in Nepal for birdwatching are Koshi Tappu Wildlife Reserve and Chitwan National Park.

Demoiselle cranes fly down the Kali Gandaki and Dudh Kosi for the winter, before returning in spring to their Tibetan nesting grounds. In the mountains, watch for golden eagles and the huge Himalayan griffon and lammergeier (bearded vulture).

The Snow Leopard Conservancy (www.snowleopardconservancy.org) is fighting to save the endangered snow leopard from extinction across the Himalaya.

There are six species of pheasant in Nepal, including the national bird, the *danphe,* also known as the Himalayan monal or impeyan pheasant. Females are a dull brown, while males are an iridescent rainbow of colours. In areas frequented by trekkers, these birds are often quite tame, though they will launch themselves downhill in a falling, erratic flight if disturbed.

Tibetan and Himalyan snowcocks are easily seen in the Everest region. The partridge-like member of the pheasant family frequents alpine pastures and rocky hills above the treeline.

Nepal hosts 17 species of cuckoo, which arrive in March, heralding the coming of spring. The call of the Indian cuckoo is likened to the Nepali phrase *kaphal pakyo,* meaning 'the fruit of the box myrtle is ripe'. The call of the common hawk cuckoo sounds like the words 'brain fever' – or so it was described by British *sahibs* (gentlemen) as they lay sweating with malarial fevers.

While trekking through forests, keep an eye out for members of the timalid family. The spiny babbler is Nepal's only endemic species, and the black-capped sibia, with its constant prattle and ringing song, is frequently heard in wet temperate forests. In the Pokhara region, the Indian roller is conspicuous when it takes flight, flashing iridescent turquoise on its wings. Local superstition has it that if someone about to embark on a journey sees a roller going their way it is a good omen.

Another colourful character is the hoopoe, which has a retractable crest, a long curved bill, eye-catching orange plumage, and black-and-white stripes on its wings. Nepal is also home to 30 species of flycatchers and 60 species of warblers, as well as bee-eaters, drongos, minivets, parakeets and sunbirds.

Around watercourses, look out for thrushes, such as the handsome white-capped river chat and the delightfully named plumbeous redstart. Scan the surrounding trees for the black-and-white pied kingfisher and the white-breasted kingfisher with its iridescent turquoise jacket.

Different species of crows have adapted to different altitudes. The yellow-billed blue magpie and Himalayan tree pie are commonly seen in the temperate zone. Above the treeline, red- and yellow-billed choughs gather in flocks, particularly in areas frequented by humans.

Birds of Nepal, by Robert Fleming Sr, Robert Fleming Jr and Lain Singh Bangdel, is a field guide to Nepal's many hundreds of bird species. *Birds of Nepal,* by Richard Grimmett and Carol Inskipp, is a comprehensive paperback with line drawings.

Plants

There are about 6500 known species of trees, shrubs and wildflowers in Nepal, but perhaps the most famous is the *Rhododendron arboreum* (*lali gurans* in Nepali), the national flower of Nepal. It might be better described as a tree, reaching heights of 18m and forming whole forests in the Himalaya region. More than 30 other species of rhododendron are found in the foothills of the Himalaya. The rhododendron forests burst into flower in March and April, painting the landscape in swaths of white, pink and red.

The best time to see the other wildflowers of the Himalaya in bloom is during the monsoon. The mountain views may often be obscured but the ground underfoot will be a carpet of colour. Many of the alpine species found above the treeline bear flowers in autumn, including irises, gentians, anemones and the downy-petalled edelweiss.

In the foothills of the Himalaya, as well as in the plains, look for the magnificent mushrooming canopies of banyan and pipal trees, which often form the focal point of villages. The pipal tree has a special religious significance in Nepal – the Buddha gained enlightenment under a pipal tree and Hindus revere various species of pipal as symbols of Vishnu and Hanuman.

Numerous species of pines thrive at higher elevations. The drought-tolerant chir pine can be identified by its long wispy needles, while the blue pine has short needles and long pendulous cones. Other pines include the pyramid-shaped hemlock and the Christmas-tree-shaped silver fir (the name comes from the silvery undersides of its needles). Around the tree line, look for stunted juniper bushes, whose leaves are burnt as incense. Sal, a broad-leaved, semideciduous hardwood, dominates low-lying forests.

Bird Conservation Nepal (www.birdlifenepal.org) is an excellent Nepali organisation based in Kathmandu that organises bird-watching trips and publishes books, birding checklists and a good quarterly newsletter.

National Parks & Reserves

Nepal has 10 national parks, three wildlife reserves, three conservation areas and, somewhat incongruously, one hunting reserve, protecting 18%

of the land in Nepal. Entry fees apply for all the national parks and reserves, including conserved areas on trekking routes in the mountains.

The main agency overseeing national parks and conservation areas is the Department of National Parks & Wildlife Conservation (www. dnpwc.gov.np). However, the last few years have seen a shift in the management to international NGOs and not-for-profit organisations with a degree of autonomy from the government of Nepal. The National Trust for Nature Conservation (www.ntnc.org.np), formerly the King Mahendra Trust for Nature Conservation, runs the Annapurna Conservation Area Project and Manaslu Conservation Area. The Mountain Institute (www.mountain.org) runs a number of conservation projects in the Himalaya.

The government imposed the first protected areas with little partnership with locals and initially without their cooperation. Recent initiatives have concentrated on educating local people and accommodating their needs, rather than evicting them completely from the land.

The community forest model has been particularly successful in Nepal – many protected areas are surrounded by buffer zones of community-owned forests, whose owners harvest natural resources and thus have a stake in their continued existence. See the website of the Federation of Community Forest Users, Nepal (www.fecofun.org.np) for more information.

Himalayan Flowers and Trees, by Dorothy Mierow and Tirtha Bahadur Shrestha, is the best available field guide to the plants of Nepal.

ENVIRONMENT & WILDLIFE NATIONAL PARKS & RESERVES

NATIONAL PARKS & CONSERVATION AREAS

CA = Conservation Area, HR = Hunting Reserve, NP = National Park, WR = Wildlife Reserve

NAME	LOCATION	FEATURES	BEST TIME TO VISIT	ENTRY FEE (RS)
Annapurna CA	north of Pokhara	most popular trekking area in Nepal, high peaks, diverse landscapes, varied culture	Oct-May	2000
Dhorpatan HR	west-central Nepal	Nepal's only hunting reserve (access is difficult), blue sheep	Mar-Apr	3000
Kanchenjunga CA	far eastern Nepal	third-highest mountain in the world, blue sheep & snow leopards	Mar-Apr, Oct-Nov	2000
Khaptad NP	far western Nepal	core area is important religious site, with musk deer, boar, danphe pheasant and Asiatic dog	Mar-Apr	3000
Langtang NP	northeast of Kathmandu	varied topography, culture, migratory birds	Mar-Apr	3000
Makalu-Barun NP & CA	eastern Nepal	bordering Sagarmatha NP, protecting diverse mountain landscapes	Oct-May	3000
Manaslu CA	west-central Nepal	rugged terrain, 11 types of forest, bordering Annapurna CA	Mar-Apr, Oct-Nov	2000
Rara NP	northwestern Nepal	Nepal's biggest lake, little visited, migratory birds	Mar-May, Oct-Dec	3000
Sagarmatha NP	Everest region	highest mountains on the planet, World Heritage Site, monasteries, Sherpa culture	Oct-May	3000
Shey Phoksumdo NP	Dolpo, western Nepal	Trans-Himalayan ecosystem, alpine flowers, snow leopards, blue sheep	Jun-Sep	1000

Environmental Challenges

The environment of Nepal is fragile and a rapidly growing population is constantly adding to environmental pressures. Much of the land between the Himalaya and the Terai has been vigorously modified to provide space for crops, animals and houses. Forests have been cleared and wildlife populations depleted, and roads have eaten into valleys that were previously accessible only on foot. Shangri La is not immune from the environmental challenges confronted elsewhere on our shrinking planet.

Population growth is the biggest issue facing the environment in Nepal. Increasing numbers of people need more land for agriculture and more natural resources for building, heating and cooking. Food security, economic development and tourism are providing the economic incentive for the settlement of previously uninhabited areas.

There have also been some environmental successes in Nepal. Foreign and Nepali NGOs have provided solar panels, energy efficient LED bulbs, biogas and kerosene-powered stoves, and parabolic solar cookers for thousands of farms, trekking lodges, schools and monasteries across Nepal.

A number of organisations can provide more information on environmental issues in Nepal:

Bird Conservation Nepal (www.birdlifenepal.org)
Himalayan Nature (www.himalayannature.org)
International Centre for Integrated Mountain Development (www.icimod.org)
National Trust for Nature Conservation (www.ntnc.org.np)
Resources Himalaya (www.resourceshimalaya.org)
Wildlife Conservation Nepal (www.wcn.org.np)
World Conservation Union (www.iucnnepal.org)
World Wildlife Fund Nepal (www.wwfnepal.org)

Deforestation

Almost 80% of Nepali citizens rely on firewood for heating and cooking, particularly in the mountains, leading to massive problems with deforestation. Nepal has lost more than 70% of its forest cover in modern times and travellers are contributing to the problem by increasing the demand for firewood in mountain areas.

As well as robbing native species of their natural habitat, deforestation drives animals directly into conflict with human beings. The loss of tree cover is a major contributing factor to the landslides that scar the valleys of the Himalaya and floods that hit areas downstream during every monsoon.

It's not all doom and gloom though – in recent years, a number of community forests have been established on the boundaries of national parks. The forests are communally owned and the sustainable harvest of timber and other natural resources provides an economic alternative to poaching and resource gathering inside the parks. See the website of the **Federation of Community Forest Users** (www.fecofun.org) for more information.

> Nepal covers only 0.1% of the world's surface area but is home to nearly 10% of the world's species of birds, including 72 critically endangered species.

SAGARMATHA POLLUTION CONTROL COMMITTEE

The **Sagarmatha Pollution Control Committee** (SPCC; www.spcc.org.np) is involved in a wide range of environmental and social development projects in and around Sagarmatha National Park. The SPCC mandate includes a commitment to the preservation of cultural heritage, as well as conservation, litter removal and education. An important part of the SPCC's work involves educating lodge owners and schoolchildren about fuel efficiency, health, hygiene and environmental issues. For more information on the work of the SPCC, drop into the visitor centres in Lukla and Namche Bazaar.

ENVIRONMENTALLY FRIENDLY TREKKING

Nepal faces several environmental problems as a result of, or at least compounded by, tourists' actions and expectations. Faced by environmental issues of a Himalayan scale, you may feel that one person cannot make a difference, but the reality is that every trekker who carries a piece of litter downhill and every lodge owner who switches to solar-heated hot water is making a genuine difference to the environment of the Himalaya.

Be a good trekker by following these guidelines:

➡ Minimise the use of firewood by staying in lodges that use kerosene or fuel-efficient wood stoves and solar-heated hot water.

➡ Reduce your 'firewood footprint' by eating daal bhaat instead of asking cooks to make a different meal for every trekker.

➡ Treat your drinking water chemically, with a filter or using ultraviolet light, rather than boiling it. Don't buy bottled water.

➡ On the Annapurna and Manaslu circuits, support the Safe Drinking Water Scheme – a chain of outlets selling purified water to trekkers. Its aim is to minimise the estimated one million plastic bottles that are brought into the Annapurna Conservation Area each year.

➡ Those travelling with organised groups should ensure kerosene is used for cooking, including by porters. In alpine areas ensure that all members are outfitted with enough clothing so that fires are not a necessity for warmth.

➡ Bring a couple of spare stuff sacks and use them to compact litter that you find on mountain trails, to be disposed of down in Kathmandu. Use the recycling bins that are in place in much of the Everest and Annapurna regions.

➡ Independent trekkers should always carry their garbage out or dispose of it properly. You can burn it, but you should remember that the fireplace in a Nepali home is sacred and throwing rubbish into it would be a great insult. Don't bury your rubbish.

➡ Take away all your batteries, as they will eventually leak toxins.

➡ Toilet paper is a particularly unpleasant sight along trails; if you use it, carry it in a plastic bag until you can burn it. Those travelling with organised groups should ensure that toilet tents are properly organised, that everyone uses them (including porters) and that rubbish is carried out. Check on a company's policies before you sign up.

➡ Don't soap up your clothes and wash them in streams. Instead, use a bowl or bucket and discard the dirty water away from watercourses.

Wildlife Poaching

Nepal's 10-year Maoist insurgency did not only affect human beings. Soldiers were withdrawn from national park checkpoints, leading to a massive upsurge in poaching. Nepal's rhino population fell by 30% between 2000 and 2005; elephants, tigers, leopards and other endangered species were also targeted.

The main engines driving poaching are the trade in animal parts for Chinese and Tibetan traditional medicine. Travellers can avoid contributing to the problem by rejecting souvenirs made from animal products.

Hydroelectricity

Scientists estimate that Nepal has the potential to generate 80,000 megawatts of hydroelectric power, but only 1% of this power is currently being exploited. On the face of things, harnessing the power of Nepal's rivers to create electricity sounds like a win-win situation, but the environmental impact of building new hydroelectric plants can be devastating.

Nepal is such a hilly country that the Nepali language has two different words for steep: *ukaalo* (steep uphill) and *oraalo* (steep downhill).

In recent years the Sapt Kosi, Bhote Kosi and Kali Gandaki rivers have all been dammed and several other huge projects have been signed, both with China (in the Upper Tamakoshi and the West Seti project) and India (the US$1 billion Arun River project and US$1.4 billion upper Karnali project). The amount of electricity and water earmarked for Indian consumption has become a particularly hot topic in Nepal.

Nepalis divide the year into six seasons, rather than four: Basanta (spring), Grisma (premonsoon heat), Barkha (monsoon), Sharad (postmonsoon), Hemanta (autumn) and Sheet (winter).

Tourism

Tourism has brought health care, education, electricity and wealth to some of the most remote, isolated communities in the Himalaya, but it has also had an impact on the local environment.

Forests are cleared to provide timber for the construction of new lodges and fuel for cooking and heating, and trekkers contribute massively to the build-up of litter and the erosion of mountain trails.

Even the apparent benefits of tourism can have environmental implications – the wealth that tourism has brought to villages in the Himalaya has allowed many farmers to increase the size of their herds of goats, cows and yaks, leading to yet more deforestation as woodland is cleared to provide temporary pastures.

Survival Guide

Directory A–Z

Accommodation

Kathmandu and Pokhara offer accommodation for every budget. Most hotels even have a wide range of rooms under one roof, including larger (often top-floor) deluxe rooms that are good for families and small groups. Cheaper rooms are often on the darker, lower floors and budget places may have solar-heated hot-water showers, which won't be hot in the mornings or on cloudy days. Midrange rooms have better mattresses, satellite TV and a tub. Almost all hotels offer wi-fi these days.

Most midrange and top-end places quote their prices in US dollars but you can always pay in rupees.

Most hotels have different rates for single and double occupancy, but the 'single room' may be much smaller than the double. The best deal for a solo traveller is to get a double room for a single price.

Trekking Lodges (Teahouses)

A quarter-century of hotel construction on the Everest, Annapurna and Langtang treks has resulted in an extensive system of lodge (teahouse) accommodation, with places to stay every couple of hours on the main trails. Many places offer pavement cafes, sunrooms, indoor Western-style toilets and electric lights, while kitchens churn out plate-loads of apple pie, pizza, steaks, enchiladas and spaghetti bolognese.

On lesser-trekked trails, places may be spartan – the accommodation may be dorm-style or simply an open room in which to unroll your sleeping bag.

During most of the year there's plenty of accommodation to go around. At times of heavy demand, such as during a flight back-up at Lukla or when snow has blocked the Thorung La,

accommodation can become difficult to find. Most places don't take reservations so you'll have a wider choice of rooms if you arrive early.

Committees of lodge owners in the Annapurna, Langtang and Everest regions have established fixed rates for food and accommodation so you won't save any money by shopping around. The cost of accommodation is actually minuscule compared to your food bill. You may be quoted an exorbitant price for a room in a lodge if for some reason you don't eat there.

Most trekking lodges are family operations, with the owners trying their best to make you comfortable. Often the husband of the house is away trading or working as a guide. Usually the wife manages things, with help from the children and relatives.

One uniquely Nepali institution is the loophole that allows a business to avoid tax by changing its name, meaning that lodge names change frequently.

STAYING IN A LODGE

There's often little to differentiate between rooms at different lodges so most people choose their lodge based on the quality of food and the cosiness of the restaurant. If you are trekking in the high season, many lodges will be chock-a-block and you'll just have to stay wherever there is space. We have learned the hard way to consider the

---

SLEEPING PRICE RANGES

Most lodges on the trail cost around Rs 200 per person, with midrange lodges in towns like Namche Bazaar offering rooms for US$20 or higher. For trailhead and other towns in Nepal we use the following ranges to refer to a double room with bathroom in high season. Rates generally do not include taxes, unless otherwise noted.

$ less than US$25 (Rs 2500)

$$ US$25–50 (Rs 2500–8000)

$$$ more than US$80 (Rs 8000)

following when choosing a lodge or room:

➡ The thickness of the foam mattress, especially in the middle.

➡ Whether the room walls are wood (noisier), stone or concrete.

➡ Proximity to a toilet (sometimes further away is better!) and whether it's Western or squat.

➡ Availability of direct afternoon sunlight. Corner rooms are generally brighter because they have windows on two sides (and just one neighbour) but can also be colder.

➡ Whether there are sinks or laundry facilities such as washing bowls and a clothes line.

➡ Try to avoid a room over a smoky or noisy kitchen.

➡ Ask whether there's a group due to arrive that day. Trekking groups tend to take over entire hotels, so if you don't fancy eating with a group of 20 (and waiting for their food orders to arrive first), choose a smaller lodge.

Your guide will likely have their favourite lodges where they get good treatment and free food and it's generally best to let them have their way unless the lodge is terrible (few are).

Shared toilets are the norm, normally a Western seat but sometimes an Asian squatter. Bring your own toilet paper and put it in the bucket to the side, not down the toilet. Some newer lodges have two rooms on either side of a shared toilet. You face less of a walk with this setup but you may have to put up with some farting and grunting (the walls are far from soundproof!). A few up-market facilities feature double beds and private toilets, but these are not common.

➡ The lodges at the far end of the village are often quieter, as tired trekkers tend to stick to the first couple of lodges they see.

TEAHOUSES, TEASHOPS & LODGES

In this guide we use the word 'teashop' to refer to a simple local *bhatti* that serves tea and noodles, whereas 'teahouse' refers to a tourist-oriented trekking lodge. The phrases 'trekking lodge' and 'teahouse' are used interchangably.

Note that in local Nepali usage a 'hotel' on a trekking route generally offers only food, whereas a 'lodge' offers accommodation.

Numerous lodges are mentioned by name in the route descriptions in this guide. Not all lodges are listed, though, and just because a lodge doesn't appear in the text, this does not mean it's not a great place to stay. In fact, we encourage trekkers to seek out small, lesser-visited lodges. You often get more personal service in these places, plus a better chance of scoring the best room. Use our listings as a starting point only.

➡ Most lodges offer private rooms, usually the minimum size to accommodate two beds. The walls will be wood or, in more rustic lodges, bamboo mats. This doesn't necessarily matter because the walls might not reach the ceiling anyway.

➡ You can expect some kind of blanket and pillow, though it's always nicer to snuggle up in your own sleeping bag.

➡ Solo travellers get to double up the two foam mattresses in the room for extra comfort.

➡ Most places have at least dim solar lights and can charge batteries.

➡ High altitude can make people sleepless and crabby and there's little soundproofing in lodges, so earplugs are a good investment.

➡ Most lodges offer some kind of hot shower, preferably solar heated, though you may just get a bucket of hot water and a

cup. Avoid places that use wood fires to heat water.

Bhattis (Teashops)

The Nepali word for a small teashop that offers food and simple accommodation is *bhatti*. These have existed for centuries in the hills, and in remote regions *bhattis* are still the only facilities available. Most *bhattis* only cater to porters and Nepali travellers and usually do not have any signboard at all.

Most *bhattis* offer tea, chow mein and daal bhaat (rice, lentils and vegetable curry) and stock simple food-stuffs like instant noodles and biscuits, as well as a jug or two of *chhang* (barley beer) or *rakshi* (rice wine) to provide some alcoholic diversion. Accommodation might be in a private room or a dormitory.

Conditions can be pretty rough and you can expect a night of smoke, coughing and dirt, not necessarily in that order. That said, the occasional night in a local inn can be a great experience and a

BOOK YOUR STAY ONLINE

For more accommodation reviews by Lonely Planet authors, check out http://lonelyplanet.com/hotels. You'll find independent reviews, as well as recommendations on the best places to stay. Best of all, you can book online.

good window into what trekking was like in the 1970s.

Camping

If you're used to carrying your own trekking gear in a backpack, you'll be amazed at the luxury of an organised trekking camp in Nepal. Although you'll be sleeping on foam mattresses placed on the ground, you'll be assigned a roomy A-frame or dome tent that comfortably accommodates two people and their gear. Meals are served inside a dining tent and camp staff race back and forth acting as waiters. If there's no permanent toilet near the camp, the staff dig a hole and set up a toilet tent.

Most villages on a trekking route have established camp sites, sometimes in a designated grassy area owned by the community, sometimes in the playground of the local school. There is often a fee of around Rs 100 per tent at these camp sites. Consider a donation to a school if there's no formal fee. In return you should get a water supply and some kind of toilet.

Bear in mind that the location of camp sites can vary according to the season. Many sites that are excellent in November and December are under water or full of rice plants in the growing season.

Discounts

Hotel prices in Kathmandu and Pokhara are highly seasonal, with peak season running from October to November and March to April, but even beyond this room rates fluctuate according to tourist demand. Discounts of 20% are common in many midrange hotels. Rates drop even lower during the monsoon season (June to September).

Some trekking lodges will offer free accommodation if you take your meals there, especially at the beginning or end of the trekking seasons.

Activities

Nepal offers some of the best rafting, kayaking and mountain biking in Asia, and there's also canyoning, bungee jumping, ziplining, paragliding and caving. Many adventure travel companies offer combination activity trips that include some rafting, kayaking and canyoning based in a fixed riverside camp, either between Kathmandu and Pokhara or up near the Tibetan border. Lonely Planet's *Nepal* guidebook has full details.

Nepal is a great place to spend three or four days learning the basics of kayak-

ing, rock climbing or mountaineering. See Lonely Planet's *Nepal* guide for details.

For details of mountain marathons see p88 in the Everest Region chapter.

Children

Trekking with children can be an enjoyable experience if you are already comfortable with backcountry travel and are realistic in your expectations of what your children can tolerate. Read the following suggestions, go on at least one short test trip at home before you commit to a long trek, and remember: a first trek with a child is better to be too short than too long.

We don't recommend going trekking with an infant younger than six months old. Children up to three years old in particular can become ill rapidly, with few signs to indicate how serious the illness is. It is difficult to ascertain if they are suffering from altitude sickness, as they can't always tell you whether they have headache, loss of appetite etc. It is better to plan treks under 3000m with children of this age.

➡ Stick to the main teahouse treks when trekking with children.

➡ Try to go with another family who have children of a similar age and bring toys, games and foods familiar to your children as they may not adapt readily to daal bhaat any more than you do.

➡ Prepare fair-skinned children for the experience of being stared at and doted upon, as this can be overwhelming.

➡ Children between the ages of two and eight can generally be carried in a modified *doko* (porter basket), but younger ones will need to be in a child's backpack. A good child porter, or *doko dai,* can develop a warm relationship with the child, carrying them when needed, and holding

---

LUXURY LODGES

If you demand a certain level of luxury on your trek, several companies offer deluxe lodges in the Annapurna and Everest regions.

Ker & Downey (www.trekking-nepal.com) operates treks staying in its deluxe chain of lodges in Dhampus, Ghandruk, Majgaun and Birethanti on the approaches to the Annapurna Sanctuary. Jomsom boasts the luxury **Mustang Lodge** (www.mustangresorts.com).

The best selection of luxury lodges is in the lower reaches of the Everest region (see p66), allowing you to make a pampered week-long loop around Namche Bazaar.

Priority is given to guests on these company's treks, but independent trekkers can also make bookings. You'll get the best rates through an agency rather than turning up on your own.

the child's hand when the child needs some exercise.

➡ Bring an ample supply of disposable nappies (diapers), as there is rarely an opportunity while trekking to wash and dry cloth nappies. Carry the soiled nappies in a plastic bag until you can find an appropriate place to dispose of them.

➡ If teenagers still want to go on a holiday with you, count yourself lucky, but make sure they really want to go. Bored children can be a ball and chain around the legs of even the most enthusiastic parents on a trek.

➡ Come to terms with the fact that your children may not be as thrilled as you are with yet another stunning Himalayan view.

➡ Check out Lonely Planet's *Travel with Children* for handy hints and advice about the pros and cons of travelling with kids.

Customs Regulations

All baggage is X-rayed on arrival and departure, though it's a pretty haphazard process. In addition to the import and export of drugs, customs is concerned with the illegal export of antiques. You may not import Nepali rupees, and only nationals of Nepal and India may import Indian currency. Officially you should declare cash or travellers cheques in excess of US$2000, or the equivalent.

Antiques

Customs' main concern is preventing the export of antique works of art, and with good reason: Nepal has been a particular victim of international art theft over the last 20 years.

It is very unlikely that souvenirs sold to travellers will be antique (despite the claims of the vendors), but if there is any doubt, they should be cleared and a

PRACTICALITIES

Newspapers

Nepal's main English-language papers are the daily *Kathmandu Post* (www.ekantipur.com/tkp), *The Himalayan* (www.thehimalayantimes.com) and *Republica* (www.myrepublica.com); the latter comes complete with a *New York Times* pull-out supplement. The *Nepali Times* (www.nepalitimes.com) is weekly.

Magazines

ECS (www.ecs.com.np; Rs 100) is a glossy, expat-orientated monthly magazine with interesting articles on travel and culture. *Himalaya* magazine (www.himalayamagazine.com) has a focus on trekking in Nepal. *Himal* magazine (www.himalmag.com) is also good.

Weights & Measures

Nepal has adopted the metric system of weights, alongside traditional measures used mainly in rural areas.

certificate obtained from the **Department of Archaeology** (Map p51; ☎01-4250683; Ramshah Path, Kathmandu; ⊙10am-2pm Sat, to 3pm Sun-Thu).

Electricity

Electricity is 230V/50 cycles. Sockets usually take plugs with three round pins, sometimes the small variety, sometimes the large. Some sockets take plugs with two round pins. Electrical shops in the main towns sell cheap adapters. Note that power supplies to some rural areas may be disrupted because of earthquake damage.

➡ Blackouts ('load shedding') are a fact of life across Nepal, especially in Kathmandu; these peak in the winter months of December and January with up to 12 hours a day of cuts.

➡ Power surges are also likely, so bring a voltage guard with spike suppressor (automatic cut-off switch) for your laptop.

➡ Many villages on the Annapurna and Everest treks have hydro-generated electricity and lodges will

power up your rechargeable batteries for between Rs 150 and Rs 350 per hour.

➡ If you are camping you will need to invest in a good solar charger to keep your camera and other batteries topped up.

➡ Batteries lose their juice quickly in cold temperatures so keep them in your sleeping bag overnight at higher elevations.

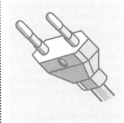

230V/50Hz

230V/50Hz

Embassies & Consulates

Travellers continuing beyond Nepal may need visas for Bangladesh, China, India, Myanmar (Burma) and Thailand.

Obtaining an Indian tourist visa in Nepal is a time-consuming process. Luckily many nationals (currently not British citizens) can now get a visa on arrival by air at select airports after applying in advance online (www.indian-visaonline.gov.in). For full details see the embassy website.

To find Nepali embassies and consulates in other countries, check out the websites of Nepal's **Ministry of Foreign Affairs** (www.mofa.gov.np) or **Department of Immigration** (www.nepal-immigration.gov.np).

Australian Embassy (☑01-4371678; www.nepal.embassy.gov.au; Bansbari, Kathmandu)

Canadian Consulate (Map p51; ☑01-4441976; canadaconsul@mail.com.np; 47 Lal Durbar Marg; ⊙9am-noon Mon-Fri) Canada maintains a consulate offering limited assistance in Kathmandu.

Chinese Embassy (Map p51; ☑01-4440286; http://np.china-embassy.org/eng;

Hattisar, Kathmandu) Visa applications are accepted on Monday to Friday from 9.45am to 11am; visas normally take three working days to be issued but can be done in just one day if you pay extra. The visa section is located in Hattisar; the main embassy is in Baluwatar.

French Embassy (Map p51; ☑01-4412332; www.ambafrance-np.org; Lazimpat, Kathmandu; ⊙9am-11.30am Mon, Tue, Thu & Fri) French embassy, but no consular section.

German Embassy (☑01-4217200; www.kathmandu.diplo.de; Gyaneshwar Marg 690, Kathmandu; ⊙9am-11.30am)

Indian Embassy (☑01-4410900; www.indianembassy.org.np; 336 Kapurdhara Marg, Lainchaur; ⊙9.30am-noon & 1.30-5pm Mon-Fri) Getting an Indian tourist visa in Nepal (or anywhere else) is a rather complicated and time-consuming process. Indian visa applications are only accepted after an online visa (https://indianvisaonline.gov.in) form has been completed. For full details on obtaining the visa see the embassy website. Tourist visas take between seven and 10 days to issue.

Israeli Embassy (Map p51; ☑01-4411811; http://kathmandu.mfa.gov.il; Lazimpat, Kathmandu; ⊙9am-5pm Mon-Thu, to 2pm Fri)

Japanese Embassy (☑01-4426680; www.np.emb-japan.go.jp; Pani Pokhari, Kathmandu; ⊙9am-1pm & 2-5pm Mon-Fri)

Netherlands Embassy (☑01-5523444; www.netherlandsconsulate.org.np; Jawalakhel, Patan; ⊙9am-4.30pm Mon-Thu, to 1pm Fri)

Thai Embassy (☑01-4371410; www.thaiembnepal.org.np; Bansbari, Maharajganj, Kathmandu; ⊙9.30am-noon & 2-4pm Mon-Fri) Most nationalities don't need a visa for stays of less than 15 days.

UK Embassy (Map p51; ☑01-4410583; www.ukinnepal.fco.gov.uk; Lainchhaur, Kathmandu; ⊙8.15am-12.30pm & 1.30-5pm Mon-Thu, 8.15am-1.15pm Fri)

US Embassy (☑01-4234000; http://nepal.usembassy.gov; Maharajganj, Kathmandu; ⊙8am-5pm Mon-Fri)

Food

On a teahouse trek in the Annapurna, Langtang, Manaslu and Everest regions, you can rely entirely on hotels for meals and not carry any food at all. Most trekking lodges also sell supplies of tinned food, chocolate bars, biscuits, toilet paper and other essentials, at a premium.

After a few days it becomes clear that lodge menus are really just every imaginable combination of the same four staples – potatoes, rice, noodles and pasta. After a hard day's walking, only a daal bhaat will truly fill you up; everything else seems inconsequential.

Interestingly, the Nepali word for eating is *khanu*, which is also used for the verbs 'to drink' and 'to smoke'.

Staples & Specialities

The staple meal of Nepal is *daal bhaat tarkari* (literally lentil soup, rice and curried vegetables). If you are lucky it will be spiced up with spicy *achar* (pickles) and maybe some *chapati* (unleavened Indian bread), *dahi* (curd or yoghurt) or *papad* (pappadam; crispy fried lentil-flour pancake). If you order daal bhaat, someone will come around offering free extra helpings of rice, daal and vegetables.

To eat daal bhaat the local way, pour the soupy daal onto the rice, mix it into balls with your fingers, add a pinch of pickle and vegetables and shovel it into your mouth with your right hand.

Most Nepalis are vegetarians, some out of choice and some out of necessity. Where you do get meat it will normally be chicken, goat or buff (water buffalo); cows are sacred to Hindus and are never eaten. You can get yak steaks at some trekking lodges.

Tibetan cuisine is a staple in many trekking lodges, with most dishes a simple variation on *momos* (dumplings, either steamed or fried, known as *kothey*), *thukpa* (long noodle soup) or *thenthuk* (torn pasta stew). A similar Sherpa speciality is *shakpa* (a stew of vegetables, bits of meat and dumplings). One cheap and cheerful dish you'll find everywhere is chow mein (thin noodles fried with vegetables or meat).

Hill people subsist on either daal bhaat or a thick paste of coarse ground corn or millet called *dhindo*. In Tibetan-influenced border regions the staple is *tsampa*, a powder of roasted and ground barley that is mixed with salty butter tea into a dough-like consistency.

A few trekkers' dishes might be new to you. *Swiss rosti* is essentially mashed potato topped with yak cheese (or, more accurately, *nak* cheese – yaks are male, so there's technically no such thing as 'yak cheese'). Probably only on a trek (or a visit to Glasgow) would you consider eating a 'Snickers roll', a chocolate bar wrapped in dough and deep fried into gooey, sickly-sweet heaven.

Apple pie appears on many menus and is often excellent, though it runs the gamut from real pie with a crust to a greasy folded taco fried over a kerosene stove. Most hotels offer something resembling a pizza, though they are hindered by a limited supply of ingredients.

Some local specialities worth trying are tart and zesty seabuckthorn juice in Manang, a breakfast of *tsampa* mixed with milk powder and sugar in any Tibetan area, and the stellar mixed vegetables made from sweet local pumpkin in Tal. Our much-coveted award for the best apple pie in Nepal goes to the Everest Bakery in Khumjung, where we once reorganised our entire Everest itinerary just to get a second helping.

Many Nepalis round off a meal with a *digestif* of *pan* (betel nut and leaf mixture). Those little spots of red on the pavement that look like little pools of blood are (generally) *pan*.

TEAHOUSE FOOD

The price of food and drink in trekking lodges rises as fast as the altitude. A cup of milk tea

EATING PRICE RANGES

A daal bhaat on the trail ranges from Rs 150 in the lowlands to as much as Rs 600 at high elevations. The following price indicators refer to a standard main course.

$ less than Rs 250

$$ Rs 250–500

$$$ more than Rs 500

GOVERNMENT TRAVEL ADVICE

Many foreign governments provide travel advice for their citizens, highlighting entry requirements, medical facilities, areas with health and safety risks, and civil unrest or other dangers. These official travel advisories should be your first port of call for up-to-date information on the travel situation in Nepal after the 2015 earthquakes. Some of this official travel advice can sound a little alarmist, but if your government issues a travel warning advising against 'all travel' or 'all but essential travel' to a specific area, then your travel insurance may be invalid if you ignore this advice. The following government websites provide travel advice for Nepal and other countries.

Australian Department of Foreign Affairs & Trade (www.smartraveller.gov.au)

Canadian Consular Affairs (www.voyage.gc.ca)

New Zealand Ministry of Foreign Affairs & Trade (www.safetravel.govt.nz)

UK Foreign & Commonwealth Office (www.gov.uk/foreign-travel-advice)

US Department of State (www.state.gov/travel)

Registration

Officials of most embassies in Nepal further recommend you register with them online before a trek. Include the contact details of your next of kin, and your travel dates, itinerary, passport number and insurance details.

Australian Embassy (www.orao.dfat.gov.au)

New Zealand Embassy (https://register.safetravel.govt.nz)

US Embassy (https://travelregistration.state.gov)

THE LOCAL FIREWATER

Out on a trek, look out for the traditional homebrews of the hills. One drink you'll find everywhere is *chhang*, a mildly alcoholic Tibetan concoction made from fermented barley or millet and water. *Chhang* is made from unpurified water so proceed with caution.

In eastern Nepal, look out for *tongba*, a Himalayan brew made by pouring boiling water into a wooden (or metal) pot full of fermented millet. The liquid is slurped through a bamboo straw and more hot water is added periodically to seep extra alcohol from the mash.

Harder spirits include *arak*, fermented from potatoes or grain, and *rakshi*, a distilled rice wine that runs the gamut from smooth-sipping schnapps to headache-inducing paint stripper.

that costs Rs 10 in the lowlands rapidly rises to Rs 100 in high places such as Lobuche and Annapurna Base Camp.

In most inns you or your guide writes down your order on pages in a notebook and tally up the bill in the morning. It's worth keeping track yourself of what you eat because other trekkers' food often makes its way onto your bill when a lodge gets busy. Lodges prefer you to order dinner and breakfast in advance and fix a rough time. In lodges, porters and guides generally eat last and separately from trekkers, often in the kitchen. Most teahouses offer porters and guides basic but free accommodation, and tea and at-cost daal bhaat. In more remote places it will probably cost Rs 300 per day for a guide to live on a trek. At lunchtime, porters and guides will generally want to eat where you do in order to get subsidised food, so bear this in mind before declaring you need some time by yourself at lunchtime.

Most Nepalis limit their breakfast to a cup of tea and have a heavy brunch of daal bhaat at around 10am. When staying in local *bhattis* or trekking with your own porters, you may find it faster to operate on the same schedule. If you wait to have lunch at noon or 1pm you will prob-

ably have to wait an hour or more while the hotel-keeper cooks rice especially for you.

SELF-CATERING

Kathmandu's supermarkets carry a wide range of staples, including chocolate bars, trekkers' muesli, granola bars, peanut butter, honey, instant noodles, packaged soups, grains, dried fruit, tinned tuna, oatmeal, nuts, instant coffee, milk powder and processed cheese.

Out in the hills you can normally find biscuits, instant noodles, vegetables, rice and beer in any decent-sized village, but that's about it. Popular trekking centres like Jomsom, Manang, Chame, Namche Bazaar and Lukla sell almost anything you could want.

You can buy *nak* cheese on several treks, including at Kyanjin Gompa and Sing Gompa in the Langtang region and at Namche Bazaar.

Where to Eat & Drink

In 1955 Kathmandu had only one restaurant. These days, every other building in Kathmandu is a restaurant, serving food from across the globe. However, travel outside Kathmandu and Pokhara and you'll find that menus quickly shrink to chow mein, fried rice, fried potatoes and daal bhaat.

At local restaurants, known as *bhojanalaya*, the custom is to eat with your right hand. Also look out for the vegetarian restaurants known as *misthan bhandar*, which serve Indian sweets and *dosas* (fried lentil-flour pancakes). A couple of *samsa* (samosas; potato curry, fried in a lentil-dough parcel) here makes a great snack.

Drinks
NONALCOHOLIC

The golden rules in Nepal are *don't drink the water* and don't buy bottled water on a trek. Cheap bottled water is available in towns but is expensive in the mountains and every bottle contributes to Nepal's growing mountain of plastic waste. Bring a water bottle and purify your own water (p348) with chemical tablets, a filer or a Steripen.

Tea is almost always safe. For proper Nepali *chiya* (sometimes called masala tea), the leaves are boiled with milk, sugar and spices. If you want Western-style tea, ask for 'milk separate'. Major trekking towns like Lukla and Namche now have cafes serving Illy or Lavazza espresso coffee. Lemon tea, ginger tea and hot lemon squash are also popular.

In Tibetan-influenced areas the drink of choice is butter tea (*soja* or *so-cha*), a soupy mix of black tea churned with salt soda and butter. It has a delicate flavour, which some travellers have likened to a mix of sump oil, boiled sweaty socks and lard. It's really not that bad and is excellent for replacing lost salts and preventing chapped lips. Locals often pour it over their *tsampa* (roasted barley flour).

ALCOHOLIC

Nepali beer is pretty good, especially after a hard day's trek. Tuborg (Danish), Carlsberg (Danish) and San Miguel (Spanish) are brewed under licence in Nepal; local brands include Gorkha and

Everest Beer. Nepal Distilleries produces a variety of bottled spirits that claim to be rum, whisky, brandy and gin. Most are pretty grim, but Khukri Rum goes down well with mixers.

Apple and pear brandies are a speciality in the Kali Gandaki region of the Annapurnas between Marpha and Tukuche, and you can even tour the distillery in Tukuche. A favourite in the Annapurna region is 'Mustang coffee', which is sweetened milk coffee with a large shot of local *rakshi*.

A few districts in Nepal are dry, including Jumla and a few villages in Helambu. Local women and other activists are agitating in several more districts to ban alcohol consumption.

Officially, alcohol is not sold by retailers on the first two days (full-moon days) and the last two Saturdays of the Nepali month.

Insurance

A travel-insurance policy to cover theft, loss and medical problems is essential for trekking in Nepal. Check how your policy defines 'dangerous activities', such as trekking, mountaineering or alpinism, or you may have a difficult time settling a claim. Some policies set an altitude limit to their coverage.

Choose a policy that covers medical and emergency repatriation, including helicopter evacuation for trekkers and general medical evacuation to Bangkok or Delhi, which alone can cost a cool US$60,000.

Rescue insurance is particularly important. An emergency helicoptor rescue can cost from US$2500 to US$10,000, depending how far you are from a major airport. Most operators won't send a chopper unless they have a guarantee of cash in hand, normally through your credit card. It's then up to you to obtain

reimbursement from your insurance company.

In Nepal, most medical treatment must be paid for at the point of delivery. If your insurance company does not provide upfront payment, be sure to obtain a receipt so you can reclaim later. Some policies ask you to call back (reverse charges) to a centre in your home country where an immediate assessment of your problem is made.

The **British Mountaineering Council** (www.thebmc.co.uk) has a range of trekking and mountaineering policies you can buy online.

Worldwide travel insurance is available at www.lonelyplanet.com/travel-insurance. You can buy, extend and claim online anytime – even if you're already on the road.

Internet Access

Internet cafes and wi-fi are now available sporadically at most places on the Annapurna Circuit and Everest treks. It's not cheap, at around Rs 200 to Rs 400 per hour or Rs 1000 for 24 hours, but connection speeds aren't bad considering where you are. Prices should fall over time as connections shift from satellite to phone.

Legal Matters

Hashish has been illegal since 1973, but it's still readily

available in Nepal. In practice, Nepali police aren't very interested in people with a small amount of marijuana on them (they're more focused on smuggling), but the technical penalty for drug possession is around five years in prison.

If you get caught smuggling something serious – drugs or gold – the chances are you'll end up in jail, without trial, and will remain there until someone pays for you to get out. Jail conditions in Nepal are not good...

Killing a cow is illegal in Nepal and carries a punishment of two years in prison.

Money

The Nepali rupee (Rs) is divided into 100 paisa (p). Banknotes come in denominations of one, two, five, 10, 20, 50, 100, 500 and 1000 rupees. Since the abolition of the monarchy in 2008, images of Mt Everest have replaced the king on all banknotes.

In general you should carry with you enough money in cash rupees to last the whole trek. It's also a good idea to bring a stash of US dollars in case you need to buy an emergency flight ticket or hire a vehicle at the end of your trek.

Away from the main teahouse treks, changing a Rs 1000 note can be difficult, so keep a chunk of your money

BARGAINING

Haggling is regarded as an integral part of most commercial transactions in Nepal, especially when dealing with souvenir shops, taxi drivers, hotels and guides or for horse or yak hire. You won't get very far haggling with lodge owners; most villages have set minimum rates.

Ideally, bargaining should be an enjoyable social exchange, rather than a conflict of egos. A good deal is reached when both parties are happy, so keep things light; Nepalis do not appreciate aggressive behaviour. Remember that Rs 10 might quite a difference to the seller, but in real terms it amounts to very little (less than US$0.10).

in small-denomination notes. Many people won't accept torn notes.

ATMs

Kathmandu and Pokhara have dozens of 24-hour ATMs; the most reliable are those of Standard Chartered Bank, Himalaya Bank and Nabil Bank. Some don't accept foreign bank cards, despite Visa signs indicating that they do.

➡ There are functioning ATMs in Jomsom, Lukla and Namche Bazaar, but power outages, mechanical faults and a lack of cash can keep them out of action for days at a time, so don't depend on them.

➡ Using an ATM attached to a bank during business hours will minimise hassle in the rare event that the machine eats your card.

➡ It's not a bad idea to inform your bank that you'll be using your card abroad, otherwise they might suspect fraud and freeze your card.

Changing Money

In Kathmandu and Pokhara, and even some trailheads like Beni, Lukla and Besi Sahar, you can change money officially at banks and authorised moneychangers. The exchange rate in larger hotels is often unfavourable.

Moneychangers are generally more convenient and efficient than banks and offer competitive rates. Most licensed moneychangers will provide an exchange receipt; if they don't you may be able to negotiate better rates than those posted on their boards.

There are banks at larger villages and trekking centres like Lukla, Namche Bazaar, Chame and Jomsom, but rates are lower than the cities. A few of the larger trekking lodges will change money and even give an advance on a credit card, but as you head further along the trail the rates drop and the commissions rise. It's far better to carry enough rupees with you.

When changing cash and travellers cheques in Nepal, US dollars are the most acceptable, although banks and moneychangers are also happy with euros, pounds sterling and Australian dollars. Travellers cheques can be exchanged in banks in Kathmandu and Pokhara for a 2% surcharge, but are not accepted on a trek. Avoid euro travellers cheques, which attract an additional US\$10 fee per cheque.

When you change money at banks, you are required to show your passport, and you are issued with a foreign-exchange encashment receipt. Hang onto these receipts to change excess rupees back into hard currency at banks; otherwise simply change your rupees back at any money-changer (no receipt required).

Credit Cards

Major credit cards are widely accepted at midrange and better hotels, restaurants, airlines and tourist shops in the Kathmandu Valley and Pokhara only. Most places levy a 3% to 4% surcharge to counter the credit card company's fees to the vendor.

Branches of Standard Chartered Bank and some other banks such as Nabil Bank and Himalaya Bank give cash advances against Visa and MasterCard, in Nepali rupees only.

Out on the trails a few entrepreneurial lodge owners give cash advances on a credit card for around 10% commission, but you should consider this in an emergency only.

International Transfers

In general, it's easiest to send money through companies such as Western Union or Moneygram, which can arrange transfers within minutes. To pick up funds at a Western Union branch you'll need your passport and 10-digit transfer code.

Note that money can often only be received in Nepali rupees, rather than US dollars.

Taxes

Most midrange and top-end hotels and restaurants add a 13% value added tax (VAT), as well as a 10% service charge. The service charge is

OPENING HOURS

Standard opening hours are listed below.

BUSINESS	OPENING HOURS
airline offices	9am-1pm & 2-6pm Sun-Fri, 9am-1pm Sat
banks	9am-4pm Sun-Fri, 10am-noon Sat
bars & clubs	generally close by 11pm or midnight, even in Kathmandu
embassies	9am-1pm & 2-5pm Mon-Fri
government offices	10am-1pm & 2-5pm (to 4pm in winter) Mon-Thu, 10am-1pm Fri (also 10am-5pm Sun outside the Kathmandu Valley)
museums	generally closed Tue
restaurants	8am-10pm
shops	10am-8pm (some shops close on Sat)

craftily calculated from the total after VAT, resulting in a whopping 24.3% surcharge to your bill. Some budget places charge only VAT or service, especially restaurants. Where hotels quote their rates including tax we mention this in the review.

Tipping

Trekking guides and porters generally expect a tip of around 15% for a job well done. Always give the tip directly to your porters rather than the guide or trek company.

On a group trek the best system is to pool the group's money and pay each member of the crew individually as a single tip from the entire group. Things get complex when you have multiple staff all on different pay grades. Have your tips worked out well in advance and bring plenty of small bills and envelopes to help the division. On larger groups the tour leader will take care of this.

Photography

Bringing an amateur video camera to Nepal poses no real problem. The exception to this is in the upper Mustang region, where an astonishing US$1000 fee is levied.

➡ Almost all flavours of memory sticks, flash cards and batteries are available in Kathmandu. Note that travellers have reported buying cheap cards in Kathmandu that do not have as much memory as the packet claims.

➡ Most Nepalis are content to have their photograph taken, but always ask permission first. Sherpa people are an exception and can be very camera-shy.

➡ Bear in mind that if a *sadhu* (holy man) poses for you, they will probably insist on being given *baksheesh* (a tip).

➡ It is not uncommon for temple guardians to not allow photos of their temple,

DASAIN STOPPAGES

Dasain (15 days in September or October) is the most important of all Nepali celebrations. Tens of thousands of Nepalis hit the road to return home to celebrate with their families. This means that while villages are full of life if you are trekking, buses and planes are fully booked and overflowing and porters may be hard to find (or more expensive than usual). Many hotels and restaurants in regional towns close down completely, and doing business in Kathmandu (outside Thamel) becomes almost impossible.

The most important days, when everything comes to a total halt, are the ninth day (when thousands of animals are sacrificed) and the 10th day (when blessings are received from elder relatives and superiors). Banks and government offices are generally closed from the eighth day of the festival to the 12th day.

and these wishes should be respected.

➡ Don't photograph army camps, checkpoints or bridges.

Post

The postal service to and from Nepal is, at best, erratic but can occasionally be amazingly efficient. Most articles do arrive at their destination...eventually. There is a porter postal service through the hills of Nepal and you'll find post offices in many remote villages.

In general you are better off sending important mail from Kathmandu or Pokhara.

Parcel Post

Having stocked up on gifts and souvenirs in Nepal, many people send them home from Kathmandu. Parcel post is not cheap or quick, but the service is reliable.

As an idea, a 2kg package to the UK/US costs Rs 1710/2010 via airmail, 25% less at 'book post' rate (a special rate for books only).

The contents of a parcel must be inspected by officials *before* it is wrapped. There are packers at the Kathmandu foreign post office who will wrap it for a small fee. The maximum weight for sea mail is 20kg;

for airmail it's 10kg, or 5kg for book post.

Postal Rates

Airmail rates for a 20g letter/postcard in Nepal are Rs 5/2; in India and surrounding countries Rs 25/20; in Europe and the UK Rs 40/30; and in the US and Australia Rs 50/35.

Public Holidays

A remarkable number of holidays and festivals affect the working hours of Nepal's government offices and banks, which seem to close every other day and certainly for public holidays and some or all festival days. Exact festival timings (and thus their public holiday dates) change annually according to Nepal's lunar calendar. Main closures include:

Prithvi Narayan Shah's Birthday 10 January

Basanta Panchami (start of Spring) January/February

Maha Shivaratri (Shiva's Birthday) February/March

Bisket Jatra (Nepali New Year) 14 April

Janai Purnima July/August

Teej (Festival of Women) August/September

Indra Jatra (Indra Festival) September

Dasain September/October

Tihar (Divali) October/November

Constitution Day 9 November

Safe Travel

For general advice on safe trekking in Nepal see the Trekking Safely chapter. In the past there has been the occasional mugging of solo walkers trekking up the Peace Pagoda and Sarangkot outside Pokhara. As ever, the advice is never walk alone. In general though, Nepal does not have serious problems with crime, though this could change with the dire economic situation in Nepal following the 2015 earthquakes.

Demonstrations & Strikes

For the last decade Nepal has been wracked by frequent demonstrations and strikes – some called by politicians, some by students, some by Maoists, and some by all three! The political situation has greatly improved in recent years but occasional demonstrations still occur.

A normal demonstration is a *julus*. If things escalate there may be a *chakka jam* ('jam the wheels'), when all vehicles stay off the street, or a *bandh,* when all shops,

schools and offices are closed. In the event of a strike the best thing to do is hole up in your hotel with a good book. In this case you'll likely have to dine at your hotel.

Telephone

The phone system in Nepal works pretty well and making local, STD and international calls is easy in most towns.

Private call centres offer the cheapest and most convenient way to make a call. Look for signs advertising STD/ISD services. Out in rural areas you may find yourself using someone's mobile phone at a public call centre. In remoter areas lodges offer calls for around Rs 100 per minute.

Note that Nepal's phone network was affected by the 2015 earthquakes, with fixed lines and mobile signals affected in some areas.

Mobile Phones

Mobile phone coverage is quite extensive in rural nepal. Mobile (cell) phone masts are dotted through the Khumbu region, including at Gorak Shep, meaning you can now get 3G coverage along the main Everest trek (though it's patchy in the side valleys).

Ncell (www.ncell.com.np) is the most popular and convenient provider for tourists, though reception in mountain areas is patchy. Ncell are currently adding towers across the Everest region so you can expect increased reception and data services by the time you read this.

To get a SIM card take a copy of your passport and one photo to an Ncell office. Ncell offers a traveller package for Rs 1000, which gets you Rs 600 worth of calls, Rs 500 of international calls and 500MB of data, for 15 days. Otherwise, local calls cost around Rs 2 to Rs 3 per minute and incoming calls free. International calls cost around Rs 5 to Rs 15 per minute depending on the destination. It's easy to buy a scratch card to top up your balance, in denominations from Rs 50 to Rs 1000. You can normally get a SIM card on arrival at Tribhuvan Airport.

For 3G internet access, you can buy a USB data card and SIM card package for Rs 2300 to Rs 2700, with which you can even get internet access on the Everest Base Camp Trek! (The first tweet from the summit of Everest was sent in May 2011...) Exact rates depend on the size of the data bundle.

SCAMS

While the overwhelming majority of Nepalis couldn't be any nicer, there are some who are impressively inventive in their range of imaginative scams. Watch out for the following:

➡ Deals offered by gem dealers that involve you buying stones to sell for a 'vast profit' at home. The dealers normally claim they are not able to export the stones without paying heavy taxes, so you take them and meet another dealer when you get home, who will sell them to a local contact and you both share the profit. Except they don't. And you don't.

➡ Children or young mothers asking for milk. You buy the milk at a designated store at an inflated price, the child then returns the milk and pockets some of the mark-up.

➡ Kids who seem to know the capital of any country you can think of; they are charming but a request for money will probably arrive at some point.

➡ 'Holy men' who do their best to plant a *tika* (a red paste denoting a blessing) on your forehead, to only then demand significant payment.

➡ Credit card scams, which are not unheard of; travellers have bought souvenirs and then found thousands of dollars worth of internet porn subscriptions chalked up on their bill.

Nepal Telecom (www.ntc. net.np) operates the Namaste Mobile network and has roaming agreements with companies such as Vodafone and Cingular, but signing up for a SIM card is a more laborious process than for Ncell. However, Namaste has a much wider reception in the mountains.

Smartcell (www.smarttel. com.np) has plans to expand into the Khumbu region.

As a general guide, Ncell is best for the Everest region, while Nepal Telecom is better for Annapurna, lower Solu Khumbu and eastern Nepal. In remoter regions such as on Manaslu Circuit and Tsum Valley, Kanchenjunga and Dolpo you won't find much mobile coverage. Organised groups generally take a satellite phone in these regions.

You will need an unlocked GSM 900 compatible phone to use local networks.

Unlike using a landline, you need to dial the local area code when making a local call on a mobile.

Time

Nepal is five hours and 45 minutes ahead of GMT; this curious time differential is intended to make it very clear that Nepal is a separate place from India, where the time is five hours and 30 minutes ahead of GMT. There is no daylight-saving time in Nepal.

Toilets

Outside of the bigger trekking lodges on the main trek routes, the 'squat toilet' is the norm.

➡ Next to a squat toilet (*charpi* in Nepali) is a bucket and/or tap, which has a two-fold function: flushing the toilet and cleaning the nether regions (with the left hand only) while still squatting over the toilet.

➡ In tourist areas you'll find Western sit-down toilets

and maybe toilet paper (depending on how classy the place is). In general, put used toilet paper in the separate bin; don't flush it down the toilet.

➡ Most rural places don't supply toilet paper, so always carry an emergency stash on you.

Visas

All foreigners, except Indians, must have a visa. Nepali embassies and consulates overseas issue visas with no fuss. You can also get one on the spot when you arrive in Nepal, either at Kathmandu's Tribhuvan Airport or at road borders: Nepalganj, Birganj/ Raxaul Bazaar, Sunauli, Kakarbhitta, Mahendranagar, Dhangadhi and even the funky Kodari checkpoint on the road to Tibet.

A Nepali visa is valid for entry for three to six months from the date of issue. Children under 10 require a visa but are not charged a visa fee. Your passport must have at least six months of validity.

You can download a visa application form from the websites of the Nepali embassy in Washington, DC (www.nepalembassyusa.org) or London (www.nepembassy.org.uk).

To obtain a visa upon arrival by air in Nepal you must fill in an application form and provide a passport photograph. Visa application forms are available on a table in the arrivals hall, though some airlines provide this form on the flight. For people with electronic passports there are now visa registration machines in the immigration hall which, after inserting your passport, will automatically fill out the visa form for you.

Nepal is moving towards an online visa application process. At the moment few people use this system as it takes longer than simply filling out the form by hand and there are few advantages to using it. However, it could become

mandatory in the future. See www.online.nepalimmigration. gov.np for details.

A single-entry visa valid for 15/30/90 days costs US$25/40/100. At Kathmandu's Tribhuvan Airport the fee is payable in any major currency, but at land borders officials require payment in cash US dollars; bring small bills.

Multiple-entry visas are useful if you are planning a side trip to Tibet, Bhutan or India. You can change your single-entry visa to a multiple-entry visa at Kathmandu's Central Immigration Office for US$20.

Don't overstay a visa. You can pay a fine of US$3 per day at the airport if you have overstayed less than 30 days (plus a US$2 per day visa extension fee), but it's far better to get it all sorted out in advance at Kathmandu's Central Immigration Office, as a delay could cause you to miss your flight.

Tourists are only allowed to spend a maximum of 150 days per calendar year in Nepal, regardless of the number of visits.

Visa Extensions

Visa extensions are available from immigration offices in Kathmandu and Pokhara only and cost a minimum US$30 (payable in rupees only) for a 15-day extension, plus US$2 per day after that. To extend for 30 days is US$50 and to extend a multiple-entry visa add on US$20. If you'll be in Nepal for more than 60 days you are better off getting a 90-day visa on arrival, rather than a 60-day visa plus an extension.

Every visa extension requires your passport, money, one photo and an application form that must be completed online first at www.online. nepalimmigration.gov.np. Visa extensions are normally available within two hours. For a fee, your trekking agency can take care of this, saving you the time and tedium of queuing.

LEECHES

If you trek on a major route during the normal trekking season from October to May, you probably won't encounter leeches, but during the monsoon leeches are everywhere, hanging from twigs and leaves. They are more an annoyance than a hazard, but they do leave an uncomfortable itching wound.

Leeches usually access your body over the top, or through the eyelets, of your boots. They secrete a Novocaine-like substance so you don't notice the bite until your boots start squelching with bloated leeches and blood-soaked socks. Be especially careful if you make a toilet stop in the bushes during leech season.

Rubbing salt, lemon juice, mosquito repellent or kerosene into ankles or socks is said to deter leeches. Leeches may be pulled off (unlike ticks, they do not leave any part of themselves behind), or made to drop off with a pinch of salt or a flame. Or try the Gurung solution: a bag of salt tied to the end of a stick. Wet the bag, tap it on a leech when it attaches itself to your shoe and it's supposed to drop off.

You can extend a tourist visa up to a total stay of 150 days within a calendar year, though as you get close to that maximum you'll have to provide an air ticket to show you're leaving the country.

You can get up-to-date visa information at the website of the **Department of Immigration** (www.nepal immigration.gov.np).

Women Travellers

Trekking as a woman in Nepal generally carries few dangers provided you take all the normal precautions you would travelling anywhere else. Nepalis have a reputation for being some of the friendliest and most helpful people on the planet and will usually go out of their way to help someone having problems.

However, women should still be cautious. Some Nepali men may have peculiar ideas about the morality of Western women, given their exposure to films portraying women wearing 'immodest' clothing. Several women have gone missing on treks in recent years and incidents of sexual assault have been reported in the Langtang region.

Safety Precautions

It makes sense never to trek alone. Two or more people walking together are a less likely target for theft, random assault or sexual harassment.

Travelling with a reliable guide can help ensure your safety, but be sure that you have a reliable person before you go, preferably an older, more experienced guide. Some lone women trekkers who hire a male guide have had to put up with repeated sexual pestering during the trek. The bigger-name trekking agencies are more likely to provide reliable guides than an off-the-street tout. **3 Sisters Adventure Trekking** (☑061-462066; www.3sistersadventure.com)

in Pokhara specialises in arranging female guides and porters for women trekkers.

What to Wear

You you will be treated better, and may even be more comfortable, if you dress conservatively while trekking in Nepal. Nepali culture is uncomfortable with the display of the female leg, and of large expanses of flesh in general. Demonstrating an effort to be culturally sensitive will gain you a greater rapport with the local people, particularly among Nepali women.

In general mid-calf-length trekking trousers are fine and short sleeves are also acceptable nowadays.

Other Hints for Women

Getting to know local people, and local women in particular, can be one of the most rewarding aspects of trekking. Two well-tested icebreakers are photographs of your family back home, and attractive jewellery – but don't wear expensive jewellery while you trek.

If you are likely to menstruate on your trek, bring a plastic bag and carry used pads and tampons with you until an opportunity arises to dispose of them properly. Don't dispose of them in outhouses; the material in outhouses is often eventually used as fertiliser, and used pads are an unwelcome sight for villagers. Household fires are considered sacred in Nepal, and are not used for burning garbage. Trekking groups occasionally build fires for burning garbage, and these are acceptable for sanitary products.

Almost all health advisories recommend not travelling above 3650m while pregnant.

Transport

GETTING THERE & AWAY

Considering the enduring popularity of Nepal as a travel destination, there are surprisingly few direct international flight connections into Kathmandu and fares are normally much higher than they are to nearby Indian cities such as Delhi. If you are coming during the prime trekking months of October and November, book your long-haul and domestic flights well in advance.

Overland and air-travel connections to India are particularly good, so it's easy to combine a dream trip to both Nepal and India, with possible add-ons to Bhutan and Tibet.

Following the 2015 earthquakes, some transport routes were disrupted, particularly in the border region between Nepal and Tibet, but at the time of publication, airports were operating as normal and travel was possible on most overland routes around and to and from Nepal.

Flights, tours and even treks can be booked online at www.lonelyplanet.com/bookings.

Entering the Country

Nepal makes things easy for foreign travellers. Visas are available on arrival at the international airport in Kathmandu and at all land border crossings that are open to foreigners, as long as you have passport photos to hand and can pay the visa fee in foreign currency (some crossings insist on payment in US dollars). Your passport must be valid for at least six months and you will need a whole free page for your visa.

Air

Airports

Nepal has one international airport, **Tribhuvan International Airport** (www.tiairport.com.np), just east of Kathmandu. In 2014 it was voted the third worst airport in the world but don't worry, it's really not that bad.

Facilities on arrival at the airport are limited – there are foreign exchange booths before and after immigration. Fill out the forms for your visa on arrival before you go to the immigration counter, as queues can be long here. A small stand provides instant passport photos, but bring some from home to be safe.

On departure, all baggage must go through the X-ray machine as you enter the terminal. Make sure that custom officials stamp all the baggage labels for your carry-on luggage. There is a branch of Himalayan Java in departures once you pass through security.

There are plans to transform Pokhara and Bhairawa airports into regional airports with flights to India, but progress on both is slow.

Airlines

Because Nepal does not lie on any major transit routes, flights to Kathmandu are relatively expensive, particularly during the peak trekking season (October to November). There are few direct long-distance flights to Nepal – getting here from Europe, the Americas or Australasia will almost always involve a stop in the Middle East or Asia.

Nepal's flagship carrier **Nepal Airlines** (✆081-520767; www.nepalairlines.com.np) is a shoestring operation. Delays and even cancellations are common; Hong Kong–Kathmandu passengers were delayed for two full days in 2011 when a rogue mouse was spotted onboard. In 2007, after a fault with one of their planes, two goats were sacrificed in order to appease Akash Bhairab, the Hindu god of sky protection. The airline has had a number of serious incidents and is, like all Nepalese airlines, banned from EU airspace. There are flights to Delhi, Dubai, Doha, Hong Kong, Bangkok and Kuala Lumpur.

Himalaya Airlines is a new joint venture between Tibet Airlines and Yeti Airlines that plans to fly to Lhasa.

Budget Indian airlines flying to Nepal include **Spicejet** (www.spicejet.com) and **IndiGo** (www.goindigo.in).

A number of other airlines serve Nepal; this list is not comprehensive and changes frequently:

Air China (☎01-4440650; www.airchina.com; Sundar Bhawan, Hattisar)

Air India (Map p51; ☎01-4429468; www.airindia.in; Hattisar) Connects Kathmandu with several Indian cities including Delhi and Kolkata.

China Eastern (☎01-4411666; www.flychinaeastern.com; Hattisar) To and from the Chinese cities of Kunming, Shanghai and Shanghai Pudong.

China Southern Airlines (☎01-4427261; www.flychinasouthern.com; Marcopolo Business Hotel, Kamal Pokhari) To Guangzhou, China,with good onward international connections, including to the US.

Dragonair (☎01-4444820; www.dragonair.com; Narayan Chaur, Naxal) Hong Kong to Nepal.

Emirates (☎01-4169048; www.emirates.com) Flights between Dubai and Nepal.

Etihad (☎01-4005000; www.etihadairways.com; Metro Park, Uttardhoka, Lazimpat) One of several high-quality airlines linking Nepal with the Middle East.

Jet Airways (☎01-4446375; www.jetairways.com; Ashadeep Bhawan, Lazimpat) Good connections to Delhi and onward to the UK.

Korean Airlines (☎01-4169192; www.koreanair.com; Heritage Plaza Block 1, Kamaladi) To and from Seoul.

Malaysian Airlines (☎01-4247215; www.malaysiaairlines.com; Marco Polo Travel, Heritage Plaza II, Kamaldi) Twice daily to Kuala Lumpur.

Oman Air (☎01-4444381; www.omanair.com; Situ Plaza, Narayan Chaur, Naxal) Flies to and from Muscat but connections to Europe aren't as impressive as some other local Middle Eastern carriers.

Qatar Airways (Map p51; ☎01-4440467; www.qatarairways.com; Sundar Bhawan, Hattisar) To Doha and with excellent onward connections to Europe.

Thai Airways (www.thaiairways.com; Annapurna Arcade, Palace Rd, Durbar Marg) The most popular route between Southeast Asia and Nepal.

Turkish Airlines (☎01-4438363; www.turkishairlines.com; Zion House, Narayan Chaur, Naxal) Good airline but often delayed leaving Kathmandu, especially in autumn and winter.

Tickets

During the autumn trekking season, from October to November, flights into and out of Kathmandu can be booked solid, and travellers sometimes have to resort to travelling overland to India to get a flight out of the region. Book well in advance. If you are booking a flight in Kathmandu, book at the start of your trek, not at the end.

Budget travellers sometimes fly to India first, and then pick up a cheap transfer to Kathmandu. If you are connecting through Delhi on two separate tickets, you will likely need to collect your luggage and check in separately for the connecting flight, for which you will need to have arranged a transit or tourist visa in advance. Indian visas are now available on arrival for nationals of Australia, Germany, Israel, Japan, New Zealand, Norway, Russia, Thailand, the US and some other countries, but only if arranged in advance online (www.indianvisaonline.gov.in).

Asia

The most popular route between Southeast Asia and Kathmandu is the daily Thai Airways flight to/from Bangkok, though Nepal Airlines also covers this connection.

There are also convenient flights to Hong Kong and Seoul. There are no direct flights to Japan. Air Asia and Malaysian Airlines fly to Kuala Lumpur, while Silk Air flies to Singapore.

Regional budget airlines connecting Kathmandu to the Gulf States include Air Arabia and Fly Dubai.

For China there are flights to Chengdu and Lhasa (Air China and Sichuan Airlines), as well as Kunming (China Eastern) and Guangzhou (China Southern Airlines). Flights are expensive, costing around US$450 to Lhasa, US$350 to US$450 to Chengdu (some flights via Lhasa!) and around US$380 to US$420 to Beijing.

You can only buy tickets to Lhasa as part of a tour group package.

Australia & New Zealand

There are easy connections from Australia and New Zealand through Bangkok, Seoul, Kuala Lumpur, Guangzhou or Hong Kong. China Southern often offers the best airfares.

Canada

Flying from Canada, you can go east or west around the globe. Fares from Vancouver through Asia tend to be slightly cheaper than flights from Toronto via Europe or the Gulf. Jet Airways offers a convenient single-airline route from Toronto through Brussels to Delhi and on to Kathmandu.

Continental Europe

There are no direct flights between continental western Europe and Kathmandu. The most direct option is via Istanbul with Turkish Airlines but be warned that through the winter months Turkish flights are often delayed by several hours ,which can play havoc with onward flight connections. Other than Turkish Airlines, most people fly via India or a Middle Eastern country.

India

Seats between Kathmandu and Delhi can be found for less than US$140, especially if you book in advance online. Jet is the best carrier, though budget Indian airlines like

IndiGo and Spicejet offer the cheapest fares. All fly daily. Fares are best booked online, though you may have trouble using a non-Indian credit card on some sites.

Air India flies from Kathmanda to Delhi, Kolkata and Varanasi. Buddha Air flies to Varanasi.

There are some good online Indian travel agencies, including **Cleartrip** (www.cleartrip.com), **Make My Trip** (www.makemytrip.com) and **Yatra** (www.yatra.com).

UK & Ireland

British Airways keeps talking about reintroducing direct flights between London and Kathmandu, but until then you will have to change in Delhi or the Gulf States.

There are good connections to Kathmandu from London and Dublin with Etihad, Emirates and Qatar Airways, changing in the Gulf. All three airlines also fly from Manchester, Edinburgh and other regional UK airports.

The fastest connection from London to Kathmandu is with Jet Airways, Virgin Atlantic or Indian Airlines, with one smooth change in Delhi's modern terminal three. Cheaper Jet connections via Mumbai require an overnight stay.

USA

North America is halfway around the world from Nepal, so you can go east or west around the globe. Flying west involves a change in Asia – Korean Airlines offers good connections through Seoul, but you could also change in Bangkok, Hong Kong or Singapore.

China Southern offers good deals flying through Guangzhou; if your transfer there is more than a few hours they will often put you up in a hotel.

Flying east normally involves a stop in Europe and, quite often, again in the Gulf or in India. Jet Airways has a convenient route from New York with stops in Brussels and Delhi.

For reasonably priced fares to Nepal, start with specialist travel agencies like **Third Eye Travel** (☏1-800 456 3393; www.thirdeyetravel.com) and **USA Asia** (☏1-800 872 2742; www.usaasiatravel.com).

Land

You can enter Nepal overland at seven border crossings – five from India and one from Tibet.

Border Crossings

INDIA

All of the land borders between India and Nepal are in the Terai, and were not seriously affected by the 2015 earthquakes. The most popular crossing point is Sunauli, near Bhairawa, which provides easy access to Delhi and Varanasi in India.

Be suspicious of travel agents in India or Nepal who offer 'through tickets' between the two countries: everyone has to change buses at the border.

Indian domestic train tickets can be booked in advance online on **Cleartrip** (www.cleartrip.com) or **IRCTC** (www.irctc.co.in).

Get timetables and fares at **Indian Railways** (www.trainenquiry.com). The **Man in Seat 61** (www.seat61.com/india.htm) is a good general resource.

SUNAULI/BHAIRAWA

The crossing at Sunauli is by far the most popular route between India and Nepal. Regular buses run from Sunauli to Gorakhpur in India from where you can catch trains to Varanasi.

Once across the border, you can visit the Buddhist pilgrimage centre of Lumbini before you continue your journey. From Bhairawa buses run regularly to Kathmandu and Pokhara, usually passing through Narayangarh, where you can change for Chitwan National Park.

MAHENDRANAGAR

The western border crossing at Mahendranagar is also reasonably convenient for Delhi. There are daily buses from Delhi's Anand Vihar bus stand to Banbassa (10 hours), the nearest Indian village to the border. Banbassa is also connected by bus with most towns in Uttaranchal.

From Mahendranagar there are slow overnight bus services to Kathmandu (15 hours), but it's better to do the trip in daylight and break the journey at Bardia National Park, Nepalganj or Narayangarh. The road sometimes gets blocked during the monsoon.

KAKARBHITTA

The eastern border crossing at Kakarbhitta offers easy onward connections to Darjeeling, Sikkim, Kolkata and India's northeast states.

NEPAL–INDIA BORDER CROSSINGS

BORDER CROSSING	NEAREST INDIAN TOWNS
Belahiya to Sunauli	Varanasi, Agra & Delhi
Birganj to Raxaul Bazaar	Patna & Kolkata
Dhangadhi to Gauriphanta	Lucknow, New Delhi
Kakarbhitta to Panitanki	Darjeeling, Sikkim & Kolkata
Mahendranagar to Banbassa	Delhi and hill towns in Uttaranchal
Nepalganj to Jamunaha/Rupaidha Bazaar	Lucknow

From Darjeeling, take a morning shared jeep to Siliguri (three hours) then another shared jeep or a taxi (one hour) to Panitanki on the Indian side of the border. Jeeps also run to the border from Kalimpong and Gangtok in Sikkim.

From Kakarbhitta there are both day and overnight buses to Kathmandu (14 to 16 hours) or domestic flights from nearby Biratnagar. You can also continue directly to Dharan, Hile and ultimately Tumlingtar to start a trek there.

BIRGANJ/RAXAUL BAZAAR

The border crossing from Birganj to Raxaul Bazaar is handy for Patna and Kolkata. Buses run from the bus station in Patna straight to Raxaul Bazaar (six hours).

From Birganj, there are frequent buses to Kathmandu (seven hours) as well as faster Tata Sumo 4WDs (five hours), plus morning buses to Pokhara (eight hours).

NEPALGANJ

The crossing at Nepalganj in western Nepal can be useful if you are meeting your trekking crew there to fly on to far western Nepal. The nearest town in India is Lucknow, where you can pick up slow buses to Rupaidha Bazaar (seven hours), near the border post at Jamunaha. You might also consider taking a train to Nanpara, 17km from the border.

From Nepalganj, there are regular buses to Kathmandu (12 hours) and Pokhara

(12 hours). Yeti Airlines and Buddha Air have flights from Nepalganj to Kathmandu (US\$187).

DHANGADHI

The little-used border crossing from Dhangadhi to Gauriphanta, Uttar Pradesh, is useful for moving on to Lucknow and New Delhi or visiting Dudhwa National Park. From Dhangadhi there are daily flights to Kathmandu and buses to Mahendranagar and Nepalganj.

CHINA/TIBET

Travel in Tibet is tightly regulated by the Chinese authorities. Officially only organised 'groups' are allowed into Tibet from Nepal and your travel agency will need to arrange Tibet travel permits and a group Chinese visa. Air China won't sell you an air ticket to Lhasa without this permit. Travel restrictions change frequently, especially at times of political tension in Tibet.

In general, travellers face fewer restrictions entering Tibet through China, so it makes more sense to visit Nepal after a trip through Tibet, not before. For full details on travelling to the plateau see Lonely Planet's *Tibet* guide.

The vast majority of travellers enter Tibet at Kodari/Zhangmu on the Friendship Highway. Other road connections, including the road from Tibet to Mustang and the new road between Kyirong and Langtang, are not open to foreigners. Although it has since reopened, the road to Kodari was severely dam-

aged by the 2015 earthquake and landslides are highly likely on this route during the monsoon months (May to August).

The only way to walk to Tibet is from Simikot in far-western Nepal to Purang in far-western Tibet, and then on by road to Mt Kailash. You will need to sign up to a pricey organised group tour to get the necessary permits and logistical support.

GETTING AROUND

Getting around Nepal can be a challenging business. Because of the terrain, the weather conditions and the condition of vehicles, few trips go exactly according to plan. Nepali ingenuity will usually get you to your destination in the end, but build plenty of time into your itinerary and treat the delays and mishaps as part of the rich tapestry that is Nepal.

The wise traveller avoids going anywhere during major festivals, when buses, flights and hotels are booked solid. The monsoon months (June to September) can also wreak havoc on transportation, as rains bring floods, landslides and destroyed bridges. Unpaved roads leading to trekking trailheads may be inaccessible during these months, especially in the far east and west of Nepal. Damage to roads from the 2015 earthquake has only exacerbated these problems.

CLIMATE CHANGE & TRAVEL

Every form of transport that relies on carbon-based fuel generates CO_2, the main cause of human-induced climate change. Modern travel is dependent on aeroplanes, which might use less fuel per kilometre per person than most cars but travel much greater distances. The altitude at which aircraft emit gases (including CO_2) and particles also contributes to their climate change impact. Many websites offer 'carbon calculators' that allow people to estimate the carbon emissions generated by their journey and, for those who wish to do so, to offset the impact of the greenhouse gases emitted with contributions to portfolios of climate-friendly initiatives throughout the world. Lonely Planet offsets the carbon footprint of all staff and author travel.

Domestic Air Routes

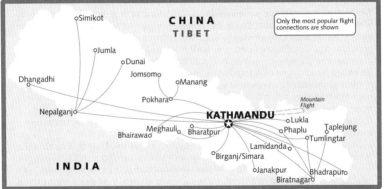

Only the most popular flight connections are shown

Air

Considering the nature of the landscape, Nepal has an excellent network of domestic flights. Engineers have created runways high in the mountains, clinging to the sides of Himalayan slopes, and all of Nepal's domestic airports are functioning after the 2015 earthquake. However, pilots must still find their way to these airstrips using visual navigation and few years pass without some kind of air disaster in the mountains.

Because flights are dependent on clear weather, services rarely leave on time and many flights are cancelled at the last minute because of poor visibility. The earliest morning flights are generally most reliable. It is essential to build extra time into your itinerary. Even if you take off on time, you may not be able to land at your intended destination because of fog. It would be unwise to book a flight back to Kathmandu within three days of your international flight out of the country.

In the event of a cancellation, airlines will try to find you a seat on the next available flight (some airlines run extra flights to clear the backlog once the weather clears). If you decide not to wait, you should be able to cancel the ticket without

penalty, though it can take a long time to arrange a refund. Private airlines are much quicker in refunding fares than Nepal Airlines, which can take weeks.

Airlines in Nepal

The largest domestic airline is the notoriously unreliable **Nepal Airlines** (www.nepal airlines.com.np). All things considered, Nepal Airlines has a comparable safety record to other domestic airlines, but if your destination is served by a private airline, this will almost always be the better option. Nepal Airlines currently has services to Biratnagar, Bhadrapur, Pokhara, Lukla, Phaplu, Lamidanda, Tumlingtar, Simikot, Dolpo, Talcha (Mugu) and Jumla, among other airstrips.

Services are more reliable on Nepal's private airlines, though fares are slightly higher. Most flights operate out of Kathmandu, but there are minor air hubs at Pokhara, Nepalganj and Surkhet in the west and Biratnagar in the southeast.

Smaller domestic airlines include **Simrik Airlines** (☑01-4106691; www.simrikair lines.com), which flies to Lukla, **Goma Air** (☑01-4007612; www.gomaair.com), which services western Nepal from hubs in Nepalganj and Surkhet, and the new **Saurya**

Airlines (☑01-4479320; www. sauryaairlines.com).

Buddha Air (☑01-5521015; www.buddhaair.com; Hattisar) One of the safer, and more reliable, airlines but it doesn't fly to many trekking trailheads. Destinations include Pokhara, Bhadrapur, Bharatpur, Bhairawa, Biratnagar, Simara, Tumlingtar and Nepalganj.

Tara Air (☑01-4493426; www. taraair.com; Tilganga) Subsidiary of Yeti Airlines. Among other destinations, it flies from Kathmandu to Lukla, Lamidanda, Phaplu and Dolpo; Pokhara to Jomsom and Kathmandu; and Nepalganj to Jumla, Simikot, Dolpo and Talcha.

Yeti Airlines (☑01-4465888; www.yetiairlines.com; Thamel Chowk) Sherpa-owned and the largest private airline with, for Nepal, a reasonable safety record; destinations include Pokhara, Biratnagar, Nepalganj, Lukla, Bhadrapur, Janakpur, Bhairawa, Tumlingtar and Bharatpur.

Air Safety

Nepal's domestic airlines have unimpressive safety records. In 2014 the website www.airlineratings.com listed Tara Air and Nepal Airlines as two of the world's four most dangerous airlines. Lukla is regularly listed as one of the world's most dangerous airstrips. No Nepalese airline is currently permitted to fly

FUN & GAMES AT THE DOMESTIC TERMINAL

Getting hold of a ticket and a confirmed seat is just the start of the game of roulette that is domestic aviation in Nepal. On the day of departure, you will arrive at the domestic terminal in Kathmandu to be greeted by a scene of absolute chaos, as hundreds of trekkers, porters and guides struggle to get mountains of luggage through the disorganised check-in procedures. Somehow, you must negotiate this melee and find the check-in desk for your flight (which might be marked as for another flight, or even airline).

Once you succeed in checking in your luggage (you must stow any sharp objects and place trekking poles inside your hold bag), the real fun begins. The flight number on your ticket is unlikely to bear any relation to the flight number on your boarding pass. The number of flights and the destinations served are permanently in flux as airstrips open and close down with the changing weather.

Departure announcements are almost nonexistent, so you must rely on a combination of luck and diligence to make it onto your plane. The prevailing wisdom is to hover by the departure gate and surge forward whenever an official from your airline walks past. It is a rare day when a flight leaves on time, but somehow, amazingly, most passengers make it onto the right aircraft.

Once on board, you will be given a boiled sweet and a bung of cotton wool to jam in your ears to dim the noise of the engines, then it's off into the great blue yonder. With any luck you should reach your destination a little shaken, but certainly stirred by what has to be one of the most surreal, maddening, exhilarating experiences in Nepal.

within EU airspace because of safety concerns.

The disturbing number of fatal domestic crashes involving foreign tourists includes two en route to Lukla (2012 and 2008; Sita Air and Yeti Airlines), one mountain scenic flight (2011, Buddha Air) and flights to Jumla (2014, Nepal Airlines) and Jomsom (2012, Agni Air). In 2013 there were nonfatal crashes on flights to Jomsom (Nepali Airlines) and Jumla (Sita Air).

Tickets

Airlines come and go and schedules change, so it's best to make reservations through a travel agent or trekking agency.

Reservations for flights in the hills rely on handwritten manifests. Whenever possible, reconfirm your return flight before you start trekking and again the day before you fly.

Changing the date of your return flight to Kathmandu is rarely a problem (and free of charge) as long as there are seats, though some remote airstrips are only served by one or to flights a week.

➡ Residents and Nepali citizens pay approximately 40% of the tourist price, which helps if you are flying your guide or porters out to a remote airstrip.

➡ Fares generally include an insurance surcharge of US$2 per leg, as well as a fuel surcharge.

➡ Domestic airlines have a 15kg allowance for hold baggage – and on some flights you cannot pay to carry excess baggage.

➡ Knives, cigarette lighters and trekking poles are not permitted in carry-on luggage. Gas cylinders are not allowed on flights.

➡ There is a penalty of around 10% to 20% for cancellations made before departure.

Helicopter

Helicopters play a vital support role in Nepal, transporting freight to remote mountainous locations and ferrying injured trekkers and locals downhill to receive hospital treatment. No companies offer scheduled passenger services, so you must charter a helicopter

(around US$1800 per flying hour, depending on the size of the chopper and the destination). You can sometimes hitch a paid ride on cargo helicopters in remote areas.

Helicopter charter companies based in Kathmandu include the following:

Air Dynasty (☎01-4497418; www.airdynastyheli.com)

Fishtail Air (☎01-4112463; www.fishtailair.com)

Mountain Helicopters (☎01-411031; www.mtn helicopters.com)

Simrik Air (☎01-4155341; www.simrikair.com.np)

Bicycle

There are plenty of places to rent bicycles in Kathmandu and Pokhara, and this is a cheap and convenient way of getting around. Mountain bike agencies in Kathmandu and Pokhara rent out imported front suspension mountain bikes for around US$12 per day. Some even organise supported mountain bike rides along such trek routes as the Annapurna Circuit.

Bus

Buses run pretty much everywhere where there is a road in Nepal and will stop for anyone, but you'll find it much easier to get a seat if you catch a bus at its source rather than mid-run. For longer-distance buses it's best to book a day or two in advance. Travelling by bus to distant rural trailheads like Tumlingtar or Taplejung in eastern Nepal is only recommended for masochists and nervous flyers. Note that schedules may be affected by damage to roads and falling demand following the 2015 earthquakes.

Public Buses

Many trekking trailheads in central, mid-western and eastern Nepal are accessible by bus from Kathmandu or Pokhara. Nepali buses are slow, noisy and uncomfortable, and breakdowns are almost guaranteed, even on the so-called 'deluxe' buses. Fortunately, services are frequent enough that you can always hop onto another bus if your first bus dies on a lonely stretch of highway. On longer journeys, buses stop regularly for refreshments and toilet breaks.

Travel after dark is not recommended – drivers take advantage of the quiet roads to do some crazy speeding, and accidents and fatalities are depressingly common. In fact, you are 30 times more likely to die in a road accident in Nepal than in any developed country. Some night buses stop for a few hours' sleep, en route, but others keep blazing through the night with the music blaring at full volume. The single best thing you can do to stay safe is to avoid travelling by road at night.

Myriad private companies run 'ordinary buses' and faster, more expensive 'express buses' that offer seats with more padding and luxuries such as curtains to keep out the sun. Tickets can be purchased in advance at the relevant counter (ask locals where to go as signs are often in Nepali) or on board from the driver. 'Deluxe' buses often come with air-conditioning and some claim (but rarely do) to offer nonstop services between two centres.

Large pieces of baggage go on the roof. Theft from luggage is not unheard of so padlock your bags shut and tie the straps to the railings. Always keep an eye on your belongings at rest stops – backpacks are extremely easy for thieves to walk off with.

At trailheads you might find any combination of buses, minibuses or 4WDs to take you to the end of the road. Prices for foreigners are often bumped up by unscrupulous conductors on these buses, especially in the Annapurna region.

Note that road travel in the far east and west of Nepal can be impossible after the monsoon. Every year the rains lead to floods that destroy stretches of road and wash away bridges.

Tourist Buses

Travel agencies can book seats on 'tourist' buses (locals use these services as well), leaving from the Tourist Bus Park in Pokhara and the Thamel end of Kantipath in Kathmandu. These are more comfortable, faster and less crowded than local buses but cost 30% more.

Greenline (www.greenline.com.np; Tridevi Marg) has deluxe, air-con buses between Kathmandu, Pokhara and Sauraha (for Chitwan National Park).

Car & Motorcycle Hire

There are no drive-yourself rental cars available in Nepal, but you can easily hire a car or 4WD with a driver through a trekking agency. Expect to pay between US$60 and US$100 per day, including fuel. Shared between three or four trekkers it's a worthwhile investment. Taxis are cheaper but less comfortable and you must negotiate a fare directly with the driver. Remember that you'll have to pay for the driver's return trip whether or not you return, as well as their food and accommodation for overnight trips.

Motorcycles can be rented in Kathmandu and Pokhara for around Rs 600 to Rs 1500 per day depending on the

---

ENCROACHING ROADS

New road construction in rural Nepal is affecting treks across the country. New roads have shaved off the first day or two of treks such as Around Manaslu and Makalu Base Camp, while sections of the Annapurna Circuit (p139) are now in sight of roads or road construction (notably from Beni to Jomsom and from Besi Sahar to Manang. Roads are also nibbling away at the beginning and end of the Shivalaya to Lukla trek.

Road links with China/Tibet are increasing at a particularly furious pace, with roads under construction from Simikot to the Tibet border and in the upper Tsum Valley. A rough road already traverses Mustang from Jomsom to the Tibet border.

The bottom line is that you can expect the first day or two of many of the treks in this book to change over the next few years, so enquire with your trekking agency when making your itinerary.

type of bike. You'll need a motorcycle driver's licence and must leave your passport as a deposit.

Insurance

If you are planning to drive a motorbike in Nepal you should double-check to see if you are covered by your travel insurance. Rental companies rarely offer insurance and you will be fully liable for the vehicle and damage to other vehicles in the event of an accident.

Road Rules

If you do drive, be aware that (in theory) you drive on the left-hand side of the road, left turns are allowed without stopping, and that traffic entering a roundabout has priority over traffic already on the roundabout. Locals rarely signal and other vehicles will pull out regardless of whether or not anyone is coming – drive defensively. Try to avoid any dealings with traffic police; locals are routinely stung for bribes and foreigners are increasingly being targeted.

Local Transport

Cycle-Rickshaw

Cycle-rickshaws are common in the old part of Kath-mandu and they provide an atmospheric way to explore the crowded and narrow streets. It's essential you negotiate a fare in advance.

Taxi

Taxis are found in larger towns such as Kathmandu and Pokhara, and these can be hired for both local and long-distance journeys. Metered taxis have black licence plates; private cars that operate as taxis for long-distance routes have red plates. Almost no taxi drivers use the meter these days so negotiate a fare beforehand.

Health

Kathmandu has the best health facilities in the country, but standards at clinics and hospitals decline the further you get from the capital. In mountainous areas, there may be no health facilities at all. Trekkers who become unwell in the mountains are generally evacuated to Kathmandu, or overseas in the event of something really serious. Always take out travel insurance to cover the costs of hospital treatment and emergency evacuations.

Most treks in Nepal are remote and inaccessible, so you should read up on the possible health risks. While trekking, it makes sense to carry a comprehensive emergency medical kit so that you can treat any symptoms until you reach medical care.

Before You Go

Insurance
Considering the terrain, potential health risks and high cost of medical evacuation, it is unwise to trek into Nepal without adequate health and evacuation insurance (p331).

Recommended Vaccinations
You do not officially require any immunisations to enter the country, unless you have come from an area where yellow fever is present – in which case, you must show proof of immunisation.

It is best to seek medical advice at least six weeks before travelling, since some vaccinations require multiple injections over a period of time.

Note that some vaccinations should not be given during pregnancy or to people with allergies.

Vaccinations you might consider:

Diphtheria and tetanus Vaccinations for these two diseases are usually combined and are recommended for everyone. After an initial course of three injections (usually given in childhood), boosters are necessary every 10 years.

Hepatitis A The vaccine for hepatitis A (eg Avaxim, Havrix 1440 or VAQTA) provides long-term immunity (possibly lifelong) after an initial injection and a booster at six to 12 months.

Hepatitis B Vaccination involves three injections, the quickest course being over three weeks with a booster at 12 months.

Influenza 'Flu is considered by many to be the most common vaccine-preventable illness in travellers. This vaccine is annual.

Japanese encephalitis This is a mosquito-borne viral encephalitis that occurs in the Terai and occasionally in the Kathmandu Valley, particularly during the monsoon (August to early October). The vaccine is given as three injections over three to four weeks and is usually boosted at three years. It's recommended only for prolonged

stays to the Terai (especially the west) or Kathmandu Valley.

Meningococcal meningitis A single-dose vaccine boosted every three to five years is recommended only for individuals at high risk and for residents.

Polio This serious, easily transmitted disease is still found in Nepal. Everyone should keep up to date with this vaccination, which is normally given in childhood. A booster every 10 years maintains immunity.

Rabies Vaccination should be considered for long-term visitors, particularly if you plan to travel to remote areas. In Nepal the disease is carried by street dogs and monkeys. Vaccination is strongly recommended for children. Pretravel rabies vaccination involves having three injections over 21 to 28 days. If someone who has been vaccinated is bitten or scratched by an animal they will require two vaccine booster injections, while those not vaccinated will require more. The booster for rabies

WARNING
Self-diagnosis and treatment can be risky, so you should seek medical help if you become ill. Although drug dosages appear in this text, they're for emergency treatment only. Correct diagnosis is vital.

vaccination is usually given after three years.

Tuberculosis (TB) This disease is highly endemic in Nepal, though cases are extremely rare among travellers. Most people in the West are vaccinated during childhood.

Typhoid Drug-resistant typhoid fever is a growing problem in Nepal, particularly in the Terai, and vaccination is recommended. The vaccine is available as a single injection or oral capsules – ask your doctor for advice.

Yellow fever This disease is not endemic in Nepal and a vaccine for yellow fever is required only if you are coming from an infected area. The record of this vaccine should be provided in a World Health Organization (WHO) Yellow Vaccination Booklet and is valid for 10 years.

Other Preparations

Visiting Nepal may take you to some very remote areas, so it makes sense to visit the doctor before you travel for a general check-up.

➡ If you have any pre-existing medical conditions, bring any medication you need from home and carry it with you, not in your checked-in luggage.

➡ Ask your physician to give you a written description of your condition and your medications with their generic names in case you have to visit a doctor in Nepal.

➡ It pays to get a dental check-up well before embarking on a trek. One of our previous authors cracked a molar on a particularly tough piece of dried beef while on a research trek and had to walk for five days to reach a dentist who performed an emergency root canal operation without anaesthetic! Be warned.

➡ Contact-lens wearers should bring plenty of solution and take extra care with hygiene to avoid eye infections.

➡ Carry backup prescription glasses and sunglasses in case you can't wear your lenses at some point.

➡ A very useful website for diabetics wishing to go up to high altitude is www.mountain-mad.org.uk.

➡ People over the age of 50 often worry about altitude and potential heart problems. There is no evidence that altitude is likely to bring on previously undiagnosed heart disease. If you are able to exercise to your maximum at sea level, you should not have an increased risk of heart attack while trekking at altitude. However, if you have known heart disease and your exercise is already limited by symptoms at

---

MEDICAL CHECKLIST

Following is a list of items you should consider including in your medical kit – consult your pharmacist for brands available in your country.

➡ aspirin or paracetamol (acetaminophen in the USA) for pain or fever

➡ anti-inflammatory (ibuprofen) for muscle and joint pain, headache and fever

➡ antibiotics, particularly if travelling off the beaten track; in Nepal, antibiotics are sold without prescription, which has led to widespread resistance to some common antibiotics

➡ promethazine (Phenergan) for relief of severe nausea

➡ rehydration mixture to prevent dehydration during bouts of diarrhoea; particularly important when travelling with children

➡ antihistamine for allergies, eg hay fever; for skin conditions, carry hydrocortisone 1% cream

➡ cold and flu tablets, throat lozenges and nasal decongestant

➡ antifungal cream such as clotrimazole 1% for fungal skin infections and thrush

➡ antiseptic (such as povidone-iodine) for cuts and grazes

➡ bandages, crêpe wraps, Bandaids (plasters), gauze pads and tape

➡ water purification tablets or filter

➡ scissors, tweezers and an electric thermometer (mercury thermometers are prohibited by airlines)

➡ sterile kit in case you need injections; discuss with your doctor

➡ motion-sickness tablets, such as Dramamine, for long bus rides

➡ laxative, in case you get blocked up with daal bhaat

low altitude, you may have trouble at altitude. If you have a history of heart disease, you should consult a doctor who has knowledge about high altitude before committing to a trek.

Websites

Medex (www.medex.org.uk) offers a free download of the useful booklet *Travel At High Altitude*, aimed at laypeople and full of good advice for staying healthy in the mountains. A Nepali translation of the booklet is also available on the website.

Centers for Disease Control & Prevention (www.cdc.gov)

Fit for Travel (www.fitfortravel. scot.nhs.uk)

International Society for Mountain Medicine (www. ismm.org)

Kathmandu CIWEC Clinic (www .ciwec-clinic.com)

MASTA (www.masta-travel-health.com)

Nepal International Clinic (www. nepalinternationalclinic.com)

Further Reading

Lonely Planet's *Healthy Travel Asia & India* is packed with information such as pre-trip planning, emergency first aid, immunisation and disease information, and what to do if you get sick on the road. *Travel with Children* from Lonely Planet includes advice on travel health for younger children. A useful health-care overview for travel in remote areas is David Werner's *Where There Is No Doctor*.

Specific titles covering trekking and health:

➡ *Medicine for Mountaineering & Other Wilderness Activities* (James A Wilkerson) covers many medical problems typically encountered in Nepal.

➡ *Mountain Medicine* (Michael Ward) has good background info on cold and high-altitude problems.

➡ *Altitude Illness: Prevention & Treatment* (Stephen Bezruchka) is essential

EMERGENCY TREATMENTS WHILE TREKKING

While trekking it may be impossible to reach medical treatment, so consider carrying the following drugs for emergencies (the concentrations in which these drugs are sold in Nepal are noted next to the drug):

➡ azithromycin 250mg – a broad-spectrum antibiotic, useful for traveller's diarrhoea; take the equivalent of 500mg per day for three consecutive days

➡ norfloxacin 400mg or ciprofloxacin 500mg – for traveller's diarrhoea; the usual treatment is two tablets daily for one week

➡ tinidazole 500mg – the recommended treatment for giardiasis is four pills all at once for two days; for amoebiasis, take four pills at once for three days, then diloxanide furoate 500mg three times a day for 10 days

➡ potent painkiller, such as acetaminophen with hydrocodone, or acetaminophen with codeine (eg Vicodin, 20 tablets)

reading for high-altitude trekking, written by an experienced Nepal trekker.

➡ *Wilderness First Aid & Wilderness Medicine* (Dr Jim Duff and Peter Gormly) is an excellent portable companion, published abroad by Cicerone.

In Nepal

Availability & Cost of Health Care

Kathmandu has several excellent clinics, including the Nepal International Clinic and CIWEC Clinic (which has a branch in Pokhara).

While trekking, your only option may be small, local health posts, and even these are few and far between.

In remote areas, you should carry an appropriate medical kit and be prepared to treat yourself until you can reach a health professional.

Infectious Diseases

HEPATITIS

There are several different viruses that cause hepatitis (inflammation of the liver). The symptoms are similar in all forms of the illness and include fever, chills, headache, fatigue, feelings of weakness as well as aches and pains, followed by loss of appetite, nausea, vomiting, abdominal pain, dark urine, light-coloured faeces, jaundiced (yellow) skin and yellowing of the whites of the eyes.

➡ Hepatitis A and E are transmitted by contaminated drinking water and food. Hepatitis A is virtually 100% preventable by using any of the current hepatitis A vaccines. Hepatitis E causes an illness very similar to hepatitis A and there is at present no way to immunise against this virus.

➡ Hepatitis B is only spread by blood (unsterilised needles and blood transfusions) or sexual contact. Risky situations include having a shave, tattoo or body piercing with contaminated equipment.

HIV & AIDS

HIV and AIDS are growing problems in Nepal, with an estimated 75,000 Nepalis infected with the virus, so insist on brand-new disposable needles and syringes for injections.

Blood used for transfusions is usually screened for HIV/AIDS but this cannot always be done in an emergency. Avoid blood transfusions unless absolutely necessary.

MALARIA

Antimalarial tablets are only recommended if you will be spending long periods in the Terai, particularly during the monsoon. There is no risk in Kathmandu or Pokhara or on typical Himalayan trekking routes.

It makes sense to take measures to avoid being bitten by mosquitoes, as dengue fever, another mosquito-borne illness, has been sporadically documented in the lowlands.

RABIES

The rabies virus causes a severe brain infection that is almost always fatal. Feral dogs and monkeys are the main carriers of the disease in Nepal.

Rabies is different from other infectious diseases in that a person can be immunised after having been exposed. Human rabies immune globulin (HRIG) is stocked at the CIWEC clinic and the Nepal International Clinic in Kathmandu.

In addition to the HRIG, five injections of rabies vaccine are needed over a one-month period. Travellers who have taken a pre-immunisation series only need two rabies shots, three days apart, if they are bitten by a possibly rabid animal.

If you receive a bite or a scratch from an animal in Nepal, wash the wound with soap and water, then a disinfectant, such as povidone-iodine, then seek rabies immunisations. Considering the risk, it makes sense to keep your distance from animals in Nepal, particularly street dogs and monkeys.

RESPIRATORY INFECTIONS

Upper respiratory tract infections (such as the common cold) are common ailments in Nepal, especially in polluted Kathmandu. Respiratory infections are aggravated by high altitude, cold weather, pollution, smoking and overcrowded conditions, which increase the opportunities for infection.

Most upper respiratory tract infections go away without treatment, but any infection can lead to complications such as bronchitis, ear infections and pneumonia, which may need to be treated with antibiotics.

WATER PURIFICATION

Don't drink the water in Nepal. Ice should be avoided except in upmarket tourist-oriented restaurants. While trekking, purify your own water rather than buying expensive purified water in non-recyclable and non-biodegradable plastic bottles.

➡ The easiest way to purify water is to boil it for one minute, which is effective even at altitudes as high as 6000m. Lodges can supply boiling water (umaleko pani in Nepali) but charge for it because it uses fuel and takes up space on the stove.

➡ Chlorine or chlorine dioxide tablets kill many pathogens, but some are not effective against giardia and amoebic cysts. Follow the directions carefully – filter water through a cloth before adding the chemicals and be sure to wet the thread on the lid to your water bottle. Once the water is purified, vitamin C or neutralising tablets can be added to remove the chemical taste.

➡ Iodine is effective and cheap water purification, either as drops of liquid Lugol's solution (5%) or in tablet form such as Potable Aqua. Iodine should not be used long term; by anyone allergic to iodine or with thyroid problems; or by pregnant women. Iodine water purification is no longer available for sale in the EU. Iodine is not effective against cryptosporidium.

➡ Note that chemical water purification is less effective when water is silty or particularly cold; in that case add a stronger dosage or wait longer to drink the water.

➡ Trekking filters take out all parasites, bacteria and viruses, and make water safe to drink. A pore size of at least 0.2 microns is considered necessary to successfully filter bacteria and protozoa. You need a mechanical filter with iodine resins to produce safe water in Nepal.

➡ Another option is a UV light–based treatment such as a Steripen. They are light to carry and provide drinking water quickly (1L in around 90 seconds) but you need to make sure you have enough batteries for your entire trip (two CR123 batteries purify around 50L of water). There's always an inherent risk when relying on an electronic machine, so it would be wise to bring a backup method of purification.

FEVER

If you have a sustained fever (over 38°C) for more than two days while trekking and you cannot get to a doctor, an emergency treatment is a course of the broad-spectrum antibiotic azithromycin (500mg twice a day for seven days), but seek professional medical help as soon as possible.

TRAVELLER'S DIARRHOEA

Even veteran travellers to South Asia seem to come down with the trots in Nepal. It's just one of those things. The main cause of infection is contaminated water and food, due to low standards of hygiene. However, diarrhoea is usually self-limiting and most people recover within a few days.

➡ Dehydration is the main danger with diarrhoea, particularly in children, pregnant women or elderly people. Soda water, weak black tea with a little sugar, or soft drinks allowed to go flat and half-diluted with clean water will help you replace lost liquids.

➡ In severe cases, take oral rehydration salts made up with boiled or purified water. In an emergency you can make up a solution of six teaspoons of sugar and half a teaspoon of salt to a litre of boiled or bottled water. Stick to a bland diet as you recover.

➡ Loperamide (Imodium) or diphenoxylate (Lomotil) can be used to bring temporary relief from the symptoms, but they do not cure the problem.

➡ In the case of diarrhoea with blood or mucus (dysentery), any diarrhoea with fever, profuse watery diarrhoea and persistent diarrhoea not improving after 48 hours, you should visit a doctor for a stool test. If you cannot reach a doctor, the recommended treatment is norfloxacin 400mg or ciprofloxacin 500mg twice daily for three days.

➡ These drugs are not recommended for children or pregnant women. The preferred treatment for children is azithromycin in a dose of 10mg per kilogram of body weight per day (as a single dose each day for three days).

AMOEBIC DYSENTERY

Caused by the protozoan *Entamoeba histolytica*, amoebic dysentery is characterised by a gradual onset of low-grade diarrhoea, often with blood and mucus. Infection persists until treated.

If medical treatment is not available, tinidazole or metronidazole are the recommended drugs. Treatment is a 2g single dose of tinidazole daily or 250mg of metronidazole three times daily for five to 10 days. Alcohol should not be consumed while taking these medications.

CYCLOSPORA

This waterborne intestinal parasite infects the upper intestine, causing diarrhoea, fatigue and loss of appetite lasting up to 12 weeks. Fortunately, the illness is a risk in Nepal mainly during the monsoon, when few tourists visit. Iodine is not sufficient to kill the parasite but it can be removed by water filters and it is easily killed by boiling.

The treatment for *Cyclospora* diarrhoea is trimethoprim and sulfamethoxazole (sold commonly as Bactrim) twice a day for seven days. This drug cannot be taken by people who are allergic to sulphur.

GIARDIASIS

Also known as giardia, giardiasis accounts for around 12% of the diarrhoea among travellers in Nepal. The disease is caused by a parasite, *Giardia lamblia*, found in water that has been contaminated by waste from animals.

Symptoms include stomach cramps, nausea, a bloated stomach, watery and foul-smelling diarrhoea, and frequent sulphurous burps and farts but no fever.

The best treatment is four 500mg tablets of tinidazole taken as a single dose each day for two consecutive days. Tinidazole cannot be taken with alcohol.

Environmental Hazards

ACUTE MOUNTAIN SICKNESS (AMS)

Above 2500m, the concentration of oxygen in the air you breathe starts to drop off markedly, reducing the amount of oxygen that reaches your brain and other organs. Decreasing air pressure at altitude has the additional effect of causing liquid to leak from the capillaries into the lungs and brain, which can be fatal. The human body has the ability to adjust to the changes in pressure and oxygen concentration as you gain altitude, but this is a gradual process.

The health conditions caused by the effects of altitude are known collectively as altitude sickness or acute mountain sickness (AMS). If allowed to develop unchecked, AMS can lead to coma and death. However, you can avoid this potentially deadly condition by limiting your rate of ascent, which will allow your body to adjust to the altitude. There is also a 100% effective treatment if you do experience serious symptoms: descend immediately.

If you go trekking, it is important to read up on the causes, effects and treatment of altitude sickness before you start walking. Attend one of the free lectures on altitude sickness given by the **Himalayan Rescue Association** (HRA; Map p56; ☎01-4701223; www.himalayan-rescue.org; 1st fl, Mandala St, Thamel; ⊙2-5pm Sun-Fri) in Kathmandu.

The onset of symptoms of AMS is usually gradual, so there is time to adjust your trekking schedule or retreat off the mountain if you start to feel unwell. Most people who suffer severe effects of AMS have ignored obvious warning signs.

Acclimatisation

The process of acclimatisation is still not fully understood, but it is known to involve modifications in breathing patterns and heart rate and an increase in the oxygen-carrying capacity of the blood. Some people have a faster rate of acclimatisation than others, but almost anyone can trek to high altitudes as long as the rate of ascent does not exceed the rate at which their body can adjust.

AMS is a notoriously fickle affliction and it can affect trekkers and walkers who are accustomed to walking at high altitudes as well as people who have never been to altitude before. AMS has been fatal at 3000m, although 3500m to 4500m is the usual range.

Symptoms

On treks above 4000m, almost everyone experiences some symptoms of mild altitude sickness – breathlessness and fatigue linked to reduced oxygen in the blood being the most common.

Mild symptoms usually pass if you stop ascending and give your body time to 'catch up' with the increase in altitude. Once you have acclimatised at the altitude where you first developed symptoms, you should be able to slowly continue your ascent. Serious symptoms are a different matter – if you develop any of the symptoms described here, you should descend immediately.

Mild Symptoms

Mild symptoms of AMS are experienced by many travellers above 2800m. Symptoms tend to be worse at night and include headache, dizziness,

lethargy, loss of appetite, nausea, breathlessness, irritability and difficulty sleeping.

Never ignore mild symptoms of AMS – this is your body giving you an alarm call. You may develop more serious symptoms if you continue to ascend without giving your body time to adjust.

Serious Symptoms

AMS can become more serious without warning and it can be fatal. Serious symptoms are caused by the accumulation of fluid in the lungs (high-altitude pulmonary odema, or HAPE) and brain (high-altitude cerebral odema, or HACE). Telltale symptoms of HAPE include breathlessness at rest and a dry, irritative cough, which may progress to the production of pink, frothy sputum. Symptoms of HACE include severe headache, lack of coordination (typically leading to a 'drunken walk'), confusion, irrational behaviour and vomiting. If ignored, this can progress to unconsciousness and eventually death.

Two symptoms deserve prime attention. People with the cerebral form of altitude sickness (ie headache, nausea, vomiting and fatigue) must be checked for lack of coordination while walking, known medically as ataxia. Have the person stand up and walk in a straight line while putting the heel of the front foot against the toe of the back foot (the classic 'drunk test' administered to drivers by police looking for signs of alcohol intoxication). If the person steps off the imaginary line, or falls altogether, they have developed severe HACE and must descend immediately. That person is only hours away from unconsciousness. They should be treated with oxygen, if available, or in a pressurisation bag.

The other significant symptom to watch for is breathlessness at rest, the key sign of HAPE. No mat-

ter how hard you have to breathe while trekking uphill at altitude, your breathing rate should return to normal after five to 10 minutes' rest. If you continue to feel breathless after 10 minutes at rest, you are developing HAPE, and you should immediately descend.

Prevention

If you trek above 2500m, observe the following rules:

➡ **Ascend slowly** Where possible, do not sleep more than 300m higher than the elevation where you spent the previous night. If any stage on a trek exceeds this increase in elevation, take at least one rest day to acclimatise before you start the ascent. If you or anyone else in your party seems to be struggling, take a rest day as a precaution.

➡ **Climb high, sleep low** It is always wise to sleep at a lower altitude than the greatest height reached during the day. If you need to cross a high pass, take an extra acclimatisation day before you cross. Be aware that descending to the altitude where you slept the previous night may not be enough to compensate for a very large increase in altitude during the day.

➡ **Trek healthy** You are more likely to develop AMS if you are tired, dehydrated or malnourished. Drink extra fluids while trekking. Avoid sedatives or sleeping pills and don't smoke – this will further reduce the amount of oxygen reaching your lungs.

➡ **If you feel unwell, stop** If you start to display mild symptoms of AMS, stop climbing. Take an acclimatisation day and see if things improve. If your symptoms stay the same or get worse, descend immediately. If on an organised trip make sure your tour leader is aware of your conditions. Don't feel pressured to continue ascending just to keep up with your group.

→ If you show serious symptoms, descend

If you show any serious symptoms of AMS, descend immediately to a lower altitude. Ideally this should be below the altitude where you slept the night before you first developed symptoms. Most lodges can arrange an emergency porter to help you descend quickly to a safe altitude.

Treatment

Treat mild symptoms by resting at the same altitude until recovery. Take paracetamol or aspirin for headaches.

Diamox (acetazolamide) can be used to reduce mild symptoms of AMS. However, it is not a cure and it will not stop you from developing serious symptoms. Even if you are taking Diamox, it is still essential to follow the acclimatisation rules to avoid altitude sickness. Diamox works by increasing the respiratory rate and depth, mimicking the breathing of a good acclimatiser. Thus, if you feel better on diamox, you truly are better; Diamox doesn't mask the symptoms of AMS. The usual dosage of Diamox is 125mg to 250mg twice daily. The medication is a diuretic so you should drink extra liquid to avoid dehydration. Diamox may also cause disturbances to vision and the sense of taste and it can cause a harmless tingling sensation in the fingers.

If symptoms persist or become worse, descend immediately – even 500m can help. If the victim cannot walk without support, they may need to be carried down. Any delay could be fatal; if you have to descend in the dark, seek local assistance.

In the event of severe symptoms, the victim may need to be flown to a lower altitude by helicopter. Getting the victim to a lower altitude is the priority – get someone else from the group to call for helicopter rescue and start the descent to the pick-up point. Note that a helicopter rescue can cost you US$2500 to US$10,000.

Emergency treatments for serious symptoms of AMS include supplementary oxygen, nifedipine, dexamethasone and repressurisation using a device known as a Gamow bag (this should only be administered by health professionals), but these only reduce the symptoms and they are not a 'cure'. They should never be used to avoid descent or to enable further ascent.

The only effective treatment for sufferers of severe AMS is to descend rapidly to a lower altitude.

To read more about altitude sickness visit www.treksafe.com.au, www.altitude.org and www.altitudemedicine.org

TREKKERS KNEE

Many trekkers suffer from knee or ankle strains, particularly if they are carrying their own pack. Anti-inflammatory pills such as ibuprofen are helpful (unless you are allergic to aspirin). Take ibuprofen with food to avoid stomach pain and don't take more than 3200mg in one day. The use of trekking poles can take 20% to 30% of the weight off the knees during descent.

FROSTBITE

Frostbite is the injury resulting from frozen skin tissue. If you develop frostbite, your digits will appear waxy and whitish in colour, in addition to being numb.

The one acceptable way to warm up frozen extremities is by a process of rapid rewarming, submerging the frozen extremity in water at a temperature of around 34° to 37°C (91° to 97°F) until it rewarms and a red flush of circulation returns. This process can be very painful. Blisters may form, and the foot or hand will then have to be protected from further trauma.

Frostbitten parts should not be rubbed.

SNOW BLINDNESS

Snow blindness is a temporary painful condition resulting from a sunburn of the clear surface of the eye (the cornea). It results from intense exposure to ultraviolet radiation, almost exclusively in situations where someone is walking on snow without sunglasses.

The treatment is simply to try to relieve the pain. Cold cloths held against the outside of the eyelids help relieve the pain and swelling. There are no long-term consequences of this injury.

SKIN INFECTIONS

An isolated, painful, red swelling that keeps getting worse over several hours is probably a bacterial skin infection. Staphylococcal infections that cause boils are common in travellers. If the boil is tense and painful, it may need to be opened and drained by a physician. Antibiotics are necessary to get rid of the infection. Cephalexin is the best choice (if you are not allergic to penicillin). Azithromycin is a reasonable alternative.

A round red patch, clearing in the centre and advancing at its edges, is usually a fungus and can be treated with an antifungal cream.

Language

Nepali belongs to the Indo-European language family and has about 35 million speakers. It's closely related to Hindi and is written in the Devanagari script (also used for Hindi). Although Nepali is the national language and is used as a lingua franca between Nepal's ethnic groups, many other languages are also spoken in the country. The Newars of the Kathmandu Valley speak Newari. Other languages are spoken by the Tamangs, Sherpas, Rais, Limbus, Magars, Gurungs and other groups. In the Terai (bordering India), Hindi and Maithili are often spoken.

It's quite easy to get by with English in Nepal. Most people visitors have to deal with in the Kathmandu Valley and in Pokhara will speak some English. Along the main trekking trails, particularly the Annapurna Circuit, English is also widely understood.

Most Nepali consonant sounds are quite similar to their English counterparts. The exceptions are the so-called retroflex consonants and the aspirated consonants. Retroflex sounds are made by curling the tongue tip back to touch the roof of the mouth as you make the sound – they are indicated in this chapter by a dot below the letter, eg ṭ or ḍ as in *Kaṭhmaṇḍu*. Aspirated consonants are pronounced more forcefully than in English and are made with a short puff of air – they are indicated by adding h after the consonant, eg ph is pronounced as the 'p' in 'pit', and th is pronounced as the 't' in 'time'.

As for the vowels, a is pronounced as the 'u' in 'hut', ā as the 'ar' in 'garden' (no 'r' sound), e as in 'best' but longer, i as in 'sister'

but longer, o as in 'sold', u as in 'put', ai as in 'aisle' and au as the 'ow' in 'cow'. The stressed syllables are indicated with italics.

BASICS

Even if you learn no other Nepali, there is one word every visitor soon picks up – *namaste* (pronounced na·ma·*ste*). Strictly translated it means 'I salute the god in you', but it's used as an everyday greeting that encompasses everything from 'Hello' to 'How are you?' and even 'See you again soon'. It should be accompanied with the hands held in a prayer-like position, the Nepali gesture equivalent to Westerners shaking hands.

Hello./Goodbye.	na·ma·*ste*
How are you?	ta·*pāi*·lai *kas*·to chha
Excuse me.	ha·*jur*
Please (give me).	*di*·nu·hos
Please (you have).	*khā*·nu·hos
Thank you.	*dhan*·ya·bad

Unlike in many other countries, verbal expressions of thanks are not the cultural norm in Nepal. Although neglecting to say 'Thank you' may make you feel a little uncomfortable, it is rarely necessary in simple commercial transactions – foreigners saying *dhanyabad* all the time sound distinctly odd to Nepalis.

Yes. (I have)	chā
No. (I don't have)	*chhai*·na
I	ma
OK.	*theek*·cha
Wait a minute.	ek chhin *par*·kha·nos
good/pretty	*ram*·ro
I don't need it.	ma·lai cha·*hi*·ṇa
I don't have it.	ma *san*·ga *chhai*·na

WANT MORE?

For in-depth language information and handy phrases, check out Lonely Planet's *Nepali Phrasebook*. You'll find it at **shop.lonelyplanet.com**, or you can buy Lonely Planet's iPhone phrasebooks at the Apple App Store.

LANGUAGES OF NEPAL

Language	Estimated % of the Population
Nepali	47.8
Maithili	12.1
Bhojpuri	7.4
Tharu	5.8
Tamang	5.1
Newari	3.6
Magar	3.3
Rai	2.7
Awadhi	2.4
Limbu	1.4
Gurung	1.2
Sherpa	0.7
Other	6.5

Do you speak English?	ta·*pāi* an·*gre*·ji *bol*·na *sak*·nu *hun*·chha
I only speak a little Nepali.	ma a·li a·li ne·*pā*·li *bol*·chhu
I understand.	ma *bujh*·chu
I don't understand.	*mai*·le bu·*jhi*·na
Please say it again.	*phe*·ri *bha*·ṇu·hos
Please speak more slowly.	ta·*pāi* bi·*stā*·rai *bol*·nu·hos

ACCOMMODATION

Where is a ...?	... *ka*·hā chha
campsite	*shi*·vir
guesthouse	*pā*·hu·na ghar
hotel	*ho*·ṭel
lodge	laj

Can I get a place to stay here?	*ya*·hā bās *paun*·chha
Can I look at the room?	*ko*·thā *her*·na *sak*·chhu
How much is it per night?	ek *rāt*·ko *ka*·ti *pai*·sā ho
Does it include breakfast?	bi·*hā*·na·ko *khā*·na *sa*·met ho

clean	sa·*fā*
dirty	*mai*·lo
fan	*pan*·khā
hot water	*tā*·to *pā*·ni
room	*ko*·thā

EATING & DRINKING

I'm a vegetarian.	ma sāh·*kā*·*ha*·ri hun
I don't eat spicy food.	ma *pi*·ro *khan*·di·na
Please bring me a spoon.	*ma*·lai *cham*·chah *lyau*·nu·hos
Can I have the bill?	bil *pau*·na *sak*·chhu

banana	*ke*·rah
bread	*ro*·ṭi
cauliflower	*go*·bi
chicken	*ku*·kha·ra/murgh
egg	phul
eggplant	*bhaṇ*·ṭa
fish	*mā*·chha
lentils	daal
meat	*ma*·su
mutton	*kha*·si
okra	ram·*to*·ri·ya
peanut	*ba*·dam
potato	a·lu
(cooked) rice	bhāt
spinach	sag

cold beer	*chi*·so *bi*·yar
boiled water	u·*māh*·le·ko *pa*·ni
hot lemon	*ta*·to pa·ni·mah *ka*·ga·ti
lemon soda	*so*·ḍa·mah *ka*·ga·ti
milk	dudh
sugar	*chi*·ni
tea	*chi*·ya
yoghurt	*da*·hi

EMERGENCIES

Help!	gu·*hār*
It's an emergency!	*ā*·paṭ *par*·yo
There's been an accident!	dur·*gha*·ṭa·nā *bha*·yo
Please call a doctor.	*dāk*·ṭar·lai bo·*lāu*·nu·hos
Where is the (public) toilet?	shau·*chā*·la·ya *ka*·hā chha
I'm lost.	ma ha·*rā*·ye

HEALTH

Where can I find a good doctor?	*rām*·ro *dāk*·ṭar *ka*·hā *pāin*·cha
Where is the nearest hospital?	*ya*·hā as·pa·tāl *ka*·hā chha
I don't feel well.	ma·*lāi san*·cho *chhai*·na

SIGNS

खुला	Open
बन्द	Closed
प्रबेश	Entrance
निकास	Exit
प्रबेश निषेध	No Entry
धूम्रपान मनाही छ	No Smoking
मनाही/निषेध	Prohibited
शाचालय	Toilets
तातो	Hot
चिसो	Cold
खतरा	Danger
रोक्नुहोस	Stop
बाटो बन्द	Road Closed

I'm having trouble breathing.	sās pher·na sak·di·na
I have altitude sickness.	lekh lāg·yo
I have a fever.	jo·ro ā·yo
I have diarrhoea.	di·shā lāg·yo

medicine	au·sa·dhi
pharmacy/chemist	au·sa·dhi pa·sal

I have ...	ma·lāi ... lāg·yo
asthma	dam·ko bya·thā
diabetes	ma·dhu·me·ha
epilepsy	chā·re rog

SHOPPING & SERVICES

Where's the market?	ba·zār ka·hā chha
What is it made of?	ke·le ba·ne·ko
How much?	ka·ti
That's enough.	pugyo
I like this.	ma·lai yo ram·ro lag·yo
I don't like this.	ma·lai yo ram·ro lag·en·a

cheap	sas·to
envelope	kham
expensive	ma·han·go
less	kam
little bit	a·li·ka·ti
money	pai·sa
more	ba·dhi
stamp	ti·ka
bank	baink

... embassy	... rāj·du·tā·vas
museum	sam·grā·hā·la·ya
police	pra·ha·ri
post office	post a·fis
tourist office	tu·rist a·fis

What time does it open/close?	ka·ti ba·je khol·chha/ ban·da gar·chha
I want to change some money.	pai·sā sāt·nu man·lāg·chha
Is there a local internet cafe?	ya·hā in·tar·neṭ kyah·phe chha
I'd like to get internet access.	ma·lai in·tar·neṭ cha·hi·yo
I'd like to check my email.	i·mel chek gar·nu·par·yo
I'd like to send an email.	i·mel pa·ṭhau·nu·par·yo

TIME & DATES

What time is it?	ka·ti ba·jyo
It's one o'clock.	ek ba·jyo

minute	mi·nat
hour	ghan·tā
day	din
week	hap·tā
month	ma·hi·nā

yesterday	hi·jo
today	ā·ja
now	a·hi·le
tomorrow	bho·li

What day is it today?	ā·ja ke bār
Today is ...	ā·ja ... ho

Monday	som·bār
Tuesday	man·gal bār
Wednesday	budh·bār
Thursday	bi·hi·bār
Friday	su·kra·bār
Saturday	sa·ni·bār
Sunday	āi·ta·bār

TRANSPORT & DIRECTIONS

Where?	ka·hā
here	ya·hā

NUMBERS

0	sun·ya	शून्य
1	ek	एक
2	du·i	दुइ
3	tin	तीन
4	chār	चार
5	panch	पाँच
6	chha	छ
7	sāt	सात
8	āṭh	आठ
9	nau	नौ
10	das	दस
11	e·ghār·a	एघार
12	bā·hra	बाह्र
13	te·hra	तेह्र
14	chau·dha	चौध
15	pan·dhra	पन्ध्र
16	so·hra	सोह्र
17	sa·tra	सत्र
18	a·ṭhā·ra	अठार
19	un·nais	उन्नाईस
20	bis	बीस
21	ek kais	एककाईस
22	bais	बाईस
23	teis	तेईस
24	chau·bis	चौबीस
25	pach·chis	पच्चीस
26	chhab·bis	छब्बीस
27	sat·tais	सत्ताईस
28	aṭ·ṭhais	अट्ठाईस
29	u·nan·tis	उनन्तीस
30	tis	तीस
40	chā·lis	चालीस
50	pa·chās	पचास
60	sā·ṭhi	साठी
70	sat·ta·ri	सत्तरी
80	a·si	असी
90	nab·be	नब्बे
100	ek say	एक सय
1000	ek ha·jār	एक हजार
10,000	das ha·jār	दस हजार
100,000	ek lākh	एक लाख
200,000	du·i lākh	दुइ लाख
1,000,000	das lākh	दस लाख

there	ṭya·hā
What is the address?	the·gā·nā ke ho
Please write down the address.	the·gā·nā lekh·nu·hos
How can I get to ...?	... ko·lā·gi ka·ti pai·sā lāg·chha
Is it far from here?	ya·hā·ba·ta ke tā·dhā chha
Can I walk there?	hi·ḍe·ra jā·na sa·kin·chhu

boat	nāu
bus	bus
taxi	ṭyakh·si
ticket	ṭi·kaṭ

I want to go to ...	ma ...·mā jān·chhu
Where does this bus go?	yo bus ka·hā jān·chha
I want a one-way ticket.	jā·ne ṭi·kaṭ di·nu·hos
I want a return ticket.	jā·ne·āu·ne ṭi·kaṭ di·nu·hos
How much is it to go to ...?	... jā·na ka·ti par·chha
Does your taxi have a meter?	ta·pāi ko ṭyakh·si mā me·ter chha

TREKKING

Which way is ...?	... jā·ne ba·to ka·ta par·chha
Is there a village nearby?	na·ji·kai gaun par·chha
How many hours to ...?	... ka·ti ghan·ṭā
How many days to ...?	... ka·ti din
Where is the porter?	bha·ri·ya ka·ta ga·yo
I want to sleep.	ma·lai sut·na man lag·yo
I'm cold.	ma·lai jā·ḍo lag·yo
Please give me (water).	ma·lai (pa·ni) di·nu·hos

bridge	pul
cold	jā·ḍo
downhill	o·rā·lo
left	bā·yā
right	dā·yā
teahouse	bhaṭ·ti
uphill	u·kā·lo
way/trail	sā·no bā·ṭo

GLOSSARY

Beware of the different methods of transliterating Nepali and the other languages spoken in Nepal. There are many and varied ways of spelling Nepali words. In particular, the letters 'b' and 'v' are often interchanged.

ACAP – Annapurna Conservation Area Project

Aditya – ancient *Vedic* sun god, also known as Suriya

Agni – ancient *Vedic* god of the hearth and fire

Agnipura – Buddhist symbol for fire

AMS – acute mountain sickness, also known as altitude sickness

Annapurna – the goddess of abundance and an incarnation of *Mahadevi*

Ashoka – Indian Buddhist emperor who spread Buddhism throughout the subcontinent

Ashta Matrikas – the eight multi-armed mother goddesses

Avalokiteshvara – Buddhist bodhisattva of compassion, known in Tibetan as Chenresig

bagh chal – traditional Nepali game

bahal – Buddhist monastery courtyard

ban – forest or jungle

bandh – strike; see also *julus* and *chakka jam*

Bhadrakali – Tantric goddess who is also a consort of *Bhairab*

Bhagwati – a form of *Durga*, and thus a form of the goddess *Parvati*

Bhairab – the 'terrific' or fearsome Tantric form of *Shiva* with 64 manifestations

bhanjyang – mountain pass

Bhimsen – one of the Pandava brothers, from the *Mahabharata*, seen as a god of tradesmen

bhojanalaya – basic Nepali restaurant or canteen

Bhote – Nepali term for a Tibetan, used in the names of rivers flowing from Tibet

Bodhi tree – a pipal tree under which the *Buddha* was sitting when he attained enlightenment; also known as 'bo tree'

bodhisattva – a near-*Buddha* who renounces the opportunity to attain *nirvana* in order to aid humankind

Bön – the pre-Buddhist animist religion of Tibet

Brahma – the creator god in the Hindu triad, which also includes *Vishnu* and *Shiva*

Brahmin – the highest Hindu caste, said to originate from *Brahma's* head

Buddha – the 'Awakened One'; the originator of Buddhism

chaitya – small *stupa*

chakka jam – literally 'jam the wheels', in which all vehicles stay off the street during a strike; see also *bandh* and *julus*

chakra – *Vishnu's* disc-like weapon; one of the four symbols he holds

Chandra – moon god

chautara – stone platforms around trees, which serve as shady places for porters to rest

Chhetri – the second caste of Nepali Hindus, said to originate from *Brahma's* arms

chörten – Tibetan Buddhist *stupa*

chowk – historically a courtyard or marketplace; these days used more to refer to an intersection or crossroads

daal – lentil soup; the main source of protein in the Nepali diet

Dalai Lama – spiritual leader of Tibetan Buddhist people

danda – hill

deval – temple

Devi – the short form of *Mahadevi*, the *shakti* to *Shiva*

dhaka – hand-woven cotton cloth

dharma – Buddhist teachings

dhoka – door or gate

Dhyani Buddha – the original Adi *Buddha* created five Dhyani Buddhas, who in turn create the universe of each human era

doko – basket carried by porters

dorje – Tibetan word for the 'thunderbolt' symbol of Buddhist power; *vajra* in Nepali

durbar – palace

Durga – fearsome manifestation of *Parvati*, *Shiva's* consort

gaida – rhinoceros

Ganesh – son of *Shiva* and *Parvati*, instantly recognisable by his elephant head

Ganga – goddess of the Ganges

Garuda – the man-bird *vehicle* of *Vishnu*

Gautama Buddha – the historical Buddha, founder of Buddhism

Gelugpa – one of the four major schools of Tibetan Buddhism

ghat – steps beside a river; a 'burning ghat' is used for cremations

gompa – Tibetan Buddhist monastery

gopi – milkmaids; companions of *Krishna*

gufa – cave

Gurkhas – Nepali soldiers who have long formed a part of the British army; the name comes from the region of Gorkha

Gurung – western hill people from around Gorkha and Pokhara

Hanuman – monkey god

harmika – square base on top of a *stupa's* dome, upon which the eyes of the *Buddha* are painted

hathi – elephant

himal – range or massif with permanent snow

hiti – water conduit or tank with waterspouts

hookah – water pipe for smoking

howdah – riding platform for passengers on an elephant

Indra – king of the *Vedic* gods; god of rain

Jagannath – *Krishna* as Lord of the Universe

janai – sacred thread, which high-caste Hindu men wear looped over their left shoulder

jatra – festival

jayanti – birthday

jhankri – faith healers who perform in a trance while beating drums

Jogini – mystical goddesses and counterparts to the 64 manifestations of *Bhairab*

julus – a procession or demonstration; see also *bandh* and *chakka jam*

Kali – the most terrifying manifestation of *Parvati*

Kalki – *Vishnu's* tenth and as yet unseen incarnation during which he will come riding a white horse and wielding a sword to destroy the world

Kam Dev – *Shiva's* companion

karma – Buddhist and Hindu law of cause and effect, which continues from one life to another

KEEP – Kathmandu Environmental Education Project

Khas – Hindu hill people

khat – see *palanquin*

khata – Tibetan prayer scarf, presented to an honoured guest or Buddhist *lama*

khola – stream or tributary

khukuri – traditional curved knife of the *Gurkhas*

kosi – river

kot – fort

Krishna – fun-loving eighth incarnation of *Vishnu*

Kumari – living goddess; a peaceful incarnation of *Kali*

kunda – water tank fed by springs

la – mountain pass

lama – Tibetan Buddhist monk or priest

lingam – phallic symbol signifying *Shiva's* creative powers

Machhendranath – patron god of the Kathmandu Valley and an incarnation of *Avalokiteshvara*

Mahabharata – one of the major Hindu epics

Mahadeva – literally 'Great God'; *Shiva*

Mahadevi – literally 'Great Goddess', sometimes known as *Devi*; the *shakti* to *Shiva*

Mahayana – the 'greater vehicle' of Buddhism; a later adaptation of the teaching, which lays emphasis on the *bodhisattva* ideal

makara – mythical crocodile-like beast

Malla – royal dynasty of the Kathmandu Valley responsible for most of the important temples and palaces of the valley towns

mandala – geometrical and astrological representation of the path to enlightenment

mandir – temple

mani – stone carved with the Tibetan Buddhist chant *om mani padme hum*

Manjushri – Buddhist *bodhisattva* of wisdom

mantra – prayer formula or chant

Mara – Buddhist god of death; has three eyes and holds the *wheel of life*

math – Hindu priest's house

mela – country fair

misthan bhandar – Indian-style sweet house and snack bar

naga – serpent deity

Nagpura – Buddhist symbol for water

namaste – traditional Hindu greeting (hello or goodbye), with the hands brought together at chest or head level, as a sign of respect

Nandi – *Shiva's vehicle*, the bull

Narayan – *Vishnu* as the sleeping figure on the cosmic ocean; from his navel *Brahma* appeared and went on to create the universe

Narsingha – man-lion incarnation of *Vishnu*

Newar – people of the Kathmandu Valley

nirvana – ultimate peace and cessation of rebirth (Buddhism)

om mani padme hum – sacred Buddhist *mantra*, which means 'hail to the jewel in the lotus'

padma – lotus flower

pagoda – multistoreyed Nepali temple, whose design was exported across Asia

palanquin – portable covered bed usually shouldered by four men; also called a *khat*

Parvati – *Shiva's* consort

pashmina – goat-wool blanket or shawl

Pashupati – *Shiva* as Lord of the Animals

path – small, raised platform to shelter pilgrims

phanta – grass plains

pipal tree – see *Bodhi tree*

pokhari – large water tank, or small lake

prasad – food offering

prayer flag – square of cloth printed with a *mantra* and hung in a string as a prayer offering

prayer wheel – cylindrical wheel inscribed with a Buddhist prayer or *mantra* that is 'said' when the wheel spins

Prithvi – *Vedic* earth goddess

puja – religious offering or prayer

pujari – priest

purnima – full moon

rajpath – road or highway, literally 'king's road'

Ramayana – Hindu epic

Rana – a hereditary line of prime ministers who ruled Nepal from 1846 to 1951

rath – temple chariot in which the idol is conveyed in processions

rudraksha – dried seeds worn in necklaces by *sadhus*

SAARC – South Asian Association for Regional Cooperation; includes Bangladesh, Bhutan, India, Nepal, Pakistan and Sri Lanka

sadhu – wandering Hindu holy man

Sagarmatha – Nepali name for Mt Everest

sal – tree of the lower Himalayan foothills

saligram – a black ammonite fossil of a Jurassic-period sea creature that is also a symbol of *Shiva*

sankha – conch shell, one of *Vishnu's* four symbols

Saraswati – goddess of learning and creative arts, and consort of *Brahma;* carries a lute-like instrument

seto – white

Shaivite – follower of *Shiva*

shakti – dynamic female element in male/female relationships; also a goddess

Sherpa – Buddhist hill people of Tibetan ancestry famed for work with mountaineering expeditions; with a lower-case 's' it refers to a trek staffer or high-altitude porter

shikhara – Indian-style temple with a tall, corn-cob-like spire

Shiva – the most powerful Hindu god, the creator and destroyer; part of the Hindu triad with *Vishnu* and *Brahma*

sindur – red vermilion powder and mustard-oil mixture used for offerings

sirdar – leader/organiser of a trekking party

stupa – bell-shaped Buddhist religious structure, originally designed to hold the relics of the *Buddha*

Sudra – the lowest Nepali caste, said to originate from *Brahma's* feet

sundhara – fountain with golden spout

tabla – hand drum

tahr – wild mountain goat

tal – lake

Taleju Bhawani – Nepali goddess, an aspect of *Mahadevi* and the family deity of the *Malla* kings of the Kathmandu Valley

tappu – island

Tara – White Tara is the consort of the *Dhyani Buddha* Vairocana; Green Tara is associated with Amoghasiddhi

teahouse trek – independent trekking between village inns (ie no camping)

tempo – three-wheeled, automated minivan commonly used in Nepal

Thakali – people of the Kali Gandaki Valley who specialise in running hotels

thali – literally a plate with compartments for different dishes; an all-you-can-eat set meal

thangka – Tibetan religious painting

third eye – symbolic eye on *Buddha* figures, used to indicate the *Buddha's* all-seeing wisdom and perception

thukpa – noodle soup

tika – red sandalwood-paste spot marked on the forehead, particularly for religious occasions

tole – street or quarter of a town; sometimes used to refer to a square

tonga – horse carriage

topi – traditional Nepali cap

torana – carved pediment above temple doors

Tribhuvan – the king who in 1951 ended the *Rana* period and Nepal's long seclusion

trisul – trident weapon that is a symbol of *Shiva*

tunala – carved temple struts

tundikhel – parade ground

Uma Maheshwar – *Shiva* and *Parvati* in a pose where *Shiva* sits cross-legged and *Parvati* sits on his thigh and leans against him

Upanishads – ancient *Vedic* scripts; the last part of the *Vedas*

vahana – a god's animal mount or *vehicle*

Vaishnavite – follower of *Vishnu*

Vaisya – caste of merchants and farmers, said to originate from *Brahma's* thighs

vajra – the 'thunderbolt' symbol of Buddhist power in Nepal; *dorje* in Tibetan

Vedas – ancient orthodox Hindu scriptures

Vedic gods – ancient Hindu gods described in the *Vedas*

vehicle – the animal with which a Hindu god is associated

vihara – Buddhist religious buildings and pilgrim accommodation

Vishnu – the preserver; one of the three main Hindu gods, along with *Brahma* and *Shiva*

wheel of life – Buddhist representation of how humans are chained by desire to a life of suffering

yak – cow-like Nepali beast of burden (only pure-blood animals of the genus *Bos grunniens* can properly be called yaks; crossbreeds have other names)

yaksha – attendant deity or nymph

Yama – *Vedic* god of death; his messenger is the crow

Yellow Hats – name sometimes given to adherents of the *Gelugpa* school of Tibetan Buddhism

yeti – abominable snowman; mythical hairy mountain man of the Himalaya

yogi – yoga master

yoni – female sexual symbol, equivalent of a *lingam*

zamindar – absentee landlord and/or moneylender

Behind the Scenes

SEND US YOUR FEEDBACK

We love to hear from travellers – your comments keep us on our toes and help make our books better. Our well-travelled team reads every word on what you loved or loathed about this book. Although we cannot reply individually to your submissions, we always guarantee that your feedback goes straight to the appropriate authors, in time for the next edition. Each person who sends us information is thanked in the next edition – the most useful submissions are rewarded with a selection of digital PDF chapters.

Visit **lonelyplanet.com/contact** to submit your updates and suggestions or to ask for help. Our award-winning website also features inspirational travel stories, news and discussions.

Note: We may edit, reproduce and incorporate your comments in Lonely Planet products such as guidebooks, websites and digital products, so let us know if you don't want your comments reproduced or your name acknowledged. For a copy of our privacy policy visit lonelyplanet.com/privacy.

OUR READERS

Many thanks to the travellers who used the last edition and wrote to us with helpful hints, useful advice and interesting anecdotes:

A Ah Yew Lim, Alan Bahl, Anat Werbner, Andrea Gillarduzzi, Andreas Stimm, Andrew Whitmarsh, Anne Forget-Levasseur, Artur Wróbel, Avishai Green **B** Bill Prime, Brandon Hausmann **C** Charles Ruechel, Chelsea Phillilppe, Corlius Jooste, Curtis Miller **D** Daniel Jones, David Galloway , David Kleinberg, Don Buckley **E** Evie Lim **G** Guillaume Roberge **H** Henry Coulter, Henryk Blasinski **I** Ian Macdonald, Inbal Frankenstein **J** Jake Strauss, Jane Corrie, Jay Thompson-Westra, Jean-Pierre Mélon, Jeffrey Grabow, Jenny Morgan, Jessica Alderman, Jochen Schuhmacher, John Sanderson, John Wall, Jonathan Wickens **K** Kitty Duncan **L** Larry Gems, Lauren Ruff , Laurence Wilbraham, Lydia Murphy **M** Marleen Lin, Mazlina Tahir, Michael Schindler, Mikael Persson, Mizio Matteucci, Muzzi Hoole **N** Natalie Francis, Nicholas Kanaan **P** Paul Clements, Pete Thomas, Peter Bidstrup, Peter Diffey, Peter March, Petra Bolfing, Pierre Gaspart **R** Raanan Greenman, Robert Thomas, Robert Kincaid, Robert Thomas, Roberto Martinez, Roger Ray, Roland Eger, Ronald Gallagher, Roshidah Hashim, Rosie Amesbury **S** Sabrina Laminger, Salvatore Cambria , Sam Miller, Scott Haggmark, Sebastian Sievers, Shai Roth, Simon Gamache, Susan Longman **T** Thomas Joller, Toby Frankenstein, Toby McAdams, Tom Stuart **W** William Chan **X** Xavi Pérez **Y** Yuval Yitzhak.

AUTHOR THANKS

Bradley Mayhew

Thanks to Kim Bannister of Kamzang Treks and Lhakpa Sherpa of Khumbu Adventures. Thanks to Niraj Shrestha and Rajesh Karki of the always professional Himalayan Encounters. Dawa Gyaljen Sherpa and his father gave great Rolwaling tips. Tejanath Pokharel in Khandbari was helpful with Makalu information. Phurba Gyaltsen Sherpa was a great porter-guide in the Khumbu, as ever. Cheers to Mukhiya and Maya, and to Dave, Cecile and Nieves, who were fine trekking companions in Manaslu and Tsum. Namgyal Ngodup generously offered lots of info on his native Tsum. Love to Kelli and thanks for coming to Kathmandu to see me!

Lindsay Brown

I am very grateful for the guidance of Stan Armington, Nepal trekking pioneer and author of the first eight editions of this book. I also thank Durga Bandari, Dawa Lama (Big), Dawa Lama (Small), Ram Roka, Narendra Lama (ACAP), Vimal and Vijay from nature-treks.com, and Ben Cester and Sinead Brown for accompanying me on the Khopra Ridge trek. Cheers to fellow authors Bradley Mayhew and Stuart Butler, and last but not least, thanks to life and travelling companion Jenny Fegent.

Stuart Butler

First and foremost I must, once again, thank my wife Heather, and children Jake and Grace for their patience with this long project, which involved so much time up in the mountains and out of touch. In Nepal, huge thanks to Thiley Lama and Ghyalbu Tamang for a memorable ascent of Yala Peak. Thanks to Durga Tamang for advice with the Tamang Heritage Trail and the Helambu treks. For an amazing Kanchenjunga trek thanks to Lakpa Dorje Sherpa, Gelu Sherpa, Geljen Sherpa, Aug Dawa Sherpa, Pemba Sherpa, Pasang Sherpa, Dipak Rai, Rames Lama, Pemba Tamang, A and Jun Tamang, Sankar Karki and, at Himalayan Glacier, thanks to Naba Raj Amgai for organising it all. Thanks also to Anna Hindmarsh and Radko for tips on Kanchenjunga North. Finally, thanks to Ben Clift and John Gray for accompanying me on the mountain trails, but clearly Ben it would be you who would be eaten by a jaguar first...

POST-EARTHQUAKE UPDATE

Special thanks are due to the journalists and Nepal experts who helped to update our content following the 2015 earthquakes, specifically: Suraj Shakya, Ajay Narsingh Rana, Nabin Baral, Rabik Upadhayay, Abhi Shrestha, Niraj Shrestha, Robin from Rural Heritage, Tony Jones from Himalayan Encounters and Jennifer Berry from Kathmandu Inside Out.

ACKNOWLEDGEMENTS

Climate map data adapted from Peel MC, Finlayson BL & McMahon TA (2007) 'Updated World Map of the Köppen-Geiger Climate Classification', Hydrology and Earth System Sciences, 11, 163344.

Cover photograph: Gokyo Ri, Sagarmatha National Park. Feng Wei Photography/Getty

THIS BOOK

This 10th edition of Lonely Planet's *Trekking in the Nepal Himalaya* guidebook was researched and written by Bradley Mayhew, Lindsay Brown and Stuart Butler. The ninth edition was written and researched by Bradley Mayhew and Joe Bindloss, while the eighth edition was written by Stan Armington. This guidebook was produced by the following:

Destination Editor Joe Bindloss

Product Editors Kate Kiely, Martine Power

Senior Cartographer David Kemp

Book Designer Wendy Wright

Assisting Editors Nigel Chin, Peter Cruttenden, Victoria Harrison, Gabrielle Innes, Lauren O'Connell

Assisting Cartographers Hunor Csutoros, Corey Hutchison, Gabriel Lindquist

Cover Researcher Naomi Parker

Thanks to Imogen Bannister, Kate James, Catherine Naghten, Claire Naylor, Karyn Noble, Angela Tinson

Index

Map Legend

Sights

- Beach
- Bird Sanctuary
- Buddhist
- Castle/Palace
- Christian
- Confucian
- Hindu
- Islamic
- Jain
- Jewish
- Monument
- Museum/Gallery/Historic Building
- Ruin
- Shinto
- Sikh
- Taoist
- Winery/Vineyard
- Zoo/Wildlife Sanctuary
- Other Sight

Activities, Courses & Tours

- Bodysurfing
- Diving
- Canoeing/Kayaking
- Course/Tour
- Sento Hot Baths/Onsen
- Skiing
- Snorkelling
- Surfing
- Swimming/Pool
- Walking
- Windsurfing
- Other Activity

Sleeping

- Sleeping
- Camping

Eating

- Eating

Drinking & Nightlife

- Drinking & Nightlife
- Cafe

Entertainment

- Entertainment

Shopping

- Shopping

Information

- Bank
- Embassy/Consulate
- Hospital/Medical
- Internet
- Police
- Post Office
- Telephone
- Toilet
- Tourist Information
- Other Information

Geographic

- Beach
- Hut/Shelter
- Lighthouse
- Lookout
- Mountain/Volcano
- Oasis
- Park
- Pass
- Picnic Area
- Waterfall

Population

- Capital (National)
- Capital (State/Province)
- City/Large Town
- Town/Village

Transport

- Airport
- Border crossing
- Bus
- Cable car/Funicular
- Cycling
- Ferry
- Metro station
- Monorail
- Parking
- Petrol station
- Subway station
- Taxi
- Train station/Railway
- Tram
- Underground station
- Other Transport

Note: Not all symbols displayed above appear on the maps in this book

Routes

- Tollway
- Freeway
- Primary
- Secondary
- Tertiary
- Lane
- Unsealed road
- Road under construction
- Plaza/Mall
- Steps
- Tunnel
- Pedestrian overpass
- Trekking Route
- Alternative Trekking Route
- Path/Walking Trail

Boundaries

- International
- State/Province
- Disputed
- Regional/Suburb
- Marine Park
- Cliff
- Wall

Hydrography

- River, Creek
- Intermittent River
- Canal
- Water
- Dry/Salt/Intermittent Lake
- Reef

Areas

- Airport/Runway
- Beach/Desert
- Cemetery (Christian)
- Cemetery (Other)
- Glacier
- Mudflat
- Park/Forest
- Sight (Building)
- Sportsground
- Swamp/Mangrove

OUR STORY

A beat-up old car, a few dollars in the pocket and a sense of adventure. In 1972 that's all Tony and Maureen Wheeler needed for the trip of a lifetime – across Europe and Asia overland to Australia. It took several months, and at the end – broke but inspired – they sat at their kitchen table writing and stapling together their first travel guide, *Across Asia on the Cheap*. Within a week they'd sold 1500 copies. Lonely Planet was born.

Today, Lonely Planet has offices in Franklin, London, Melbourne, Oakland, Beijing and Delhi, with more than 600 staff and writers. We share Tony's belief that 'a great guidebook should do three things: inform, educate and amuse'.

OUR WRITERS

Bradley Mayhew

Coordinating author; Kathmandu; Everest Region; Langtang, Helambu & Manaslu; Eastern Nepal A self-professed mountain junkie, Bradley has been trekking in the Himalayas for 20 years now, from north Pakistan and Zanskar to Tibet and Bhutan. For previous editions of this guide he's trekked in Nar-Phu, Dolpo, Langtang and the Annapurnas. For this edition he concentrated on the Everest region and Manaslu. Bradley is also the coordinating author of Lonely Planet's guides to Nepal, Bhutan, Tibet, and Central Asia, as well as the Odyssey guide to Uzbekistan. He has lectured on Central Asia to the Royal Geographical Society and was the subject of two Arte/SWR documentary series, one retracing the route of Marco Polo, the other hiking Europe's ten best long-distance trails. See what he's currently up to at www.bradleymayhew.blogspot.com.

Lindsay Brown

Annapurna Region; Western Nepal The Nepal Himalaya is a favourite destination for Lindsay, a keen trekker and former conservation biologist. Lindsay first visited Nepal over 25 years ago and has spent the last decade or so regularly visiting the country to hit the trails. He has trekked, jeeped, ridden and stumbled across many a mountain pass while contributing to Lonely Planet's *Bhutan*, *India*, *Nepal*, and *Pakistan & the Karakoram* Highway guides, among many others.

Stuart Butler

Langtang, Helambu & Manaslu; Eastern Nepal Stuart first travelled to Nepal over twenty years ago and has been a frequent visitor to both Nepal and the greater Himalaya region ever since. From the far north of Norway to the mountains of Yemen and the forests of the Congo, he has walked in many mountain and wilderness areas around the world. Today he lives with his wife and young son and daughter on the beaches of southwest France, right at the foot of the beautiful Pyrenees mountains. He's the author of Lonely Planet's *Hiking in Spain* guide. His website is www.stuart butlerjournalist.com.

Read more about Stuart at:
http://auth.lonelyplanet.com/profiles/stuartbutler

Published by Lonely Planet Publications Pty Ltd
ABN 36 005 607 983
10th edition – Jan 2016
ISBN 978 1 74179 272 0
© Lonely Planet 2016   Photographs © as indicated 2016
10 9 8 7 6 5 4 3 2 1
Printed in Singapore